W9-BHS-539

Advanced Praise for Inside LightWave 7

"Dan's comprehensive tome of knowledge has been an invaluable resource in navigating through the wild and woolly world of LightWave. When nobody knows the answer, chances are it's in here somewhere."

—**Aram Granger,** *Animation Supervisor, Foundation Imaging*

"Dan Ablan makes the hardest concepts easy to learn."

—**Paul Oberlander,** *Computer Teacher — Los Angeles Unified School District*

"Dan Ablan is possibly the best LightWave artist working in 3D CG at this time. I've learned everything I know from him."

—**Will Harrison,** *LightWave User*

"Hands down the best LW resource!"

—**Charles Meyer,** *Technical Director, Wet Cement Productions*

"If you're new to LightWave this will open a lot of doors for you. If you're an old school user, Dan's books take the hassle away from learning the new tools."

—**Kyle Toucher,** *Visual Effects Animator, Foundation Imaging*

"Dan Ablan's Inside LightWave books have set a new quality standard when it comes to in-depth tutorials. They are a cornerstone in the deeper understanding of LightWave 3D."

—**Eki Halkka,** *VFX supervisor, AKMP-Program Oy Finland*

"Once again, Dan Ablan transcends LightWave with version 7's inner workings and delivers inspiring techniques. Inside LightWave 7 is a powerhouse of LightWave knowledge."

—**Michael Hardison,** *CG Supervisor, Pixel Magic*

Dan Ablan's "Inside Lightwave" books are, quite simply, indispensable guides for unlocking the power of LightWave 3D, for both new and experienced users. They are not only a great reference to what tools are present in LightWave, but they also supply the deep understanding of techniques that the user needs in order to make the efficient and effective use of these powerful modeling, animation, and rendering tools. We've made sure to add each edition to our Technical Support Staff Library as they are released. I repeat, indispensable.

—**Chuck Baker,** *Director of Customer Support and Services, NewTek, Inc.*

INSIDE LIGHTWAVE® 7

BY
Dan Ablan

201 West 103rd Street, Indianapolis, Indiana 46290
An Imprint of Pearson Education
Boston • Indianapolis • London • New York • San Francisco

Contents at a Glance

Inside LightWave® 7

Copyright © 2002 by New Riders Publishing

All rights reserved. No part of this book shall be reproduced, stored in a retrieval system, or transmitted by any means—electronic, mechanical, photocopying, recording, or otherwise—without written permission from the publisher. No patent liability is assumed with respect to the use of the information contained herein. Although every precaution has been taken in the preparation of this book, the publisher and author(s) assume no responsibility for errors or omissions. Neither is any liability assumed for damages resulting from the use of the information contained herein.

International Standard Book Number: 0-7357-1134-8

Library of Congress Catalog Card Number: 2001087446

Printed in the United States of America

First Printing: January 2002

06 05 04 03 02   7 6 5 4 3 2

Interpretation of the printing code: The rightmost double-digit number is the year of the book's printing; the rightmost single-digit number is the number of the book's printing. For example, the printing code 02-1 shows that the first printing of the book occurred in 2002.

Trademarks

All terms mentioned in this book that are known to be trademarks or service marks have been appropriately capitalized. New Riders Publishing cannot attest to the accuracy of this information. Use of a term in this book should not be regarded as affecting the validity of any trademark or service mark.

The NewTek LightWave icon, used throughout the book in Notes, Tips, and Warnings, is a trademark of NewTek and is used with permission.

Warning and Disclaimer

Every effort has been made to make this book as complete and as accurate as possible, but no warranty of fitness is implied. The information provided is on an "as is" basis. The authors and the publisher shall have neither liability nor responsibility to any person or entity with respect to any loss or damages arising from the information contained in this book or from the use of the CD or programs accompanying it.

Publisher
David Dwyer

Associate Publisher
Stephanie Wall

Production Manager
Gina Kanouse

Marketing Manager
Kathy Malmloff

Managing Editor
Kristy Knoop

Acquisitions Editors
Linda Bump
Deborah Hittel-Shoaf

Development Editor
Audrey Doyle

Project Editor
Suzanne Pettypiece

Copy Editor
reVisions Plus, Inc.

Technical Editor
Doug Nakakihara

Publicist
Susan Nixon

Cover Designer
Aren Howell

Compositor
Jeff Bredensteiner
Damon Muzzy
Amy Parker

Proofreader
Jeannie Smith

Indexer
Lisa Stumpf

Media Developer
Jay Payne

Table of Contents

About the Authors

 **Dan Ablan** is president of AGA Digital Studios, Inc., a 3D animation company in the Chicago area. AGA has produced 3D animation for broadcast, corporate, and architectural clients since 1994, as well as post-production services. Dan holds a B.A. in broadcast journalism from Valparaiso University, with a minor concentration in photojournalism. He is the author of four best-selling international LightWave 3D books from New Riders Publishing: *LightWave Power Guide* (v5.0), *Inside LightWave 3D* (v5.5), *Inside LightWave [6]*, and *LightWave 6.5 Effects Magic*. He has released an on-going series of LightWave training videos through Christie Entertainment (*www.classondemand.net*) and has written columns and articles for *LightWave Pro* magazine, *Video Toaster User* magazine, *3D Design* magazine, *3D World* magazine, and *NewTek Pro* magazine. In addition, Dan was Technical Editor for Jeremy Birn's *Digital Lighting & Rendering* from New Riders Publishing. Dan has been teaching LightWave seminars across the country, since 1995 including at AGA Digital Studios, Inc., an authorized NewTek LightWave training facility. Visit *www.danablan.com* and *www.agadigital.com*.

Dan authored Chapters 1, 2, 3, 4, 5, 6, 7, 9, 10 (revisions for LightWave 7), 11, 12, 13, 16, 17, 18, 19, 20, 21, and the appendixes.

 For the past seven years, **Jarrod Davis** has spent almost every waking moment slaving away at the computer, constantly trying to improve his skills in 3D animation and effects. And what has it gotten him? A fantastic job at Foundation Imaging working on shows, such as *Roughnecks, Max Steel,* and *Dan Dare,* nationwide commercials, and the fulfillment of his dream to work on *Star Trek*. With the support of his wonderful fiancée—herself an aspiring animator—he intends to proceed with his plans to conquer the world...when he gets some free time. Jarrod Davis is affectionately known as J-Rod. Jarrod authored Chapters 14, "Expression Applications," and 15, "Animation with Expression."

Stuart Aitken is currently head of 3D at Axis animation—a company he co-founded along with several colleagues in 1999 with the aim of eventual total world domination of the 3D CG industry. Although often plagued by the lingering notion he really should be somewhere else by now, he still lives and works amid the gritty iron and sandstone landscape of Glasgow, Scotland. Stuart has been using LightWave for nigh on seven years now and amazingly still isn't bored. His particular emphasis is on organic 3D modeling, texturing, character setup, and expanding waistlines. Stuart created the cover image for *Inside LightWave [6]* and 7, and he authored Chapter 10, "Organic Modeling," for *Inside LightWave [6]*. That chapter has been updated for LightWave 7.

Randy Sharp is currently a 3D animator at Digital Domain in California. He spent two and a half years at Foundation Imaging working on a number of productions, and was a supervising modeler for his last year there. Prior to working at Foundation Imaging, Randy worked at Applied Materials for 10 years, leaving as a manufacturing engineer. Randy authored Chapter 8, "Architectural Environments."

There are many people that Randy could thank for the opportunities he's been given, but none of it would have happened without the love and support of his wife, Kathleen. Spending countless hours behind a computer monitor is hard, but having someone that supports him in every way imaginable is what gives him the strength to do it. Without her, Randy says, he would never have had the success and opportunities he has enjoyed. Randy would like to say thanks to Kathleen for helping him realize a dream.

Bob Cazzell holds a degree in electronic engineering and is the chief information officer for REZN8 Productions, Inc., an Emmy Award-winning graphic design, animation, and visual effects studio in Hollywood. Bob has been fooling around with computer graphics since the early 1990s and joined REZN8 in 1997 when he decided that the healthcare industry was not a fun and exciting career choice. He also thinks Bugs and Daffy are the greatest comedy duo in history. Bob supplied the technical references located at the end of Appendix B, "Lightwave 7 Plug-in, Tool, and Technical List."

About the Technical Editor

 **Douglas J. Nakakihara** is the documentation manager for NewTek. Although he graduated with a degree in accounting and gained a CPA certificate, his real interest was always computers. He freelances as a 3D animator and has written for many computer publications through the years. He also is a web designer and has written several PC utilities. For more information, see *www.dougworld.com*.

Dedication

I'd like to dedicate this book to my wife Maria. Without her love and support, this couldn't have been done. Maria, without you, nothing is worth doing.

—**Dan Ablan**

Acknowledgments

So, I'm sitting here, trying to think of who to acknowledge, while trying to not make it sound like every other book's acknowledgments. But I can't. I'm thinking about how the words "3D animation" didn't exist when I was growing up on the south side of Chicago. And I must thank all my friends at New Riders Publishing without sounding insincere, so here goes: To Linda Bump for really pushing my buttons and making me work—thanks Linda; Jennifer Eberhardt for everything; Steve Weiss and David Dwyer for believing in me, again; Audrey Doyle—you're the best! Deborah Hittel-Shoaf, thanks for keeping my deadlines in check! I needed it. Big huge thanks again to my friend Doug Nakikihara at NewTek. Doug is the best tech editor we could ask for. Also at NewTek, my appreciation and thanks go out first to Phil Nelson, who has really helped tie the knot between our books and NewTek. Thanks Phil—go Spurs! Also, thanks to Art Howe and Brad Peebler for the great "inside" info for creating this book. Major thanks goes to the entire LightWave development team in San Francisco—your software has matured beyond belief. Now, can you get it to run on my Amiga? Paul Holtz at Christie Video Entertainment—thank you for your always-positive support. Big thanks to my little girl for understanding the many missed visits to the park. Lastly, thanks to my fantastic wife for understanding my extremely long hours every night and on weekends to get this book done. The coffee is appreciated. Sagapo Agape.

New Riders Acknowledgment

New Riders would like to thank NewTek for allowing us to include the NewTek LightWave icon throughout this book. (The NewTek LightWave icon is a trademark of NewTek and is used with permission.)

A Message from New Riders

As the reader of this book, you are our most important critic and commentator. We value your opinion and want to know what we're doing right, what we could do better, in which areas you'd like to see us publish, and any other words of wisdom you're willing to pass our way.

As the Associate Publisher of New Riders, I welcome your comments. You can fax, email, or write me directly to let me know what you did or didn't like about this book—as well as what we can do to make our books better. When you write, please be sure to include this book's title, ISBN, and author, as well as your name and phone or fax number. I will carefully review your comments and share them with the authors and editors who worked on the book.

Please note that I cannot help you with technical problems related to the topic of this book, and that due to the high volume of email I receive, I might not be able to reply to every message. Thanks.

Email: stephanie.wall@newriders.com

Mail: Stephanie Wall
         Associate Publisher
         New Riders Publishing
         201 West 103rd Street
         Indianapolis, IN 46290 USA

Visit Our Web Site: *www.newriders.com*

On our web site, you'll find information about our other books, the authors we partner with, book updates and file downloads, promotions, discussion boards for online interaction with other users and with technology experts, and a calendar of trade shows and other professional events with which we'll be involved. We hope to see you around.

Email Us from Our Web Site

Go to *www.newriders.com* and click on the Contact Us link if you

- Have comments or questions about this book.

- Want to report errors that you have found in this book.

- Have a book proposal or are interested in writing for New Riders.

- Would like us to send you one of our author kits.

- Are an expert in a computer topic or technology and are interested in being a reviewer or technical editor.

- Want to find a distributor for our titles in your area.

- Are an educator/instructor who wants to preview New Riders books for classroom use. In the body/comments area, include your name, school, department, address, phone number, office days/hours, text currently in use, and enrollment in your department, along with your request for either desk/examination copies or additional information.

Contact Dan's Web Sites

Dan Ablan keeps a regular web site for book information, video training, personal on-site training, tutorials, and links at *www.danablan.com.* For up-to-date information on all Inside LightWave books to date, please check *www.insidelightwave.com.*

Call Us or Fax Us

You can reach us toll-free at 800-571-5840 + 0 (ask for New Riders). If outside the U.S., please call 1-317-581-3500 and ask for New Riders. If you prefer, you can fax us at 1-317-581-4663, Attention: New Riders.

Technical Support and Customer Support for This Book

Although we encourage entry-level users to get as much as they can out of our books, keep in mind that our books are written assuming a non-beginner level of user-knowledge of the technology. This assumption is reflected in the brevity and shorthand nature of some of the tutorials.

New Riders will continually work to create clearly written, thoroughly tested and reviewed technology books of the highest educational caliber and creative design. We value our customers more than anything—that's why we're in this business—but we cannot guarantee to each of the thousands of you who buy and use our books that we will be able to work individually with you through tutorials or content with which you may have questions. We urge readers who need help in working through exercises or other material in our books—and who need this assistance immediately—to use as many of the resources that our technology and technical communities can provide, especially the many online user groups and list servers available.

- If you have a physical problem with one of our books or accompanying CD-ROMs, please contact our customer support department.

- If you have questions about the content of the book—needing clarification about something as it is written or note of a possible error—again please contact our customer support department.

- If you have comments of a general nature about this or other books by New Riders, please contact the Associate Publisher.

To contact our customer support department, call 800-571-5840 + 1 + 3567 + 7.

Introduction

New Riders Publishing is a leader in the graphics publishing industry. Its *Inside* series of books has been at the forefront of the creative community. *Inside* books live on just about all artists' desks as permanent residents. Usually the *Inside* series of books is updated when software is upgraded, but *Inside LightWave 7* is a completely new book. NewTek, Inc., maker of LightWave 3D, has again revamped one of the 3D industry's most popular and powerful animation programs. Because of that, it is only fitting that this book has been thoroughly updated to provide the most complete, up-to-date information.

Getting the Most from *Inside LightWave 7*

Inside LightWave 7 is designed differently from other books on the market. Each chapter is tuned to provide key information about a specific topic. The project-based chapters in Parts II, "A Project-Based Approach to Creating and Building 3D Scenes," and Part III, "A Project-Approach to Animating Scenes," teach you how to create entire animations, not just portions of them. Because of this approach, you'll model, texture, light, and animate—all within one chapter! However, taking the book as a whole from start to finish will allow you to make the most of the information it provides.

About the Creation of This Book

Inside LightWave 7 was written on a Dell Dimension XPS 600, Pentium III. The system has 512MB of RAM and a 32MB NVidia GeForce 256 video card. This book's tutorials were tested on this system, as well as on a Macintosh G4 733Mhz, with 512MB of RAM and a 32MB GeForce video card. The authors worked hard to ensure that Macintosh LightWave users are just as informed as the Windows users, and you'll see this reflected in Tips and Notes throughout the book. And although with LightWave 3D version 7 very few differences exist between the platforms, we've made note of any variances that you should be aware of.

Use the LightWave 7 Software with This Book

Due to a complete rewrite of the LightWave architecture from versions previous to 6.0, and the additions and changes made to version 7, it is recommend that you have the most current version of the LightWave software so that you can take full advantage of the information within these pages. You will not be able to apply the tutorials in this book to LightWave versions prior to 6.0.

In addition, you should check the NewTek web site (*www.newtek.com* and *www.lightwave3d.com*) for any current updates. Also be sure to check *www.insidelightwave.com* for the latest updates and links.

Read the LightWave Manuals

Inside LightWave 7 is designed for use along with the manual that was supplied with your LightWave software from NewTek. Be sure to read through the NewTek-provided manual before working through this book. When you're comfortable with the information there, dive into this book to become the best LightWave animator on your block. Although previous LightWave books, such as *LightWave Power Guide, Inside LightWave 3D 5.5*, and *Inside LightWave [6]*, have a tremendous amount of information, the changes in LightWave 7 make the information in this book unique. The *Inside LightWave* series from New Riders always brings you the best, and will continue to do so in the years to come! Don't be fooled by imitations!

To get the most out of this book, it is strongly recommended that you study your software manuals and keep them nearby for quick reference.

Start at the Beginning of the Book

Unless you are somewhat familiar with LightWave 6 and/or 6.5, it is important for you to start at the beginning of this book and not skip directly to a project chapter. Although it's tempting to dive right in, LightWave 7 has a new structure and there are changes throughout LightWave's Modeler and Layout modules that you should be familiar with before you begin. Do yourself a favor and read about these changes.

Experiment with the Software

One of the best things you can do as an animator learning LightWave is to experiment. This is stressed throughout this book. However, consider this a warning: Experimentation takes you to places within the program that you might not normally go. That's why this book provides many screenshots of the topic at hand. It is important to have not only a comprehensive understanding of techniques, but also a visual reference as well.

Practice Your Craft

There is no substitute for practicing your craft. If you happen to be driving down the road and notice an interesting tree, practice re-creating it in LightWave. If you decide that you'd love to visualize your dream house, build it in LightWave. Don't wait until you have a paid project or assignment to work in LightWave. All the extra time you spend modeling and animating will help give you that extra edge.

Use Other Books with This Book

No single book can deliver it all, although we'll try! And because no single book has all the answers, it's to your advantage to use additional and, sometimes, more specific references. For example, character animation is a driving force for many of the changes within this program, as well as the reason many of you got into 3D animation in the first place. *Inside LightWave 7* covers as much of this topic as possible, but a great number of other resources also are available to you. Some of these resources include books on facial muscles, character design, motion and body studies, figure drawing, and lighting. Books and magazines, along with the Internet, can provide much information; study as much as you can. The Internet also provides many downloadable animations that you can study and/or use as references, or from which you can simply gain ideas. Be sure to visit *www.danablan.com* for updates and information on this book, and visit *www.insidelightwave.com* to help you learn. Remember, knowledge is power!

Checking Out the Organization of This Book

Inside LightWave 7 is organized into five parts.

Part I, "Getting Started with LightWave 7," is an overview of the new features and functions of LightWave 7. This includes 3D terminology, methodology (such as the HUB and Spreadsheet Scene Manager, and Motion Mixer), and other important information about the many changes in the new version. This section introduces you to creating 3D objects, the Layout and Modeler interfaces, and customizable buttons.

Part II, "A Project-Based Approach to Creating and Building 3D Scenes," takes you through the real-world process of creating animations. The chapters in this section bring you through the necessary steps in LightWave 7's modeling functions and features, surfacing techniques, lighting, and cameras.

Part III, "A Project-Based Approach to Animating Scenes," shows you how to push your LightWave software even further through the use of LightWave 7's Expression engine, and advanced Inverse Kinematics (IK). You'll learn compositing techniques and work through a real-world project, creating broadcast-style graphics.

Part IV, "Animation Post and Effects," is dedicated to helping you output your animations and apply post-processing effects to them. In this section, you add to the information you need to create a killer demo reel, from content information, length, and many other important considerations. Also you learn about getting your animation to videotape, getting it to the web, and working with various recording formats.

Part V, "Appendixes," includes information on plug-ins and on some necessary LightWave-related information on the Internet.

Identifying the Conventions Used in This Book

Throughout this book, you'll come across Warnings, Tips, and Notes. These areas are marked with a small NewTek LightWave icon, similar to the one that appears on your desktop when you install LightWave. Any control area that opens is referred to as a *panel*. Fields where you enter values are referred to as *requesters*, and buttons that have a small upside-down triangle are referred to as *drop-down menus*. That's simple enough, isn't it?

There's one more thing to remember—always work with the Caps Lock key off! Throughout this book, you will come across many keyboard shortcuts, and there are significant differences between a lowercase shortcut and an uppercase shortcut. The essential and immediate shortcuts used regularly are assigned to lowercase keys, while less-used commands are assigned to uppercase keys. What's important to remember is that some of the uppercase commands are more complex functions, and if you're not prepared to execute such a command, you might cause problems for yourself.

System Considerations

LightWave 7 is definitely a more robust program than any previous version of LightWave. Because of this, a good strong system is your best bet for enjoying the full benefits of the program. However, LightWave still takes fewer resources to run effectively than its competing applications. As always, the more RAM (system memory) you have, the better. *Inside LightWave 7* recommends that you have at least 256MB of RAM in your system. This is the bare minimum! This greatly enhances your workflow. Larger memory requirements are needed because computations in LightWave 7 are done with floating-point accuracy rather than integers. What this means for you is better renders! Please note that you should consult your LightWave 3D Reference Guides supplied by NewTek for specific requirements.

If you are planning to buy a new system or upgrade your existing one, you can get help through a number of resources. The Internet is your best bet for finding the most up-to-date pricing, power, and performance information. You also can find recommended systems through 3D workstation vendors such as Dell or Hewlett-Packard. The graphics and computer industry is constantly changing, and if the price you find for a system is too high, just wait a few months and the costs will most likely decrease. However, you should not be too frugal when upgrading or purchasing a system. Be smart, but don't wait thinking that a new and faster processor will be out soon. There will always be a faster, cheaper, and stronger system. Inevitably, you could be waiting forever! Buy a good system, and start making great animations now.

Video Memory

Don't think that because you have the latest processor on the market, or the fastest Mac available, you'll have the best computer for animation. Processing power is only one part of the computing process when it comes to creating with LightWave. Your system memory—in this case, 256MB of RAM or more—is very important to a productive system. However, your video memory is just as important.

Given LightWave 7's expansive interface enhancements, you should have a good OpenGL-compatible video card with at least 32MB of RAM. LightWave's Modeler and Layout allow great control over viewports, shading, and interface color, all of which will rely heavily on your video memory. Not only can you model in full color in a perspective window, but you also can see your texture maps, UV maps, specularity, transparency, reflections, lights, and more, all in real time. Take advantage of the ridiculously inexpensive video cards available today and upgrade your system. Some recommended cards are the GeForce, Oxygen VX1, and Matrox G400 Max. These cards from NVidia are among those that give you the best bang for the buck. Also Oxygen VX1 from 3D Labs or the Matrox G400 Max, both of which are designed for 3D graphics and cost less than $300, work very well.

The Matrox G400 and the more expensive Evans & Sutherland Tornado support dual monitors from one computer. What this means is that you can have two monitors side by side with your information panels open on one, while you work on the other. Or set up one monitor with Modeler and the other with Layout; the choice is yours. Other programs such as Adobe Photoshop, In-Sync's Speed Razor, Apple Final Cut Pro, and NewTek's Aura2 can definitely benefit from a dual display. With a strong video card, you can move, rotate, and select with instant feedback and no delays. Primarily, you'll want a video card that is fully OpenGL compliant. Also video cards change often, so be sure to check with NewTek about any new card recommendations the company might have.

Dual Monitors

LightWave 7's non-modal panels might not mean much to the single-monitor user. But if you have installed a video card such as a Matrox G400 Max or better, you can take full advantage of the non-modal feature. A non-modal panel is one that can remain open while you work. For example, if you've ever worked in Adobe Photoshop, you can leave certain panels, such as the Brush panel, open so that you can choose different brush styles as you go. With a dual-monitor setup, you can open any of LightWave 7's panels and move them over to your second monitor, leaving the primary monitor full screen for optimal visibility. As you work, the panels are updated in real time. Ask your computer dealer for more information on dual-monitor setups.

Note

Windows 2000 supports multiple monitors natively, so you might not need to invest in an expensive video card to have dual display. For example, you can run one AGP card for the main monitor on your Windows 2000 system. Add a PCI card, install the driver, and Windows then will enable a button in the Display Settings panel to "Extend my desktop to this monitor." Simple and very cool. Check with your system manufacturer and operating system developer for more details.

You also can set up dual monitors on your Macintosh system as well. Macs have been using dual-monitor setups for years, and it's proven to be a great working environment for video editors, graphic artists, and animators alike.

Words to Work By

It wasn't too long ago that most of you didn't even know what 3D animation was all about. Now if you're one of the lucky ones, it's your hobby, or better, your livelihood. I've seen LightWave grow from a fun and cute little Amiga program to a rich, powerful, and robust animation package.

Like many of you, my background in video and photography has helped me excel with LightWave to create the types of images I couldn't create in the real world. For others just starting out, you've come on board at a marvelous time.

LightWave 7 is for all of you—experienced and new users alike. This book was written to help you learn the nuances of LightWave 7, from its keyboard shortcuts to its powerful character animation and modeling tools, to its smart scene creation through the new nonlinear animation control of Motion Mixer and its scene management capabilities. But more importantly, you'll gain a valuable resource for just about any project that comes across your desk with the information on these pages. Whether you are a continuing reader from my first four LightWave books, or are brand new to the game, welcome to *Inside LightWave 7*.

Part I

Getting Started with LightWave 7

Chapter 1

Introducing LightWave 7

LightWave 7 has many new features and improvements. Just when you thought it couldn't get any better, NewTek released version 6.5. Then, as soon as you thought it was safe to go back in the water, *bam*! Version 7 hits! But before you dig into the new features in this version, take a quick look at the new user interface and the historical and architectural changes within the program. When you purchase LightWave 3D, you actually get two programs that NewTek calls Modeler and LightWave. Modeler is where you build and create 3D objects. LightWave is where you put objects into motion and create animations. For clarity, this book will refer to the two programs as *Modeler* and *Layout*.

Specifically, this chapter teaches you about the following:

- Layout's interface
- Layout's groups
- The Layout Preferences panel
- The Modeler Preferences panel
- Metaball and SubPatch resolution
- Undo levels

A Brief Look at the History of LightWave

LightWave 7 is the 11th release of the program, which is in its third generation. The first generation of LightWave was available only on an Amiga computer bundled with a video card called the Video Toaster. That first generation of LightWave introduced 3D animation to an entirely new group of users who could not previously afford the technology (like the guy who's writing this book!).

The second generation of LightWave occurred with version 4.0, when NewTek modified the architecture of the program to work independently of the Video Toaster board as well as run identically on multiple platforms, such as Macintosh, IBM PC or Silicon Graphics. That second generation of LightWave also opened up the software to third-party developers with a plug-in architecture, greatly enhancing LightWave's position in the marketplace as well as strengthening its power by allowing small programs to be added on a user-by-user basis. These plug-ins included image filters for post-processing renders, particle systems, motion effects, and more.

A Brief Look at Layout and Modeler

To start your relationship with LightWave 7, look at the two user interfaces: Layout and Modeler. Figure 1.1 shows Layout, and Figure 1.2 shows Modeler.

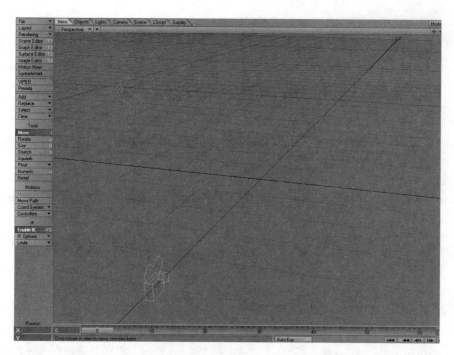

Figure 1.1   This is the Layout program at startup on both PC and Mac.

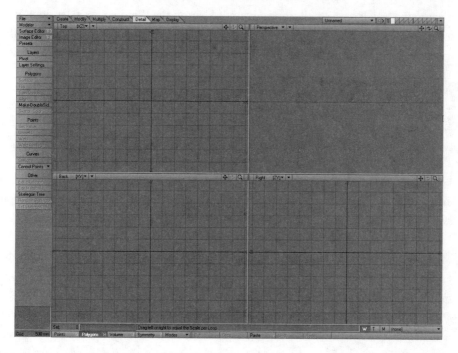

Figure 1.2   This is the Modeler program at startup on both PC and Mac.

Note
Whether you're running LightWave on a Macintosh or a PC, the interfaces are identical. Button locations and keyboard equivalents also are identical.

These interfaces might look similar to previous versions of LightWave, but don't let the similarities fool you—they are actually quite different. What's more is that the interfaces can look different from the ones pictured here. LightWave 7's interfaces are customizable and partially removable. The look of the interfaces can vary, depending on the project at hand. You might use a full-frame shaded Perspective mode in Modeler, using a Quad view in Layout, or a Tri view with an added Schematic view—this is all possible. You learn how to customize interfaces in Chapter 3, "LightWave 7 Modeler," and Chapter 4, "LightWave 7 Layout."

A Brief Look at the Architecture of LightWave

When you install LightWave, you'll see multiple executable files in the LightWave\ Programs\LightWave_Support directory, such as LightWav.exe (LightWave Layout), Modeler.exe (LightWave Modeler), Hub.exe on the PC, and LightWave and Modeler on the Mac. The HUB program runs automatically when you start Modeler or Layout. Once it's running, you'll see a small icon in your taskbar on the Windows or extensions Mac interfaces. When you right-click this icon (or press the Ctrl/Command key and click the mouse button on your Mac), you can launch it, or you can launch Layout or Modeler. The HUB is an active link between Layout and Modeler.

Tip
After you start Layout, you can simply press F12 on your keyboard to start up Modeler. From that point on, pressing F12 will switch between the two programs.

Before LightWave version 6, you had to use the Get and Put commands in Modeler to load and save objects from Layout. Now, the HUB automatically keeps information available in both programs. For example, suppose that you've loaded your scene into Layout and you realize that some objects you created need modification. Jump into Modeler by pressing F12 (or pressing the Alt and Tab keys together), and next to the Layers buttons on the top-right corner of the screen you'll see a drop-down or "pop-up" menu. This menu shows you the objects that are loaded in Layout. Select an object, adjust it, and your object is modified—when you make an adjustment to your model, it is automatically updated in Layout. You also can use the Send Object to Layout command, found in Modeler under the tiny drop-down at the top-right corner of the interface. Finally, you can use the Switch to Layout command and the Synchronize Layout command to sync up objects loaded into both Layout and Modeler. You'll use these tools and others throughout the book's tutorials. There's nothing like using a tool to understand how something works!

Tip

Mac users: To simulate the right-click commands used in Windows, you need to hold down the Ctrl/Command key while you click the mouse button. Better yet, go get a two-button mouse and save yourself from some unnecessary keyboard work!

The HUB also allows you to monitor LightWave activities, including how many processes are currently running, how many times LightWave and Modeler have been launched, Memory Block Synchronization records, and File Asset Synchronization records. You have the option to choose how long the HUB runs: 5 Minutes, 30 Minutes, 1 Hour, or Never. By default, Never is selected; you do not need to set any of these options for LightWave or Modeler to run. You also can set an Automatic Save from the Hub properties. Most of the time, you won't need to access this panel.

Note

You must run Layout and Modeler at least once to get them to "see" each other using the HUB.

NewTek, Inc. has been working on this version of LightWave since the release of version 6. The company has rewritten the software from the ground up and has established a significant programming force. NewTek still listens to user requests, and the feedback is reflected in the functionality and customization of this very robust new version. Of particular value are these changes:

- Customizable interfaces
- Groupable interfaces
- Multiple viewport configurations
- Schematic view and the Spreadsheet Scene Management tool
- Shortcut navigation
- Redesigned panels

The sections that follow discuss these architectural changes.

Customizable Interfaces

The user interface is at first the most noticeable change. With completely configurable buttons and toolbars and an updated look, both Layout and Modeler are streamlined but offer enhanced workflow. Once again, NewTek, Inc. has kept to its original workflow pattern and not succumbed to nonsensical icons but has, yet again, changed the menu configurations. This is a good thing, as the workflow has been greatly enhanced. LightWave 6.0 introduced a new menu configuration and smarter workflow over previous versions; however, many functions and tools in that version were deeply buried within drop-down menus and lists. Version 7 brings out all the tools and puts them right in front of you. It might seem overwhelming to look at so many buttons and commands, but they will soon make sense. You will work better because you'll be aware of—and be able to access easily—all the tools in your toolbox.

The buttons are clearly named but now are even easier to access. Toolbars are customizable, as they were in version 6.0, and can be moved to the left or right side of the screen or hidden completely for maximum visibility as well. Figure 1.3 shows Layout's toolbar at startup, and Figure 1.4 shows a customized version of the toolbar.

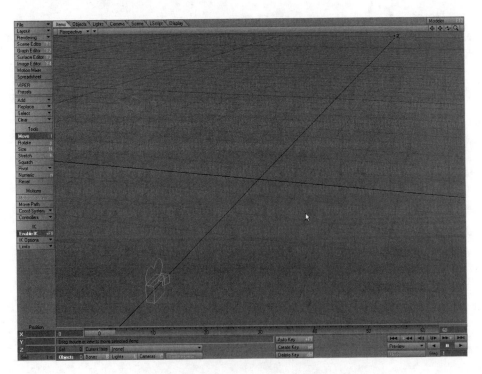

Figure 1.3   Layout's default toolbar is located at the left of the interface.

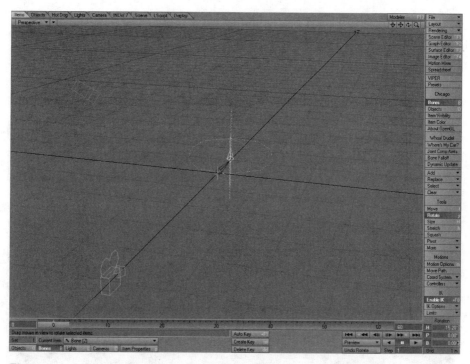

Figure 1.4   You can customize Layout's toolbar with your own tabs and favorite commands.

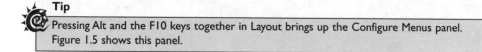

Tip

Pressing Alt and the F10 keys together in Layout brings up the Configure Menus panel. Figure 1.5 shows this panel.

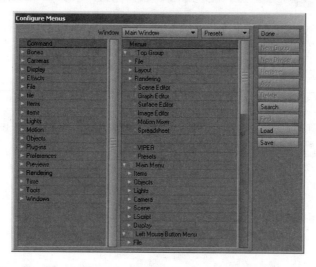

Figure 1.5   Pressing Alt and the F10 keys together calls up the Configure Menus panel.

Groupable Interfaces

Not only are the toolbars customizable, but you also can customize or create your own groupings. Imagine starting up LightWave and seeing only the tools you use. Figure 1.6 shows the default menu groups in Layout at the top of the interface on startup with an additional customized menu group. Both Layout and Modeler's customization work the same.

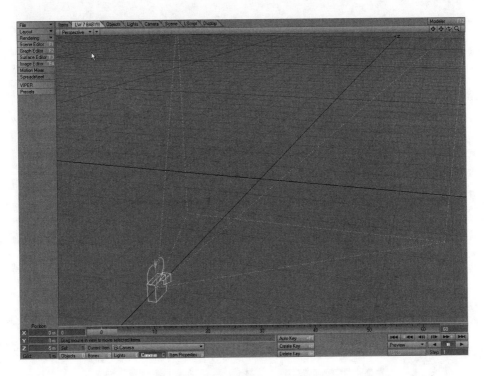

Figure 1.6   Menu groups can be customized, and new menu groups can be created to house only the specific tools you need.

Warning

To ensure that you can follow the exercises and projects in this book, please use the default program settings for all groups and menus unless otherwise specified. If you open the Configure Menus panel (press Alt and F10) and then select the Presets drop-down menu at the top right of the panel, you'll find the Default selection.

Multiple Viewport Configurations

The new Layout and Modeler offer more to you than simple customization. You also can work in any interface, in any mode, such as Wireframe, Sketch, or even Smooth Shaded. Figure 1.7 shows Layout with multiple independent views.

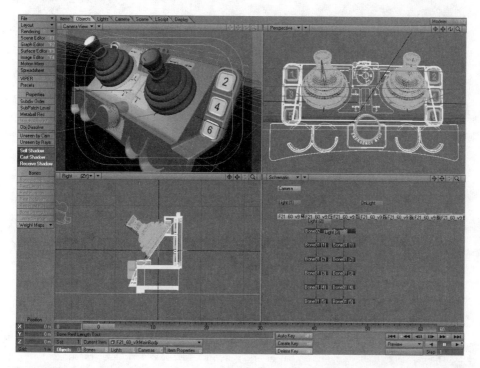

Figure 1.7   Layout now supports multiple independent viewports.

Viewports (or quadrants) in Modeler have multiple configurations and can have varying modes, such as Wireframe, Sketch, Weight Shade, and more. Access these modes by selecting your choice from the drop-down list in the Viewport title bar. Turn on the Viewport title bar through the Display Options panel (press the d key). Figure 1.8 shows the LightWave 7 Modeler with its four viewports reconfigured with various modes set to each view. You can do the same in Layout.

You can reconfigure the modes through the Display Options panel (the d key). However, if your title bars are active, you can quickly change each view without using the Display Options panel. This choice is yours.

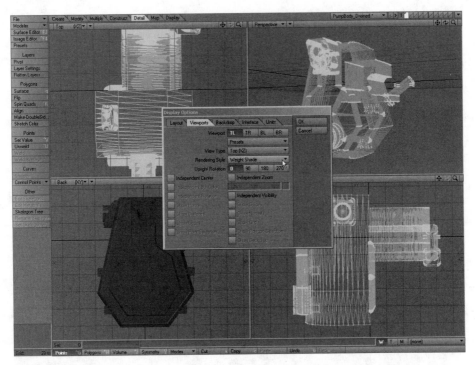

Figure 1.8 The viewports in this configuration of Modeler have a different mode set to each view.

Note

The capability to have multiple configurations in both Layout and Modeler means that you can make each viewport different. Each viewport's varying mode is its render style, such as Wireframe, Color Wireframe, Sketch, Smooth Shaded, Texture, and so on. You can easily select the Viewport Style by clicking the drop-down arrow atop each viewport, as in Figure 1.9.

Don't let the similarities between LightWave 7 and previous versions of the software fool you. The new user interface of LightWave 7 has much more to it than meets the eye. Over the years, NewTek has taken some heat for having two separate programs, Layout and Modeler, rather than one combined interface. By developing the HUB as the link and giving Layout and Modeler similar tools (such as the Surface Editor), NewTek has made LightWave easier to use. Having two programs allows your system resources to be better utilized and keeps the interface clutter to a minimum.

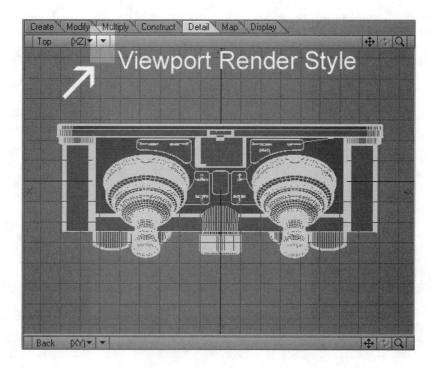

Figure 1.9   Each viewport can have its own specific render style, found in the small drop-down list, available in each viewport.

Schematic View

Within Layout's new viewport configurations is a welcomed addition for the serious animator. A Schematic view has been added to help aid in the organization of your scenes. A Schematic view, shown in Figure 1.10, is blueprint of your scene. Items within your scene are represented by colored boxes that you can arrange as you like. This can help show the overall flow of your scene as well as provide an instant way to select items.

Note

To access the Schematic view in Layout, click and hold the drop-down label at the top of the Layout display window to access the viewport display styles. You also can press the d key to access the Display Options panel, set up multiple viewports, and make one viewport your Schematic view. Figure 1.10 shows the selection.

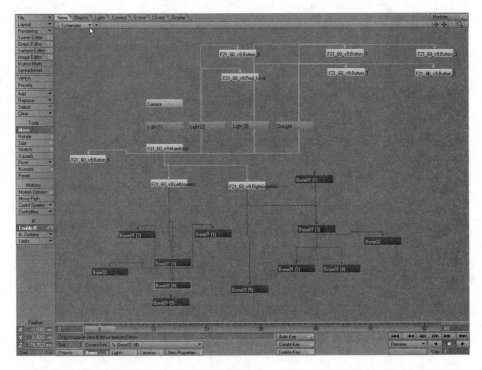

Figure 1.10   The Schematic view provides an outline of your scene, allowing you to select items, clear them, clone them, parent them, and set their wireframe color. You can make these changes by right-clicking an item in the Schematic view. Use Ctrl to parent items.

> **Tip**
>
> One of the coolest uses for Schematic view is setting parents for items. To parent in Schematic, select an item, such as an object or light. Hold the Ctrl key and click another item to set a parent relationship to that item. To unparent, hold the Ctrl key, and click a blank area of the screen. Additionally, you can use a multiple viewport configuration to show your Camera view, Orthogonal views, Perspective, and Schematic all at the same time. Pressing the a key while in Schematic view will "fit all" to view, just as it does in Modeler.

Additional controls for the Schematic view can be found in the Display Options panel by pressing the d key. You'll see the Schematic View tab at the bottom of the panel. Here, you can determine link variables and visibility options, as shown in Figure 1.11. Additional Schematic tools can be found directly in Layout by clicking on the Scene tab, and then choosing Schematic View Tools from the Generics drop-down list, as shown in Figure 1.12. The Schematic view is available only in Layout.

These tools include options for setting grid size, grid snap, and view types.

Figure 1.11   Controls for the Schematic view can be found at the bottom of the Display Options panel.

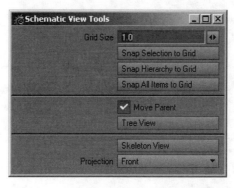

Figure 1.12   Additional Schematic tools can be found under the Scene tab in Layout.

Shortcut Navigation

Part of the power to reconfigure your user interface also includes the capability to hide all tools and access the commands through mouse and keyboard strokes. To hide the tools and reduce interface clutter, follow these quick steps:

1. Open Layout and press the o key to access the General Options tab.

2. Click Hide Toolbar.

3. Close the Options panel.

4. To access any of the buttons you've just hidden, hold down both the Control and Shift keys, and click the left mouse button. Or to take the more direct route, use Alt and the F2 key.

You will see a list of the file commands, such as Load Scene and Save Scene, and actions such as Load Object, Save Object, and so on.

Holding down the Control and Shift keys while clicking the right mouse button gives you access to window commands, such as Scene Editor or Graph Editor. Holding down the Ctrl and Shift keys also functions with the middle mouse button to access the Command History, selection options, as well as the Hide Toolbar command.

Using the mouse to access the hidden tools might take some getting used to, but the pay-off can be an uncluttered user interface. Figure 1.13 shows what's visible when you press Ctrl+Shift and click the left mouse button while working in Layout.

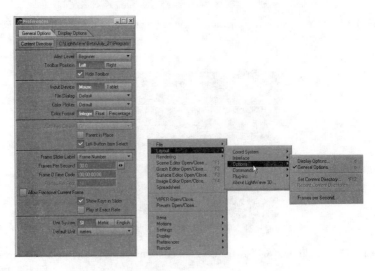

Figure 1.13   Holding the Ctrl and Shift keys and clicking the left mouse button brings up the shortcut navigations.

Redesigned Panels

In addition to the customizable menu groups or the easily configured viewports, the panels have been redesigned throughout the program as well. The panels in LightWave are the information areas you'll access often to control item properties, such as light or camera settings. You can have many panels open at once, which is where dual monitors come in handy.

Figure 1.14 shows the new Surface Editor panel, which looks similar to the other panels throughout the program, and is identical in both Modeler and Layout. Chapter 2, "LightWave 7 Surface Editor," is dedicated to enlightening you on the functionality of the new Surface Editor. If you take a look at Figure 1.15, you can see many panels open at once. You probably wouldn't have this many panels open at at the same time—you wouldn't be able to see your Layout! But keeping a few panels open while you work, such as the Surface Editor, Motion Mixer for nonlinear animation, or the Graph Editor, can be quite beneficial.

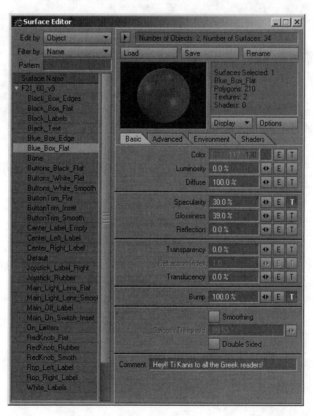

Figure 1.14   Here is Layout's Surface Editor panel. The panels throughout LightWave 7 are similar in design and functionality.

Note
In addition to keeping multiple panels open when you're using dual monitors, you also can keep them open during rendering. The main control panels—Scene Editor, Graph Editor, Surface Editor, Image Editor, Motion Mixer, and Spreadsheet—can always be found at the top left of the Layout interface. These are global functions used throughout the entire program.

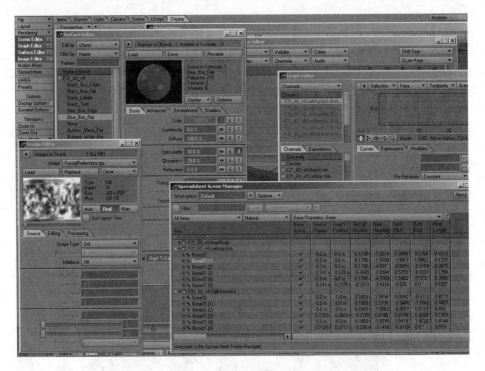

Figure 1.15   Layout now supports multiple independent panels that can remain open while you work.

Although the new panel design throughout the program appears streamlined, panels in version 7 are more functional than ever before. As you read on through this book, you'll discover how intuitive this new design truly is.

Notable Enhancements to Layout

Layout has many enhancements that can help you streamline your creative process.

Graph Editor

The Graph Editor within LightWave's Layout always has been the black sheep of the program—but no longer! Figure 1.16 shows the Graph Editor expanded to full screen for version 7.

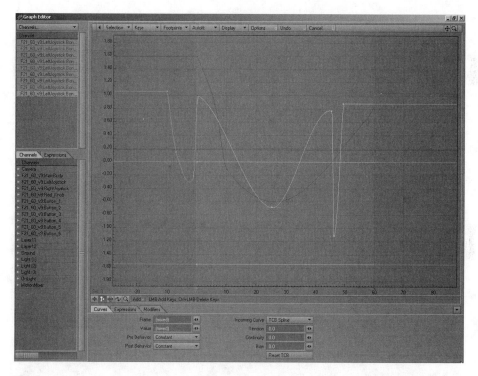

Figure 1.16   Here is LightWave 7's Graph Editor. You'll be spending a lot of time here.

With the new Graph Editor, you'll have more control over your motions than you'll know what to do with. Keyframes can be copied, pasted, and modified in a variety of ways. You can store sets of keyframes for use in other projects. You can adjust or set offsets by dragging entire groups of keyframes.

The Graph Editor supports multiple curve types in a single animation channel, such as TCB (Tension, Continuity, and Bias), Hermite, Bézier, Linear, and Stepped. The Graph Editor has a multiple curve evaluation and modification function so that you can have control over dissimilar items. For example, you simultaneously can view and edit any curve in a scene. With an interactive cut and paste of keyframes, you can adjust any keyframe within the scene with little time and effort. LightWave 7's Graph Editor is resizable so you can expand the window to full screen for maximum visibility. You also have the ability to collapse the left side of the Graph Editor as well as the bottom section, leaving only the curve area visible. You do this by clicking the small triangle in the bottom right of the curve area and the top left of the curve area. Conversely, you can squeeze the Graph Editor down and squeeze up Layout to have both on screen while you work, as in Figure 1.17.

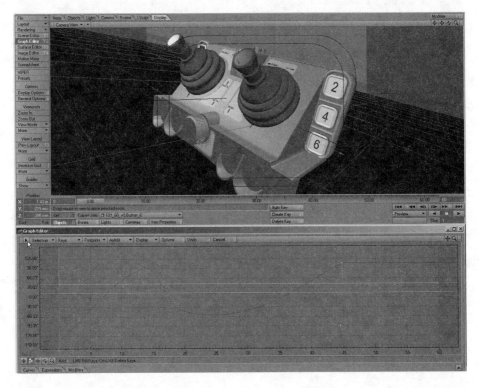

Figure 1.17   Use the Graph Editor to your advantage by keeping it open while working in Layout.

As you update your curves in the Graph Editor, your changes happen in real time in Layout. Are you thinking about setting up a dual-monitor system now? Okay, I'll stop bugging you.

Don't worry about how complex this new area of LightWave is; we'll discuss the Graph Editor in detail and step you through some tutorials in Chapter 5, "LightWave 7 Graph Editor." You'll be up to speed in no time.

Groups

Layout's new design is definitely confusing at first to new users. If you're familiar with a previous version of LightWave, you'll see that many of the controls buried within panels are now easily accessible from the left side of the screen. The many panel buttons across the top of the interface, such as Items, Objects, Lights, and so on, have been simplified. You now have seven default tabs, which are called *groups*, and are labeled Items, Objects, Lights, Camera, Scene, LScript, and Display, as seen in Figure 1.18.

Figure 1.18   The Default tabbed groups across the top of the Layout interface make tool access easy.

LightWave 7 Groups in Layout

Rearranging the groups and the tools within the groups can help you bring up a setting that is buried deep in the default interface, such as a generic plug-in you often use. You can create your own groups and assign only the controls and functions you like to that group. For example, try the following:

1. In LightWave Layout, select Clear Scene from the drop-down File menu at the top-left side of the screen.

2. From the Layout drop-down at the top left of the screen, select Interface and then Edit Menu Layout, as in Figure 1.19. You also can press Alt+F10 to access the panel.

Tip

> LightWave 7 has "sticky menus." What that means is anytime you need to click a small downward triangle on a button to display a list, you don't have to hold the mouse button down! Simply click once and let go—LightWave's menu set will "stick" open until your next selection.

Figure 1.20 shows the Configure Menus panel. The left column of the panel is home to the commands, or functions, and the right column, the menus. At the top of the panel, you can change your presets, such as default (LightWave 7 command style), 6.0 Style, or 5.6 Style menu configurations. Commands that are ghosted are already assigned to a menu or group; commands that are bold are not. Take a close look at the right column. The first item listed is Top Group. These are the group of command tabs along the top left of the Layout interface: File, Layout, Rendering, and so on.

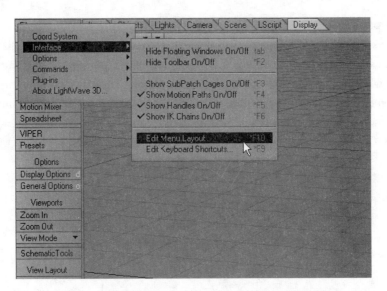

Figure 1.19   You can access the Configure Menus panel by selecting Edit Menu Layout.

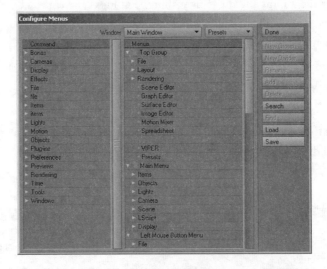

Figure 1.20   The Configure Menus panel pops up when you press Alt+F10.

3. Create your own group tab by selecting File on the right and then clicking the New Group button on the right side of the Configure Menus panel. You'll see that a line labeled New Group now sits between File and Layout at the top left of the interface.

4. Select the New Group listing in the Configure Menus panel, and then click Rename. Rename the group to whatever you like. Click OK, and you'll see the new group tab appear on the top of the Layout interface (see Figure 1.21). You can rearrange the groups by simply clicking and dragging them—you'll see a small line appear as a guide.

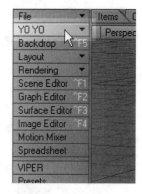

Figure 1.21
A new group now lives with the others at the top of the LightWave Layout.

You need to assign some commands to the group that you've just created. You can do this by first pressing Alt+F10 on the keyboard, then selecting a command in the left column (your desired Group in the right column), and then clicking Add. Or, you can drag a command to the menu window. Instantly, the command will now be included with the new group. Note that even if a command is ghosted, you can assign it to another location if you like. If you use the Display Options often, you might want to create a button or group for it on every tabbed area.

Note
At any time you can return to LightWave's default grouping configuration by pressing Alt+F10 to call up the Configure Menus panel and selecting Default from the Presets drop-down list. Once you're happy with the working configuration, quit Layout (or Modeler) and start up again. This saves the configuration for future use.

Creating a group is only one way to customize your Layout interface. You also can reconfigure the interface by adding or removing commands from existing groups and menus. In the right column of the Configure Menus panel, you'll see a small white triangle before each group. Clicking this expands the group, allowing you to see the commands set for each. You can add, remove, or even rename any one of these. Also you can save and load different configurations as you like. Click around, create new groups, and don't worry; you can always click Default to return to your original configuration. Play around and create some fun arrangements.

Note
These grouping instructions apply to LightWave Modeler as well, also by pressing Alt+F10. Configure menus in Modeler by selecting the Modeler drop-down list at the top left of the screen, selecting Interface, and then choosing Edit Menu Layout.

Tip

If you're adventurous, set up some new configurations for your co-workers. Or, simply rename and/or remove a button or two. It'll drive them mad!

Enhanced Layout Display Options Tab

Pressing the d key in both Modeler and Layout brings up the Display Options tab within the Preferences panel, shown in Figure 1.22.

The Display Options tab allows you to adjust, activate, or deactivate settings for LightWave Layout's appearance. At the top of the panel, you can tell Layout what the viewport should look like, such as a single panel or quad view. You also can set your favorite Viewport Layout as a default so that the next time you start LightWave, your settings will be applied. Figure 1.23 shows the drop-down menu choices for Viewport Layout settings.

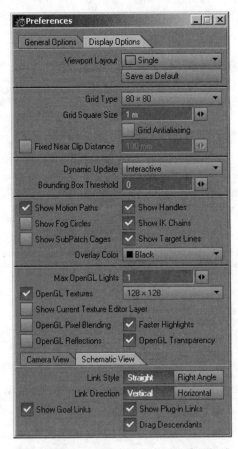

Figure 1.22   Pressing the d key in Layout brings up the Display Options tab within the Preferences panel.

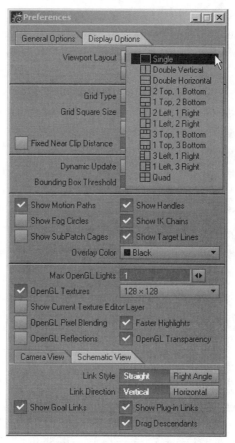

Figure 1.23   Within the Display Options tab, you can choose from many Viewport Layout configurations.

Grid Types

Within the Display Options tab in the Preferences panel, you can change the Grid Type and Grid Square Size, and set the Grid Antialiasing. Grid Type allows you to increase the size of the visible grid in Layout. This is handy for larger scenes such as landscapes, cityscapes, or space shots. Grid Square Size sets the individual grid square. For example, the default Grid Square Size is 1m. This means that every square within the visible Grid in Layout is 1 meter is size. This is extremely important when it comes to modeling and setting up surfaces, camera shots, and more. You'll reference the Grid Square Size throughout the tutorials in this book. Clicking on Grid Antialiasing eliminates the jagged lines often associated with the grid lines farther from view in Layout.

Fixed Near Clip Distance

When an object gets too close to the camera in Layout, it starts to clip, or become unseen. This doesn't affect the object or the final render, but it can be irritating when you are trying to work. By turning on Fixed Near Clip Distance in the Display Options panel, you can tell Layout the distance at which to begin clipping an object's visibility. The only other way to adjust for clipping is to change the grid size, which then affects your working environment. Fixed Near Clip Distance is a direct control for the "too close to camera" clipping problem.

Additional Controls

You have the option of choosing six check boxes and one selector for additional view properties:

- **Show Motion Paths.** Shows a visible line representing the motion of an object, light, or camera.

- **Show Fog Circles.** Shows a visual representation of the fog radius settings.

- **Show SubPatch Cages.** Shows the SubPatch cages of your objects created in Modeler with the Tab key.

- **Show Handles.** Displays the visible control handles of a selected item's X, Y, Z or H, P, B movements on items in the viewport that you can drag.

- **Show IK Chains.** Displays a thin dotted line in Layout, which represents the relative setup of your Inverse Kinematics (IK) chain. Figure 1.24 shows a Wireframe view of a simple IK robotic arm with Show Handles and Show IK Chains turned on.

- **Show Target Lines.** Displays a line from an item to its target, if a target item has been assigned.

- **Overlay Color.** Allows you to change the color of various overlays in Layout, such as the wireframe outline when the Show Safe Areas is selected.

Note

LightWave 7 allows you to load SubPatch objects directly into Layout. You no longer need to change the objects (or freeze the curves) into polygons. This means you can work with a low-data object for fast interaction, while maintaining a high-data object for superb renders. These controls are discussed in Chapter 4.

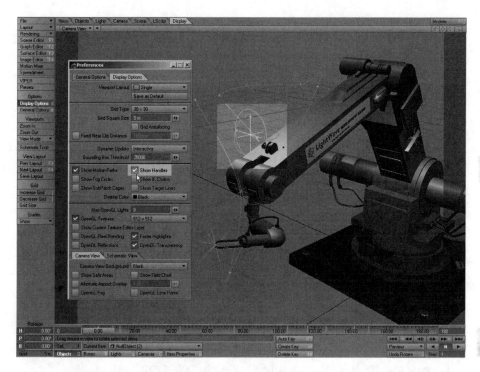

Figure 1.24   Setting Show Handles helps control each element's movements and direction during an animation.

When you select Show Handles and you select Move for the object, you'll see three arrows—one green, one blue, and one red—extending from the specific selection. You'll notice this throughout LightWave 7. Essentially, there are different handles for the Move, Rotate, and Stretch tools. The green arrow that points upward (for Move) is pointing toward the positive y-axis. Clicking and dragging it limits the selected items' motions to y-axis movements only. Similarly, clicking and dragging on the blue arrow (which points toward positive z) limits movements to just the z-axis. The red arrow points toward the positive x-axis, and limits movements to just the x-axis. This is very helpful and time-saving, compared to previous versions of LightWave in which you needed to lock and unlock the certain axes with which you wanted to work. If you want to have free movement in all axes, you can click and drag off of the pivot point of the joined arrows. Figure 1.25 shows a simple ball object with move handles showing.

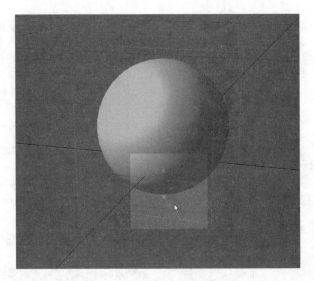

Figure 1.25   Selecting Move for any Layout item displays handles for axis control.

Like the handles that appear for movement of a Layout item, a rotation handle will appear as well. Figure 1.26 shows the same ball object when Rotate is selected. Clicking and dragging on the colored circular handles limits its axis rotations.

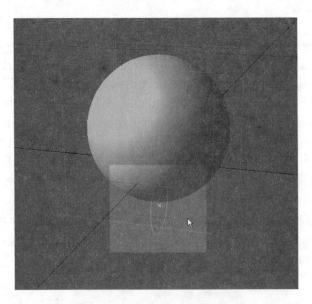

Figure 1.26   Selecting Rotate for any Layout item displays round handles for axis control. You can see them at the pivot point of the object because they are located at the base of the ball.

Additional Display Properties

Because LightWave 7 is essentially two programs, Modeler and Layout, users often confuse the function of each program. LightWave 7 integrates the two programs, yet each has very different functions. Each has display properties, as well, that can be similar in both Modeler and Layout.

For example, the Modeler portion of LightWave is where you create and build your models. You have full access to the Surface Editor in Modeler as well! The Layout portion of LightWave is where you set up your scene. Setting up a scene not only requires that your objects are in place, but that lights, textures, and atmospheres are set as well. Typically, you have to render a frame or two to see many of these settings. LightWave 7 Layout gives you the option to turn on OpenGL Textures (from the Display Options panel, press d) in your Camera view to see how your textures are being applied. Setting the Size (from the drop-down menu) tells LightWave the pixel resolution to display textures, from 64×64 to 1024×1024.

Note

Enabling Textures under the Display Options tab within the Preferences panel in Layout and setting a specific size has no bearing on your final render. This size setting is for display purposes only, but applies to all the settings that are available under the Display Options tab. The resolution of the textures when rendered depends on the initial resolution of the image map. This applies to all the OpenGL display options as well.

You also can Enable Reflection Mapping in Layout to view reflections on your object above 50 percent. If you have fog added to a scene, Enable OpenGL Fog under the Camera View tab turns on visible fog in Layout—a great timesaver. Enable Lens Flares allows you to see your lens flare settings in real time. You'll also see a button called Faster Highlights, which speeds up the display of specular highlights, but might make them less accurate.

If you're working with OpenGL-shaded objects in Layout, it's handy to see how the lights in your scene are working. Within the Display Options panel, you can tell LightWave to display up to eight lights when using OpenGL. You might have more than eight lights in a scene—perhaps as many as twelve. In each light's Properties panel, you can set Affect OpenGL, essentially telling Layout which light to use for OpenGL previews.

Note

As a rule, the Layout display settings for OpenGL Textures, OpenGL Reflection Mapping, and so on, are only approximations. You should get in the habit of test rendering everything before you commit to a final render.

Dynamic Update

In the center of the Display Options panel is a drop-down menu labeled Dynamic Update. Here, you can tell Layout to update interactively, with a delay, or not at all. Dynamic Update offers more control to you as an animator. If you are working with a strong computer system, a decent amount of system memory (RAM), and a powerful video card, setting Dynamic Update to Interactive will show you your panel changes instantly. For example, if you have the Surface Editor panel open and change the color of a surface on an object, you'll see the change right away. If your system resources are limited, having Interactive set might make panel adjustments sluggish. If you have a sluggish response, change your Dynamic Update setting to Delayed, which will not update Layout until you finish making changes within the panels. Or, you simply can turn this feature off. By doing so, your Layout display will update after any open panels are closed.

Bounding Box Threshold

A key Layout component is the Bounding Box Threshold. LightWave, by default, creates a bounding box, or bounding region to represent your object. Setting this value tells Layout when to draw bounding boxes for your objects and when not to. If you create an object that is 6500 polygons and need to see your texture placement in real time, set a Bounding Box Threshold value of 6501. Any object that is less than 6501 points or polygons will not be displayed by a bounding box and remain solid. Any object made up of more than 6501 points or polygons will be displayed by a bounding box when selected and adjusted. The value here is just an example and will vary depending on your models. Keep in mind that if your object is large in size, setting a larger Bounding Box value will slow down your system. This will affect all objects in a scene.

You can determine what Bounding Box Value to set by selecting the particular object in Layout, and pressing the w key. This brings up the Statistics panel for your scene. Or, with the current object selected, you can press the p key to call up the Object Properties panel to see its specific point and polygon values.

 Note

Often, the best way to work is with a Bounding Box Threshold set to 0. This gives you very quick feedback and redraw speeds in Layout. Also, Bounding Box is shown only when the object or view is moved or rotated.

Camera View Tab

A simple but notable new Display Options feature in LightWave 7 has to do with the Camera View Background in Layout. When you are in Camera View mode in Layout, you tell LightWave to show a blank background, a colored background, an image, or a LightWave preview file. These settings are handy for compositing, text and logo placement, or simple reference. The Alternate Aspect Overlay feature enables you to see an additional visible marker in Layout. This helps as a reference to your camera's visibility with set aspect ratios. Note that this overlay, like Safe Areas, is visible only through the camera panel. Show Safe Areas adds two rounded squares to the Camera view. These represent a video safe area (outer line) and a title safe area (inner line). Safe areas serve as valuable references when you are setting up animations for video or broadcast.

Schematic View Tab

With more control for your scene than previous versions, the Schematic view available in Layout has display controls found in the Display Options panel. In this tabbed area of the Display Options panel, you can specify your schematic view to have Straight or Right Angle link styles. This represents how the connecting lines are viewed between items in the Schematic view. These items can be listed in Horizontal or Vertical fashion. Additionally, you can set various visible properties, such as Show Goal Links (for IK), Show Plug-In Links (for items using plug-ins), and Drag Descendents (for parented items).

Notable Enhancements to Modeler

This section guides you through the many options and setup features available in LightWave 7 Modeler. You'll learn that having the capability to customize the interface is a great asset to your creative workflow. As you work through this book, you can refer to this section as a reminder.

The Modeler Display Options Panel

With the enhancements to each LightWave interface, you will find similar functions in both Modeler and Layout. Pressing the d key in Layout brings up the Layout Display Options tab within the Preferences panel, as previously discussed. The d key in Modeler also brings up the Display Options panel. This area allows you to set up and configure your Modeler interface. Figure 1.27 shows the Modeler Display Options panel.

This panel gives you complete control over Modeler's appearance, viewports, backdrop, interface, and the units of measurement. When the panel comes up, you'll see five tabs labeled Layout, Viewport, Backdrop, Interface, and Units.

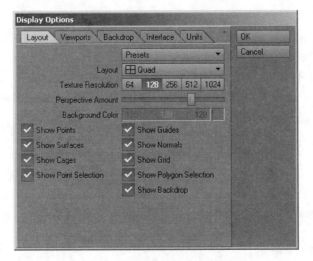

Figure 1.27   Pressing the d key in Modeler brings up the enhanced Modeler Display Options panel. Here the Layout tab is selected, referring to Modeler's Layout views, not to be confused with the Layout portion of LightWave.

Layout Tab

As a default, the Layout tab is selected. Here, you can set the initial layout of Modeler, such as a Quad view, Single view, Double Vertical, and more. Figure 1.28 shows the Layout drop-down selections from which you can choose.

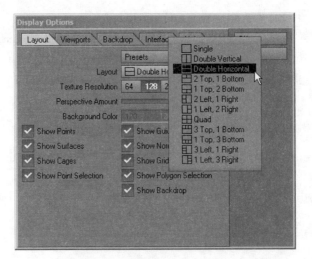

Figure 1.28   The Layout drop-down menu within Modeler's Display Options panel lets you select from many Viewport Layout options just like LightWave's Layout.

Directly above the Layout drop-down menu is a presets drop-down menu. This menu allows you to choose presets for your Modeler's layout, such as a Quad Logo (XY) view, which puts the XY or Back view in the bottom-left quad; the XZ or the Top view in the upper-left quad; and the ZY or Right view in the bottom-right quad. The upper-right quad is a Preview or Perspective view. Experiment with the presets to see some different configurations. Two important groups of options on this tab are as follows:

- **Texture Resolution.** These options let you set the resolution of surface textures visible in Modeler. This resolution setting is helpful for creating objects on images where there is fine detail. Setting a higher resolution here shows finer detail, but it will use up more system resources.

- **Perspective Amount.** This simple slider adds a wider or flatter view to your perspective window. Load up an object, drag this slider, and watch the results.

- **Background Color.** These options let you change the Background Color for all viewports. If you're an experienced LightWave modeler, you know that always working in a wireframe mode can sometimes slow you down. When you set any viewport in LightWave 7 to a shade mode, such as Wireframe Shade or Smooth Shade, you now will see the background color. This option is simple, but gives you the control you need to model better and faster.

More Display Options

Among the Layout tab options within the Modeler Display Options panel are nine additional selections that give you choices for greater control over your Modeler setup. Remembering that this is the Display Options panel, you have the choice to Show Points, Show Surfaces, Show Cages, or Show Point Selection, which are all display functions. Selecting or deselecting any of these settings will show the change in each Modeler view.

These Display options are visibility options that, depending on the model at hand, you might decide to use. For example, when working with a complex model, you can deselect the Show Surfaces option, which shows only the points of the object. Additionally, you can set Show Guides, which will help you see and work with your SubPatch cage better. Note that the more complex your model is, the less likely it is that you would use this function because it might clutter your view. Because this feature is independent of the cage, however, you can turn off Show Cages and work with only the guides to shape your model. The choice is yours!

Within the Display Options panel, you can turn the grid on or off for better visibility, use Show Normals to see in which direction your surface is facing, and also use Show Backdrop to view backdrop images. In addition, you have the option to Show Polygon Selection. Turning this feature off also turns off the visible yellow highlights that appear when a polygon is selected. You would do this to save time when selecting large, high-detail models. Models with an extreme amount of polygons can take time to redraw. Using this alternative, turning visibility on or off, saves time.

Note

Select Show Cages refers to SubPatch models. SubPatch will be discussed throughout the modeling chapters in this book. Chapter 3 will get you started.

At first, the multiple options available to you throughout Modeler and Layout might be overwhelming, but as you work through models and projects, you'll come to appreciate their control. Commonly, you'll use 20 percent of Modeler's tools 80 percent of the time, but it's good to know what else you can cut your teeth with!

Viewports Tab

The second tab option available to you within the Modeler Display Options panel controls the viewports. Although previous versions of LightWave Modeler didn't allow for much variation, LightWave 7 Modeler gives you independent viewport control. Figure 1.29 shows the Display Options panel with the Viewports tab selected.

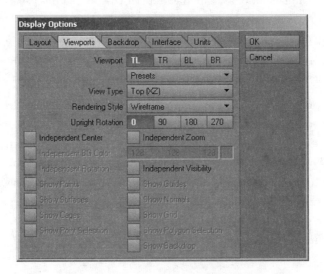

Figure 1.29   The Viewports tab in the Display Options panel allows for independent control over Modeler's viewports.

Note

Settings within the Viewports tab can override the global settings on the Layout tab, such as the Enable commands.

When you are working with a quad layout and have selected the Viewports tab, you'll see four selections across the top labeled (clockwise from the top-left viewport): TL (Top Left), TR (Top Right), BL (Bottom Left), and BR (Bottom Right). When you are not using a quad layout mode, names will be given to each viewport. You can customize each viewport in this area. Try it yourself by following these steps:

1. In LightWave Modeler, press the d key to call up the Display Options panel. Then, select the Viewports tab.

2. Select the first Viewport button, labeled TL. This controls the top-left quadrant, which until LightWave version 6, was typically the Top (XZ) view only.

    You can choose a preset for this quadrant from the drop-down preset menu list in the Display Options panel, or set up a customized viewport to your liking.

3. The third selection area from the top in the Viewport tab is the View Type selection. Use this area to determine whether the selected quadrant will be a Top (XZ) view, Bottom (XZ) view, or Perspective view. Choose Perspective view.

Tip

If you choose to set the current viewport to any of the orthogonal view types (Bottom XZ, Left ZY), the Upright Rotation options appear. Use these to rotate your view 90, 180, or 270 degrees. This is helpful for visual control depending on the model at hand.

4. Next, tell LightWave Modeler what Rendering Style to make the viewport. The choices are Wireframe, Color Wireframe, Sketch, Wireframe Shade, Flat Shade, Smooth Shade, Weight Shade, and Texture. Set the current viewport to Smooth Shade.

Note

To set the color for Color Wireframe rendering style, go to the tab labeled Detail from the main Modeler screen, then click Sketch Color from the commands on the left side of the interface. This also affects the Sketch rendering style.

Experiment with different options and different views. You will find that as your projects change, you'll appreciate the flexibility of configuring each viewport. But there is more control here for you to investigate. Read on to learn more.

Note

If you have Viewport Titles selected from the Interface tab, you can change the View Type
and Rendering Styles directly at the top of each viewport. This is enabled by default.

Display Options—Independent Controls

There are additional controls you can set for each viewport that go beyond the visuals
listed previously. LightWave Modeler understands independent control over each viewport. You have the choice of setting Independent Zoom, Independent Center, and
Independent Background Color and exercising independent control over the layout
visuals listed earlier, such as Show Guides, Show Surfaces, and so on. These "Show" settings are available only when Independent Visibility is enabled.

With Independent settings enabled, such as Independent Zoom, you can specifically
control keyboard commands by placing the mouse pointer in the specific viewport. If,
for example, Independent Zoom is active, you move the mouse into a viewport, and
press the period (.) key to zoom into the view, only the current viewport will zoom. If
you move the mouse pointer outside of this independent-enabled view, the zoom
function will apply to all views as it normally does. As you work, you'll discover which
settings work best for you, whether only select viewports are independent, wireframe,
shaded, and so forth.

The Backdrop Tab

Next on the list of tabs within the Modeler Display Options panel is the Backdrop tab.
Figure 1.30 shows the selection.

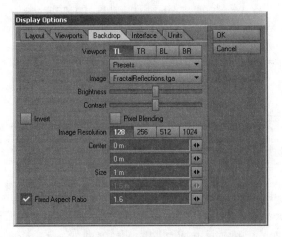

Figure 1.30   The Backdrop tab within the Display Options panel allows you to load images to
be placed in each viewport.

The Backdrop panel is straightforward. It allows you to load an image and select the viewport in which it will be seen. You would do this if, for example, you had to build a 3D logo from artwork or you needed to create a character from an artist's sketch. Within this panel, you can adjust the brightness and contrast and set the size and image resolution. You'll use this feature later in Chapter 3.

Note

If you are using the UV Texture view type, the render style drop-down list shows images that can be loaded into the specific viewport's background. This saves you the step of entering the Display Options panel.

The Interface Tab

The Interface tab has a few key functions for your working Modeler environment. This is the place to tell Modeler how good you are—at modeling, that is. You can choose an Alert level for various warnings, such as improper object vertices and so on. Also you can tell Modeler whether you're using a mouse or tablet input device in the Interface tab area. You can select the position of your toolbar—the right or left side of the screen. You also can turn off the toolbar, increasing Modeler's screen visibility.

The Interface tab has a few more options. These options, however, are often set and left alone.

- **Viewport Titles.** This feature should be on all the time. Having it on displays each viewport's ViewType and Rendering Style at all times. This means that you can quickly and easily change your perspective window from Smooth Shaded to Wireframe, or make it a Top view with Smooth Shaded, and so on. Having Viewport Titles on saves a lot of time by eliminating the need to go deep into panels and menus to make interface changes.

- **Fine Detail Cursor.** Checking this box leaves the cursor at the normal crosshair and doesn't change when you use different tools.

- **VBFileRequester.** This is LightWave's varied File Dialog requester when loading and saving elements such as objects or images. Figure 1.31 shows the default file requester for a Windows-based system. Figure 1.32 shows the new VBFileRequester option, using a more robust selection method.

Note

When using the VBFileRequester, you can choose to view your files as a list, or as icons, making navigation and selection fast and easy.

Figure 1.31   The Interface tab within the Display Options panel offers the choice of a standard system file requester by choosing default. Either PC or Mac, default uses your system's normal file requester.

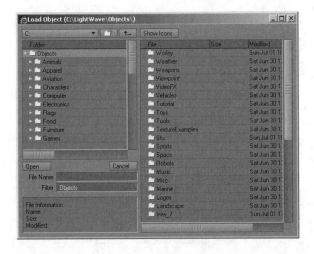

Figure 1.32   In addition to the default file requester, LightWave 7 offers a newer, visually enhanced file requester.

Tip

When using the new VBFileRequester in Modeler, you can resize the window for better visibility. Additionally, you can choose from a File view or Icon view. What's better, when using either your system file requestor or the VBFileRequester, you can load multiple objects into Modeler. When using the VBFileRequester, right-click on file names for additional controls. Remember that to right-click the Mac, you need to press and hold the Apple key.

- **LW_ColorPicker.** Along the lines of a newer file requester, you also can use the LightWave color picker instead of your system's standard color picker. This setting also is found under the Interface tab in the Display Options panel. Figure 1.33 shows a default Windows color picker, and Figure 1.34 shows the new LW_ColorPicker option.

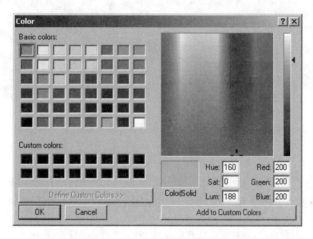

Figure 1.33   The default Windows color picker is available to you through the Interface tab in the Display Options panel. If you're working on a Macintosh, you'll see the default Mac color picker instead.

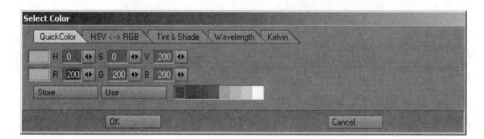

Figure 1.34   LightWave's new color picker offers much more control over the type of selection, such as this Quick Color view for instant RGB or HSV color values.

The LW_ColorPicker offers the Quick Color picker, as shown in Figure 1.34, or an HSV to RGB visual selector. In addition, you have the choice of Tint & Shade, Wavelength, or Kelvin. Using Kelvin as a color picker allows you to put in the degree of a Kelvin temperature, such as the sun, which is 6000 degrees Kelvin, or in technical terms, "really hot." This is an excellent way to match real-world lighting. Figure 1.35 shows the Kelvin color selection.

Tip

The Color Picker appears when you choose to edit colors from wherever there is a color selection swatch, such as the Surface Editor.

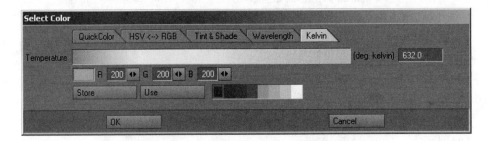

Figure 1.35 Using the new LW_ColorPicker, you can choose to set colors in degrees Kelvin to match real-world light temperatures.

- **Color Format.** The final option available to you under the Interface tab within the Display Options panel is the Color Format selection. You can choose between Integer, Float, or Percentage options. This affects the display units for color triplets. Integer is 0–255, Float is .00 to 1.00, and Percentage is 0 percent to 100 percent. These functions give you even greater control over the way Modeler handles your color selection. This color format changes the RGB/HSV color units and is shared through the HUB.

- **Simple Wireframe Edges.** This option allows you to decrease the number of lines drawn for wireframe views. This is helpful for cleaner display.

- **Simple Wireframe Points.** Turning this feature on gives you the option to increase the size of selected points. This is for better visibility, and easier selection when needed.

The Units Tab

Throughout this book, you'll be instructed to set specific measurements and refer to the Grid size often. To set up your Modeler with a unit of measurement, you can select the Units tab in the Display Options panel (see Figure 1.36).

The Units tab is important for you to understand. First, you have the choice of selecting a Unit System of measurement. Your choices are Metric, English, or SI measurement. SI is the System International unit of measurement, which is the recommended default setting. This measurement system uses microns, millimeters, meters, kilometers, and mega meters. You can choose any of these as your default unit. As you begin the tutorials later in the book, you should use the default unit of 1 meter, unless otherwise instructed.

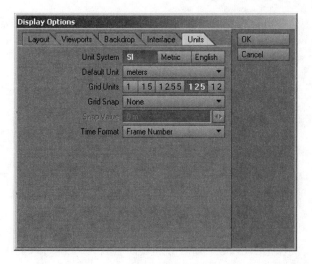

Figure 1.36   The Units tab within the Display Options panel enables you to set your system measurements.

You also can set the Grid Units in this tab area. You'll see settings of 1, 1 5, 1 2.5 5, 1 2 5, and 1 2. These settings refer to the way your grid increases or decreases when zooming in or out. If you set the Grid Unit to 1 5, for example, when you zoom in, your Modeler grid squares will increase by one, then five, then by one again, and so on. Lastly, you can define the Grid Snap as None, Standard, Fine, or Fixed. This is used for controlling your mouse movements while moving or dragging points and polygons. If you have a fixed value set, you can enter a setting of 1mm, for example. Dragging a point around in Modeler would make the point snap in place every 1mm. Use this setting for more precise modeling.

You also can set the Time Format for Frame Numbers, SMPTE Time Code, Film Key Code, and Time in Seconds to match your setup in Layout. This only affects how time is formatted when used in Modeler. You'll rarely use this feature.

 Tip

If you are modeling more organic objects, such as a character, you should turn the Grid Snap off. Having this feature enabled will hinder your control when shaping your curves by not allowing you to precisely position selections.

The Modeler General Options Panel

Earlier in this chapter, the General Options tab from the Preferences panel in Layout was discussed. Pressing the O key in Layout brings up the panel that allows you to change various settings for your Layout workflow. Although you'll visit the General Options in

Layout often, you'll only use the General Options in Modeler to set a few key options. Figure 1.37 shows the General Options panel in Modeler. Pressing o in Modeler also calls up this panel.

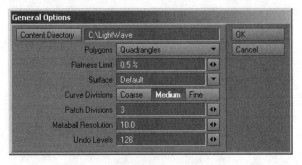

Figure 1.37   The General Options panel in Modeler gives you access to initial polygon creation values, curve divisions, as well as the Content Directory similar to Layout. You'll also find the all-important Undo Levels setting.

Polygons

The Polygons selection allows you to tell Modeler what type of polygons you would like to create, such as quadrangles or triangles. This is good for creating primitive shapes. As a recommended rule for this book, work with quadrangles. Why? Because you can always turn a quadrangle into a triangle by using the Triple command. You can turn triangles into quadrangles, but it's difficult to do, and it's time-consuming to work backward. Also you will have much better control over the shape and contour of your models in LightWave by working with quadrangles. (Quadrangles are simply polygons that are made up of four points. Triangles are made up of three points.) You also can set this option to Automatic, and Modeler will generate the necessary polygons depending on your model.

The other options within the General Options panel are usually set once, and most of your modeling is done with these variables. Try making a few objects with various settings to see the differences.

- **Flatness Limit.** When polygons are created, they have a general flatness to them. The Flatness Limit is the minimum angle before a polygon is considered nonplanar. You can change the value of this through the Flatness Limit option. In most cases, this value stays at its default of 0.5 percent.

Tip

Unless a polygon is perfectly flat (0 percent Flatness Limit in the General Options panel), you still can have render errors. Flatness Limit sets a usable threshold for those times when a polygon is likely to show errors.

- **Surface.** Each time you create polygons in Modeler, whether you create them from points, extrusions, or text, a default surface is applied. This default surface is typically slate gray and is named Default. If you choose, you can set a specific name to all default surfaces. Within the Change Surface dialog box (q), you can make any existing surface a default. You can find the Change Surface button under the Polygons tab. This default name will be applied to any unnamed surfaces. However, it's a good idea to leave this setting named "default" for clarity. If you decide to be clever and name your default surface something like "Cannoli," you can easily confuse things later when you add multiple surfaces.

Curve Divisions

When you build curves in Modeler for objects such as rail extrusions, you can set an initial Curve Division. As a common value, the Curve Division is left at Medium, but you also have the choice of Coarse or Fine. Depending on the complexity of your spline curve, you can set this value to increase or decrease smoothness of the curve.

Patch Divisions

This is the one area of the General Options panel that you will access regularly. When building objects with SubPatch (which will be discussed further in Chapter 3), you need to set the Patch Divisions. A SubPatch smoothes an object by subdividing the selected polygons. The Patch Division determines the amount of subdivision. Each region or patch of an object will be subdivided by the value you set in the General Options panel for Patch Division. For example, a Patch Division value of 4 will subdivide one selected polygon four times. A typical setting is about 3 or 4. The lower the value, the less smooth your object will be. The higher the value, the smoother and more complex your model will be. Patch Division also affects the smoothing you see in viewport displays.

Tip

LightWave 7 can load SubPatched objects into Layout for animating. There are two Patch Division settings in Layout as well, which can greatly help workflow. This feature allows you to set a Display SubPatch Level, which can be a low value to help save system resources. You can set a Render SubPatch Level for rendering for smoother objects. These settings can be set to any level.

Metaball Resolution

LightWave 7 has a creation method called Metaballs. Yes, there were Metaballs in previous versions of Modeler, but not as mature as the feature in this version. Think of a Metaball as a sphere of lava from a lava lamp—as it moves toward another Metaball, they begin to blend together and become one. A tip for using Metaballs is to see what HyperVoxels will look like. HyperVoxels, discussed later in the book, display only when rendered, except for when using LightWave 7's new Sprite display in Layout. HyperVoxels is part of LightWave's volumetric rendering engine. It allows you to render surfaces and volumes around points; it is great for use with particles. Metaballs appear in OpenGL. These Metaballs are interactive and definitely much more powerful. You can set a Metaball resolution in the Data Options panel. The default value is 10.0, but you can increase this value for smoother, cleaner Metaball shapes. Be sure to read more about Metaballs in Chapter 3.

Undo Levels

Undo Levels is a control that you really don't need to set more than once. Having the option to set undo levels is handy, but most likely you'll want to set Undo Levels to the highest level possible (128) and leave it there. For example, setting the undo level at 5 could be a mistake—what if you need to undo something you did 6 or 7 steps back? For best results, set this value to a high value. You never know when you'll need all the undo levels available to you.

When you quit Modeler, the value set here is recorded, and remains the same the next time Modeler is started. The only reason you'd need to set a lower undo level than the maximum of 128 would be due to memory problems. If you're working with larger objects and undo dozens of times, Modeler will use up memory to store the data. Most of the time, this is rarely a problem —jack up those undo levels!

Content Directory

If you're an experienced LightWave animator, you are familiar with the Content Directory in Layout. LightWave 7 has a Content Directory in Modeler. It tells LightWave where to look for scenes, objects, images, and any other necessary content. Because Modeler directly integrates with Layout through the HUB and you have complete surfacing control in Modeler, you need to set up a Content Directory. You need to set the Content Directory only once for both Modeler and Layout, as the HUB will update both programs for you.

The Next Step

When you are preparing to create, one last bit of advice is to be comfortable. Yes, it's been said before, but it is something that is often overlooked by animators and employers. 3D animation is one of the hottest growing markets in the world, from kiosks to video games to television and of course movies. It is a very creative industry and as any creative person knows, the surroundings and mood of your environment play a key role in your creative success.

So, turn off the nasty green overhead fluorescent lights, adjust your chair so you're not hunched over your keyboard, crank up the coffee pot, and head on into Chapter 2.

Summary

You've just been through the key preparation and configuration you'll need to get rolling in LightWave 7 Layout and Modeler. The similarity between the two programs will help you greatly, even when it comes to keyboard commands.

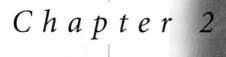

Chapter 2

LightWave 7
Surface Editor

What was the first thing that piqued your

interest in 3D? Was it a movie? Maybe it was

a video game. Perhaps you took a class in

school, or a friend or colleague introduced

you to 3D. Whatever the case may be, it is often the realism of 3D animation that is so eye-catching. Realism in 3D is created by two key factors, lighting and surfacing. Both of these factors play an extremely important role throughout your 3D creations, and they will help bring your animations to life.

This chapter introduces you to LightWave 7's Surface Editor. Specifically, you will learn about the following:

- Organizing surfaces
- Setting up surfaces
- Working with image map references on surfaces
- Using the Image Editor

If you are familiar with the Surface Editor in previous versions of LightWave, you'll find the Surface Editor not that much different, but definitely improved. Figure 2.1 shows the Surface Editor interface at startup.

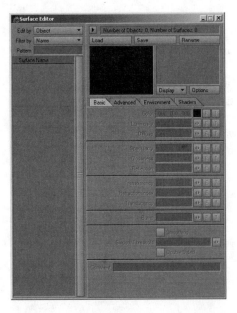

Figure 2.1   This is LightWave 7's Surface Editor at startup.

LightWave 7's Surface Editor is part of the software you'll use often. In LightWave versions previous to 6.0, the process of setting up surfaces for your models began in Modeler, when you were building the models. You could make only basic surface changes in Modeler, which meant essentially just naming selected polygons. From there, you needed to apply any image maps or procedural textures in Layout. Now you have the choice of using the Surface Editor in either Modeler or Layout. The panel is the same in both programs, so this chapter applies to both Modeler and Layout.

You'll always find the Surface Editor in Modeler at the top left side of the interface. The Surface Editor button is the third button from the top (see Figure 2.2).

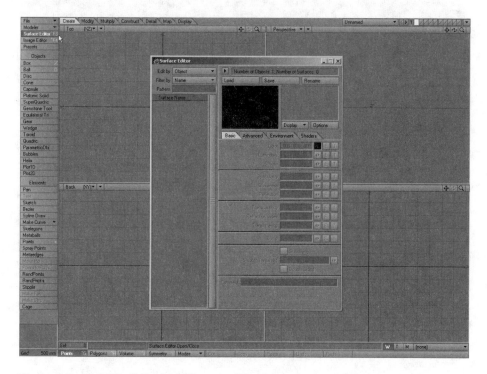

Figure 2.2   LightWave's Surface Editor can always be accessed at the top left in Modeler.

When you access the Surface Editor in Layout, you'll also find it at the top left side of the interface, but it's the sixth button from the top (see Figure 2.3). You also can press Ctrl+F3 in both Modeler and Layout to access the Surface Editor panel.

Tip

Using the Surface Editor in Modeler does not give you access to LightWave's VIPER (Versatile Interactive Preview Render), which is discussed in detail later in this chapter. So for major surfacing projects, use the Surface Editor in Layout and take advantage of VIPER. VIPER requires rendered data to work, and you can only render in Layout. VIPER uses information stored in LightWave's internal buffers for instant feedback.

Note

Remember that LightWave 7 enables you to customize completely the user interfaces in both Modeler and Layout. However, you should be working with the LightWave default Configure Keys (Alt+F9) and Menu Layout (Alt+F10) settings throughout this book.

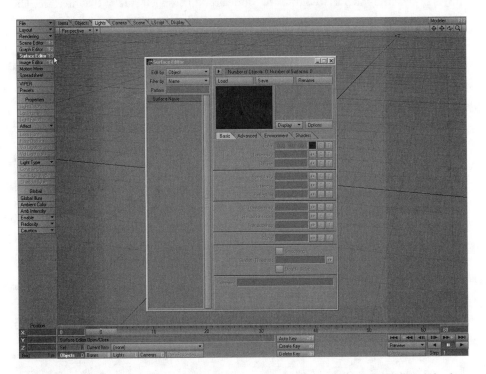

Figure 2.3   You access the Surface Editor in Layout by clicking the button in the top left of the interface.

Using the Surface Editor

As you begin to explore and use the Surface Editor either in Layout or Modeler, you should be familiar with its features. Enhancements have been made to make surfacing your objects easier.

Organizing Surfaces

The Surface Editor makes it easy for you to manage your surfaces. Figure 2.4 shows the Surface Editor with an object loaded that has multiple surfaces.

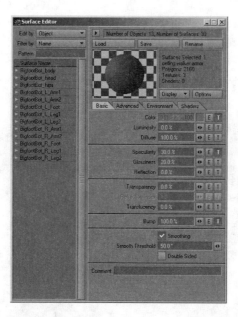

Figure 2.4   The Surface Editor allows you to manage your surfaces easily, on an Object or Scene basis. You also can Filter your surface names for organization.

If you enter the Surface Editor after a scene has been loaded, the scene's surface names are listed alphabetically, as you can see in Figure 2.4. The Surface Name list enables you to manage your surfaces easily by grouping individual surfaces in a drop-down list for each object. Clicking the small triangle next to the object name expands the list, showing the surfaces associated with that object. Figure 2.5 shows the same scene as in Figure 2.4, but with a surface of the first object selected. Note that in this setup, Edit By Object is selected, which lists the surfaces with their appropriate objects.

When you display a surface list of an object, your surface settings, such as color, diffusion, or texture maps, won't be available until you click a surface name. You must select one of the surfaces in the list before you can begin to work with it. When you select a surface, you see the surface properties change. Working with a hierarchy like this is extremely productive, enabling you to access quickly any surface in your scene.

Figure 2.5
Surfaces are grouped with their respective objects when Edit By Object is selected.

LightWave 7's Surface Editor allows you to collapse the Surface Name list, saving desktop real estate. Figure 2.6 shows the way the Surface Editor appears when you collapse the Surface Name list. When the list is collapsed, you can choose your selected surface through the drop-down selection at the top of the list, as Figure 2.7 shows.

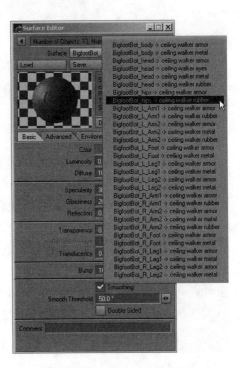

Figure 2.6 Click the small triangle at the top of the Surface Editor to collapse the Surface Name list.

Figure 2.7 Select surface names in a collapsed view by using the Surface drop-down list.

Selecting Existing Surfaces

Do you like to be in control? If so, that's good, because LightWave 7 is *all* about control. The program gives you these three modes to aid you in quickly selecting the surface or surfaces you want:

- Edit By
- Filter By
- Pattern

Note

On a larger scale, the Edit By feature is not really so much about how you select surfaces, but rather determining whether they are global to the scene or local to the object. Depending on which one you select, the options available to you will change—but don't get used to changing the Edit By mode just to change the options that are listed. Also, remember that if you are working with the Surface Editor and have the surface name list collapsed, you won't have access to the Edit By feature.

The Edit By mode, found in the top-left corner of the Surface Editor panel, has two selections: Object and Scene. You use the Edit By mode to tell the Surface Editor to control your surfaces by either Objects or the Scene. For example, suppose that you have 20 buildings in a fantastic-looking skyscraper scene and eight of those buildings have the same surface on their faces. If you choose to Edit By Object, you would need to apply all the necessary surface settings eight times.

Tip

LightWave saves the Edit By setting from session to session. You might accidentally overwrite previously saved surfaces by switching between Edit By Object and Edit By Scene settings. To avoid this, always make each surface name unique.

In contrast, you can set the Edit By feature to Scene, and the changes you make will be applied to any surface with the same name in the scene, which requires you to set the surface only once. This means that in the case of the 20 buildings with eight identical surfaces, one setting will take care of all eight surfaces. For this reason, be sure to name your surfaces accordingly when building objects; this way, there is no confusion when using the Surface Editor. In addition, creating and naming surfaces properly in Modeler makes surfacing easier and you end up using the Edit By feature as an organization tool, not a search engine.

Note

Any surface settings you apply to objects are saved with the object. Remember to choose Save All Objects as well as Save Scene. Objects retain surfaces, image maps, color, etc.; Scenes retain motion, items, lighting and so on. Be sure always to save both objects and scenes before you render. Make it a habit.

In the top-left corner of the Surface Editor panel, you'll see Filter By listing. Here, you can choose to sort your surface list by Name, Texture, Shader, or Preview. Most often, you'll select your surfaces by using the Name filter. Suppose, for example, that you have 100 surfaces and out of those 100, only two have texture maps. Instead of scrolling through a long list of surfaces, you can quickly select Filter By and choose Texture from the drop-down list. This displays only the surfaces that have textures applied. You also can select and display surfaces that use a Shader, or Preview. Preview is useful when working with VIPER because it lists only the surfaces visible in the render buffer image.

Below the Filter By setting, you see a space for typing a pattern. Pattern enables you to limit your surface list by entering a specific name. The setting works with Filter By. Think of Pattern as an "include" filter. Any surface that does not "include" the Pattern won't show up in the Surface list. Have you ever created an object with multiple surfaces and found yourself wasting time looking for one of those surfaces? You probably spent quite a bit of time scrolling up and down a Surface list, but now you can simply type in a keyword. For example, suppose that you created a scene with 200 different surfaces. You have six surfaces named carpet, and for some crazy reason you can't find them. By entering "carpet" into the Pattern requester, only the surfaces named carpet will appear in the Surface Name list. Pretty cool, eh?

Working with Surfaces

After you select an existing surface, you are ready to work with it. LightWave has four commands at the top of the Surface Editor panel that are fairly common to software programs: Load, Save, Rename, and Display.

The first command, Load, does what its name implies: It loads surfaces. You can load a pre-made surface and quickly apply it to a new surface or even modify it. For example, you made a shiny silver surface for a corporate client and you know that this client comes in every quarter and wants a big animated silver metallic logo. The client tells you "make it just like last time!" and you suddenly draw a blank. By having that surface saved, you can load it and not have to worry about matching something you did three months earlier.

The second command, Save, tells the Surface Editor to save a file with all the settings you've set. This includes all texture maps, bump maps, image maps, and so on. Having the capability to save your surfaces is handy because you can create an archive of surfaces. For example, suppose that you've been working hard to surface a nice wood-planked wall, and it took hours of tweaking to make it look just right. You can reuse this surface again on different objects. To do so, you need to first save the surface.

Note

A visual representation is always a good choice for previewing surfaces, over just a text listing. Because LightWave 7's Preset Shelf saves and organizes all your surface samples, it might be more productive to use it instead of Save because with the Preset Shelf you can see what your saved surfaces look like. The Preset Shelf, which is found in the upper-left portion of the Layout window (11 buttons from the top), is discussed in more detail later in this chapter.

Often, you'll create a complex object with dozens, even hundreds of surfaces. This, again, stresses the importance of organization. With the third command, Rename, you can rename any of your surfaces. This helps you keep things in order.

The fourth command is Display. While you're working with the Surface Editor, you'll often want to see how your surface and textures are coming along. Without going through the process of a full-frame render, you can simply glance at the Display window at the top of the Surface Editor interface. There you can see your surface changes instantly. This is useful especially for luminosity and specularity, as well as for procedural texture settings.

In some cases, however you might need to look at these or other channels independently. The Display command allows you to choose the type of display you'll see. Figure 2.8 shows a sample surface in the Display window.

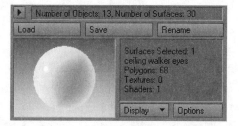

Figure 2.8   The Display window within the Surface Editor can show you your selected surface.

The drop-down list for the Display command offers many choices, the first of which is Render Output mode. This is the default display, and it is the most common. The Render Output mode shows what the rendered surface will look like. This includes color, texture, bump, and any other surface settings you've added. Figure 2.9 shows the full surface sample of a loaded object, with Render Output selected in the Display drop-down list.

Figure 2.9   Choosing Render Output as the Display shows the current surface's attributes, such as Color, Diffuse, Specularity, and Glossiness.

Perhaps you have a situation in which you don't want to preview the entire render output in the Surface Editor's display window. Maybe you just want to see the Color Channel. You can do this by selecting the Color Channel option from the drop-down list (see Figure 2.10). The Color Channel shows the color component of the surface. This component can be a texture image, gradient, procedural, or a combination. You'll see that color appear, rather than a complex surface with specularity, bumps, and more. Being able to select only the item you want to display enables you to concentrate on a specific aspect of a surface.

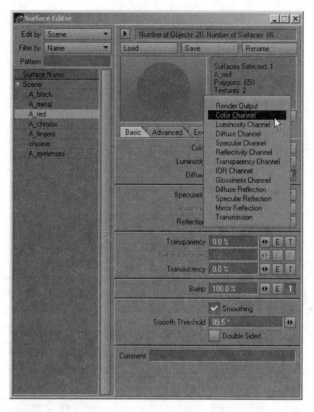

Figure 2.10   The same surface in the Display window with the Color Channel selected. Notice that the bump texture and specularity do not display as in Figure 2.9.

Selecting the Luminosity Channel shows only the amount of luminosity of the surface, as shown in Figure 2.11. If you are using a procedural texture for luminosity, you might want to display just the Luminosity Channel.

Note

Except for Render Output and Color, all the channels are grayscale, with pure white representing 100 percent of that surface attribute and black being 0 percent.

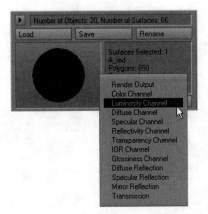

Figure 2.11   The same surface in the Display window with the Luminosity Channel selected. No luminosity is set for the object, so you will not see anything in the Display other than a black circle.

When creating surfaces, you can use LightWave's Preset Shelf to save and load surfaces visually and instantly. In the top left of the Layout window, click the Presets command to open the Surface Preset panel (see Figure 2.12). To save a surface to the Preset shelf, double-click the display window, and the currently selected surface is added. To copy a surface setting from the Surface Preset panel to another selected surface, first select the new surface name in the Surface Editor panel, and then double-click in the preset surface in the Surface Preset panel. Double-click in the preview window to use the Save Surface Preset function. Be sure to have the Preset window open so that you can see the saved surface. Presets are found in the left side of the interface. Double-click that surface preset to load it to a new surface. Similarly, you can right-click the preview window for additional options such as Save Surface Preset.

If you right-click in the Surface Preset panel, you can create new libraries for organizing your surface settings. You also can copy, move, and change the parameters.

Setting Up Surfaces

The main functions you use to set up and apply surfaces in the Surface Editor are located under four tabs. These tabs are Basic, Advanced, Environment, and Shaders (see Figure 2.13).

Each tab controls varying aspects of the selected surface. This section introduces you to the most commonly used tab areas—the Basic and Environment tabs.

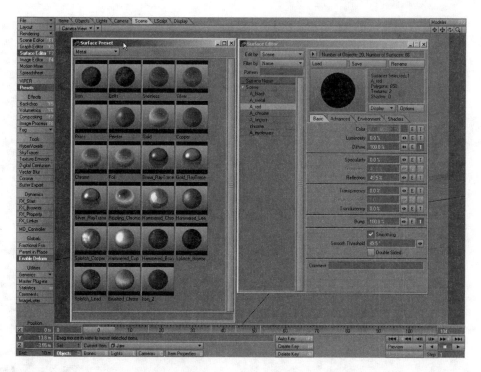

Figure 2.12   The Surface Preset panel is home to a number of NewTek-provided surfaces, as well as any you decide to add.

Tip

As a quick reference, keep the LightWave Reference Manual available while working through this book's tutorials.

Aptly named, the Basic tab is home to all your basic surfacing needs. These are the most commonly used surface attributes, and they usually act as a basis for any advanced, environmental, or shaded surface (see Figure 2.14).

Within the Basic tab, you can assign the following:

- **Color.** The color of the selected surface.
- **Luminosity.** The brightness, or self-illumination of a surface.
- **Diffuse.** The amount of light the surface receives from the scene.
- **Specularity.** The amount of shine on a surface.
- **Glossiness.** The spread of the shine on a surface. A High-Glossiness setting keeps the specularity, or shine, to a tight hotspot, similar to glass.

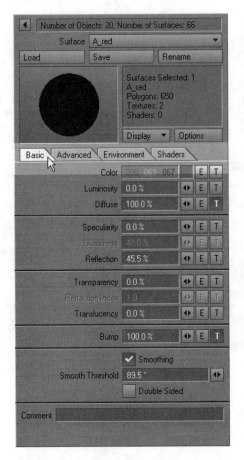

Figure 2.13 The Surface Editor consists of four primary tabbed areas of control.

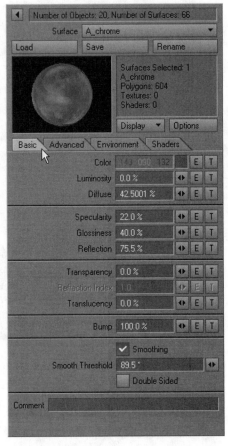

Figure 2.14 The Basic tab area in your Surface Editor is home to the most common surface settings.

- **Reflection.** The amount of reflection of a surface.

- **Transparency.** The amount of transparency in a surface.

- **Refraction Index.** The amount of light that bends through a surface, such as water or glass.

- **Translucency.** The ability of light to pass through a surface, such as a thin leaf or piece of paper.

- **Bump.** A visual displacement based on procedural textures or image maps.

- **Smoothing.** A shading routine to make a surface appear smooth.

- **Smooth Threshold.** This is how much smoothing will be applied to the surface. Generally, the default of 89.5 is too high.

- **Double Sided.** The placement of a front or back on single-sided surfaces.

- **Comment.** Make notes for particular surfaces as reminders or more detailed descriptions.

If you were familiar with LightWave 1.0 through 5.6, you'd know to click the Reflection Options button next to Reflection for setting values. In LightWave 7, that option has been replaced by Environment, an entire tab of settings (see Figure 2.15).

Remember, Reflection tells a surface to reflect its surroundings, like a mirror or piece of glass. Refraction, on the other hand, is the bending of light, such as light through a thick window or a glass of water. Both reflection and refraction look to their surrounding environments.

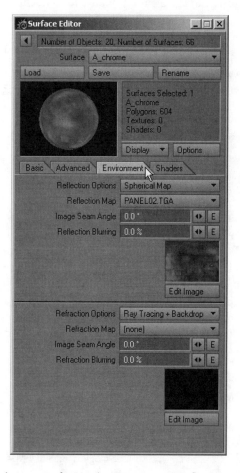

Figure 2.15   The Environment tab area gives you access to reflection and refraction controls.

Within the Environment tab, you can assign the following:

- **Reflection Options.** The type of reflection applied to a surface, either spherical, raytrace, or backdrop.
- **Reflection Map.** What image will be reflected.
- **Image Seam Angle.** You can control where the seam of a reflected or refracted image will appear.
- **Reflection (and Refraction) Blurring.** The amount of blur your reflections and refractions will have.
- **Refraction Options.** The type of refraction applied to a surface, either spherical or raytrace.
- **Refraction Map.** The image file used (if any) for refraction.

Note

Take a moment and play with the Reflection and Refraction blurring options, which are brand new to LightWave 7.

The best way for you to get a feel for using the Surface Editor and the Basic and Environment tabs is to try them out for yourself. For an excellent way to observe the effect of the settings you choose, use the LightWave 7 VIPER feature.

Exercise 2.1   Using VIPER with Basic Surfacing

VIPER was a new feature introduced in LightWave 6 that many users have learned to appreciate. LightWave 7 has improved VIPER's usefulness. VIPER stands for Versatile Interactive Preview Render. This feature gives a preview of your scene within certain areas of adjustments in Layout, such as Volumetric settings or the Surface settings. It's important to point out that because VIPER does not do a full-scene evaluation, some aspects of your surfacing are not calculated, such as UV Mapping and shadows. However, VIPER is very useful for most of your surfacing needs such as color and texture. As you adjust your surfaces, you'll be able to see what's happening without re-rendering and know how the object's surface looks. VIPER is available in Layout only.

Note

With LightWave 7, VIPER has been separated from the various plug-ins from which it used to be called. Now it is a more general server, which is why the button has been moved onto the main interface from the Surface Editor. The controlling client depends on the active plug-in. This setup will allow a greater number of plug-ins to use VIPER. Some of these plug-ins are, of course, surface plug-ins such as Hypervoxels or Volumetrics.

Note

Surfacing objects can be as simple or as complex as you want. A key role in how your surfaces appear when rendered has to do with the light and surroundings in the 3D environment. In this chapter, you learn about the key features in the Surface Editor. Later in the book you will use these techniques, along with proper lighting, for realistic-looking 3D images.

To get an idea of how useful VIPER is, try this quick tutorial:

1. Start Layout, or if it is already running, select Clear Screen from the File drop-down menu at the top left of the Layout screen (or press Shift+n). Be sure to save any work you've completed thus far.

2. Load the CD.lws scene from the Chapter 2 folder within this book's CD Projects directory.

   The image shows a couple of music CD cases sitting on a simple set. The scene is lit with basic stage lighting.

Note

You don't always need to clear the scene before loading a scene. Simply loading a scene overrides your current scene. This two-step process is here to familiarize you with the available tools and Layout's workflow.

3. Click the VIPER button found in the upper-left area of the Layout window (see Figure 2.16).

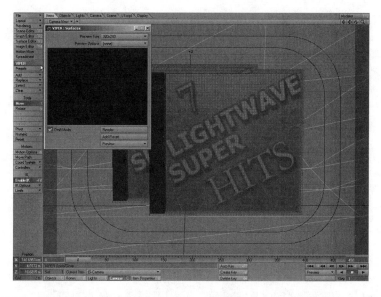

Figure 2.16   The VIPER command is always found in Layout in the top left of the interface.

4. With the VIPER window open, click the Render button at the bottom of the panel. Nothing happens. Click the Surface editor button from the left of the interface, and then click the Render button again from VIPER. An error will appear stating the VIPER has no surface data to render.

This is normal. VIPER needs you to render a frame so that it can store information from a buffer; otherwise, VIPER has no idea what's in your scene.

5. Press F9 to render a single image of the current frame.

6. Once the frame renders, press the ESC key to close the Render Status window. Then, click the Render button again in the VIPER window. You'll see your last rendered frame appear.

Note

Be aware that VIPER opens using the last client that accessed it during the session. (A client is a part of Layout that uses VIPER.) This means that if you just started LightWave, VIPER won't show surface previews until you display the Surface Editor and render a frame (F9). If you had last used VIPER with, say, Volumetric Lights, it would open in that mode. Remember that you can update VIPER by simply rendering a frame while using the desired client.

Note that the covers of the CD will be black because VIPER does not show transparency. Because of this, the CD's cover, which is transparent, is also a separate object that can be dissolved out. Figure 2.17 shows the VIPER window, now with buffer information of the render, such as specular, diffuse, color, and more. The cover case of the CD object is set up like a transparent plastic.

Figure 2.17 Pressing F9 renders the current frame and stores the information in LightWave's internal buffer. Because of this, you can see your surface changes through VIPER.

7. Select the LWCD_Set surface from the Surface Name list within the Surface Editor. You might need to expand the LW_CD_Set object by clicking the small white triangle to the left. This is the surface of the background object.

You'll see the surface settings appear throughout the commands on the right, on the Basic tab. The T button, which stands for Texture, is available throughout LightWave. Here in the Surface Editor, you can apply a texture map to every surface property.

8. Click the T button to the right of the Color listing to enter the Texture panel for the LWCD_Set surface. Take a look at the existing surface settings.

You'll see that the Layer Type at the top of the commands is set to Procedural. A procedural texture is computer-generated, meaning that it has no end, no seams, and can often be just what the doctor ordered for organic-looking surfaces.

The Blending Mode is set to Normal, which tells LightWave to add this procedural texture to the selected surface.

The Layer Opacity is set to 100 percent, telling LightWave to use this procedural texture to the fullest extent.

The Procedural Type is set to Fractal Noise, used by LightWave animators for years.

Adding Fractal Noise to the current surface color of the set, which is a dull gray, adds color variances to the surface.

9. Make sure the VIPER window is open and visible to the side of the Texture Editor.

If VIPER is not open, click the VIPER button on the left side of the Layout interface. You rendered the scene in step 5, and LightWave remembers that by storing the data in its internal buffers.

10. Now you can make changes to surface settings and see your changes in real time. Figure 2.18 shows the two panels open.

Note

Remember that if you change the Preview Size resolution in the VIPER window, you'll need to re-render the image by pressing F9.

11. Make certain that the Texture Editor is still open (you got to the Texture Editor by clicking the T button next to Color in the Surface Editor).

12. The Procedural Fractal Noise texture was a little too busy, so you need to change some of the parameters—in this case, Size, found under the Scale tab at the bottom of the Texture Editor panel. Click and drag the X, Y, and Z values, and watch VIPER redraw your image with the surface changes.

13. Experiment with the other procedural settings for Fractal Noise. From there, try to use other procedurals and adjust their properties as well. Save any of your settings you come up with for later use!

Note

To the left of the Texture Color setting in the Texture Editor window is a small square display. This area shows your procedural pattern. The base background color for the procedural is black. When combined with a dark Texture Color, this makes a very hard-to-see swatch. To make the swatch more visible, right-click the swatch, and set a new background color. Figure 2.19 shows a close-up of the setting. Mac users, remember to use the Apple key along with the mouse for right-mouse button commands.

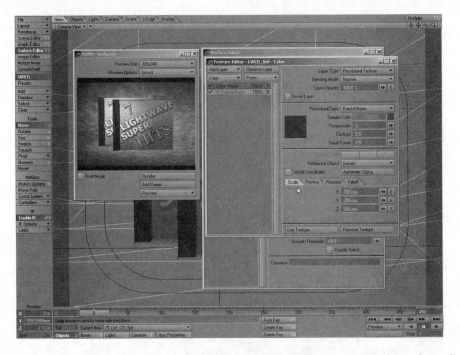

Figure 2.18   Because you made a render of a frame (F9), VIPER now can display the render, and you can make surface changes in the Texture Editor (among other places) and see them in real time.

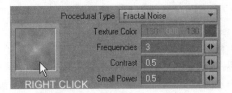

Figure 2.19   You can change the base background color for your procedural texture display by right-clicking in the display window.

Tip

When setting up procedural textures, you can right-click the Display window to change the background color display of the procedural. In addition, you can click with the left mouse button on the Display window and drag the preview around. Doing this helps you see more of the procedural pattern.

VIPER will quickly become one of your best friends *inside* LightWave 7 (no pun intended!). VIPER saves you time. And beyond that, many of you are not mathematical wizards and do not know what every value means within the surface settings. Explaining all these values would defeat this book's purpose—to teach you LightWave. Using VIPER can answer many of your questions when it comes to surfacing because you can instantly see the results from changed values. It's likely that during your practices, you'll utter a loud "Oh, *that's* what that does!" from time to time.

Final VIPER Tips

Here are a few more VIPER tips before you move on:

- Never trust VIPER as your final render. That is to say, if something looks odd, always make a true render (F9) for final surfacing.

- You can use VIPER to see animated textures by selecting Make Preview from the Preview drop-down list in the VIPER window.

- Pressing the ESC key will abort a VIPER preview in progress.

- Clicking Draft Mode on the VIPER window helps decrease redraw time.

- Clicking on a particular surface in the VIPER window will instantly select it in the Surface Editor's Surface Name list. This is a great feature in that it can save a lot of time on complex textured scenes.

- Lastly, VIPER is available only in Layout, not Modeler.

Using the Environment Tab Settings

To take you even further into the Basic tab of the LightWave 7 Surface Editor, try the following exercise.

Exercise 2.2   Creating Everyday Surfaces

You often may have a project that requires you to use, for instance, a vehicle, machine, or household item. This could be an object that you've created yourself, or purchased from third-party companies such as Viewpoint Corporation (*http://www.viewpoint.com*) or

Zygote (*http://www.zygote.com*), or downloaded from public archives on the Net. Follow these steps to apply a simple reflection to a surface:

1. Be sure to save any work you've completed thus far. Start Layout, or if it is already running, choose File, Clear Scene.

Note

At this point, it's a good idea to assign LightWave's Content Directory to the book's CD. Insert this book's CD into your computer's CD-ROM drive. You can either install the project files, or if you'd prefer to work from the CD, click the Cancel button if the CD auto-starts. Press the o key in Layout to access the General Options tab of the Preferences panel. At the top, click Content Directory, and set it to the Projects folder on the CD. Now LightWave knows where to look for this book's tutorial files (see Figure 2.20).

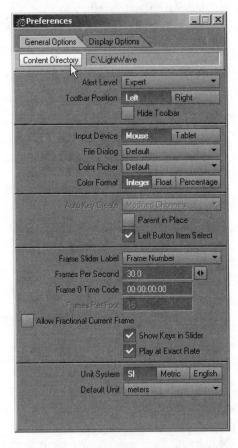

Figure 2.20   The Content Directory tells LightWave where to look when you load Scenes, Objects, or Images.

2. Next, load the BlankCD.lwo object from the Projects/
Objects/Chapter2 folder of the CD. To load the object,
click the Items tab, select Add from the drop-down list on
the left side of the interface. Click Objects, and then select
Load Object (see Figures 2.21 and 2.22). LWO stands for
LightWave Object.

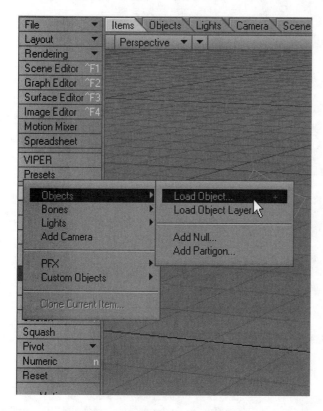

Figure 2.21
To loading an object,
begin with the Items tab
at the top of Layout and
then select the Add drop-
down list on the left side
of the screen.

Figure 2.22   Once you select Add, you can tell LightWave Layout what you'd like to add, such
as an Object.

Tip

Cool tip here folks: You can hide all the toolbars and menus in Layout and work with
only the keyboard and mouse. Press the letter o on the keyboard to access the General
Options tab of the Preferences panel. Select Hide Toolbar (see Figure 2.23). Now when
in Layout, you can access the Surface Editor (or any other panel) by holding the Ctrl and
Shift keys together, and then clicking either the left or right mouse button. Doing this
will pop up the list of commands and menus you've just hidden away (see Figure 2.24)!
Press o again to access the General Options panel to unhide the toolbar. Now that you
know where things are located, simply use Alt+F2 to hide and unhide the toolbar.

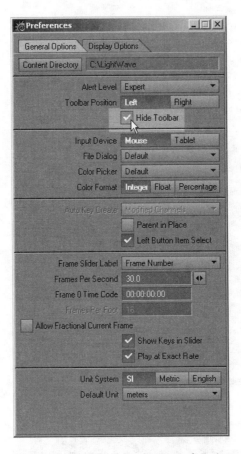

Figure 2.23   You can hide Layout's toolbars from the General Options tab.

Note

Remember that you should be using LightWave 7's default interface configuration for all tutorials in this book. To make sure that you are using the defaults, press Alt+F10 to call up the Configure Menus panel. Click the Default button from the Presets drop-down list at the top right side of the panel's interface. If it is ghosted, you have already set the default interface. Select Done to close the panel.

3. After the BlankCD. lwo object has been loaded, open the Surface Editor panel by clicking the Surface Editor button on the left side of the interface.

   By default, the name of the object appears in the Surface Name list when you are using Edit By Object mode.

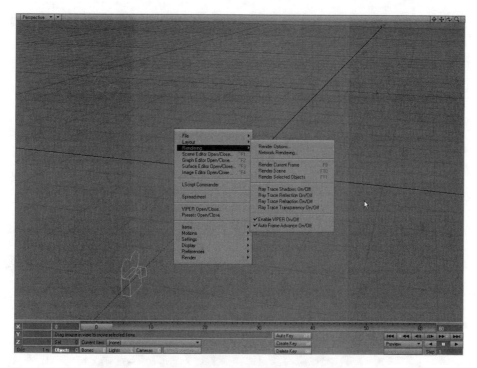

Figure 2.24   Load objects into Layout from the Add drop-down menu, found under the Actions tab, or by holding the Ctrl and Shift keys, and then clicking in the Layout window with the left mouse button, as show in this example.

4. Clicking the small triangle to the left of the BlankCD.lwo filename opens and closes the surface list.

   All the surfaces associated with the BlankCD object appear, as shown in Figure 2.25.

Note

If you have more surfaces than you do space in the Surface Name list, a scroll bar will appear. Simply click and drag the scroll bar to view the entire surface list.

5. LightWave 7 allows you to resize the Surface Editor panel simply by clicking and dragging the edge of the panel. Click and drag the bottom edge to stretch out the panel. Conversely, you can collapse the panel by clicking the small triangle centered at the top of the interface. You can then select your surfaces from the drop-down Surface list.

Tip

Naming your surfaces—a task you use Modeler to do—is half the battle when building 3D models. If you name your surfaces carefully, you'll save oodles of time when you have many surface settings to apply. Remember that organization is key!

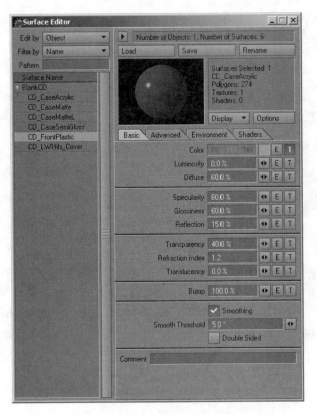

Figure 2.25   When an object is selected in Layout and the Surface Editor is opened, the selected objects' surfaces are listed.

6. Switch to Camera view by selecting the drop-down list at the top-left side of the viewport title bar (see Figure 2.26). Then select the CD_FrontPlastic surface from the list within the Surface Editor.

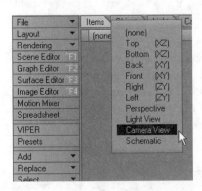

Figure 2.26   You can choose a view type from the drop-down list at the top of the Layout interface.

When a surface is selected, the name appears in the information display to the right of the surface preview. The number of polygons associated with that surface will also appear. In this case, the selected surface, CD_FrontPlastic, has one polygon, as shown in Figure 2.27. You'll also see a display at the top of the surface panel that shows the number of objects and surfaces in the scene.

Because this BlankCD is from your favorite discount music store, there is no cover image! Given that, you need to make the plastic surface transparent, and add a cover image. You'll want the color of the plastic to be a soft gray color (RGB: 180,180,180).

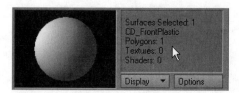

Figure 2.27   Information about the selected surface is displayed in the top-right portion of the Surface Editor panel.

Note

Don't worry about glass and plastic surfaces too much at this point. They are easier to create than you might think, and quite cool to look at, too! A glass-surfacing tutorial is coming up later in Chapter 8, "Architectural Environments."

There are a few ways to set a color to the CD case. Under the Basic tab of the Surface Editor, you'll see the Color listing at the top. There is an RGB value indicator, with a small color sample. This small area offers you a lot of control:

- Left-clicking on the small, colored square next to the RGB values makes the standard system color palette appear. Here, you can choose your color through RGB (Red, Green, Blue), HSL (Hue, Saturation, Luminance), or from custom colors you might have set up previously.

- Right-clicking on the small colored square next to the RGB values in the Surface Editor changes all three values at once. This is great for quickly making black-and-white surfaces.

- Clicking and dragging the left mouse button on either the red, green, or blue numeric value and dragging left or right increases or decreases the color value. You will instantly see the small color square next to the RGB values change. You'll also see the sample display update.

Note

Your surface preview window has a number of options, and you may need to set them up so that you can see your color surface adjustments. Be sure to check the settings by right-clicking directly in the Preview window, as shown in Figure 2.28.

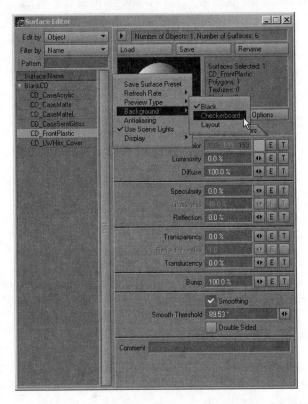

Figure 2.28   Right-clicking on the Surface Preview window in the Surface Editor offers you more control over the display of the surface. Here, you can set a checkerboard background, which is great for dark surfaces.

- If you're not keen on setting RGB values and you prefer HSV values instead, rest easy. Right-clicking once on the RGB values changes the selection to HSV. Figure 2.29 shows the change.

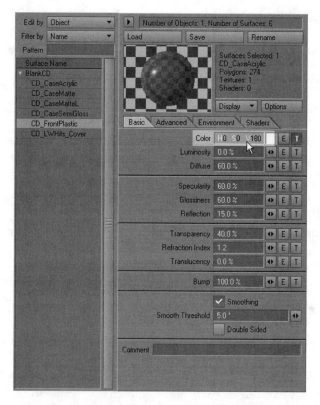

Figure 2.29   Right-clicking on the RGB value in the Surface Editor (Basic tab) changes the settings to HSV values.

Note

HSV is an acronym for Hue, Saturation, and Value. This setting describes colors by their overall color directly, unlike RGB values, which are three discrete subcolors. HSV is another way to define color values.

With the CD FrontPlastic surface set to the soft gray color, you still need to make the plastic transparent and shiny. This next part of the tutorial shows you how to surface the case, while introducing you to the rest of the Surface Editor. Throughout the rest of this book, you will continue to use the Surface Editor to create many more exciting and interesting surfaces.

7. Make sure VIPER is opened and positioned off to the side of the Surface Editor so that you can see your changes in real time. With the CD FrontPlastic surface still selected as the current surface in the Surface Editor, go down the list of options and set each one to match the settings in the following steps.

8. Make sure that the value of Luminosity (the option just below Surface Color) is 0.

   Luminosity is great for objects that are self-illuminating, such as a light bulb, candle flame, or laser beam. Note, however, that this does not make your surface cast light unless radiosity is applied. Learn about radiosity in Chapter 9, "Realistic Lighting Environments."

9. Set the value of Diffuse to roughly 60 percent to tell the CD FrontPlastic surface to accept 60 percent of the light in the scene.

   The Diffuse value tells your surface what amount of light to pick up from the scene. For example, if you set this value to 0, your surface would be completely black. And although you want the glass to be black, you also want it to have some sheen and reflection. A zero Diffuse value renders a black hole—nothing appears at all.

10. Set the value of Specularity to 60 percent.

   In simple terms, Specularity is a shiny reflection of the light source—0 percent is not shiny at all, whereas 100 percent is completely shiny.

   When you set Specularity, you almost always adjust the Glossiness as well. Glossiness, which becomes available only when the Specularity setting is above 0 percent, is the value that sets the amount of the "hot spot" on your shiny (or not so shiny) surface. Think of Glossiness as how much of a spread the hot spot has. The lower the value, the wider the spread. For example, Figure 2.30 shows a simple object with a Specularity setting of just 10 percent and Glossiness set to 10 percent. The result resembles a soft and silky fabric.

   On the other hand, Figure 2.31 shows a Specularity setting of 80 percent and a Glossiness setting of 20 percent. The result looks closer to a shiny metallic surface. A higher Glossiness setting looks like polished metal in this case. There will be a lot of surfacing ahead in this book for you, such as glass, metal, human skin, and more. This section, however, should give you a brief understanding of the toolset.

Figure 2.30 A low Specularity and a low Glossiness setting results in a surface that looks like a silky fabric.

Figure 2.31 Higher Specularity settings combined with moderate Glossiness settings results in a copper or metal-type surface.

11. Now back to the CD object. Set the value of the Glossiness for the CD FrontPlastic surface to 60 percent.

    This gives you a good, working glass surface for now.

12. Set the value of Reflection for the CD FrontPlastic surface to 40 percent.

    Glass and clear plastic surfaces generally reflect their surroundings. In this case, the plastic case has no surroundings, so instead, it can reflect a sky.

 Tip

It's a good idea when setting reflections to balance the Reflection value and the Diffuse value to roughly 100 percent. The CD FrontPlastic surface has Diffuse at 60 percent, and Reflection at 40 percent, for a total 95 percent. This is not law, but just a guideline to follow. If your Diffuse setting remained at 100 percent and you added a reflection of 40 percent or more, you'd end up with an unnaturally bright surface.

13. To see the image below the plastic case, you need to make it transparent. Set Transparency to 70 percent. There's one more option—Smoothing. Leave this feature off. You would use this setting to apply Phong Shading to smooth the surface. Because the CD FrontPlastic surface is flat, no smoothing is necessary. With objects that are rounder, this will take away any visible facets in the geometry.

Tip

Flatter surfaces are often simply too smooth, thereby creating odd renders. A lesser smoothing threshold fixes those problems. More information on smoothing is explained in Chapter 17, "Broadcast-Style Animation."

Note

Phong is a shading method developed by Bui Tuong-Phong in 1975. Essentially, it interpolates the vertex normals of an object, rather than the intensity. The result is a smooth surface that is good for plastics, metals, or glass.

14. Click the Environment tab in the Surface Panel.

Figure 2.32 shows the Environment tab.

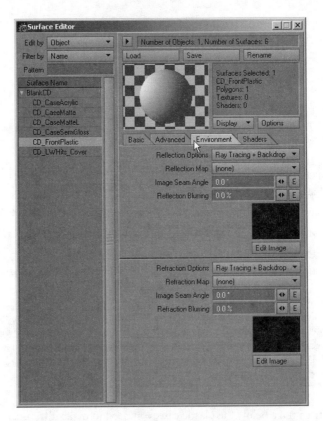

Figure 2.32   The Environment tab is where you set up Reflection Options in LightWave 7.

15. Set the Reflection Options to Spherical Map.

This sets an invisible sphere around your entire scene, which is wallpapered with whatever image you choose. In this case, use the Sky.jpg image from the Projects/Images/Chapter2 folder on the CD.

16. Click the Reflection Map drop-down list, select Load Image, as shown in Figure 2.33. Choose the Sky.jpg image from the Chapter2/Images directory.

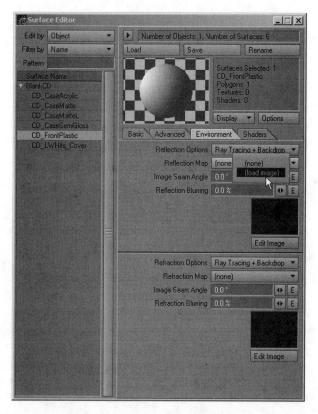

Figure 2.33   You can easily load an image for your surface to reflect by clicking the drop-down list for Reflection Map and selecting Load Image.

Because LightWave can calculate realistic reflections, setting a reflecting image helps create a more realistic surface. A small thumbnail image appears in the panel.

You should see the texture sample update in the top of the Surface Editor interface.

Tip

LightWave allows you to adjust the image properties—such as contrast, brightness, and more—through the Image Editor. This saves time by allowing you to change image properties without using a third-party image-editing program. Additionally, the information is stored with the LightWave scene file, which means that it's nondestructive to your original image. You can access the Image Editor by clicking on the Edit Image button just below the thumbnail image.

Exercise 2.3   Adding a Cover Image to the CD Case

With an object such as a CD case, one of the toughest things to do is match the real-world properties of the clear plastic. Believe it or not, this is very easy to do with LightWave 7. The right amount of transparency, specularity, glossiness, and reflection helps create the visual effect. But if the surface is transparent, what's behind it? In this particular instance, a cover image is needed for the CD case. This next section takes you through the steps required to surface the cover image. Figure 2.34 shows the CD without a cover.

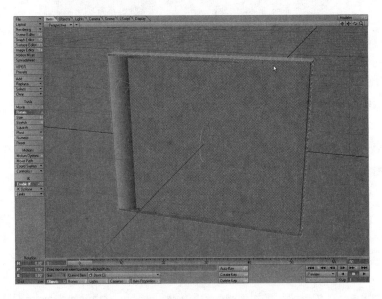

Figure 2.34   This CD case needs some surfacing!

1. Select the CD_LWHits_Cover surface of the BlankCD.lwo object. You can leave the Color alone because you're going to override it with an image.

2. Leave the Diffuse set to 100 percent, the Specularity to 20 percent, and the Glossiness to 10 percent.

3. No reflection is needed, so make sure Reflection is set to 0 percent.

At this point, the CD doesn't look that much different than it did when you loaded it. Remember that other factors play a role in surfacing, such as surroundings and lighting, but right now you need to apply the cover image.

4. Select the CD_LWHits_Cover surface, and click the T button to the right of Color under the Basic tab (see Figure 2.35).

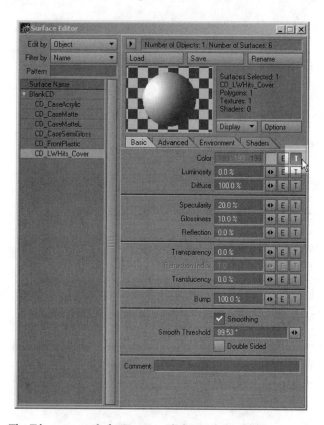

Figure 2.35   The T button stands for Texture. Click it to open the Texture Editor. Because the button is next to the Color setting, you're applying a Texture to the Color.

5. Make sure that Layer Type is set to Image Map.

6. Leave Blending Mode set to Normal, to have the image map override the Surface Color. You want to display only the image.

7. Layer Opacity should be left at 100 percent. This applies 100 percent of the image's brightness.

8. Projection should be set to Planar. Planar is flat. This is the front cover image, so you want to apply it flat, not curved.

9. Now you need to tell LightWave which image to apply. Click the Image drop-down list and select Load Image, as shown in Figure 2.36.

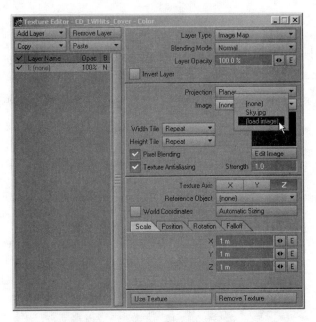

Figure 2.36   After you have set Image Map properties, you need to tell LightWave which image to apply by selecting Load Image.

10. Select the LWHitsCD.psd image from the Projects/Images/Chapter2 folder on the book's CD. The image will load and you'll see a tiny thumbnail in the Texture Editor panel.

11. If you take a look in Layout, you'll see the loaded image repeating across the surface (see Figure 2.37). Set Width Tile and Height Tile to Reset. Right now, they are set to Repeat.

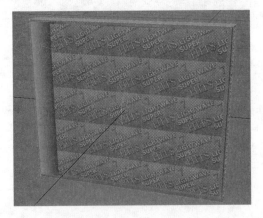

Figure 2.37   When an image map is first applied, the Width Tile and Height Tile are set to Repeat by default, making the image tile. Sometimes this is good for carpet or bathroom designs, but not for CD covers.

Note

If you can't see your texture in the Layout view, as shown in Figure 2.37, make sure that you have OpenGL Textures turned on under the Display Options tab within the Preferences panel (see Figure 2.38).

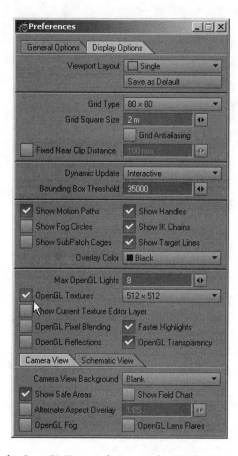

Figure 2.38   Clicking the OpenGL Textures button in the Display Options tab allows you to see applied image maps in Layout.

12. Set the Texture axis to z, and then click Automatic Sizing. The z-axis is in the front and back of the camera, therefore the image will appear in this view.

Automatic Sizing adjusts the texture based on the geometry available, usually creating a perfect fit for the image. You'll see the X, Y, and Z values change under the Scale tab at the bottom of the Texture Editor panel.

 Note

Automatic Sizing computes a 3D bounding box around the surface. The bounding box dimensions are used to fill the Scale XYZ fields.

You now can see your image applied to the cover, as shown in Figure 2.39. This is possible because transparency is shown in Layout. In versions previous to LightWave 6.5, you could not see through transparent surfaces until you rendered. Bonus!

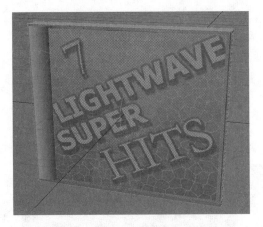

Figure 2.39   Width Tile and Height Tile are set to Reset, and with Automatic Sizing applied in the Texture Editor, the cover image is properly mapped.

13. Press F9 to render a frame to see the clear plastic over the cover image. Figure 2.40 shows the render.

Figure 2.40   Pressing F9 renders a single frame showing the clear plastic and its reflections over the applied image map cover.

From this point, you can work with the other surfaces and apply a similar clear plastic to the CD_CaseAcrylic surface, black plastic to the CD_CaseMatte, and so on. There is a final surfaced CD (LW_CD) in the Projects/Objects/Chapter2 folder, on the CD from which you can study and make Presets. To use Presets for your surfaces, read on.

Note

Remember that simply saving a LightWave scene file does not save your surfaces. You must save your object (File drop-down list, Save, Save All Objects) in addition to saving your scene, if you want to keep the surfaces applied.

You'll often come across a situation in which you need to use the same surface settings on multiple surfaces. Because so many variables are set within the Surface Editor, keeping track of identical surfaces could be a problem. And wouldn't it be nice to have a quick reference to the changes you've made to the current surface? This is where the Preset Shelf comes in.

Exercise 2.4   Using Preset Shelf

The CD object you've been working with is comprised of multiple surfaces. A few of the surfaces, such as CD_FrontPlastic and CD_CaseAcrylic, are similar. Instead of redoing all the surface parameters, you can use the Preset Shelf to save and apply the same surface, and then simply make any necessary changes to the surface properties.

Tip

Loading and saving surfaces accomplishes the same goal, but the Preset Shelf shows you a small thumbnail of the surface. Nice!

The Preset Shelf defaults to a tall thin column that appears when you access the Surface Editor, as shown in Figure 2.41.

Note

All the Presets from this chapter's tutorials are on the CD that has been packaged with this book. Go to the Projects/Scenes/Presets/ directory on the CD, and you'll find the Chap2 Preset category. Be sure to copy these Presets to LightWave/Programs/Presets/Surface Editor/Surface Preset directory. When you go back to Layout and click in the Preset window, the new category will appear.

If your Preset Shelf does not appear, you can access it from the toolbar. If you are working with the Default Menu Configuration, you'll always find the Presets button in the top-left third of the Layout interface, as you see in Figure 2.42.

Figure 2.41
The Preset Shelf by default opens as a tall window, but you can resize it to fit your screen.

Figure 2.42   The Presets are found by clicking the button at the top-left third of the Layout interface.

If you don't care for the tall narrow look of the Preset Shelf, you can click and hold one of the corners of the panel and resize it to your liking. A good option is to stretch the shelf out across the interface from left to right, and move it to the bottom of the screen. Because all your Preset Shelf samples remain in the shelf, you also can open up the panel to fit your entire screen. The choice is yours.

Tip

Using LightWave with a dual-monitor system is great when you are setting up surfaces. Simply set the Preset Shelf wide open on the additional monitor, maximizing the visibility of the Preset Shelf and giving you more real estate for your work.

If you set up a surface you'd like to keep, you can simply save it in the Preset Shelf. To do this, just follow these steps:

1. Open the Surface Editor and select the CD_FrontPlastic surface. Double-click the sample render display in the Surface Editor.

    You'll see that surface sample appear on the Preset Shelf (see Figure 2.43).

Tip

Although double-clicking the sample display is one way to add a surface to the Preset Shelf, you also can right-click the preview window and select Save Surface Preset or press the s key in the Surface Editor. There's one more way to add a surface to the Preset Shelf: Click Add Preset from the VIPER window.

2. Select the second surface to which you need to apply surfacing, such as the CD_CaseAcrylic.

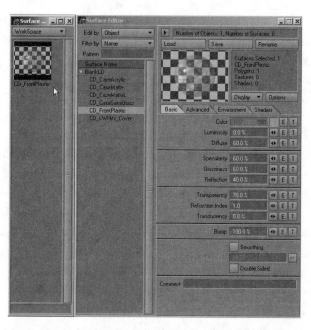

Figure 2.43   Double-clicking the display sample in the Surface Editor, shown on the right, instantly adds those surface settings to the Preset Shelf, shown on the left.

3. Go back to the Preset Shelf, and double-click the sample you recently added.

   A small window appears asking you to load the current settings. This question is asking whether you want the settings from the Preset Shelf sample to be applied to the currently selected surface in the Surface Editor. In this case, you do.

4. Click Yes, and all the surface settings are set for the CD_CaseAcrylic. For any small changes, adjust as needed.

   By using a preset to copy and paste a surface, it's much easier to change one simple parameter, such as more reflection, than it is to reset all the surface and reflection properties.

Tip

Just in case you're really lazy, you don't even have to use the Preset Shelf to copy and paste a surface. Simply right click the Surface Name in the Surface Editor, and select Copy. Select a new surface, right click, and select Paste. Easy enough!

As you can see from the previous examples, the CD case is starting to look like a useable object. The next step is to continue surfacing it on your own, using the few simple parameters outlined in the previous pages. If you like, you can load the LW_CD object from the Projects/Objects/Chapter2 folder on the book's CD-ROM to study.

Color, diffuse, specularity, glossiness, and reflection will be the base for just about all the surfaces you create. Once you have a handle on setting up the basics, you are ready to create surfaces that are more advanced.

Making a 3D Surface from a 2D Image

Too often when you are working on a project, your client will demand, or politely ask, for a particular surface. And although you might have many texture CD-ROM surface collections (such as Seamless Textures from Marlin Studios, *www.marlinstudios.com*), they might not match your exact needs and might instead serve as only a base from which to start. For example, suppose that your big corporate client comes in and needs its new testing division's logo animated. "No problem," you say in your best corporate-ladder voice. The client tells you it needs to be completed in three days. Again, "No problem," you reply. Then the client tells you that it must be on green marble. You scramble for words as the hard drive in your head scans your memory for any images of green marble. As you begin working on the project, you realize you have no images of green marble! What will you do to complete the project in that timeframe? You can use LightWave's Surface Editor and all will be well.

In your archives, you find a high-resolution earth-tone marble image. That's helpful—but the client needs green. Toning the image in an imaging program like Photoshop could work, but by adjusting the image in LightWave, you'll have more control over the final scene. Follow along in this next tutorial to take a single 2D image and make it a different colored 3D image.

Exercise 2.5   Using the Texture Editor for Bump and Specularity Maps

Marble, granite, and stone are great surfaces for 3D animation. Terrific images for logo backgrounds, floors, sidewalks, and more, these textures are often easy to find on the Internet and in the world around you. Figure 2.44 shows the earth-tone marble image used as the base for the animation.

In this project, you'll start with a picture and use it to create bumps and specular highlights on a surface. To do this, follow these steps:

1. Select Clear Scene in Layout from the File requester. Remember to save any work.

2. Next, load the MarbleBoard.lwo object from the Projects/Objects/Chapter2 folder on this book's CD. This is a flat polygon in which you'll apply an image map, just like you applied the CD cover earlier.

3. Select the Camera button at the bottom of Layout, and then press 6 on the numeric keypad to switch to Camera view.

Figure 2.44 This everyday earth tone marble image was scanned from a sample that would be available at any home store.

Selecting Camera first told LightWave that you want to work with cameras. Conversely, selecting Lights would have told LightWave you wanted to work with lights, and so on.

4. Move the camera in toward the MarbleBoard.lwo object so that it fills the frame. Press Enter twice to create a keyframe at frame 0, which will lock the camera in place. Go to the Surface Editor and select the MarbleBoard surface, and set the RGB Color value to deep green, RGB 105, 130, 085.

5. With the proper color set, look to the Diffuse area, and click the T button to access the Texture Editor.

Note

Earlier in this chapter you used the Texture Editor to apply an image map to Color. The Texture Editor for Diffuse looks identical, but because it's for Diffuse, not Color, its effect will be completely different. This is the same throughout LightWave. The panels look the same, but the point at which you access them is key to the results you achieve.

6. Starting at the top of the Texture Editor, make sure that the Layer Type is set to Image Map.

You're selecting an image map because you're using an image to enhance the surface. Image maps can be used on all types of surfaces as an alternative to procedural textures that are strictly computer generated.

Here, you are mapping an image onto the flat object—think of image mapping like wallpapering. Other layer types you can set are Procedural, computer-generated surfaces that do not use image maps. You also can choose to set a Gradient layer type, which on a small scale enables you to use a spectrum of colors as a texture.

Note

A gradient allows you to control an attribute based on an Input Parameter, like bump height, distances, weight maps, and so on. The real power of gradients is that you can control how the Input Parameter is applied using the gradient bar, which acts as a filter.

Gradients in LightWave 7 are quite complex and will be used throughout the book. They are surface translation filters. Figure 2.45 shows the Diffuse Texture Editor interface.

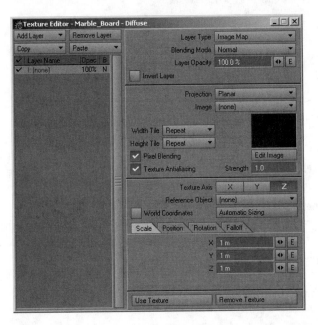

Figure 2.45   All the small buttons labeled with a T throughout LightWave take you to this panel, the Texture Editor.

7. Set the Blending Mode to Normal from the drop-down list.

    You can also select other blending modes: Additive uses the texture to its full extent for the selected surface. Subtractive subtracts the full extent of the image from the selected surface. Choosing Difference as the Blending Mode determines how a layer affects underlying layers, similar to Adobe Photoshop.

8. Experiment with blending modes to see what results you can come up with.

Note

Every surface layer can have a different blending mode.

9. Return the Blending Mode to Normal, and keep the Layer Opacity set to 100 percent for now.

    A setting of 100 percent tells LightWave to use this texture map completely. Because you are in the Texture Editor for Diffuse, you are using the brightness values of the image for the diffuse channel, and the Color data is disregarded.

10. Leave Invert Layer turned off.

    In this example of an image map, inverting the layer would reverse the image.

11. Set the Projection to Planar.

    Remember, with an Image Map layer type, you are wallpapering. Planar tells LightWave to keep the wallpaper flat. You also can choose to set Projection to Cylindrical, Spherical, Cubic, Front, and UV. These additional values enable you to surface on tubes, balls, boxes, composited backgrounds, and organic surfaces.

    Now you need to tell LightWave which image you want to image map as a diffusion texture.

12. Next to the Image drop-down list, select Load Image and from the book's CD-ROM, select the EarthMarble image file from Chapter 2's Image directory.

    You'll see the image appear in the small thumbnail window.

13. Keep Pixel Blending turned on to smooth out the pixelization that can occur if the camera gets too close to the surface.

14. Because you are using Auto Sizing, you don't need to set Width Tile and Height Tile to Reset—so leave those settings alone. These settings allow you to repeat or mirror the image map and might be used, for example, to tile a floor on which you want a texture to repeat.

15. Uncheck Texture Antialiasing.

    Turning this off is important when applying textures. When you render animations, you will turn on Antialiasing in the Camera Properties panel. This setting smoothes out jagged edges throughout your scene. Setting Antialiasing within the Texture Editor will smooth your texture. When you add that to a final render that is antialiased, however, you end up with a blurry image. Too much antialiasing can sometimes be a bad thing.

    You told LightWave to set an image map and keep it flat (planar). Because this is a 3D animation program, you also need to identify to which axis you want to apply this image.

16. Set the Texture Axis to z, the axis that is in front (positive z) and in back (negative z) of you.

Note

You do not need to set a Reference Object for this surface. Setting up a Reference Object, such as a null object, allows you interactively to control the position and size of the image map in Layout. However, LightWave enables you to animate a texture's Position, Scale, and Rotation. The choice is up to you.

17. Click the Automatic Sizing button.

LightWave looks at the polygons of the selected surface and applies the currently selected image to them. The size parameters change under the Scale tab at the bottom of the Texture Editor interface. In most cases, Automatic Sizing works like a charm. When it doesn't work the way you want it to, use a null object as a reference object to obtain precise image placement.

18. Leave World Coordinates unchecked.

When you tell LightWave to Image Map, you are wallpapering an image onto the surface of an object. If you move the object, the image should move with it. But imagine what would happen if you wallpapered a bumpy wall and decided to move the wall. When you did this, you wanted the wall to move, but not the wallpaper, making the bumpy wall move through the wallpaper. Clicking on World Coordinates does just that.

Now your texture surface is set up, but you have a few more things to do.

19. Go to the top of the Texture Editor interface and choose the Copy drop-down list. Select the Current Layer choice, and then click Use Texture to close the panel. Copying the Current Layer enables you to apply all these settings to another aspect of the surface, such as a Bump Map.

20. In the Layout window, select the single light in the scene, press y to rotate, and point it toward the MarbleBoard object. It often helps to set the light from Light View.

Move the light up and back slightly to fully illuminate the object. Press Enter twice to create a keyframe and lock the light in place at frame 0. Because this is a distant light, its rotation—not its position—matters. However, moving the light into place from the Light View allows you to change the light type later without the need to adjust the light position.

Press F9 on your keyboard to see the marble image blended with the green color set earlier, as shown in Figure 2.46.

Tip

Be sure that your Render Display is set to Image Viewer within the Render Options panel so that you can see the F9 render. This will make the full frame appear after the render is complete.

Figure 2.46   Applying an image map in the Texture Editor for Diffuse mixes the image with the green color.

Note

Be sure to check out the color images for all of the book's figure references on the accompanying CD.

21. Before you go any further, click the File drop-down list at the top of the Layout interface, and select Save All Objects from the Save drop-down list on the left side of the screen (see Figure 2.47).

This saves the surface properties to your object thus far.

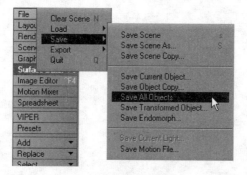

Figure 2.47   Make sure you select Save All Objects to keep the surface settings attached to the object for future use. If you don't do this, the next time you load the object, it will be blank, as it was when you started this section.

Exercise 2.6   Applying Bump and Specularity to a Surface

The rendered result at this point doesn't look like much, does it? It looks like you just went through a lot of steps to create a rendered image that looks just like the original image, only green. But, in LightWave, you can apply as many textures as you'd like and you can use the Texture Editor in other areas to do so. To use the Texture Editor for Bump mapping, follow these steps:

1. In the Surface Editor, click the T button next to Bump.

   The Texture Editor appears again. And although this is the same editor you used to apply a Diffuse texture, it has different results. Instead of resetting all the same parameters, you need only to paste them. Remember the Copy Current Layer command you selected earlier? This copied all the Texture Editor settings for Diffuse.

2. From the top of the Texture Editor interface, choose Paste and then select Replace Current Layer.

   All the parameters are now aligned.

   You'll see that the same EarthMarble image has been loaded into the thumbnail window. Changes need to be made to only two areas, which is easier than changing all the settings. This is why you copied and pasted the settings.

3. Click the Image Editor button in Layout and then select the EarthMarble image, as shown in Figure 2.48. You also can click the Edit Image button from the Texture panel within the Surface Editor.

Figure 2.48   The Image Editor allows you to manipulate imported images and animations in a variety of ways.

Instead of going through a drawn-out task of creating separate images for bump maps in an image editing program like Adobe Photoshop, you can do everything you need right here in LightWave.

4. At the top of the Image Editor interface, select Clone, and choose Instance to create a copy of the EarthMarble image. You'll see a second image in the Name list on the left side of the panel labeled EarthMarble.tif(1). Select this copy.

5. Click the Editing tab, and bring the Saturation down to –1.0, all the way to the left. The color will be stripped from the image (see Figure 2.49).

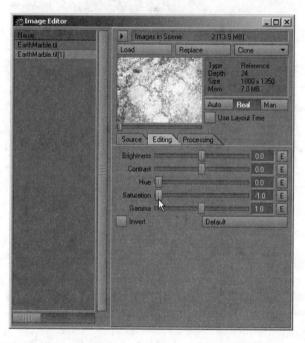

Figure 2.49   A clone of the original image is created and its color is stripped, quick and easy in the Image Editor.

6. Close the Image Editor, and return to the Texture Bump Map panel for the MarbleBoard surface. Go to the Image selection, and change the original EarthMarble image to the newly cloned EarthMable[1] image, as shown in Figure 2.50.

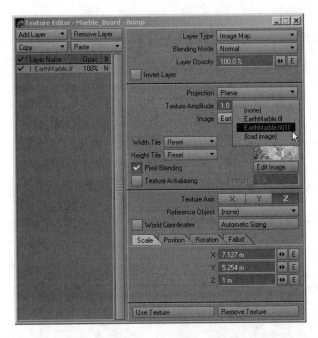

Figure 2.50   The cloned image is now selected within the Bump Map Texture Editor.

The next step is to set the Texture Amplitude for the Bump Map.

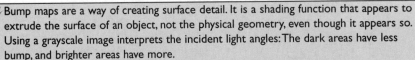

Note

Bump maps are a way of creating surface detail. It is a shading function that appears to extrude the surface of an object, not the physical geometry, even though it appears so. Using a grayscale image interprets the incident light angles: The dark areas have less bump, and brighter areas have more.

You also can apply LightWave's Bump Displacement feature. This will take the bump map, which changes only the surface appearance, and apply a physical change to the surface, thereby enhancing the 3D effect even more. You can access this feature in the Deformations tab of the Object Properties panel. However, it's best to have at least a multi-segmented object—or better, a SubPatched object—for this feature. The object you've been using in this chapter is only one polygon and can't benefit from Bump Displacement. You'll learn about SubPatches in Chapter 3, "LightWave 7 Modeler."

7. Set the Texture Amplitude to 8.0. Essentially, this is the amount of Bump the Texture Editor applies.

8. Copy this surface as you did earlier, and then click Use Texture.

9. Be sure to select Save All Objects again; then press F9 to render a test frame.

    Figure 2.51 shows the surface with both Diffuse and Bump maps applied.

Figure 2.51   When you add a bump map to the surface, it starts to take on more depth.

 Tip

It is not always necessary to use a grayscale image for bump mapping. If your color image has good variations in contrast, it will often work well as a bump map image.

10. With the bump texture copied, now enter the Texture Editor (T) for Specularity.

    This is where you can take an average surface and make it exceptional. Because you copied the bump texture, simply paste it here. You are not trying to apply the bump map as a Specularity texture; that isn't how it works. By copying, you are taking the grayscale value of the image and its settings, such as size and position. Copying saves you the trouble of resetting all the values.

11. Paste the copied surface to the current layer in the Specularity Texture Editor. This will use the same settings, but make the surface shinier where the image is brighter and less shiny where the image is darker. Click Use Texture to close the panel.

    The last step you need to take to make this surface look great is to adjust the Specularity and Glossiness.

12. After reading more about LightWave's lights in Chapter 7, "Lighting and Atmospheres," change the single light in the scene to a spotlight. This will help direct the light more accurately on the marble surface. For now, simply make sure your default Distant light is shining on the object. Leave the Specularity at 0 percent, and set the Glossiness to roughly 15 percent or 20 percent.

    Because the Specularity Texture Layer Opacity is set to 100 percent, the base (the 0 percent setting) is meaningless. This creates a nice wide gloss on the surface. However, you can play with the amounts to find a setting you might like more.

Figure 2.52 shows the three textures applied to the single surface, which is just one polygon. You can load this scene, named EarthMarble.lws on the book's CD-ROM.

Note

In the Camera panel, Antialiasing was set to Medium for Figure 2.52's render. This will help clean up any noise you might see in your render.

Figure 2.52   Adding a Specularity texture map helps bring this surface to life, all from a flat image.

Note

You also can use LightWave's gradients to apply specularity maps and help control contrasts. Look for more on gradients in Chapter 8, "Architectural Environments."

Specularity maps are useful any time you have bump maps. If you look at even the slight imperfections on your desktop, or your computer monitor, you can see that there are bumps, but the light falls in and out of them. This is what a Specularity map will do for your surface. And similar to the bump map properties, it also bases its calculations on the grayscale image—the darker areas do not allow as much Specularity, where the lighter areas allow more.

These techniques provide a foundation for your entire real-world surfacing projects. Anything from a plastic toy, to a telephone, to a dirt road can benefit from setting these three texture maps. As another example, read on to create a dirty metal surface with a few more involved steps.

Applying Image Maps to Surfaces

Surfacing that CD object earlier in this chapter was no big deal. You used basic, everyday surfacing techniques and a couple of simple reflection images. This is great for logos and colored balls, but in today's marketplace, if you want to stay competitive, you need to make things look not so clean. In the early days of 3D animation, shine and reflection were big crowd pleasers, but now it's a different story and you need to be aware of the change. The trick is to use LightWave's Surface Editor to apply texture maps, bump maps, and procedurals to achieve the "not so perfect" surface.

What happens when you need to create a dirty and rusty piece of metal pipe? Fortunately, you can apply these surfacing techniques to anything you want, such as metal grates, steel, wood, fences, bricks, and much more. How? You can use image maps.

When you begin creating a 3D object, you most often work from some sort of reference, whether it's a physical model or a photograph.

The same would apply to surfacing your model, but most people don't consider that fact. When you begin to surface an object, you will save yourself hours of frustration and headaches by having a photograph or digital image of the surface you want to create. In this particular case, an image has been photographed and scanned into a computer at a high resolution. This single image is used as a reference to create an entire 3D surface. Essentially, you'll use the steps to create a 3D surface presented earlier, but take it further by adding noise and dirt. Figure 2.53 shows an image you can use as a reference.

Figure 2.53   The starting point to any decent surface is a decent image.

There are a number of resources available to you for gathering image maps. One of the best resources is your own eye and a camera. Taking photographs of the world around you is the best way to get the original and real textures into your 3D environment. Not to mention, photos you take yourself are *your* images and they're royalty free. You don't need an expensive digital camera; you can certainly use a traditional 35mm film camera. Most digital cameras today have excellent quality. If you are using images in 3D for surfacing, you should always go for the highest quality. However, the quality of the film sometimes has a much nicer look to it than the digital, especially when applied as image maps. Not to go unmentioned is the Kodak PhotoCD. You can have any of your photographs created on a PhotoCD that can be read in your computer's CD-ROM drive. Check your local photo shop, or search the web for more information.

If you can't take your own photos, you can buy some wonderful sets of real-world textures. Marlin Studios (*www.marlinstudios.com*) has more than half a dozen CDs available with some of the best-looking rocks, foliage, wood, and more, available today. You can buy these discs from Safe Harbor computers at 1-800-544-6599 or online at *www.sharbor.com*. A few sample images are provided on this book's CD-ROM for you to try.

To achieve a complex look from a base image, you can use LightWave's Layered surfaces in combination with your base image. This next exercise shows you the techniques needed to use LightWave's powerful texture layers to blend multiple textures on a single surface.

In the previous exercise, you mixed Surface Color with an image map through a Diffuse texture map. In this instance, you are going to go a step further with procedural textures.

Exercise 2.7   Setting Up the Image Map and Layers

LightWave's Texture Editor looks simple at first, but it actually runs deep with control. This next tutorial steps you through setting up a base image and adding layers of procedural textures to create a rocky surface.

1. Save any work you want to keep, and then select Clear Scene from the File drop-down menu.

2. From the book's CD, load the BrickPic.lwo object into Layout.

   This is a simple polygon box just like the EarthMable background earlier. The textures will be applied to the entire object.

3. Open the Surface Editor, select the BrickPic surface, and click the T button next to Color.

All the default values in the Texture Editor are settings you can use. The Layer Type is an image map, the Blending Mode is Normal, Layer Opacity is 100 percent, and because the object is flat in front of the camera, set the Projection to Planar.

4. From the Image drop-down menu, select Load Image. Load the Brick image file.

   A thumbnail image appears as representation.

5. Select z as the Texture axis. You don't need to set Width Tile and Height Tile because these settings aren't affected due to Automatic Sizing. Click Automatic Sizing.

6. Press F9 to draw a quick render preview of your surface.

   The image should be mapped out, similar to Figure 2.54. Now you can add layers to this surface for more complex surfacing. You can move your camera in for a closer view for rendering, as you did for the EarthMarble object earlier in this chapter.

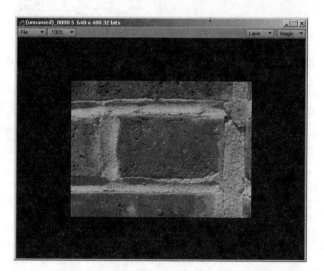

Figure 2.54   The flat image is now applied as a texture map to the surface. This is only one layer of surfacing.

7. From the top of the Texture Editor interface, click and hold down the mouse button on the Add Layer button, and then select Procedural.

   You'll see the right side of the interface change, and a small thumbnail of fractals appears, as shown in Figure 2.55.

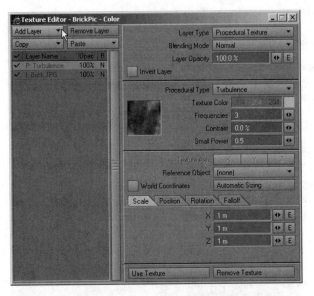

Figure 2.55   Adding a Procedural Layer to your surface displays a similar Texture Editor display.

As you add layers to your surfaces, you'll see a list begin on the left side of the Texture Editor interface, as shown in Figure 2.56.

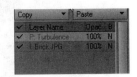

 Note

LightWave's surface layers are stacked on top of each other. You can obscure lower layers if the upper layers show through either by using Layer Opacity or setting certain procedural textures. All procedurals have some portion of the texture that is less than 100 percent. Otherwise, they would be solid. Essentially, the darker parts are less than 100 percent and allow the underlying layers show through.

Figure 2.56
You can easily select which layer you want to work on by selecting the Layer Name from the list on the left side of the Texture Editor interface.

If you look at the Layer Type selection, you'll see that it is set to Procedural. Blending Mode is still set to Additive, because you want to add this procedural on top of the Image Map layer.

8. Set the Procedural Type to Fractal Noise.

   This is a random fractal pattern that can be used for creating dust, dirt, rust, or just a simple variation in a surface. At this point, it's a good idea to turn on VIPER to preview your surfacing.

9. Press F9 to render one frame.

   This puts the render into LightWave's buffer, for use with VIPER.

10. After the render is complete, click the Render button on the VIPER window. Your render appears, as shown in Figure 2.57.

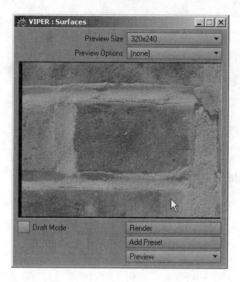

Figure 2.57   A quick F9 single frame render gets the buffer information necessary for VIPER to display.

11. Back in the Texture Editor, you can begin adjusting the Fractal Noise procedural color. Because this will be dirt, select an RGB value close to 100, 100, 75.

12. Move down to the bottom of the Texture Editor panel, and select the Scale tab to change the size of the procedural texture, making the X value 150mm and leaving the other values at their 1m defaults.

    You'll see the updated image appear instantly in VIPER. Notice that the fractal noise now looks streaked across the image.

13. Click the Rotation tab, and set the B (bank adjustment) to 12 degrees.

    The procedural texture is now slightly angled across the surface.

14. Click the Falloff tab, where you can tell the texture to simply end—fall off.

    Because the texture is primarily on the y-axis (up and down), you want to make the dirt look like it's dripping.

15. Set the Y falloff value to –15 percent, and set Linear Y from the drop-down Type list. You'll see the texture fade toward the bottom of the image. Figure 2.58 shows the image.

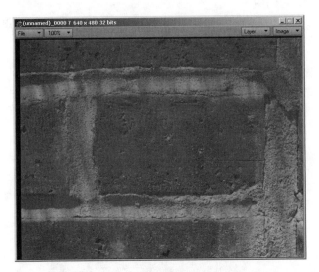

Figure 2.58   Add a little Fractal Noise and the brick image looks weathered. This is only one layer of texture—you can continue with many more for added depth.

From this point, try copying the brick surface and creating a bump and specularity map, as you did with the marble surface earlier. Then, go a step further and create bump maps for the procedural textures, not forgetting the specularity maps for those as well. Simply copy and paste the procedural texture layer into the texture panel for Bump.

Experiment with Glossiness maps as well. Remember, all of the Texture Editor panels are the same—they simply have different effects based on where they are applied.

Note

Falloff is the rate at which the texture decreases from the center to the edge of the texture.

The Next Step

Using VIPER in combination with the Scale, Position, Rotation, and Falloff tabs is a great way to work. Now you can interactively set these values.

From this point on, you can experiment on your own. Add more layers. As a matter of fact, add as many as you like. Your only limitations are time and system memory! Try adding some of the other procedural surfaces, such as Smokey, Turbulence, or Crust. Keep adding these to your rusty metal surface to see what you can come up with. Now if you remember the copy and paste commands you used earlier with the Bump mapped marble tutorial, you can repeat those same steps. Try selecting the Copy All Layers from the Color Texture and applying them as Bump and Specularity textures. The results are endless. In addition, try applying LightWave's powerful surface shaders. For a complete list of the Shader plug-ins, refer to Appendix B, "LightWave 7 Plug-in, Tool, and Technical List."

Summary

This chapter gave you a broad overview of the main features within LightWave 7's Surface Editor, including the Texture Editor. There are literally countless surfaces in the world around us, and it's up to you to create them digitally. As the book progresses, you will use the information and instructions in this chapter to create even more complex and original surfaces such as glass, skin, metal, and more. But from here, read on to Chapter 3 to begin the object creation process.

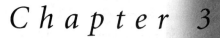

C h a p t e r 3

LightWave 7 Modeler

It's been said that necessity is the mother of invention, and when you get into LightWave Modeler 7, you'll see that this statement has never been truer.

The LightWave 7 Modeler has all the features, ease of use, and control you'd want in any 3D-modeling package. With it you can create everything from simple shapes, to famous architecture, to complex characters.

Of course, a combination of necessity and significant suggestions from the LightWave community has made this version of Modeler what it is today. There are enhancements upon enhancements in Modeler, from a customizable interface to interactive controls to brand-new modeling tools. This chapter guides you through Modeler with practical working examples. Some major issues discussed in this chapter include

- Points, polygons, and volume
- Objects
- Weight Modeling mode
- Texture Modeling mode
- Morph Modeling mode with endomorphs
- SubPatching objects
- Bevels and Symmetry mode
- Skelegons
- Cool tools you should know

The exercises in this book are not only a simple cookbook of techniques, but also a thorough explanation of what is happening when you choose a specific command. Don't mistake this for a long, drawn-out description of the Modeler toolset, however—that's what the manuals are for! Building anything requires that you start with a good working knowledge of your software and what you are trying to accomplish.

How you work, where you work, and the people you work with all play a part in your projects. When you sit down to create a 3D model, you choose to expand your creative sense and style. Interruptions can block your creative process. Try to make your work environment as comfortable as possible, even if 3D modeling is just a hobby to you.

Just as important as your working environment is your model management. Although you can just sit down to see what you can create with LightWave Modeler, it is always more productive to know where you are going. For example, if you decide to build and animate a dancing chicken, you first need to decide what the chicken should look like. You don't need to be an artist to make a simple sketch of your idea. Flush out any variations on paper before you start your modeling. (Of course, *why* you'd want to create a dancing chicken is another chapter entirely.)

From there, what will the character do in the animation? LightWave 7's modeling tools are designed for ease of use when it's time to animate. This means that you need to plan your animation so that your model can be animated appropriately. Realizing what you are trying to do and where you are trying to go will help you get there that much faster. There is nothing worse than trying to make a bad model move the way you want it to. Plan your motions, and know how the character will react to its surroundings.

For some, getting a new software package and diving right in is a common practice. For others, reading the manuals cover-to-cover is the norm. As with anything, moderation is the key, and either of these extremes may not be the best way to tackle this new program. But more than anything else with this version, plan, plan, plan! Logos, industrial designs, characters, architecture, or anything else you create—plan it out.

Understanding Modeler 7

Before you begin to figure out where you are going with your models and animations, it's a good idea to be familiar with the tools you have available to you. Although this chapter cannot take you through each panel in Modeler, it does describe how you can quickly create any type of model you want. You'll use the information in this chapter (and your LightWave manual) as reference for the remainder of this book. Figure 3.1 shows the LightWave 7 Modeler interface at startup.

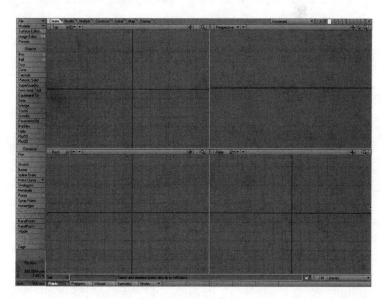

Figure 3.1   LightWave 7 Modeler at startup looks similar to previous versions of LightWave, but don't let that fool you.

LightWave 7 Modeler is more powerful than ever. It is a better way to work, not only because of the many new tools, but also because you can work faster through numerous interactive tools. You can customize keyboard shortcuts and menu bars to fit your specific needs. Refer to Chapter 1, "Introducing LightWave 7," for more information on customizable menus in LightWave.

To begin, you should be familiar with the way Modeler 7 creates objects. Although points, polygons, and splines are all still a part of the object creation process, Modeler now integrates many animation setup routines. These routines were left for Layout before version 6, but now you can fully build, surface, and set up hierarchies for your objects directly in Modeler. If you're already familiar with LightWave Modeler 6 or 6.5, you're ahead of the game.

Note

LightWave 7 Modeler enables you to create full skeletal structures for your objects, which you can save with your objects. Learn more about bones in Chapter 11, "Character Construction," and Inverse Kinematics in Chapter 13, "Inverse Kinematics."

Click around the Modeler interface and try to make a few simple objects, even if they are only boxes and balls. You'll learn, even from these simple tasks, that this version of the software is different from any other version of LightWave. Aside from interactive tools and a streamlined interface, you should be aware of LightWave's object structure. Objects have their own layers, allowing a single object to have multiple independent parts. Features commonly used in Layout are now updated and available in Modeler, such as a robust Surface Editor and the creation of bones (Skelegons). Click further to see what buttons are hidden within panels and try them. Doing so will spark your curiosity when reading through your reference guides and through this book.

Note

Here's a very important rule when working in Modeler—always work with the Caps Lock off. Keyboard shortcuts in Modeler are case sensitive, and most common commands by default are on lowercase keys.

Points, Polygons, and Volume

At the bottom left of the Modeler interface, you'll see three selections available to you: Points, Polygons, and Volume. By selecting Points, you are telling Modeler that you want to work with the *points* of an object. By selecting the Polygons button, you're telling Modeler that you want to work with the *polygons* of an object. Points make up polygons, sort of like connecting the dots. You can't have polygons without points. Although moving points that make up an object also moves the polygons, there are times when you will work with one selection over the other. Working in Points mode, you gain finer control over adjusting details of a model. You'll be instructed to work in both of these modes throughout the exercises in this book.

Volume mode allows you to make a selection either within a set-bounding region or outside of it. With Volume mode set, you can drag out a region for your object, press the w key to bring up the Volume Statistics, and select the points to include or exclude polygons on the border of the volume. You will constantly move between Points and Polygons modes, but will only occasionally work in Volume mode. Instead of using the Volume Statistics, you can select an area in any view. But know that Volume Statistics is there when you want it! Please read through your LightWave 7 manuals for more information on these selection modes. It is important for your success with Modeler to understand the difference between the Points, Polygons, and Volume selection modes.

Objects

3D modeling must begin somewhere, either with a few points, a curve, or more commonly, a primitive object. Look around you—most everyday shapes are based on primitive geometric shapes. The desk you work at can be created from a box. The walls around you, the windows, all can be created from boxes—even your significant other! Cups, plates, and other kitchen items can be created from discs. You see, the more you pay attention to something—even something as simple as a coffee mug—the more you will understand how to re-create it in LightWave Modeler. You can use the Primitive Objects, Box, Ball, Disc, and Cone tools as the basis for even the most complex 3D models.

With an upgrade like LightWave 7, it can be a challenge to find a starting point for creating. In LightWave, objects are created in specific ways, and understanding this is vital to your success with LightWave.

Loading, Saving, and Creating Objects

Loading objects has not changed since previous versions of LightWave. Pressing l on the keyboard opens the Load Object command window. Here, you can load LightWave objects (lwo), 3D Studio objects (3ds), AutoCAD objects (dxf), and Alias|Wavefront objects (obj). You also can choose to use the mouse to load objects. With the Objects tab selected, you can select Load Object from the File drop-down menu.

Although loading objects is straightforward, you must be aware of the changes made to Modeler in respect to its multidocument capability. Modeler 7's objects have their own set of layers. If you've created a big red ball and decide to create a big yellow box, you need to tell Modeler that you are creating a new object using the File menu. This moves the existing object and sets up a new object layer set. The existing object is still loaded but not selected.

As you read through this book, many of the tutorials will use LightWave Modeler's new object standard, MultiMesh. MultiMesh is what LightWave calls an object with multiple layers.

The File menu also lets you save objects, close objects, import objects, save layers as objects, and create new objects, as well as execute a few other commands. By the way, pressing Shift+n creates a new object instantly. Figure 3.2 shows the File drop-down list of commands.

Because objects themselves have layers, you need to inform LightWave that you want to begin creating a new object. You can select New Object from the File menu. Doing so will create a fresh set of layers. A single object file can have unlimited layers, so don't be confused when your current object suddenly vanishes—it is still loaded in Modeler, but it is not within the new object's layer set. Creating a new object does not delete any other work. As the modeling tutorials progress, you'll understand how this functionality is used. When you create new objects, you'll see the object selections are added as "Unnamed 1," "Unnamed 2," and so on. You can find these in the object selection drop-down menu at the top right of the Modeler interface, to the left of the Layer buttons (see Figure 3.3).

Figure 3.2
The File drop-down list of commands is where you can find the basic object loading and saving functions.

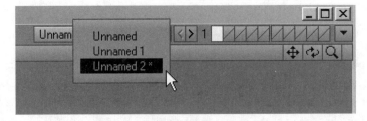

Figure 3.3   Objects loaded into Modeler can be selected from the drop-down list in the upper-right corner of the interface.

Versions of LightWave Modeler previous to version 6 only required you to either clear or delete an object to discard it for good. LightWave 7 requires you to select Close Object from the File menu, just as 6 and 6.5 did. The functionality of the layers is significant to the way you build objects. Every object you create will have its own set of unlimited layers, which is good for objects with many separate moving parts, such as a car with doors and wheels or a house with windows and doors. Selecting Close Object removes the object and closes its layers. Later in this chapter, you'll learn more about managing objects, interface enhancements, and functionality to streamline your workflow. For now, read on to learn about how Modeler 7 creates objects.

 Note

If you delete an object instead of closing it and then decide to save the object, you've just saved an empty object. Be careful!

Creating Object Layers

The layer buttons you'll use to work with layers are positioned atop the Modeler interface in the upper-right corner. Before Modeler 6, you could create different objects or parts of objects on each layer. Essentially, each layer in previous versions was its own object. All layers now relate to the current object.

If you're familiar with Adobe Photoshop, you often use layers in that program to build your images. The same idea applies to Modeler. For example, you've created a large mechanical robotic arm. The base and main arm of the robot are complete, but to build the extended arms that move on their own pivots, you need to create a separate part of the same object—this is where the use of layers in Modeler is key.

A secondary use for layers relates to references. Using layers, you can set one or more layers as a background reference layer and work in a clean foreground layer without harming your other model(s). Modeler still works like this, but the functions run much deeper. Now, each object has its own layer set, and you can have unlimited layers. Figure 3.4 shows the Modeler interface with objects loaded in both the foreground and background layers.

The layers in Modeler have more than just one function. They also are used for modeling using Booleans, creating curve extrusions, slicing up objects, and more. You will use multiple layers later in this chapter to create various objects.

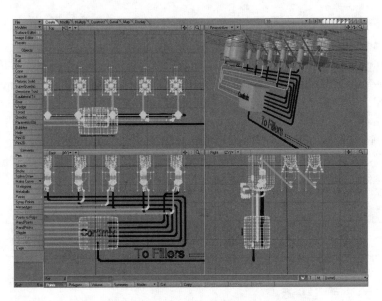

Figure 3.4   Objects can be put in different layers for reference and safety.

Layers can be visible or invisible. To help control layer visibility, you can open the Layer Browser window (Figure 3.5). This panel enables you to select (or multiselect with the Shift key) any and all layers. A check mark under the F heading refers to the geometry in a foreground layer, and a check mark under the B heading refers to the geometry in a background layer. You can find this window in two ways:

- From the Modeler drop-down list at the top left of the interface, select Windows and then choose Layer Browser Open/Close (see Figure 3.6).
- Press CTRL and the F5 key.

When you move beyond the basics, the layers within Modeler are very powerful and can be confusing at first. As with anything, the best way to understand this is to try it out. Before that can happen, you need to know how Modeler creates different types of objects.

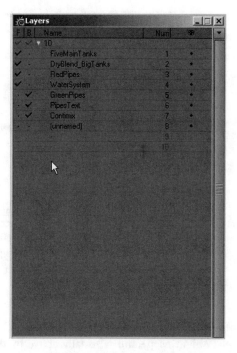

Figure 3.5   The Layer Browser window will show you all of your layers for every object in Modeler.

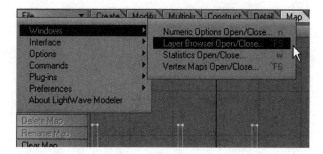

Figure 3.6   The Layer Browser window can be opened via the Modeler drop-down list.

Modeling Methods

Modeler is more than a tool used to create geometric shapes. Many of the tasks performed in Layout also can be done in Modeler, such as surfacing, morph targets, and skeletal setups. This is because Modeler offers various types of vertex maps. At the lower-right side of the Modeler interface, you'll see three small buttons labeled W, T, M (see

Figure 3.7). These letters stand for Weight Map, Texture, and Morph, respectively. These three types of vertex maps are easily accessible directly on the Modeler interface. Other vertex maps, such as Color Vertex are quite useful as well but are found under the Map tab.

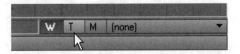

Figure 3.7   Three of LightWave's vertex maps can be created easily from the Modeler interface: Weight, Texture, and Morph.

Note

A vertex map is additional data that can be hung on points. This additional data is an instruction that is attached to the points of an object, such as an endomorph, which is information about a change in the position of points. Points make up polygons. Polygons make objects.

Weight Modeling Mode

The first button is W (Weight Map) and is usually active by default when you start Modeler. However, the default vertex map is "none," as seen in the Weight Map drop-down list. "None" signifies that the particular Weight Map is not selected. This applies to all three vertex maps—W, T, or M.

In a basic sense, a Weight Map is a set of values associated with the points in an object. A point can have a value, 0, or no value in a map. There are two types of Weight Maps: General and SubPatch Weight. If you create a General map, you can assign different values to points for this map. Then you can do things like bend an object with bones using the map to control the influence of the bones. Maps can also be used for falloff with most modeling tools. The SubPatch Weight Map is a predefined special map that controls the bias of a control point. Weights can be used everywhere for motion, modeling, surfacing, and more. See Exercise 3.1 for an example of using weights. (Also see Chapter 11 for further information about using Weights.)

Note

A SubPatch is a surface that is subdivided until it is smooth. Pressing the Tab key creates results exact to MetaNURBS in previous versions of LightWave. SubPatch in LightWave 7, however, is like a real-time MetaForm (the complex subdivision tool in older versions of LightWave), allowing you to create smooth organic objects from simple primitives such as automobiles, humans, or even flowers. SubPatch is discussed later in this chapter.

Exercise 3.1   Using Weights

Weights are mentioned often throughout this book, but to give you a good head start, create your own object with a SubPatch weight map.

1. Start Modeler and be sure that you are using the default interface settings. You should have the Create tab selected at the top of the Modeler interface.

   You'll see the buttons change on the left side of the screen. These are all the commands that allow you to create objects.

2. Click the W button at the lower-right corner of the interface.

   This puts Modeler in Weight Creation mode.

3. In the drop-down menu next to the W, T, and M buttons, click and hold down the mouse button to select SubPatch Weight from the list.

   Your other choices are None or New, which will be used later. Figure 3.8 shows the SubPatch selection.

Figure 3.8
The SubPatch Weight is selected from the drop-down menu at the bottom-right corner of the interface.

4. Select the Box command under the Create tab.

5. In the top Left viewport in Modeler, click and drag to draw a box. The box at this point is flat, so click in the Back viewport (bottom-left quad) above and below the flat box. The box object expands to meet your mouse (see Figure 3.9).

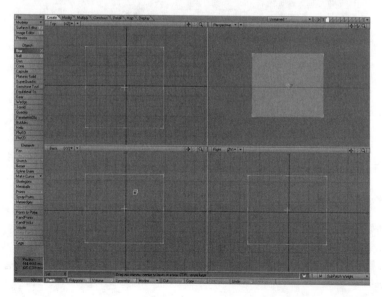

Figure 3.9   Create a simple box by dragging out in the Top view, then in the Back view.

6. Once the box has depth, press the spacebar to turn off the Box command. If you accidentally click in a blank area before you turn off the Box command, you'll lose your object.

Note

The box you just created was LightWave's way of building objects. When you draw out a box as you did here, you are in Setup mode. Turning off a tool keeps the object and deselects the tool.

7. Press the comma (,) key once to zoom out. Press Tab to apply a SubPatch to this box.

You'll see the square box turn into a control cage for a smooth-surface object. This is the SubPatch at work, as shown in Figure 3.10.

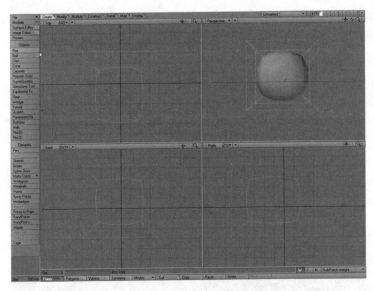

Figure 3.10
Pressing the Tab key activates SubPatch for the current object. This is a simple box, but SubPatch smoothes it out.

8. Be sure that one of your Modeler views is set to Perspective, such as the upper-right. Make that Perspective view's render style Weight Shade, as shown in Figure 3.11. You can do this through the Viewport Titles or through the Display Options (d) panel.

9. Select the Map tab from the top of the Modeler interface.

Toward the bottom on the left side of the interface, you'll see the Weight and Color commands. Figure 3.12 shows the toolbar.

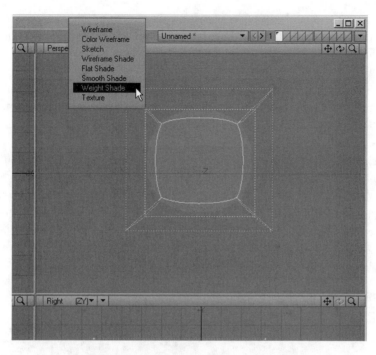

Figure 3.11   You can specify a Weight Shade mode in any of the Modeler views from the Viewport title bar.

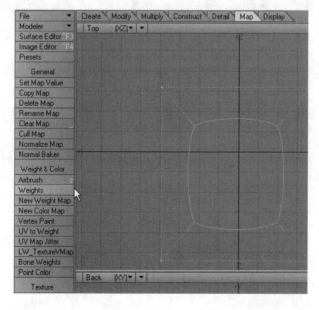

Figure 3.12   When a SubPatch Weight is active, the Weights tool becomes available.

10. Select Weights, and move your mouse over to the Perspective viewport. With the left mouse button, click and drag to the right on one of the corners of the SubPatch box. (You also can rotate the view for a better angle. To rotate, click and drag the small rotate button in the viewport title bar within the view.)

    When you click and drag on the SubPatch box, you'll see three things happen: a percentage change will appear in the info display, the corner will sharpen, and it will turn red.

11. To see the Weight Shade being applied, you need to have your Viewport Rendering Style set to Weight Shade. This is not necessary for Weight control to work, but it is necessary for color representation.

    Now if you click and drag a point to the left of the box, you'll see the SubPatch object smooth out and turn blue. Access the Viewport Rendering Style through the small drop-down arrow atop each viewport.

A Weight object enables you to sharpen or smooth a SubPatched object without the need to create more geometry. Figure 3.13 shows a simple box with Weights applied. This shape uses only six polygons.

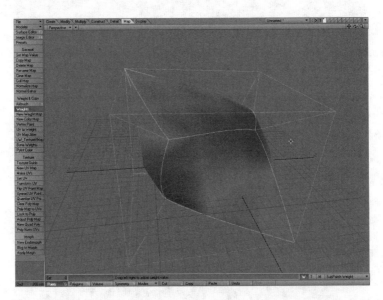

Figure 3.13   Using Weights to adjust your SubPatch model allows for complex shapes with a very low geometry count.

If the object in Figure 3.13 did not have Weights applied, however, it would take nearly 400 polygons to create this shape. It is easy to create a shape like this by using Weights. The type of weighting used in Figure 3.13 is a SubPatch weight. What this technique does is shift the curves at the various control points, which changes the shape of the object. Because the object is made up of curves, it remains smooth throughout. Without using

Weights on your objects in your scene, you'll find that there is a lot of wasted geometry. The more geometry there is, the longer it will take to render your animation. The redraw speed in Layout will also be affected. Additionally, Weights give you precise control in areas of your model not previously possible.

This is the most basic of Modeler's Weights. Regular objects can have Weights, and you can change UV maps to Weights, Paint Weights, and more.

Texture Modeling Mode

Not to be confused with the Texture Editor or an applied texture, the Texture button in Modeler offers to you another control for creating models. Figure 3.14 shows the T button at the bottom of the Modeler interface.

Figure 3.14
The Texture modeling mode button is located at the lower-right area of the Modeler interface.

Texture enables you to create a texture map for your object. This is not a traditional texture map, but a texture UV map. UV mapping was a new addition to LightWave 6 and is improved in version 7. UVs can be useful for applying images to complex objects, as you'll see later in this book. UV maps are used in Chapter 9, "Realistic Lighting Environments," and bonus UV mapping tutorials can be found on the web at *www. danablan.com* and *www.insidelightwave.com*.

Morph Modeling Mode with Endomorphs

You may be familiar with the term "endomorphs." An endomorph is an embedded morph. A morph is a displacement of points from one position to another, like a marching band forming different shapes. Points, of course, make up an object and, in turn, morphing reshapes your object. In previous versions of LightWave, morphing between objects required that you model separate objects for each target. In LightWave 6 and later versions, morph targets can be all part of one single object via the Morph Modeling mode, also known as endomorphs.

Figure 3.15
The Morph modeling mode button is located at the lower-right corner of the Modeler interface.

Figure 3.15 shows the M button at the lower-right corner of the Modeler interface. Select this mode to begin creating an object with endomorphs.

Exercise 3.2   Preparing an Endomorph Object

Creating a morph object is easy. You don't need to make a new object to create endomorphs—any existing object will work. The first step is that you need to be sure that you are in Morph mode. Be sure to select the M button pictured in Figure 3.15 before you begin modeling. The next step is to understand the difference between Absolute and

Relative morph settings. An Absolute morph setting tells Modeler that any newly created endomorph stands on its own and is not affected by any changes to the base model. A Relative morph setting then reflects any changes made to the base model. Follow along with this next example to see how easy it is to create morph objects.

Now that you know the difference, here's a rule of thumb—never use Absolute. Using Absolute negates the benefits of creating endomorphs. Let's say you have a complex character you've built, and it's taken you some time to complete. Toward the end of production, and after countless cans of Coke, your client asks you in a sort of mousey voice, "Can you make the nose bigger?" You cringe. But then you realize that you simply can make the change to the nose of the base model, which in turn updates all the endomorphs. If you had used Absolute to create one or all of the endomorphs, you'd have to make the change to the nose on each endomorph. So, never use Absolute.

Note

You create morph objects with endomorphs to be animated in Layout. A primary use for endomorphs is animating character expressions. This will be covered in detail in Chapter 12, "Deformations and Movement."

1. With your default Modeler configuration active, start Modeler and press the l key (lowercase L).

   The l key opens the Load Object command window.

Tip

The Grid is part of LightWave's coordinate system. Its size determines the scale with which you'll be building objects. In Modeler, the Grid size is visible through the information panel at the lower-left corner of the interface. For more information on the Grid, refer to your LightWave reference manual.

2. Load the Face.lwo object from the Projects/Objects/Chapter3 directory.

3. Press the a key to fit the model into all views.

4. Click the M at the lower-right portion of the screen to tell Modeler you'll be working with endomorphs.

5. To the right of the M key selection, you'll see the word "base" in the drop-down menu.

   This tells Modeler that the current object, and the way it looks right now, is the base morph target.

6. Click and hold the same drop-down menu for M and you'll see the selection labeled "new." From this drop-down menu, you can select your "base" as well as any new endomorphs you create, and you can select "new" to create a new endomorph. Select the option labeled "new," and you'll see the Create Morph Map panel come up, as shown in Figure 3.16.

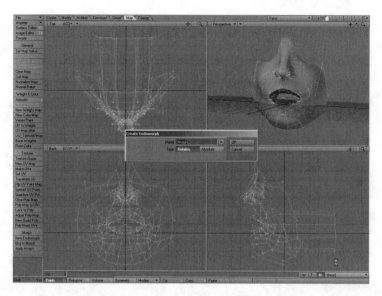

Figure 3.16   Choosing to make a new endomorph calls up the Create Morph Map requester.

7. In the Create Morph Map requester, type a new name, such as Mouth.open.

It's important to add the period between the name and the control, because this creates a group called Mouth, which has a control called Open. When you use the MorphMixer plug-in in Layout, you'll be able to see your groups and control your morphs. It's not necessary for the endomorph to work, but it helps organize things.

Note

MorphMixer is a Layout Displacement plug-in that enables you to morph between any of the morph targets you've created. It produces a window of morph sliders that you can adjust and keyframe.

Before you click OK in the Create Morph Map panel, choose a Relative Morph Map that will be affected if you make any changes to the base object. Of course, any changes you make to the geometry, such as adding or deleting, will affect all morph targets. You will use a Relative type setting most of the time when creating endomorphs.

8. For the Mouth.open Morph Map, choose Relative, and click OK.

9. Now, select the points encompassing the lower portion of the mouth and jaw, as shown in Figure 3.17. With the lower jaw points selected, in the Right view (lower right) move the mouse to the back of the face. Press the y key to select the Rotate command.

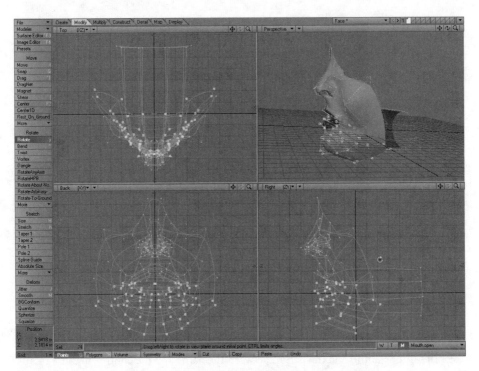

Figure 3.17 After you have created a new Morph Map, adjust the model's points to a new position. This becomes an endomorph—an embedded morph target.

10. When your mouse cursor changes to two small curved arrows, click and drag slightly in the jaw area of the model, within the Right viewport. Rotate the group of points to open the mouth.

11. After you've moved the points into a position you like, deselect them by first tapping the spacebar to turn off the Rotate command and then clicking a blank area of the interface, or by pressing the ?/ key.

12. Now, from the drop-down menu next to the M button, select "new" as you did in Step 6 and create additional Morph Targets. Set the new name to Mouth.pucker. You'll see that this reflects the base object state. Keep the Type set to Relative.

13. Select the points of the mouth area and move them into a pucker position using the Size tool (Shift+h) in the Back view (bottom-left view). Feel free to use the Stretch and Move tools to get the pucker into the position you like.

14. Once you've puckered the lips, you may need to Move the selection forward to make sure the puckered lips are not too far back into the face. Figure 3.18 shows the face with a pucker.

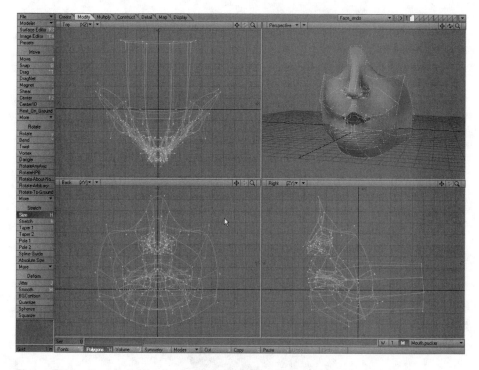

Figure 3.18   By simply selecting groups of points and using the basic modify tools, such as Size, a pucker face is created.

Note

If you create a new Morph Map and do not adjust the model in some way, and then select another Morph Map, the new Morph Map will not be created. This happens because vertex maps can have a value (including zero) or no value. A map has to have at least one value for at least one point to exist.

You've now created two Morph Maps.

15. Save the object as a new object, making sure not to save over your original.

16. Continue making new Morph Maps, and save your changes as you go. Experiment with this feature, with modifications to a simple ball just to get the hang of it.

Exercise 3.3   Testing Morph Maps

To test your Morph Maps, select a map from the drop-down list. In the previous example, you created Mouth.open and Mouth.pucker. You should now see these names in the list, along with "base" and "new."

You can use endomorphs to make phonetic shapes for lip-syncing and speech animation. You also can make changes to eyelids, cheeks, brows, and so on. Of course, the model in this example has no eyes or brows, so you'll need to use a different object. Having individual Morph Maps for these things allows greater flexibility when animating.

1. You can put each Morph Map into motion at any time. If you decide to animate another part of the face, such as the cheeks, set your Morph Map name to Cheeks.xxx, where the cheeks will become a group, and the xxx will be the position you choose to name.

2. Load the face_endo.lwo object into Modeler to see additional Morph Maps. When this object is loaded, select the name list at the lower-right corner of the Modeler interface. You'll see the list of endomorphs created, as shown in Figure 3.19.

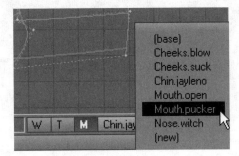

Figure 3.19   As you create various endomorphs, you'll see them in the list to the right of the M button, which is at the bottom right side of the Modeler interface.

3. Select any of the morph targets to see a particular object's various facial positions.

SubPatching Objects

You'll hear the term *SubPatch* a lot throughout this book. As a matter of fact, you might get sick of hearing about it, but the truth is that this is one of the most powerful tools within LightWave Modeler. SubPatches are what used to be MetaNURBS. MetaNURBS were LightWave's version of Non-Uniform Rational B Splines. In LightWave 7, a SubPatched object turns quadrangles (polygons made of four points) and triangles (polygons made of three points) into curves. Think of SubPatch as digital clay, which enables you to mold objects.

Exercise 3.4   Creating SubPatches with Symmetry

Perform the next steps to get a feel for how LightWave's SubPatch system works. Remember that you've already worked with SubPatched objects earlier in the chapter. This section expands on functionality.

1. From the File drop-down menu in Modeler, select Close All Objects.

Note

There is no Clear button in Modeler. You must select Close All Objects. Be sure to save any work you want to keep before you do this.

2. Press the a key to fit all views. Because no objects are loaded, the Modeler views will return to the default 1m grid size, and the Perspective view will reset with the positive z-axis in front of you. (This will ensure that any measurements in this book match up with your system.) Slightly rotate the Perspective view to see the grid.

3. Be sure that you are using the Default Modeler configuration and select the Box primitive from the Create tab, or press Shift+x at the same time. From the Perspective view (top-right quadrant), hold the Ctrl key and draw out a box, similar to Figure 3.20.

   Notice that the rectangle is already visible in the viewports. This is because LightWave Modeler does not require you to "make" an object. Once you draw out the tool, the box is generated. Because you are creating the object in the Perspective view and holding the Ctrl key while you do so, the box is equal on all sides.

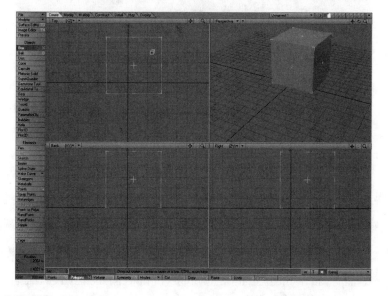

Figure 3.20   The Box primitive can be used to draw out a box or rectangular shape in any view, even Perspective.

4. Once you've drawn a box, press the spacebar to turn off the Box tool.

   Your box has been created. All you need to do to create a box, ball, or any other primitive is to select the particular tool, draw it, and turn off the tool. A "make" button no longer exists.

5. Press F2 to center the object on the 0, 0, 0 xyz-axis, and then press the a key again to fit the box to view.

Note

Attention Mac users: If you press F2 and the box does not center and a system message appears, you need to assign your Function keys. You also can use the Center function, found under the Modify tab.

6. Next, press the Tab key. Your rectangle will suddenly become an oval, as shown in Figure 3.21.

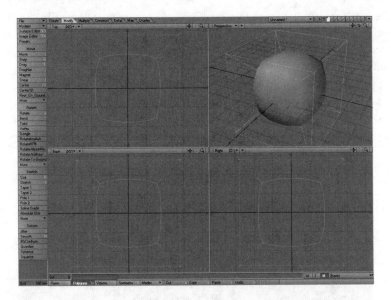

Figure 3.21   Pressing the Tab key activates SubPatch mode, smoothing active polygons.

Note

SubPatched polygons require either three- or four-sided polygons. However, try to always work with four-sided polygons for best results. Three-sided polygons can sometimes create undesirable results when rendering smooth surfaces.

This shape can be the basis for many types of objects, such as a character, car, or spaceship.

7. At the bottom of the Modeler interface, select Symmetry mode (Shift+y), as in Figure 3.22.

Figure 3.22   Symmetry mode will allow you to work on one side of an object while LightWave works on the other!

8. Make sure that you're in Polygon mode, and then in the Perspective view, click once on the right side of the box object. This is the positive X side (see Figure 3.23). Two polygons will be selected with one click, due to Symmetry mode being turned on.

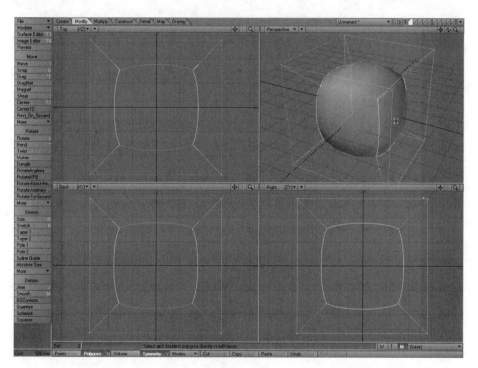

Figure 3.23   When Symmetry mode is enabled, you only have to worry about selecting and working with points and polygons on the positive x-axis.

Note

Symmetry mode works only on the x-axis. If you leave Symmetry on when not intending to work on a symmetrical object, you will run into problems. Whatever you do on the positive x-axis is mirrored on the negative X. Also your object must be identical on both sides of the x-axis for Symmetry to work.

9. Press b to activate the Bevel tool (also found under the Multiply tab). Now click and drag the selected polygon of the box in the Right view to begin beveling, similar to Figure 3.24.

Note

For Bevel, up and down movements with the mouse apply Shift to the bevel, while left and right movements with the mouse apply Inset. Shift moves the polygon outward or inward, while Inset moves the polygon up or down.

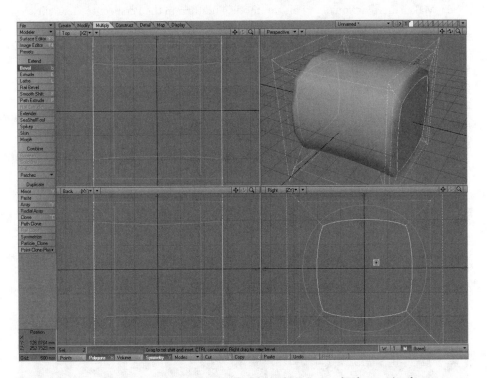

Figure 3.24   Applying a bevel to the SubPatched box object instantly changes its shape. Beveling is a multiply function, and you've now added more geometry to the object, which changes the way the SubPatch sees the polygons.

10. Right-click once to add another bevel to the selected surface and then use the left mouse button to move it outward and size it down, as shown in Figure 3.25.

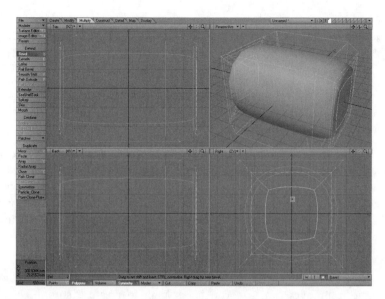

Figure 3.25   Right-clicking when the Bevel tool is active adds another polygon to the already selected polygon. This is great for creating bevels with multiple segments.

11. Repeat this process again, sizing down the selected polygon as you go. Use the Stretch tool from the Modify tab to flatten the selected polygon, as shown in Figure 3.26.

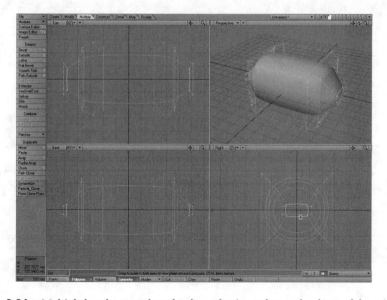

Figure 3.26   Multiple bevels on a selected polygon begin to change the shape of the original SubPatched box. Stretching a selection down as you go also modifies the shape.

Note

You might need to press the comma (,) key to zoom out the views slightly to see the object as you build.

From this point on, continue with more bevels and various sizing to create the wings of a simple spaceship, as shown in Figure 3.27. Symmetry mode has helped by allowing you to concentrate on only one side of the object.

This quick example showed you how a simple box can be made into something organic, such as a generic spaceship. Of course, more time and detail would have created a more complex object. Although this is just a hint of what SubPatch can do, the principles are the same regardless of the complexity of your object. You start with a simple primitive, such as a box or a ball. Using SubPatch you can mold and shape your model into anything you can imagine.

Later in Chapter 8, "Architectural Environments," you'll learn how to build more complex objects and surface them. And Chapter 10, "Organic Modeling," will show you how these simple techniques can take you far enough to create a stunningly realistic human head.

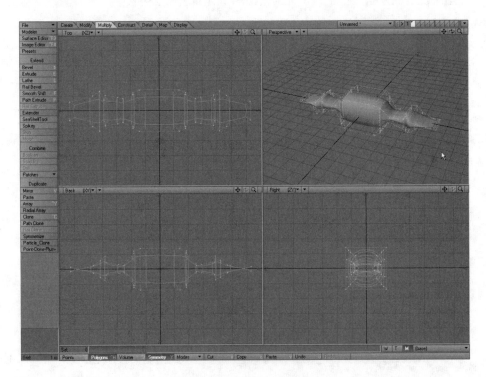

Figure 3.27   A few quick bevels and you've made the base for a simple spaceship.

Splines

With LightWave's SubPatch mode, rich toolset, and full OpenGL interface, it is easy to create any shape you can imagine. However, there is yet another way for you to create and shape your models. A *spline* is a curve defined by mathematical functions such as Bezier, B-Spline, Hermite, and NURBS. Spline modeling can help you create additional shapes like tubes, tunnels, staircases, and more. It is also useful for creating 3D geometry from background images. The next two exercises show you how to create and shape a spline and build a simple object from a background image.

Before the capability was available to mold shapes with SubPatch, splines were often used to create smooth-flowing objects, such as curtains or the hull of a boat. This type of modeling is still available in LightWave and might be more useful for your specific modeling needs. This next tutorial shows you how to create a rowboat with spline curves.

Exercise 3.5   Creating a Rowboat using the Skin Command

In this exercise, you will build a rowboat using splines and the Skin tool. Its curves are simple, but too complex for primitive shapes. These techniques also can be used to create cloth, landscapes, or even characters.

1. Save any work in Modeler, and then select Close All Objects from the File menu. Press the a key to fit all views. Don't forget to turn off Symmetry mode.

2. Select the Points command from the Create tab (Figure 3.28).

    This enables you to create points—points that make up a curve.

3. In the Top view (top left), click with the right mouse button (hold the Apple key on a Mac) to instantly create a point to the right of the x-axis.

    You can line up a point with the left mouse button and then click the right button if you like.

4. Create five points, similar to Figure 3.29.

    These points will represent an outline of one-half of the rowboat. LightWave's splines will make the curve, and the Skin feature will be used to create a surface.

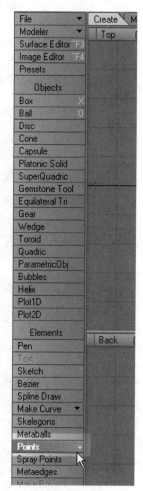

Figure 3.28
The Points command is at the bottom left of the Create tab.

Note

Depending on the quality of your video card and screen resolution, you might have trouble viewing your newly created points. You can adjust the point visibility by going to the Display Options panel (d). Under the Interface tab, click Simple Wireframe Points and enter a new pixel size.

5. Press Ctrl+p to create an open curve. You can find this tool under the Create tab at the bottom left, as in Figure 3.30.

   If you had pressed Ctrl+o, you would have created a closed curve.

6. With the single open curve created, call up the Clone tool by pressing Ctrl+c (the Clone tool also is found under the Multiply tab). Using the Clone tool, duplicate the spline curve for the rest of the boat's right side.

7. For Number of Clones, enter 4.

   This creates four more splines in addition to the original, totaling five.

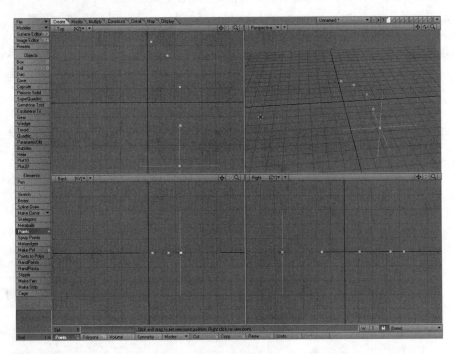

Figure 3.29   Five simple points are created in the Top view.

8. Set the Offset Y to 250mm.

   This spreads the curves up 250mm from the original.

9. Set the Offset Z to 150mm.

   This shifts each clone down the z-axis, creating the curve needed for the front of the rowboat. Figure 3.31 shows the Clone tool's interface.

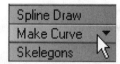

Figure 3.30   Once points are created, you need to make a curve, either open or closed.

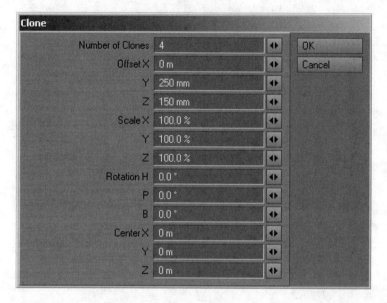

Figure 3.31   The Clone tool, as shown here, can be used on curves or on objects.

10. Click OK to see your curves.

    Feel free to adjust the curves, if you like, and to try various Offset values. Figure 3.32 shows the cloned curves.

11. Making sure that no curves are selected, select the Mirror tool (Shift+v) from the Multiply tab and with the left mouse button, click and drag the mouse on the center x-axis in the Top or Back views. You're using one of these particular views so that you can mirror the curves on the x-axis. The right view looks down the x-axis, therefore not giving you much control.

    LightWave's tools are interactive, and holding the mouse down while slightly moving the mouse shows where the mirrored objects will be placed.

12. Line up the mirrored curves with the original curves.

13. Release the mouse button to set the new curves.

14. Press the spacebar to turn off the Mirror tool. Figure 3.33 shows the mirrored curves.

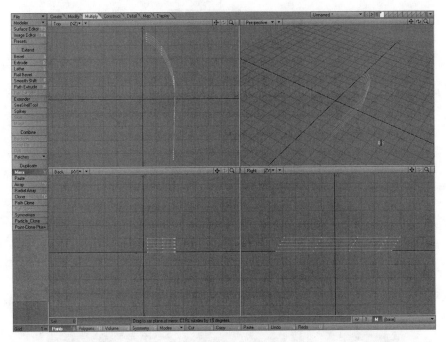

Figure 3.32   The Clone tool duplicated the single curve, creating a framework for the rowboat.

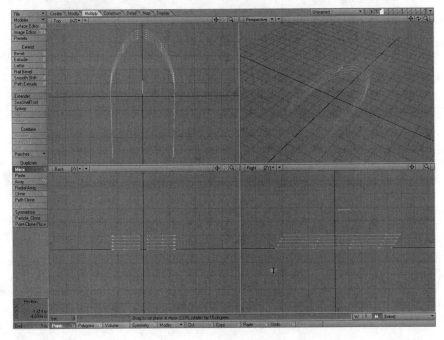

Figure 3.33   The interactive Mirror tool is used to create a duplicate of the curves on the opposite side of the x-axis.

If the front points of the curves do not line up and connect on the 0 x-axis, don't worry—you can align them to make sure your boat won't have any leaks.

15. Switch to Points mode at the bottom of the Modeler interface, and select the 10 points that make up the curves in the front of the boat, as shown in Figure 3.34.

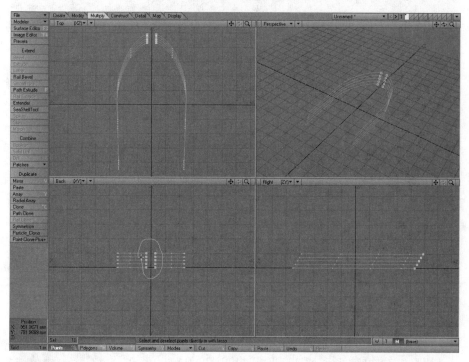

Figure 3.34 Working in Points mode, make sure that the 10 points in the front of the boat are selected.

Note

By right clicking and dragging around the desired points, you're lassoing the selection. This works for both points and polygons. You'll see a blue line drawn around the points as you select.

16. With the 10 points selected, go to the Detail tab and select the Set Value command (also Ctrl+v).

This enables you to set precisely any selected points to a specific location.

17. Select the x-axis, and set the Value (the Modeler measurement you want to move the points to) to 0, as shown in Figure 3.35.

18. Click OK.

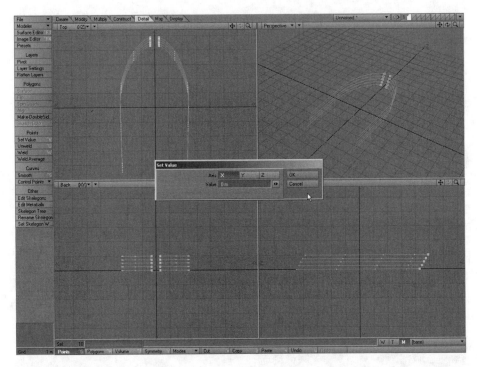

Figure 3.35   Using the Set Value command, you can move any selected points or polygons to a specific position.

Even though it looks like only five points are now remaining, if you look at the small information window above the Points mode button at the bottom of the Modeler interface, you'll see that it reads Set 10. This tells you that you have 10 points selected. Figure 3.36 shows this area.

Keeping the 10 points in the exact location does you no good. When you create a surface for the boat, the front side will not connect. Modeler still sees the curves as separate entities. You can see only five points after the SetValue command was applied, meaning that the points now occupy the same space.

Figure 3.36
The information area above the Point selection at the bottom of Modeler shows that 10 points are selected.

19. Now eliminate the duplicate points by pressing the m key for Merge Points.

20. When the Merge Points panel comes up, select Automatic, and click OK. A message should instantly pop up telling you that five points were eliminated. Press the / key to deselect the points.

21. From here, all you need to do is create a surface on top of the curves. You do this by using the Skin tool, found under the Multiply tab. But first, you need to tell Modeler what to skin.

22. In any of the Modeler viewports, select half of the curves in order, one after the other, being sure not to skip any.

Make sure that you are working in Polygon mode by checking the bottom of the Modeler interface (see Figure 3.37). The curves are highlighted with bright yellow when selected (see Figure 3.38).

Figure 3.37   You can choose Polygon mode (at the bottom of the Modeler screen) to tell Modeler to work with Polygons.

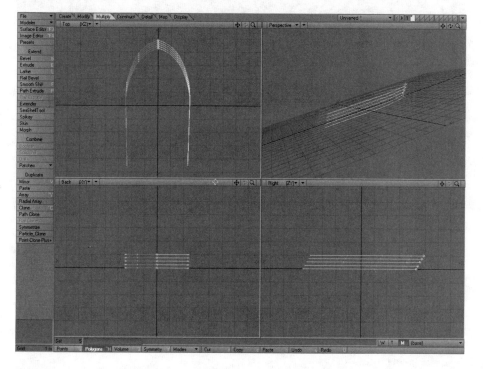

Figure 3.38   When selected, the curves highlight yellow.

23. Once the first set of curves is selected, select the Skin tool from the Multiply tab, and Modeler will generate a surface or skin for the curves.

Because these were open curves, Modeler will try to connect the end of the curve with the starting point. You'll see a straight section of new polygons on the inside of the boat.

24. Press the / key to deselect the curves and then select the extra polygons on the inside of the boat, as shown in Figure 3.39.

25. With the extra inside polygons selected, press the Delete key to delete them.

> **Note**
> LightWave 7 allows you to see color wireframes. From the Detail tab, select Sketch Color, and pick a color. Then, in one of the viewports, set the render style to Color Wireframe.

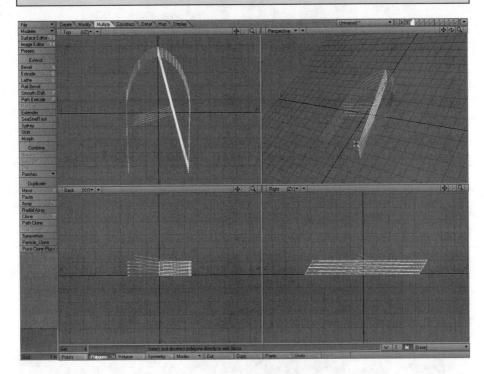

Figure 3.39   To eliminate the unneeded polygons, simply select them, and press Delete.

26. Press the f key to flip the existing surface outward, if the polygons don't seem to be facing outward.

If your polygons were facing inward when you skinned the curves, you mostly likely selected the curves from the bottom up. Next time, select the curves in order from the top down, and they'll face outward.

Also when surfacing, you can make the boat's surface double-sided so that both the inside and outside have visible polygons. Figure 3.40 shows some smoothing and basic surfacing on one side of the rowboat in a full-frame Perspective view.

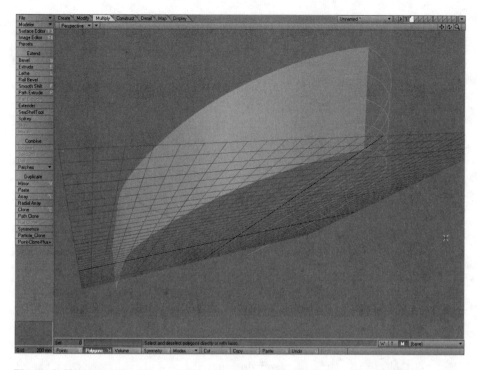

Figure 3.40   Once the unwanted polygons are removed, pressing the f key flips the remaining polygons outward if needed. Here you can see that half of the boat now has a surface.

There's nothing glamorous about spline modeling. It's tedious and not often the best method to use when creating specific shapes. The idea here is that you have all the tools you need to create whatever you can imagine. This section introduces you to the basic tools and functions that will be used throughout this book. LightWave 7 Modeler has even more features—read on to learn about a few more cool functions.

Notable Functions

Even if you are a seasoned veteran in LightWave Modeler, there will always be some tool or function that you don't use or didn't know about. Version 7 is no exception, and as your modeling hours accumulate, you may find that there are even more functions you weren't aware of. We could write an entire book on the powerful functions within Modeler 7! For now, here is a mention of a few cool tools. You'll learn about more tools throughout the tutorials in the book.

HUB Commands for Modeler

At the very top right corner of the Modeler interface is a small downward-pointing triangle. Click it and you'll see three commands: Switch to Layout, Synchronize Layout, and Send Object to Layout. Figure 3.41 shows the selection from the drop-down list.

Figure 3.41
The Modeler HUB commands live at the top right of the Modeler interface in a small drop-down selection.

Switch To Layout

Switch to Layout does what it says—even if Layout is not currently running. Selecting this option will run Layout and bring it forward.

Synchronize Layout

Directly below Switch to Layout is the Synchronize Layout command. This automatically updates Modeler and Layout so that your project is current in both programs. You wouldn't want to be working with an older model in Modeler and override the newer model in Layout by mistake. Synchronization is automatic as you switch between Layout and Modeler. Therefore, you generally don't need to select this option.

Send Object to Layout

The Send Object to Layout command does just that—sends your object to Layout. However, it is ghosted until you save the current object. Once the object is saved, the command becomes available and you can instantly send the object to Layout for animation. This is a command for which you might consider creating a button, or better yet, a hotkey on the keyboard.

> **Note**
> Send to Layout and Sync Layout work only if the HUB is active. You also must save an object before you can use the Send to Layout command.

Bone Weights

Bone Weights are a powerful tool in LightWave 7. Because you can set up full skeletal structures for your characters directly in Modeler, you also can assign Bone Weights. These are just general weight maps used for bone influences. When you create a character and set up a skelegon structure in Modeler, which will later be converted to bones in Layout, the bones deform the geometry to create a moving character without any seams. Often, areas like fingers are troublesome to animate due to influences bones have on surrounding geometry. Now with Bone Weights, you can tell each Skelegon to have a certain amount of falloff and influence. This subject will be covered with a detailed tutorial later in Chapter 11, "Character Construction." Figure 3.42 shows the Make Bone Weight Map panel which appears when you select the tool from the Map tab.

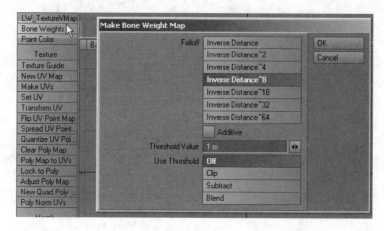

Figure 3.42   Bone Weights can be found under the Map tab and offer more control over bone influences when skelegon structures have been created.

Box Tool Enhancements

The Box tool has undergone a makeover for version 7. Figure 3.43 shows the Numeric panel (n) for the Box tool. An added edge control allows you to create rounded edges on boxes as they're created. In addition, you can now create a box by defining its width and height, rather than the cumbersome method of defining positions of two corners in previous versions of LightWave.

Commands and Tools and More Commands

There are so many handy tools in Modeler, from Capsule creation to the Gemstone tool, to UV Maps and more. As you find free moments while working with Modeler, be sure to click around and check out the tools available to you. Find your favorites, and make a note of them. Try everything! The more familiar you are with the tools in your tool chest, the more prepared you'll be on your next project. For example, you can use the Capsule tool to create tanks, pills, or rounded caps for various objects instantly. You can use the Gemstone tool to create jewel-shaped objects. A combination of all these primitives can really set you on your way to modeling complex objects.

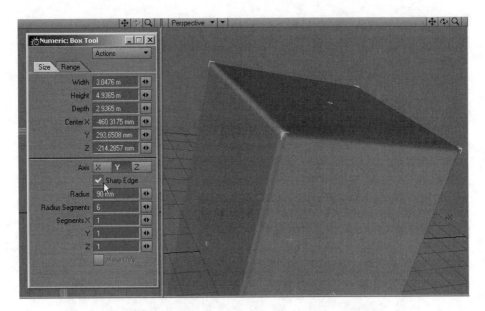

Figure 3.43   Boxes with rounded or beveled edges can be created instantly.

You might even have projects that require you to create a complex object or shape from nothing more than an image. And although it would be nice to have a command in the Additional list that was labeled "Make Cool Object," you're simply not going to find it. Learn the tools, and you will know how to make tons of cool objects.

The Next Step

Throughout this chapter, you were introduced to Modeler's functionality through a few brief tutorials. You created objects with primitive shapes, points, and curves. Later in Chapter 17, "Broadcast-Style Animation," you will create high-quality graphics from fonts. Certain fonts can be shapes such as arrows, road signs, and more, which all can be imported into Modeler. Often, a client will have an EPS or AI (Adobe Illustrator) file of his original artwork. This is an excellent way to import artwork into Modeler to create instant and perfect geometry. If you happen to use Adobe Illustrator or a similar program, try loading some of the EPS files you've created using the EPSF loader in Modeler (select File, then Import at the top left of the interface). This is just one more way to create objects in Modeler.

Summary

The exercises in this chapter took you through some of the key features of Modeler 7. You were introduced to many new functions and revisited old ones as well. The steps provided here will help guide you through the upcoming chapters and the tutorials within them. It is important that you understand the methods and principles of how LightWave 7 Modeler functions and how objects are created. If you're okay with that, turn the page and head on into Chapter 4, "LightWave 7 Layout."

Chapter 4

LightWave 7
Layout

Just about everything can be animated in
LightWave 7. Because of this, it is crucial
for you to plan your projects. Knowing
ahead of time what you want to create

helps you decide how to create it. The tools in Layout are extraordinary and powerful, and knowing what they can do and how they do it is a benefit to you and your projects. Before that, however, you need to be familiar with the basic Layout environment, keyframing, and animation setup types. This chapter steps you through the simpler aspects of Layout. Specifically, this chapter discusses the following:

- The animation environment
- Keyframing
- Constructing scenes
- Using the Scene Editor
- Understanding Motion Mixer for nonlinear animation

Although these aspects are simple, the concepts here are the foundation for moving ahead and creating more complex objects and animations.

In the simplest terms, 3D objects are created in LightWave's Modeler. LightWave's Layout is used to put these objects in motion.

Understanding the Animation Environment

Understanding the environment in which you are creating animations is key to your success as an animator. Knowing how to create an effect, or where to make the right adjustments, saves you not only time but also aggravation.

LightWave 7 has a lot of power and it's up to you to harness it. If you are familiar with LightWave version 6.5, the LightWave 7 Layout interface should look familiar and you should think of Layout as your very own television studio. It is uncluttered, yet functional. While many other programs fill up the screen with useless icons, LightWave names buttons clearly. By default, one camera and one light are used in the scene. Figure 4.1 shows the Layout window at startup. The default interface is in Layout's Perspective view—sort of a bird's-eye view of the environment.

 Note

The colored arrows visible on selected items represent axis control handles. Clicking and dragging the green arrow limits movements to the y-axis. Clicking and dragging the blue arrow limits movements to the z-axis, and clicking and dragging the red arrow limits movements to the x-axis.

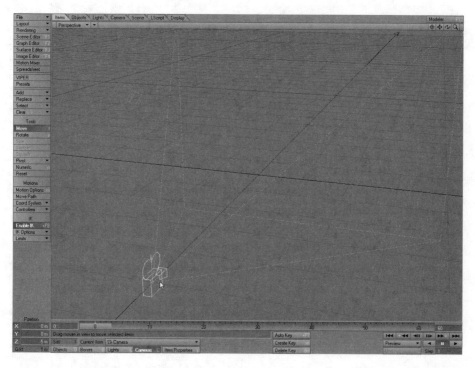

Figure 4.1   Layout opens to the Perspective view at startup.

The Layout Interface

Too often when a program opens, it seems as though you're staring at a blank canvas. Where do you go from here? What's next? Or even if you know what's next, what should you create? If you look at the default startup of the tabs across the top of Layout, you'll notice that seven tabs are available: Items, Objects, Lights, Camera, Scene, LScript, and Display. When you select any of these tabs, various controls appear on the left side of the interface. The toolbar across the top of the interface will show a different set of tools. Think of the tabs across the top as your steps to creating by asking yourself the following questions:

- What items will you need in your scene?

- How will you control objects?

- What lights and cameras do you need?

- Do you need to set any scene parameters?

- Are you adding and executing LScripts to your scene?

- How will you display your Layout view?

Note

You should be using LightWave's default interface settings for this chapter. By default, the controls are displayed on the left side of the interface, but you can move them from left to right or hide them, if you choose. Later you can use Chapter 1, "Introducing LightWave 7," or your LightWave 3D reference guide to find out how to add your own tabs and controls and rearrange everything to your liking. For now, however, stick with these default settings.

The Timeline and Fractional Frames

At the bottom of the Layout interface, you'll see more controls. The timeline for your animations, referred to as the *frame slider* in LightWave 7, appears here and cannot be moved. Don't think of this as just a timeline for your animations; think of it as your lifeline. All the elements of 3D animation are important, from lighting, to cameras, to special effects, but the timing and movement you employ is what brings it all to life. Figure 4.2 shows the default Layout timeline.

Figure 4.2   The Layout 7 frame slider at the bottom of the interface is the lifeline of movement and timing for your animations.

If you click and drag the frame slider, you can shuttle through your animation. By default, the timeline ends at frame 60. In most cases, you'll need more than 60 frames for your animations. In the General Options tab within the Preferences panel, accessed by pressing o, the frames per second (fps) is set to 30. NTSC video is 30fps, which is the most common setting for rendering in the United States. If the timeline ends at 60, and there are 30fps, you have a 2-second animation. To change this, double-click the number 60 at the end of the timeline to highlight it, and enter a new number, such as 300. At 30fps, 300 frames will give you a 10-second animation. Once entered, the numbers in the timeline adjust automatically, as shown in Figure 4.3.

Figure 4.3   The Layout timeline adjusts accordingly when you make the total animation length longer.

Note

LightWave allows you to set a different starting frame as well as an end frame. To change the starting frame, simply double click the numeric value at the front end of the timeline and enter a new starting frame. Additionally, you can add a negative value, so your animations start before frame 0. There's no rule that says you have to start your animation at frame 0. You would set negative keyframes to begin a motion of an item before the entire animation begins. Using pre 0 keyframes is great for character animation—your character can already be in motion as the scene begins.

Although the default fps value is 30, you can change this to whatever you like. For example, if you're creating animations for film, change this value to 24. You might need an animation rendered at 15fps for a corporate Microsoft PowerPoint presentation. Whatever fps you set, the default value will be used the next time you run Layout. Saved scenes with different fps values retain the information.

Note

You can also set a higher fps if you like for strange and cool visual effects.

LightWave 7 offers the capability to view fractional frames in the timeline. Activating Allow Fractional Current Frames enables you to input frame numbers and keyframes with decimals, like frame 10.23. Back under the General Options tab in the Preferences panel, click the Allow Fractional Current Frame button and you'll see values appear between the increments in the timeline (see Figure 4.4).

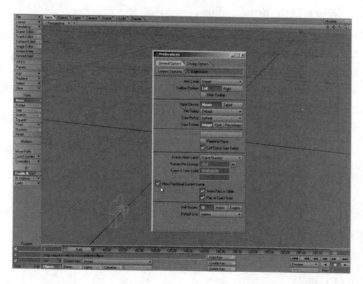

Figure 4.4   Fractional frames can be turned on in the Preferences panel and will be displayed in the timeline for specific control and timing.

The Coordinate System

Animating in 3D takes some getting used to. You need to realize that although you are looking at a flat computer monitor, elements in a 3D environment have x, y, and z-axes. This is the 3D world in which your animations live. The world, per se, is the environment around your animation. Each animation you create will have its own environment and its own coordinate system. LightWave 7 allows you to choose between three coordinate systems: World, Parent, and Local. The Local coordinate system eliminates any movement problems by allowing an object to be moved or rotated upon its own axis.

The Coordinate System setting affects movements and determines what happens when you drag your mouse. The easiest way to see this is to add a null, rotate it on Heading (H), Pitch (P), and Bank (B), and then parent the default light to it. You can turn on the Show Handles option to indicate the movement axes. If World is used, the axis will be along the grid. With Parent, it will be the same as the null's local axes. With Local, it will be the light's own axes. Only World is really new. If an item is deep within a hierarchy of rotated parents, movement along its parents or local axes can be confusing. The capability to move the item along the world axes is a lifesaver.

Pivots

Every item in Layout has a pivot. Think of a pivot as an item's root. Movements, rotations, parenting, or targeting all work based on an object's pivot. As in previous versions, LightWave 7 enables you to interactively move pivots in Layout as well as rotate them. To understand this further, follow along with this next exercise.

Exercise 4.1   Moving Pivots

Building multiple objects in Modeler, such as machinery or industrial equipment, requires you to have individual parts that rotate independently but remain assembled to a single object. A tractor, for example, requires that the wheels rotate upon their own pivots and the main lift rotates upon its own pivot. The arm extending from the main lift also needs to rotate, as does the main body of the tractor. The main body also needs to move and rotate upon its own pivot. This tutorial shows you how to load a single object with multiple pivot points (something you couldn't do before version 6) and move each pivot into place. Doing this will allow you to animate your model correctly.

1. You have three ways to load objects in Layout. You can select Load Object from the File drop-down menu and then select Load>Load Object. You can press + on the keyboard, or you can select Add from the Items tab; then Objects, and Load Object. Load the Tractor object from the Projects/Objects/Chapter4 folder on the book's CD-ROM.

2. At the bottom of the Layout interface, click and hold the Current Item drop-down list, as shown in Figure 4.5.

   You'll see that the single object you loaded is comprised of five layers. Each layer contains a separate part of the object.

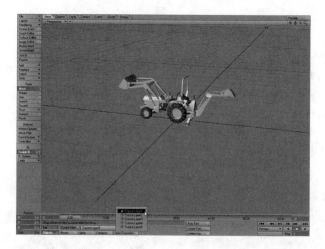

Figure 4.5   The Tractor object has five layers, which means there are five parts (four wheels and the main body) to the object, each with separate pivoting parts.

3. Press 1 on the numeric keypad to switch to the Back view.

   This is the view looking down the z-axis. Figure 4.6 shows the view.

Figure 4.6   The Back view in Layout is an orthogonal view that looks down the z-axis, toward the back of the Layout view. Only the Camera view is rendered.

Note

The numeric keypad is preprogrammed in Layout. You can switch among views easily, as follows: press 1 for Back view (z), 2 for Top view (y), 3 for Right view (x), 4 for Perspective view, 5 for Light view, 6 for Camera view, and 7 for Schematic view.

You can use the period key (.) to zoom in to the view, or the comma key (,) to zoom out.

4. From the top right of the viewport, click the small target icon to select Center Current Item.

The view centers on the currently selected item's pivot. If you move your view, the currently selected item will remain centered. Figure 4.7 shows the Center Current Item function. Note that this feature toggles on and off—select it again to turn it off.

Figure 4.7   The Center Current Item function helps you align your view.

To place the pivots correctly, start with the wheels.

5. Select Layer 2 of the Tractor object from the Current Item selector for objects at the bottom of the Layout Interface, as shown in Figure 4.8.

Figure 4.8   Select a layer of a particular object from the Current Item drop-down list at the bottom of the Layout interface.

When Layer 2 is selected, you'll see that the front-left wheel is highlighted yellow.

Tip

If your object continually jumps to the representational Bounding Box mode when object layers are selected, increase the Bounding Box Threshold. Press d on the keyboard to enter the Display Options panel. Set the Bounding Box Threshold to 42000. This value is slightly higher than the amount of points and polygons, whichever is higher. This keeps all layers drawn when selected. Also, if you'd like to see your object's pivots more clearly, you can change the view to Front Face Wireframe, as shown in Figure 4.9.

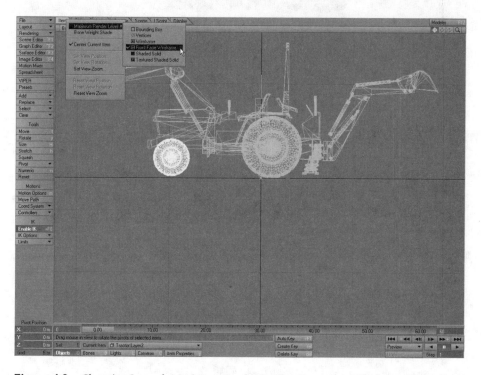

Figure 4.9   Changing Layout's Maximum Render Level to Front Face Wireframe shows all objects as only the front facing wireframe for better visibility.

Warning

Higher levels of the Bounding Box Threshold can slow system resources.

At this point, you can begin to move the item's pivot into position. Positioning pivots in orthogonal views is important for accuracy. This is why you are in the Back (xy) view.

6. With Layer 2 of the Tractor selected, select Move Pivot Tool from the Pivot command under the Items tab (see Figure 4.10).

Figure 4.10   With the Items tab at the top of Layout selected, choose Move Pivot Point Tool from the Pivot drop-down list.

The object's handles, shown as arrows, will appear: a green arrow pointing upward, a red arrow pointing from left to right, and a blue arrow pointing away (which is not visible in the Front view). The handles are centered on the object's origin along the x-, y-, and z-axes. The wheel is off to the left of its origin. The 0 axis is where the x-, y-, and z-axes meet, similar to an intersection. Each axis has 0, represented in Modeler by the dark line in the center of the grid. For example, in the Back view, the dark line running up and down is the 0 y-axis. To the right of the 0 y-axis is the positive x-axis, and to the left of the 0 y-axis is the negative x-axis. Rotating the wheel in this position would rotate the wheel around the 0 axis, and not its center. Figure 4.11 shows the wheel rotated with the existing pivot.

7. With the wheel in its original position, move the pivot to the center of the wheel by dragging the red arrow.

This moves the pivot on the x-axis. Use the period key (.) to zoom in if needed.

Tip

Make sure Auto Key is off when you're working through these exercises. If you have moved the wheel, simply click the u key to undo the move. Undo works only one time.

Tip

To move quickly into a closer view of the wheel, position the mouse pointer over the wheel, making sure that Center Current Item is off (upper right Layout). Press the g key to instantly center the mouse position. Then, zoom in by pressing the period key (.). Note that this works only in the Front, Side, or Top view.

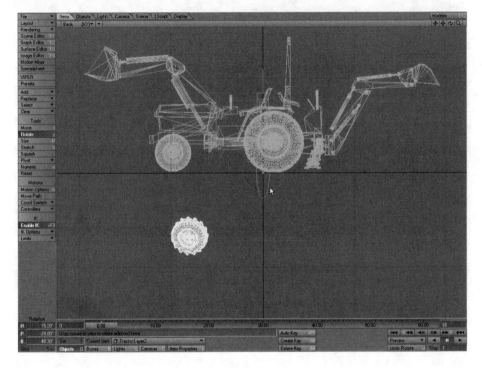

Figure 4.11   Rotating the wheel's pivot instead of moving it produces a wide rotation around the 0 axis. The wheel should rotate around itself.

Be as precise as possible centering the pivot.

8. When the x-axis pivot movement is in place, press 3 on the numeric keypad to switch to the Side view (x).

9. Select the green arrow and move the pivot up and over, centering it on the wheel for the z and y positions. If you like, you can move the y position from the Back view. Try dragging directly on the handles to constrain an axis. Figure 4.12 shows the movements in Bounding Box mode.

10. If you cannot get your pivot movements to be precise enough, you might need to adjust your Grid Square size.

   You can do this through the Display Options panel (d) or press the left-bracket key ([) for a smaller grid and the right-bracket key (]) for a larger grid.

Tip

> If you do create a smaller grid square size, you'll need to zoom out by using the comma (,) key. A smaller grid square size allows you to create more precise movements.

Figure 4.12

Use the Side view to align the pivot's position for the y- and z-axes. This view shows the selection in Bounding Box mode for better visibility.

   You've just moved the pivot for the front wheel, Layer 2.

11. To test its position, select the Rotate command for the selected item and then use the right mouse button to click and drag to rotate the wheel on its bank position.

   Because the tractor is positioned on the x-axis, selecting Bank for rotation makes the tire rotate upon its center.

If you notice that the spinning of the wheel is unaligned, reposition the pivot point. When you have it to your liking, save your scene and your objects. From here, select the other layers of the Tractor object and move the pivot points into place. Experiment with different pivot point positions, and even try rotating them for various results. You can load the Tractor object into Modeler, select the scoop area, and place it on another layer. Resave the object, and you'll be able to set a pivot point for the rotation of the scoop. You can do this for any object.

Remember that pivot points are the roots of the object and/or layer. All movements, centering, and even rotation are based on the pivot. For example, the pivot for a door swinging on a hinge would be the edge of the door where it meets the frame. The door rotates on this pivot point.

Setting Pivot Points in Modeler

You also have the capability to set a pivot point in Modeler. Setting the pivot point in Modeler is much easier than in Layout. To do so, choose the object you want to adjust and follow these steps:

1. Under the Detail tab, select Pivot, and you'll see a blue crosshair appear in your Modeler views.

2. You'll see a blue crosshair. This is your pivot point. Move it into your desired position, and save the object. This is a smart way to create complex objects with many moving parts. Once you have a pivot point set, it will be saved with the object.

Tip

To Rotate the pivot in Layout, use the Rec Pivot Rot (Record Pivot Rotation) command to lock the new pivot location, which records Pivot Rotation. Pivot Rotation is for resetting the rotation values to zero and allowing full axis rotation from something other than HPB 0,0,0. Actually, with the new coordinate system feature this option is not often used.

This eliminates rotation problems often found in complex hierarchies and works well for LightWave's multilayer objects.

Understanding Keyframing

Many of the features in LightWave 7 are discussed and used throughout the projects in this book. Because this is the first chapter to dive into Layout, it's necessary that you understand the importance of keyframing and timing. After you've mastered proper keyframing, you'll be equipped to move into more advanced techniques and concepts.

Keyframing is the act of setting or marking an animatable attribute in time. When you want a ball to move from point A to point B over two seconds, you need to set keyframes to tell the computer "stay here" at this point in time. You quickly will get a feel for timing the more you set keyframes. You can set keyframes yourself or let LightWave manage them for you.

Keyframing goes beyond just animating position and rotation. It encompasses light intensity, color, various surface attributes, and virtually anything in Layout that has a value that can be changed.

Exercise 4.2   Auto Key

By default, LightWave's Layout turns on the Auto Key button at the bottom of the Layout interface. It will adjust the values of existing keyframes. For the Auto Key feature to automatically create keys, you need to turn on Auto Key Create (General Options tab), which is off by default. Any commands such as Move, Rotate, Size, or Stretch will be remembered for selected items at the current frame. The following exercise explains this feature further.

1. Clear your scene in Layout, and load the Capsule object from the book's CD-ROM (Projects/Objects/Chapter4 folder).

2. With the Capsule object loaded, be sure the frame slider at the bottom of the Layout interface is at 0, be sure Auto Key is enabled, and activate Auto Key Create under the General Options tab within the Preferences panel (o) to have keyframes created automatically.

3. Select Modified Channels from the selection area of the Auto Key Create command. Modified Channels creates keyframes for those channels that have been changed, whereas setting Auto Key Create to All Motion Channels will create keyframes for everything in your scene.

   In the Layout window you'll notice that there is always a key at frame 0 by default. Thus, an object is locked in place, even without Auto Key. Auto Key merely lets you make an adjustment at frame 0 without having to re-create the key.

4. Move and rotate the capsule in Layout (see Figure 4.13). It's fine to stay in Perspective mode to do this. The Move and Rotate tools can be found on the left side of the Layout Interface, when the Items tab at the top of the screen is selected.

5. Move the timeline slider to frame 10.

6. Rotate the object to a different angle.

7. Click and drag the timeline slider forward.

   The object doesn't move. This is because Layout has automatically locked it in place at frame 10 (the previous position of the slider), thanks to Auto Key.

8. Drag the timeline slider to frame 20.

9. Move the object to a different position, and give it some rotation.

Note

When setting up keyframes, LightWave automatically draws a motion path. When the keyframe is set at frame 20, you will see a line appear representing the object's path of motion, if Show Motion Paths is enabled from the Display Options panel (d).

10. Move the timeline slider to frame 40, and then move and/or rotate the object again.

11. Press the Rewind button (see Figure 4.14); and then press Play Forward. (The button with the right-pointing triangle, located above the step value entry.)

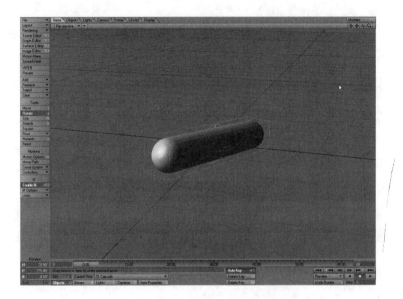

Figure 4.13   The Auto Key is on, and when you rotate the capsule object, it will remain in the new position without needing a keyframe to lock it in place.

Figure 4.14   The Rewind button and its associated controls can be found on the lower-right side of the Layout interface. Clicking the button on the top left, takes you back to frame 0 and resets your timeline.

The three buttons underneath the Rewind button are the Play Forward, Play Reverse, and Pause buttons. You should see the Capsule object move and rotate between keyframes 20 and 40. You can shuttle through the animation by grabbing the timeline slider and dragging.

Auto Key can make your animation work go smoother, but if you're not careful, it can damage your work. There may be situations where your keyframing needs to be precise. Having Auto Key enabled and accidentally moving the wrong object, or moving the right object the wrong way, could potentially cause you more work. Although you can undo an action like an accidental move, you have only one undo level, so be cautious using Auto Key.

Tip

A great time to use Auto Key is when setting up character animation.

Exercise 4.3   Manual Keyframing

Manual keyframing is more common than using Auto Key, but of course the choice is yours. Keyframing requires that you develop a keen sense of timing—although this can't be done overnight, a few practice animations can get you started.

Tip

A good way to work is to turn off Auto Key Create under the General Options tab (from within the Preferences panel), and work only with Auto Key enabled. Auto Key adjusts existing keyframes without the need to create them again after any changes are made.

1. Load the LWLogo object from the Projects/Objects/Chapter4 folder on this book's CD-ROM into a clear Layout scene. Be sure to turn off Auto Key, at the bottom of the Layout interface.

2. Press 6 on the numeric keypad to switch to Camera view.

   If the logo object is not selected, click it with the left mouse button. A bounding box highlights around the logo, and its handles show, as shown in Figure 4.15.

3. With the left mouse button, click and drag the green arrow up out of view, moving the logo up on the y-axis.

   Move the logo until it just leaves the frame. This is where you want the object to start off in the animation. Now you need to tell LightWave to make the logo stay at this location.

4. Press the Enter or Return key once to call up the Create Motion Key requester.

   The current frame will be highlighted, as shown in Figure 4.16. You also can select the Create Key button at the bottom of the interface.

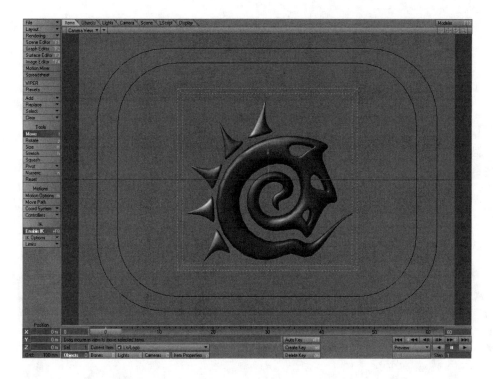

Figure 4.15   Selecting the LWLogo object shows the bounding box representation and the object handles. The box in the upper-left portion of the screen is a light.

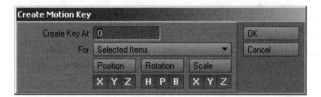

Figure 4.16   Pressing Enter or Return calls up the Create Motion Key command.

If the timeline slider was at frame 0, a 0 will appear in the Create Key at Command window.

5. If the timeline slider is not at frame 0, enter 0 and press the Enter or Return key again.

The keyframe is now set.

There are a few things you should know about the Create Motion Key requester. In it, you can specify that you wish to create a keyframe for selected items, which you just did: Current Item Only, Current Item and Descendants for parented items, or for All Items. Additionally, you can set keyframes for specific channels of motion. For example, suppose that you have a logo keyframed to make a continuous loop. Then you realize you need to move it to a new location, while not disturbing the rotation. To solve this, you can create a keyframe only for the new position, not rotation. Try it out!

Tip

You might be in the habit of clicking in each numeric window, erasing the existing values, and then reentering them. This is not necessary. When you open the Create or Delete Key requester, the existing value is already selected. All you need to do is enter the desired value. This saves time.

Note

You do not need to move the timeline slider to set keyframes throughout an animation if you are manually setting keyframes. However, moving the slider manually helps you keep yourself organized and aware of the current animation frame.

6. Move the LWLogo down to the grid plane where it originally was, as shown in Figure 4.17.

Note

If you can't see the object to grab it, you can switch to the Back view by pressing the number 1 on the keyboard. You also can constrain movement on the x- and z-axes by using the right mouse button for just the y-axis. Mac users, remember that Apple key for right mouse-button commands.

7. Press the Enter or Return key to call up the Create Motion Key command.

8. Type 60 from the numeric keypad and press Enter.

   Too often, users are in the habit of using the number keys across the top of the keyboard. Although this works just as well, you will save time by using the numeric keypad.

Tip

Because you want the LWLogo to end at frame 60 where it originally was positioned, you could have created a key for frame 60 when it was in that position. You can use the single position of an object to create various keyframes by entering the desired keyframe values in the Create Motion Key dialog box.

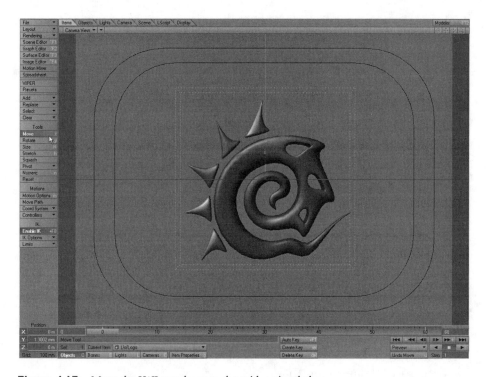

Figure 4.17   Move the LWLogo down to the grid, or just below.

9. Click the Play button (right pointing triangle) at the bottom right of the Layout interface.

The LWLogo should drop into the screen and land.

Okay, that was really basic and will be the simplest thing in this book, but it's important for you to get the hang of how to keyframe and understand what you are doing. You told the LWLogo to be at a certain position at frame 0, the beginning of the animation. Then, you moved the object to its resting position at the end of the animation. You told LightWave that the last position of the LWLogo is frame 60, creating a 2-second animation. LightWave will interpolate the frames between 0 and 60. Like magic, you made an animation.

Deleting Keyframes

You also can delete keyframes just as easily as you create them. Pressing the Delete key on the keyboard calls up the Delete Motion Key dialog box, with the cursor set at the Delete Key At requester and the current frame already selected, as shown in Figure 4.18.

Figure 4.18 Delete unwanted keyframes by pressing the Delete key on the keyboard to call up the Delete Motion Key command.

As with creating keyframes, the timeline slider does not need to be on the specific keyframe when you delete a key. Enter the key you want to delete when the Delete Motion Key command window opens. Again, use your numeric keypad to save time! And, remember, just as you can create keyframes for specific channels, you can delete them as well.

Note

You can make the LWLogo object you created in the last exercise land more gently using spline controls. Chapter 5, "LightWave 7 Graph Editor," explains it all.

Following the Keyframing Rule

You should know a few more things about keyframing in LightWave. A common misunderstanding with keyframes is that the more you have, the more control there will be in a scene—wrong! Thank you for playing!

Setting up keyframes creates a motion path. That motion path is a curve, controlled by the keyframes you set. A good rule of thumb to use when setting keyframes initially is to make two keyframes: your first keyframe and your last one. Then set your frames that fall in-between. You want an object to move down a path, for example, and around an obstacle. The movement needs to be smooth, and trying to guess the timing might be tough to do. Set the beginning keyframe, and then set the ending keyframe to create the initial motion path. If you drag the timeline slider, the object moves between the two keyframes. If you move the timeline slider to the point where the object would move around the obstacle, you'll have the exact frame to set your next key. By creating the keyframe at this point in time, you've adjusted the motion path evenly. You can load the 2Keyframes and 5Keyframes scenes as examples from the Projects/Scenes/Chapter4 folder on the accompanying CD-ROM. Also, load the LWLogoTwist scene to see a variation on the previous exercise. In this scene, the LWLogo had two mid-keyframes added, but notice that the motion is smooth and even between each of the keyframes.

Later, in Part III, "A Project-Based Approach to Animating Scenes," you'll have many more opportunities to work with advanced keyframe techniques.

Constructing Scenes

With the necessary basics on keyframing out of the way, it's time for you to begin learning how to build 3D scenes in LightWave. A scene in LightWave is comprised of objects, lights, and cameras, similar to a real-world television set. But with LightWave, you have no limitations—it's a virtual world you can call your own.

Setting up scenes often requires that you plan what it is you are trying to accomplish. Plan it, organize, and you'll be much better off. Remember the motto, "Work smarter, not harder."

Surfacing Objects

Sometimes starting a big project can be overwhelming. Where do you begin? What should you do first? How much are they paying? All of those questions play a role in how you approach a project. From the start, you should know where you want to end up. This is, of course, if you're creating an animation for a client or your boss. There is much to be said about letting your creativity flow and see where it takes you—just don't do this on paying jobs. Time is money! Nevertheless, you should be aware of the entire project and begin by creating models.

When you set up a scene, a good place to start is to load your objects into Layout. However, because LightWave's object files retain their surface information (surfacing is not saved with a scene file), it's a good idea to load an object, surface it, save it, and then continue. Don't load all your objects at once, and don't try to surface them all together. Surface objects one at a time. From there, you can concentrate on movements and lighting.

 Note

LightWave's Modeler supports surfacing and texture mapping. So much of your object's surfaces can be created there, as well as in Layout. The choice is yours. Be sure to check out Chapter 10, "Organic Modeling," for more surfacing information.

Loading and Saving Objects

Earlier in this chapter you followed the steps to load objects into Layout. However, you also can load objects from other scenes, load recently loaded scenes, or load a specific object layer. Additionally, because you have the capability to change object properties and shapes, you can save objects as well. Figure 4.19 shows the options available to you in LightWave 7 for loading objects into Layout, while Figure 4.20 shows the options for saving.

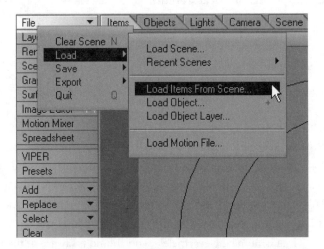

Figure 4.19   Load functions, such as Load Items From Scene, are found under the File drop-down list at the top left of the Layout interface.

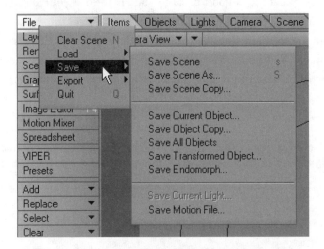

Figure 4.20   There are various save options available to you in Layout, found in the File drop-down list, under Save.

At some point in your career as an animator, you will come to know the Load Items From Scene command. This handy option enables you to load just the objects and their motions from one scene into another. You also have the option to load another scene's lighting into your existing scene.

For example, let's say you've set up a complex scene of a scary haunted house and grave-yard. Now you need to add a bat or two flying about the front of the house. You could load the bat and its wings into this scene and set it in motion. However, you'd need to do that twice, once for each bat, and you'd be working in a crowded scene, which might slow things down and make it confusing to see what you're doing.

Additionally, you don't want to accidentally change any of the other objects' settings, such as the house. Instead, you can set up the bat in a scene all its own. You can test the wings, make sure they flap, and so on. From there, you can save the scene, and load the complex haunted house scene. Then, all you need to do is select the Load Items From Scene command to load the bat and its motions into your current scene.

When using Load Items From Scene, LightWave will ask you whether you'd like to load the lights as well. In most cases, you won't load the lights because you already have a scene with active lights. You really want only the objects and their motions to be added into your current scene. But there are times when all you do want is the lights, such as a scene where the light source is a key element. You can create a scene with only the specific lights you need, and load those lights with their motions into your current scene, also with the Load Items From Scene command. For example, you can spend an afternoon creating lighting setups for various sets, such as a traditional three-point lighting scheme or a daylight scene. When it's time to light your scene, you'll already have it done. Just use Load Items From Scene to import what you've already created.

Adding Cameras to a Scene

Without a camera in your scene, you would never see anything render. LightWave lets you add multiple cameras. Adding additional cameras is very useful for animations that need multiple angles of a single animation event. For example, perhaps your client has contracted you to re-create a traffic accident. It is required that you show the animation from all views: top, side, front, back, and a traveling aerial view. You can add five cameras and place them all once, in their respective positions. This eliminates the need to move the camera to different angles. Instead, you can simply switch between any of the multiple cameras. Chapter 6, "LightWave 7 Cameras," explores multiple cameras further.

Note

It's important to remember that in LightWave, rendered animations are always seen through whichever camera is selected at the time of rendering. Therefore, it's a good idea to get into the habit of using camera views to set up your scenes and keyframes.

Exercise 4.4   Adding Multiple Cameras

This next exercise will use multiple cameras. You'll learn how easy it is to load and set up different cameras for renders from different angles.

1. Clear the scene by selecting Clear Scene from the File menu.

2. From the Items tab, click the Add drop-down menu.

3. Select Add Camera, as shown in Figure 4.21.

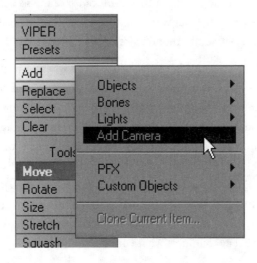

Figure 4.21   Adding a camera is as easy as adding objects.

Before the camera is added, a requester comes up asking you to name the camera. If you choose not to name the camera, LightWave names it Camera (1) (additional cameras are automatically named Camera (2), Camera (3), and so on). If you are creating a scene with more than two cameras, take the extra three seconds and name them. Figure 4.22 shows the MultiCam scene's cameras (found in the Projects/Scenes/Chapter4 directory of the book's CD-ROM).

If you want to rename your existing camera, you can do so by first selecting the specific camera and then selecting the Items tab, clicking the Replace drop-down menu, and choosing Rename Current Item.

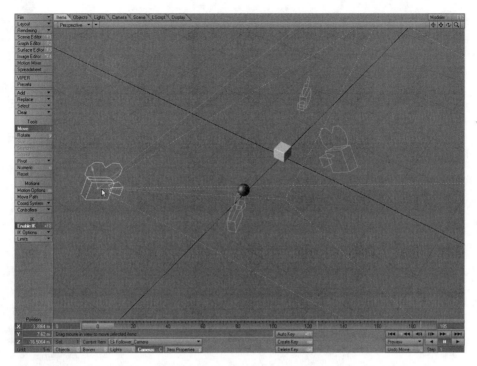

Figure 4.22   When scenes have multiple cameras, rename the cameras so that you can keep track of each camera.

Adding Lights to a Scene

Even if your scene is a virtual set, you need to add a light or two to see what's going on. By default, Layout has one light, which cannot be removed. It can be turned off, but cannot be deleted from the scene. To add a light to a scene, select the Add drop-down list under the Items tab, choose the Lights listing, and select the type of light you want to add.

When you have selected a light, you can display the Light Properties panel by pressing p. In the Light Properties panel, you can color each light, change the type of light, and add lens flares, volumetrics, and more. However, you can quickly access the individual light controls from under the Lights tab, shown in Figure 4.23.

Lights in Layout respond the way objects do when selected. They can be moved or rotated, and they, too, will show control handles. You can also select lights (as you can with objects) directly in Layout by clicking them. If you hold down the Shift key, you can select multiple lights. When you have selected multiple lights or objects, your movements and rotations apply to each selection. Multiple selections are great if you have to place your lights or objects perfectly and need to adjust their positions. However, if you were smart and planned out your scene, you would have parented the items to a null object.

Parenting

Parenting your lights or objects in Layout is a good way to help keep things organized and save time. This next brief tutorial will show you how to parent a few lights to a null object. *Parenting* is the process of making objects "belong" to one another. For example, a car is one object that has four wheels, each being objects in their own right. Parenting the four wheels to the car will make the wheels follow the car if it is moved. Once parented, the wheels are "children" and a hierarchy is born.

A *null object* is nothing more than a representational point in Layout used for various control issues. It does not show up in the render, and it is very useful for texture references, visual references, motion tracking, parenting, or targeting. The following exercise shows you how it works.

Exercise 4.5   Parenting Lights

Lights, in many ways, work like objects. They have a property panel, can be animated on any motion channel, and can also be parented.

1. Clear the scene.

   Start by adding two more lights, making a total of three, including the existing default light. Do this from the Items tab.

2. Select Add, then Lights, then Add Distant Light, as shown in Figure 4.24.

Figure 4.23
Instead of opening the Lights panel to set parameters for your selected light source, you can directly select commands from under the Lights tab.

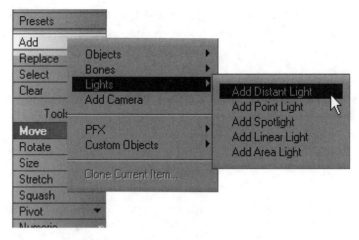

Figure 4.24   Add lights directly from Layout.

 Tip

Remember that you also can access the Add menu by pressing the Ctrl and Shift keys, and clicking directly on the Layout interface with the left mouse button. This brings up the mouse button menus.

Note

When you add a Light to a scene, a name requester appears asking you to give the light a name. You also can choose not to name the light and click OK, or press the Enter key.

The second light appears directly in the middle of Layout at the 0 xyz-axis. Now it's time to add a null object.

3. Select Add, then Objects, and then Add Null.

4. Just like adding a camera or light, a name requester appears. Click OK or press Enter to leave the default name Null.

5. The Null object also loads at the 0 xyz-axis. Select the second light in the center of the screen and move it off center, similar to Figure 4.25.

    Don't forget to create a keyframe for the light after you've moved it to lock it in place! Otherwise, it will jump back to the previous position once the timeline slider is adjusted.

Figure 4.25   The second light is moved off center to make the Null object more visible.

Note

If the Left Button Item Select feature is turned on from the General Options tab (o) in the Preferences panel (see Figure 4.26), you should be able to click and select the light directly in Layout. However, because both the light and the null object are located at the 0 xyz-axis, LightWave might not select the desired item. If this is the case, simply select Lights at the bottom of the Layout interface, and select the particular item from the Current Item list, also at the bottom of the interface.

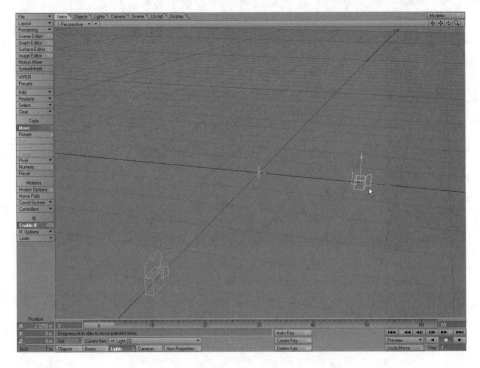

Figure 4.26   The Left Button Item Select function allows you to directly select items in Layout.

6. With the second light still selected, press the m key to access the light's Motion Options panel.

7. Select Null for the Parent Item, as shown in Figure 4.27.

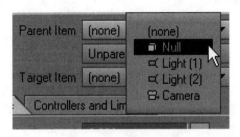

Figure 4.27   The Motion Options panel holds the commands for parenting and unparenting your objects.

8. Keep the Motion Options panel open, and in Layout, select the next child item, such as the first light in Layout (the item that is to be parented). You may need to move the Motion Options panel off to the side to see your Layout.

9. Parent the first light and the camera to the same Null object.

10. Back in Layout, select the Null object, and move and rotate it.

    You'll see that the items parented to it move along with it.

Parenting items is useful in so many ways. You can create great variations in reflections by parenting objects and rotating them during an animation. You can organize your scene and group items, such as lights and cameras.

This is a traditional way of selecting and parenting objects. However, LightWave also allows you to parent items directly in the Scene Editor, and in Modeler when you build your objects. In addition, you can parent multiple items at once, which is handy for characters with bone structures, or other complex hierarchies. Later in Chapter 12, "Deformations and Movement," you'll discover how parenting is essential to properly setting up skeletal structures for character movement, and more. But for now, you can load the SimpleParent scene from the Projects directory of the book's CD-ROM as an example of parenting described here. Use this scene to parent items to other objects and even to unparent items to get a feel for parenting.

Targeting

Targeting is different from parenting in that parenting attaches one item to another. Targeting only points one item to another. For example, if you parented a camera to a moving car, the camera would move with the car wherever it traveled. If you target a camera to a car, the camera will remain stationary, but it will always point at the car, following it wherever it goes.

Although targeting is different from parenting, the two processes are similar. From the Motion Options panel of a selected item, you can choose to have an item target another. Figure 4.28 shows the Motion Options panel and Target Item selection.

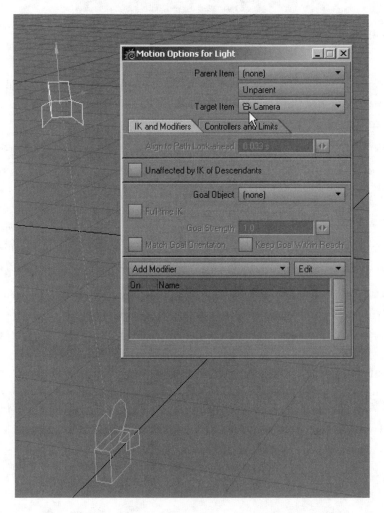

Figure 4.28   The Motion Options panel for the selected item allows you to target other items.

When setting up targets, the camera's pivot will point at the pivot of the object. This is great for many types of animations, such as a character's eye movements, a simulation rifle to target animation, and much more. Try targeting the camera to a null object and move the null around. The camera will point at the null no matter where it goes. When you target something in Layout, you'll see target lines between the two items. You can turn this on or off from the Display Options tab in the Preferences panel. Remember that any parent or target looks to the pivot point of an object. If your object's pivot makes your targeting look odd, you can add a null object and parent the items to it. Then, target the camera to the null.

The exercises in this chapter have given you an idea of the relationship between objects in that each individual item, such as an object, camera, or light can be grouped together or used individually through parenting and targeting. Larger scenes incorporate the same usefulness of hierarchies, but managing them becomes difficult in Layout. No worries, though—the LightWave 7 Scene Editor keeps track of your complex setups.

Tip

LightWave 7 allows you to parent and target anything to anything. A light can target a camera, a camera can be parented to a light, an eyeball can target a camera, and so on.

Using the Scene Editor

Managing any scene you put together requires that you are aware of everything going on in your animation. From time to time, however, you will need a visual reference of your setup and the capability to control items and make changes to them. Figure 4.29 shows the LightWave 7 Scene Editor with a scene loaded.

The Scene Editor also can be considered the scene outline. You can use this to parent and unparent items, instead of the Motion Options panel. To do so, drag the selected item underneath the item to which you want to parent it. Figure 4.30 shows the line that appears representing the parenting position.

Tip

Although the Motion Options panel can be used to parent items, the Scene Editor is a better way to do so. By working in the Scene Editor, you have a hierarchical view of your object. The Scene Editor also allows for multiple parenting of items.

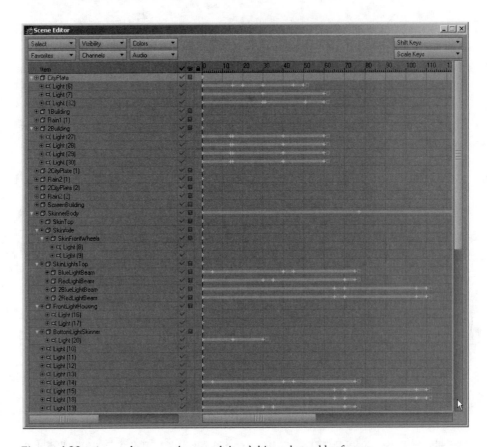

Figure 4.29   A complex scene shows each item's hierarchy and keyframes.

In Figure 4.30, the highlighted item has been selected and dragged underneath another item. The line represents where the selected item will be parented. If you move the mouse slightly over the parent, the line will indent, signaling to you that the selected item will become a child of the parent. Otherwise, you are simply re-arranging an item, which also makes the Scene Editor useful. Any item that is parented to another will be indented.

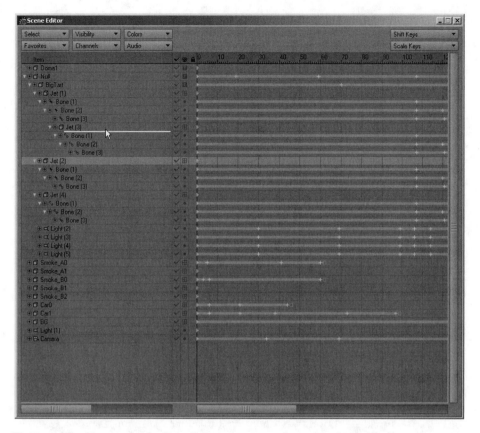

Figure 4.30   You can use the Scene Editor to parent and unparent items. The line represents the parenting position.

Keyframe Adjustments

In addition to the organization of your Layout items, the Scene Editor also can help you change the pace of your entire animation, or just one item. Figure 4.31 shows the Scene Editor with a small scene loaded. The shaded lines on the right side of the interface represent items that are in motion. The small plus signs within them represent keyframes.

Also, you can see in Figure 4.31 that the BlueBall object and the Follower_Camera have been expanded. By clicking the small plus sign in front of any item, you can expand the item's properties to show its XYZ values for Position, Rotation, and Scale. Across the top of the main Scene Editor window, you'll see numbers. These numbers represent time in your animation. If your scene is 185 frames long, you'll see these numbers listed through 185. The Scene Editor is similar to the Graph Editor, without the ability to change keyframes.

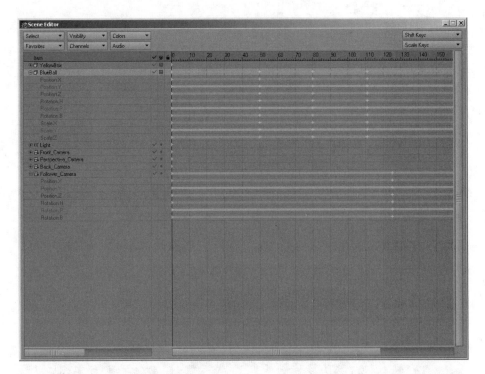

Figure 4.31   The Scene Editor displays items that are in motion (the shaded lines on the right side of the interface) as well as keyframes (small plus signs).

You can click a shaded motion track and drag it to adjust its timing. Figure 4.32 shows the BlueBall object with its motion now starting 40 frames into the animation, rather than at 0. This was accomplished by dragging the motion track.

You also could move this motion to negative 40 frames. Perhaps you've set up a perfect motion for a flying logo. The only problem is, you need it to animate to its resting place much sooner. If you set up new keyframes, the perfect rotations and timing with other elements will be off. Instead, you can drag the motion to a value less than 0. When you begin rendering the scene at frame 0, the flying logo would already be in motion.

Later in Chapter 17, "Broadcast-Style Animation," you'll use the Scene Editor in a project to adjust the timing of animations.

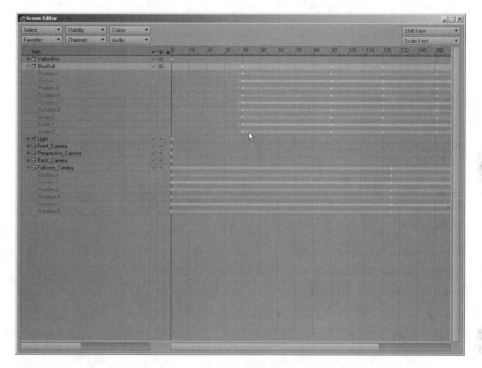

Figure 4.32   The Scene Editor allows you to move the entire motion of an item simply by dragging the shaded areas.

Control Options

The Scene Editor also provides control for various options, such as the visibility of your Layout items, selection sets, colors, and Scene Editor channel control. You can choose to view which items are seen as wireframes, points, or shaded. Also, you have the ability to expand or collapse various channels. Figure 4.33 shows the section of menus available for adjusting your scene's visibility at the top of the Scene Editor panel.

Figure 4.33   The Scene Editor gives you the power to adjust any item's visibility.

With these menus, you can choose what to select, such as Objects, Lights, Cameras, or Bones, and how to view them, such as Wireframe or Solid. You can select various items and hide them to help keep Layout clutter to a minimum. Also, you are given the capability to make each item a separate color for organization.

Although the visibility controls in the Scene Editor are straightforward, take some time and click around in there. Try various selections and colors. Expand and collapse the channels of items while experimenting with parenting and rearrangement.

Audio Files

Audio files also can be loaded from the Scene Editor panel. Figure 4.34 shows the Audio drop-down menu requester.

When you load an audio file (WAV file), you can instantly play it by choosing the selection from the menu list. By default, the Fixed Frequency option is turned on (checked). This keeps the pitch of the audio file constant as you scrub through it on the timeline. You will use this feature extensively in Chapter 11, "Character Construction."

Figure 4.34
Audio files can be loaded from the Scene Editor panel.

Shift and Scale Keys

The Scene Editor also allows you to Shift or Scale selected keyframes. For example, suppose that your client loves the animation you've created and is ready to sign the check. But, before that happens, the entire animation needs to be exactly five seconds shorter. By using the Scale Keys function, you can scale the entire scene to exactly the length you need. This is handy because throughout the animation, elements have varying keyframes, and resetting each of them would be quite tedious. Shift and Scale allow you to adjust timing without resetting keyframes. Chapter 16, "Nonlinear Animation" will give you a step-by-step explanation of these features.

Note

There are a few other cool features in the Scene Editor, such as the ability to toggle items on and off. Do this by using the small checkmark. You also can shrink the horizontal size of the Scene Editor panel by dragging the left border. Add LightWave's Item Picker and you have a good amount of control for your scene setup.

Spreadsheet Scene Manager

New to LightWave 7 is the Spreadsheet Scene Manager. Imagine if you took the Scene Editor and pumped it with steroids—you'd have this new monstrous scene control panel. Figure 4.35 shows a scene loaded and viewed through the Spreadsheet Scene Manager.

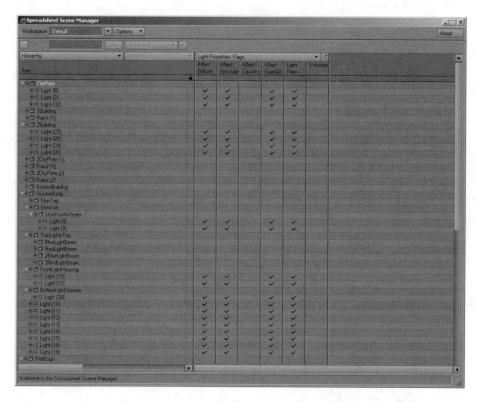

Figure 4.35   LightWave 7's Spreadsheet Scene Manager takes your scene control to the next level.

This panel of controls is quite extensive and will be covered more in Appendix A, "Motion Capture and LightWave." In it, you can choose how to view your scene, taking a look at what's loaded in alphabetical order, reverse order, and more. You can look at the properties for every single item in your scene, view channel values, look at file locations and polygon sizes, see which lights have what types of shadows, and so much more. You can even set up automated tasks, such as opening the Graph Editor after applying envelopes.

Using a dual-monitor setup is ideal for this control panel. You can keep it open and use it to select items, and even set light colors. The best way to learn this new tool is by using it, so we've implemented it into a few tutorials in the book. Keep an eye out for it!

The Next Step

This chapter introduced you to LightWave 7's Layout and its core functionality. There is much, much more to learn within this program, and the rest of this book will help take you there. LightWave's object format introduced here will be a stepping-stone for all the objects you create in Modeler. The keyframing information can be applied to any project you encounter, while the coordinate system information is important for every model and animation you create. Another great tool that you'll soon learn about is Motion Mixer, LightWave 7's nonlinear animation tool. You can use this feature to blend motions together for fast and great results. For now, use the information in this chapter as reference for the rest of this book, and any future projects you take on. You can never have enough information!

Summary

In this chapter, you learned about keyframing, both manual and automatic; the importance of pivots and how to adjust them; parenting and targeting; adding multiple cameras; and the Scene Editor. All these elements are foundations for the projects you'll work on in LightWave, but there's just one more area you need to be familiar with before you really get into the meat of things. Chapter 5 introduces you to the motion control you can have over every aspect of your scene with the Graph Editor. You will learn about modifiers, curves, channels, and footprints. Once you've worked through Chapter 6, step up to Part II, "A Project-Based Approach to Creating and Building 3D Scenes."

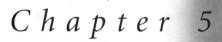

C h a p t e r 5

LightWave 7 Graph Editor

LightWave 7's powerful Graph Editor offers

you complete control over a specific item's

motion and timing. This can be a camera,

object, light, or any other type of parameter

that can be enveloped, or changed over time. The Graph Editor also gives you control over every channel of an item, such as the Position.X, Position.Y, Rotation Heading, and so on. Each channel can be controlled through the use of expressions, modifiers, or even keyframes, all from within the Graph Editor. The Graph Editor is used to edit any type of parameter that can be enveloped, from surface color, light intensity, object dissolves, and more. In this chapter, you will learn about the following:

- Using the Graph Editor
- Multi-curve editing with the Graph Editor
- Exploring additional commands
- Editing color channels

Navigating the Graph Editor

From Layout's interface, you can access the Graph Editor by clicking the Graph Editor button at the top left of the screen, under any tab. Figure 5.1 shows the Graph Editor at startup.

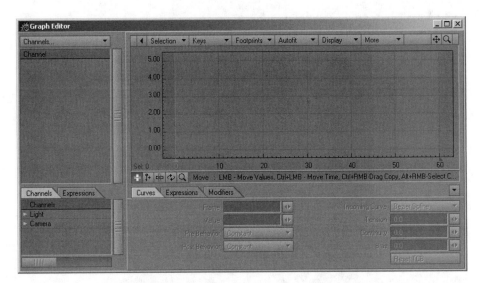

Figure 5.1   The LightWave 7 Graph Editor is greatly enhanced over the editor in previous versions of LightWave. The Graph Editor shows all the items in Layout on the bottom left, and individual channels to be edited are available in the upper left.

Note

Any of the small buttons labeled E throughout LightWave Layout also can access the Graph Editor. You can find them next to the values of items that can be edited in the Graph Editor, such as Surface Color.

When you open the Graph Editor, you'll notice four general areas.

- The Curve Bin zone is in the top-left quadrant. This is the area of the Graph Editor where you select the specific channels you want to edit (see Figure 5.2).

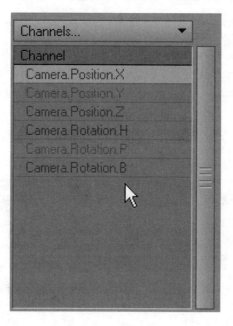

Figure 5.2   The Curve Bin zone houses specific editable channels.

- The Curve Window zone is in the largest area, the top-right quadrant. This is the area where you edit curves. You can adjust values, edit keyframes, and more (see Figure 5.3).

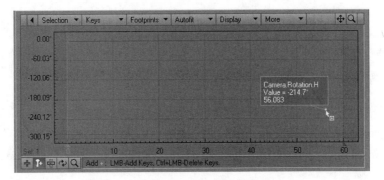

Figure 5.3   The Curve Window zone is the main large area of the Graph Editor where all curve editing will take place. Here you can see your keyframes, motions, and more.

- The Curve Controls zone is in the bottom-right quadrant. Here you can set frames, values, behaviors for keys, and modifiers, as well as set expression plug-ins, spline controls, and so on (see Figure 5.4). The settings on the Curves tab is explored further in Chapter 14, "Expression Applications," and Chapter 15, "Animation with Expressions."

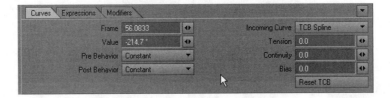

Figure 5.4   The Curve Controls zone at the bottom-right quadrant of the Graph Editor is where you set specific controls, such as expressions, modifiers, spline controls, and more.

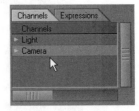

- The Scene List zone is in the bottom-left quadrant and shows your current scene elements. Lights, cameras, and objects are listed here. You can select any or all of their channels, bring them into the Curve Bin, and begin editing. This area also shows you any expressions that might be applied (see Figure 5.5).

Figure 5.5
The Scene Display zone in the bottom-left corner of the Graph Editor shows a list of items in your currently loaded scene in Layout. You also can access any expressions loaded by clicking the tabbed area.

Work with each zone to adjust, modify, or create various motions, timing, and values for LightWave elements. Here you can control all Layout items—from the camera, to lights, to objects—including color, light intensities, morph envelopes, and more. You might be asking yourself where you should begin with the Graph Editor and wondering what it really does. Good questions! The Graph Editor is a complex part of Layout, one that is best explained through examples.

> **Note**
>
> An envelope in LightWave is an animatable feature that you access via the Graph Editor. Many settings throughout Layout have a button labeled with an E. This E stands for "envelope," and when you press such a button, you are led into the Graph Editor where you can envelope whatever setting you're accessing. For example, suppose that you have set a Light Intensity value somewhere in your scene. Clicking the E button for Light Intensity (Lights panel) lets you envelope the Light Intensity value. This goes for any of the E buttons you see throughout LightWave.

The following exercise provides an illustration of how to navigate through the Graph Editor interface.

Exercise 5.1   Working with Channels

When you begin creating an animation, you often will need specific control over one keyframe or a group of keyframes. The Graph Editor gives you this control, but you first must understand how to set up the channels with which you want to work. This exercise introduces you to working with the position and rotation channels for a light and a camera.

Figure 5.6
The Scene list in the lower-left quandrant of the Graph Editor shows the items in your scene. Clicking the small white triangle next to an item expands to show all of its channels.

1. Open Layout, and select the default Distant light.

2. Click the Graph Editor button on the toolbar to enter the Graph Editor.

   You don't need to load anything into Layout as you follow along here.

   Look at Figure 5.6 and you'll see that the attributes in the Scene list (lower-left quadrant) relate to the items in Layout, such as the Light. Click the small white triangle next to the Light listing under the Channels tab to expand to see the appropriate channels listed .

> **Tip**
>
> You can maximize the Graph Editor window by clicking the standard system maximize button next to the X in the top-right corner of the panel. Clicking this square opens the Graph Editor to full view. Mac users can resize the window as well.

Tip

You can rearrange the order of items in the Curve Bin by clicking and dragging them. This does not affect your scene.

3. Hold down the Shift key and double-click the Camera label in the Scene list area. This is in the lower-left corner of the Graph Editor interface.

    Double-clicking the Camera label adds all its channels to the Curve area, overriding any channels already in the bin. Doing this now makes those channels available for editing.

    You also can just click and drag a channel from the Scene list to the Curve area. This is great if you just want to add a selected channel or two. If you hold the Shift key, select a channel, and then select another channel, all channels in-between will be selected. You can then drag those channels to the Curve area. And, like the Scene Editor, pressing the Ctrl key while selecting allows you to select noncontiguous channels.

4. Go back to the Scene list area and expand the Camera's channels by clicking the small white arrow to the left of the Camera label.

Note

You can resize the individual quadrants in the Graph Editor by simply placing your mouse cursor on the line that separates the areas and clicking and dragging (see Figure 5.7).

5. Double-click any of the Camera's channels.

    The channel is now added to the Curve Bin and overrides any other channels. However, you can add more channels to the Curve Bin without overriding the existing channels by using the Shift key.

6. To add the Position.X and Rotation.H channels to the Curve Bin, hold down the Shift key and select the two channels. Then drag the selected channels up to the Curve Bin. You've now added channels instead of replacing them.

Note

If you have noncontiguous channels (channels not in order) to select, use the Ctrl key rather than the Shift key to make your selections in the Scene list.

Now that you know how channels are added to the Curve Bin, the next thing you can do is modify or edit them in many different ways.

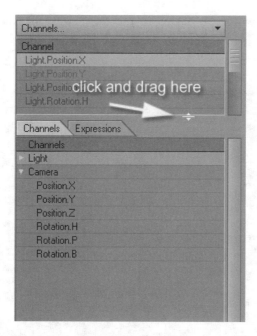

Figure 5.7 When you expand an item's channels, you can use the scroll bar on the right of the Scene Display quadrant to access them, but a better thing to do is resize the display area.

Working with the Graph Editor

Navigating through the Graph Editor is straightforward. You select the channels you want to edit from the Scene list and add them to the Curve Bin. From the Curve Bin, you select the desired channels and then edit their curves in the Curve Window, the main area of the Graph Editor. Editing curves is one of the primary functions of the Graph Editor. Think of your workflow from bottom left, to top left, to top right, to bottom right to help understand the flow of editing curves.

Editing Curves

The Graph Editor is used to edit curves. Editable curves are values that you've created in Layout to control lights, objects, cameras, and other animatable Layout attributes, such as textures or intensities. The preceding section talked about the Scene Display area and the Curve Bin. The Curve Window is discussed in this section.

Figure 5.8 shows the Graph Editor in full frame with the same LWLogo scene (LWLogoTwist.lws) from Chapter 4, "LightWave 7 Layout," loaded. You can find this scene in the Projects/Scenes/Chapter5 folder on the book's CD.

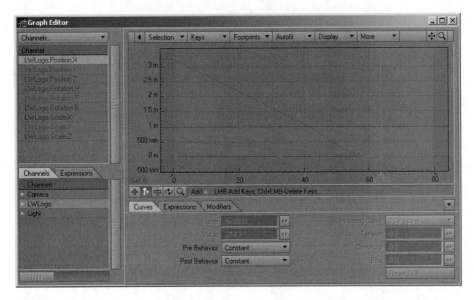

Figure 5.8   With a scene loaded into Layout, opening the Graph Editor reveals in the Curve Bin all motion channels already in place for the selected LWLogo object.

In Figure 5.8, the first channel (Position.X) in the Curve Bin is selected. In the Curve Window, the channel that represents the logo's X position is highlighted. On your computer, you'll notice that each channel has a specific color in the Curve Bin: X is red, Y is green, and Z is blue. The same color represents the corresponding curve in the main Curve Window. If you move the mouse pointer over one of the small colored dots (which represent keyframes) on an active curve, (also the item's motion path) numeric information will appear, as shown in Figure 5.9.

Your LightWave manual takes you step-by-step through the necessary buttons in the Graph Editor. *Inside LightWave 7* takes you further with practical tutorials. Exercise 5.2 (later in this chapter) requires you to load a scene from this book's CD and adjust various channels. You will create and delete keyframes in the Graph Editor, adjust timing, and even adjust multiple channels at once. Later, you will apply Graph Editor Modifiers to existing keyframes.

 Note

Remember that there are complete full-color versions of all the book's figures on the enclosed CD-ROM.

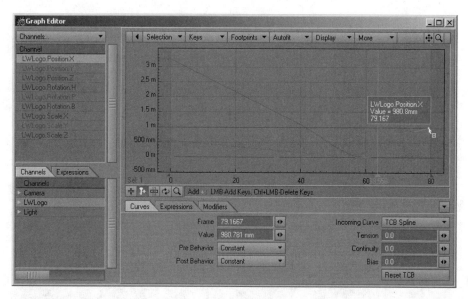

Figure 5.9 Moving the mouse pointer over a keyframe instantly displays the keyframe number, the value, and the channel (such as Position.X) you're working with.

Positioning the Graph Editor

Before you begin working with the Graph Editor, you should know that you can configure the window so that it is visible along with Layout. Figure 5.10 shows a possible interface configuration.

To resize the Graph Editor:

1. Drag the lower-right corner of the Graph Editor window. Make sure that the window is not maximized.

2. Click and drag the Layout window from the top of the panel, and move it to the upper-left portion of your screen, as shown in Figure 5.10.

3. Open the Graph Editor and resize it as well. Move it below the Layout window.

Additionally, you can keep the Surface Editor and Preset Shelf open while you're working in Layout if you like, perhaps also using the Spreadsheet Scene Manager. This is beneficial because you can make a change, see the result in Layout, and continue working. You do not have to continually open and close panels—simply leave them open. Either a large monitor or a dual-monitor setup is helpful for screen real estate when setting up configurations like this.

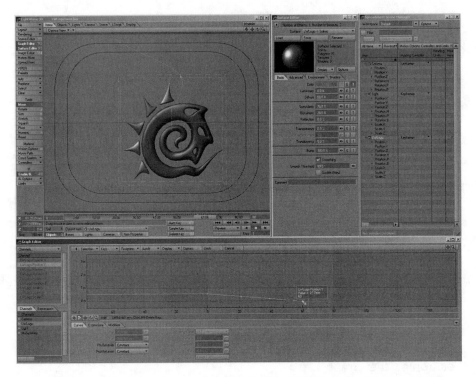

Figure 5.10   You can resize Layout and the Graph Editor, keeping both of them open while you work, thanks to LightWave's resizable non-modal panels.

Graph Editor Timing

The Graph Editor enables you to do many things, such as create, delete, or adjust keyframes for specific channels. You can also modify various entities within LightWave, such as surface color and light intensities. One of the more common uses for the Graph Editor is for timing. You can use the Graph Editor to adjust the timing of elements in your LightWave scenes.

Exercise 5.2   Adjusting Timing in the Graph Editor

The Graph Editor has many uses, which you will inevitably take advantage of at some time during your career as an animator. One of the more common uses of the Graph Editor is the ability to adjust the timing of your Layout animations.

1. Load the BlueBKD scene into Layout from the Projects/Scenes/Chapter5 folder on this book's CD.

    This loads a simple background animation that can be used for animated logos.

2. The HexLogo_Flat object should already be chosen because the scene was saved with it selected. Open the Graph Editor.

You'll see that all the object's channels are automatically loaded into the Curve Bin. However, in this tutorial, you are adjusting only the object's timing on the x-axis; therefore, the remaining channels are not needed. Figure 5.11 shows the Graph Editor with Position.X selected. If you have the Graph Editor open, the channels will have the same curves. If so, you can use the Selection > Get Layout Selected command (Shift+g) to update the Graph Editor.

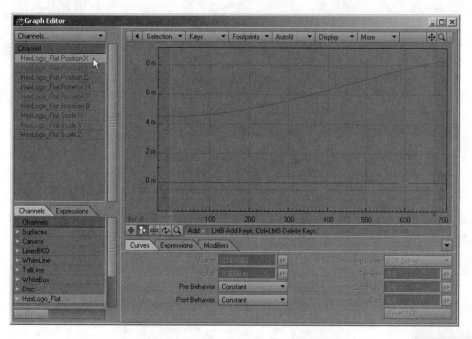

3. To remove the remaining channels, first select Position.Y in the Curve Bin. This is identified in green and should be the second channel in the list.

4. Holding down the Shift key, select the Scale.Z channel, the last channel in the list.

   This selects all the channels between Position.Y and Scale.Z, as shown in Figure 5.12.

5. To remove these selected channels, you can right-click the selections and choose Remove from Bin, as shown in Figure 5.13. Or, as an alternative, you can choose Remove Channel from Bin from the Selection drop-down list at the top of the Graph Editor panel. Figures 5.14 and 5.15 show the commands. As an option, you can use the Clear Unselected Channels option from the Selection drop-down list.

Figure 5.12
Selecting the Scale.Z channel selects all the channels between Position.X and Position.Y.

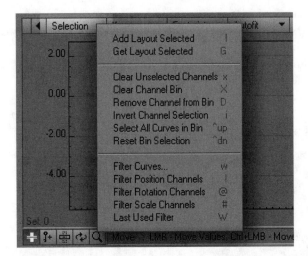

Figure 5.14   The Selection drop-down list at the top of the Graph Editor gives you access to a number of controls.

Figure 5.13
To remove selected channels, right-click the selections and choose Remove from Bin.

Tip

If you take a close look at the functions available in the Selection drop-down list, you'll see that you can do much more than simply remove channels. You can clear the Channel Bin, invert selections, Select all curves in Bin, and more. Experiment with these options to get a feel for their usefulness.

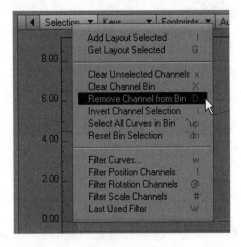

Figure 5.15   Choosing Remove Channel from Bin from the Selection drop-down list removes selected channels from the Curve Bin.

> **Tip**
>
> You don't need to remove channels if you're making changes to only one specific channel. However, it's a good idea to keep just the specific editable channel in the Channel Bin to keep things uncluttered and organized. It keeps you from accidentally editing the wrong curve.

You are now be left with only the Position.X channel in the Curve Bin.

6. Select the Position.X channel to highlight it in the Curve Window.

   This represents the motion of the X position for the object. The tall vertical line is the current frame.

7. Move your mouse over the first small dot (the first keyframe) on the curve for Position.X to see the information for that keyframe (see Figure 5.16).

   The information tells you what curve it is, which in this case is Position.X for the HexLogo_Flat object. It also tells you the current frame and the value. The value is the object's position. For example, the value in Figure 5.16 reads 1.045m. You are working with the Position.X channel, so this means the object is –1.045m away from the 0 axis on the positive x-axis.

   It's probably hard to identify that first keyframe in the curve. To simplify this, use the Graph Editor's Custom Point Color function.

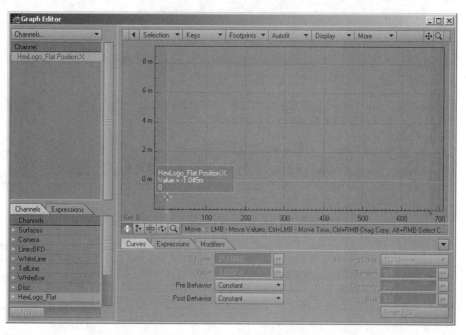

Figure 5.16 Holding the mouse over any keyframes in the Curve Window shows the channel, value, and frame number.

8. While still in the Graph Editor, press the d key to call up the Display tab of the Graph Editor Options panel. Click Custom Point Color at the bottom of the list, and the color selector will become active (see Figure 5.17). The default color white is fine, so simply click OK to close the panel. Your keyframes in the Curve Window will now be easier to identify.

Tip

A number of other commands within the Options panel can help you when working with the Graph Editor. You can also access these commands and others by easily clicking the Display drop-down list from the top of the Graph Editor interface. Figure 5.18 shows the list of commands for Display.

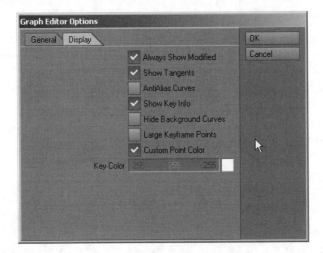

Figure 5.17   Setting the Custom Point Color in the Graph Editor Options panel helps make a curve's keyframes more visible.

9. In the Curve Window, click the first keyframe to select it. Be sure that the Move edit mode button is selected. It is the first button located above the Curves tab and below the Curve Window. Directly click the key to select it, or use the right mouse button to draw a region of selection. This second method is good for selecting multiple keyframes.

You'll see the keyframe highlight slightly, and the values throughout the Curves tab at the bottom of the screen appear, as shown in Figure 5.19.

Figure 5.18
The Display drop-down list atop the Graph Editor interface gives you controls for working in the Graph Editor Options panel.

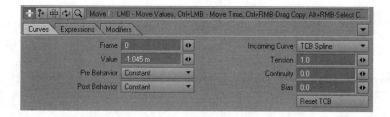

Figure 5.19   When a keyframe is selected, the commands in the Curves tab area become available.

The middle of the Graph Editor interface offers four tools for you to choose: Move, Add, Stretch, Roll, and Zoom. These are small icons. When you select them, information is displayed to the right, explaining what the function does through a keyboard legend. Figure 5.20 shows the area.

Figure 5.20   Selecting a specific tool displays the appropriate keyboard legend. Here, the Move tool is selected, allowing you to move selected keyframes in the Curve Window.

The Move tool can be used to select and move single or multiple keyframes in the Curve Window.

10. Select the Move tool, and click and drag the first keyframe in the Curve Window.

    Notice that you can move only its value. Doing this changes the position of the object in Layout.

11. Move the keyframe to set the value around 2m.

    Perhaps you do not want the HexLogo_Flat object to move until frame 100. This kind of delayed movement is easy to do in the Graph Editor.

12. Make sure that the Move tool is selected. While holding down the Ctrl key, click and move the 0 keyframe to the right. You'll see the frame number appear over the keyframe, as shown in Figure 5.21.

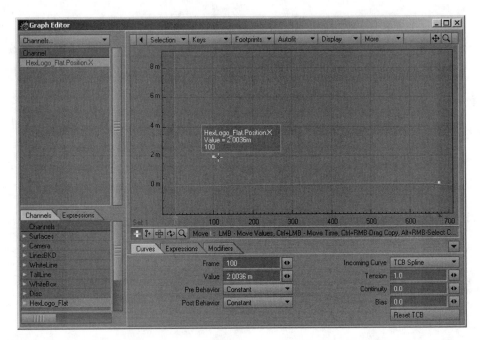

Figure 5.21   Holding the Ctrl key and moving selected keyframes adjusts timing. You didn't realize it was this easy, did you?

Tip

If you don't care to hold down the Ctrl key and use the mouse, you can numerically enter the specific keyframe. At the bottom of the screen under the Curves tab, enter the selected keyframe by clicking in the Frame field and typing the number. You also can set the value numerically by typing it in the Value field.

13. Adjust the value and keyframes of selected objects and return to Layout to see the effects. You can adjust values by dragging the keyframes in the Curve Window or entering them numerically under the Curves tab area.

Additionally, you have a number of key controls available from the Keys drop-down list atop the Graph Editor panel. Figure 5.22 shows the Move Keys selection, which allows you to numerically set offset values. You soon will get the hang of editing in the Graph Editor.

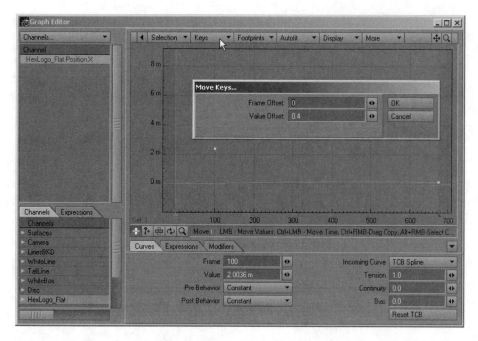

Figure 5.22   The Move Keys selection allows you to set a specific numeric value to move a key.

There's much more to the Graph Editor than this. The first part of this chapter guided you through basic navigation and editing of channels and keyframes. Moving forward, you have the capability to move groups of keyframes, adjust curves, and add modifiers.

Copy Time Slice

Another cool feature of the Graph Editor's Keys functions is the Copy Time Slice command. Let's say that you have your scene all set up, and the timing of a motion is just right. However, you'd like to copy the object's position at a point where there is no keyframe. What do you do? You could numerically in Layout write down the Move and Rotation values, and then go to a new keyframe and enter them. A much easier way is to use Copy Time Slice in the Graph Editor. Here's how it works:

1. Select the curve you want to edit, such as the Position.Y channel. Drag the timeline bar to the desired frame of motion you want to copy, as shown in Figure 5.23.

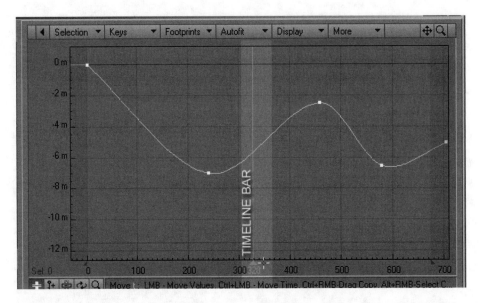

Figure 5.23   Use the timeline bar in the Graph Editor to move through your item's motion.

2. From the Keys drop-down list, select Copy Time Slice, as shown in Figure 5.24.

3. Drag the timeline slider to a new desired position.

4. From the Keys drop-down list, select Paste Time Slice, and a new keyframe will be created with the values from the previous position.

Tip

You can also use the keyboard shortcuts for Copy Time Slice: Ctrl+c for copy, and Ctrl+v for paste. This is the same for Macintosh and PC systems.

Copy Time Slice is an extremely handy function of the Graph Editor. If you set two keyframes in Layout for an item—at frames 0 and 60, for example—LightWave will interpret the motion for the frames between those two keys. Using Copy Time Slice allows you to copy the motion of any one of those interpreted keys and paste them somewhere else on that existing curve.

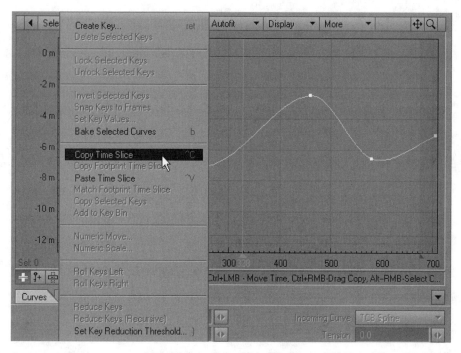

Figure 5.24   The Copy Time Slice command, accessed from the Keys drop-down list, records the current position of the timeline slider.

Multi-Curve Editing

Multi-curve editing is useful when you want to edit multiple curves simultaneously or use curves of different items as references. By selecting desired curves in the Curve Bin (as demonstrated earlier in this chapter), you can edit them together as one in the Curve Window. You easily can drag and drop curves from the Scene Display window into the Curve Bin. For example, you might combine the Position.X of an object with the Rotation.Y of a light, and add in the Scale.Z of a camera. You can use any channel you want.

Foreground and Background Curves

When you add selected curves to the Curve Bin, you can see them in the Curve Window, and view them as either foreground or background curves. Curves that are selected in the Curve Bin will become editable foreground curves in the Curve Window. Conversely, the curves unselected are uneditable background curves in the Curve Window.

There are benefits to working with foreground and background curves. You can interactively cut and paste keyframes from one curve to another. You also can replace an entire curve with another, or lock areas of curves together. By having multiple curves selected when you create keys, the curves can be identical at those selected areas during an animation. Additionally, you have the capability to compare one curve to another, such as a light intensity to the H rotation of a camera. This next tutorial demonstrates some of these features.

Exercise 5.3   Adding Keys to Multiple Curves

1. Clear Layout and open the Graph Editor. If the Graph Editor was already open, it will automatically be cleared with the Clear Scene command.

2. Move Camera Position.X and Light Position.Y to the Curve Bin. Do this by expanding the item in the Scene Display (bottom left) and then dragging the desired motion channel up into the Curve Bin.

3. Once loaded, hold down the Shift key and select both channels in the Curve Bin.

    You'll see both curves highlight in the Curve Window. Right now there are only straight lines as the channels have no motions applied.

Note

You can click and drag on the bar between the Curve Bin and the Scene Display windows in the Graph Editor to quickly resize the two windows.

4. Select the Add Keys button beneath the Curve Window, as shown in Figure 5.25.

Figure 5.25   You can choose to add a key from the Graph Editor window, as well as Move, Stretch, Roll, and Zoom.

5. Click once in the top area of the Curve Window, and once near the bottom right, similar to Figure 5.26. You'll see the two curves adjust to the keys you just created.

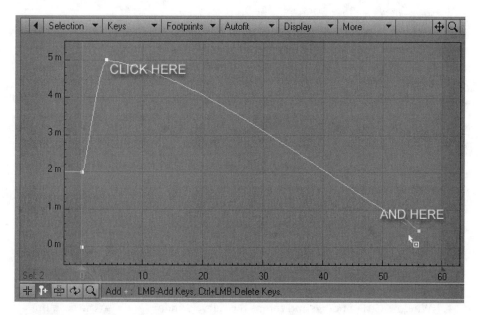

Figure 5.26   You can create keyframes for the selected motion channels directly in the Curve Window.

Navigating the Curve Window

When you select Multiple Curves, you can edit them together, create keyframes together, and so on. However, you also can adjust one of these curves based on the background curve: Simply select only the curve you want to adjust in the Curve Bin. The remaining curves in the Curve Bin appear slightly darkened in the background of the Curve Window. From there, you can select the Move tool, and click and drag a keyframe to change its value. Following are just a few quick steps to remember when working in the Graph Editor:

- Select the Move keyframe button (in the center of the Graph Editor) and click and drag to adjust the selected key(s).

- Select the Move keyframe button and click and hold the Ctrl key to adjust the selected key's position in time—for example, to move a keyframe from frame 5 to 15.

- Hold the Alt key and click in the Curve Window to adjust the entire Curve Window view.

- Press the period (.) key to zoom into the Curve Window; press the comma (,) key to zoom out.

- Press the a key to fit the Curve Window to view—for example, if you zoom into the Curve Window, press the a key to instantly fit all keyframes of curves to the full window.

- You can import curves into the Graph Editor by pressing Shift+g. Many animators think you need to close the Graph Editor, select your next item in Layout, and then re-open the Graph Editor to add the particular curve. Instead, move the Graph Editor aside, select an item in Layout, and then use Shift+g back in the Graph Editor to update.

- Select Numeric Limits from the Display drop-down list at the top right of the Graph Editor window to set the minimum and maximum frame for the Curve Window. Ctrl+alt drags and zooms the Curve Window. You also can set a minimum and maximum value. Alt drag options are similar to their use in Layout's Perspective viewport. Figure 5.27 shows the Numeric Limits panel.

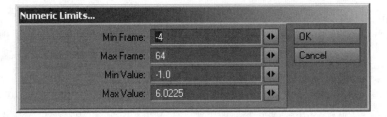

Figure 5.27   You can set Numeric Limits to control the frame and value settings in the Curve Window.

Exploring Additional Commands in the Graph Editor

In addition to the commands you'll use most often as you animate your scenes, you need to know about the Graph Editor commands that can increase your efficiency. As you've learned in other areas of LightWave 7, clicking the right mouse button in certain areas gives you access to additional tools, which enable more control.

Key Pop-Up Menus

In both the Curve Bin and Curve Window, you can access additional controls by using the right mouse button. Figure 5.28 shows the key pop-up menu in the Curve Bin. Figure 5.29 shows the pop-up menu in the Curve Window. All of these controls are available in one location as well as through the Keys drop-down list at the top of the interface. The right-click popup appears in the Curve Edit window only if your mouse cursor is positioned directly over a key.

Selecting a specific channel and right-clicking it in the Curve Bin gives you control to perform a number of tasks. You can replace a channel with a pre-existing one. You also can save a specific channel's properties, which is useful when you want to save and reuse motions like a flickering light or a rotating globe. Instead of setting up new keyframes, you can save the channel motion and reload it later.

You also can copy and paste a specific channel's motion if you want to create a duplicate. Other controls include Show Velocity, which you can use to add a visual representation of the selected channel's velocity in the Curve Window; Show Speed, to make the speed of the selected channel visible in the Curve Window; and Remove from List, to delete a channel from the Curve Bin.

Footprints

Part of the charm of the LightWave 7 Graph Editor is the capability to create Footprints for a selected channel. Because you are not always sure of the adjustments you might make to a keyframe or curve, setting a Footprint helps you visually remember the shape of your curve before it is adjusted. You can then return your curve to the Footprint if you choose. Follow this next tutorial to learn more about Footprints.

Figure 5.28
Right-clicking a selected channel opens the key pop-up menu for additional control.

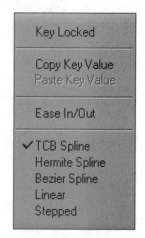

Figure 5.29
Right-clicking a selected keyframe opens the key pop-up menu for control in the Curve Window.

Exercise 5.4   Working with Footprints

1. Open Layout, clear the scene, and open the Graph Editor.

2. Select the light in the Scene Display, and drag it to the Curve Bin.

    All the motion channels for the light are added to the bin, as shownin Figure 5.30.

3. Select the Light Rotation.P, which is the Pitch rotation for the Light. Of course, any selected channel will do for this exercise.

    When a channel is selected, you'll see it highlight in the Curve Window.

4. Select the Add Keys command, and click throughout the Curve Window to create some keyframes for the Rotation.P channel. Figure 5.31 shows the channel with a few keys added.

5. Go back to the Curve Bin, and with the Rotation.P channel still selected, right-click it to open the pop-up menu.

6. Select Footprints, and then select Leave Footprints. You also can do this through the Footprints drop-down list at the top of the Graph Editor, as shown in Figure 5.32.

    Figure 5.33 shows the selection. It won't look like much has happened in the Curve Window, but wait.

Figure 5.30   Selecting just the Light from the Scene Display area and dragging it to the Curve Bin adds all its motion channels.

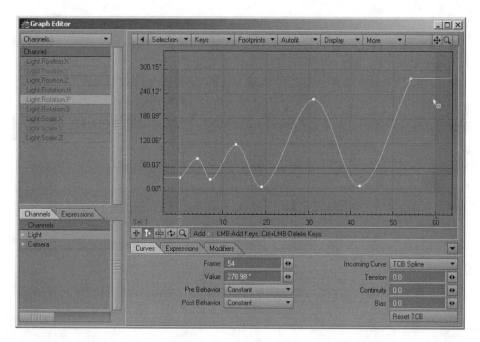

Figure 5.31 A few keyframes are added to the Light's Rotation.P channel in the Curve Window.

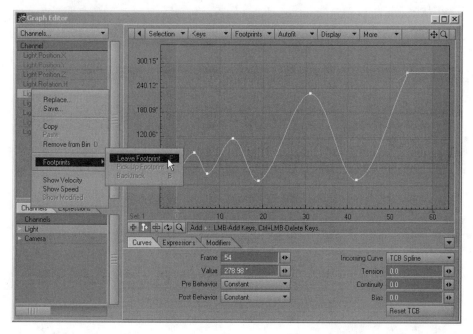

Figure 5.32 Right-clicking a selected channel lets you select the Footprints option.

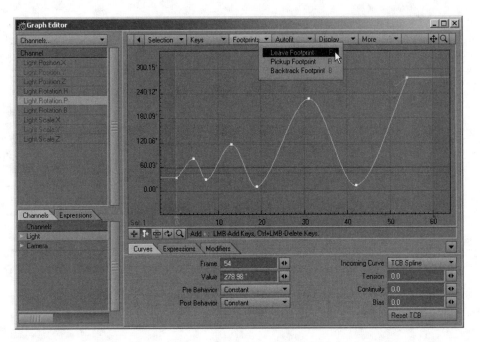

Figure 5.33   All Footprint commands are available at the top of the Graph Editor interface through the Footprints drop-down list.

7. With the right mouse button, click and drag to select a region over all your keyframes in the Curve Window.

This selects all keys, as shown in Figure 5.34.

Note

You also can hold the Shift key and double-click in the Curve Window to select all keys. Move mode must be selected to do this. Clicking once in the blank area of the Curve Window deselects keyframes.

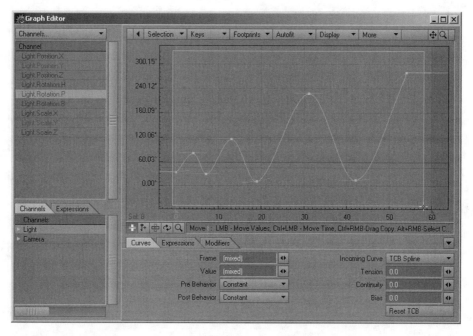

Figure 5.34   Right-clicking and dragging in the Curve Window lets you select multiple keyframes. Mac users, don't forget—holding the Apple key while clicking the mouse button performs a right mouse button function in LightWave.

8. With all the keyframes selected, click and drag in the Curve Window to move the entire motion curve up, as shown in Figure 5.35.

   You'll see a faint line below the curve you just moved. This is the footprint that tells you where your curve was.

9. Go back to the Curve Bin, right-click again, and choose Pick Up Footprint or Backtrack. Or use the command from the Footprints drop-down list.

   Picking up the Footprint removes it from the Curve Window. Selecting Backtrack resets any channel adjustment to the original Footprint position.

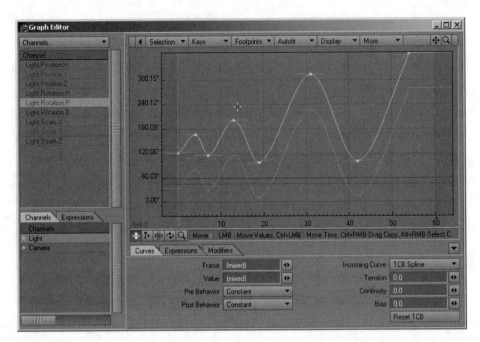

Figure 5.35   After a Footprint is created, moving either single or multiple keyframes reveals the Footprint.

Footprints provide a simple way for you to keep track of what you're doing and where you've been while working in the Graph Editor. It is easy to make too many changes and lose your place when adjusting various channels. Using the Footprint option helps you organize your steps by allowing you to get back to your original curve if you need to.

Using the Curves Tab

At the bottom of the Graph Editor interface is the Curves tab. Here you can adjust the value of a selected keyframe and its pre- and post-behaviors. This area is ghosted until a keyframe is selected. For example, suppose that you have created a spinning globe that takes 200 frames to make a full 360-degree revolution. Your total scene length is 600 frames and the globe needs to rotate throughout the animation. Instead of setting additional keyframes for the globe, you can set the post-behavior to repeat. Once the globe completes its 200 frames of motion, the Graph Editor's post-behavior takes over. You can also set pre-behaviors. A pre-behavior is what happens before the first keyframe.

You can set either pre- or post-behaviors to the following settings:

- Reset, which resets the current value to 0.

- Constant, where values are equal to the first or last key's value.

- Repeat, which will repeat the motion from the first to the last keyframe.

- Oscillate, which mirrors the channel repeatedly. For example, you can make a spotlight rotate from frame 0 to frame 30 on its heading rotation. Set post-behavior to Oscillate, and the motion will sway back and forth between the two keyframes, like a searchlight.

- Offset Repeat, which is similar to Repeat, but offsets the difference between the first and last keyframe values.

- Linear, which keeps the curve angle linearly consistent with the starting or ending angle.

The Curves tab also is home to Spline controls. If you are familiar with versions of LightWave prior to 6, you may have used either Tension (T), Continuity (C), or Bias (B) to control keyframes' splines. LightWave offers more control than simple TCB splines.

Spline Controls

Spline controls come in many varieties, and they give you the control you need over your curves. When an item is put into motion in LightWave, it instantly has a curve. The Graph Editor gives you control over the individual channels of an item's motion. You can adjust the keyframes of the curve that is created with various types of splines. Figure 5.36 shows the Incoming Curve types. An Incoming Curve is the type of curve that precedes a keyframe.

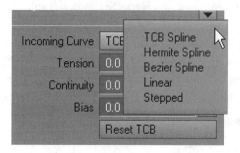

Figure 5.36   LightWave 7 has numerous curve types from which to choose.

TCB Splines

Easy to set, TCB splines are useful for creating realistic motions. The values for each spline range from 1.0 to –1.0.

A Tension with a value of 1.0 is often the most commonly used TCB spline because it allows items to ease in or out of a keyframe. For example, a 3D-animated car needs to accelerate. Setting it in motion would make the car move at a constant rate. By adding a Tension setting of 1.0, the car would ease out of the keyframe and gain speed. By setting a negative value, the car would speed away toward the keyframes.

Setting Continuity enhances a break or change in an item's path. You might not really use a positive continuity setting, as it overcompensates an item as it passes through a keyframe. Negative Continuity, however, can be used to create a sharp change in an item's motion between keyframes, such as a bouncing ball.

Bias is great for anticipation. A positive Bias creates slack after a keyframe—great for a car moving fast around a corner. A negative Bias creates slack before a keyframe. This could be used for keyframing a roller coaster around a sharp turn.

TCB Shortcuts

LightWave 7 allows you to quickly and easily control Tension, Continuity, and Bias controls in the Graph Editor. You don't even need to select a key! Select the keyframe for which you want to set a tension value (or hold the Shift key and double click in the Curve window to select all keyframes) and press F1, then click and drag in the Curve window. Press F1 and drag the mouse to the left to set a negative Tension, or drag to the right to set a positive Tension. Do the same for Continuity with F2, and Bias with F3. Cool stuff.

TCB splines are not the only spline controls you have over keyframes in LightWave 7. This version of the software employs Hermite and Bezier spline curves as well.

Hermite and Bezier Splines

Although TCB splines are often used for common, more everyday animated elements, such as flying logos or animated cars, Hermite and Bezier splines offer a wider range of control. Hermite splines have tangent control handles that give you control over the shape of a curve. Figure 5.37 shows three keyframes with Hermite splines added to the middle keyframe. Its handles are adjusted.

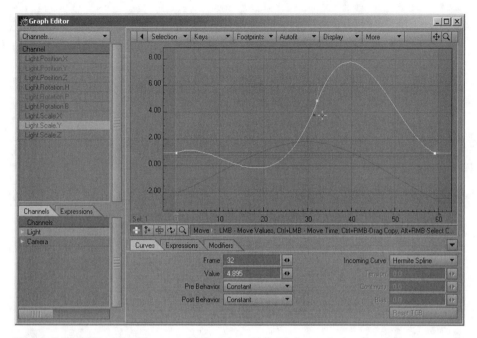

Figure 5.37   Hermite splines are added to the middle keyframe. Such splines offer more control than regular TCB splines.

Figure 5.37 shows three keyframes—one low, one high, and one low again—in a sort of bell shape. However, the middle keyframe has a Hermite spline applied and the left handle of it has been pulled down quite a bit. The figure shows how an adjustment to one keyframe can have a drastic effect on the shape of a curve.

Now if you apply a Bezier curve, you will have different control than you would over a Hermite spline. A Bezier spline is a variant of a Hermite spline and shapes the curve. Figure 5.38 shows the same bell curve of three keyframes with one handle of the Bezier curve pulled down drastically.

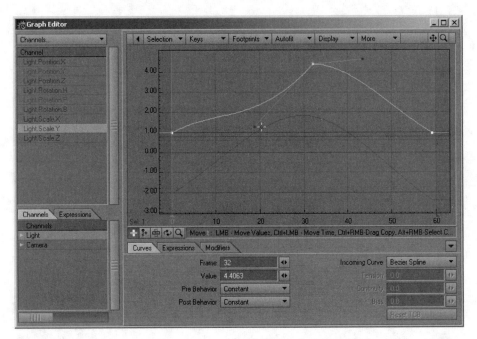

Figure 5.38   Bezier splines, although a variant of Hermite splines, work when the next key is also set to Bezier.

Note

The biggest difference between Hermite and Bezier is that Bezier lets you change the length of the tangent, which also affects the curve shape.

Both Hermite and Bezier splines can help you control your curve. It's up to you to experiment and try both when working with the control of an item's motion. Knowing when to apply curve controls such as these is important. As you work through the tutorials throughout this book, the necessary controls will be used so that you can see the direct effect. Keep an eye out for their use.

Stepped Transitions

Using a stepped transition for an incoming curve simply keeps a curve's value constant, and abruptly jumps to the next keyframe. Figure 5.39 shows a few keyframes with a stepped transition applied.

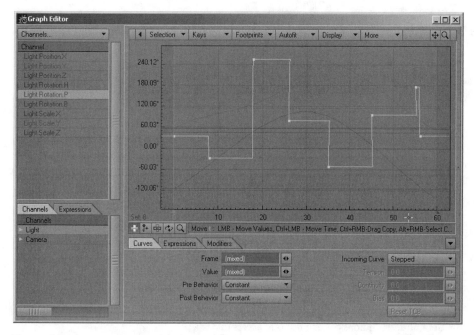

Figure 5.39   Stepped transitions for curves abruptly change your motion from one keyframe to the next.

Use stepped curves when you want to make drastic value changes between keyframes for situations such as lightning, interference, or blinking lights.

Whether you create motions in the Graph Editor or simply adjust preexisting ones, you should understand the amount of control the Graph Editor gives you. The Graph Editor in LightWave 7 even allows you to mix and match spline types for individual channels. Follow along with Exercise 5.5 to make and adjust curves in the Graph Editor.

Tip

Although you have many options for curve control in LightWave's Graph Editor, using the TCB controls can provide the most natural motion for your animations.

Note

Pressing the o key in the Graph Editor opens the General Options tab of the Graph Editor Options panel. Here, you can set the Default Incoming Curve as well as other default parameters (see Figure 5.40).

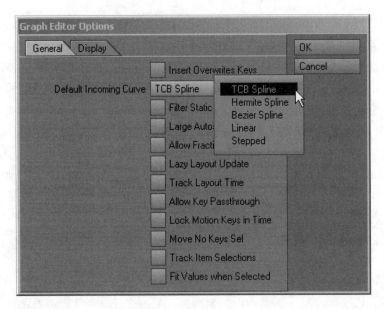

Figure 5.40   You can define the Default Incoming Curve under the General Options tab of the Graph Editor Options panel. Press o to access this tab.

Exercise 5.5   Creating Matching Curves

Start by saving anything you worked on in Layout, and clear the scene. These next few steps provide information about creating curves and adjusting them so that certain areas match perfectly. These techniques can be used with any of your projects.

1. Open the Graph Editor, and in the Scene Display, double-click the Position.Z channel for the Camera.

   The Camera's Z position is now added to the Curve Bin and your Graph Editor interface should look like Figure 5.41.

2. Expand the channels for the light in the Scene Display by clicking the small white triangle.

3. Hold down the Shift key and double-click the Light's Position.Z channel to add it to the Curve Bin. If you didn't hold the Shift key while double-clicking, the new selection would override anything already added to the Curve Bin.

4. In the Curve Bin, hold down the Shift key and select both the Camera Position.Z and Light Position.Z channels.

5. Select Add mode, and in the Curve Window create three keyframes to the right of the first keyframe at zero.

   Figure 5.42 shows the Graph Editor with the additional keyframes.

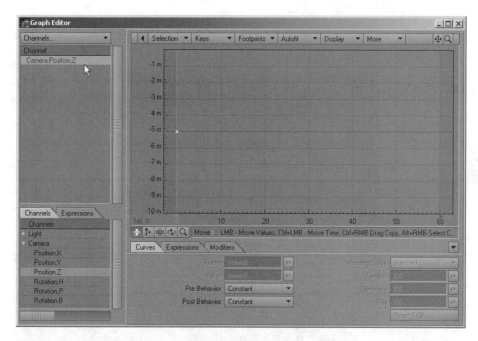

Figure 5.41   Double-clicking the Camera's Z position channel adds it to the Curve Bin.

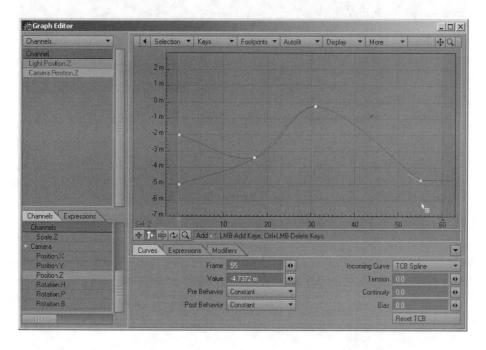

Figure 5.42   With multiple curves selected, you can create identical keyframes for both keyframes at once.

6. Select just the Camera Position.Z channel in the Curve Bin. This automatically deselects the Light Position.Z channel.

7. Select Move mode, and move up the last keyframe.

You'll see the Light Position.Z channel in the background. What you've done here is create similar motions on the z-axis for both the camera and light, but toward the end of the motion, the value has changed. Figure 5.43 shows the adjusted channel.

Note

When modifying identical channels on one keyframe, you'll need to compensate surrounding keyframes slightly. Due to the spline curves, one keyframe affects another. You can see the slight shift in the curve in Figure 5.43.

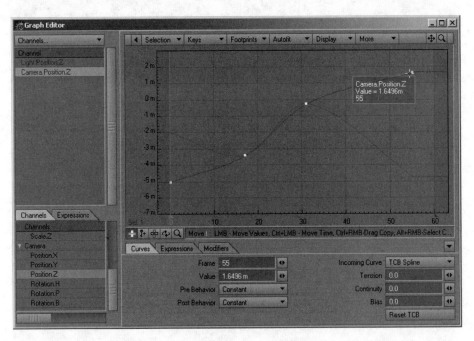

Figure 5.43   One keyframe of matching channels is adjusted.

A more realistic example of matching curves is a formation of flying jets. Each jet flies in unison, swooping, looping, and twisting in perfect sync. After the formation, one or two jets might need to fly off from the pack. Using the preceding example, you can easily select the appropriate channel, and adjust the value at the desired keyframe.

It's easy to see where you would move the jet in Layout, but in the Graph Editor, translating the visual motion to a value might take a little more work. Don't worry; this next exercise helps you adjust values in the Graph Editor.

Exercise 5.6   Adjusting Graph Editor Values

1. Select Clear Scene from the File drop-down menu.

2. In the Graph Editor, click the small white triangle to expand the Camera channels in the Scene Display window.

3. Double-click the Camera Position.Y channel.

    Because only one channel is in the Curve Bin, it is automatically selected.

4. In the Curve Window, create a few keyframes. Figure 5.44 shows the additional keyframes.

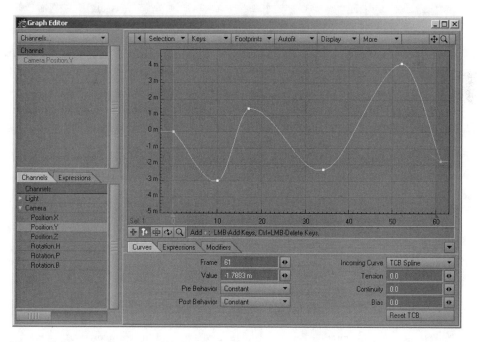

Figure 5.44   One channel is added to the Curve Bin and additional keyframes are created in the Curve Window.

5. With Move mode selected, hold the Shift key and double-click in the Curve Window to select all keyframes, as shown in Figure 5.45. When the keyframes are selected, you'll see small lines extending out from each. These are control handles for the particular incoming curve setting.

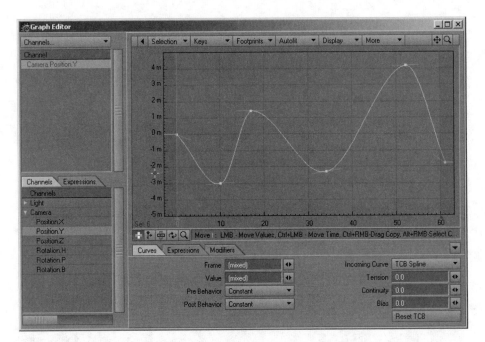

Figure 5.45   Hold the Shift key and double-click in the Curve Window to select all keyframes. Also you can use the right mouse button to draw a bounding box to select multiple keyframes in the Curve Window.

Take a look at the Frame and Value areas under the Curves tab. Instead of values, they are highlighted with the word [mixed], as shown in Figure 5.46. This means that the currently selected keyframes have different values.

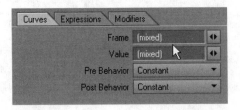

Figure 5.46   Because multiple keyframes are selected, the word [mixed] represents the Frame and Value areas.

6. In the Value area, type the value 10 and press Enter.

   You'll see all selected keyframes jump to the same value. This is useful when you need to adjust many keyframe values. Instead of selecting a keyframe and adjusting individual values, you can change values in one step as long as multiple keyframes are selected.

If you choose to set a value that seems to make your curves disappear, they're probably just out of view. Simply press the a key to fit them to view.

Note

By selecting multiple keyframes with the bounding box selection, you also can set all spline controls at once.

Editing Color Channels

A cool feature in LightWave's Graph Editor is the capability to animate color channels, in addition to motion channels, texture channels, and more. This is great for animating colored lights for animations such as stage lighting or a gradually changing sunset.

Exercise 5.7   Animating Color Channels

1. Close the Graph Editor, and then clear the LightWave scene and select the scene's default light.

2. Press the p key to enter the light's Properties panel.

    You will see a series of small buttons labeled E. These are envelopes, and anywhere you see them throughout LightWave they will guide you right back to the Graph Editor. However, when you access the Graph Editor in this manner, you will have control over only the specific area from which you have selected an envelope, such as Light Color.

    It's important to note that entering the Graph Editor by using the E buttons tells LightWave that you want to perform a specific function. For example, if you click the E button next to Light Color, you are telling LightWave that you want to animate the Light Color, and the Graph Editor opens accordingly. Entering the Graph Editor on its own from the Layout interface would not enable you to animate the Light Color initially. Once you have entered the Graph Editor using any E button, the value you enter will remain there until you clear it; therefore, you need to enter the Graph Editor from particular E buttons only once.

3. Click the E button next to Light Color, as shown in Figure 5.47.

    Once you've clicked the E button, you are in the Graph Editor. It looks similar to the Graph Editor you've been reading about in this chapter, but there is a strip of color along the bottom. LightWave enables you to use the Graph Editor's capabilities on color channels as well as motion channels. Figure 5.48 shows the Graph Editor with the color channel.

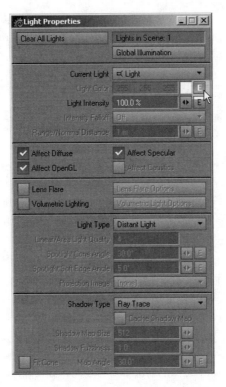

Figure 5.47   The E button (envelope) guides you to the Graph Editor for specific control over Light Color.

In Figure 5.48, the Curve Bin doesn't show position, rotation, or scale channels, but rather, color channels.

4. Select a color channel such as LightColor:G. You also can select all color channels at once by selecting LightColor.R, then holding down the Shift key and selecting LightColor.B (if they are not already selected).

5. Create a few keyframes in the Curve Window and then right-click over a key, and choose Open Color Picker.

   Click and drag the Value slider for a particular keyframe. Figure 5.49 shows what just one color channel looks like when it's been adjusted.

6. You also can change the value of a key as well. From the Curves tab at the bottom of the Graph Editor, adjust the value and watch how the curve changes.

   You'll see the color you've selected appear as a gradual change in the Curve Window.

7. Set colors for the other keyframes, and adjust their values accordingly to set precise timing. Experiment with these values to see the different types of results you can achieve.

   You can cycle colors like this for lights, backgrounds, textures—just about anything!

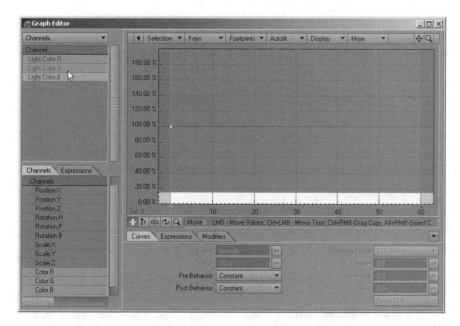

Figure 5.48 Color channels can be animated in the Graph Editor, along with motion channels. Here you can see the separate RGB channels in the Curve Bin, while the default Light Color, white, is visible in the Curve Window.

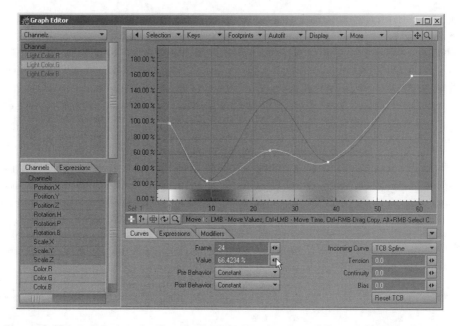

Figure 5.49 Scaling the value for a particular RGB color channel changes the color channel for a set keyframe.

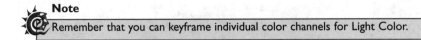

Note

Remember that you can keyframe individual color channels for Light Color.

The Next Step

The Graph Editor is a home base for your animations and envelopes. Before long, you will be using it with most of your animations, and you might even consider keeping it open while you work. Try using the Selection drop-down list above the Curve Window to access more control over your keyframes. LightWave's panels are non-modal, which means that you don't have to be in a certain "mode" to keep them open. Additionally, you can shrink the size of Layout, and configure your computer screen to show Layout, the Graph Editor, and even the Surface Editor all at once. Remember that you can collapse the left side and lower portion of the Graph Editor to reveal just the Curve window too.

You'll find yourself using the Graph Editor for adjusting timing, clearing motions, saving motions, creating object dissolves, or animating color channels more often than you think. Practice creating, cutting, and adjusting keyframes and channels in the Graph Editor. When you're confident of your ability, read on to begin creating amazing models and animations with LightWave 7.

Summary

Don't let the Graph Editor overwhelm you. Although much of this chapter introduced you to the many features and functions of the Graph Editor, you don't always need to use it for keyframing. A good way to work is to use traditional keyframing methods directly in Layout so that you can see what you're doing. Then, use the Graph Editor for tweaking and adjustments. As with much of LightWave, you have multiple ways to achieve the same result. Refer to this chapter any time you need to control your keyframes with splines or specific modifiers, or you need specific control over individual channels. The power of the Graph Editor will become more evident throughout this book, specifically in Chapters 14 and 15.

Chapter 6

LightWave 7 Cameras

Learning the art of 3D animation involves more than creating models, applying textures, and setting keyframes. 3D animation is an art form all its own, and it's still in its infancy. But part of learning this new and fascinating art form is understanding the digital camera. Not the kind of camera you use to take snapshots of your family, but the kind *inside* the computer—your digital eye.

This chapter introduces you to everyday camera techniques that you can apply to your LightWave animations. The camera in LightWave is a significant part of every animation you create, from simple pans, to dollies and zooms, to dutch angles. If you have any experience in photography or videography, the transition to "shooting" in LightWave will be smooth.

The title of this chapter is plural because LightWave offers multiple cameras. LightWave always has been a digital studio, and just like in a television studio or movie set, you can set up multiple cameras in your scenes. This chapter instructs you on the following:

- The Camera Properties panel
- Basic real-world camera principles
- Setting up and using LightWave's cameras
- Applying various camera techniques to animations

Setting Up Cameras in LightWave

As you work through LightWave, you'll become familiar with the various item properties panels associated with objects and lights. The Camera Properties panel controls camera settings, such as resolution, focal lengths, and more.

Take a look at the Camera Properties panel in Layout. Figure 6.1 shows the Camera Properties panel, accessed by first selecting Cameras at the bottom of the Layout interface, and then clicking the Item properties button.

Close to the top of the Camera Properties panel, you'll see an item labeled Resolution. Figure 6.2 shows the selections that are available in the Resolution drop-down list.

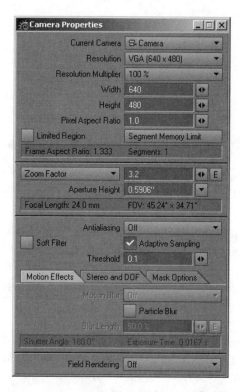

Figure 6.1   The Camera Properties panel gives you the control you need to set up cameras in Layout.

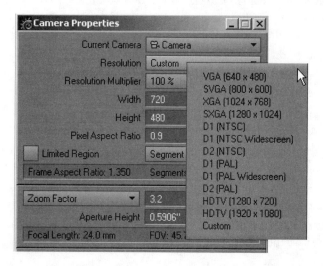

Figure 6.2   From the Resolution window, you can automatically set the width, height, and pixel aspect ratio for your renders.

Multiple Cameras

Multiple cameras in LightWave are easy to set up, and they can be very useful for any type of scene. More specifically, multiple cameras can be used when you have a large scene that has action that needs to be covered from various angles, such as an accident re-creation. Exercise 6.1 shows you how to add multiple cameras to Layout.

Exercise 6.1   Adding Multiple Cameras to Layout

Multiple cameras can help you save time setting up animations that need to be viewed from different angles. And although you can't switch between specific cameras during rendering, you can render passes from any camera in the scene. Here's how to add cameras to Layout:

1. From the File menu in Layout at the top left of the interface, select Clear Scene.

2. Select the Add drop-down list, and choose Add Camera, as shown in Figure 6.3.

   Figure 6.3
   You can add more cameras to your scene from the Add drop-down list in Layout.

   You now have two cameras in the scene: the default camera that's always in a blank scene, and the camera you just added.

   When you select Add Camera, a small requester comes up, asking you for a name. Clicking OK keeps the camera name as "Camera," which appears with a number next to it, such as "Camera (2)," for the second camera added, and so on.

   You can choose whether to rename the cameras you add. You can always rename them later if you don't want to rename them now. Clicking OK sets the default name, Camera, and adds another camera to Layout.

3. Click OK to add an additional camera to Layout.

   Now you want to tell Layout that you want to set up your cameras, but first you must select a specific camera.

   With multiple cameras in a scene, you need to choose which camera you are currently using. Adding, selecting, or deleting cameras is the same as selecting any other scene item, such as objects or lights.

4. Select the camera by first clicking the Cameras button at the bottom of the interface.

5. From the Current Item selection, choose which camera you want to use.

6. To rename a camera, select the camera and choose Replace, and then select Rename Current Item from the Items tab.

> **Note**
> Remember that there are complete full-color versions of all the book's figures on the accompanying CD-ROM.

Working with multiple cameras is as easy as working with one camera. Simply point and shoot! To get the most out of multiple cameras, set them up in a way that will be most beneficial to your animation. For example, suppose that you need to re-create a traffic accident and the client wants to see the accident from a bystander's viewpoint, an aerial viewpoint, and the driver's point of view. By adding three cameras to your scene and setting them in the desired positions, you can render the animation from any view. Try it!

Resolution

After you choose the current camera, Resolution is the first selection within the Camera Properties panel you'll want to work with, and for good reason. It is the width and height of your rendered images. LightWave also sets the appropriate pixel aspect of your rendered images when a specific resolution is set.

Note

Rendering is a generic term for creating or drawing an image. This is done in LightWave by pressing the F9 key for single frames (Render Current Frame) and F10 for multiple frames (Render Scene).

The resolution you set here determines the final output size of your images and animations. The default resolution is VGA mode, which is 640 pixels wide by 480 pixels tall. This resolution is of a medium size, common for most computer work. You also can choose SVGA, which is 800 by 600 pixels, or XVGA, which is 1024 by 768 pixels. These are good resolutions to work with if your images or animations are being used in a computer environment, such as in QuickTime or Audio Video Interleaved (AVI) formats. Although these three resolutions might be too large for most QuickTime or AVI files, you can use the Resolution Multiplier to change the output size. This is discussed later in this chapter.

Note

QuickTime is Apple Computer's animation format, now common on both Macintosh and Windows computers. Rendering an animation to a QuickTime movie creates a playable computer file. AVI, developed by Microsoft is another type of animation format. Each has varying levels of compression, so check with your particular computer system for your ideal setting.

If you are creating animations that will eventually end up on videotape, you'll want to use the D1 or D2 NTSC resolution settings (in the United States), or the D1 or D2 PAL resolution settings (in Europe).

> **Note**
> In 1953, the National Television Standards Committee (NTSC) developed the North American television broadcast standard. This standard is 60 half frames, or fields, per second, with 525 lines of resolution. PAL stands for Phase Alternate Line. This standard, which most of Western Europe uses, is 625 lines of resolution at 50 fields per second.

Resolution Multiplier

The Resolution Multiplier is a nice feature in LightWave because it can help you more accurately set up animations in different sizes. The feature is handy in instances in which you've created an animation in low resolution (to work faster) but then you begin rendering in a higher resolution (for quality) and you do not achieve the same results. For example, suppose that you've created a scene that uses a lot of stars, made with small individual points. You set your resolution to a low setting to make sure that your test renders quickly. The individual points are modified and adjusted to look right. But when you choose a higher resolution, the stars are barely visible. This happens because the actual resolution of the image is changing. What looks large on a small image is not the same size on a larger image. This problem also occurs when setting up lens flares. LightWave's Resolution Multiplier, as shown in Figure 6.4, keeps the same resolution settings but multiplies the value by 25 percent, 50 percent, 100 percent, 200 percent, or 400 percent. An image rendered at 100 percent is the exact size of the set width and height, whereas 50 percent renders an image half the size.

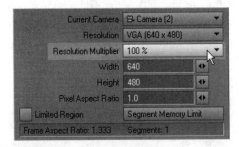

Figure 6.4   The Resolution Multiplier increases or decreases resolution while keeping the width, height, and pixel aspect ratios correct.

Pixel Aspect Ratio

The difference between VGA modes and D1 or D2 modes, aside from the resolution difference, is the pixel aspect ratio. The *pixel aspect ratio* is the shape of the individual pixels the computer draws. A *pixel* is a tiny picture element that is square or rectangular and is comprised of colored dots that make up the computer graphic image. Computer images use square pixels, which means a pixel aspect ratio of 1.0. Television images, generally 720×486, or 349,920 pixels, use rectangular pixels. NTSC D1 video is 0.9 pixel tall. Because the pixel aspect ratio is the ratio of the width to the height, 0.9 is narrower than it is tall. Try Exercise 6.2 to get a better idea of pixel aspect ratios.

Exercise 6.2 Working with Pixel Aspect Ratios

Throughout most of your animations, setting the appropriate resolution automatically sets the proper pixel aspect ratio. By default, LightWave shows the Perspective view. To see the change in camera settings, you need to switch from Layout to Camera view. Pixel aspect ratio (PAR) is merely the shape of the pixel on the target display device. If the images will be viewed on a PC, you always want 1.0 because PCs use square pixels. If the images will be shown on a video device, such as television with a 4 to 3 screen ratio, you need a PAR that is .86 to .9.

For example, suppose that you have a perfect square in your image. If you use a PAR of 1.0, LightWave will render the square using the same number of pixels for its width and height. This looks cool on your PC monitor, but if you showed the image on a TV, it would look tall. This is because televisions have tall pixels. Although the same number of pixels make up the square's height and width, because they are "tall" they make the box tall. You need to compensate for this. If you use a PAR of .9, LightWave automatically scales the pixels it uses to make the image with the assumption of "tall" pixels. A television pixel aspect ratio might not always be exactly .9, but it won't be 1.0. To give you an idea of how the different aspect ratios work, open LightWave Layout and perform the following steps:

1. Select Camera View in the selection mode at the top of the Layout window, as shown in Figure 6.5.

   Remember that although resolution settings can be seen directly in Layout, you won't see the stretching due to an incorrect PAR in Layout. Rather, it merely shows you what portions of the scene will be in the rendered image. It is the projection of this image on the display device that causes the stretching, if any.

Figure 6.5
Resolution and the results of setting the pixel aspect ratios can be seen only through the Camera View in Layout.

2. Make sure that Show Safe Areas is selected, and then press the d key to enter the Display Options tab.

3. Select Show Safe Areas under the Camera View tab at the bottom of the interface, as shown in Figure 6.6.

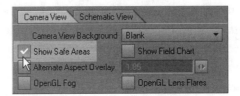

Figure 6.6   Selecting Show Safe Areas from the Display Options tab turns on a visible outline through the Camera View in Layout.

4. Close the Display Options panel by pressing the d key again, or p (for panel).

Figure 6.7 shows the Camera View with the safe areas enabled. This represents the Title Safe and Video Safe areas of your view. You should set up animations with this feature enabled to ensure that your animation is viewed properly when recorded to videotape.

Note

Safe areas are important to use as shot reference. The outer line represents the Video Safe area—any animation elements outside this area will not be visible on a standard 4 to 3 ratio television monitor. The inner line represents the Title Safe area—any text in your animations should not travel beyond this bounding region. Video has something called "overscan," and the area you're not seeing is within this region. Broadcast monitors allow you to view overscan, but standard 4 to 3 televisions do not. Keeping within these guidelines will help your relationship with video editors as well.

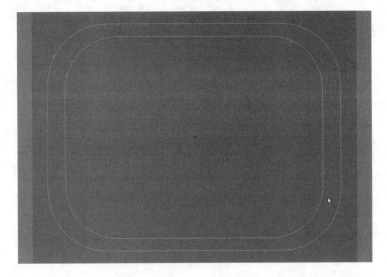

Figure 6.7   When Show Safe Areas is enabled, you'll see a television-style shape around your field of view through the camera.

Tip

You can change the color of the safe area outlines by changing the Overlay Color selection in the Display Options tab of the Preferences panel. Doing this also changes the color of any overlays seen in the Camera View, such as Field Chart.

5. Select Camera from the bottom of Layout, and then choose the Item Properties panel, or press the p key. Move the Item Properties panel over to the far right of the screen, revealing more of your Layout window.

6. Go to the Resolution drop-down list and select D1 NTSC Widescreen, as shown in Figure 6.8.

This resolution changes the width to 720 and the height to 486, with a pixel aspect ratio of 1 to 2.

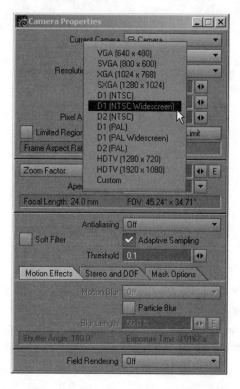

Figure 6.8   You have a number of choices when it comes to resolution, such as LightWave's Widescreen settings.

7. Press the p key to close the Camera Properties panel.

Figure 6.9 shows the safe areas with a different pixel aspect ratio. Notice how the view looks stretched?

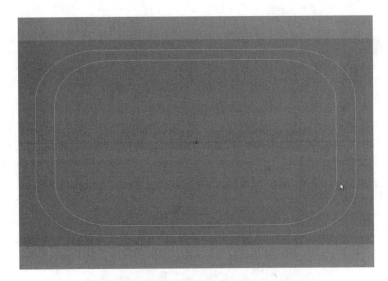

Figure 6.9   Setting a resolution to D1 NTSC Widescreen changes the pixel aspect ratio to 1.2, making the safe area viewed through the Camera panel appear stretched.

8. Press p again to open the Camera Properties panel. Grab the slider button next to Pixel Aspect Ratio, and drag it back and forth.

   Figure 6.10 shows the slider button. You should see the safe area field of view changing in Layout.

Figure 6.10   You can interactively control pixel aspect ratio by clicking and dragging the small slider buttons.

It's important to note that the pixel aspect ratio will affect your renderings. Changing the resolution changes the size of the image, whereas changing the pixel aspect ratio changes the target pixel shape—which also can distort your final output if it is not set properly. As an animator, it's important for you to remember what the target display device is, such as a video recorder, and set your resolution and aspect ratio accordingly. For example, if you are rendering an animation for video and accidentally set to D1 NTSC Widescreen resolution, your final animation when imported into an animation recorder or nonlinear editor will appear stretched. The computer will take the full image and squeeze it to fit the television-size frame your nonlinear editor or animation recorder uses. This happens because Widescreen resolution is the incorrect resolution for the standard video recorder. And because setting resolution also sets the pixel aspect ratio, both are the wrong version for widescreen to video.

Limited Region

Every now and then, there might be a situation in which the resolution settings are not the exact size you need for rendering. You sometimes might need to test-render just an area of an animation, saving valuable time rendering. For example, if you have an animation that has many objects, textures, reflections, and more, test-rendering the full image might take up too much of your time—especially if you want to see how one small area of the scene looks in the final render. Using the Limited Region setting helps you accomplish this. Figure 6.11 shows the selection in the Camera Properties panel.

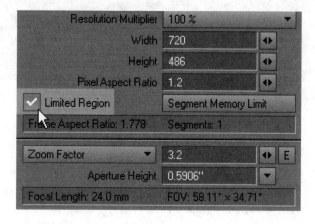

Figure 6.11 Limited Region lets you control the area of the screen to be rendered.

When using Limited Region, you can easily turn on a limited region directly in Layout by pressing the l key. A yellow dotted line appears, encompassing the entire Layout area. From here, you can click the edge of the region and resize it to any desired shape. Figure 6.12 shows a limited region for a small area of a scene. Figure 6.13 shows how the image renders in the Render Display window and how this Limited Region setting would look.

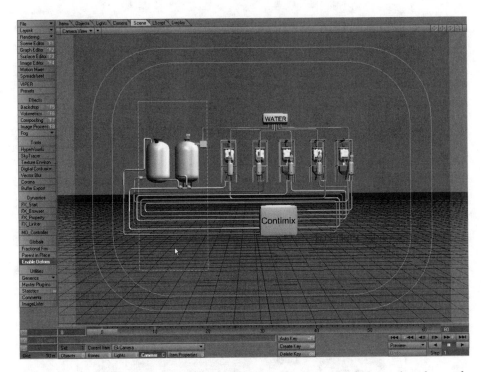

Figure 6.12   You can resize the Limited Region directly in Layout to render a selected area of the animation.

Limited regions also are useful for creating images for web sites using LightWave. Perhaps you want to animate a small spinning globe or a rotating 3D head. Rendering in a standard resolution draws unwanted areas, creating images that are not only the correct size, but also larger as well. Setting up a limited region can decrease file size and create renders in the exact size you need, such as a perfect square. Limited region essentially renders a portion of what normally would be a larger image. Try using a web GIF animation program and render out a series of small GIF files, set up with a limited region. The GIF animation program imports the sequence of images to create one playable file. Limited Region works differently from a custom resolution. A limited region can be made to any size visually and set for any area on the screen. Setting a custom resolution sets only the specific size for the center of the screen. Also, Limited Region enables you to render limited regions of very high-resolution images. A custom resolution would not work this way.

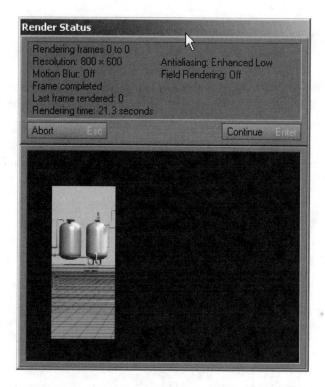

Figure 6.13   The Limited Region-rendered image is just the area assigned in Layout.

Segment Memory Limit

Too often, you'll run out of RAM while you are creating animations. RAM, or the memory in your computer, is used quickly by many images, large objects, and hefty render settings. The Segment Memory Limit feature lets you tell Layout the maximum amount of memory to use for rendering. Lower values will render a frame in segments, which means they might take a bit longer to load and execute. The tradeoff is that you don't need as much memory.

For faster renders, you can increase the segment memory. Setting the segment memory to 20 Megabytes, or 20MB of RAM, will often enable you to render D1 NTSC resolution in one segment. Although this setting is only an example, LightWave 7's Segment Memory setting is a maximum setting. This means you can set this value to the same amount of RAM in your system, and LightWave will only use what it needs, often eliminating the need for your system to use virtual memory or a scratch disk.

Note

Remember that higher resolution settings require more memory.

When you click the Segment Memory button, a small requestor pops up, asking you to enter a value. You can enter a value as large as you want, provided you have the memory in your system. When you click OK, LightWave will ask you whether you want to make this value the default. Click Yes, and you won't have to change this value when you start creating another animation scene. Figure 6.14 shows the Segment Memory selection in the Camera Properties panel.

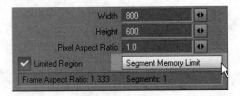

Figure 6.14   Setting a Segment Memory Limit tells LightWave how much memory is available for rendering. Setting a higher value allows LightWave to render animation frames in one pass.

Current Camera

Because LightWave allows you to add multiple cameras to your scene, you'll need a way to select them to adjust each item's properties. The Current Camera selection list is at the top of the Camera Properties panel. If you have not added any cameras to your scene, you will see only the item "Camera." If you have added multiple cameras, they will be listed here, displayed as Camera (1), Camera (2), and so on, if you have not set a name for them. Cameras added with names also appear in the list, as shown in Figure 6.15. These cameras listed are all available for selection in the Current Item selection list at the bottom of the Layout interface. You don't need to enter the Camera Properties panel to select a different camera.

Figure 6.15   All your scene's cameras can be selected from within the Camera Properties panel, from the Current Camera selection list.

Zoom Factor

The Zoom Factor option is probably one of the most overlooked features when it comes to working with cameras in LightWave. The zoom factor is essentially the camera's lens. Have you ever worked with a telephoto zoom lens on a real camera? This is the same thing, only in a virtual world. Pretend that you are videotaping a family party with your camcorder. You probably pan around and constantly zoom in and out to cover the action. In LightWave, you can do the same thing! Changing the zoom factor over time not only gives your animation a different look, but also adds variation to your animations.

The default zoom factor is 3.2, as shown in Figure 6.16.

Figure 6.16   LightWave's default zoom factor is 3.2, or the equivalent of a 24mm focal length.

This setting is fine for most projects, but to make something come alive in 3D, you should lower this value. The setting 3.2 is equivalent to a focal length of 24mm, or an average camera lens. Figure 6.17 shows a scene with the default zoom factor setting. The image looks good, but the scene lacks depth. But take a look at Figure 6.18, where the same shot has a zoom factor of 1.5. Notice how wide the shot looks and how much depth is in the image. Now the image looks three-dimensional. This setting is only an example, and you should try different zoom factors on your own to see what works best for you.

The cameras in LightWave are just as important as your objects. Don't overlook the possibilities of changing the zoom factor over time, either. Using LightWave's Graph Editor, you can animate the zoom factor with stunning results.

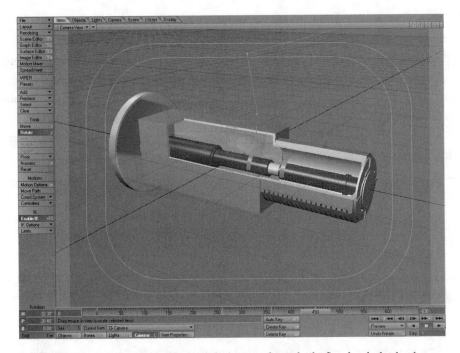

Figure 6.17   A scene rendered with the default zoom factor looks fine, but lacks depth.

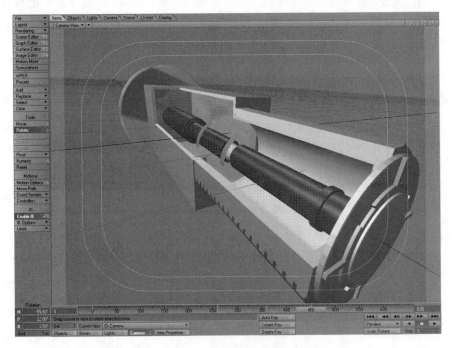

Figure 6.18   The same scene with a zoom factor of 1.5 gives the shot a lot more dimension and makes it much more interesting.

Focal Length

Zoom factors directly relate to lens focal lengths. Focal length is measured in millimeters. The larger the focal length value, the longer the lens. For example, a telephoto lens might be 180mm, and a wide-angle lens might be 12mm. Because focal lengths represent everyday camera settings, just like your 35mm camera, you might be more comfortable working with lens focal lengths instead of zoom factors. You can do this by selecting the desired option from the Zoom Factor drop-down list, as shown in Figure 6.19.

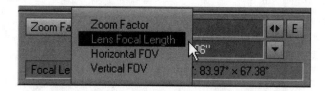

Figure 6.19   You have the option to choose Lens Focal Length instead of Zoom Factor in the Camera Properties panel.

Note

Each camera you add to Layout can have different zoom factors. For example, in the Camera Properties panel, you can select one camera and set the zoom factor so that it renders like a telephoto lens. Then, you can select another camera in the Camera Properties panel and make it render like a wide-angle lens. Each camera in LightWave can be set differently.

Field of View (FOV)

In addition to zoom factor and lens focal length, you can set up a camera's field of view (FOV) using the Horizontal FOV or Vertical FOV settings. Changing the values for zoom factor automatically adjusts the lens focal length, the horizontal FOV, and the vertical FOV. The horizontal and vertical fields of view give you precise control over the lens in LightWave. The two values listed next to FOV are the horizontal and vertical fields—horizontal being the first value. Working with FOV is useful when you are working in real-world situations and need to match camera focal lengths, especially when compositing.

Don't let all these settings confuse you, however. The Zoom Factor, Lens Focal Length, Horizontal FOV, and Vertical FOV settings all enable you to set the same thing. Simply use the one you're most familiar or most comfortable with—or choose whatever is called for to match a real-world camera. There is no inherent benefit in using one over the other.

Antialiasing

When you render an animation, it needs to look good. The edges need to be clean and smooth, and no matter how much quality you put into your models, surfaces, lighting, and camera technique, you won't have a perfect render until you set the antialiasing. *Antialiasing* cures the jagged edges between foreground and background elements. It is a smoothing process that creates cleaner-looking animations. Figure 6.20 shows a rendered image without antialiasing. Figure 6.21 shows the same image with a low antialiasing setting applied.

Figure 6.20   Without antialiasing, the rendered image looks jagged and unprofessional. Notice the case lines on the left side of the CD. They're jagged and appear uneven. This is because no antialiasing has been applied.

Figure 6.21   After antialiasing is applied, even at a low setting, the image looks cleaner and more polished. Take a look at the case lines on the left side of the CD. With Enhanced Low Antialiasing, the lines are clean and sharp.

Antialiasing can really make a difference in your final renders. Figure 6.22 shows the available antialiasing settings.

The higher the antialiasing setting, the more LightWave will clean and smooth your polygon edges. But of course, higher values mean added rendering time. The Enhanced Antialiasing setting smoothes your image at the sub-pixel level, which takes a bit more time to render, but it produces better results. In most cases, Medium to Enhanced Medium antialiasing produces great results.

Figure 6.22   You can choose to add a Low antialiasing setting to your animations, all the way up to Enhanced Extreme.

Adaptive Sampling

Although you can set up an antialiasing routine for your renders, you still have to tell LightWave how it should be applied. Adaptive sampling is a flexible threshold that LightWave employs to evaluate the edges in your scene. Lower values evaluate more, enabling a more accurate antialiasing routine. Higher values evaluate less. A default setting of 0.1 is an average threshold value. Changing this to 0.01, for example, adds to your render times but helps to produce a cleaner render. A good way to work with adaptive sampling is to set a higher antialiasing, with a not-so-low threshold. For example, Enhanced Medium antialiasing, with a threshold of 0.1, renders reasonably well (depending on your scene) and produces nice-looking images. For more details on adaptive sampling, refer to your LightWave manual.

Soft Filter

As an additional help to eliminate sharp, unwanted edges in a scene, you can turn on the Soft Filter option in the Camera Properties panel. As an alternative to setting higher antialiasing routines, you can set a lower antialiasing with Soft Filter applied. Soft Filter will add a small blur to your render, creating a soft look.

Motion Effects

At the bottom of the Camera Properties panel, there are three tabs. Each tab offers even more control over your camera's settings. The first tab, Motion Effects, is home to some common, everyday functions.

Motion Blur

When antialiasing is turned on (set to at least Low), the Motion Blur option becomes available. From time to time, you might need to create motions that mimic real-world properties, such as a speeding car or a fast-moving camera. To give things a more realistic look, you can apply motion blur to your scene. Motion blur in LightWave combines several semi-dissolved images on each frame to give the effect of blurred motion. Motion blur mimics real-world actions. Remember that the multiple rendering passes used with antialiasing are needed in order to compute the dissolved images, which is why antialiasing needs to be set at Low or above. You can see an example in Figure 6.23.

Figure 6.23   Motion blur is applied to a fast-moving logo scene. Motion blur helps add the feeling of movement because in real-world cameras, the shutter speed is not fast enough to freeze the action.

Motion blur should be used anytime you have something fast-moving in your scene. Even if it's only a slight motion blur, the added effect will help "sell" the look. If your animation is perfectly clean, perfectly smooth, and always in focus, it will look better with some inconsistencies, such as motion blur.

Motion blur also is important to set for things like a bee's wings flapping, an airplane's propellers, and so on. Many animated objects moving at this speed will require you to set Motion Blur. If you look at spinning propellers in the real world, all you see is a blur. To re-create that look in LightWave, turn on Motion Blur in the Camera Properties panel.

Blur Length

Simply put, blur length is the amount of motion blur you want to use. The default is set to 50 percent, which produces nice results. Depending on the animation, you may want to set this value slightly higher—say, to 60 percent or 65 percent—for more blurring. When you apply the Blur Length setting, corresponding Shutter Angle and Exposure Time values appear beneath the Blur Length window. Most of your motion-blurred animations should have a 50 percent blur length set. This is because the blur length relates to the amount of time the theoretical film is actually exposed. Because of the physical mechanism, a film camera can't expose a frame for 1/24 of a second, even though film normally plays back at 24 frames/sec. It turns out that this rotating shutter mechanism exposes the film for only 50 percent of the per-second rate; thus, 50 percent blur length is right on.

Particle Blur

Along the lines of motion blur is particle blur. Use this setting anytime you have an animation whose particles need to blur, such as explosions, fast-moving stars, snow, rain, and so on. A blur length of 50 percent works well for particle blur.

Field Rendering

At the bottom of the Camera Properties panel is the Field Rendering selection. In NTSC video, there are 30 frames per second, or 60 fields per second. Applying field rendering to your animations is useful when your objects need to remain visible when moving swiftly and close to the camera. This setting is targeted for video, and it allows you to mimic the effect of video's interlaced fields. Motion will seem smoother on the video display. Field rendering makes the final output crisp and clean, especially when there are visible textures. Video draws half the frame first, or one field, and then the other half, or the second field. There are two fields per frame. You can set LightWave to render the even or odd fields first. Motion can occur between the time it takes to display these fields, just as it does from frame to frame, and applying field rendering accounts for this.

Stereo and DOF

Setting up additional camera properties can further enhance the final look of your animations. The second tab area at the bottom of the Camera Properties panel is the Stereo and DOF tab, as shown in Figure 6.24.

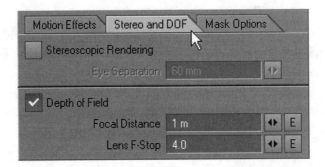

Figure 6.24   The Stereo and DOF tab offers stereoscopic rendering and depth of field functions to your cameras.

Stereoscopic Rendering

Within the Stereo and DOF tab in the Camera Properties panel, you can turn on Stereoscopic Rendering. Stereoscopic rendering is yet another way for you to change the look of your animations. Applying this setting to your camera results in an image that looks separated, as though two images are blurred together. Simply put, this setting creates left and right stereoscopic image files. Changing the Eye Separation value tells LightWave how far apart to render the left and right stereo images.

Depth of Field

You see depth of field every time you look through a camera lens. It's used in movies, television, your own eyesight, and even animation. *Depth of field* (DOF) is defined as the range of distance in front of the camera that is in sharp focus. Depth of field is a fantastic way to add real depth to your animations. Without DOF, everything will be in focus, as Figure 6.25 shows.

Figure 6.25 Without depth of field applied, everything in your scene will be in focus.

By adding a DOF setting, you tell the camera where to focus. Anything before or after that focal point will be out of focus. Figure 6.26 shows the same image with DOF applied. Notice how the background is out of focus.

Depth of field can dramatically add to your LightWave renders because it enables you to set a focal distance for any of your LightWave cameras. The focal distance tells the camera in Layout where to focus when DOF is applied. The default setting is 1m. To use depth of field in your animations, you must have selected an antialiasing setting of at least medium quality.

Figure 6.26   With DOF applied, the image is out of focus farther away from the set focal point.

Using LightWave's grid, which is the system of measurement in Layout, you can easily determine the focal distance from the camera to your objects in a scene. Figure 6.27 shows the information window in the bottom-left corner of the Layout interface. You'll see the grid measurement at the bottom. The default of 1m appears.

X	2.0543 m
Y	1.4736 m
Z	-744.52 mm
Grid:	1 m

Figure 6.27
Using LightWave's grid measurement, you can easily determine where to set the focal distance from the camera to the objects in the scene.

The grid measurement relates to every square in the Layout grid. If the default grid size of 1m is present, each square of the grid in Layout equals 1m. Therefore, you can count the number of grids between the camera and the focal point in the scene. If you had a scene where the camera is 4 grid squares away from the front of the object, with a grid measurement of 1m, the focal distance setting should be 4m. This makes any object before or after the 4m mark out of focus.

Range Finder for DOF

You also can use a custom object to set depth of field. Under the Items tab, you can select Add, then Custom Objects, to select Add Range Finder (see Figure 6.28). This will add a null object to your scene with a visible numeric value. In the numeric Range Finder pop-up that appears, you can set the Item to Camera, and then select Draw Link, as shown in Figure 6.29.

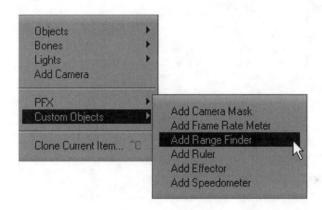

Figure 6.28   You can add a custom object to quickly measure distances in Layout from any item, such as the camera for setting depth of field measurements.

Figure 6.29   The Range Finder pop-up allows you to set the Camera as a link.

You'll see a line between the camera's pivot point and the Range Finder null. Make sure that Auto Key is enabled, and move the null. You'll see the measurement values change, as shown in Figure 6.30. This value is your distance from the camera that you can easily use to set DOF. If you're specifically trying to set the focus on an object, simply put this Range Finder null on the object, and take the measurement. This is a really good way to calculate rack focuses for animated DOF as well.

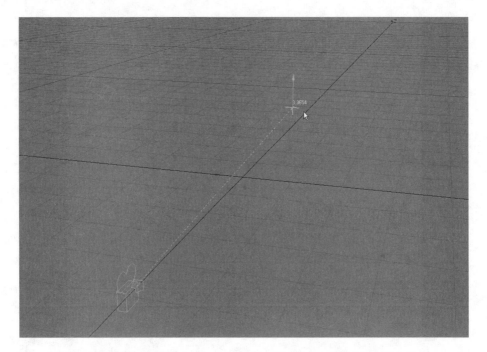

Figure 6.30   With the Range Finder custom object added, when Auto Key is on, you'll see a target line between the selected item (Camera) and the Range Finder. Cool stuff.

F-stop

In addition to focal distance, you also can set an f-stop for any of your LightWave cameras. You do this through the Stereo and DOF tab.

The human eye automatically adjusts to brighter or darker lighting situations. Under low light, the human eye's iris and pupil open to allow in the maximum amount of light. Bright sunlight, on the other hand, makes the human eye close to protect the eye.

By the same token, cameras also have an iris and pupil that allow in more or less light. While the human eye smoothly opens and closes to control incoming light, cameras need to have this control set. This is done through f-stops.

F-stops are numerical values that represent the amount of varying degrees of light transmission. A smaller f-stop allows more light into the camera, while higher values allow less light into the camera. Here are the common f-stop numerical values used in the real world:

- 1.4 Softest focus, allowing a lot of light into the camera
- 2.0

- 2.8
- 4.0
- 5.6
- 8
- 11
- 16
- 22   Sharpest focus, allowing little light into the camera

Here's how it all comes together. When you have a higher f-stop number (which equates to a smaller iris opening), your DOF-value will be greater. So, the DOF on a LightWave camera set to an f-stop of 11 will be larger and less blurred, creating a flatter image. If you set an f-stop of 2.0, you will have a smaller depth of field, making items behind and in front of the focal distance out of focus. Be sure to check out Appendix B, "LightWave 7 Plug-in Tool, and Technical List," for valuable camera setting information.

Mask Options

The final tab available for enhancing the LightWave camera is the Mask Options tab. Here, you can tell the camera in LightWave to render certain areas while masking out others. The remaining areas are defined by a color. This option is great for setting up pseudo wide-screen renders, or a letterbox effect. You can set values for left, top, width, and height, as well as the mask color. Figure 6.31 shows the Mask Options tab. Figure 6.32 shows a rendered image with the Mask option applied. You can use the Mask option for making letterboxed images, simulating a 16 to 9 or widescreen look on a 4 to 3 television.

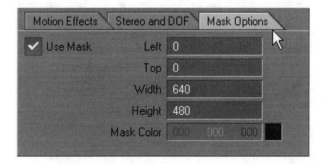

Figure 6.31   The Mask Options tab within the Camera Properties panel enables you to mask areas of your camera view for rendering.

Figure 6.32   Mask options are great to use for rendering only portions of animations while setting a color for the unmasked area.

Note
Remember that masking covers up your rendered image based on the parameters you set. It does not resize your image.

You can see that the control available to you for LightWave's cameras can be a significant element in the animations you create. Too often, the camera is ignored and left in place. This is a crime—remember the camera when you animate! Animate it as well as your objects.

Camera Concepts

So, you want to incorporate the camera more into your animations, but don't know where to begin? You might find yourself in situations where you don't know how to frame a shot or decide where to place the camera. This next section will provide you with some basic instruction that you can use throughout any of your animations.

View in Thirds

To many animators, looking through a camera lens is like looking at a blank canvas. Where should you begin? How should you view a particular shot? Your first step in answering these questions is to get a book on basic photography and cinematography. References such as these can be invaluable to animators as well as a great source of ideas.

When you look through the camera in LightWave, try to picture the image in thirds. Figure 6.33 shows a sample scene as viewed through LightWave's default camera; however, lines have been painted in to demonstrate the concept of framing in thirds.

Figure 6.33   Framing your shot in thirds can help you to place the camera more accurately.

By framing your shot in thirds in the vertical and horizontal views through the camera, you have areas to fill with action. Now remember, you need to visualize this grid when setting up camera shots in LightWave. There is not an option to do this. By visualizing, you can begin to think more about your shot and framing. Figure 6.34 is an example of a bad camera shot. Figure 6.35 is the same scene with a decent camera angle.

Figure 6.34   Here is a good scene gone bad because the camera is set up poorly. The city is not centered in view, a common mistake many animators make. This is bad because there is too much open or "dead" space on the top and right of the frame.

If you visualize in thirds, you can see that the action in Figure 6.35 feels better—it is aesthetically pleasing. Although Figure 6.34 had the main focus, the cityscape, off and below center, the rest of the frame was ignored. Figure 6.35 takes into account not only the main focus, but also the surrounding areas of the frame. If you visualize the image in thirds, as in Figure 6.36, you can see that areas of the scene fit into place.

Figure 6.35   The same scene looks much better because the camera is set up properly, placing action within the frame. Notice that the dead areas at the top and right of the frame are now filled with subject matter.

Figure 6.36   This shows Figure 6.35 with lines drawn in thirds for the horizontal and vertical views. Notice that all areas of the scene seem to have a place in view.

When thinking in thirds while setting up a shot, don't be too literal. Your objects don't need to line up exactly into each third area. Visualizing your camera shot in thirds is a way to help frame the entire field of view. Don't be afraid to try different camera angles and different perspectives.

Camera Angles

After you get the hang of framing a scene, the next thing you should think about is the camera angle. Consider what you are trying to portray in the render. Do you want the subject to look small, or should it be ominous and looming? What you do with the camera in LightWave helps sell the mood of your animations to the viewer. As good as your models and textures might be, your shot needs to work as part of the equation as well. Figure 6.37 shows the city from a bird's-eye point of view.

But perhaps you need to convey that the city is not a pleasant place to be. You want to convey a feeling that the city is overpowering. Figure 6.38 shows how a different camera angle changes the feel of a shot.

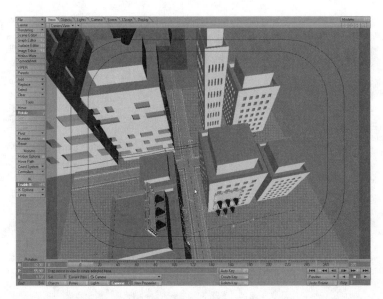

Figure 6.37   Setting your camera to a bird's-eye point of view makes the shot unthreatening.

Figure 6.38   A wider camera angle, set low in front of the city, gives a grander look and feel to the shot.

Taking your scenes one step further, you can also employ dutch angles to your cameras. Adding a dutch angle will convey the feeling of uneasiness, or a creepy mood. Figure 6.39 shows a shot similar to Figure 6.38, with the camera rotated on its bank, or dutched.

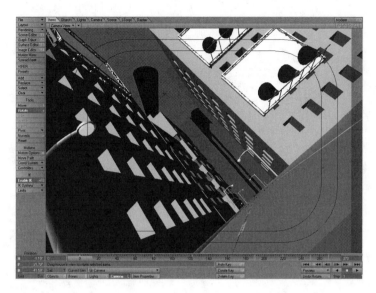

Figure 6.39   Rotating the camera on its bank sets up a dutch angle that conveys the feeling of something being wrong, creepy, or uneasy.

The Next Step

The cameras in LightWave are as powerful as the software's modeling tools. When you model, you create shapes and animate them. When you animate, your motions create a mood, and without the proper camera angles, your work will not be as powerful. Practice setting up different types of shots. Load some of the scenes from your LightWave directory that installed when you loaded the program. Study the camera angles used there and try creating your own. Use reference books from real-world situations, mimic the cinematography in movies, and most importantly, experiment. Hopefully this chapter got you thinking about the cameras in LightWave and the shots you can create and animate.

Summary

This chapter introduced you to the cameras in LightWave Layout. You learned how to add multiple cameras and set their parameters. Concepts were presented to you to change the way you look through the camera to make your animations more powerful and expressive. And, you read about navigating the interfaces, surfacing, cameras, and using the Graph Editor.

A large portion of what goes into a shot deals with lighting and environments. The next section of this book discusses just that. So, when you are ready and feel that you have a solid grasp on the concepts in this section, move ahead into Part II, "A Project-Based Approach to Creating and Building 3D Scenes," where you will put this information to the test with real-world projects.

Part II

A Project-Based Approach to Creating and Building 3D Scenes

Chapter 7

Lighting and Atmospheres

You might consider lighting to be one of
the less important aspects of your 3D animations, or perhaps it is an area with which
you are just not comfortable. Lighting is

crucial to your success as an animator. Lighting can be used for so much more than simply brightening a scene—it can convey a mood, a feeling, or even a reaction. Lighting is vital in film, photography, and 3D animation.

Project Overview

Basic lighting can add warmth to or cool off your animations. It can improve your animations. But you need to be aware of some basic real-world principles before you can put it all together. This chapter instructs you on these topics:

- Basic lighting principles
- Using LightWave's Global Illumination
- Using different light sources
- Animating lights
- Adding atmospheres

Before you begin working through lighting setups in this chapter and throughout this book, you should be aware of the types of lights LightWave has to offer as well as their uses. At the top of the Layout interface is the Lights tab, from which you can access all the lighting properties listed in this chapter.

Lighting for Animation

The great thing about LightWave is that its lights work in a fashion similar to lights in the real world. They aren't exact duplicates of real-world lights, but with a few settings and adjustments, you can make any light appear realistic.

Five lights are available in LightWave Layout. Each has a specific purpose, but each is not limited to that purpose. They are

- **Distant lights.** Used for simulating bright sunlight, moonlight, or general lighting from a nonspecific source.
- **Point lights.** Used for creating sources of light that emit in all directions, such as a candle, light bulb, or spark.
- **Spotlights.** Used for directional lighting such as canister lighting, headlights on cars, studio simulation lighting, and more. Spotlights are the most commonly used types of light.
- **Linear lights.** Used to emit light in elongated situations, such as fluorescent tubes.

- **Area lights.** The best light to use for creating true shadows, area lights create a brighter, more diffuse light than distant lights and therefore can create the most realism. They do, however, take longer to render than spotlights, distant lights, or point lights.

Note

Lights are available only in Layout.

The environment in which your animation lives is crucial to the animation itself. Color, intensity, and ambient light are all considerations that you should be aware of each time you set up a scene. Light and the use of shadows are as much an element in your animation as the models and textures you create.

Light Intensity

By default, there is always one light in your LightWave scene. It has a light intensity of 100 percent, and it is a distant light. The light intensity of 100 percent is a placeholder for you to adjust. Although you can use this one light and its preset intensity as your main source of light for images and animations, it's best to adjust the light intensity to more appropriately match the light and the scene at hand.

Light intensities can range from values in the negative range to values in the thousands. Yes, thousands! You can set a light intensity to 9000 percent if you want! The results might not be that desirable, unless you're animating a nuclear holocaust. In general, if you were to create a bright, sunny day, a point light, which emits light in all directions, can be used with a light intensity of 150 percent or so for bright light everywhere. Conversely, if you were lighting an evening scene, perhaps on a city street, you can use spotlights with light intensities set to around 60 percent.

Negative lights also can be handy depending on the scene you're working on. Just as lights with a positive light intensity can brighten a scene, negative lights can darken a scene. You might be asking why you would darken a scene with a negative light instead of simply turning the lights down. For example, you might have to add a lot of light to make areas appear properly lit. Depending on the surfaces you've set, the extra light might make one area look perfect, while making other areas too bright. This is where negative lights come into play. Adding a negative light (any light with a negative light intensity value) will take away light from a specific area.

Light Color

The color of the light you use is important and useful in your images and animations because it can help set tone, mood, and feeling. No light is ever purely white, and it's up to you to change LightWave's default 255 RGB light color.

In LightWave, you can even animate colored lights. Suppose that you're animating a rock concert, for example, and you need to have fast-moving lights shining on the stage. By animating the light color, you can change the colors over time at any speed you want. The light color in LightWave can be enveloped, meaning that you can use the Graph Editor to make changes to the color over time.

Note

Be sure to check the end of Appendix B, "LightWave 7 Plug-in, Tool, and Technical List," for color temperatures of light, for settings such as candle light, sunlight, and more.

Adding Lights

Adding lights in LightWave 7 is easy. Follow these simple steps to add lights to LightWave Layout and get a feel for how they work. And remember, unless you are working with Auto Key enabled, you'll need to create a keyframe to lock your lights into position after they're moved.

1. Open Layout or select Clear Scene from the File drop-down menu.

   This sets Layout to its default of one distant light.

2. Make sure that you are in Perspective view so that you have a full view of Layout. Under the Items tab, select the Add drop-down button, Lights, and then Add Spotlight. Figure 7.1 shows the menus.

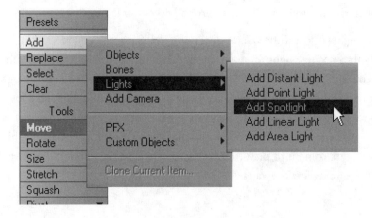

Figure 7.1   You can add lights directly in Layout under the Items tab.

You have the choice to add any type of light you want.

3. Before the light is added to Layout, a Light Name requester appears, as shown in Figure 7.2.

Figure 7.2   After a light is added, the Light Name requester appears, enabling you to set a specific name for your light.

4. Type in the name you want to give the new spotlight.

Note

You don't have to change the name of a new light. Instead, you can accept LightWave's default light name by clicking OK when the Light Name requester appears. By default, LightWave names new lights as follows: Light (1), Light (2), Light (3), and so on.

The added light is placed at the 0 axis, also called the *origin*, as shown in Figure 7.3.

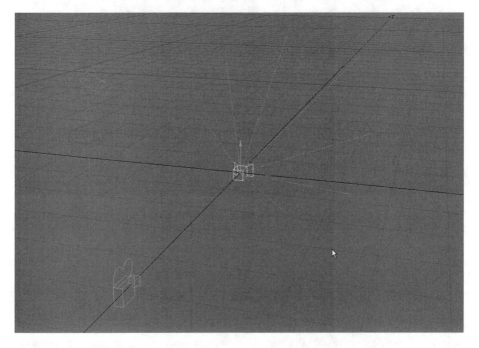

Figure 7.3   Added lights are placed at the 0 axis (the origin) in Layout.

Adding lights is intuitive. In addition to adding lights like this, you also can clone lights. Cloning a light creates an exact duplicate of a selected light. This includes the light's color, intensity, position, rotation, and so on. Any parameter you've set will be cloned. Cloning lights is as easy as adding lights. To clone a light, first select the light to be cloned, and then select the Add drop-down list under the Items tab, but instead of selecting Lights, and then Add Light, select Clone Current Item. The selected light is cloned. This process works the same way for cloning objects or cameras.

Global Illumination

The space around you, whether that space is at your desk, in your living room, or outside, has global luminosity properties. The following global properties—Global Light Intensity, Global Lens Flare Intensity, Ambient Light, Ambient Color, Radiosity, and Caustics—can be controlled in the Global Illumination panel. You can find the Global Illumination panel under the Lights tab in Layout. Figure 7.4 shows the panel.

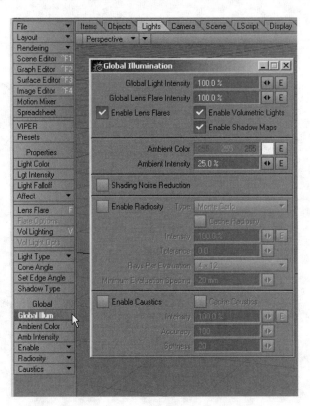

Figure 7.4   The Global Illumination panel, found under the Lights tab in Layout, is where you can control such properties as Global Light Intensity, Global Lens Flare Intensity, Ambient Light, Ambient Color, Radiosity, and Caustics.

Global Light Intensity and Global Lens Flare Intensity

Global Light Intensity is an overriding volume control for all lights in a scene. This can be useful for scenes that have multiple lights that need to get brighter or dimmer over time. Consider the earlier example of the rock concert. You have 20 spotlights shining on the stage. All their intensities are randomly and quickly changing to the beat of the music. At the end of the song, you want all the lights to fade out equally. Instead of setting the light intensity 20 times for each light, you can ramp down the Global Light Intensity. Similarly, if you have lens flares applied to these lights, you can change the Global Lens Flare Intensity.

Ambient Light and Ambient Color

The light around you is either direct or ambient. Direct light comes predominantly from a light source. Ambient light has no specific source or direction.

Within the Global Illumination panel, you can set the intensity of your ambient light. A typical setting is around 5 percent. LightWave defaults to 25 percent, which is often too high a value for most situations. It is better to lower the value, sometimes to 0 percent, and use additional lights for more control. Don't rely on ambient light to brighten your scene. Instead, use more lights to make areas brighter.

You also can set the color of your ambient light so that the areas not hit by light still have some color to them. For example, you might have a single, blue light shining on an actor on a stage. You can make the side of the actor not hit by any light visible by using an Ambient Light setting; with the Ambient Color set to blue (like the light), the shot will look accurate. Remember, ambient light hits all surfaces, not just those that are unlit by actual lights, which is why knowing about Ambient Intensity is important. You'll use the Ambient Light and Ambient Color settings later in this chapter.

Note

Ambient light is often considered a poor man's radiosity. You can use it to brighten areas not directly lit by lights.

Radiosity and Caustics

Also within the Global Illumination panel are the Radiosity and Caustics settings. These two features in LightWave enable you to take your 3D creations even further by adding more real-world lighting properties.

Radiosity is a rendering solution that calculates the diffused reflections of lights in a scene. It is the rate at which light energy leaves a surface. This also includes the color within all surfaces. In simpler terms, radiosity is bounced light. A single light coming through a window, for example, can light up an entire room. The light hits the surfaces of the objects and bounces, lighting up the rest of the room, in turn creating a realistic image. You'll use radiosity and learn more about the setting in Chapter 9, "Realistic Lighting Environments."

Caustics are created when light is reflected off a surface or through a refracted surface. A good example is the random pattern often seen at the bottom of a swimming pool when bright sunlight shines through the water. Another example of caustics is the ringlets of light that can appear on a table as light hits a reflective surface, such as a gold-plated statue. The light hits the surface and reflects. Chapter 9 walks you through an exercise explaining this technique further.

Lens Flares

Introduced in LightWave 3.0, lens flares are a popular addition to animated scenes. Too often when you add a light to a scene, such as a candlestick, the light source emits, but no generating source is visible. By adding a lens flare, you can create a small haze or glow around the candlelight. Other uses for lens flares are lights on a stage, sunlight, flashlights, and headlights on a car. Anytime you have a light that is in view in a scene, you should add a lens flare so that the viewer understands the light has a source. Lens flares in LightWave can be viewed directly in Layout before rendering. You'll be setting up lens flares later in this chapter.

Volumetric Lights

You need to be aware of one more area of LightWave lighting before you start working through exercises. Volumetric lighting is a powerful and surprisingly fast render effect that can create beams of light. Have you ever seen how a light streaks when it shines through a window? The beam of light that emits from the light source can be replicated in LightWave with *volumetrics*. Volumetric settings give a light source volume. Additionally, you can add textures to a volumetric light to create all sorts of interesting light beams. Coverage of volumetric lighting can be found in Chapter 9.

Applying Lights in LightWave

You will encounter many types of lighting situations when creating your animation masterpiece. This next section steps you through a common lighting situation that you can use for character animation tests, product shots, or logo scenes.

Lighting for Video

One of the cool things about LightWave is that you don't have to be a numbers person to make things happen. You can see what's happening throughout the creation process from object construction, to surfacing, to lighting. This exercise introduces you to basic three-point lighting often used in everyday video production. You can apply this lighting style to LightWave and create a photographer's backdrop (or *psych*) to act as a set for your objects. Creating a set in LightWave is a good idea so that even simple render tests are not produced over a black background. By rendering objects on a set, you add more depth to your animation.

Exercise 7.1   Simulating Studio Lighting

The goal of this project is to introduce you to a common lighting setup that can be useful in just about any type of render situation when you are simulating studio lighting. You'll use a pre-made set object that was created in LightWave Modeler with a segmented box, which is smoothed out by applying a SubPatch.

1. In Layout, load the ChairRoom.lwo object from this chapter's folder on the accompanying CD.

   This loads the MultiMesh object, which includes two layers: the room and a simple chair object. Figure 7.5 shows the object loaded in Layout from the Perspective view.

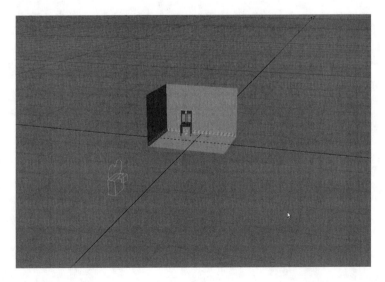

Figure 7.5   The pre-made room object loaded from the book's CD into Layout is a perfect object onto which to cast different lights.

2. Select the default light that is already in the scene. This is a distant light and is not useful for the current lighting situation.

3. Switch to the Lights tab at the top of the Layout interface to access the light controls.

4. Change the Light Type to Spot, as shown in Figure 7.6. You can also do this directly from the Lights Properties panel as well. When you are changing a multitude of settings for lights, it's sometimes faster to just do everything directly in the Light Properties panel.

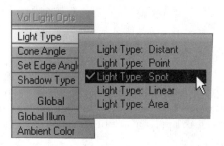

Figure 7.6   For studio lighting, spotlights often work best. Start by changing the default distant light to a spotlight.

The spotlight becomes the key light, or the main light in the scene setup. You'll be creating a three-point lighting situation in this scene.

5. Change the Light Intensity to 95 percent. You can do this by selecting the light intensity button labeled Lgt Intensity on the left side of the interface. When you click this button, the numeric value becomes available at the bottom-left corner of the interface.

Then set the Light Color to off-white, about 245, 245, 220 RGB.

You've set the Light Color to off-white because light is never purely white. In a studio setting, the key light burns with a slight off-white tint.

Note

Three-point lighting is a common lighting setup used in most studios. It consists of a key light, which is the primary source of brightness; a fill light, which is less bright than the key and used opposite the key; and a backlight, sometimes referred to as a *hair light*, which is used to separate the subject from the background.

6. Set the Spotlight Cone Angle to 40 and the Spotlight Soft Edge Angle to 40. This creates a nice edge falloff for the key light.

7. Lastly, set the Shadow Type to Shadow Map, which creates softer shadows than ray-traced shadows.

8. Change the Shadow Map Size to 2000. This setting is the size of the pixels of the shadow map. Leave Shadow Fuzziness set to 1.0. Set these settings from within the Light Properties panel because there is no direct control button in Layout.

9. Be sure the Fit Cone option is selected, and press p to return to Layout.

Warning

You can use shadow maps only with spotlights. This is because LightWave uses the same procedure to calculate areas that are hidden from the Camera view by objects as it does for a spotlight. Because a spotlight's position and rotation both matter to LightWave, they are useful for calculating shadow maps. Other lights work differently in that only one element, such as position or rotation, is needed. The result of a shadow map is a soft shadow.

Note

The larger the Shadow Map size, the more memory LightWave uses to calculate the shadow. Larger Shadow Map Sizes produce cleaner shadows, but increase render times. A Shadow Map size of about 1000 to 2000 is a good size to work with. If you want to increase the Shadow Fuzziness to, say, 8, you should increase the Shadow Map size to 3000 or higher. This is high, and you'll need a good amount of memory just for this light, but will result in cleaner shadows.

10. Back in Layout, press 5 on your numeric keypad to switch to Light view. Looking through the light to set it in position is the quickest and most accurate way to set up lights.

11. With the current light selected, press the t key to select Move; then right-click directly in Layout view and move the light up on the y-axis about 30m. Mac users, don't forget that using Apple key with the mouse button enables you to access right mouse button functions.

When you load the ChairRoom object, the Grid Size in Layout changes to 20m. You're now moving the light up 1 grid square. LightWave shows the grid squares for the y-axis when you are working in the Side and Front views. You can lower the grid size to your liking for more control over your items.

12. On the numeric keypad, press 1 for Front view or 3 for Side view to see the light position.

13. Switch back to the Light view (5). With the left mouse button, move the light back away from the set so that it has a larger coverage area, as shown in Figure 7.7.

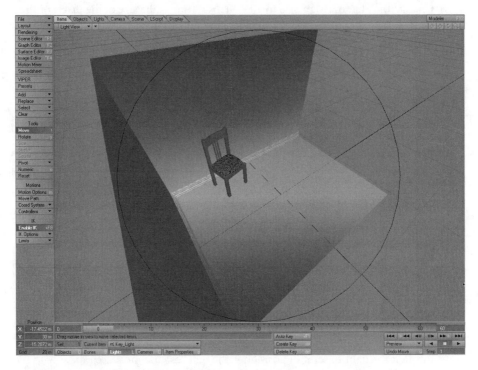

Figure 7.7   Setting the position of the spotlight from the Light view is quick and easy. Because of the way the object is shaded, you can see that the light is in front and to the upper left of the set.

14. Save your scene as LightSetup.lws.

    Before you add the other lights, you need to rename this light to keep your scene organized.

15. With the existing light selected in Layout, click the Items tab, choose Replace, and then select Rename Current Item. Rename the light to Key_Light, and click OK.

    Now you need to add another light to create the fill light.

16. From the Items tab, select Add, then Lights, and then Add Spotlight. After you add the light, LightWave asks you to name it. Name this light Fill_Light (or Phil light if your name is Phil).

17. For the Fill_Light under the Lights tab, change the Light Intensity to 65 percent. Change the Light Color to a soft blue with the settings 135, 170, 230 RGB.

Adding a blue light as a fill light is often a nice touch when setting up lights, either in a studio or in outside situations. This type of light helps create a subtle feeling of distance in your animation.

18. Change Shadow Type to Shadow Map for this spotlight, as you did with the Key_Light; change the Spotlight Cone Angle to 40; and change the Spotlight Soft Edge Angle to 40.

19. Move the Fill_Light to X 40m, Y 7m, Z –18m, and Rotate the light to H –60, P 0.0, B 0.0. To do this, make sure the Fill_Light is selected, press t to move, and then n to access the numeric values at the bottom-left corner of the interface. Type the value, and press Enter on the keyboard. Press y for rotate, and then press n for numeric again. Create a keyframe at zero to lock the light in place. Figure 7.8 shows a view of the set from the Fill_Light. Figure 7.9 shows a Perspective view of the Layout setup.

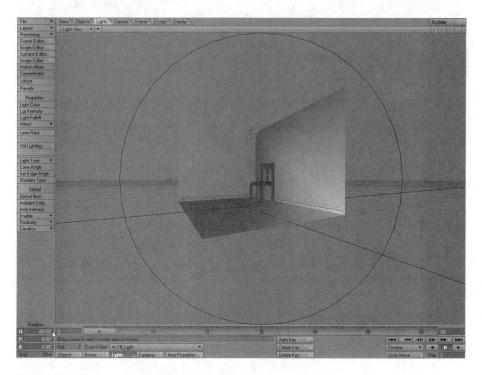

Figure 7.8   Here you see the Fill_Light's view of the set.

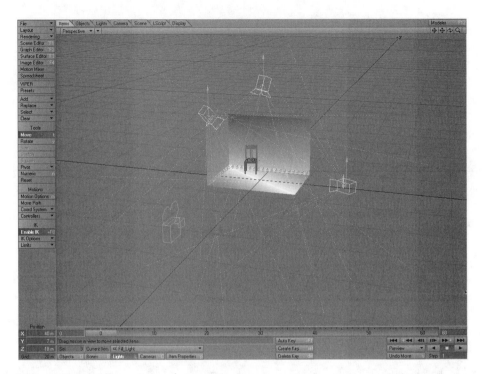

Figure 7.9   In this overview of the scene thus far, you can see the Key_Light to the left and the Fill_Light to the right.

You need to add one more light to the scene to set up the backlight. This light also will be a spotlight.

20. Based on the settings for the Key_Light and Fill_Light, add another spotlight and set the values similar to the Key_Light. Position the new spotlight above and to the back of the room, slightly above the chair, facing into the room. Be sure to create keyframes at zero to lock the lights in place. Save the scene.

Note

You also can clone a light in Layout by first selecting the particular light, and then selecting Clone Current Item from the Add drop-down menu.

21. Now select the camera and move it in so that the room fills the frame, as shown in Figure 7.10. Be sure to create a keyframe at frame 0 to lock the camera in place.

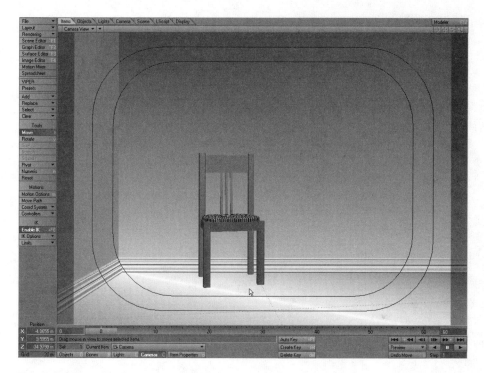

Figure 7.10   Move the camera in to fill the frame with the room.

22. Press F9 to render, and you'll see a nicely lit, simple set, as shown in Figure 7.11.

You can load the CameraLightSetup scene from the book's CD to see everything to this point.

Note

The view in Figure 7.10 shows the Camera view with Safe Areas enabled to help frame the shot for video. You can find out more about Safe Areas in Chapter 6, "LightWave 7 Cameras." To turn on the Safe Areas, press the d key for the Display Options tab, and click Show Safe Areas under Camera view.

Exercise 7.2   Finishing Touches for Studio Lighting

Now that you have some basic lighting set up, you need to create some drama and depth. You have a set and lights, but no textures, no life. This exercise shows you how to adjust your lighting situation using ambient light as well as textures to enhance the lighting environment.

Figure 7.11   Although the set is boring, and the walls are bare, the render looks pretty good, thanks to a basic three-point lighting rig.

1. Be sure that the scene you've been working on is loaded in Layout. If not, use the one from this book's CD, labeled BlankRoom scene.

2. From the Lights tab, open the Global Illumination panel. Set the Ambient Intensity to 5 percent.

   The default Ambient Intensity is 25 percent. This is much too bright and can make your renders appear flat and washed out. Ambient is the area in your scene not affected by light. LightWave allows you to make this brighter or darker based on the Ambient Intensity setting. As a good rule of thumb, keep this setting low, often as low as 0. If you need more light, add it with a light—don't just use Ambient Intensity.

3. Press F9 to render the frame. The dark areas are darker, and the shot begins to take on depth. But you still need to do something about those walls!

4. With LightWave 7, you can replace specific layers of objects. For now, the chair is fine, but the walls need a makeover. Go to the Items tab, and select Replace, and then choose Replace With Object Layer, as shown in Figure 7.12.

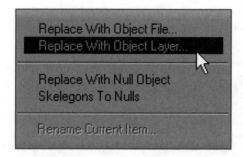

Figure 7.12   You can tell LightWave to replace only the layer of an object with the Replace command.

5. When you select Replace With Object Layer, and then select an object for replacement, a requester comes up asking you which layer you want to replace. Select the ChairRoom_Texture object as the replacement. In this case, layer 1 was the room, and layer 2 was the chair. Replace layer 1, as shown in Figure 7.13.

Figure 7.13   When you select Replace With Object Layer, a requester pops up, asking which layer you want to replace. It's a good idea to remember which objects are in each layer.

At this point, you can finesse the scene with light adjustment.

6. Press the d key to open the Display Options tab for Layout. Set the Max OpenGL Lights to 4 or higher.

This setting enables you to set the effects of lights directly in Layout. The maximum number of lights you can set for OpenGL visibility is 8.

7. Close the Preferences panel.

8. To get a feel for how your lighting looks, press the F9 key to render a frame. You should see something similar to Figure 7.14. Although the three point spotlights work great for studio-type lighting, you can create a softer, more natural look simply by changing the lights. This figure shows the same wall with one image-mapped texture applied, for added effect.

Figure 7.14   This initial render of the setup shows lighting that is good for studio lighting, but you can change the look and feel by changing the lights, and adding a texture.

Projection Images with Spotlights

Exercise 7.2, although basic in design, is the core lighting situation with a slight variation for many of your LightWave projects. Simple stage sets, equipment, figures, generic objects, or any element can benefit from this basic three-point lighting setup. But you are not limited to using just three lights for these types of situations. You can start with the basic three, and then add or remove lights to highlight certain areas, brighten dark areas, or use additional lights as projection lights.

Exercise 7.3   Creating Gobo Lights

This exercise will show you how to use LightWave's Projection Image feature. This is a useful lighting tool that mimics real-world lighting situations where "cookies" or "gobos" are used to throw light onto a set. A *gobo* is a cutout shape that is placed in front of a light, sort of like a cookie cutter. Certain areas of the gobo hold back light, while other areas let light through. For this exercise, you will use a gobo that creates the look of light coming through a window.

Figure 7.15 shows the gobo you'll use to create the effect. This image is nothing more than six white squares on a black background. When this image is applied to a spotlight, the white areas allow light to shine through, and the black areas do not.

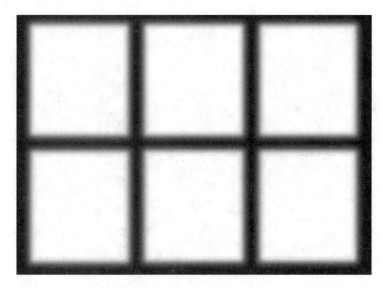

Figure 7.15   A painted image with white squares can be used as a Projection Image in the Lights panel to create window lighting effects.

Note

Gobo images can be created with a paint package such as Adobe Photoshop, Jasc Software's Paint Shop Pro, or better, NewTek's Aura 2. The image should be 24 bits and the size should match your render resolution. For example, video-resolution gobo images should be a pixel size of 720×486. Images smaller than 320×340 resolution do not produce the best results.

1. Select Fill_Light and press 5 on the keyboard to switch to Light View mode.

2. Move the Fill_Light up and inward toward the room and chair objects so that the light is focusing down, toward the object, as shown in Figure 7.16. Create a keyframe at 0 to lock the Fill_Light in place.

3. Select the Back_Light, and press the – key to delete it from the scene.

4. Now select the Key_Light and change it to a point light. Also change its Light Intensity (in the Lights tab) to 30 percent. This light will be a general soft light to fill up the room.

   The Fill_Light in the upper right will become light from a window.

5. To project the image from the fill light, select Fill_Light and press the p key to open the Light Properties panel. Change the light color to a warm sunny color, about 255, 255, 220 RGB. Set the Light Intensity to 150 percent.

6. In the Light Properties panel for the Fill_Light, select the drop-down list next to Projection Image, and select Load Image, as shown in Figure 7.17. Load the 07windowGobo.tga from the book's CD.

Figure 7.16   The Fill_Light is moved inward to encompass only the object.

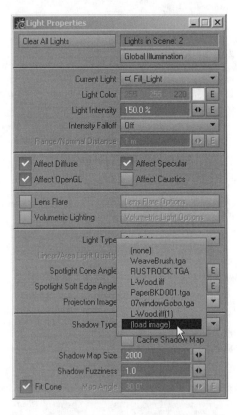

Figure 7.17   You can add a projection image to a spotlight directly from the Lights panel. Doing this will simulate light coming in through a window.

7. Once the image has been loaded, press F9 to render. You'll see what appear to be window panes across the room. The light is now projected through the black and white image (see Figure 7.18). You can take a closer look at the gobo image in the Image Editor. Note that your image might appear slightly different due to variances in light placements.

Figure 7.18   Now with just two lights in the scene, a gobo on a spotlight gives the room a different lighting environment.

You can load this final scene into Layout from the book's CD and take a look at the final settings. The scene is called WindowRoom. Take a look at it and modify it for your own scenes.

Adding gobos is easy. But it's probably a more powerful feature than you realize. Creating window panes on a set is nice, but you can accomplish much more with gobos. For example, consider the following:

- Use a black and white image of tree branches to simulate shadows from a tree.
- Use color images for added dimension. Darker areas will hold back more light, and lighter areas will shine more light. For example, you can create the effects of light through a stained-glass window.
- Use softer, blurry images for added effects.
- Use animation sequences as projection images.

You also can apply volumetric effects for projection images. Later in this book, you'll learn about volumetric lighting and the cool things you can create with this feature. Combine those techniques with these lighting techniques and you're ready to rock!

Area Lights

Distant lights and point lights produce hard-edged, ray-traced shadows. Ray-traced shadows take more time to calculate, which of course means more time to render. Spotlights also can produce ray-traced shadows, but with spotlights you have the option of using Shadow Maps, which take less time to render than ray-traced shadows. Softer than ray-traced shadows, Shadow Maps use more memory to render than ray-traced shadows; but ray-traced shadows use more processing power.

Area lights also can produce realistic ray-traced shadows, but to do so they require more rendering time. For example, suppose that a person is standing outside in bright sunlight. The shadow that the person casts has sharp edges around the area by the subject's foot, where the shadow begins. As the shadow falls off and away from the subject, it becomes softer. Ray-traced shadows from distant lights, point lights, and spotlights cannot produce this effect—and neither can Shadow Maps. Area lights can produce these true shadows and give a softer overall appearance to animations.

Exercise 7.4   Applying Area Lights

As you learned earlier in this chapter, spotlights are the most common lights, and they are the most useful for your everyday animation needs. But on occasion, the added rendering time generated from area lights is worthwhile. An area light is represented in Layout by a flat square and emits light equally from all directions except for the edges, producing very realistic shadows. This next exercise introduces you to using area lights.

1. Load the AreaSetup.lws scene file from the book's CD. This is the scene created for the previous exercises, and it has only one default distant light.

2. Select the light and press p to go to the Item Properties panel. Change the Light Type to Area. Change the Light Intensity to 75 percent. Keeping the default 100 percent Light Intensity would be too bright, and the image would appear washed out.

3. Close the Item Properties panel and return to Layout.

4. If the new area light is not selected, select it and change your Layout View to Perspective to get an overall view of the scene. The area light appears as a small box outline. Position this above and in front of the chair object and create a keyframe to lock it in place.

Note

To help set up lights in Layout, change the Maximum Render Level to Solid Shaded or above. Make sure that Max OpenGL Lights is set to one or above, and turn on Affect OpenGL for the light in the Light Item Properties panel. This makes the light source's effect visible in Layout, and helps you line up the direction of the light source.

After the light is in place, you need to tell LightWave to calculate the shadows. The Item Properties told the light what kind of shadow to use, Ray Trace by default, but now you need to turn on the feature.

5. Under the Rendering drop-down list, select Render Options, and then click Ray Trace Shadows to have LightWave calculate shadows for the Area Light, as shown in Figure 7.19.

Figure 7.19   You tell LightWave to calculate Ray Trace Shadows while rendering from the Render Options panel.

 Tip

While you're in the Render Options panel, make sure that the Show Rendering in Progress feature is checked. This enables you to see the render as it's being drawn.

6. Close the Render Options panel. Press F9 to test-render the current frame. You'll see that the shadow has a hard edge.

7. Back in Layout, select the area light, and then select Size from the Items tab. Size the light up (click and drag) to about 18m. You also can type the numeric values by pressing n on the keyboard to access the numeric values and directly entering the size change. Figure 7.20 shows the render with an area light applied.

Figure 7.20   Adding just one area light to the scene creates a soft, realistic-looking light with shadows. Notice the soft shadows under the folds of the chair, and how the shadow and light fall off onto the wall and floor.

Tip

If you increase the size of the Area Light, the shadow will soften. However, it might appear grainy or jagged. If so, simply increase the Area Light Quality in the Light Properties panel. The default is 4—good for most renderings. Often a value of 5 or 6 works slightly better but takes more render time. Isn't it always the case?

Sizing a light might seem odd, but for an area, it helps spread the amount of light and thereby the shadow as well. Notice that in Figure 7.20, the shadow is soft and very realistic. Area lights take a long time to render, but they produce the best results.

Area lights can give your animations a professional look. The time it takes to render such lights will be increased, but the results are often worth it. Here are a few more things to remember when using area lights:

- Quality settings can be adjusted. The default Area Light Quality of 4 results in 16 samples per area light. Values of 2 and 3 result in 4 and 9 samples per area light, respectively.

- Linear lights perform like area lights but emit light from a two-point polygonal shape, similar to a fluorescent tube.

- You can mix spotlights, distant lights, point lights, and linear lights with area lights for added effects.

Adding Atmospheres

When you create scenes in LightWave, whether they consist of logos, characters, or architecture, you can create an atmosphere for added value. Atmospheres in LightWave can be created through various methods, such as backdrops, fog, or LightWave's SkyTracer plug-in, to name a few. These next sections introduce you to the different types of atmospheres you can create in LightWave.

Backdrops

The Backdrop panel in LightWave is where you can set up background and gradient colors or add environmental shaders. Setting a backdrop creates an infinite world inside Layout. By default, the backdrop color is set to black, as you can see in Figure 7.21.

Figure 7.21   The default backdrop color is black; however, this can be easily changed.

Think of LightWave Layout as one infinite world. When you set a backdrop color, the color is, in effect, wallpapered to this world. You cannot cast shadows onto it, nor can you pass through it or have it affected with lights. To use a gradient as a backdrop instead of a solid color, all you need to do is click the Gradient backdrop button. This turns off the solid backdrop color and creates a gradient backdrop, defined by four color variables:

- **Zenith Color.** This is the top-most region of the "infinite world." If you were setting up a daytime scene, this color would be deep blue, simulating space through Earth's atmosphere.

- **Sky Color.** This is just what it implies: the color of the sky. This color blends smoothly with the zenith color.

- **Ground Color.** This setting, by default, is brown, simulating a ground plane below the 0 y-axis. However, because it's labeled Ground Color does not mean that this is all it's used for. If you set the color values of Ground Color to those of Sky Color, you'll create a smooth transition of color.

- **Nadir Color.** This is the bottom-most region of the "infinite world." The Ground Color will blend smoothly with the Nadir Color.

If you look through the Chapter 7 scene folder on this book's CD, you'll find a few scenes with backdrop settings. Take a look and explore some of the variations possible.

Sky Squeeze and Ground Squeeze

Because the backdrop color is applied as an infinite world, you might need to shrink the world from time to time. The Sky Squeeze and Ground Squeeze settings default to 2.0, but if you increase them, the ground color and sky color will, in essence, squeeze together. This is useful for sunsets, for example, where you can set a larger Ground Squeeze to make the ground color smaller, while the sky color remains larger. Check out the 07Sunset.lws scene on the book's CD for some examples of Sky Squeeze and Ground Squeeze.

Adding Environments

Add Environment, a selection available in the Backdrop panel of LightWave 7, is an environmental setting that enables you to add environmental shaders to your backdrop. Figure 7.22 shows the drop-down list.

Note

Be sure to use the SkyGen plug-in for instant pre-made LightWave background environments using gradients. Find this gem under the Scene tab's Generics drop-down list. Select SkyGen, pick a sky, and then click OK. Press F9 to render.

LW_ImageWorld

This handy environment plug-in enables you to use an image as a backdrop within LightWave's virtual world. You can use LW_ImageWorld as an environmental mapping solution often used in radiosity situations. This feature adds the capability of applying an image using a spherical warp technique used by high dynamic-range images as an environment wrap. Although this is the most common application, you don't have to use HDRI images. Any image will work as well. Radiosity is covered in Chapter 9.

To set up LW_ImageWorld, select it from the Add Environment tab under the Backdrop tab. After LW_ImageWorld is loaded in the list, double-click it. This calls up a requester enabling you to apply an image.

LW_ImageWorld creates a spherical image map around your entire LightWave scene. This is not visible in Layout, but it will be when rendered. It's useful for creating reflections and radiosity lighting.

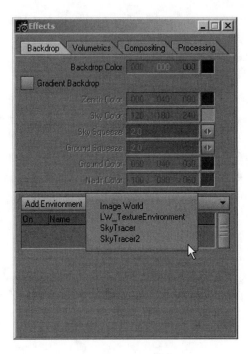

Figure 7.22   The Add Environment selection in LightWave 7 offers more control for creating various backdrops.

LW_TextureEnvironment

Wouldn't it be cool if you could do more with your backdrop than add color and a single image to it? Wouldn't it be useful to apply LightWave's powerful procedural texture engine to the backdrop or apply complex layers of gradient colors? All this is possible with the LW_TextureEnvironment handler. Adding this environment gives you access to LightWave's Texture Editor. The results are put into the backdrop.

Exercise 7.5   Adding a Texture Environment

This feature is simple to use, but powerful. You can create realistic-looking backdrops for your animations, or cool computer screen backgrounds, or textures that can be reloaded and mapped onto surfaces of your objects. To begin, save any work you've been doing, and then choose Clear Layout.

1. Under the Scene tab, select Backdrop from the Effects heading on the left side of the screen. First select the LW_TextureEnvironment plug-in from the Add Environment list, and then double-click it to open the interface control.

   You'll see a set of controls appear just below the listing, as shown in Figure 7.23.

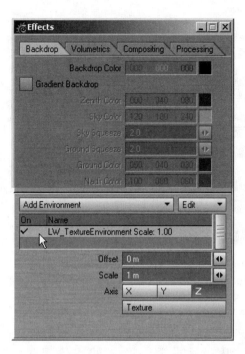

Figure 7.23   Double-clicking the LW_TextureEnvironment listing brings up its controls.

2. Leave the Offset at 0m and the Scale at 1m. The z-axis should be selected because you want the texture to be applied down the z-axis.

3. Begin to set up the texture environment by clicking the Texture button for the LW_TextureEnvironment.

   LightWave's Texture Editor appears.

4. Change the Layer Type to Procedural Texture. Leave Blending Mode set to Normal and Layer Opacity to 100 percent.

5. Change the Procedural Type to RigidMultiFractal and the Texture Color to something other than white, such as bright orange. Also change the Scale setting for the X, Y, and Z to 200mm at the bottom of the Texture Editor interface. Press F9 to see what happens. Figure 7.24 shows the fractal pattern texture applied as a background.

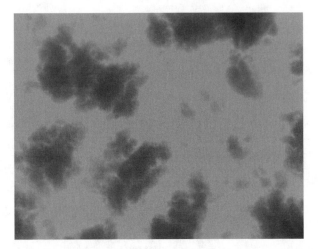

Figure 7.24   The LW_TextureEnvironment plug-in enables you to use LightWave's Texture Editor as backgrounds for your animations. Here, a procedural texture, RigidMultiFractal, has become an animated backdrop.

This is just a taste of what the LW_TextureEnvironment can do. You can use multiple images, gradient textures, and other procedural textures, such as Ripples, Puffy Clouds, and of course, more Fractal Noise. You also can animate these textures. This is a great way to make complex textures as well. If you have a large scene with lots of surfaces, for example, you can use the LW_TextureEnvironment feature to create full-screen procedural texture images. Render the images, and then map them onto your surfaces. LightWave will not have to calculate multiple procedural textures—image maps render much faster than procedurals. Try experimenting with these settings and various combinations!

SkyTracer

Too often, you'll need to create a realistic sky. Sure, you can load in an image map or sequence of a sky or clouds, but it's more fun to generate your own. This next exercise takes you through setting up a SkyTracer sky.

Exercise 7.6   Using SkyTracer

SkyTracer can add beautiful clouds and skies to your LightWave environments. It's cool because it creates more than a pretty backdrop—it actually creates a full environment so that wherever you rotate the camera in Layout, you'll see the sky. This is why the feature is found under the Add Environment listings in the Backdrop panel.

Note

When you install LightWave 7, SkyTracer can be found in the Legacy plug-ins folder. You might need to add this plug-in to use SkyTracer. However, SkyTracer2 will be installed with your LightWave 7 configuration automatically.

1. Begin by saving any work and selecting Clear Scene in Layout.

2. Under the Scene tab, go to the Backdrop panel, and from Add Environment select SkyTracer to add it. Double-click the listing to start SkyTracer. Figure 7.25 shows the SkyTracer panel at startup.

The SkyTracer control panel contains numerous controls that you can use to set up SkyTracer and quickly generate great-looking environments. First, look at the default settings by clicking the Refresh button below the Preview window. Notice how a sky with some clouds appears. Figure 7.26 shows SkyTracer with the preview pane refreshed.

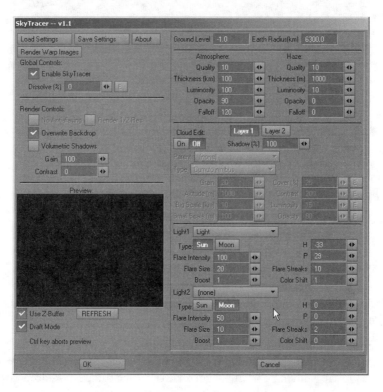

Figure 7.25   Here is the SkyTracer control panel at startup.

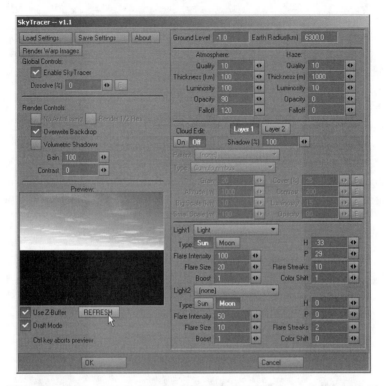

Figure 7.26   By pressing the Refresh button underneath the Preview window in SkyTracer, you can see a nice blue sky.

You'll use this Preview window to see how your sky is coming along. Notice that in this window, the sky appears only in the top half. This is because LightWave sees the ground plane, and SkyTracer is generating the sky from above the 0 y-axis. It's up to you to create a ground in Layout.

The next step is to adjust your settings. The best method for setting up a decent sky with SkyTracer is to utilize the Preview window. Make an adjustment, and see the result in the Preview window. This is your fastest route to animated skies.

3. Adjust the Atmosphere settings by changing the Quality to 50 at the top of the interface and changing the Thickness to 50.

This makes the sky a clearer and deeper blue.

4. Change the Luminosity to 80, which lessens the overall brightness of the sky. The Opacity should be set at 90, but a lower setting can create a deep, rich-looking sky.

5. Set the Falloff to 50, and click the Refresh button under the Preview window to see how the sky looks at this point.

It needs some clouds! The following settings show your how to create an overcast day with SkyTracer.

6. Click the On button for Cloud Edit, and you'll see the controls become active, as shown in Figure 7.27.

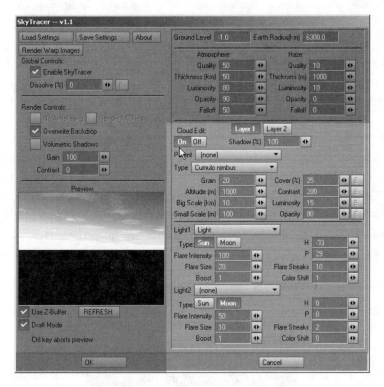

Figure 7.27   Turning on Cloud Edit enables the Cloud Edit controls.

7. Select Cumulo nimbus as the Cloud Type.

   Cumulous clouds are big and puffy; sometimes they're tall when a storm is near.

8. Set the Grain to 10.

   This adds nice variations to the clouds.

9. The Earth Radius set by default at the top-right corner of the screen is 6300km. Therefore, set the Altitude in the Cloud Edit area to 1500m.

   This creates a low-lying cloud layer.

10. To change the cloud's size, set Big Scale to 30km and Small Scale to 10m. Set Cover to 75 percent because you want things mostly cloudy.

11. Set Contrast to 50 to add contrast between the sky and the cloud layer. Set Luminosity to 15 to make the clouds duller and less bright. And then, set Opacity to 75 to set the strength of the cloud layer. Click the Refresh button under the Preview window to see the clouds.

> **Note**
> When using the Preview window in SkyTracer, you can stop any Refresh by pressing the Ctrl key. Also you can speed up the Refresh previews by clicking Draft mode. The Use Z-Buffer button remembers the last render you performed in Layout.

SkyTracer takes a little getting used to, but the advantage is that you can create full environments with it. The downside is that it can be an exhaustive render process. To make your life a little easier, SkyTracer has a feature called Render Warp Images.

Render Warp Images

The Render Warp Images feature at the top left of the SkyTracer interface enables you to create your sky environment and save out five seamless images. Instead of rendering every frame, SkyTracer can generate a front, back, left side, right side, and top image that it seamlessly maps together on a cube. Simply import this cube into Layout, and you have your rendered sky. Figure 7.28 shows the Render Warp Images interface, which reads Warps Render Parameters.

Figure 7.28   Render Warp Images creates a rendered view of your environment from SkyTracer.

After you have the sky settings the way you like them, you can click Render Warp Images and tell it where to save the files. From there, use LightWave's Load Items From Scene feature to load the scene it generates. Then, add your objects!

SkyTracer2

LightWave 7 has another variation of SkyTracer called SkyTracer2. Figure 7.29 shows the interface.

Figure 7.29   SkyTracer2 is streamlined and easier to manage over the original SkyTracer.

SkyTracer2 allows you to quickly and easily add beautifully rendered skies in LightWave. There are a few tabbed areas within the SkyTracer2 panel that control all the necessary parameters. First, SkyTracer2 works similarly to SkyTracer in that it renders an entire environment in your scene. When you turn your camera around, the sky will be all around you. Figure 7.30 shows a render from SkyTracer2.

Figure 7.30   Opening SkyTracer2 and pushing two buttons achieves a result like this sunset sky.

To create this environment, follow these few simple steps:

1. From the Scene tab in Layout, click the SkyTracer button on the left side of the screen. Click the VIPER button on the left side of the interface to see an automatic preview of your SkyTracer settings as you work.

2. You also can access SkyTracer2 from the Backdrop tab within the Effects panel, by clicking the Add Environment drop-down list, as seen in Figure 7.31.

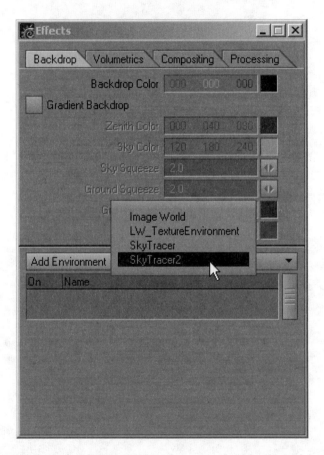

Figure 7.31   Add SkyTracer2 from the Add Environment tab under the Backdrop tab in the Effects panel.

3. Once SkyTracer2 is loaded, double-click it to open its interface. The first tabs you see are the Atmosphere tabs. For now, leave all these settings at their default values.

4. Click over to the Clouds tab, and click Enable Clouds, as shown in Figure 7.32.

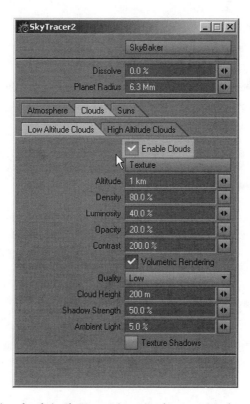

Figure 7.32   Creating clouds in SkyTracer2 is as simple as turning them on.

5. Close the SkyTracer2 panel and press F9. Voila, instant sky, faster than regular SkyTracer and a lot easier to set up.

Another cool feature about SkyTracer2 is that it allows you to "bake" the settings. In a way, this is similar to SkyTracer's Render Warp Images feature, where LightWave calculates the sky only once, and image-maps them from then on.

You can bake motions, textures, and even skies. You'll learn more about "baking" in LightWave 7 later in this book.

The Next Step

The information in this chapter can be applied to any of the exercises and projects in this book. These basic lighting setups and core functions will apply to all your LightWave work in some way. Use the information here to branch out on your own and create different lighting environments. Use lights to your advantage—remember, there are no wires or electric bills to worry about when creating virtual lighting situations. You won't need to worry about light bulbs burning out either! Experiment by adding more lights to your everyday scene or perhaps take some away. Use negative lights, colored lights, dim lights, overly bright lights, and whatever else you can think of to make your animations stand out.

Summary

This chapter guided you through common lighting situations, including three-point lighting, area lights, and environments. In Chapter 9, you'll create more advanced lighting situations with volumetric lighting, lens flares, and radiosity. This chapter can be a good reference for you in any of the lighting situations you may encounter. To go further, use the information in the other chapters to fully enhance your lighting environments. The combination of textures, motion, models, and light is what makes great animations.

Chapter 8

Architectural Environments

3D animation is so much fun. If you don't
think so, the information in this chapter will
give you enough knowledge and insight that
you will change your mind! This book was

created to help you stop scratching your head and concentrate on a goal—creating with LightWave. Up to this point, you've learned about many of LightWave 7's cool features and powerful creation tools. Now you'll learn how to use the toolset to create an architectural environment. You can use this knowledge for any type of structure. This chapter gives you a chance to use many of those tools and introduces you to some new ones.

Project Overview

Too many books just tell you how to create one object in an animation, such as a cup; but what about the saucer? Or they instruct you on creating trees; but what about the landscape? This chapter takes you step-by-step through the creation of a 21st-century skyscraper and its surrounding environment. In this chapter, you'll do the following:

- Model the skyscraper
- Apply basic lighting
- Texture the skyscraper
- Create the environment for the skyscraper

That's a lot to cover, so stock up on the caffeine and let's get started!

Exercise 8.1   Building the Skyscraper

The first portion of this project begins in LightWave's Modeler. The skyscraper design is simple and is based on similar structures you'd find in many science fiction films and books.

Before you begin any real-world project like this, you must have an outline for your project. What is the final output? Video? Film? Television broadcast? What should the model look like? How will it be used in its final form? All these questions are important to answer up front because the answers can help you determine the level of complexity you need to add to the model. For this project, the goal is to create a weathered, high-tech looking building (see Figure 8.1).

You will approach this project as though it were for television. It would be considered a medium resolution model. You will be able to get fairly close to it for your animations. The final rendering shown in Figure 8.1 is about as close as you want to get to the sides of the building.

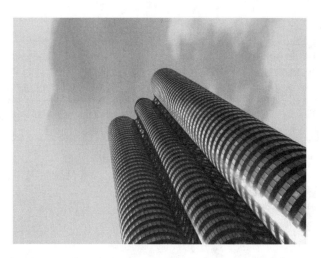

Figure 8.1   In this chapter, you'll learn how to model, texture, and render a model skyscraper.

1. Open Modeler and change the Grid size to 10m. Do this by pressing the a key to set Modeler to its default grid size, and then repeatedly press the comma key (,) until the numeric display in the lower-left corner reads 10m.

    To create the skyscraper, you will start with a simple top-down profile and build from there. When you complete the work, you will look back and be surprised at how such a simple shape can be the basis for something that looks so complex.

2. Select Disc from the Objects section under the Create tab, and press n (for numeric). The Disc tool should be activated by default. Enter the following values:

Axis	Y
Sides	48
Segments	1
Bottom	0m
Top	0m
Center X	−50m
Center Y	0m
Center Z	0m
Radius X	16m
Radius Y	0m
Radius Z	16m

Tip

When you are using a tool such as Disc, pressing n opens the Numeric panel. It should be activated when you open the numeric window. If you select the n key to open the numeric window *without* a tool selected, it will open; however, it will be blank and you will have no options available. To fix this, you can leave the numeric window open then select a tool, such as the Disc tool; then activate the numeric window by pressing n key again. Alternatively, you can select Activate from the pull-down menu at the top of the numeric window.

Note

The width of the windows in your building will be based on the number of sides you use when you create the discs. If you choose too few sides, in later steps the windows might appear to be too wide; if you use too many, they might appear to be too narrow.

These values were used to simulate real-world dimensions, although on a very grand scale.

3. Close the numeric window by pressing n. Press the spacebar to keep these measurements.

4. Now you will use the Mirror tool to duplicate the disc you just made. This will be the second of four lobes of your skyscraper. Select Mirror from the Duplicate heading under the Multiply tab and press n to activate the numeric panel. Enter the following values:

Axis	X
Center X	0m
Center Y	0m
Center Z	0m

5. Close the numeric window and press the spacebar to drop the tool.

6. You will now create the remaining two lobes of the skyscraper using the Copy and Paste functions followed by the Rotate tool. First, select the two discs that you created previously.

7. With the polygons selected, copy them to the internal buffer by pressing the c key or by clicking the Copy button at the bottom of the Modeler interface. This will copy the selected geometry to the buffer so you can paste them to a new layer or to the same layer. Do not deselect the discs.

8. Paste the discs in the buffer to the same layer. To paste, press the v key or click the Paste button at the bottom of the Modeler interface (it is to the right of the Copy button you clicked previously). The discs will be pasted right on top of the geometry that you have selected. Again, do not deselect the discs that currently are selected.

9. Select the Rotate tool. It is located under the Modify tab under the Rotate heading, or you can activate it by pressing the y key.

10. Rotate the selected discs 90 degrees along the y-axis, as seen from Top view (see Figure 8.2).

Tip

When using the Rotate tool, you can perform an action a number of ways. You can click and drag the mouse until you are satisfied with the rotation. You can hold the Ctrl key while you click and drag the mouse to restrict the rotation to 15-degree increments; or you can press the n key to be more precise and enter the specification numerically.

You also can use the r key to rotate an object or selection set. To do this, you simply place the mouse pointer in the respective view and press the r key and the geometry will be rotate, counter-clockwise, in 90 degree increments.

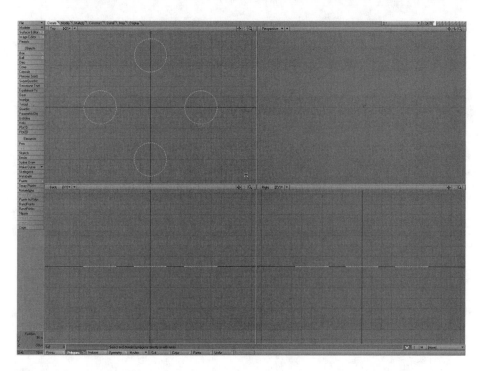

Figure 8.2   You should have four, 32-meter discs, two on the x-axis and two on the y-axis.

11. With the four lobes of the cross-section profile now completed you will create four more discs to connect them.

12. Select the Disc tool again, press the n key to activate the Numeric panel, and enter the following values:

Axis	Y
Sides	48
Segments	1
Bottom	0m
Top	0m
Center X	−50m
Center Y	0m
Center Z	50m
Radius X	34m
Radius Y	0m
Radius Z	34m

13. Press the n key again to close the numeric window and press the spacebar to drop the tool.

14. You will now duplicate the large disc you just created four times, but you will use the Array tool instead of the Mirror tool. Before starting make sure that you are in Polygon Selection mode and the large disc you just created is selected.

Note

The Array tool was used this time to show you that there are different ways to approach modeling. As you develop your skills, you will notice that you use some tools more frequently, while someone else might use different ones. The end result might be the same, but the path leading to it might be very different. You should explore each tool to see how it works for you.

15. Activate the Array tool by selecting it under the Duplicate heading under the Multiply tab, or use the keyboard shortcut of Ctrl+y.

16. The Array tool has its own window that opens automatically. When it opens, use the following options:

Array Type	Radial
Number	4
Axis	Y
Center X	0m
Center Y	0m
Center Z	0m

This will create four copies, including the original, of the large disc you created earlier.

17. After completing this function, you will have some duplicate points where the small and large discs overlap. To eliminate these, use the Merge Points tool, found under the Reduce heading under the Construct tab; or, you can simply press the m key and click the OK button. Modeler will tell you "8 points eliminated." You should have something that looks like Figure 8.3.

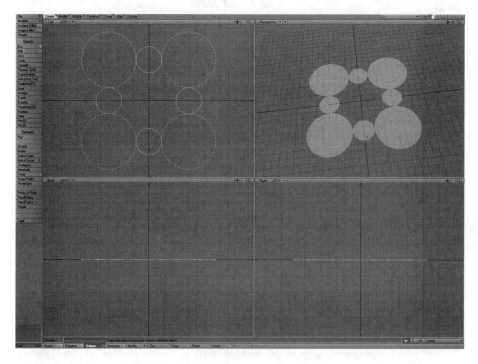

Figure 8.3   You should have a total of eight discs, four large and four small.

18. The discs you have created are templates that you will use to complete the Top-view profile. To help with point selection, maximize Top view to fill Modeler by moving the mouse cursor over Top view and pressing the 0 (zero) key on the numeric key pad.

19. You do not need the polygons that make up the disc, so go ahead and kill them by pressing the k key.

20. With Top view maximized, make sure that you are in points selection mode.

 Tip

You can change quickly between selection modes by pressing the spacebar or by using the hotkeys listed on the buttons on the lower-left of the Modeler interface. Select Points mode by pressing Ctrl+g, and Polygon mode by pressing Ctrl+h.

21. Start selecting the points in a counter-clockwise order, as shown in Figure 8.4.

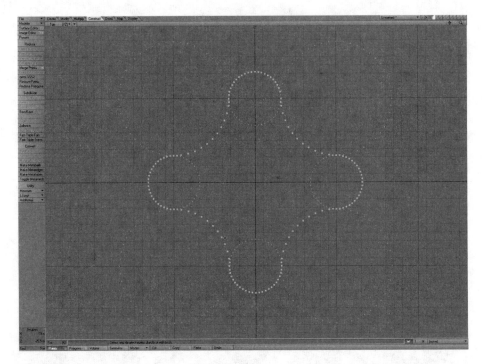

Figure 8.4   Select points in a counter-clockwise order to ensure that the polygons will be facing the correct direction.

Tip

If you accidentally select a point out of order, release the mouse button. Select the point, or points, that are incorrect, and they will deselect. Then press Shift and begin to select the proper points in order, starting where you left off. Once you start selecting points again, you can release the Shift key.

22. With the points selected, create a polygon by clicking on the Make Pol menu item under the Elements heading under the Create tab, or press the p key.

23. Switch Modeler back to its default four-pane layout by pressing the 0 (zero) key on the numeric key pad.

24. Zoom all the windows to show all the points and the polygon by pressing the a key.

25. You do not need the remaining extra points. To select them for deletion, activate the Point Statistics window by pressing the w key.

26. To select the points not affiliated with the polygon you just created, click the + sign next to the line that reads, 0 Polygons. There should be 226 points.

27. Cut the points you have selected by pressing the x key. You should have something that looks like Figure 8.5.

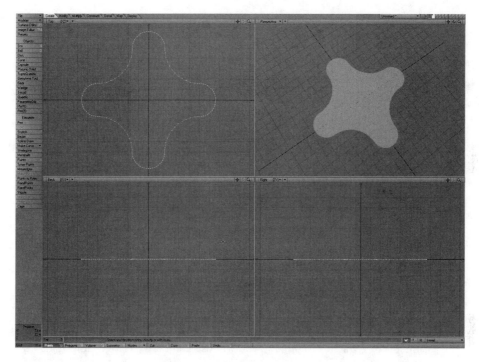

Figure 8.5   Here is the completed Top-view profile of the base of the skyscraper.

Next you will extrude the profile to the height of the building. You will have a number of segments in the extruded shape. These segments will represent the windows and interior of the skyscraper.

Note

The height of the windows will be based on the distance between each segment during the extrusion process; therefore, it is very important that you select an appropriate number of segments. If you select too many segments, the windows will be too short; if you select too few, the windows will be too high.

28. Select the Extrude tool from the Extend heading under the Multiply tab, or press the Shift+e key combination.

29. Press the n key to activate the numeric panel and enter the following values:

Extent X	0m
Extent Y	550m
Extent Z	0m
Sides	120

30. Next, you will put a temporary surface on the skyscraper. This is done primarily to help you when you need to select certain groups of polygons. Press the q key to bring up the Change Surface panel.

> **Note**
> Creating a temporary surface enables you to assign base generic surface attributes to the model.

31. With the Change Surface panel open, enter the following:

Name	Skyscraper_Base
Color	51, 63, 77
Diffuse	80
Specularity	60
Smoothing	On (Checked)

32. After entering the values, click the OK button to apply the surfaces and close the panel.

33. You now will add a smoothed radius to the top of the building. Rather than using lots of geometry to build it, you will use LightWave's smoothing angle calculation to do the work for you. Start by selecting the top polygon of the building.

34. Activate the Bevel tool by choosing it under the Extend heading under the Multiply tab, or by pressing the b key. Activate the numeric panel, and enter the following:

Shift	1m
+/−	0m
Inset	0m
+/−	0m
New Surface	Unchecked
Edges	Inner

35. After creating the first bevel, drop the tool by pressing the spacebar or the b key again.

36. Select the Bevel tool again, call up the numeric panel, and enter the following:

Shift	1m
+/−	0m
Inset	1m
+/−	0m

New Surface	Unchecked
Edges	Inner

37. As before, drop the tool by pressing the spacebar, reselect it, and call up the numeric panel. Enter the following:

Shift	0m
+/–	0m
Inset	1m
+/–	0
New Surface	Unchecked
Edges	Inner

When that task is completed you should have something that looks like Figure 8.6.

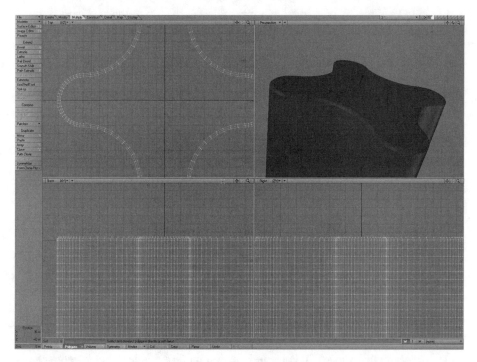

Figure 8.6   The beveling of the top of the skyscraper gives the appearance of a rounded corner.

Note

> Beveling three times is very important. The first and last bevels are used to eliminate smoothing errors while rendering in Layout. If they were not created, and instead only the bevel with both shift and inset were created, you might get a smoothing error during rendering. The first and last bevels act as a mathematical calculation "buffer" for LightWave to create easily the smooth, rounded corner effect. This technique also can be used, as you will see later, to create inner bevels for recessed areas.

At this point, you should be ready to create some details on top of the skyscraper. You'll accomplish this in the next exercise.

Exercise 8.2   Adding Details to the Skyscraper

This exercise focuses on adding details to the roof of the skyscraper, starting with additional room areas on the top of each lobe you created in the Top-view profile.

1. Go to layer two by pressing the number 2 key at the top of the keyboard, and select the Ball tool under the Object heading under the Create tab. Enter the following into the numeric panel:

Type	Globe
Axis	Y
Sides	32
Segments	18
Center X	50m
Center Y	567m
Center Z	0m
Radius X	13m
Radius Y	13m
Radius Z	13m

2. After entering the data, close the numeric panel and drop the tool. You should now have a ball floating above the right-most lobe on the roof of the building. To verify this, make layer one a background layer.

3. Make sure that you are in Polygon Selection mode and select the polygons that construct the bottom portion of the sphere. Once they are selected, delete them, leaving a hemisphere.

4. Switch to Point Selection mode and, using the Lasso selection technique, select the bottom points that make up the hemisphere (see Figure 8.7). These are the points that are the flat part of the hemisphere. Make sure that you select them by making a loop around them. The direction of the loop is not important.

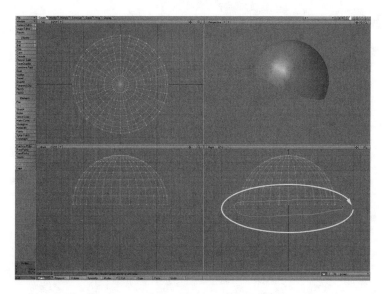

Figure 8.7   Select the bottom points of the hemisphere for capping.

5. Once you have selected the points, create a polygon by pressing the p key. After creating the polygon, switch to Polygon Selection mode and, if the polygon normal is directed toward the inside of the hemisphere, flip its direction by pressing the f key.

6. With the flat circular polygon still selected, activate the Bevel tool and call up the numeric window for it. Enter the following:

Shift	13.5m
+/–	0m
Inset	0m
+/–	0
New Surface	Unchecked
Edges	Inner

This creates the sides of the additional room areas.

You are now going to add a little lip, or flange, detail to the bottom of the object to make it look like it is integrated into the building. Without this detail, the room area would look like it was just shoved into the building—because it would be!

To do this, you will use the same beveling technique you used earlier, but it is slightly different.

Rather than insetting the polygon the way you did earlier, you are now going to perform a Shift, Shift and negative Inset, followed by a negative Inset.

7. You will do three beveling operations as before, but now enter the following:

Bevel 1

Shift	200mm
+/–	0m
Inset	0m
+/–	0m
New Surface	Unchecked
Edges	Inner

Bevel 2

Shift	200mm
+/–	0m
Inset	–200mm
+/–	0m
New Surface	Unchecked
Edges	Inner

Bevel 3

Shift	0m
+/–	0m
Inset	–200mm
+/–	0m
New Surface	Unchecked
Edges	Inner

8. You created the bottom rounded corner that joins the room area to the flange area that will connect it to the building. Before you create the outer corner of the flange, add a little more depth to the flange by adding a bevel with the following:

Shift	0m
+/–	0m
Inset	–200mm
+/–	0m

New Surface	Unchecked
Edges	Inner

9. Now you will create the outer corner of the flange by doing the Bevel operation yet again, three times with the following:

Bevel 1

Shift	0m
+/−	0m
Inset	−200mm
+/−	0m
New Surface	Unchecked
Edges	Inner

Bevel 2

Shift	200mm
+/−	0m
Inset	−200mm
+/−	0m
New Surface	Unchecked
Edges	Inner

Bevel 3

Shift	200mm
+/−	0m
Inset	0m
+/−	0m
New Surface	Unchecked
Edges	Inner

10. Now that you have created the outer corner of the flange, you will do one final bevel operation on the circular disc shape to give the flange some depth. Bevel the disc using the following:

Shift	1.6m
+/−	0m
Inset	0m
+/−	0m
New Surface	Unchecked
Edges	Inner

11. Now that this portion of the object is completed you can delete the disc, that was used to create the beveling. You could retain it, but it is inside the building and would never be seen, so save some system memory and delete it. Your object should look like Figure 8.8.

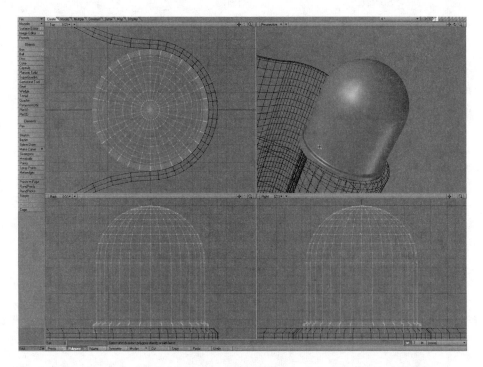

Figure 8.8   Here is the base of the room area for the skyscraper. This image reflects the beveling operations that were used to form the flange that connects the room to the rest of the building.

12. The dome section of the room area is a bit too round. Use the Stretch tool to flatten it out a bit.

    First, select the points that are part of the domed top but do not include the points where it joins the sides (see Figure 8.9).

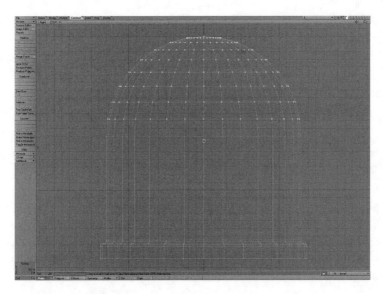

Figure 8.9   Select the points on the domed section of the room area.

13. Activate the Stretch tool by clicking its name under the Stretch heading under the Modify tab. With the Stretch tool selected, call up the numeric panel and enter these values; then press the Apply button:

Horizontal Factor	100%
Vertical Factor	65.0%
Axis	X
Center X	50m
Center Y	567m
Center Z	0m

Now that you have flattened the top of the dome, you need to add some windows to the room area. To do this, you will use the Knife tool to add polygons so that you can construct them.

14. Start by making Right view a single, large panel. As before, you will move the mouse cursor over the view and press 0 (Zero) on the numeric keypad.

15. Switch to Polygon Edit mode, and with Right view enlarged, select the Knife tool by clicking on its name under the Subdivide heading under the Construct tab, or by pressing the k key.

16. You want to create windows that are two meters high, and two meters apart. To use the Knife tool, click and hold the mouse button to the left or right of the geometry. Then drag the cursor over the geometry and the Knife tool division line will appear between the start and end of the tool. When you release the

mouse button, you can move either end of the Knife tool and drag it (or both, in sequence) to your desired location. Start by cutting the geometry 2m below the domed area.

To make your cuts easier while you are using the Knife tool, press and hold the Ctrl key. This will constrain the tool to a vertical or horizontal axis.

Tip

To assist you in this process, you can set the grid size to 2m by pressing the comma key (,) to zoom out or the period key (.) to zoom in. You can do this even while a tool is activated.

17. With the first cut completed, you can speed things up by leaving the Knife tool active, and right-clicking your mouse button at the next location, two meters below your first cut. Make sure that when you right-click you do not click the horizontal line that defines the cut line. Continue to right-click until you have made six cuts in the geometry (see Figure 8.10).

Tip

While using the right-click method to retain the current Knife tool settings and add more cuts, you still are able to make adjustments. If you hold the right mouse button after you click the new location, you will be able to move the Knife tool around until you are satisfied.

If you release the right-click, you still are able to adjust the Knife tool be selecting its center, or by selecting it on either end.

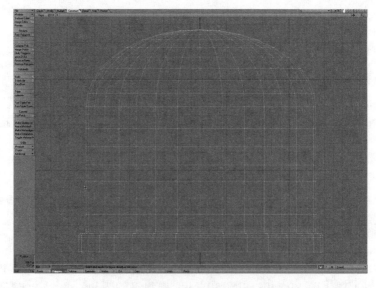

Figure 8.10   The Knife tool is used to cut the room area geometry for the creation of the windows.

18. Using the Lasso selection, select three rows of polygons to make the windows of the room area, as shown in Figure 8.11.

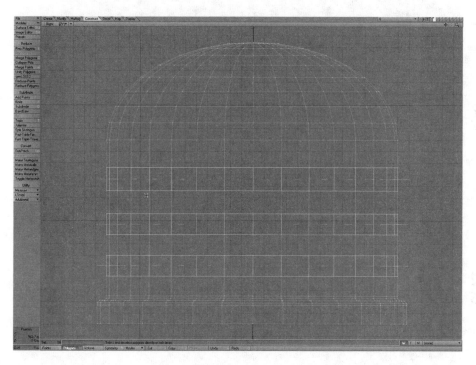

Figure 8.11 Select the polygons that will become the windows of the room area.

19. Give the selected polygons a surface name by activating the Change Surface panel. Press the q key to open the panel and add the following:

Name	Skyscraper_Windows
Color	255, 255, 128
Diffuse	80
Specularity	60
Smoothing	On (Checked)

20. After entering the surface attributes, click OK to assign them to the selected polygons. Your room area should look like Figure 8.12.

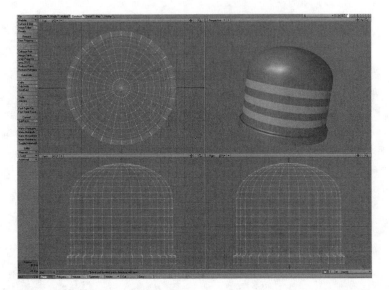

Figure 8.12   Here is the temporary window surface applied to the polygons that will make the windows of the building.

The top of the dome needs something else to give it a little more kick—it's a bit too plain the way it is. You will now add some details to the top of the room area.

21. Start by selecting the top three rows of polygons at the top of the room area, as shown in Figure 8.13.

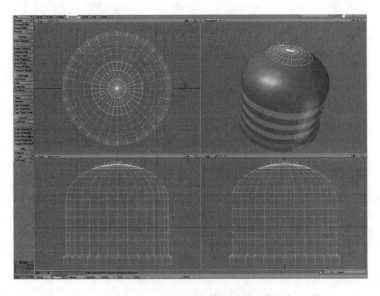

Figure 8.13   Select the top three rows of polygons for adding details to the room area.

22. You need to merge the selected polygons into one large, flat polygon. Do this by using the Merge Polygon tool. Activate it by clicking the Merge Polygons name in the Reduce heading under the Construct tab or by pressing the Shift+z (capital Z) key combination.

23. Switch to Point selection mode and activate the Point Statistics panel by pressing the w key.

24. With the panel open, click the plus sign next to the name listed as O Polygons. It should be the second row in the list.

25. Delete the selected points; they are not needed.

You will now create a recess in the top of the room area dome to fill with nurnies.

Note

Nurnies is a term coined by Ron Thornton, co-owner of Foundation Imaging, describing details that are added to a model that give the appearance of affecting the model. They are critical to creating models that look real.

26. Start by changing to Polygon selection mode; the large flat disc polygon should still be selected. If it is not, re-select it.

27. Now activate the Bevel tool and add a small bevel that follows the contour of the dome area on the room area.

As before, this row of polygons is used only as a mathematical buffer to prevent smoothing errors (see Figure 8.14).

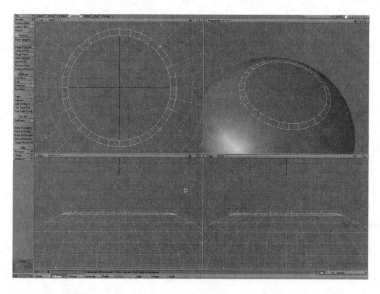

Figure 8.14   The top row of polygons, highlighted for clarity, is added to prevent smoothing errors.

You now will do a number of bevel operations to add a recessed area on the top of the dome. This area will then be filled with some nurnies to complete the room area.

28. With the large disc polygon still selected, perform the following bevel operations:

Bevel 1

Shift	0m
+/–	0m
Inset	200mm
+/–	0m
New Surface	Unchecked
Edges	Inner

Bevel 2

Shift	–200mm
+/–	0m
Inset	200mm
+/–	0m
New Surface	Unchecked
Edges	Inner

Bevel 3

Shift	–200mm
+/–	0m
Inset	0m
+/–	0m
New Surface	Unchecked
Edges	Inner

Bevel 4

Shift	−1m
+/−	0m
Inset	0m
+/−	0m
New Surface	Unchecked
Edges	Inner

Bevel 5

Shift	−200mm
+/−	0m
Inset	0m
+/−	0m
New Surface	Unchecked
Edges	Inner

Bevel 6

Shift	−200mm
+/−	0m
Inset	200mm
+/−	0m
New Surface	Unchecked
Edges	Inner

Bevel 7

Shift	0m
+/−	0m
Inset	200mm
+/−	0m
New Surface	Unchecked
Edges	Inner

Tip

When you do multiple Bevel commands, you can use the right-click method you used while working with the Knife tool. Rather than calling up the numeric panel, entering the data, dropping the tool, and then re-using it, you can use the right-click method along with the numeric feedback given in the lower-left corner of the Modeler interface to get the exact amount of beveling. Using this technique will greatly enhance your productivity.

After completing the seven bevels, your room area should look like Figure 8.15.

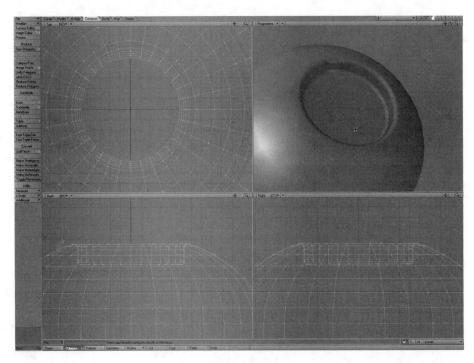

Figure 8.15   Here is the completed recess on the top of the room area after your seven beveling operations.

29. Now it is time for you to add some nurnies to the inside of the recess you just created. Switch to a new, empty layer and start by clicking the Box tool, which is located under the Objects heading under the Create tab, or press the Shift+x combination.

30. After clicking on the Box tool, bring up the numeric panel.

If you are familiar with previous versions of LightWave 3D, you will notice that the numeric panel for the Box tool is different in LightWave 7. The lower half of the numeric panel now has an area for creating rounded corners! This is something that will increase your efficiency quite a bit. In the past, you had to create a box and use the Bevel tool to break the edges. Not anymore!

31. With the numeric window open, select the Size tab and enter the following:

Width	2.05m
Height	680mm
Depth	4.04m
Center X	48.5m
Center Y	572.85m
Center Z	1.45m
Axis	Y
Sharp Edge	Off
Radius	50mm
Radius Segments	1
Segments X	1
Segments Y	1
Segments Z	1

> **Note**
>
> The most important part of the new feature, as it pertains to this segment of modeling, is the Radius tool. It is pretty self-explanatory as to what the options do; but you want to use around 50mm for the radius. This will provide you with just enough beveled edge to give a specular highlight when the light hits the object at the right angle.

32. After dropping the Box tool, add a surface to the box by pressing the q key to call up the Change Surface panel, and enter:

Name	Skyscraper_RoofNurns1
Color	255, 255, 255
Diffuse	80
Specularity	40
Smoothing	Off (Unchecked)

33. Now you want to add a little detail to the box you just made. Select the next empty layer and select the Ball tool by clicking on its name. This tool is found under the Objects heading under the Create tab, or you can call it up by pressing the Shift+o key combination. Then call up the Numeric window and enter the following:

Type	Globe
Axis	Y
Sides	12
Segments	8
Center X	48.5m
Center Y	573.17m
Center Z	500mm
Radius X	800mm
Radius Y	800mm
Radius Z	800mm

34. After creating the sphere, delete the bottom half of it. Do this from either the Back/Front view or the Side view.

35. After deleting the bottom half, use the Stretch tool to flatten the sphere a bit. Activate the Stretch tool by clicking its name under the Stretch heading under the Modify tab or by pressing the h key. With the tool active, bring up the numeric panel and enter the following values:

Horizontal Factor	100%
Vertical Factor	52%
Axis	Z
Center X	48.5m
Center Y	573.17m
Center Z	500mm

36. Click the Apply button when you are finished entering the values and the sphere should stretch down a bit.

37. Now flatten the top of the sphere by selecting the top row of polygons. They are the only three-point polygons on the object. Now use the Merge Polygons tool to merge the polygons into one (Shift+z). Switch to Point Selection mode, select the single point that is no longer connected to the object, and delete it.

38. Switch back to Polygon Selection mode, and select the top two rows of polygons. Make sure that you do not include the polygon you just created using the Merge Polygon tool. Next, activate the Bevel tool, call up the numeric window, and enter the following:

Shift	10mm
+/−	0m

Inset	10mm
+/–	0m
New Surface	Unchecked
Edges	Inner

39. Unselect the polygons and add a new surface to this piece by activating the Change Surface panel and entering these values:

Name	Skyscraper_RoofNurns2
Color	70, 70, 70
Diffuse	80
Specularity	40
Smoothing	On (Checked)

40. The default value for the smoothing angle (threshold) is 89.53 degrees. With this value, the bevels you created are being smoothed, and they do not look good, so you will want to change the value. To change it, open up the Surface Editor by clicking its name. Its listing appears at the top of any of the tabs, or you can press the Ctrl+F3 key combination to open it.

41. With the panel open, select the name of the surface you just created (Skyscraper_RoofNurns2) and change the Smoothing Threshold to 44.5 degrees. Next, press the Enter or Tab key; then close the window.

42. Now duplicate the spherical nurnie by using the Mirror tool. Activate the Mirror tool, open the numeric panel, and enter these settings:

Axis	Z
Free Rotation	Unchecked
Center X	0m
Center Y	0m
Center Z	1.5m
Merge Points	Checked

43. Now make sure that you are in Polygon Selection mode and select all the polygons. Copy and paste them to the same layer. As before, they are pasted right on top of your originals. Do not deselect the polygons.

44. With the original set still selected, use the Rotate tool to rotate them 90 degrees on the y-axis (as seen from Top view). As with other tools, if you press and hold the Ctrl key before you rotate, the rotation will be in increments of 15 degrees. As discussed earlier, you also can use the r key in Top view to rotate them.

45. With the selection still active, move the nurnie block down and to the left until it matches Figure 8.16.

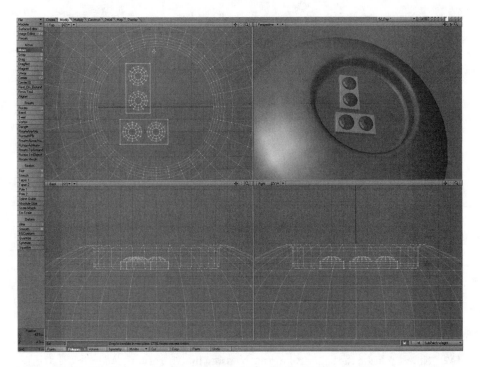

Figure 8.16   The first set of nurnies is placed in the final position.

With the first set of nurnies complete, you will now create a second type that you will put in the same cavity to fill it in a bit more.

46. First, switch to a new layer. Then, start construction with the Box tool, bring up the numeric panel, and enter the following:

Width	3.3m
Height	2.2m
Depth	3.8m
Center X	51.65m
Center Y	573.7m
Center Z	1.2m
Axis	Y

Radius	20mm
Segments X	10
Segments Y	1
Segments Z	12

The Skyscraper_RoofNurns2 surface should be assigned to the box for you. This is because it was the last surface assigned to an object, and by default LightWave will assign the last assigned surface to all new geometry that is created. However, if you had unchecked the Make Default button, LightWave would not have assigned it to the box.

47. To add more detail, you now will use the Knife tool. Select it and enter the following:

Start X	53.45m
Start Y	574.6m
Start Z	1.2m
End X	49.75m
End Y	574.6m
End Z	1.2m
Axis	Z

48. After using the Knife tool, drop it. Then select all the polygons at the very top of the box, excluding any bevel edges (there are a total of 120). Then use the Merge Polygon tool to make them into one polygon.

49. Switch to Point Selection mode and activate the Point Statistics panel. In that panel, select the points that are connected to zero polygons and delete them.

Because the bottom of the box will be inside the room area, below the recess bottom, you can select the points and delete them. This step, and the previous one, helps keep the polygon count down. Although the model will ultimately be fairly heavy in polygons, it's a good idea to try and remove unneeded polygons whenever possible.

50. Select the polygons that make up the lower portion of the box, but omit the corners, as shown in Figure 8.17.

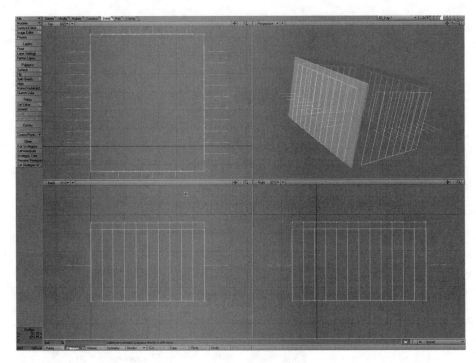

Figure 8.17   Polygons are selected to add more detail to the second nurnie type.

51. Use the Bevel tool to add further detail to the polygons selected in the previous step. Using a Shift amount of –100mm and Inset of 35mm should be sufficient to get the detail required.

52. Do not deselect the polygons. Use the Select Connected selection technique— press the right bracket (]) once (this bracket key is two keys to the right of the p key on your keyboard).

53. Using the Change Surface panel, assign a surface to the polygons and name them Skyscraper_RoofNurns2.

54. Deselect the polygons, and then cut and paste the box nurnie to the layer that contains the previously made nurnies.

55. Using the same Copy/Paste, Rotate, and Scale tools, make smaller versions of the first nurnie type and place three copies on top of the second nurnie type (see Figure 8.18).

Figure 8.18   Nurnie type one is copied, pasted, scaled, and rotated into place.

56. Now cut and paste both types of nurnies and place them on the same layer as the dome. This is an additional area of the skyscraper that is called the room area, as shown in Figure 8.19.

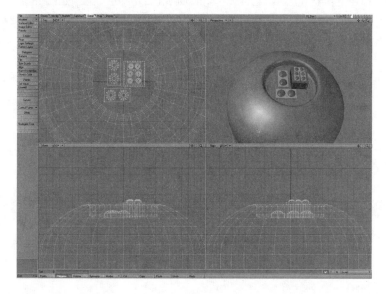

Figure 8.19   Both nurnie types are placed in their final locations.

Exercise 8.3   Creating Additional Details

In this exercise, you create a set of three antenna/warning lights for the top of the room area. They will be placed around the nurnies you created in Exercise 8.2.

1. Change to a new layer and select the Disc tool, call up the numeric panel (n), and enter the following:

Axis	Y
Sides	8
Segments	1
Bottom	572.5m
Top	575m
Center X	53.9m
Center Y	573.75m
Center Z	–1.1m
Radius X	200mm
Radius Y	1.25m
Radius Z	200mm

2. After dropping the Disk tool you will select the top disk polygon and use the Bevel tool to add a little taper to the antenna/warning light. With the Bevel tool selected, and with the numeric panel open, enter the following:

Shift	250mm
+/–	0m
Inset	100mm
+/–	0m
New Surface	Unchecked
Edges	Inner

3. Now you will add some height to the antenna/warning light. Reselect the Bevel tool, call up the numeric panel, and enter the following:

Shift	11.3m
+/–	0m
Inset	0m
+/–	0m
New Surface	Unchecked
Edges	Inner

Tip

It is strongly recommended that you use the right-click method and the numeric read-out in the lower-left corner of Modeler when using the Bevel tool. As mentioned previously, this approach is much more efficient. From here on out this chapter will provide what you need for basic beveling, but the steps for calling up the numeric panel will be omitted.

4. Now use the Bevel tool (b) to taper out the antenna/warning light. This will be where the blinking light is housed. Activate the Bevel tool and bevel until you have the following:

Shift	70mm
+/–	0m
Inset	–70mm
+/–	0m
New Surface	Unchecked
Edges	Inner

5. Bevel again, but this time with just a Shift value of 700mm.

Tip

Don't forget that holding down the Ctrl key while beveling will constrain it to a single axis.

6. Bevel one last time with the following:

Shift	50mm
+/–	0m
Inset	50mm
+/–	0m
New Surface	Unchecked
Edges	Inner

7. Deselect all the polygons and assign a texture name to the antenna/warning light by calling up the Change Surface panel and entering the following:

Name	Skyscraper_WarningLights
Color	177, 189, 203
Diffuse	80
Specularity	100
Smoothing	On (Checked)

8. Now you will make two cuts on the warning lights to make the glass area that houses the lights. Activate the Knife tool (Shift+k) and, using the numeric panel or by doing it by hand and paying close attention to the numeric read out in the lower-left corner of the Modeler interface, enter the following:

Cut 1

Start X	54.17m
Start Y	586.68m
Start Z	–1.1m
End X	53.61m
End Y	586.68m
End Z	–1.1m
Axis	Z

Cut 2

Start X	54.17m
Start Y	587.27m
Start Z	–1.1m
End X	53.61m
End Y	587.27m
End Z	–1.1m
Axis	Z

9. After knifing the warning light, select the polygons between the two cuts and, using the Change Surface panel, assign them a name of Skyscraper_Warning Lights_Glass. Assign them also a slight yellow color.

The top of your antenna/warning light should look something like Figure 8.20.

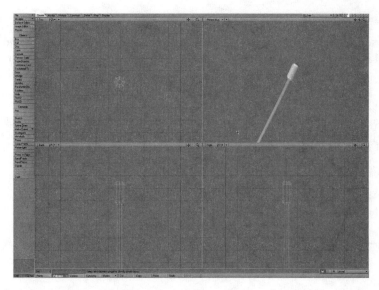

Figure 8.20   Here is the completed antenna/warning light.

10. You will now duplicate the antenna/warning light two times and move both copies to different positions within the recessed top of the room area. Using the Copy/Paste technique, make copies and move them into place. Go to Point Selection mode and select the top of the antenna/warning lights and vary their heights. Your screen should look similar to Figure 8.21.

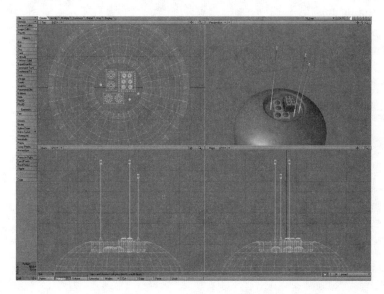

Figure 8.21   Here are the completed nurnies for the top of the room area.

Exercise 8.4   Creating the Second Structure

The skyscraper looks a little plain with only a central building shooting up into the air. You will now create a second structure that will be placed next to, and then be connected to, the main building.

1. Switch to an empty layer.

2. Start with the Disc tool to create a cylinder with many segments. These segments will later become windows. Create the cylinder with the following:

Axis	Y
Sides	48
Segments	120
Bottom	0m
Top	550m
Center X	50m
Center Y	275m
Center Z	−50m
Radius X	25m
Radius Y	275m
Radius Z	25m

3. Select the top circular polygon and delete it.

   Now you will add a sphere, similar to the way you did on the room area, to maintain the overall look of the building.

4. Switch to a new layer and create a ball with the following:

Type	Globe
Axis	Y
Sides	48
Segments	18
Center X	50m
Center Y	550m
Center Z	−50m
Radius X	25m
Radius Y	25m
Radius Z	25m

5. Select and delete the bottom half of the sphere.

6. Select the top five rows of polygons that make up the top of the hemisphere, and use the Merge Polygon tool to make them into one polygon.

7. Switch to Point Selection mode and activate the Point Statistics panel. Using the statistics panel, select the points listed as 0 Polygons and delete them.

8. Switch back to Polygon Selection mode. The polygon you created by merging the top five rows should still be selected. If it is not, select it.

9. Use the Bevel tool on the polygon to create a rounded edge. There will be three bevel operations and they should be done as follows:

Bevel 1

Shift	400mm
+/−	0m
Inset	400mm
+/−	0m
New Surface	Unchecked
Edges	Inner

Bevel 2

Shift	400mm
+/−	0m
Inset	1m
+/−	0m
New Surface	Unchecked
Edges	Inner

Bevel 3

Shift	800mm
+/−	0m
Inset	0m
+/−	0m
New Surface	Unchecked
Edges	Inner

10. With the bevel operation complete, cut and paste the dome to the same layer as the cylinder and merge the points.

11. Give this part of the building a temporary surface using the Change Surface panel. Make sure that you activate smoothing. You should have something like Figure 8.22.

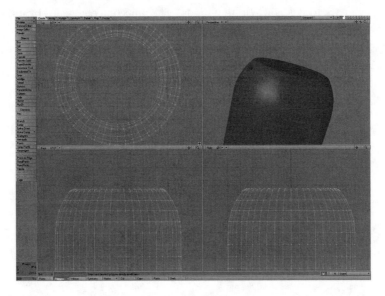

Figure 8.22   Here is the base geometry for the secondary skyscraper structure.

You will now create the geometry to connect the two types of buildings.

12. Switch to a new layer and make a flat square using the Box tool with the following:

Width	0m
Height	320mm
Depth	300mm
Center X	−21.5859m
Center Y	2.16m
Center Z	−50.15m
Axis	X
Radius	60mm
Segments X	1
Segments Y	1
Segments Z	1

13. After creating the flat square, with chopped corners, select all the polygons and use the Merge Polygons tool to make them into one polygon.

14. Switch to Point Selection mode, call up the Point Statistics panel, select the 0 Polygons points, and delete them.

15. Move the polygon using the Move tool and assign the following settings:

Offset X	5.9m
Offset Y	600mm
Offset Z	0m

16. With the polygon moved, extrude it out to make a box tube. Extrude it on the negative x-axis a distance of –9.9 meters.

17. Select the two polygons that are the "caps" of the box tubes and clear them by pressing the Delete key.

18. Use the Mirror tool twice to make rails for the support structure. Assign the following in the numeric panel:

Mirror 1

Axis	Z
Free Rotation	Off
Center X	–21.203m
Center Y	1.26m
Center Z	–49.375m
Merge Points	On

Mirror 2

Axis	Y
Free Rotation	Off
Center X	–21.203m
Center Y	1.985m
Center Z	–49.88m
Merge Points	On

When completed, your rails should look something like Figure 8.23.

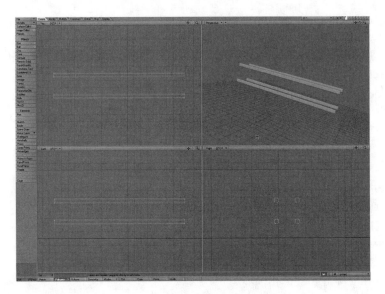

Figure 8.23   The rails for the support structure should look like this.

19. In Right view, select the polygons that make up the rail in the upper-left corner. Copy and paste the rail to a new layer and scale it by 80 percent.

20. In Back view, rotate the scaled rail down 45 degrees, and using the Move tool, move it to the right side of the rails, as shown in Figure 8.24.

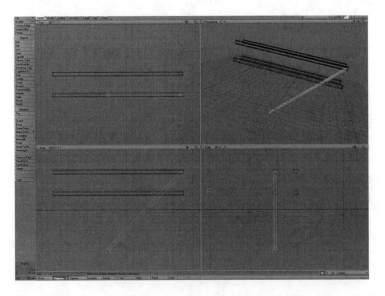

Figure 8.24   The first cross-member of the support structure should look like this.

21. Using the Knife tool, slice the rail you just rotated at a point that is halfway through the bottom rail. Delete the bottom portion, as you see in Figure 8.25.

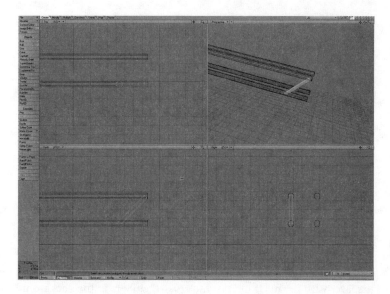

Figure 8.25　Here is the first cross-member trimmed to the correct length.

22. With the cross-member trimmed, use the Mirror tool to duplicate it, as shown in Figure 8.26.

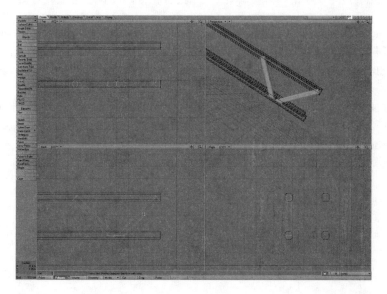

Figure 8.26　The first cross-member is now mirrored.

23. Use the Array tool to duplicate the cross-member over the length of the rails. Use the following settings:

Array Type	Rectangular
X Count	3
Y Count	1
Z Count	1
Jitter X	0m
Jitter Y	0m
Jitter Z	0m
Offset Type	Manual
Offset X	–3.6m
Offset Y	0m
Offset Z	0m

24. You should now notice that the cross-members are a bit longer than the rails. Go to the layer with the rails, and put the cross-members in the background layer for reference.

25. Select the points on the left side of the rails, as seen in Back view, and use the Move tool to move them –950mm on the x-axis.

26. Reverse the layers by pressing the single quote key ('). Use the copy and paste technique to duplicate the cross-members. Then use the Rotate tool, in Right view, to rotate them 180 degrees, or press the r key twice to rotate the geometry 180 degrees.

27. After rotation, use the Move tool to move the cross-members in to place so that your model looks like Figure 8.27.

28. Repeat step 27 to duplicate all the cross-members for the top and bottom, but rotate by only 90 degrees.

    Your screen should now resemble Figure 8.28.

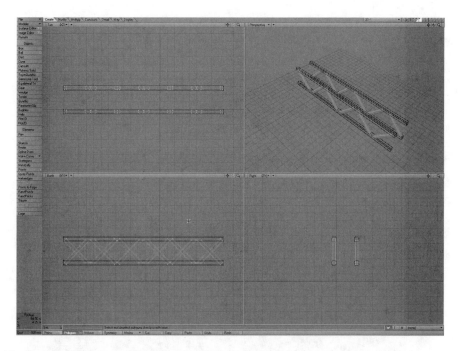

Figure 8.27   The cross-members are copied, rotated, and moved into place.

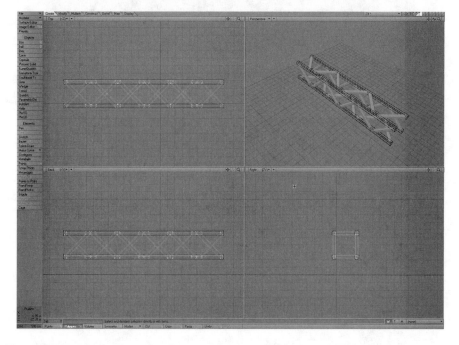

Figure 8.28   The top cross-members are copied, rotated, and moved into place.

29. Cut and paste the cross-members into the layer with the rails.

30. The support structure currently is too short to span the gap between the two buildings when they are rotated into position. To lengthen the buildings, use the Copy/Paste technique with the Move tool to extend them the length of the support structure. After moving them, use the Merge Points command to ensure that you have them in the correct position.

    When completed, your model should look something like Figure 8.29.

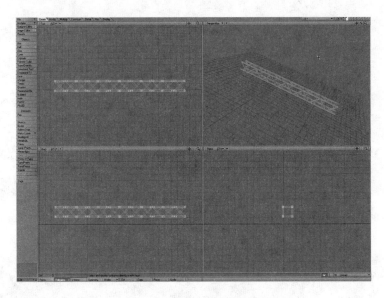

Figure 8.29   The extended support structure looks like this.

31. In Back view, rotate the support structure up (clockwise) –45 degrees. The rotation point should be on the right side, halfway between the top and bottom rails.

32. With the support structure in its final resting place, clean up the geometry by using the Knife tool twice. Slice the geometry and discard the extra polygons.

    Use the following to slice the geometry:

    Knife Cut 1

Start X	–15.6m
Start Y	580mm
Start Z	–49.375m
End X	–15.6m
End Y	4.32m
End Z	–49.375m
Axis	Z

Knife Cut 2

Start X	−25.6m
Start Y	10.6m
Start Z	−49.375m
End X	−25.6m
End Y	13.95m
End Z	−49.375m
Axis	Z

33. After knifing the geometry, select the polygons on either end of the slice areas and clear them. Use the Change Surface panel to assign them a name of Support Girders with no smoothing. You should have something that looks like Figure 8.30.

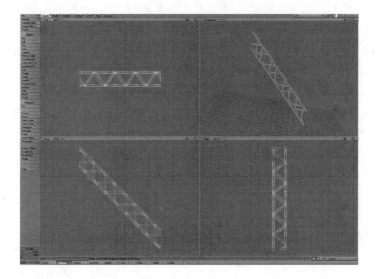

Figure 8.30   Here is the final support structure.

You will now create some cement pads that the support structures would be connecting to if this were a real building. You will be using the Box tool to create three of them.

34. Switch to a new layer.

35. Create the pads using the following settings:

Pad 1

Width	2.05m
Height	6.05m
Depth	4.65m

Center X	−16.625m
Center Y	4.275m
Center Z	−49.325m
Axis	X
Radius	50mm
Segments X,Y,Z	1

Pad 2

Width	2.05m
Height	11.84m
Depth	4.65m
Center X	−24.975m
Center Y	13.72m
Center Z	−49.325m
Axis	X
Radius	50mm
Segments X,Y,Z	1

Pad 3

Width	2.05m
Height	11.84m
Depth	4.65m
Center X	−16.625m
Center Y	26.59m
Center Z	−49.33m
Axis	X
Radius	50mm
Segments X,Y,Z	1

36. After creating the pads, select the polygons that will be on the inside of the building, and delete them. They will not be seen by LightWave's render engine, and only add more polygons to the model. Use the Change Surface panel to give them a surface of Girder Pads with no smoothing. Refer to Figure 8.31 to determine which polygons to select.

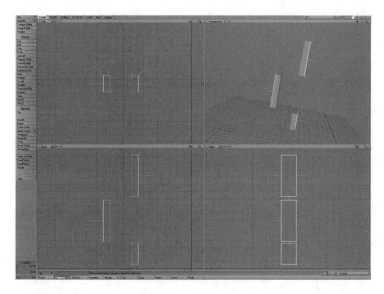

Figure 8.31   Polygons on the pads are selected for deletion.

37. Now it is time to set up the structure for the Array tool. To do this, switch to the layer with the angled support structure.

38. Using the Mirror tool (Modify tab) in the Back view and the following settings, mirror the support structure:

Axis	Y
Free Rotation	Off
Center X	–25.4m
Center Y	13.8m
Center Z	–49.375m
Merge Points	On

39. Cut and paste the structure to the same layer as the pads.

40. Select everything on the structure and pads layer, except the bottom pad.

Tip

To make selecting easier, select a polygon on the bottom pad, use Select Connected (right bracket,]), and then reverse your selection set. See Figure 8.32.

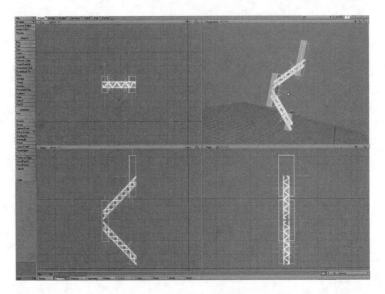

Figure 8.32   Support and pad geometry are selected for use with the Array tool.

41. Use the Array tool with the following settings to clone the geometry:

Array Type	Rectangular
X Count	1
Y Count	21
Z Count	1
Jitter X	0m
Jitter Y	0m
Jitter Z	0m
Offset Type	Manual
Offset X	0m
Offset Y	25.5m
Offset Z	0m

42. The structure was built on the opposite side of the other geometry. To correct this, use the Mirror tool with the following settings:

Axis	X
Free Rotation	Off
Center X	0m
Center Y	0m

Center Z	0m
Merge Points	On

43. Select the polygons that are the original structure and then clear them. You should be left with the structure on the right side.

44. Use the Copy/Paste technique on the support structure, followed by the Rotate tool, with the following settings:

Angle	90
Axis	Y
Center X	50m
Center Y	0m
Center Z	–50m

Your structures should look like Figure 8.33.

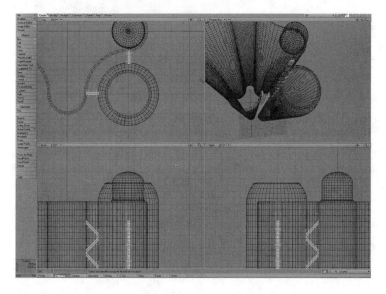

Figure 8.33   The structures are duplicated and rotated into place.

Exercise 8.5   Creating the Windows

Now it is time for you to get some wrist exercise by way of the Lasso tool. You will be selecting a number of rows of polygons to create the windows of the buildings.

I. Make sure that you are in Polygon Selection mode and are on the layer with the second cylindrical-style building part.

2. With the Lasso tool, start selecting every other row of polygons. Start at the bottom and work your way up. Do not start with the bottom row (windows resting on the ground is not too practical). The Lasso tool is a good choice for this task because polygons are easy to miss in Wireframe view. Figure 8.34 shows what you should have when you get to the top of the building.

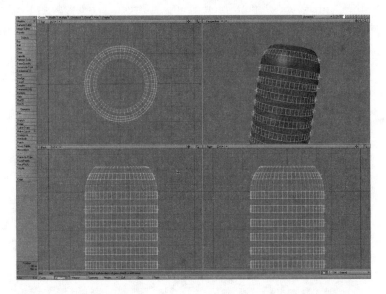

Figure 8.34   These are the polygons for the windows on the cylindrical building.

3. Before assigning the window surface to the selected polygons, deselect the columns of polygons that intersect the cement pads. Cement pads through windows are a bit unsightly.

4. With the correct polygons selected, assign them the Window surface, using the Change Surface panel that you created earlier.

5. With the window surface polygons selected, cut and paste them to the next empty layer.

6. Select all the polygons you just pasted into the new layer.

7. Using the Bevel tool, bevel them with an inset of 200mm.

8. Reverse the selection set by pressing the double quote (") key. This will select the polygons that the bevel operation created. Change the surface of these polygons to the surface you assigned to the cylindrical building. These will be the window frames.

9. Cut and paste the window frames to the layer containing the cylindrical building. Merge the points. Your screen should look like Figure 8.35.

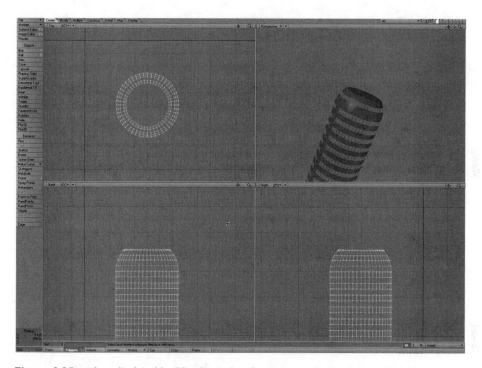

Figure 8.35 The cylindrical building's window frames are pasted and merged back into the main building.

10. Switch back to the layer with the windows on it. Copy and paste all the windows to the next empty layer.

11. Now bevel all the objects with the following settings:

Shift	−1m
+/−	0m
Inset	500mm
+/−	0m
New Surface	Unchecked
Edges	Inner

12. Using the Change Surface panel, assign them a surface named Interior1 and make sure that smoothing is activated. You should get something like Figure 8.36.

It looks a bit funny, don't you think? Don't worry, it is supposed to!

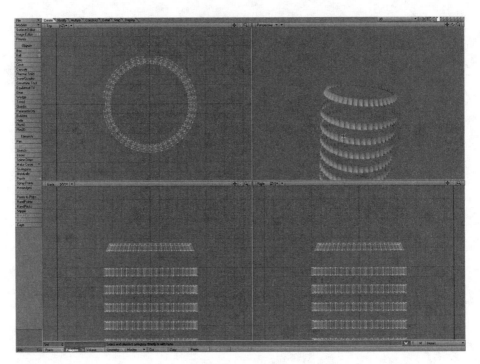

Figure 8.36   These are the cylindrical building's interior polygons.

13. Now for the fun part: Select polygons at random to create different interior sets. When completed, you want to have a total of five interiors.

How you do this is up to you. Here are some hints for getting good looks:

- After selecting a number of random polygons, press the right square bracket (]) to select the connected polygons. This will give you a good idea as to how your current interior set looks.

- Stay away from selecting groups of interior sets that are adjacent to one another; breaking it up will make it look much better.

- When you are happy with a current set that you think would be about 1/5 of the total interior, give it a new surface name: Interior2, Interior3, etc., until you have worked through all of the polygons.

14. After you are happy with an interior set and have assigned a surface to it, hide the polygons by pressing the hyphen (-) key. This will make selecting what is remaining much easier. Be patient; don't rush through it.

When you are finished, you should have something similar to Figure 8.37.

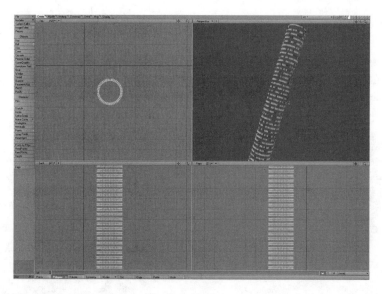

Figure 8.37   The interior polygons are now complete.

15. Now cut and paste the interiors and windows from their layers and paste them in the layer with the rest of the cylindrical tower.

16. If you care to see the interiors of the building through the windows, open the Surface Editor and add a little transparency.

When completed, your screen should look something like Figure 8.38.

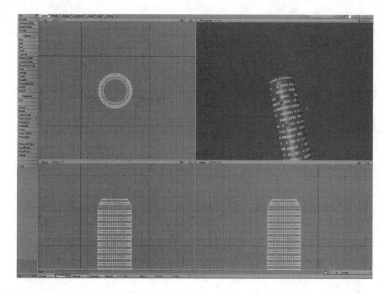

Figure 8.38   Here are the cylindrical building's interiors and windows.

17. Now that you have completed the secondary tower, use the same technique to add the windows and interior to the main tower and room area.

18. Switch to the layer with the room area. Copy and paste it to a new layer.

19. Put the secondary, cylindrical tower in the background. Use the Scale tool and the Move tool to place the new room area so that it fits nicely on top of the cylindrical tower. Cut and paste into the cylindrical tower's layer (see Figure 8.39).

Figure 8.39   Here is the cylindrical building with its new room area.

20. Now cut the girders and pads from their layer and paste them in the layer with the cylindrical tower.

21. Use the Array tool to duplicate this assembly. Use the following settings:

Array Type	Radial
Number	4
Axis	Y
Center X	0m
Center Y	0m
Center Z	0m
Merge Points	Off

Figure 8.40 shows the structure in its current state.

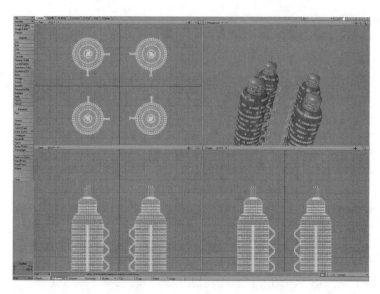

Figure 8.40   The completed cylindrical towers should look like this.

22. Switch to the layer that has the room area for the main building. Use the Array tool again, with the same settings you used in the previous step, to clone them for the top of the main building.

23. Now cut and paste the cylindrical buildings to the layer with the main building. You should have something similar to Figure 8.41.

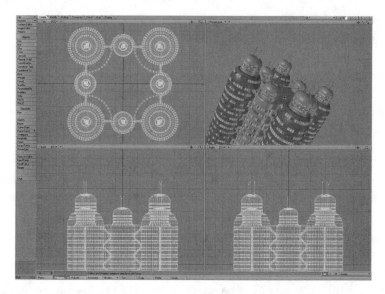

Figure 8.41   The main building and the cylindrical building are now combined.

24. The roof needs a helicopter landing pad. To create one, select the large top polygon of the main building. Turn off all the other polygons by pressing the equal sign key (=).

25. With the large top polygon isolated, switch to a new layer.

26. Using the Box tool, create a box with the following settings:

Width	40m
Height	37.31m
Depth	40m
Center X	0m
Center Y	560.655m
Center Z	0m
Radius	0m

27. Switch back to the rooftop and put the box in the background layer.

28. Access the Solid Drill panel by clicking its name from the Combine heading under the Multiply tab or by pressing Shift+c.

29. Select the Stencil button and enter RoofTop HeliPad in the Surface field. Click OK.

30. Once the operation is complete, reverse the layers and delete the box. After deleting the box, reverse the layers again and select the square polygon that was stenciled on the rooftop.

31. After selecting the polygon, use the Bevel tool to push up the landing pad. Use the following settings:

Shift	200mm
+/–	0m
Inset	400mm
+/–	0m
New Surface	Unchecked
Edges	Inner

Now you're ready for the last part of the modeling stage. You are going to copy some of the nurnies from within the recesses of the domed areas and place them on the rooftop around the helipad.

32. Copy the nurnies from the recessed area on the right side of the room area that is attached to the main building. Do not copy the antennas/warning lights.

33. Paste them to a new layer.

34. Use the Move tool to place them on the rooftop close to the helipad and to one side of the x-axis.

35. Copy and paste the nurnie set and move it the same distance on the opposite side of the x-axis.

36. Now use the Array tool with the following settings to duplicate them:

Array Type	Radial
Number	4
Axis	Y
Center X	0m
Center Y	0m
Center Z	0m
Merge Points	Off

37. Cut and paste them to the same layer as the rest of the skyscraper.

38. Before you can complete the model, make sure that you are in Polygon Selection mode, and unhide all the hidden geometry by pressing the backslash (\) key.

Call up the Polygon Statistics panel and select the polygons with the name you gave the glass for the Antennas/Warning Lights.

With the polygons selected, cut and paste them to layer 2.

Your completed model should have all of the geometry on layer 1, except for the antennas/warning lights glass, which should be on layer 2. Your screen should look like Figure 8.42.

Figure 8.42   The skyscraper, after completing the modeling phase, should look like this.

Building an Architectural Scene in Layout

Building a skyscraper is only one aspect of a complete project. While it's an important aspect, the texturing, lighting, camera placement, and environment that your building lives in are just as important.

Exercise 8.6   Creating the Skyscraper Environment

If Modeling is the ying, then Texturing and Lighting are the yang. All of these elements are connected. If you have a great model but poor textures and surfaces, the model will look poor. If you have a poor model and great textures, the model will still look bad.

For this reason, you need to make sure that you learn and excel at working with both models and textures. Do not rush—if you speed through either phase of the project, it will show. If you take your time and methodically work through the entire process, the care and quality of your work will stand out.

To develop your surfaces and textures adequately, you will need a good light kit. A *light kit* is a set of lights used for a particular scene. Many times you might develop a generic light kit that you can use over and over again. But, your generic light kit is only a starting point, a jumping-off place from which you can develop your scene. The light kit is not the end of your journey; it is the beginning.

This exercise will bring your model to Layout. You'll create an environment for the Skyscraper object, as well as position the camera. You can make the skyscraper appear more impressive with the proper camera positioning. From there, you'll apply lights and textures to bring the building to life.

1. Start Layout and make sure that your Content Directory is set to Skyscraper.

2. Load the skyscraper model you created by pressing the plus key (+) or by clicking the Add button and choosing Object and then Load Object. This command is located under the Items tab.

Tip

The performance of your computer will determine how you should set the display of your objects in Layout. If you have a computer with the fastest CPU and the best graphics card available, you may be able to display very complex models with OpenGL textures turned on.

Experiment with the different display modes to find the one that best suits your needs and does not bring your system to a halt.

3. After loading the skyscraper model, set a keyframe for the Camera. Doing this now will keep the camera at its current location.

   If you did not set a keyframe for the Camera, when you load the skyball the camera will move along the negative z-axis to frame all of the object.

4. Next, load the Skyball.lwo object, provided on the accompanying CD.

5. With the skyball and skyscraper loaded, make the Camera the active item by clicking Cameras at the bottom of the Layout interface or by pressing Shift+c.

6. Make sure that your view is looking through the camera by pressing the 6 key on the top row of numbers on the keyboard (not the numeric keypad) or by selecting Camera view in the upper-left corner of the view border.

7. With the Camera active, change its location and rotational values as follows:

Position

X	40.5264m
Y	10m
Z	−190.8049m

Rotation

Heading	−15.20°
Pitch	−70.40°
Bank	−32.60°

Tip

To move the camera, select the Move tool under the Tools heading under the Items tab or press the t key.

To rotate the camera, select the Rotate tool under the Tools heading under the Items tab or press the y key. The hot keys in Layout are the same as they are in Modeler, which makes them easier to use because you do not have to learn a new set of hot keys for each module of the software.

8. Set a keyframe for the camera.

Note

After moving and rotating your camera, you object might look clipped. This is because your Grid Size is set too high.

To make your Grid Size smaller, use the left square bracket key ([). To make your Grid Size larger, use the right square bracket key (]).

9. Rotate the skyball on its Heading to place the bright area of the image map in the appropriate place in the scene. Why this particular angle was chosen will be described later when you create your lighting kit. Use the following settings:

Heading	144.00°
Pitch	0°
Bank	0°

10. Make a keyframe for the skyball.

With the skyball rotated to the correct location, you will want to change its rendering properties. If you were to add your light kit and start rendering, the skyball would affect the lighting in the scene. You do not want that.

The skyball is used to give the scene some background. It also is used to indicate where the light is coming from.

11. Change to Object Selection mode and make sure that your skyball is the object that is activated.

12. Once the skyball is the active object, activate its Object Properties panel by clicking the Item Properties button at the bottom of the Layout interface or by pressing the p key.

Approximately one quarter of the way down on the Object Properties panel, there are four tabs:

Geometry

Deformations

Rendering

Edges

13. Select the Rendering tab. Then deselect all of the Shadowing Options for the skyball. They are Shelf Shadow, Cast Shadow, and Receive Shadow.

By deselecting all of the shadowing options, the skyball will not block the lights in the scene. Your view should look like Figure 8.43.

Figure 8.43   The camera and skyball have been moved and rotated into their correct positions.

Exercise 8.7   Adding Lights to the Skyscraper Environment

This next exercise takes your architectural environment one step further by creating the lighting for the scene. By adding the environment first, as you did in Exercise 8.6, you'll now be able to better visualize the light placement and color.

1. Before creating the light kit, activate the Global Illumination panel by selecting it from the Global heading under the Lights tab.

2. With the Global Illumination panel open, set your Ambient Intensity to 0 (zero), and then close the panel.

Tip

Use ambient light with care. Ambient light tends to flatten an image and wash out its depth. This is not what you want because you are working in the 3D realm.

Instead of using ambient light, use distant lights and spotlights as fill lights to lighten areas that are too dark. This takes some practice, but with patience you will soon be able to re-create ambient light settings without flattening your scene.

With the skyball prepared, you will now start creating your light kit.

3. Start with the key light. Switch to Light Selection mode. The default light should be selected.

4. Activate the Light Properties the same way you did for the skyball.

5. Change the light from a Distant light to an Area light, and set its Intensity to 90 percent.

6. Change the light's color by clicking on the color swatch on the Light Properties panel. For its Red, Green, and Blue colors, enter the following:

Red	255
Green	255
Blue	232

Note

From here on out, Red, Green, and Blue values will be referred to as RGB and expressed as XXX, XXX, XXX (Red, Green, Blue). As an example, the previous setting would be expressed as 255, 255, 232.

7. After changing the color, close the panel.

8. Click the Items tab at the top of the interface, select the Replace button, and then Rename Current Item.

    As an alternative, you could open the Scene Editor panel, select the Light, and right-click it. When the menu appears, select Rename.

9. With the Light 1 Name panel open, rename it to Sun.

10. Move and rotate the light into position. Using the same technique you used for placing the camera, enter the following values:

Position

X	−906.8326m
Y	1.0895km
Z	−343.8673m

Rotation

Heading	75.80°
Pitch	35.00°
Bank	0.00°

11. Set a keyframe at frame 0.

12. To view the scene through the light you just moved, press the 5 key or select Light View from the pull-down in the upper-left corner of the view window.

13. Switch back to viewing from the camera.

14. Activate the Render Options panel and make sure Ray Trace Shadows, Ray Trace Reflection, and Extra Ray Trace Optimization are checked.

15. Close the panel and save the scene. Get in the habit of saving the scene before you perform any test renders.

16. If you are like most animators, you want to see what this is starting to look like! Press F9. This is a good thing. When your render completes, it should look like Figure 8.44.

Figure 8.44   The scene after your first render with the camera and light set up should look like this.

Now would be a good time to talk about the key light. Yours is called Sun.

The main purpose of a key light is illumination of the subject; in this case, the skyscraper. There are certain guidelines you should follow when you place your key light:

- Do not put the key light directly behind the camera, because it will flatten your image and look very boring. As a basic rule of thumb, you want to put between 45° and 60° to one side of your camera and the same in height.

- The color should be dictated by the scene. This is a very simplistic example, but it is the truth. In this case, the driving force is the color of the light in the sky-ball. If it were a nighttime shot, you would gravitate toward the blue spectrum. Daybreak and sunset gravitate toward the red and orange tones. Feel free to refer to Chapter 7, "Lighting and Atmosphere," for more lighting information.

The key, or Sunlight in this scene was place at an angle to provide a decent amount of illumination and provide a nice specular kick off of the building.

Now you will add a fill light. The purpose of a fill light, as the name implies, is to soften or lighten the darker areas of the scene.

In most cases, fill lights are used without specularity and shadowing options. Because of their purposes, they usually come from the opposite side of the key light; so if they were to have specularity and shadows it would give the impression that there are two lights. An outdoor building having two suns is not very realistic, unless it were to be on a different planet.

17. Add the fill light by selecting Add, choosing Lights, and selecting Add Distance Light, which is located under the Items tab.

18. When the Light Name panel opens, name the light Fill. *Phil*, if you have a sense of humor.

19. Move the fill light to its correct position and rotation by using the following data:

Position

X	945m
Y	1.015km
Z	−312.5m

Rotation

Heading	−68.00°
Pitch	34.10°
Bank	0.00°

Note

Although the position of distant lights does not affect the lighting of your model(s), sometimes it is easier to visualize how they will affect your scene if you move them.

20. After orienting the fill light, set a keyframe at frame 0.

21. Call up the Light Properties for the fill light and use the following:

Color	234, 232, 255
Intensity	20%
Affect Specularity	Off
Shadow Type	Off

All other options set to default

You gave the fill light, which is acting as an ambient fill, a slight blue color to simulate the bluish color of the sky.

To see the result of the fill light, press F9. Your screen should look like Figure 8.45.

Figure 8.45   Adding the fill light should give you this result.

You can see in the second render that the fill light has added the look of some ambient blue light coming from the sky. The areas that were very dark are now a bit lighter and the shadows are not as dark.

Now you will add a second fill light. Its only purpose, as the other fill light, is to add the ambient feel to the image.

22. Add the second fill light as you added the first, and name it Ambient.

23. After adding the Ambient light, change its location and rotation using the following values:

Position

X	0m
Y	3.363km
Z	0m

Rotation

Heading	0°
Pitch	90°
Bank	0°

As you can see, the ambient light is placed directly above the building, facing straight down on to it. This will help with filling in the darker areas not filled before.

24. Change its settings as follows:

Color	188,255, 255
Intensity	13%
Affect Specularity	Off
Shadow Type	Off

All other options set to default

To see the effect of the lighting on the scene, press F9. Your scene should look like Figure 8.46. While it's not so noticeable in print, the final animation will benefit from this added light.

Figure 8.46   Adding the second fill light adds subtle detail to the side of the building.

The effect of the ambient light is very subtle, but it lightens the shadows in the very interior area, where the two buildings are connected.

Exercise 8.8   Adding Blinking Accent Lights

Now you will add the accent, blinking lights at the tip of the antenna/warning lights. The process of making them look similar, but different is fairly simple. You'll use LightWave's Graph Editor to animate the light's brightness.

1. Create the first light, taking time to get the light intensity, intensity falloff, blinking rate, and flare size correct. Next, clone the light for placement within the particular area of the skyscraper.

2. You then can clone it again, but change or offset some of the settings, and do it for the next set. There are three sets in the model, but you would do the same if you had 100.

3. To help you see where your lights are being placed, open the Scene Editor and change the skyball to either Wireframe or Bounding box. Then, in Perspective view set the Maximum Render Level to Front Face Wireframe. You then can rotate, zoom, and pan the view to see how the lights are set in the scene even before you press the F9 key.

4. Change Perspective view to Right view by pressing the 3 key.

   Take a look at Figure 8.47 to see how Layout looks during this phase. You will notice that the Scene Editor is open and placed in the upper-left corner because you will be doing some parenting. The Side view is zoomed out fairly far so that when you add the first light, you will be able to place the light roughly above the building using the numeric display in the lower-left corner.

5. Once you get the light placed in the general area, use the mouse to get it closer. Then get closer to the light and the antenna/warning light to make the final placement.

6. Add a point light and name it Warning.

7. In the Scene Editor, click the new light, and hold the mouse button down. With the mouse button still depressed, drag the mouse cursor up until it is on top of the main layer of the skyscraper (layer 1). Release the mouse button. The light should be parented to the main part of the building.

8. Move the point light up on the y-axis 600m.

9. Zoom in Right view so you can get a closer look, and place your light more accurately (see the Figure 8.48).

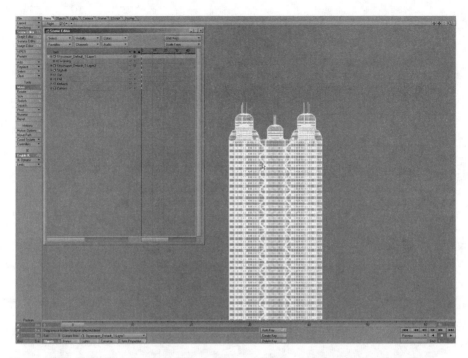

Figure 8.47   Here is the layout of the view in preparation of placing the first point light.

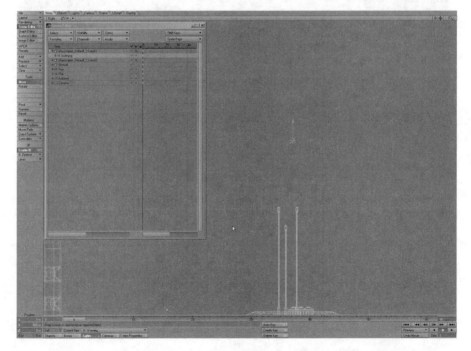

Figure 8.48   Zoom into Side view to help place the point light more accurately.

10. Now move the light so that it is inside the antenna/warning light, as seen in Side view.

11. Now switch to Front view by pressing the 1 key.

12. Nudge the light over on the x-axis until it is centered in the antenna. Create a keyframe at frame 0 to lock it in place. You will have to pan around in Layout to keep the light in view while moving it.

13. When you move the light, you can lock the view to keep the selected item centered. To do this, click the down arrow next to the view name in the upper-left corner of the view and select Center Current Item from the menu that appears.

14. To ensure that you have placed the light correctly, switch to Perspective view by pressing the 4 key (see Figure 8.49).

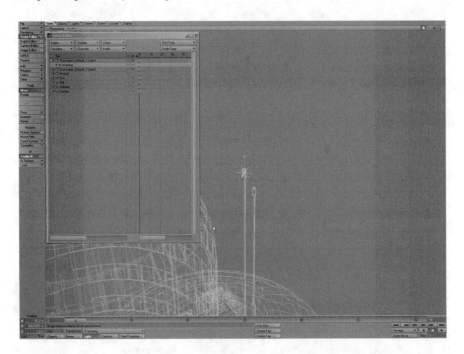

Figure 8.49   Here is Perspective view showing the final placement of the first point light.

15. Change the light properties for the point light by pressing the p key while the light is selected. When the Light Properties panel opens, enter the following details:

Color	255, 255, 128
Intensity Falloff	Linear
Range/Nominal Distance	28.3 m

All other options set to default values

The Intensity Falloff was used for the point light to add a sense of scale. If it were not used, the point light would cast light off to infinity. This is not true to life. The value for the Range/Nominal Distance was chosen so that enough light would be cast to cover most of the room area.

16. With the Light Properties panel still open click in the E button next to the Light Intensity field. Clicking this button will open the Graph Editor for the point light and will automatically set the current channel to be the light's intensity.

    You are going to use the Graph Editor to make the light blink.

17. With the Graph Editor open, right-click and hold the mouse button, and then drag a bounding box over the keyframe at frame 0. Alternately, you can left-click the keyframe. Both methods will select this as the current keyframe to be edited; however, there's less chance of accidentally moving the key if you use the right mouse lasso. Mac users, remember to hold the Apple key for right mouse button functions.

    Once the keyframe is selected, you will notice that the values at the bottom of the panel will become active, allowing you to edit them.

18. Make sure that the Frame reads 0 and change the Value to 0 percent.

19. Add a keyframe for the light at frame 15 by clicking on the small button at the bottom of the Graph window that shows a key with a plus sign (+) next to it.

    Currently the Graph is a straight light that extends out from frame 0 with a value of 0 percent.

20. Click the graph line at frame 15. Once you do this, the fields in the lower portion of the window will become active again. If the frame is listed as something other than 15, change it to read 15.

21. Change the Value to 150 percent. The graph will go from a value of 0 percent at frame 0 to 150 percent at frame 15.

22. Using the same technique, add a keyframe at frame 30 with a value of 0 percent.

    You will now have a curve that looks like a bell. There is a small problem, though—if you look at frames 0 and 30 the graph comes to a sharp point. To show just how sharp it is, you will change the Pre Behavior and Post Behavior.

23. Set both behaviors to Repeat by clicking on the drop-down menu and selecting them.

    The sharp, abrupt change in the graph should now be very evident. It would be much better if the lights had a smooth transition at this point.

24. To make the transition smoother, click the Move Keyframe icon in the lower-left corner. It is just to the left of the Add keyframe button. You want to do this so you don't accidentally add a keyframe while making adjustments.

25. Now drag a bounding box with the right mouse button over the keyframes at frame 0 and 30. Once you do this, you will see that the Frame filed reads (mixed).

26. With the two keyframes selected, right-click and hold over one of the keyframes. From the menu that appears, select Ease In/Out.

    The graph will now update with a smooth transition at those points (see Figure 8.50).

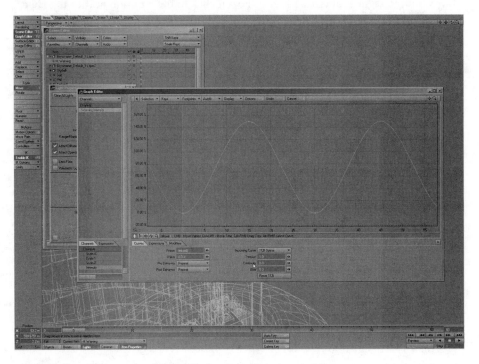

Figure 8.50   Here is the Graph Editor for the first blinking light.

27. Close the Graph Editor.

28. Now you will set up the lens flare options for the blinking light. To do so click the Lens Flare check box and then the Lens Flare Options button.

29. With the Lens Flare Options panel open, add the following settings:

Fade Behind Objects	On
Fade With Distance	On
Nominal Distance	300m
Central Ring	Off
Red Outer Glow	Off
Random Streaks	Off
All others	default

You now need to create an envelope for the flare intensity, just like you did for the light's intensity.

30. Click the E button next to the Flare Intensity field.

31. After the Graph Editor panel opens, move the Intensity channel to the curve bin for the light intensity by selecting "Intensity" in the Channel Listing in the lower-left corner and dragging it up in to the Channel Window, which currently shows the Flare Intensity. When done correctly, your screen will look like Figure 8.51.

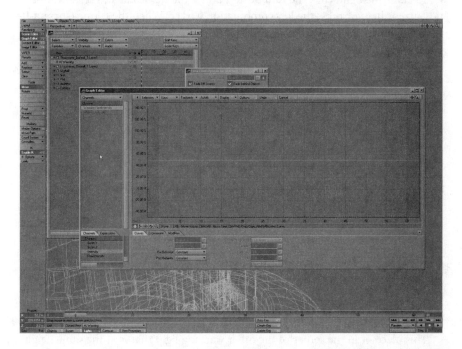

Figure 8.51   The Graph Editor shows that the Light Intensity channel has been added to the Channel Window so that you can copy the Flare Intensity.

32. To copy the Light Intensity settings, left-click its name in the Channel Window to highlight it, then right-click it. When the menu appears, select Copy.

33. Once you have copied the settings, left-click the Flare Intensity listing in the Channel Window to highlight it. Then right-click it and select Paste from the menu.

The graph should be updated to be an exact copy of the Light Intensity graph. The only problem with this is that the peak intensity is 150 percent. A setting that high would be too bright and blow out the scene's visibility completely.

34. Left-click the keyframe at frame 15 and change the value at the bottom of the window to 4.5 percent. This will give a nice subtle glow to the light. The key here is subtlety; you want the light to have just enough kick to make it look like the light bulb inside is glowing. Too much glow and it will blow the sense of scale in the scene. Too little and, well obviously, you would not see it.

35. Close the Graph Editor, the Lens Flare Options panel, and finally, the Light Properties panel.

Exercise 8.9   Cloning Lights

You will now use this light, its settings, and the Clone tool to create the remainder of the blinking lights.

1. To clone the light, click the Add button under the Items tab and select Clone Current Item or press the key combination Ctrl+c. When the Clone Current Item panel opens, click OK to make one clone.

2. Now move the cloned light, which should be the selected item, to its final position. To do this, click in the X Position field, make the number –52.2m, and press the Tab key three times.

3. Create a keyframe at frame 0 for this light.

4. Clone this light one time. Change its Positional values to X: –2.2m, Y: 589.6751m, Z: –52.2m.

5. Create a keyframe at frame 0 for this light.

6. Clone this light one time. Change its Positional values to X: –2.2m, Y: 589.6751m, Z: 52.2m.

   The first set of blinking lights is now complete. Once you get the first one done, you'll see that setting up the other three was pretty easy!

7. Now you will create the second set. To do this, select the first blinking light. Its name is Warning (1).

8. Clone it once and move it to X: 46.5m, Y: 589.6751m, Z: 600mm.

9. Create a keyframe for this light at frame 0.

   This places it in the center of the other warning light that is at the same height as the first set of lights.

10. Activate the Light Properties panel.

11. Click the Light intensity envelope button which will activate the Graph Editor.

12. Once the Graph Editor is open, right-click and drag a window across all the keyframes or press Shift and double-click in the border (there are only three).

13. With the keyframes selected, press the Ctrl key and use the left mouse button to drag the keyframes in time to the right by 15 frames.

14. You should see the whole graph shift by 15 frames.

    This will make the second set of lights blink on when the first set is off, and blink off when the first set is on.

15. Do the same for the Flare Intensity.

16. Close all panels.

17. Clone this light one time.

18. Change the clone X position to -46.5m.

19. Set a keyframe for the light at frame 0.

20. Clone this light one time.

21. Change its position to X: 600mm, Y: 589.6751m, Z: –46.5m. Set a keyframe for this light at frame 0.

22. Clone this light one time.

23. Change its Z position to 46.5m.

You have now completed the second set of blinking lights.

24. Now, select the first blinking light again. It is named Warning (1).

25. Switch to Top view by pressing the 2 key.

26. Clone this light one time.

27. Working in Top view, move the light to X: 53.9m. Leave Y the same for now. Change the position numerically, from the Top View, Z: –1.1m.

28. Now switch to Front view by pressing the 1 key.

29. Move the light down on the y-axis, until it is positioned at 586.9752m.

30. Create a keyframe for this light at frame 0.

31. To verify that the light is in the correct position, switch to Perspective view by pressing the 4 key. If you rotate the view around, you will see that the light is in the correct position.

If you do this on your own building or project of any sort, you will want to display Perspective view occasionally to verify the position of your lights.

32. Using the same steps you did before, call up the Graph Editor for the light's Light Intensity.

33. Now, instead of shifting the keyframes to the right by 15 frames, shift them to the right by 7 frames.

34. Do the same for the Flare Intensity.

35. Clone the light one time.

36. Change its X position to –53.9m.

37. Set a keyframe at frame 0 for the light.

38. Clone the light one time.

39. Change the new lights position to X: –1.1m and Z: –53.9m. The Y position will remain the same.

40. Set a keyframe at frame 0 for the light.

41. Clone the light one time.

42. Change the light's Z position to 53.9m.

43. Create a keyframe for the light at frame 0. Figure 8.52 shows the cloned lights from Perspective view in Layout. Note that the visibility has been set to Wireframe for easier viewing.

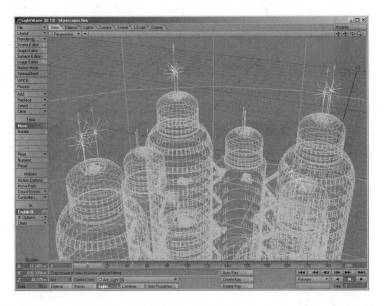

Figure 8.52   Simply cloning the point lights atop the skyscraper completes the blinking accent light setup.

This completes the lighting portion of the scene. You did a bit extra by creating blinking lights at the top of the building. This is a good idea because if you choose to move the camera to the top of the building, the blinking lights will be seen. Even during the day, lights of this nature are blinking.

If you choose to use the building in a night scene, your blinking lights are ready to go!

Now you will move on to the texturing phase of the project. This is where it all really comes together, and at some point you will do a test render and say, "Wow! This is starting to look really nice!"

This is a great motivator. At times, modeling and lighting can get a bit mundane because of the repetitious tasks—selecting all of those polygons to make the windows or cloning all of the blinking lights. But, when you see that one render and realize that all the pieces are starting to come together, you will find yourself reenergized and ready to keep going.

So, with that said, let's jump right to it!

Exercise 8.10   Surfacing the Skyscraper Walls

Now that your environment and lights are in place, you need to surface the skyscraper. This exercise guides you through the proper surfacing for an architectural scene, taking into account the surrounding area, such as the sky and clouds. The tools and process used to surface the skyscraper in this tutorial can be applied to any type of building.

1. Switch back to Camera view by pressing the 6 key.

2. Open the Surface Editor.

3. With the Surface Editor open, click the surface name you assigned to the main building. When you click the name, it should become highlighted.

4. The first step is to assign the surface some texture on the color channel. To assign a texture map to the surface, click the T button to the right of the color swatch and the envelope button.

   When you click the texture button the Texture Editor will open. This is where you assign textures to the surface. They can be image maps, procedural, or gradients. In this case, the first texture will be an image map.

5. By default, the texture editor is set to image map as the Layer Type, with a Blending mode of Normal. To load an image, click the Image button in the middle section on the right side of the panel. When the menu pops up select load image.

6. When the mini-browser appears, select the image named DarkMETAL-seamless.iff and click OK.

   The image will be loaded as the active image in the Texture Editor.

7. Switch the Projection type to Cubic. This will apply the image from all axes from both directions.

8. Uncheck both Pixel Blending and Texture Antialiasing.

9. Click the Automatic sizing button towards the bottom-right of the Texture Editor. This is done to center the image map on the surface. You will manually set the scale in which it is applied to the surface.

10. To set the scale of the image map application, make sure that the Scale tab is selected on the bottom of the interface. When it is set to the Scale tab, change the scale to reflect the following values, as shown in Figure 8.53.

    Texture Scale

X	33m
Y	148.085m
Z	33m

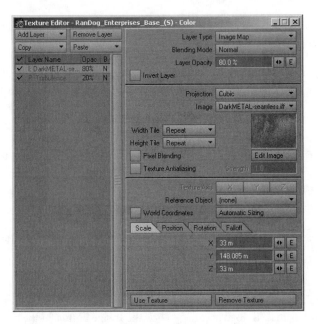

Figure 8.53   A cubic image map is applied to the Base texture of the skyscraper, using a seamless metal image.

This will stretch the texture along the y-axis, and apply it evenly on the x- and z-axes.

11. Set the Layer Opacity to 80.0 percent. This means that the image map will contribute to 80 percent of the color of the surface.

Because this is a tileable image, it should look nice on the surface; however, some tileable images show a pattern if the surface area is rather large. Because the building is large, you may detect a bit of repeating. To help reduce that, you will put a bit of a procedural texture on top of the image map.

12. To apply a procedural texture on top of the cubic metal image map, click the Add layer button in the upper-left corner of the Texture Editor, and select Procedural from the list.

13. By default you should receive a procedural texture layer with a Procedural Type of Turbulence. This is good—it is what you want. Edit the settings as follows (see Figure 8.54).

Texture Color	076, 056, 025
Frequencies	3
Contrast	80.0%
Small Power	.5

Scale X   10m

Scale Y   50m

Scale Z   10m

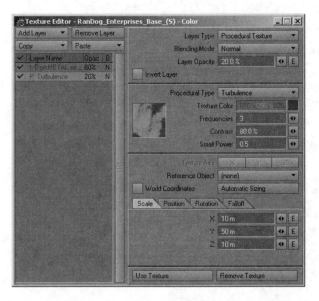

Figure 8.54   A procedural texture is applied to the base metal texture of the skyscraper for a weathered look and added realism.

 Tip

When setting a procedural texture, you can right-click the texture preview to change the background color display. This will make setting the dark procedurals easier. You also can left-click and drag on the preview display in the texture panel to see more of the texture.

---

14. When you are done, click the Use texture button at the bottom of the Texture Editor.

Next you will add two diffuse textures. Diffuse is the area of an object that shows the color of the object. It is flat, and it has no specularity. If you were to have a sphere with no specularity at all, you would see only the diffusion of the surface. The less diffuse the surface the darker it appears. A very diffuse surface will appear to suck up light. As a rule of thumb, if you are not using any diffuse textures, set the value at 80.0 percent; however, it is strongly recommended that you use a texture at all times. This gives you a lot of control over the way your object will look. Having no diffuse texture at all makes the surface look too regular—obviously computer generated.

15. To create the two diffuse layers, click the T next to the Diffuse line on the Surface Editor.

16. When the Texture Editor opens, set your layers up as follows:

Layer 1

Type	Image Map
Layer Opacity	50.0%
Projection	Cubic
Image	DreadHullSpec.tga
Pixel Blending	Off
Texture Antialiasing	Off
Scale X	8.75m
Scale Y	8.75m
Scale Z	8.75m

Layer 2

Type	Image Map
Layer Opacity	100.0%
Projection	Cylindrical
Image	metal_scuffed_color.iff
Pixel Blending	Off
Texture Antialiasing	Off
Texture Axis	Y
Scale X	33m
Scale Y	148.085m
Scale Z	33m
Position X	0m
Position Y	296.17m
Position Z	0m

17. When you are done entering the textures, click the Use texture button.

With the diffuse portion set, you will now move on to the specularity channel. Like diffuse, specularity defines the material of which the surface is made.

Specularity is what creates the highlights on a surface when light strikes it. Tighter highlights will give your surface a shinier feel, while broader highlights will give it a more flat look.

18. Click the T button on the Specularity area.

When the Texture Editor opens enter the following:

Layer 1

Type	Image Map
Layer Opacity	20.0%
Projection	Cubic
Image	DreadHullSpec.tga
Pixel Blending	Off
Texture Antialiasing	Off
Scale X	8.75m
Scale Y	8.75m
Scale Z	8.75m

Layer 2

Type	Image Map
Layer Opacity	100.0%
Projection	Cylindrical
Image	Lgtrust4_Spec.iff
Pixel Blending	Off
Texture Antialiasing	Off
Texture Axis	Y
Scale X	33m
Scale Y	148.085m
Scale Z	33m
Position X	0m
Position Y	296.17m
Position Z	0m

These settings will break up the specularity of the surface nicely. Instead of having a consistent, even specular highlight, it will have broken edges.

19. Next, click the Advanced tab in the Surface Editor and set the Color Highlights to 45.0 percent. This will color the highlight with 45 percent of the color you defined using the textures.

20. Lastly, click the Shaders tab.

21. Then click the Add Shaders bar, and select Fast Fresnel from the list. The fresnel effect is best explained by example.

    If you look directly at your computer monitor, the glass that makes the tube looks clear. As you move to the side and continue to look at the glass surface it will become more and more reflective and will have a higher specularity.

    Here's another example: When you drive down the road, look at the cars as they pass you. Notice the windows of the car. As the cars go by, the windows become more reflective, and at a certain point, they almost look mirror-like. This is the fresnel effect.

    Don't forget to look back at the car in front of you and slam on the brakes to keep from rear-ending them because you were not paying attention to the road!

22. Double-click the Fast Fresnel listing in the Shader list, and you will see the variables appear below it, as shown in Figure 8.55.

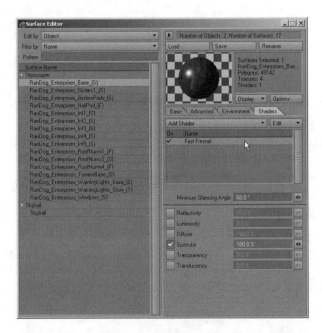

Figure 8.55   Adding the Fast Fresnel shader will help add realism to the base surface of the skyscraper.

23. Turn all options off, except the Specular field. Set it to 100.0 percent and set the Minimum Glancing Angle to 60.0 degrees.

24. That is it for the main part of the building. To copy the settings to the cylindrical part of the secondary building, right-click the name in the Surface Name list that is your source surface and select Copy. Conversely, you can double-click the surface preview to add the surface settings to the Preset shelf.

25. Select the name of the other surface by clicking it. Then right-click it and select Paste.

That is all there is to it.

26. Do the same for the surface of the antenna/warning lights as well.

> **Note**
>
> Rather than going through the model surface by surface and defining how everything is created, you can cut to the chase and see how the final scene looks by loading it from the CD. You have only a few minor changes to make, and these are covered in the following exercises.

Exercise 8.11   Surfacing the Skyscraper Window Interiors

To help the building look realistic, you created interiors during the modeling process. They are very simple, yet as you'll see, extremely effective. Placing smoothing on the surfaces of the interiors gives the appearance that there is some depth behind the windows.

It is very common to see beautiful buildings with flat, lifeless windows. There is a way to keep this from happening, and you already have taken the first steps in Modeler when you created the interiors with depth. By activating smoothing on the beveled interiors, it creates a virtual cup to which the images can be mapped. As you view the model from various locations in your scene, or when the camera moves past the building in an animation, the cupped effect makes it look like you have modeled interiors to the building.

1. To get started with surfacing the windows, first make sure that the basic settings for all of the Interior surface channels, in the Surface Editor, are as follows. These are labeled with the Int1 through Int5 extension:

Color	255, 255, 215
Luminosity	0%
Diffuse	80.0%
Specularity	0%
Reflection	0%
Transparency	0%
Bump	0%

As you can see from the parameters in the Surface Panel, there is not a lot going on here. This is because the interior surfacing is created mainly by using textures instead of overall, basic values.

2. To start the texturing, select the Color Texture button for the first interior and open the Texture Editor.

3. With the Texture Editor open, as you see in Figure 8.56, set the following:

Type	Image Map
Layer Opacity	65.0%
Projection	Cubic
Image	Building_Interior_1.jpg
Pixel Blending	Off
Texture Antialiasing	Off
Scale X	20m
Scale Y	20m
Scale Z	20m

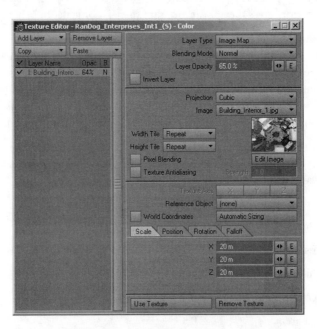

Figure 8.56   The basic color texture for the window interior surface uses a cubic image map.

4. Before closing the Texture Editor, click the Copy layer button (found below the Add Layer button at the top-left corner of the Editor). Select Current Layer from the menu.

5. Then click the Use texture button at the bottom of the panel.

6. Next, open the Texture Editor for the Luminosity channel.

7. Click the Paste button, which is found to the right of the Copy button you clicked previously, and select Replace Current Layer from the menu.

8. The only change you need to make is to set the Layer Opacity to 40 percent.

9. To break up the luminosity a bit more, click the Add layer button and select Procedural from the list.

10. For this layer, input the following, as shown in Figure 8.57.

Layer Opacity	50.0%
Procedural Type	Fractal Noise
Texture Value	32.0%
Frequencies	3
Contrast	1.63
Small Power	.5
Scale X	5m
Scale Y	5m
Scale Z	5m

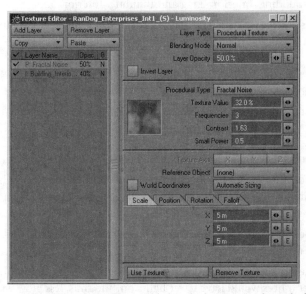

Figure 8.57   A small bit of Fractal Noise is added to the luminosity channel of the window interior surface. This will help "muck up" the surface.

11. When finished setting the values, click the Use texture button.

12. Click the texture button for Diffuse, and paste the layer like you did before, replacing the default layer.

13. Change the Layer opacity to 60 percent. Click the Use texture button.

14. To add a little more realism to the interior, switch to the Advanced tab in the Surface Editor, and set the Glow Intensity to 20 percent.

Even though this scene takes place during the day, lights will be on inside the building. Because of this, they need a bit of a glow. This is why you are adding it to the scene.

15. That completes the first interior of the building. Make sure that the first interior surface of the building is selected on the left side of the Surface Editor. Right-click its name and select Copy.

16. Click the remaining interiors one at a time, right-click, and then Paste the surface from the first interior. This will give you a great place to start the other interiors.

During the course of the creation of the other interior surfaces you will want to use a different interior image map—having the same one, even if it is modified in the various surface channels, will look repeated. Your image maps don't all have to be completely different; three total, one for each of the interiors, should be sufficient.

There are two other interior image maps to use. They are named, appropriately enough, Building_Interior_2.jpg and Building_Interior_3.jpg.

There also are other areas of the surface that you want to change to get the required variation across the whole building:

Diffuse	Vary on Surface Editor by +/–40%
Diffuse	Vary the Layer Opacities by +/–50%
Luminosity	Vary the Layer Opacities by +/–20%
Glow Intensity	Vary the Intensity by +/–10%

Keep the following guidelines in mind when you are adding variations to surfaces:

- Surfaces that reduce the amount of overall Diffuse also should have their Luminosity Layer Opacity and their Diffuse Layer Opacity reduced. Reducing these settings darken the surface.

- It would not make a lot of sense to lower the Diffuse value, and raise the others. The effects would be fighting each other.

- As the surfaces get darker, reduce the amount of glow. This makes sense, as darker offices would have fewer lights on, and thus, less glow would be emitted from the it.

- Do not make any office completely black.

Exercise 8.12   Surfacing the Skyscraper Glass

This last portion of texturing is very important because it involves the glass windows that cover the office interiors. Creating a realistic surface here is more involved than simply turning up the transparency. Sure, increasing the transparency value will enable you to see the interior of the building, but that effect alone will not look very real.

1. Begin by adding a touch of realism to the color channel amounts of the windows surface by using the following values (see Figure 8.58):

Color	199, 213, 214
Luminosity	0%
Diffuse	80.0%
Specularity	90%
Glossiness	60%
Reflection	20%
Transparency	75%
Bump	100%

    There is nothing particularly special about these settings. The fun begins when you add some Bump channel and start adding the fresnel effect.

2. With that said, open the Texture Editor for the Bump channel.

3. With the Texture Editor open, set the following values:

Layer Opacity	100.0%
Procedural Type	Fractal Noise
Texture Value	8.0%
Frequencies	3
Contrast	.5
Small Power	.5
Scale X	10m
Scale Y	10m
Scale Z	10m

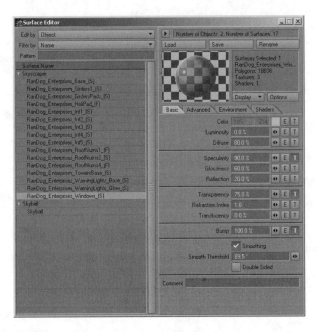

Figure 8.58   The basic surface properties are applied to the window surface.

The Bump texture is important. Having a very subtle, broad bump effect will give the windows just enough variation to make them look real and help with the reflection of the environment.

4. Speaking of environment, click the Environment tab so that you can set up the reflection options.

5. Under the Environment tab, change the Reflection Options to Ray Tracing + Spherical Map. For the Reflection Map, choose the skyball image.

6. After changing the reflection options, switch over to the Shaders tab. Similar to the procedure you used with the building, add the Fast Fresnel shader.

7. Double-click the Fast Fresnel listing in the shaders list to display its options. Enter the following values, as shown in Figure 8.59.

Minimum Glancing Angle	50°
Reflectivity	90.0%
Luminosity	Unchecked
Diffuse	Unchecked
Specular	100%
Transparency	0%
Translucency	Unchecked

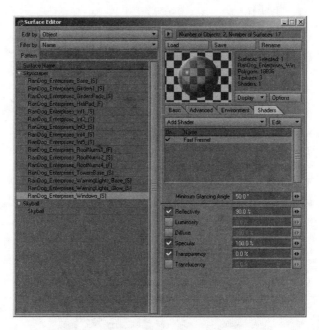

Figure 8.59   Adding the Fast Fresnel shader to the surface of the windows aids in the realism of the surface by varying the specularity, reflectivity, and transparency as seen through the camera.

It is important that you do not set the unchecked values to 0. This will tell the renderer that you want the channel affected and that at that glancing angle, you will see the effect.

Reflectivity is increased as the glancing angle increases. Specularity increases as well. Transparency on the other hand, is reduced.

Remember back in Modeler when you took the glass surfaces for the antenna/warning lights and cut and then pasted them to layer two? This was done for a reason!

8. To make sure the point lights can be seen, not blocked by the glass change to Object Selection mode, select the antenna/warning lights glass objects (layer 2). Be sure to save this glass surface setting for future projects.

9. Activate the Object Properties panel by pressing the p key.

10. With the panel open, disable all shadowing options for the glass objects, as you see in Figure 8.60.

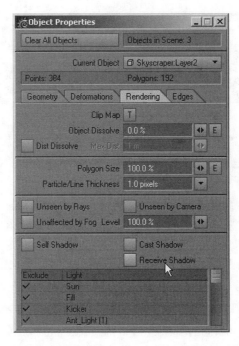

Figure 8.60   As you make sure that the lights shine through the glass surfaces on top of the skyscraper, the object does not have any ability to cast or receive shadows, as seen here in the Object Properties panel.

With the texturing completed, there are a few things you should do to your scene to make sure that it looks the best it possibly can.

To give the building more scale, add some fog to the scene. This will help tie the building to the background image.

To activate fog and change its parameters, open the Volumetric panel by selecting its name from the Effects heading under the Scene tab or by pressing the key combination of Ctrl+F6.

With the Volumetric Effects panel open, input the following:

Fog Type	Linear
Min Distance	0m
Max Distance	1.03km
Min Amount	10%
Max Amount	40%
Fog Color	160, 197, 201

The fog color was chosen here by bringing the skyball image into Adobe PhotoShop and using the color picker to select a color that best represented the fog in the image. If you want to adjust the amount of fog in the scene and get real-time feedback, open the Display Options panel by pressing the d key.

With the panel open, enable OpenGL Fog. You should now see the fog in Layout without having to render.

Lastly, you want to enable the glow effect. With the Volumetric panel still open, just select the Processing tab.

Check the Enable Glow button, set the Intensity to 60 percent and the Glow Radius to 8.0 pixels.

The Next Step

Guess what. That's it! You've now modeled, textured, surfaced, and lit a structure, and even added some fog to the scene. The techniques applied throughout this chapter apply to many types of scenes you'll encounter in your animation journeys. The advanced OpenGL architecture of LightWave 7, such as Fog in Layout, will make your job so much easier.

Summary

This chapter introduced you to modeling concepts that are common, everyday tools. For example, your created a basic profile of the skyscraper and used the Extrude tool to make the basic shape for the building.

The key is to take the example that you have worked through in this chapter and apply it to your own projects. Start with the key concepts and use the new tools you have learned to make your project come to life.

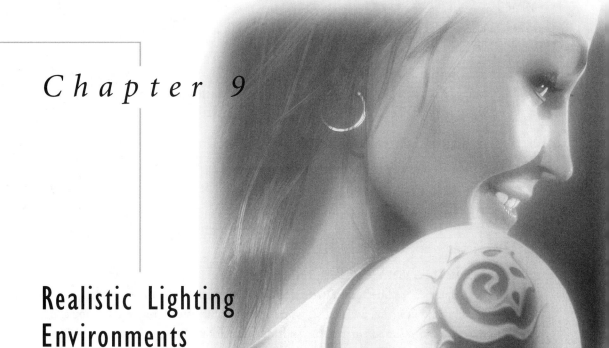

Chapter 9

Realistic Lighting Environments

Perhaps at one point in your career, you've

dabbled in photography or video. If so, you

know how important lighting is to a shot.

Light is everything. It can lift an atmosphere

or darken a mood. Light can warm a shot or make it feel cold. This chapter introduces you to the powerful lighting techniques available in LightWave 7. Specifically, you'll learn about the following:

- Proper light setups for radiosity effects
- Baking radiosity for walkthrough animations
- Creating caustics for glass
- Setting up lighting for sunlight

Project Overview

In Chapter 8, "Architectural Environments," you built a structure—a skyscraper. You surfaced and lit it. You added a sky and fog, and you created a realistic-looking scene. But you can go even further by utilizing the various light properties available in LightWave, and this chapter will help you do that.

In this chapter, you will light the interior of a simple room with radiosity and learn to "bake" it. This technique enables you to take the millions of calculations needed for rendering any apply them to an entire scene by rendering only one frame. The result is very realistic lighting produced in a 3D environment. The effect happens this way because in the real world, light bounces. If you have a window open in your room during the day, sunlight enters and bounces everywhere, lighting up the place. In the computer, without radiosity, the light only comes in the window. Unless additional lights are added in the scene, the other areas of the shot will remain dark.

You'll also learn about the caustics feature in LightWave 7, which is a real-world property that happens every day. A good example is the small area of light that a magnifying glass produces when light is refracted through it. Another example would be the patterns of light that reflect off of a shiny metal object onto another surface. Caustics add a realistic touch to your scene.

In addition to understanding and applying radiosity and caustics, you'll learn how to add volumetrics to your lights for an added effect.

Understanding Radiosity

You need to understand radiosity before you begin using it in your project. *Radiosity* is a rendering situation that calculates diffuse reflections of color and light from all surfaces in a scene. In 1984, a team at Cornell University published a paper called "Modeling the Interaction of Light between Diffuse Surfaces." This paper described a new rendering process called radiosity, a type of global illumination. You'll find a Global Illumination panel in the Lights tab in Layout that contains the radiosity controls.

Radiosity is the calculation of the rate at which light leaves a surface. This process calculates the diffused light of an entire surface, unlike ray tracing. Figure 9.1 shows a simple room with light coming through a window. This is a typical render. Figure 9.2 shows the same setup with radiosity turned on—a not-so-typical render. You don't always need lots of geometry and complex surfaces to achieve a realistic look when applying radiosity.

Figure 9.1   A simple room with a light shining through a window. The rest of the room is dark without radiosity.

Figure 9.2   Turning on radiosity makes the light bounce off of the floor and walls, lighting up the entire room. The light is soft and diffused.

Faking Radiosity

Although LightWave's radiosity feature can produce realistic results, you might want to fake radiosity effects so that you can cut down on the time you spend rendering your animations. The calculations LightWave needs to process for radiosity effects can often be time-consuming. When rendering multiple frames for an animation, your computer might be tied up calculating for days! But by "baking" the radiosity calculations, which you'll do later in the chapter, you can achieve radiosity effects without the cost of heavy render times.

You can fake radiosity effects by shining colored lights on the areas where the bounced light would be. For example, suppose that a light is shining through a window onto a wood floor. The walls are white. In the real world, the light would hit the brown wood floor and bounce to hit the walls and ceiling. A soft light matching the color of the floor can be pointed up toward the ceiling from the floor to simulate the bounced effect. Additionally, a smaller colored light can be pointed to the wall surface to give the appearance of the brown wood color bouncing.

Faking radiosity is common in many animation houses, and it is often quite effective. However, with processor speeds on PCs and Macintoshes reaching beyond 1,000MHz, you eventually won't need to worry about render times. Won't that be nice?

Understanding Caustics

Caustics are all around you. A caustic happens when light is reflected off a surface or shines through a transparent surface and creates a small area of light. A glass of water on a table in the sunlight will have caustics on the table because the light that is refracting through the glass, and then the water, focuses onto a small area of light. The reflections of light at the bottom of a pool or the hotspot generated from a magnifying glass are caustics. In this chapter, you'll place objects on a simple set and enable caustics to add to the scene's realism. Figure 9.3 shows glass objects lit on a set without caustics. Figure 9.4 shows the same setup with caustics turned on. Like radiosity, this feature is found in the Global Illumination panel (Lights tab).

Figure 9.3   Here are glass objects on a set, without caustics. Nothing happens to the light when it passes through the glass surfaces.

Figure 9.4   Turning on caustics takes the refracted light through the glass and creates an area of small light on the set.

Understanding Volumetrics

Volumetrics are lighting effects used for special effects and dramatic scenes. In the world around you, volumetrics can be seen on a sunny afternoon, when light streaks through a living room window. The visible beams from car headlights on a foggy road are volumetrics. Animators use volumetric lights to mimic real-world properties. Setting up volumetrics in LightWave is as easy as pushing the Volumetrics button, found within the Lights panel. Later in Chapter 17, "Broadcast-Style Animation," you'll use volumetric lighting for enhanced shots.

Interior Daylight

One of the great things about using radiosity is that it makes your job a lot easier when you are simulating indoor lighting. Wherever you are—at home, at work, in the car—the light from sources around you bounces off everything. In the daytime, the light shining through your window can easily light up the entire room. To simulate this in a 3D environment requires a lot of lights, which are cleverly diffused and set up to light all the areas in your 3D environment. A scene with radiosity not only makes your project look more real, but also saves you the headache of setting up multiple lights.

The lighting you choose to create in your 3D animations does more than simply light your scene. It also creates a mood. Mood lighting is used in films; it's that soft, hazy light shining through a café window in the morning. This light is warm and creates a mood that otherwise would be hard to produce. This next exercise guides you through creating a mood in a 3D environment using radiosity and volumetrics.

Exercise 9.1   Using Radiosity Lighting

This exercise requires only that you be patient and have a room with a view. That is to say, you need an object that has some surfacing inside and a window to the outside. This exercise uses the skyscraper object created in Chapter 8, which also is on the book's CD-ROM.

1. Open LightWave Layout, and load the scene labeled SimpleRoom_setup from the book's CD.

   The model on the CD is set up for you to work quickly and easily through these exercises. With some added detail and extra work, the room can be greatly enhanced.

Warning

This exercise uses a lot of processing power to handle the number of calculations needed for radiosity. Be sure that you have other programs closed when working with this scene to save on resources.

Figure 9.5 shows the room interior with a table and some colored boxes.

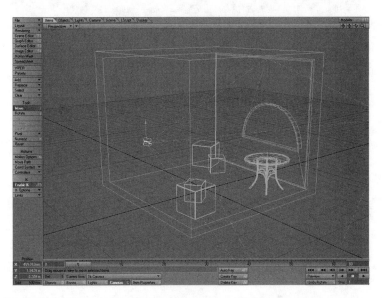

Figure 9.5   The interior of a simple room as seen through Layout, with some boxes and a table added.

2. Switch to Light Edit mode by selecting the Lights button at the bottom of the Layout window. There is only one light in the scene, so it will automatically be selected from the current item list at the bottom of Layout. Press 5 on the numeric keypad to select Light view. Select Move from the Items tab, press n to activate the numeric entry at the bottom left corner of the interface, and set the light to the values listed below.

Move:

Position X	–700mm
Position Y	3m
Position Z	5m

Then set the values for Rotate as follows:

Rotate:

Heading X	152°
Pitch Y	30°
Bank Z	0°

Figure 9.6 shows the view from the light source now in position with the preceding settings.

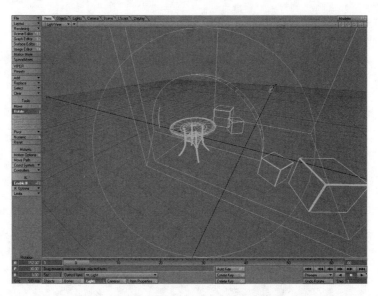

Figure 9.6   One spotlight in position, ready to calculate some radiosity lighting inside the room.

This light source will simulate sunlight coming through the window inside the room. The position you've set for the light is a good working position because it will shine through the window and cast shadows from the table and elements inside the room. Be sure to create a keyframe to lock the light's position in place.

3. With the light still selected, press the p key to enter the Light Properties panel. The tools you'll use also can be found directly in Layout under the Lights tab. You might find that it's most convenient, however, to see all of your lighting controls in one set place, like the Light Properties panel.

   A single spotlight exists in this scene and is the best light to use in this situation.

   Point lights do not direct the light with as much intensity as a distant light or spotlight. The controlled direction of a distant light or spotlight helps "charge up" the surface, meaning it will bounce light better. A point light will emit light in all directions.

4. Change the Light Intensity to 110 percent.

   Although the Light Intensity slider only brings the setting to 100 percent, you can manually enter values much higher. Remember that the sun is really bright (that's a technical term). Because this light needs to simulate sunlight, a brighter light is needed. In addition, the brighter light will help the radiosity solution.

   The objects—walls, floors, table, and so on—in this scene can't have pixel colors that are brighter than 100 percent (which is 255, 255, 255 RGB, or pure white), but with an intense light source (such as the one in this scene set at 110 percent), the bounced light fills the room. What happens is that the RGB values can exceed what would be 255 in a 24-bit image. A 0.0 to 1.0 range is encoded as 0 to 255. High dynamic range support allows pixel intensities to exceed this range. For example, you could have something like RGB 3.0, 0.5, 90.0. Internally, LightWave always uses HDR. Because HDR uses floating-point values, it can account for even more subtleties than possible within the 0 to 255 range.

Radiosity is merely the bouncing of light. LightWave's Radiosity feature allows you to light surfaces using light bouncing from other surfaces. Remember, too, that even if the RGB values don't exceed 1.0, the surface is still bouncing light, albeit very little. The only relationship between HDR data and radiosity is that HDR data lets you exceed the maximum amount of bounced light possible using 24-bit intensities. Even without HDR data (which can't really be turned off), you could still have radiosity. They are independent.

5. Set the Light Color to 250, 240, 200 RGB for a warm, off-white color.

6. Make sure that Shadow Type is set to Shadow Map. Also set both the Spotlight Cone Angle and the Spotlight Soft Edge Angle to 40 degrees. This will create a nice, soft falloff for the edge of the spotlight.

If you were to render the frame now, you would see something similar to the example shown in Figure 9.7. The light is falling nicely through the window of the room, but the rest of the interior is still dark. Now you need radiosity.

Figure 9.7 A single spotlight on the outside of the room works well to cast light through the window and light some of the interior objects. However, the rest of the room needs more light.

7. Click the Global Illumination panel, from either the Light Item Properties panel or the Lights tab directly in Layout (labeled Global Illum).

8. Click Enable Radiosity, which is in the middle of the Global Illumination panel.

This tells LightWave to calculate the diffused lighting when rendering. You won't see the effects in Layout's OpenGL display.

There are three types of Radiosity settings:

- Backdrop Only evaluates only rays that hit the backdrop.
- Monte Carlo and Interpolated are the same, except that Monte Carlo uses a zero tolerance and Interpolated lets you adjust tolerance.

9. Change the type to Interpolated. Make the Intensity 550 percent, and set the Tolerance to 0.25.

The Intensity setting is a setting you need to understand. You'll change the other values for the quality, and adjust the Intensity based on the how the render looks to you. Like many values in LightWave, this one can go well beyond 100 percent.

Without Intensity, you'll find yourself cranking up Light Intensity values to unrealistic levels. Radiosity Intensity gives you more control over your radiosity values. Try it out with different values to see the effects.

Note

Notice that there is an E button next to Intensity for Radiosity. You can envelope, or change the intensity over time, by clicking this button.

When Tolerance is less than zero, LightWave interpolates radiosity using previously calculated (stored) values instead of calculating radiosity for each "evaluation ray." Tolerance determines how much LightWave relies on these stored values. Using a lower number yields more accurate results.

10. Change the Rays Per Evaluation (RPE) to 11×33.

The Rays Per Evaluation setting determines the density of how many evaluation rays are sent off when radiosity is computed to shade a pixel. It's only a theoretical "hemisphere" used to determine the angles of the evaluation rays. You can set values from 1×3 to 16×48. This determines the number of radiosity rays sent out for evaluation. With a higher value, the quality is much better because LightWave is sending out more radiosity rays for evaluation—this, of course, requires more render time.

For example, suppose that you have a pixel that needs to be lit with radiosity. This is done after all other normal lighting and surface rendering is computed. The pixel says, "Okay, I'm going to send an evaluation ray off in this direction and see how much light I'm getting from there. I'll send another in that direction and see how much I'm getting from there." The Rays Per Evaluation setting determines how many and at what angle the evaluation rays are sent out. If RPE is set to 11×33, then 363 eval rays (11×33=363) are sent out for each evaluation pixel. If you have a scene with a lot of nooks and crannies, you need to use a lot of rays or the eval rays are likely to miss some spots.

Now, the Min Eval Spacing setting determines how close these evaluation points are set apart. Closer is more accurate, but renders longer.

Radiosity is bounced light. So, in the example of, say, the cover image of this book, a luminous polygon is placed in front of the face. The polygon isn't really a light source. With radiosity applied, the surface has additional lighting from the polygon. This feature places these hemispheres on surfaces that shoot out rays to detect illuminated surfaces. The Rays Per Evaluation setting determine the number of rays, and the Min Evaluation Spacing controls the spacing of these hemispheres. The hemisphere data is evaluated and the surface is lit accordingly.

Note

A good rule of thumb is to set up your radiosity scene with a low Rays Per Evaluation setting, and then increase the value for final renders.

The higher the setting for Rays Per Evaluation, however, the better the quality. Of course, this comes with a price. A higher value also will generate higher render times. Often, the results are worth it.

11. Set the Minimum Evaluation Spacing to 10mm.

The default setting is 20mm, and a lower value will make a better image but create longer render times.

12. Turn on Cache Radiosity.

This is useful when rendering an animation because it caches radiosity data for multiple render passes and frames. If you are antialiasing your final render (which you should do), cache radiosity will help save time during antialiasing passes.

When lights or objects are moving, however, this setting might produce inaccurate results because it is using the radiosity information from the initial rendered frame. If you are animating only the camera, the radiosity will still be the same.

13. Save the scene.

The settings you've applied here are for high quality, so you might want to set a lower resolution for testing. Press F9 to test the frame. Figure 9.8 shows the final frame.

Radiosity can add realism to your scenes. This example shows how one single light source can help illuminate the interior of a simple room or office. Often, certain structures are dark inside, and because of the way LightWave's radiosity engine works, you might need to add a few fake radiosity lights to help illuminate an interior. This is occasionally needed because the textures can be dark and not very luminous. You should work with brighter surfaces when possible and also try adding additional light sources. Your experimentation is key to the final image!

Figure 9.8   The interior of the room is now lit to photorealistic quality, thanks to radiosity. One spotlight outside the window is creating all the lighting in this shot. Cool, huh?

Volumetric Lighting

With radiosity being such a cool thing, it's hard to imagine that you can enhance the visuals of a scene even more. But you can further improve things by using volumetric lighting. This feature enables your light to have physical volume. Some examples of this are the huge search beams soaring into the sky at a movie premier or a searchlight in a storm. You also can use volumetric lights for stage-lighting a rock concert or even to create simple hazy atmospheres.

Volumetrics can have shadows, which is especially cool for realistic effects. For example, a spotlight behind a logo with volumetrics applied can have the beam of light broken where the geometry is—in effect, making the light "spill" out from behind the logo. Figure 9.9 shows a simple volumetric example with one spotlight.

Exercise 9.2   Applying Volumetric Lighting

This exercise continues using the same scene from the first exercise in this chapter. The use of volumetric lighting along with radiosity can produce realistic images.

1. In Layout, load the SimpleRoom_rad scene from the book's CD-ROM. This is the simple room scene from Exercise 9.1 with radiosity applied.

2. Make sure that Enable Radiosity is off, in the Global Illumination panel (Lights tab).

3. Back in Layout, select the light and go to the Lights tab, or choose the light's Item Properties (p).

Figure 9.9   A single spotlight with volumetric lighting applied. Notice how the beam of light is visible but breaks through the text object.

4. Click Volumetric Lighting for the light (listed as Vol Lighting in the Lights tab in Layout). When the Light Properties become available, click the Volumetric Light Options button to enter the Volumetric Options for Light panel, as seen in Figure 9.10.

   Instead of adjusting the settings in the panel and guessing what the outcome will be, you can use VIPER to see firsthand what the values do.

Note

You can find more info on using VIPER, the virtual interactive preview renderer, in Chapter 2, "LightWave 7 Surface Editor."

Figure 9.10   You can display the Volumetric Options for Light panel from the Lights tab in Layout or through the Light Properties panel.

5. Click the VIPER button at the left of the Layout interface. Move the open Volumetric panel to the side of the screen so that both panels are visible, and click the Render key within the VIPER window to see the volumetric light in VIPER.

   Don't be alarmed when the image looks washed out—remember that shadows do not show up in VIPER. Because the light source is outside the window, the rendered volumetric will be partially blocked by the window and wall of the room—this helps create the streaks of light.

   Now, when you make changes to the volumetric settings, the result will update in VIPER, giving you instant feedback.

6. In the Volumetric Options panel, set the Quality to Good.

   You'll always want to start out at low quality, test the render, and then increase the quality as needed. The Good setting is neither low nor high quality—sort of right in the middle. The higher the quality, the more render time you'll need.

   Now it's time to adjust the Cone Base to see how large the volumetric light will be. The Grid Square Size for this scene (found in the information panel at the bottom left of the Layout interface) is 500mm.

7. Set the Cone Base to 1m to make the volume light glare a little more than halfway into the VIPER frame. This also will set the start of the volumetric toward the base of the light. You'll see a white cone outline representation on the light source in Layout.

   The Cone Base setting is available because a spotlight is being used in the scene. If you had used a point light, this setting would be listed as Radius, not Cone Base. A point light is omnidirectional, so it requires a radius. Distant lights also will use a radius setting along with height, while a spotlight uses only height values. Radius and height determine the size of the volumetric light.

8. The Height Value setting should be set to 10m. You can change this value lower or higher and instantly see the effects in the VIPER window. Change Luminosity to 180 percent.

   This will make the volumetric source nice and bright.

9. Bring the Opacity setting to 160 percent.

   This setting tells LightWave how transparent the volumetric is. The setting of 0 percent tells LightWave to create solid volumetrics. A setting of 100 percent would make a transparent volumetric. As before, adjust this setting and watch the change in the VIPER window.

10. Change Attenuation to 20 percent.

    This setting is a falloff setting for the volumetric. Attenuation makes the volumetric effect fade off from the origin. In this scene, the volumetric light needs to be bright at the window, but then dissipate as it reaches the other side of the room. A fair Attenuation setting fits the bill for this exercise.

11. In conjunction with Attenuation, set the Red Shift to 10.

Red Shift controls the activity of the light, similar to the real world. Essentially, during a sunset, for example, the atmosphere does not diffuse the red colors, nor do they have attenuation—they don't fall off. Setting the Red Shift above 0 percent tells the volumetric to allow the color red from the source to bleed through.

12. Set the Density to 40 percent. This setting tells the volumetric light to be more or less dense, like a thick fog.

13. Leave the Specify Medium Color setting for the volumetric at its default white. For special effects, such as green oozing light coming from a dungeon, you can set the color of the volumetric. Press F9 to render-test the volumetric in the scene.

Note

Volumetrics add some time to rendering, so from the Camera panel, set your resolution Multiplier to 25 percent and turn of Antialiasing. This will help you see quickly the volumetric effects in the scene. When the settings render just the way you want, render the frame at a higher resolution with Antialiasing turned back on.

Figure 9.11 shows the render with the volumetric lighting applied. If you apply radiosity to the image, you add significantly to your render times, but enhance the image. Using volumetric lighting in a scene also is a great way to add brightness and atmosphere without adding more lights to the scene. In addition, add some interior lights, such as candles and real or faked radiosity lights, for an even greater appeal.

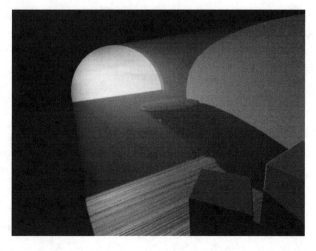

Figure 9.11   Volumetric lights are applied to a spotlight, creating glares of light streaking through a window.

You can apply volumetrics quickly in LightWave, especially with VIPER. Once you've test-rendered a frame of your scene by pressing F9, you'll be able to see that render in the VIPER window while setting up the volumetric. Remember, though, you won't see the shadows with VIPER; instead, you'll see only the full frame render (F9).

In addition to adding simple volumetric effects to your lights, you can add textures. At the bottom of the Volumetric Options for Light panel is the Edit Texture button. Clicking this button guides you into the ever-familiar Texture panel you see throughout LightWave. Here, you can apply procedurals, images, or even gradients to volumetric lights. Here's a great example: A movie projector is playing a film, projecting on a screen in the 3D movie house you made. You can load a sequence of frames, or a QuickTime or .AVI movie, and apply it as a projection image to the light. Turn on volumetrics and the sequence will shine through the volumetric light, picking up colors and shapes, just as it would in the real world. Try it out!

Environmental Radiosity

You're probably reading the word "environmental" often in this chapter, but it has important meaning to many aspects of LightWave. This next section sheds some light (figuratively) on the uses of environmental lighting. It also will teach you how you can quickly render full animations with Radiosity using LightWave's Baking feature.

Environmental lighting is another way to light your 3D worlds with real photographs, and the result is photorealistic lighting. Figure 9.12 shows the skyscraper from Chapter 8 rendered with some generic lights and radiosity. It's nice, and it looks great. The light is hot on the side of the building but the shadows falling in between aren't too dark. The Radiosity helps create a more even light throughout the image. The lighting in this scene uses an environmental map of a real photograph. Using radiosity, LightWave takes the millions of colors and variations in the image and uses them to light the geometry in the scene.

HDRI: High Dynamic Range Images

Computer systems represent color on a 24-bit spectrum. Each of the colors of the spectrum (red, green, and blue) are 255 at their highest values. High Dynamic Range (HDR) images can store more data than the standard 24 bits per pixel. HDRI formats can store RGB values greater than 255. So, although a normal image format maxes out at RGB 100 percent, 100 percent, 100 percent (RGB 255, 255, 255), an HDRI image (or LW internally) could have a pixel-shaded RGB of 300 percent, 50 percent, 9000 percent. You can't see this much information onscreen, but the information is used for situations, such as radiosity for added brightness from a surface. LightWave can load HDR images, such as Flexible Format, TIFF LogLuv, or Radiance HDR images. An easy way to see HDR values is to render your room scene using the Image Viewer FP. Place your mouse over the rendered image and you'll see pixel values appear such as 132.67 percent, 116.44 percent, 78.17 percent, and 100.17 percent. These will appear in the top title bar of the Image Viewer. The first three numbers are the RGB values (100 percent = 255). The fourth number is the alpha.

Figure 9.12   The skyscraper is lit with conventional lighting and some added fog. It's a great-looking image, but it also can be lit with radiosity.

LightWave always respects and internally computes RGB values greater than 255. The setting doesn't necessarily have to be pure white. It could be RGB 143 percent, 44 percent, 87 percent. To retain the extra HDRI data, you just need to save in a file format that supports it.

Using the HDR Expose plug-in from the Image Filters plug-in list "normalizes" HDR data. That is, it scales (in a nonlinear manner, of course) the HDR 0-to-infinity range to normal (0 to 255). You use this feature to brighten up HDR images instead of cranking up lights. This plug-in predates radiosity intensity. You might also increase radiosity intensity instead of using this, but both functions can be used to achieve the same result.

From the Backdrop tab of the Effects panel in Layout, you can select the Image World environment plug-in to enhance your renders. Selecting this feature allows you to place a Light Probe image into your scene. LightWave will wallpaper this image around your scene setup. By adding radiosity to the render, the image will light your scene.

This is a cool technique to apply, depending on the type of scene you're creating. Perhaps your object has very intricate facets and levels, making shadows a real problem. Using radiosity with a Light Probe image can add realism to your scene. LightWave will use the color values and brightness of the image to light your scene, rather than conventional lighting methods. The result: more realistic-looking lighting.

Baking Radiosity

The downside to radiosity is that it takes more time to render, especially when working with interiors. Interior shots truly can benefit from calculated radiosity, but often the render times are unreasonable. LightWave, however, allows you to "bake" in the radiosity calculations. What this means is that you simply render one frame with radiosity on, and LightWave will record that data for future frames. If you consider the results, it is often the best way to go for photorealistic walkthrough rendering. The process is simple, requiring only a few steps, outlined here.

Exercise 9.3   Baked Interior Lighting

1. Open Modeler, and load the SimpleRoom_Rad object from the book's CD. This is the same simple room object, except that this time, all of the objects are placed in one single layer. This is beneficial for saving time when "baking" radiosity.

2. Press the a key to fit everything to view. In the bottom right of the Modeler interface, select the T button. Then, to the right, click the drop-down list and choose New. The Create UV Texture Map appears.

3. Select Atlas as the map type. This will separate your object (visually) based on its objects—sort of unwrapping it to create a UV Map. Figure 9.13 shows the Create UV panel.

   Simply put, UV mapping enables you to tack an image onto your model. The points of the model act as tacks, and adjusting any of these tacks adjusts the UV-mapped image.

   Notice that the three layers of the simple room object were selected by default when the object was loaded into Modeler and the UV map was created.

4. Type a name, if you like, or leave the name Texture by default. Click OK once you've chosen Atlas as Map Type. Leave all other settings alone.

5. It will look like nothing happened, but don't be fooled. In the Top viewport, change the Render Style to UV Texture, and you'll see the unwrapped object appear. Press a to fit. Figure 9.14 shows the interface.

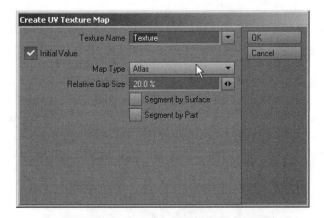

Figure 9.13   Access the Create UV Texture Map panel in Modeler to create a UV map for the simple room.

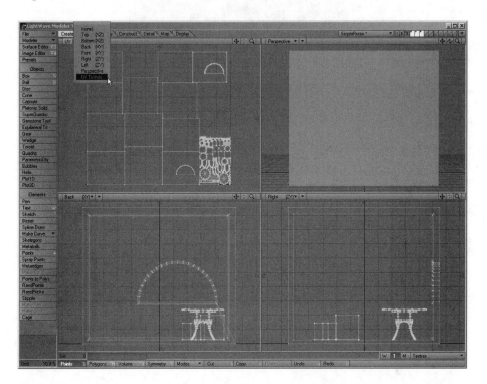

Figure 9.14   In a viewport, select UV Texture as the view type, and you'll see your unwrapped object.

6. There's one more thing you need to do, and that's to make sure that you are working only with polygons made up of three or four vertices. Select Polygon mode from the bottom of the interface, and press the w key to bring up the Statistics panel.

7. Look at the panel and you'll see that there's a bold listing for >4 Vertices (see Figure 9.15). This says that there are polygons made up of more than 4 vertices. Press the plus sign to the left to select them. Once selected, press Shift+t to triple (triangulate) those polygons. You'll see that in the Statistics panel, the listing for >4 Vertices is no longer bold.

Figure 9.15   Using the Polygon Statistics panel (w), you can quickly select polygons with more than four vertices.

8. Now save your object and return to Layout.

9. Load the SimpleRoom_rad scene from the book's CD. Then select the SimpleRoom:Layer1 listing from the bottom of the screen.

10. From the Items tab, select Replace, and then choose Replace with Object File. Replace the object with the object for which you created a UV Map in Modeler.

You're doing this because the SimpleRoom_rad scene has all the necessary lighting set up. So, instead of setting up a new scene, you can simply replace the objects in the already lit scene. Just be sure to save it under a different name.

11. Once the object has been replaced, open the Surface Editor. Select the WallsZ surface, and click the Shaders tab.

12. Select Surface Baker from the list. Double-click it to open the panel, as shown in Figure 9.16. Leave all the settings at their defaults because these are the most common.

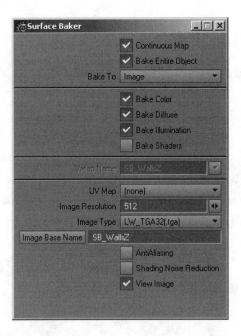

Figure 9.16   Display the Surface Baker interface from the Surface Editor. Here you tell LightWave how to "bake" your surface, where to save the image, and more.

Note

It's important to remember that you need to bake only one surface. All the surfaces for the same object get baked when you select Bake Entire Object in the Surface Baker panel.

13. However, from the UV Map listing, select the UV Map you created in Modeler for the object. Change the Image Type to LW_TGA24.

14. Click the Image Base Name to tell LightWave where to store the baked (recorded) image. Finally, set the Resolution to about 800. This is important because LightWave is creating a rendered image that then will be mapped throughout your scene, so you'll want good resolution.

15. Close the panel and push F9 to render the current frame. Remember that Radiosity was set for the scene, which is the reason you're using the Surface Baker feature.

LightWave then begins rendering. Shortly, you'll see a panel pop up giving you the status: Baking in Progress.

16. Once the baking process is complete, the baked image will appear, as shown in Figure 9.17. Note that you need to have View Image selected in the Surface Baker control options (refer to Figure 9.16) to see this. This is only a preview—the image is still saved after it's baked.

Figure 9.17   The final baked image is displayed when the View Image selection is chosen in the Surface Baker panel.

17. Now the fun part begins. Go to the Global Illumination panel, and turn off Radiosity. Be sure to remove the Surface Baker plug-in in the Surface Editor panel.

Because you just baked the radiosity, LightWave has recorded all the info of the radiosity calculations and created one large image file. This image file will be mapped on the entire scene using the UV map you created earlier. See how this works?

18. Go to the Surface Editor and select all the surfaces in the scene. You can do this by selecting the first surface, holding the Shift key, and then selecting the last surface. All the surfaces in-between will be selected.

19. Click the T button next to Color to open the Texture Editor. Set the following:

Layer Type	Image Map
Blending Mode	Normal
Layer Opacity	100%
Projection	UV
UVMap	(Whatever you named the UV in step 4, such as Texture)
Image	Select Load Image, and choose the image you just baked and saved
Pixel Blending	On
Texture Antialiasing	Off

Note

In this exercise, you've baked only an image for the room. Surface Baker bakes all of the surfaces in the same object. If the table and block layers are in different layers and thus different objects, you'll need to apply Surface Baker on one of the table surfaces and on one of the box surfaces as well. You can use those two image maps with the same UV you created earlier and get the results you want.

20. You do not need to click Automatic Sizing. A UV map is already perfectly sized. Finally, click Use Texture to close the Texture Editor panel.

21. With all the surfaces still selected, bring Luminosity to 100 percent and Diffusion to 0 percent. Doing this tells LightWave to display the applied UV image to its full brightness, while not accepting any light from the scene.

Be sure that you have the OpenGL Textures option selected in the Display Options tab (d) to see textures in Layout. You should see the baked image applied to your entire room!

Now all you need to do is set up any camera moves and render! The calculated radiosity is now applied as an image map throughout the scene.

You are essentially rendering a scene now with no lights or shadows and no radiosity, using only geometry and image maps. The result? Fast renders! Baking is cool! Figure 9.18 shows the final image, which took only seconds to render versus minutes with radiosity applied.

Figure 9.18   The final baked image is applied as a UV map to all the surfaces at once in the scene. Renders now look like radiosity was used, but the scene is merely an image map.

That's the power of Surface Baking with Radiosity. This technique, while great for walkthroughs, is not ideal for applications like character animation, although you can use it for such things. The reason it's not good for character animation is that a character would be moving in a scene. A moving character will change the shadows and amount of bounced light in a scene, adversely affecting the radiosity. What you would need to do in that case is render and bake the radiosity solution, as you did with the previous exercise. From there, you can add lights that are the same color as the radiosity and "fake" it on a character. This way, your character can move through the scene without you having to render a full radiosity solution for each frame.

As always, experiment on your own with this technique. Trust in the fact that if you do architectural renderings for a living and can offer full radiosity walkthroughs to your clients, business will skyrocket. Only you will know the secret that the radiosity is calculated only once, saving you oodles of time. Time is money, folks!

Adding Caustics

Caustics can also produce realistic results when applied correctly. This next exercise instructs you in two areas: surfacing glass objects for use with caustics, and applying caustics to objects in a scene.

Exercise 9.4   Tabletop Realism

For this exercise, you can start with the simple glass ball objects from the CD-ROM accompanying this book. You will set the parameters of the glass surface using one area light and a basic set.

1. Begin by saving any work you've done in Layout, and load the BaseCaustic scene from the book's CD. Figure 9.19 shows the loaded scene.

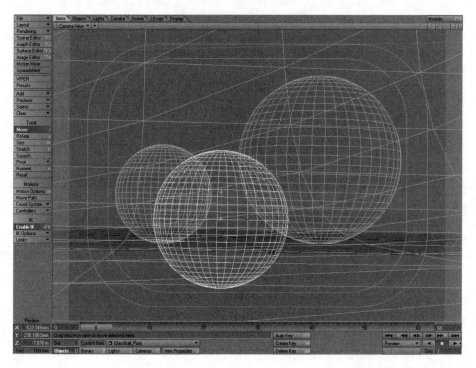

Figure 9.19   Here, glass balls sit on a set, a reflector object resides in front of the balls, and both are set and ready for refraction and caustics.

The scene contains three glass balls, a small set below them, and an area light above and in back of the objects.

2. Go to the Surface Editor and select the GlassBall_Teal surface. Set the Color to a bluish green, RGB 192, 226, 215. Leave the Luminosity at 0 percent, and change the Diffuse to 95 percent.

3. Change the Specularity to 70 percent for a shiny glass surface, and bring the Glossiness to 40 percent. This will create a medium-size hotspot on the glass ball. A higher Glossiness would create a smaller hotspot, giving the surface the appearance of highly glossed ball.

4. Set the Reflection to 5 percent.

5. Change the Transparency to 100 percent.

   You might think that a 100 percent transparent object would be invisible, right? Well, in fact it wouldn't show up at all in the render. However, an everyday glass is transparent, but what makes it visible is a combination of reflection and refraction.

6. Set the Refraction Index to 1.33. The higher the value, the more refraction will occur. Water and glass typically have a refraction value of around 1.33.

7. Bring Translucency up to 100 percent to help the light pass through the glass ball. Smoothing should be turned on.

   You need to tell LightWave to calculate the reflections and refraction. By default, the Environment tab within the Surface Editor lists the Reflection Options as Ray Tracing and Backdrop; however, this setup will use the Ray Tracing and Spherical Map option.

8. Under the Environment tab of the Surface Editor, for the GlassBall_Teal surface, set the Reflection Options to Ray Tracing and Spherical Map. Make the Reflection Map Fractal Reflections. This is a fractal image on the book's CD. Simply select Load Image from the Reflection Map drop-down list to load the image.

9. Click the Shaders tab in the Surface panel, and from the Add Shader drop-down list, select Edge_Transparency. When loaded, double-click it in the list to open its controls. Make sure that the Edge Transparency is set to Opaque, as shown in Figure 9.20.

10. Under the Advanced tab of the Surface Editor, bring the Color Filter value to 100 percent. The tools in this tabbed area allow you to set features that are not commonly used but are key for certain situations. The Color Filter setting, for example, is perfect for glass. This will color the light source traveling through the transparent surface.

11. Go to the Render Options panel and make sure that Ray Trace Shadows, Ray Trace Reflection, and Ray Trace Refraction are turned on. These are all heavy-duty render killers, meaning they take a long time to render, but the results are worth it.

Note

You can speed up render times when using Ray Tracing by changing the Extra Ray Trace Optimization value from the default 16 to 8 or lower.

12. Press F9 to render a frame. Make a low-resolution render to save on rendering time from the Camera panel if you need to. Figure 9.21 shows the rendered image.

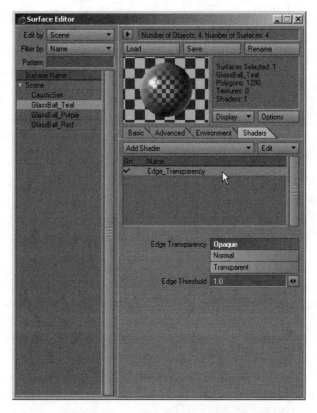

Figure 9.20   The Edge_Transparency shader for the GlassBall_Teal surface helps give the surface an opaque look.

Figure 9.21   Although only one light exists in the scene behind the objects, a transparent refractive surface on the glass ball allows the light to pass through.

13. Feel free to play with the lighting and refraction levels for different looks. When you're satisfied, save your objects and save your scene.

14. Now you can copy and paste the surface settings from the GlassBall_Teal surface to the two other glass balls. You can do this in two ways. Either double-click the surface sample preset display at the top of the Surface Editor to save the surface in the Preset shelf or simply right-click the surface listing. Right-clicking on a surface listing in the Surface Editor allows you to copy and paste. Pick a method and copy the surface for GlassBall_Teal.

> **Tip**
> You can use the Preset shelf for long-term storage and retrieval of surface settings. One-time copy and paste are best handled by using the right mouse button operation. There is a third way that involves loading and saving a surface file by using the Save and Load buttons at the top of the Surface Editor.

15. Select the GlassBall_Purple surface and paste the copy. Do this by right-clicking and selecting Paste (which will paste what you right clicked and copied). Or, you can double-click the surface preset you made for the Preset shelf.

16. Once the surface is copied, simply change the color to a soft purple, about 189, 136, 193 RGB. Copy and paste again for the GlassBall_Red surface and make the color 209, 78, 58 RGB.

    By copying and pasting the GlassBall_Teal surface, you save a lot of time resetting similar surfaces. All you needed to do is change the color. This also helps keep your objects consistent in all settings.

> **Note**
> You also could have selected all three surfaces and changed the parameters for all settings at the same time. Then, you could go back, selecting a specific individual channel and change it's specific color. If you do this, you'll need to re-add the Shader in the Shaders tab. Shaders do not apply to multiple surfaces and must be applied one surface at a time.

17. Go to the Global Illumination panel (Lights tab) and click Enable Caustics. Turn on Cache Caustics (which will save data for subsequent renders, similar to Cache Radiosity discussed earlier) and set the Intensity to 60 percent. This is a scaling factor for the brightness of the caustic.

18. Set the Accuracy to 200.

    This value can range from 1 to 10,000, and the higher it is, the more time is required to calculate the caustic. On a simple water glass, an accuracy of 120 is fine. More complex objects with multiple caustics would require a higher accuracy.

19. Finally, set Softness to 20.

This evaluates the surrounding caustic rays when rendering. A higher softness results in blurrier caustics, while a lower softness results in sharper caustics. If the caustic appears blotchy and not so smooth, the Softness setting can be increased, but the accuracy setting needs to be increased as well.

Figure 9.22 shows the final rendered image with reflection, refraction, shadows, radiosity, and caustics applied. Load up the Caustic scene from the book's CD-ROM to see the final scene.

Figure 9.22   Some of LightWave's heavy render hogs are at work: ray tracing, and caustics. Quite nice, but expensive rendering times.

 Tip

Try applying Refraction Blurring from the Environment tab of the Surface Editor. A setting of 15 percent or so is a good place to start. What this will do is blur the refraction effects, enhancing realism.

The Next Step

Although caustics and radiosity are cool tools in LightWave, using them together can cramp your style—well, at least your render times. As you work through the other examples in this book, think of ways you can incorporate the information in this chapter. *Inside LightWave 7* shows you that radiosity is good for lighting not just interiors, but 3D images of people as well, such as the cover of this book. Chapter 10, "Organic Modeling," will guide you through modeling, texturing, and lighting a human body with radiosity.

Summary

This chapter introduced you to radiosity and caustics and provided you with a number of practical, real-world examples. You've seen radiosity applied with individual lights, and you've used it to create dynamic interior lighting environments. These techniques can be taken further with the use of HDR images.

You also learned about caustics and saw how applying them can add realism to your scenes. With area lights, and additional LightWave tools such as the Image World and baking technology, your images can look amazingly real. Just imagine what you can do with more experimentation and practice! Before you send your computer off to render-render land, move on to Chapter 10 and learn how to build the best human head around.

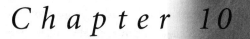

C h a p t e r   10

Organic Modeling

If you read *Inside LightWave [6]*, you might
be familiar with this chapter. Although
new tutorials are included in every other
chapter of *Inside LightWave 7*, the tutorial

in Chapter 10 of *Inside LightWave [6]* was so popular that we decided to retool it for this book. That tutorial, originally written by Stuart Aitken—who, incidentally, created the cover image for this book—has been updated for use with LightWave 7.

This chapter carefully guides you through a project containing all the stages required to build a realistic 3D model of a young woman's head. The tutorial consists of several parts, and it might take you some time to complete. It deals with advanced modeling issues, so you should be fairly comfortable modeling with LightWave 7's toolset before tackling it.

Organic modeling is the process of creating objects that can't be created with only primitive shapes. Buildings, roads, computers, and many other objects can be built with simple boxes, balls, cones, and discs. But more organic or natural objects, such as the human form, need a different approach to be created in 3D. Figure 10.1 shows a render of the head used for the cover model of this book, which is the subject of this chapter.

Figure 10.1   This chapter will teach you how to model, texture, and light a young woman's face. The finished model is shown here.

Project Overview

The face has been the most favored subject of artists—professional, budding, or otherwise—throughout history, and it's no different in today's world of 3D computer graphics. The reasons for this are fairly obvious. You are surrounded by people's faces every day of your life, and they are your primary means of communicating and showing your feelings—happy or sad, angry or serene. As such, people tend to be fascinated by looking at faces.

Ironically, it is this kind of ubiquitous interest and familiarity that makes re-creating faces realistically one of the hardest tasks for any artist, digital or otherwise. Everyone is an expert on the face, and everyone will sense when you've gotten it wrong.

In addition, a face, in a purely abstract sense, is actually a complex structure of interlocking shapes and forms. But don't worry. In the following sections, you're going to break down what might initially seem like a daunting task into manageable chunks that you should be able to follow relatively easily. With a modicum of artistic ability, you should soon have a new head to be proud of. In this chapter, you will learn to

- Create a photorealistic female head
- Use LightWave's advanced texture-mapping tools to create realistic surfaces
- Paint and create texture maps
- Set up lighting for a human head with radiosity

Using SubPatch Surfaces to Model the Head

The tutorial steps throughout this chapter are geared toward using Modeler's SubPatch surfaces.

Although they are the easiest and most intuitive methods in LightWave for modeling free-flowing organic subjects, like most 3D tools SubPatch surfaces tend to require you to work in specific ways to make the most out of them. The first few sections of this chapter outline some basic techniques for working with SubPatch surfaces. As well as heads, this chapter also gives you a good foundation for modeling any kind of organic geometry.

Organic Model Preparation

When using SubPatch surfaces, you don't have to worry about adding more geometry to make a surface smooth, as you would with normal polygonal modeling, because the software takes care of that for you. If you need the model to be smoother, you can turn up the patch resolution (particularly now that LightWave can render SubPatched objects directly in Layout). With a SubPatched object, you will create a cage, which is a simplified mesh. You can control this mesh to shape and form your object.

Controlling Curves

When modeling with SubPatch surfaces, the main way to control the curvature or tightness of a surface is to increase or decrease the number of polygons (and thus, vertices) in the control cage mesh. You can deliberately ignore point weighting here because in complex objects that method won't produce the required results (because there is no control over the direction of the effect). Figure 10.2 shows an example.

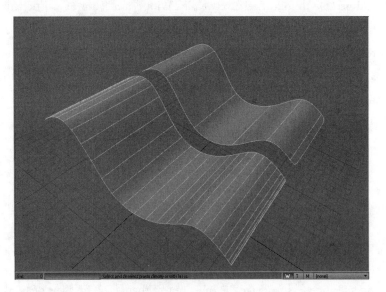

Figure 10.2   The density of the control mesh relates to the curvature of the underlying shapes.

To achieve a proper balance, tightly defined areas of a model with harder edges or a lot of detail will need several vertices to accurately define the shape. Fewer control vertices should be used to define flat or smooth areas. When working with curves, remember the following:

- Having too many control vertices in the control mesh is inefficient and makes editing or altering an object time consuming and difficult.

- Having too few vertices in the cage might make it close to impossible to accurately define the exact shape you need.

- Aim to get your model just right with just enough polygons to define the shape you want in a specific area. (This often takes a bit of trial and error.)

Both objects in Figure 10.2 are identically shaped, but the one farthest away uses fewer vertices to achieve the same result—this will be easier to adjust or sculpt. Because sculpting (basically, pushing and pulling vertices around) takes up the vast majority of modeling time (or should if you're doing things right), making the process as easy as possible should be a priority.

Following Contours

The next thing to consider when building organic models is that because SubPatched surfaces are built primarily from quad polygons (polygons made up of four points), they tend to form grid-like structures. How these grids or patches align with the underlying form of the surface is important. Generally you should get the grid to follow the natural contours of the model. This has several advantages:

- It leads to a more efficient use of geometry. (Again, the fewer polygons and vertices you can get away with using, the better.)

- It makes the underlying surface much easier to follow, and therefore edit.

To better illustrate how a grid formation should follow the contours of an object, take a look at Figure 10.3. You can see that the control mesh is easier to follow because it follows the natural contours of the polygonal shape. Figure 10.3 shows how the control mesh does not follow the natural contours of the shape, making it harder to manage and edit.

To quickly recap, an easily editable cage relies on the following:

- Getting the quad patch structure of the control mesh to flow with the contours of the model.

- Getting the right number of control polygons to achieve the appropriate curvature in various parts of the model.

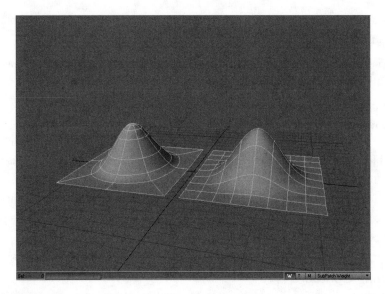

Figure 10.3   When building geometry, you should try to follow the natural contours of the model, such as the hump on the right.

Following these guidelines will make the job of shaping the forms of the human face much easier. The more ideal the control cage structure you create for the surface at hand, the more you can concentrate solely on the sculpting process of molding the surface without having to wrestle with the inherent behavior of the SubPatch itself.

Okay, enough of the textbook stuff. How does all this work in the real world? How do you achieve this mythical, "structural" balance with models, such as a human head, that have lots of smooth areas joining against areas with a lot more detail; where the contours of the model flow one way here, and a completely different way there?

Well, basically, you have to compromise. Most "real-world" approaches can be reduced to two opposing camps, with associated pros and cons.

The Box Approach

One way is to create the basic, general forms of the model first and then selectively add more detail as needed. This method is called the "box approach," as it generally entails starting with a rough box and then refining the model by dragging points, stretching, slicing, knifing, beveling, and smooth-shifting various bits as you work down to the areas of small detail.

Although generally a fast and intuitive way to model for most people, this approach also can be rather chaotic. Unless you're either very adept at it, or very careful, the polygon structure created along the way tends to favor the broader forms of the model (that is, what you started with) at the expense of the detailed areas, where things can often get a little tricky.

The Detail-Out Approach

The second way to model is to start with the detailed areas in isolation first, where it is relatively easy to construct them with an ideal polygon structure. Work your way from there, dealing with how these areas join into the whole later, as you work outward. This is called the "detail-out" method.

Modeling this way is definitely a more structured process than the box method but, again, things can sometimes get tricky when you have to join all the separate bits neatly. Despite this limitation, the detail-out approach makes modeling complex objects and, especially human head models, a bit easier. This is the approach you'll use in this chapter.

The most important parts of the human face are the mouth and eyes because they are the most expressive. For this reason, a detail-out modeling approach works well. Additionally, these parts must usually be able to deform in carefully controlled ways if you are thinking about making expressions later on. Therefore, they require an ideal control structure. By building a proper control structure, or mesh, of the expressive areas of the face first, you'll eliminate the difficulty of shaping and modifying the object to your desired shape. Properly modeling the expressive areas of the face first makes joining them with the rest of the head much easier.

Using Background Template Images

A potential drawback to modeling using the detail-out method is that by concentrating on smaller areas first, it is easy to lose a sense of the overall proportions of the model. For this reason, it's important to use background images, as shown in Figure 10.4, to guide you as you work.

For the purposes of this tutorial, two images—a front and a side view of the head—are included on the book's CD-ROM to help you get started. They are FaceFront.bmp and FaceSide.bmp (Projects/Images/Chapter10/background_template). When following these techniques on your own projects, try to make or acquire similar templates; a simple rough sketch will do, as long as the overall proportions are correct. If you are modeling from a real-life subject, try to get photographic equivalents or use a mirror.

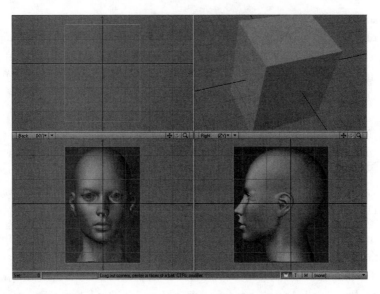

Figure 10.4   These background template images were set up in Modeler.

Exercise 10.1   Setting Up Background Images

For this exercise, begin in LightWave Modeler. You don't need Layout running right now. To set up the backdrop images in the Modeler viewports, follow these steps:

1. Select the Box tool and press the n key to open the Numeric panel. Select Activate from the Actions pop-up, click the Range tab, and input the following dimensions:

Low	X	−80mm
Low	Y	−120mm
Low	Z	−100mm
High	X	80mm
High	Y	120mm
High	Z	100mm

2. Leave Segments at 1 for all three axes, and leave all other settings at their defaults. Click the Box tool again to turn it off, or press the spacebar. This will create a box with the right dimensions for you to automatically size your images to. Press the a key to fit it to view.

3. Press d to bring up the Display Options panel and select the Backdrop tab. For Viewport BL, the bottom left (Back view), load the FaceFront.bmp image. For Viewport BR, the bottom right (Right view), load the FaceSide.bmp image of the

head. Click the Automatic Size button for each viewport. Also, set each viewport's resolution to 512 or 1024 for better display quality. Your Modeler screen should look like Figure 10.5.

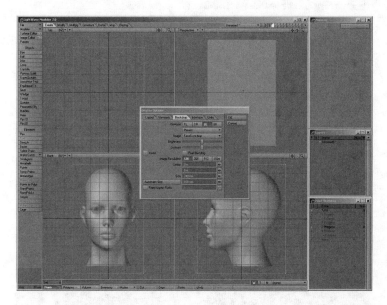

Figure 10.5 Using the Backdrop image feature in Modeler, a separate image can be placed in different viewports as references for modeling.

It's a good idea to keep the box you created as a separate object that you can load to quickly set up background images.

Building the Eyes

The first part of the face you're going to tackle is the eyelid area. But before starting the actual skin mesh, you will build an eye object. It's much easier to properly shape the eyelids if you have an eye in another layer to make sure the lids match up.

Exercise 10.2   Modeling the Eyeball and Cornea

1. Close the Box tool if you haven't already, and then click Layer 2 and select the Ball tool.

2. Using Figure 10.6 and the background images as a guide, drag out a sphere over the character's left eyeball in the Back view. It should have an approximate radius of 11mm on all three axes, which you can see in the numeric requester. Set the Axis to Z in the Numeric panel as well. Press the spacebar to turn off the Ball tool.

Note

You can hold the Ctrl key while creating the ball to force Modeler to create a perfect sphere. Also if the background images seem too bright for you, remember that you can adjust the contrast and brightness in the Backdrop panel.

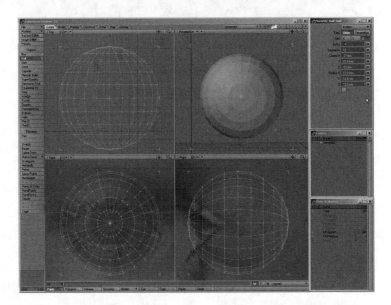

Figure 10.6   To place the eye, start by dragging a sphere over the left eyeball.

3. Creating the ball on the z-axis is important, because this will facilitate making the pupil and iris later on. Alternatively, you can rotate the ball after creation to face down the z-axis by placing the mouse pointer over the center of the object in the Right viewport and pressing the r key to instantly rotate it 90 degrees. Conversely, pressing the e key instantly rotates it −90 degrees.

4. Press q and name the sphere Surface Left Eyeball.

   It's generally convenient later in Layout to have a separate cornea surface (the shiny outer coating of the eye), so that's what you're going to make next.

5. Copy the eyeball by pressing the c key. Go to a new layer and press v to paste it.

   This will leave you with two copies, one in each layer. Switch to Polygon Edit mode from the selections at the bottom of the Modeler screen.

6. Press q to change the surface name of the copied eyeball. Call it Left Cornea.

7. Select Smooth Scale from the Modify tab (listed as Sm Scale) and scale this surface up by .25mm, which will leave the cornea slightly larger than the eyeball. You can place the Eyeball layer in the background to see the size difference.

A real cornea has a large bump where it covers the front of the eyeball over the iris, and it's important to model this feature. The change in curvature over this bump is the reason the eye tends to catch specular highlights from light sources most of the time, and it works the same way in the virtual 3D world. A highlight in the eye helps give the illusion of life to a 3D character.

8. To create the bump, select just the first two bands of polygons that face into the negative z-axis for the cornea. It's easier to select these bands of polygons in the Right viewport using the right mouse button and the Lasso Select function (Mac users, hold that Apple key!). From the Multiply tab, use Smooth Shift to multiply the selected polygons with an offset of zero. To smooth-shift with an offset of zero, right-click once, directly on the selected polygons. Do not move the mouse when you do this. If you do, you will create an offset greater than zero.

9. Press the spacebar to turn off the Smooth Shift command, and then move (t) these polygons about –3.0mm on the z-axis and size (Shift+h) them by a factor of 80 percent in the numeric panel, making sure your cursor is centered on the cornea on the z-axis. You want the cornea to sort of bubble-out in front of the eyeball.

Note

You might want to set Grid Snap to None under the Units tab in the Display Options panel. This will help you precisely size and move polygons in small amounts. Don't forget that you can add values numerically in the Numeric window for each tool.

10. Press the spacebar to turn off the Size tool.

11. Deselect any polygons, and use the Knife (Shift+k) tool from the Construct tab to slice vertically on the third row of polygons, as in Figure 10.7. To use this tool, select it, drag up, slicing the object, and then turn off the tool to keep your selection. You can click and drag on the Knife tool display line before turning off the tool to align it.

    This will add some definition to where the bump blends back into the sphere of the eye. It also will help the smoothing over the front of the cornea.

12. Select the back four rows of both the cornea and the eyeball (which are each on their own layer) and delete them. The camera will never see this side of the eyeball, so you can safely delete the geometry there for efficiency. You can hold the Shift key to select both layers, and perform the removal.

13. Use the Surface Editor to add some preliminary colors to the cornea and eyeball surfaces. Set some specularity as well, and make the cornea surface about 30 percent transparent. You'll formally surface these objects later. Remember to turn on Smoothing. This will help you see how your eyeball model is coming along.

14. Use the Metaform tool (Shift+d) to subdivide both the eyeball and cornea once to check that everything is smoothing off nicely. This is found by pressing Shift+d. Set the Subdivision Method to Metaform and leave the other settings at their defaults. The eyeball and cornea should look like the ones in Figure 10.8a. Save your work.

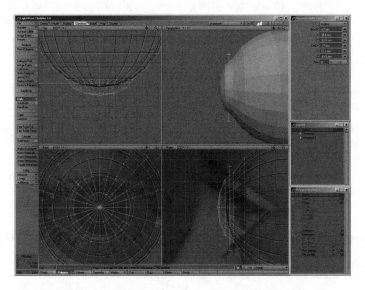

Figure 10.7   Vertically slice the cornea object at the third row of polygons.

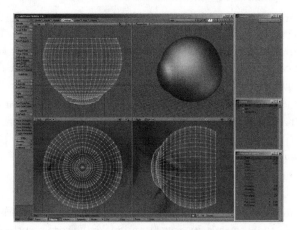

Figure 10.8a   After metaforming the eyeball and cornea, and some basic surfacing, they should look like this. Note that you're looking at two layers in this view.

Exercise 10.3 outlines the steps you need to follow to create the iris, lens, and inner cornea of the eye.

Exercise 10.3   Creating the Iris, Lens, and Inner Cornea

1. Undo the metaform you created in the preceding tutorial by pressing u. Click over to the eyeball layer, and select the front two bands of the eyeball in the Right view. Right-click to lasso select (hold the Apple key on your Mac).

2. Press Shift+z to activate the Merge Polygons command from the Polygon tab. This will merge these polygons into a flat disc. Next, at the bottom of Modeler, click the Modes drop-down list and set the Action Center to Selection (F8). This will allow you to size a selection without exactly aligning the mouse cursor. Select the Size tool (Shift+h) and size the selection 90 percent.

   Some points will be left over after you merge polygons. To eliminate these, select Point mode at the bottom of Modeler, and using the Point Statistics panel (w), click the white plus sign (+) next to the area labeled 0 Points. This will select any points not associated with polygons. After they are selected, you can press the Delete key to remove them.

3. Back in Polygon mode, change the surface name of this polygon to Left Iris by pressing the q key. Change the color a bit in the Change Surface requester to ensure your surface name change has been applied. Next, perform the following series of bevels with the Numeric tab to give the iris the right amount of inward curvature. Press the b key to activate the Bevel tool. Press n to activate the Numeric panel and enter the following for an inner bevel, remembering to press the Enter key on your keyboard after every entry. Also, press the b key to turn off the Bevel tool, and then activate it again by pressing b between each entry. Click Activate or Reset from the Actions pop-up to access the numeric fields, and enter the following:

Shift 0mm	Inset 1mm
Shift −.25mm	Inset .25mm
Shift 0mm	Inset .5mm
Shift 0mm	Inset 2mm
Shift −.25mm	Inset .25mm

4. Cut the disc polygon by pressing the x key. Then press the v key to paste it down. What you've done here is separated the polygon from any adjoining points. Reselect the polygon, and size (Shift+h) it about 130 percent. Make sure the Numeric panel is open, and you'll see the Factor where you can add the 130 percent value directly. Click Apply from the Numeric window to resize the selection. If you use the numeric requester to set the value, click in the Layout once to center the numeric panel values.

5. With the polygon still selected, change the surface name to Lens Black. This polygon stops the camera from seeing through the eyeball when it comes time to render. Figure 10.8b shows the eyeball with the bevels and lens.

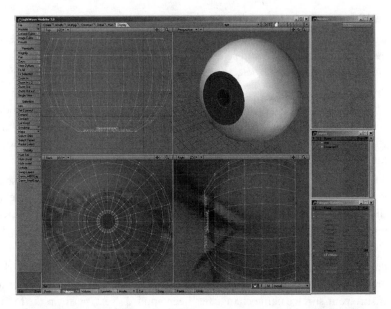

Figure 10.8b   Shown here are the eye with the front polygon beveled in, and the lens.

Now you will create a back surface for the cornea. This is important because you will ultimately render the eye with refraction turned on.

6. Click over to the layer with the Cornea object. Copy it (c), hide the original cornea object by pressing the Hide Sel button from the Display tab, and then paste (v) in the copy.

   What you're doing here is making an inside to the cornea. Right now, the surface only faces outward, and for the cornea to properly refract, an inside needs to be created, sort of like a glass.

7. Select the copied cornea and flip the polygons so that they point inward by pressing the f key. Rename this Eye Aqueous (press q).

8. Use the Size tool to scale down the Eye Aqueous until its outer edge matches up with the outer edge of the iris, just about 97 percent for the Factor in the Numeric panel for Size. Ideally the object should be the same diameter as the iris and should just butt up against it. You'll probably have to use the Move tool to properly line Eye Aqueous.

9. Unhide everything (\) and select the eyeball and cornea layers, and then select all polygons except the Lens Black surface (the flat disc) and subdivide again using Metaform (Shift+d) once to smooth out the eye.

10. Save your work.

Your eye should look like the one in Figure 10.8c. (The cornea in this image has a transparency of 30 percent set in the Surface Editor so that you can see the whole eye better.) Alternatively, compare your results with the eye layer in the final model on the CD.

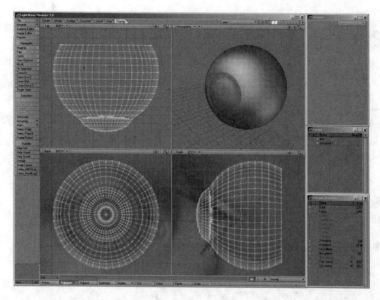

Figure 10.8c   The cornea is dissolved slightly so that you can see the whole eye better.

Building the Eye Area

Now that the eye object is finished, it's time to build the eyelids.

In real life, the actual muscle structure that gives the eyelids their shape is a circular band. Therefore, in this exercise, you will build the eyelids from a shaped circular band of polygons. Building them in this manner also will enable you to sculpt the eyelids efficiently and easily, as well as deform them in a lifelike manner when building morph targets.

Exercise 10.4   Modeling the Lids

To prepare for this exercise, switch back to Layer 1, with the eye in Layer 2 as a background layer. You can delete the initial box you created in the beginning of the chapter for scaling the background images.

Begin by building a template polygon to shape the hole between the lids. Zoom into the Back view, or press the a key to see the left eye close up.

1. Select the Pen tool from the Create tab, and lay down 15 points, as in Figure 10.9. Note how there are more points around the areas where the shape narrows in the outer corner and around the tear duct in the inner corner. This will enable you to tightly define the surface in those areas. Rename the surface Skin (q), and apply a skin color of your choice.

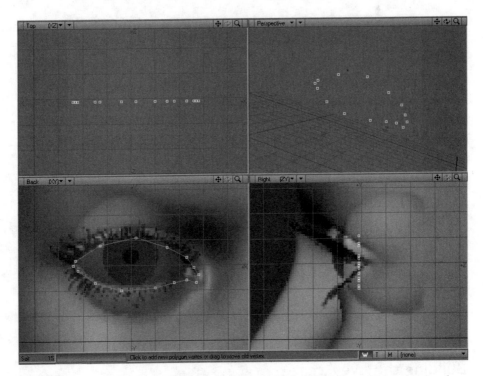

Figure 10.9   To shape the hole between the eyelids, start by laying down 15 points using the Pen tool.

Next, you will use this polygon to bevel out the bands of polygons that will form the eyelids. Don't worry about shaping the lids just yet. All you're doing here is getting the polygons in place (and in the right structure) so that you can sculpt them into nicely defined lids later.

2. Turn off the Pen tool, and make sure the polygon you've just created is selected. Then, bevel (b) the polygon four times with the following settings, remembering to turn the Bevel tool off and back on again after each Shift and Inset entry. Just press b, and b again:

Shift 1mm	Inset 0 mm
Shift −0.6mm	Inset −1.5mm
Shift −1.5mm	Inset −1.5mm
Shift 0mm	Inset −2.0mm

You might need to press the f key to flip your polygons forward. The end result should look something like Figure 10.10. Note that the Perspective view is set to Wireframe Shade mode. Delete the template, or the initial polygon. This should be the only selected polygon.

> **Note**
> To interactively bevel, press the b key to call up the Bevel command. Left-click the selected polygon, and drag. Dragging down shifts; dragging to the left or right insets. To multiply and bevel a new polygon from the selected polygon, just right-click with the mouse and then left-click to continue beveling. (Macintosh users use the Apple key with the mouse for right-click functions.)

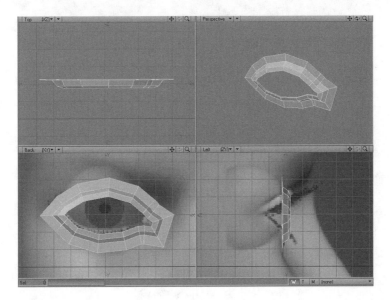

Figure 10.10   Beveling the template and flipping the polygons forward should give you this result.

Note that the Side viewport is changed to left rather than right to get a better look at the geometry in the Shaded View modes.

3. Press Tab to turn the geometry into a SubPatch surface.

4. Now select the polygons on each end of the object in turn and use Bend from the Modify tab to bend them in toward the face. The curvature should roughly match the profile of the eye in Layer 2. You can use the Move tool to help you line up the eyelid before bending if you want. You'll need to change the mode back to Action Center: Mouse (Shift+F5) for an easier time using the Bend tool.

5. Use Sheer from the Modify tab in the Top viewport to pull the top of the lids forward slightly.

6. Select points in each of the upper and lower lids, and Move and stretch the lid object in the Front viewport so that its front profile matches up again with the background image.

You should now have something that's similar to Figure 10.11.

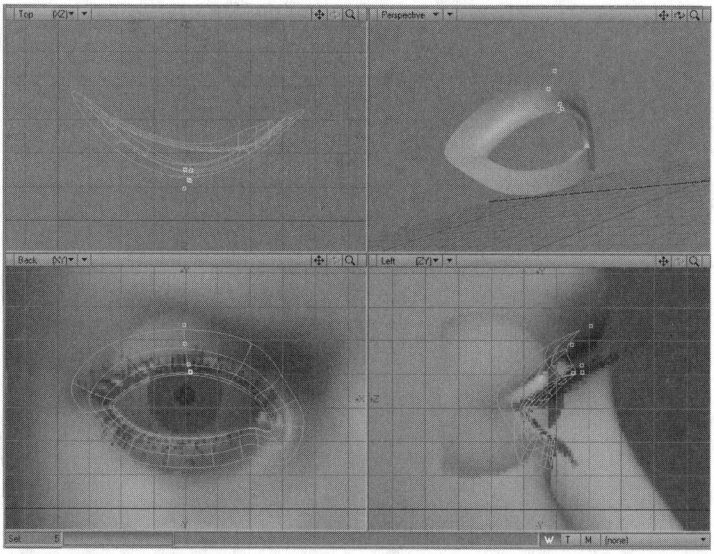

Figure 10.11   The selected points show the top lid profile.

Now it's time to sculpt the eyelid.

7. Select each radial row of points in turn on the top part of the lid and drag them in the Side viewport to shape the eyelid surface. Tackle one row at a time, and always try to work in SubPatch mode. You also can switch the Side view to Wireframe while checking your results in a shaded Perspective view. Sculpt the bottom lid in the same manner. Note that as you go from the center of the eye out, the general shape becomes softer and rounder. Aim for something that looks like Figure 10.12.

Tip

When you move the points on the inside edge of the lid, make sure you move the two innermost points on each row as a pair. The distance between them forms the thickness of the eyelid "lip" at that point, and you want to keep this fairly even along the whole of the lid surface.

Note

You'll do a lot of control-point sculpting when building the rest of the face. It's not really feasible to provide numerically exact instructions for doing these massaging operations. Just remember to match the background image and take it nice and slow. This is where your talent as a sculptor (as opposed to a technical 3D modeler) will shine.

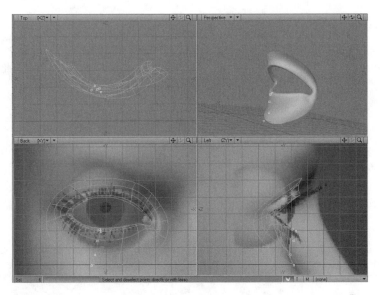

Figure 10.12   Sculpt the bottom lid by selecting each radial row of points in turn on the bottom part of the lid and dragging them about in the Side and Back viewports.

8. Tuck the bottom lid up behind the top lid slightly at the outer corner by selecting the points as shown in Figure 10.13 and moving them up and under the edge of the top lid.

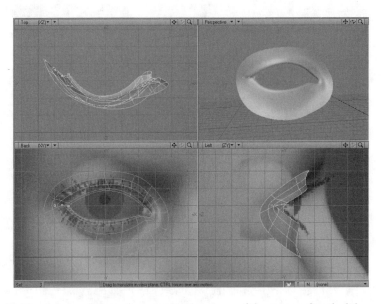

Figure 10.13   Select and move the points in the corner of the eye to refine the lids.

Note

It will probably take a bit of trial and error to refine the lid corner. If you get lost as to what point belongs to which bit of the mesh, try turning on Guides or Cages under the Display Options tab. If you get really stuck, switch the surface back to standard polygons by pressing the Tab key, select the points you need, and then go into Poly Selection mode and reactivate the SubPatch surface with the Tab key. The points still will be highlighted when you change back to point selection.

Now it's time to add a bit more geometry to make the tear duct in the inner corner of the eye.

9. Select the five innermost points on the lid that surround the tear duct area. Then press p to make a polygon.

Tip

An easy way to select only the inner points of the lid is to use the Statistics tab (w) to select only points with two polygons attached, and then deselect the ones you don't need.

10. Add a point (using the Add Points command from the Construct tab) to this polygon's inner edge and split the poly, as shown in Figure 10.14, so that you have two quads. To add a point, the polygon must be selected first. To Split, select the two points in the center of the polygon, and then click the Split button from the Construct tab.

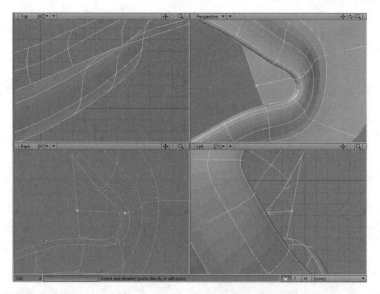

Figure 10.14   Add geometry to make the tear duct by first adding a point, and then splitting the polygon.

11. Switch to Polygon mode, and make sure the two new quad polygons are selected for the tear duct. Now smooth-shift (Shift+f) the two polygons and move them in toward the eye socket a bit.

12. You will have to manually drag a few points around to get the bump in the middle, as in Figure 10.15, and to refine the shape. The figure shows the object with SubPatch surfaces turned on (Tab key).

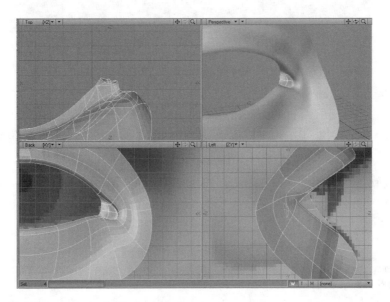

Figure 10.15 Here is the finished tear duct.

Finally, check that the eyelids are sitting just off the surface of the eyeball.

13. Select the points of the inner eyelid, first the upper, then the lower, and then hold the Shift key and select Layer 3, the Cornea layer. With both Layers 1 and 3 in the foreground, move the selected points into place so that they are resting just outside the cornea.

    The points will become transparent in any shaded view when they move behind the surface of the cornea. So, positioning them in the Perspective view is a good way to go. If the points disappear, you'll know that they've been moved behind the cornea.

14. Check the rest of the lids to make sure they look nice and smooth. Figure 10.16 shows the finished lid surface. Save your work.

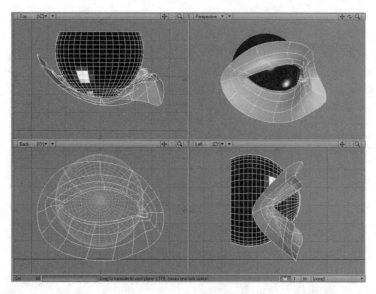

Figure 10.16   With the eye object layer in the foreground, select the eyelid surface and match the lids to the cornea.

Exercise 10.5   Extending the Lids Up into the Brow

Your next modeling task is the eyebrow. Instead of creating new geometry from scratch, you will use the Extender plug-in to expand the existing mesh.

1. Select the outer points of the top lid surface in order, working from left to right, and select the Extender tool from the Multiply tab.

    Although it appears nothing has changed, the plug-in has duplicated the points and connected them to the originals with new polygons.

2. Select the Size tool and scale the new points out from the center of the eye in the Back view.

3. Using Extender again, repeat the scaling operation two more times.

    Extender will have created three back polygons during the operations because it always forms closed loops that you don't need. These unnecessary polygons should be much longer than the other ones, spanning from one side of the selection of points to the other.

4. Select the unnecessary polygons and delete them.

> **Note**
>
> Note that some of the remaining polygons aren't facing the correct direction. You can select these polygons and press the f key to flip them forward. Additionally, you can select Align, from the Detail tab. Align will look at the polygons of your object and flip the lessor amount of polygons to match the majority polygon direction.

5. Figure 10.17 shows the results of the three Extender/Size operations after the back faces have been removed and the geometry has been aligned to face the front. Deselect any polygons and press Tab to activate SubPatch mode.

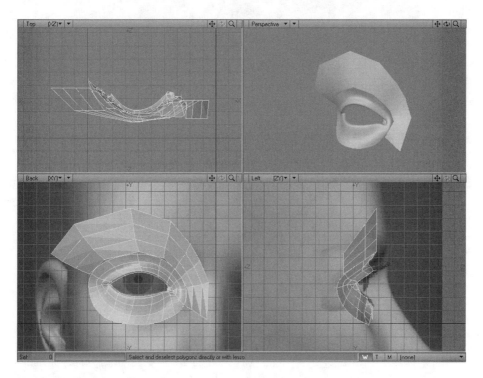

Figure 10.17   This is the new geometry created with the Extender tool.

6. Select just the new polygons and shape the brow ridge, one row of points at a time, using the Drag tool (Ctrl+t). This enables you to move the selected point around in all viewports without fear of disturbing any other parts of your model accidentally. Remember to pay attention to the background image in both the Back and Right view to shape the polygons.

You might have to switch to Wireframe mode on some viewports to select and drag all the points you need, and you might find it helpful to change the visibility options frequently (for instance, enabling Cages and Guides) while you work (Display options, d). Figure 10.18 shows the result. Save your work.

Note

By holding the Ctrl key and pressing a number on the numeric keypad, you can set up shortcuts to switch between viewport modes.

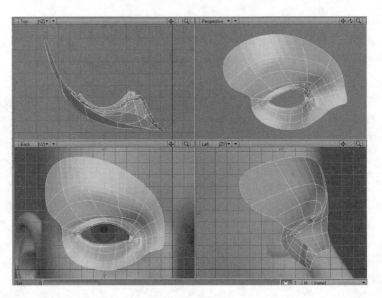

Figure 10.18   The finished brow should look something like this.

The following list offers you important points to note while you work:

- The skin around the tear duct corner turns out quite sharply as it begins to join the bridge of the nose.

- A layer of fat and muscle just under the brow tends to hang down over the top lid, creating a distinct crease. This part can be hard to get right. Don't be afraid to move the brow control points down quite a bit over the upper lid.

- Keep the horizontal ridge of the brow distinct by keeping the rows of points there fairly close together.

Don't pay too much attention to what the model looks like in Plain Polygon mode. The SubPatch surface is what's important, not the control cage (although as mentioned earlier, going back to Polygon mode is sometimes useful to select those hard-to-pick points). Make sure you switch back to SubPatch mode before sculpting by pressing the Tab key.

Exercise 10.6   Extending the Brow down to Form the Cheekbone

Looking at the reference pictures in the backdrop, you should be able to see how the outer brow curves around the eye and merges into the cheekbone below the eye, to complete the eye socket. To model this, you'll use the Extender tool again, this time on the outer edge of the brow.

1. In order, select the three vertices running between the outer corner of the lids and the second-to-last outer brow row.

2. Press your Extender key from the Multiply tab.

3. Use the Move (t) and Rotate (y) tools in the Back and Right views to bring the new vertices around the outer edge of the lower lid area so that the new row of polygons matches up with the lid surface above, as in Figure 10.19.

4. Repeat this process—Extender, Move/Rotate—another seven times, matching up the new row of cheekbone polygons with the next row in the eyelids each time until you reach the corner where the brow surface starts, as in Figure 10.20.

5. Once again, delete the back polygons. It might be a bit harder to select them this time. They're the ones that span from the top edge of the cheekbone to the bottom edge, as shown in Figure 10.20. The easiest way is to select them from the back in the Perspective window.

6. Make sure the remaining cheekbone polygons are aligned and facing the right direction, as in Figure 10.21. Then change them into SubPatch surfaces.

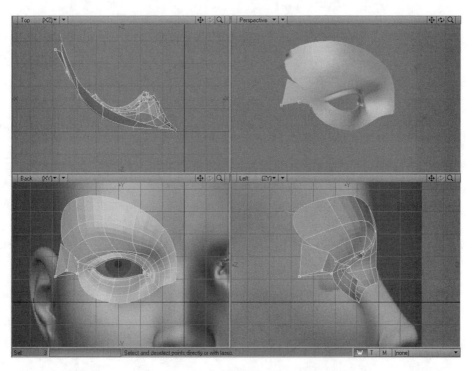

Figure 10.19   Bring the extended points down and around the lower lid.

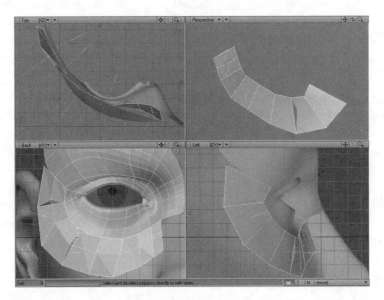

Figure 10.20   Bring the new cheekbone surface all the way around to the inner corner of the eye, and then delete the back polygons, shown selected here. You can see in the Top view that surface normals are facing the positive z-axis. You only want normals facing forward.

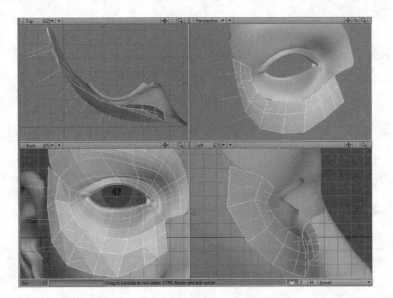

Figure 10.21   Here is the cheekbone surface after alignment.

7. Select the edge points along the border of the lower lid and the cheekbone (see Figure 10.22) and press m to access the Merge panel.

8. Click Automatic, and uncheck Keep 1-Point Polygons. By clicking Automatic, you are instructing Modeler to merge points within a general range. (Clicking Fixed enables you to merge points within a range that you specify.) Click OK and save your work.

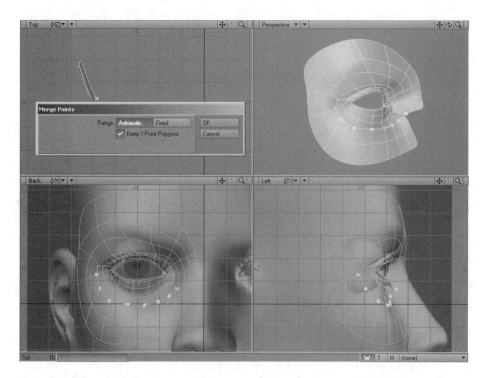

Figure 10.22   Merge the border points.

If you've been sloppy along the way (modeling, that is), the merge might have missed a few stray points or merged the wrong points. (A small kink in the merged surface around the selected points is a sure sign of this.) If this is the case, undo the merge, select nearby points, and weld (Ctrl+w) the vertices in pairs manually.

Finally, take a look at the finished surface and make sure it's nice and smooth. Use the Drag tool to reshape it, if necessary.

Exercise 10.7   Building the Bridge of the Nose

The final step in building the eye area is to build the bridge of the nose.

1. Select the first four points on the extreme right edge of the brow, and then use the Extender command to duplicate them:

2. Use the Set Value command (Ctrl+v) to bring these new points directly to 0 on the x-axis. Set Value is great for aligning multiple points to one specific location.

3. Follow the standard procedure you've been using throughout the exercises in this chapter with any new geometry—that is, kill the extra back polygon created by the Extender command, align the remaining polygons properly, use the Drag tool (Ctrl+t) to arrange points, and then press Tab to activate SubPatch mode. Your result should look like Figure 10.23.

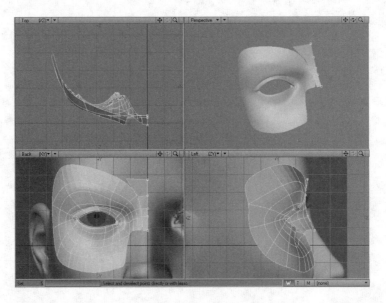

Figure 10.23   To build the bridge of the nose, kill the extra back polygon created by Extender, align the remaining polygons properly, and then press Tab.

4. Deselect any extra geometry created with the Extender tool and choose the Mirror tool (Shift+v). Activate the Numeric tab (n) and accept the default values. Mirror over the x-axis centered on zero with Merge Points on.

5. Go to Layers 2 and 3, and follow step 4 for the eye geometry to mirror the model thus far.

6. Bring both layers to the foreground. You should now have a pair of eyes and the surrounding head area staring out at you. Save your work.

The benefit of seeing both sides of the head is that you can decide whether you want to make any cosmetic changes. Hopefully, if you're using the supplied background images as a guide, there shouldn't be anything amiss, but chances are something will need to be tweaked a little. Don't be put off by any inconsistencies in your model. No matter what you create in LightWave Modeler, you'll always need some tweaking here and there.

If this is the case, LightWave has a nifty "mode" to help out with altering symmetrical objects. Look at the bottom of Modeler, and you'll see a button called Symmetry. When Symmetry is active, and as long as you have any geometry mirrored exactly over x, as you do here, anything you modify (using any of LightWave's Modify tools) on the positive x-axis will be copied on the negative side. Your final image should look similar to Figure 10.24.

Note

Although the Symmetry tool is cool, it also can mess you up! Be aware when this tool is active, as everything you do on the positive x-axis will be mirrored on the negative x-axis. Be sure to turn off this tool when you do not want your actions mirrored, such as centering the model (F2).

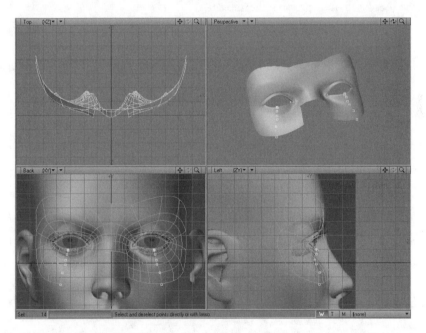

Figure 10.24   Make final modifications to the eye area with Symmetry on. For Symmetry to work properly, the X values need to match exactly.

Building the Mouth

The other main area of detail on the face is, of course, the mouth, which is what you'll be moving on to next. You'll start in a way similar to the eyelids—quickly building a suitable cage structure, and then carefully molding the resulting SubPatch surface into shape. As you can see, a few key tools can help you build just about anything! Too often,

LightWave animators think there is some hidden secret to making great models such as the one in this chapter. Instead, you're learning that with the right references, proper point placement, and a little time, you can create a great-looking model.

Like the eyelids, the mouth area also is basically a circular ring of muscles. However, when modeling the lips, the difference in thickness (the side profile) along the length of each lip is much more pronounced than in the eyelids, so it's easier to start building them from the side first rather than the front.

Exercise 10.8   Modeling the Lips

Make sure only Layer 1 is active and, hide all the existing eyelid geometry. Start with the top lip first. Be sure that you have turned off the Symmetry tool. Also if SubPatch mode is active, deactivate it by pressing the Tab key.

1. Look at Figure 10.25 and, using the Point tool (Create tab), lay down a similar group of vertices (six altogether) to make a side profile for the top lip. Try to make them in order from top to bottom. If you don't, reselect them in that order.

   Note that two points are close together at the leading edge. This is important to define the distinct ridge where the lip blends into the skin above it.

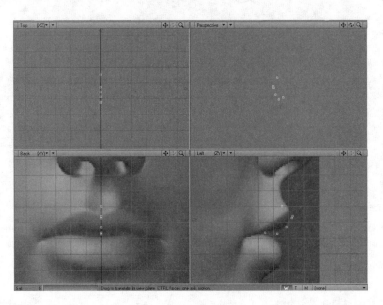

Figure 10.25   Here are the profile points for building the top lip. You can see how easy this is with a picture reference.

2. Use the Extender tool to multiply the six points, and then in the Back viewport, move the points to the left (about 6mm or so) and up slightly.

3. In the Top viewport, move the points forward a couple of millimeters as well.

4. Use the Extender tool again. This time, move the points back a few millimeters in the Top view and rotate them clockwise about 10 degrees, keeping the mouse centered as you do. You can see how important the Extender tool is!

5. Move the points down slightly in the Front view and rotate them counterclockwise a couple of degrees.

6. Squash them a bit on the z and y-axes using the Stretch (h) tool.

7. Repeat steps 4, 5, and 6 another three times, using Figure 10.26 as a guide, to roughly shape the surface with the Move, Stretch, and Rotate tools as you go. You should end up with a band of polygons five rows wide.

8. As you did in earlier exercises, delete the extra back polygons created by the Extender tool, and make sure all polygons are facing forward. Press the Tab key to activate the SubPatch mode.

9. Finally, refine the top lip shape using the Drag tool (Ctrl+t). Select each row of points in turn before tweaking. Remember to pay attention to all viewports to see how your model is shaping up. Save your work.

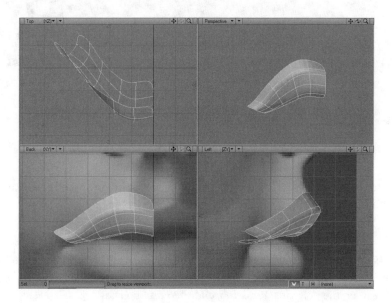

Figure 10.26   Here is the finished top lip before it's mirrored.

10. Repeat the entire process from step 1 of this exercise for the bottom lip. Hide the upper lip first (Display tab) so that you don't destroy the work you've done on it. Figure 10.27 outlines the point profile for the lower lip. Again, use the Point tool to put the vertices in order from top left to bottom.

Tip

As in the top lip, the bottom profile has two points that are fairly close together and that help define the join between skin and lip. However, here the lip blends more smoothly into the skin, so keep the selection a bit wider apart than in the top lip.

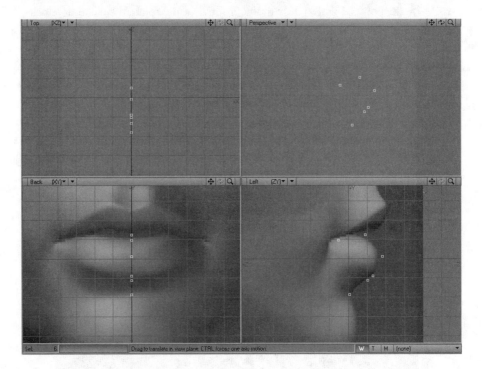

Figure 10.27   The bottom lip profile is fuller and rounder than the top.

11. Use the Extender tool to multiply the point profile in the lower lip, and then move, stretch, and rotate the selection to build out the lip surface as you did for the upper lip.

The rows of points should gradually be rotated from a vertical to a horizontal profile as you go (use the Front viewport to do this). Again, you should end up with a band of geometry five rows of polygons wide.

12. Clean up the polygons. Press Tab, and then use the Drag tool (Ctrl+t) to make sure the points are in the right position and shaped nicely based on the background reference images. Finish refining the surface. Save your object.

Remember that the bottom lip stays thicker for more of its length than the top lip.

Although the bottom lip gets thinner at the outer corner, it actually retains a bit of volume. Don't make it too thin at the far edge. Figure 10.28 shows how it should end up. The end looks a lot thinner in the Side view because its profile has been rotated.

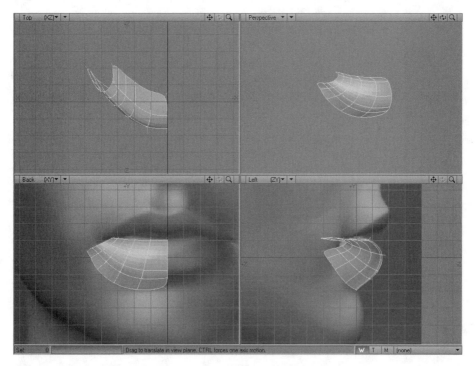

Figure 10.28   Here is the finished bottom lip before it's mirrored.

Now that the lips have been modeled, it's time to join them together.

Exercise 10.9   Joining the Lips Together

1. To begin, unhide the top lip (if you hid the polygons in the previous exercise). Make sure only the two lip surfaces are visible and then align the outer edge vertices (shown in Figure 10.29) so that the two lips match up with each other.

2. Select the last row of vertices on the top lip and rotate them counterclockwise in the Front view so that they lie on a horizontal plane. Do the same for the outer row of points on the bottom lip, this time rotating them clockwise so that they roughly match up with the top lip vertices.

3. Select both sets of edge vertices and drag them in the Top viewport so that each pair (one vertex from the top lip and the corresponding vertex from the bottom lip for each row) is aligned.

4. In the Back viewport, use Stretch (h) to compress the two sets of vertices together. Weld each pair together in turn, and use Drag to refine the join area. It helps to select the last row of polygons in the bottom lip (shown in Figure 10.30) and slightly tuck them up, under, and behind the top lip surface.

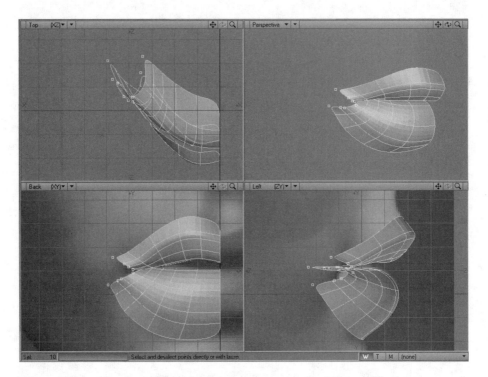

Figure 10.29   Align the two sets of outer edge vertices together before welding.

> **Tip**
>
> The lip crease at the corner can be fairly tricky to shape properly. Don't pull the points in this area too close together on the x-axis or you'll end up with an ugly pinch in the corner of the mouth. Do pull them close together on the y-axis (especially in the inner corner). The crease should be a lightly curved, well-defined horizontal line that continues the natural curve of the lips.

5. When you're happy with the corner area, select the other edge vertices of both lips and use Set Value (Ctrl+v) to make sure they are all sitting perfectly on the x-axis at 0.

6. Use the Mirror tool (Shift+v) to create the right side of the mouth. The default numeric settings should be fine. Mirror on the x-axis and make sure Merge Points is on in the Numeric Mirror panel.

7. Switch to the trusty Drag tool (Ctrl+t) again and make any last-minute refinements to the completed lip surface. Save your work. Figure 10.31 shows the finished area.

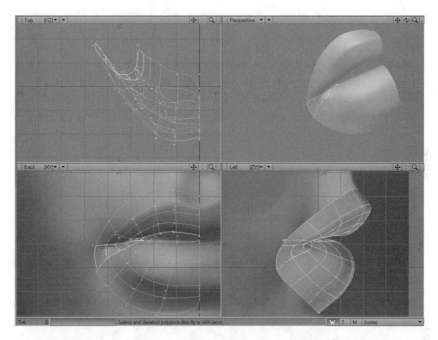

Figure 10.30   Be careful sculpting the corner of the mouth. Although it needs to be tightly defined, try not to make the area look pinched.

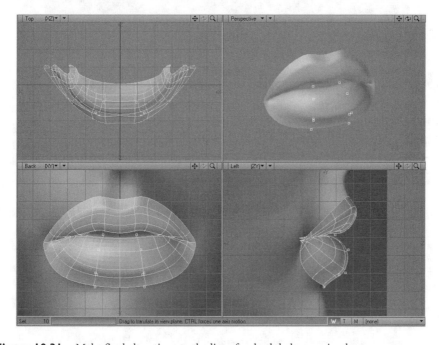

Figure 10.31   Make final alterations to the lips after both halves are in place.

Exercise 10.10   Building the Rest of the Mouth Area

To complete the mouth, you'll need a few more bands of geometry around the lips.

1. Select all the outer-edge vertices in order, going clockwise.
2. Use the Extender tool to create the first band of polygons, and then use Scale to give them some width.
3. Repeat step 2 again.

   You should now have something that looks like Figure 10.32.

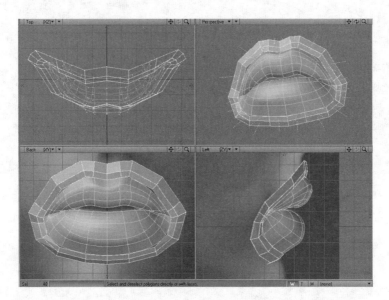

Figure 10.32   Here is the mouth after extending the outer lip points.

> **Note**
> Don't worry about any extra back polygons this time. Because you deliberately extended a closed loop of points, everything should be fine. Just make sure all the geometry is aligned, however, before switching them to SubPatch mode.

Now it's time to sculpt the outer mouth area. This procedure should be fairly familiar to you by now.

4. Select rows of points one at a time to work on.
5. Switch the Top, Back, and Side views to Wireframe if necessary for access to obscured geometry, but keep the Perspective window shaded so that you can accurately gauge your progress.
6. Switch on Enable Guides or Enable Cages in the Display Options panel (d), or switch the surface back to Polygon mode in the viewport briefly if you have trouble working out which vertices you need to be working on.

Note

You can quickly switch between viewport modes easily by setting a numeric preset. By changing the viewport to a certain display style, and then holding the Ctrl key and selecting any of the numbers on the numeric keypad, you can save a view preset.

7. The mouth sits in the middle of a raised mound. Spread the outer edges back into what would be the face, making sure they form a smooth curve around the whole mouth area, using the Drag (Ctrl+t) tool.

   A distinct notch runs from the two upper tips of the top lip all the way up to the base of the nose. Keep a bit of definition in this area by keeping the points relatively close together. There should be just the right amount of geometry to get the shape right. You can turn on Symmetry mode to mirror your actions if you want. If Symmetry does not work for you, your points are not exact on the positive and negative x-axes.

8. At either side of the mouth, there is a small raised area and a light crease where a lot of facial muscles meet. Slightly drag a couple of points out from the face here. Save your work.

   The bottom lip will blend into the start of the chin. A defined crease in the middle just under the lip will soften out quite quickly toward the outer edges of the mouth, as in Figure 10.33.

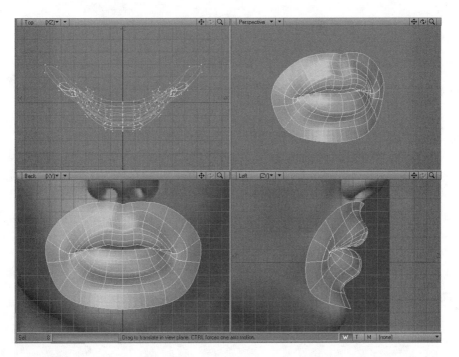

Figure 10.33   Here is the completed mouth area.

Building the Jaw

The jaw, despite being a relatively smooth structure, defines a major contour of the face and is important in terms of overall proportion. It's a good idea to add it in at this stage as you start to see more of the face coming together.

Exercise 10.11   Adding the Jaw Line

1. Hide the polygons you've created thus far before you start building the jaw. Hiding the polygons from the Display tab does not remove them. It only makes them invisible so that you don't harm the work you've already done. You also can work in another layer and then copy and paste later if you like. Make sure Symmetry mode if off at the bottom of the Modeler screen, and do not have the SubPatch mode active (Tab key).

2. Use the Points tool to lay down a row of five profile points, as in Figure 10.34. These should curve in toward the neck area at the bottom. Remember to pay attention to all viewports as you build.

3. Using the Extender tool to multiply the points, rotate (y), stretch (h), and move (t) the points to fill out the jaw line, as in Figure 10.35.

   You should have six rows of polygons, from the start of the jaw near the ear to the center x-axis.

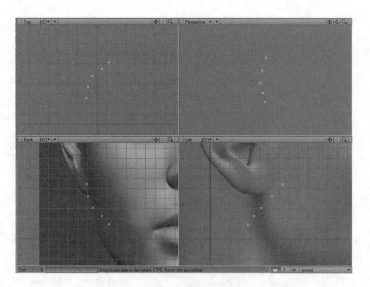

Figure 10.34   Lay down a row of five profile points for creating the jaw line.

Tip
Remember to cull those pesky back polygons from the Extender operations, and make sure the extended geometry is aligned to face the right direction.

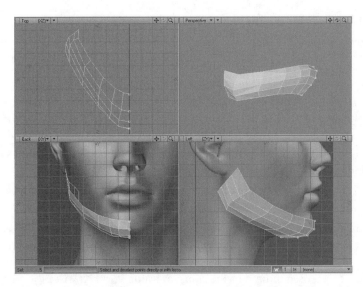

Figure 10.35   Extend the jaw line so that you have six rows of polygons, from the start of the jaw near the ear to the centerline on the x-axis.

4. Use Set Value (Ctrl+v) to make sure the last row of points sits exactly on the x-axis. Then mirror them to create the other half of the jaw.

5. Finally, use the Drag (Ctrl+t) and Stretch (h) tools to refine the jaw shape, and press the Tab key to activate SubPatch mode to see the smooth shaped jaw, as in Figure 10.36. Save your work.

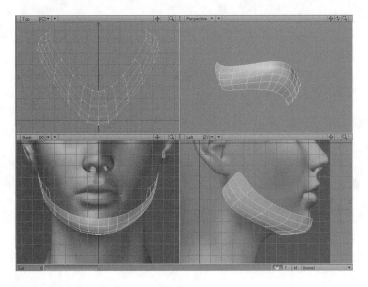

Figure 10.36   Here is the completed jaw surface.

Exercise 10.12   Joining the Jaw and Mouth to Create the Chin

With the jaw complete, it's time to create a chin. Turn off SubPatch mode by pressing the Tab key.

1. Make sure only the jaw and the mouth area are visible by unhiding the mouth polygons, and hiding the eye areas and nose bridge polygons. As a side note, you can use Modeler's Parts feature to help quickly hide and unhide sets of polygons. The Parts feature is found under the Grouping list under the Display tab.

2. Align the middle seven vertices at the lower edge of the mouth and the corresponding points on the upper edge of the jaw, as in Figure 10.37.

3. Weld (Ctrl+w) the respective pairs of points together, or use a fixed merge (m) if you think you've got them close enough together.

4. Refine the chin area if needed with the Drag tool (t), or Stretch tool (h). Pay special attention to the points highlighted in Figure 10.38. They control the surface crease where the lower mouth blends into the jaw and changes direction to become the raised mound of the chin. Save your work.

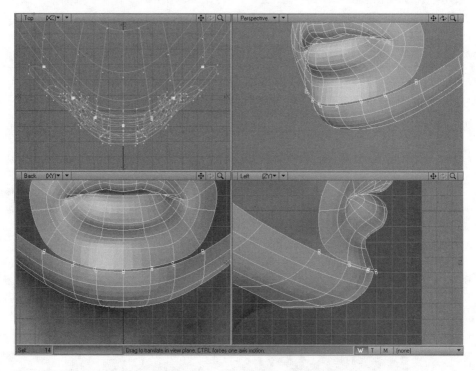

Figure 10.37   Drag the selected vertices of the mouth and the jaw so that they line up.

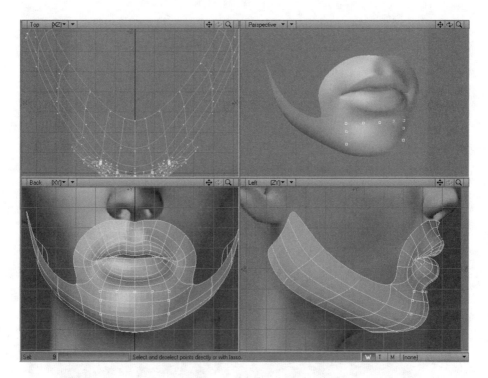

Figure 10.38   The points shown here need to be carefully positioned. Even moving them fractionally can make a big difference.

Building the Nose

The nose seemingly presents the aspiring face modeler with a few challenges, because the nose is a complex little knot of interconnecting curves and planes. Just like all the other parts of the face you have modeled so far, however, after you've broken it down into smaller, easy-to-model sections, the nose is really not that hard at all to create.

Exercise 10.13   Extending the Bridge

Start by bridging the remaining gap between the cheekbones to complete the bridge of the nose.

1. Invert the visible status of your geometry by selecting Invert from the Display tab. The previously modeled eye area should now be the only thing you can see, whereas the mouth and nose polygons become hidden.

2. Select the vertices at the bottom of the currently existing nose bridge, between the two cheekbones, in order from left to right. There should be nine of them altogether.

3. Use the Extender tool to multiply the selection, and then move (t) the points down so they match up with the next row of cheekbone points. You'll have to move them forward a bit off the face as well.

4. Repeat the preceding step so that the points match up with the bottom row of cheekbone vertices.

5. Do one last extend/move operation so that you have one more row of nose bridge polygons protruding at the bottom. Check that their profile matches up with the line of the nose in the Left viewport.

6. Weld (Ctrl+w) the border between the bridge and the cheekbones at either side of the nose and save your work. Figure 10.39 shows the results at this stage.

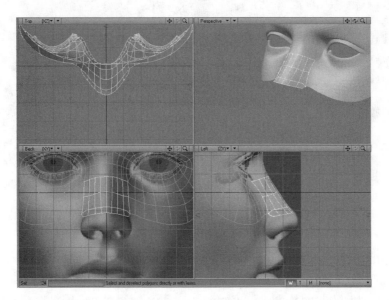

Figure 10.39   Fill in the gap between the two cheekbone sections to continue the nose line.

Exercise 10.14   Sculpting the Nostrils

Begin the left nostril by building some polygons to form the outer "wing." You should know the drill by now.

1. Lay down some profile points in order. (Five points should suffice this time.)

2. Use Extender and a combination of Move, Rotate, and Stretch to create and roughly shape the new geometry. Remember, pay attention to the geometry you're creating in all viewports to properly shape the nostrils.

3. Delete the extra back polygons, align the remaining geometry, and turn it into a SubPatch surface by pressing the Tab key. Use Drag to refine the shape, as in Figure 10.40.

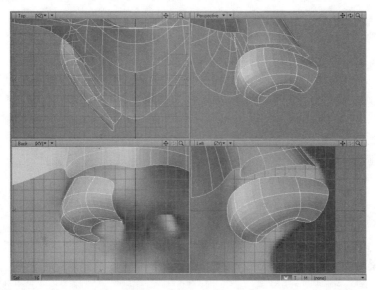

Figure 10.40   Here is the nostril "wing" surface.

4. Start at the back of the nostril wing and begin contouring the shape of the nostril. Use the Drag (Ctrl+t) tool to individually adjust the points.

5. Make the shape gradually curve around until it meets the nose tip using the Drag tool, but stop short of the center x-axis.

   The wing should be four poly rows wide. (You will join it with the corresponding nose bridge polygons shortly.)

6. Curve the lower edge of the nostril below itself to form the edge of the actual nostril hole.

7. Now mirror the nostril over the x-axis.

8. Between each upper nostril edge and the lower edge of the nose bridge, a gap exists. The quickest way to fill this gap is to just select a group of four points at a time, and then press p to make a polygon. Depending on the order in which you selected the points, you might need to flip some of them afterward. Try to select in a clockwise order.

9. Using the Extender tool, fill in the middle tip of the nose between the two nostrils, but leave a gap between the last two rows around the inner nostril edges.

10. Weld (Ctrl+w) the border points between the tip and the bridge of the nose. Your object should look like the one in Figure 10.41. Again, note that a gap should remain between the bottom nostril rows.

    On the left nostril, do the following:

11. Use the Extender tool on the two points at the gap edge of the lower row of nostril polygons. You need to do this four times altogether to expand this bottom row into a complete ring of polygons.

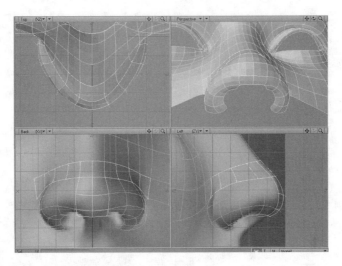

Figure 10.41   Here is the nose after filling in the gaps.

12. Use Move and Rotate to bring the points around a bit each time.

13. When the last polygon is in place, weld the seam points to make the nostril edge a continuous circle.

14. Make sure the four new polygons are properly aligned—flip them (f) to face forward, if they're not—and then select them and press Tab to activate SubPatch mode. Save your work.

   Don't worry about the back polygons. Only one polygon is created when Extender is used on just two points. Figure 10.42 should make these last few steps more clear.

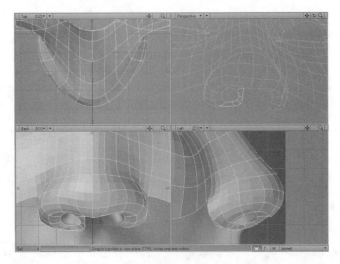

Figure 10.42   Extend four extra polygons to complete the circle at the bottom edge of the nostril.

Exercise 10.15   Joining the Nose to the Upper Lip

1. Mirror the four polygons from step 14 in the preceding exercise (the polygons highlighted in Figure 10.42) over to the right side of the nose, deselect them, and do an automatic merge to weld them in place. (You might need to weld a couple of points manually. A small kink or tear in the surface usually indicates this.)

2. Select a set of four points for the other two rows between the nostrils and press the p key to create a polygon. This will complete the underside of the nose tip.

3. Unhide the mouth/jaw assembly if it's still hidden. Move the five middle points on the upper-top lip edge to align them with the five middle points on the bottom nose edge. Weld these border points in pairs, as in Figure 10.43.

4. On the left nostril, select the innermost points in the bottom nostril ring in a clockwise order. (Perspective view is the best to use for this.)

5. Press p to make a polygon, and check that it faces downward.

6. Bevel (b) this a couple of times, moving it up into the nose each time, as in Figure 10.44.

7. Delete the temporary polygon. Select the inner nostril polygons created by the bevel. Press Tab to switch them to SubPatch surfaces.

8. Mirror these across, deselect, and merge or weld to join them to the opposite side of the nose.

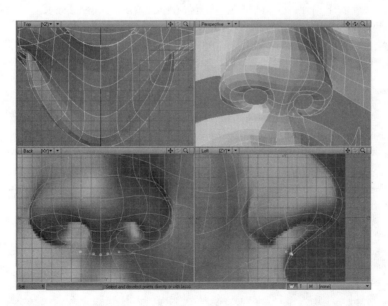

Figure 10.43   Weld the border points between the nose and the top lip surfaces.

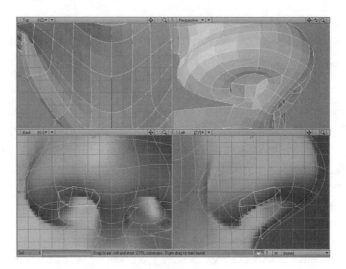

Figure 10.44   Bevel in the nostril using a temporary polygon.

Next you're going to join more of the nose to the top of the mouth. As you can probably see from the model, however, there is a geometry mismatch between the two areas—that is, there aren't any points on the top lip edge that you can easily match up to the next free points on the bottom nose edge. Rectifying this will take a bit of low-level polygon editing on the top lip.

9. Switch all your geometry back to Polygon mode by pressing the Tab key to turn off SubPatch mode.

10. Using Figure 10.45 as a guide, first select the polygons (you must be in Polygon Edit mode) around the top edge of the lip under the nose. Then add two points to the top edge of the polygon shown by first selecting the polygon and then using the Add Points tool from the Construct tab. Then split the polygon (Construct tab) so that it becomes two quads. To split polygons, select two points—the split also will activate. Click it, and you'll split the geometry.

You now have the extra geometry needed to match up the top lip with the bottom nose edge (on the left side at least).

> **Note**
>
> This kind of editing—splitting, merging, and adding points to polygons—is often required to match up two distinct surfaces that need to be joined together, but have a different number of points along the border edge.
>
> Most of the time it can be avoided if you can arrange in advance for the two surfaces to have the right amount of geometry to start with—knowing that they will need to match up at some point. That's one of the reasons you created various sections with specific numbers of polygons or points. But sometimes, either by accident or by design, it doesn't work out that way, and you will need to fiddle around with the border edges a bit to get them to match up properly, as you have here.

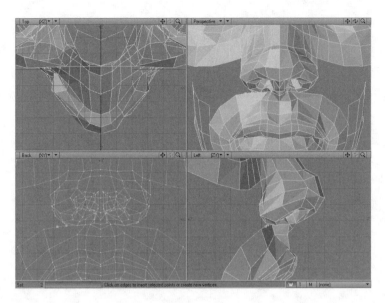

Figure 10.45   Use low-level editing to adjust the local geometry match between two surfaces.

11. Align the newly split polygon with the left side of the lower nostril using the Drag tool, as in Figure 10.46. Then weld them to the nostril.

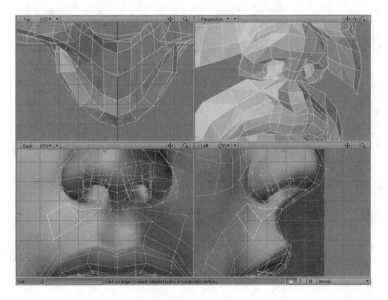

Figure 10.46   Align the new geometry to the nose.

12. Deselect and then turn everything back to SubPatch surfaces by pressing the Tab key, as in Figure 10.47.

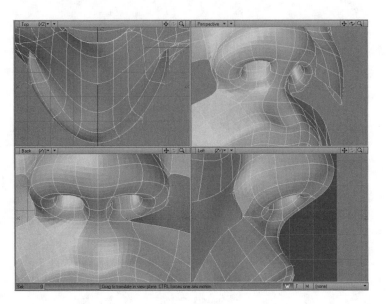

Figure 10.47   Here is the join in SubPatch mode.

13. Now perform the same operation of patching by repeating steps 10 and 11 on the right side of the nose. Save your work.

   By mirroring along the way, you can get a good sense of how your model is coming along. Many animators wait until the model is complete before mirroring, but testing along the way helps your vision.

Completing the Face

Okay, you've modeled the eyes, eye area, mouth, jaw line, and nose. But you still need to perform a few more steps to complete the face. Get some coffee, and then continue.

Exercise 10.16   Creating the Cheeks

In this exercise, you will go back to where the lower cheekbone edge joins the bridge and fill in the gap between it, the nose, and the upper lip edge.

1. Use the Extender tool to multiply and duplicate the three points from the side of the nose around the bottom of the cheek. (Don't forget to clean up after extending.)

2. Align, making sure your polygons are facing outward, and then weld the border vertices of this new geometry at both the upper edge, where it meets the cheekbone, and the lower edge, where it meets the top lip surface. Figure 10.48 shows the filled gap.

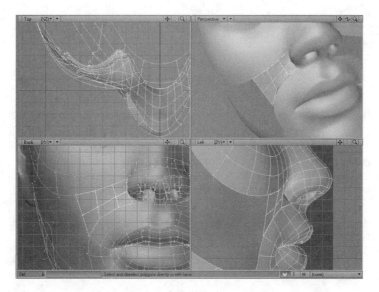

Figure 10.48 The highlighted polygons show where the gap has been filled.

Continue in a similar manner to fill in the much larger gap between the jaw and the rest of the cheekbone surface:

3. Select the five points at the left edge of the cheek/mouth area.

4. Use Extender and then move (t) the points to the left and back so that they match up with the next row of points on the jaw and the cheekbone. Weld the border vertices at the top and bottom. Your model should look like the one in Figure 10.49.

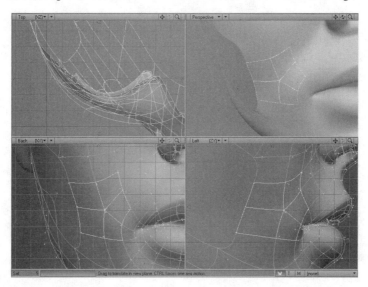

Figure 10.49 Here is the cheek surface after filling in one row of polygons.

5. Continue to use the Extender tool and move the cheek edge points so that you completely fill the gap between the jaw and the cheekbone. Remember that you can use the Drag tool on selected points as well.

6. Clean up the unwanted back polygons and align the remaining geometry.

7. Weld the edges, select the cheek polygons, and press Tab when you're done to activate SubPatch mode. Figure 10.50 shows the finished cheek structure.

> **Note**
>
> The polygon selection in Figure 10.49 marks an interesting structural feature. The point in the middle of the highlighted area is attached to *five* patches instead of the usual four. (Although you've actually created a few five-patch intersections already—look closely at the nostril area, for instance, where there are several—this one is a much clearer example.) Five-patch intersections are useful for joining areas with differing contour structures or patch densities. In this case, you have the circular area of the mouth and lips joined to three much more planar arrangements of polygons that form the jaw, cheek, and cheekbone surfaces.
>
> However, five-patch intersections also can cause a few problems of their own when sculpting a surface. Because the vertex in the middle is attached to five patches rather than the usual four it has an unduly large influence on the local shape of the surface compared to its normal neighbors (which are only attached to four polygons). So you'll have to position this point with extra care. The surface around the intersection point doesn't tend to smooth as consistently as normal and will have a much greater tendency to crease.
>
> With that in mind, it's a good idea to try to stick them in areas where you would expect to see a crease anyway. In this case, they lie at the natural crease zone between the mouth and the cheeks.

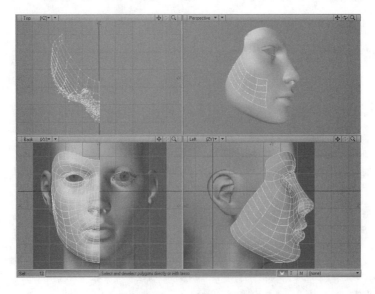

Figure 10.50   The cheek completes the face by filling the last gap.

8. Instead of repeating this for the right side, use the Volume Selection tool at the bottom of the Modeler screen to delete everything on the positive side of the x-axis. (You should be left with exactly half a face on the left side.) To do this, select the Volume tool, and drag around the desired points. With the Statistics panel open (w), press the plus key next to Points Inside, and press the Delete key.

9. Make sure all the points lying near the 0 x-axis are positioned exactly on the 0 x-axis by using Set Value (Ctrl+v).

10. Mirror the face over x with Merge Points on.

11. Finally, go over the whole face (use Symmetry mode to update both sides at once) and make changes to the shape of any areas you feel need refining with the Drag and Stretch tools. Once again, it's generally best to select small groups of points at a time to do this. You also can drag one point at a time. Save your work.

Specifically, it's highly likely that the area spanning from one edge of the face over the cheeks and nose to the other will need a bit of tweaking to get everything looking just right—and that's the key. Tweak and adjust until the model looks right to you.

Figure 10.51 shows the face after this process. The cheekbone profile has been cleaned up and smoothed where it blends into the lower mouth and jaw. The nose has been reshaped slightly to give it a bit more definition around the nostrils and where it blends into the eyes and cheeks. For future revisions of the model, you can drag these cheekbone points to make your model look heavier or gaunter.

If you still have any unwanted kinks or bumpy bits that you are finding hard to get rid of using Drag, careful use of the Smooth tool from the Deform section of the Modify tab will usually do the job. Don't go overboard with it, as overuse can remove too much definition from the face, but for the simpler areas of the face it's quite useful. Use low smoothing values/iterations, and then repeat if necessary. Also be aware that Smooth tends to have adverse effects if used with Symmetry on. It will certainly alter the exact relationship between the two sides of the face that Symmetry relies on to work properly. Remember, to use Symmetry, the point placement must be identical on both the negative and positive x-axes.

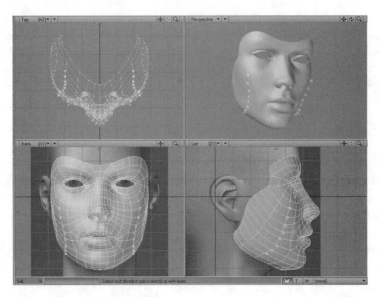

Figure 10.51   Select rows of points to refine the cheeks.

Building the Rest of the Head

Now that you have completed the face, the rest of the head should be easy by comparison. You should be familiar with using Extender, Drag, Stretch, and so on. And everything except the ears is fairly straightforward at this point.

Exercise 10.17   Extending the Forehead to Create the Skull

To build the skull, you first need to add a few extra polygons to the temple area on each side of the head.

1. Using Figure 10.52 as an example, build four similar polygons off each brow edge using Extender. Remember to clean up the back polygons and align them.

   Now you can use Extender again on the entire upper brow area to sweep out the skull.

2. Select the points at the top of the eyebrows, as shown in Figure 10.53.

3. Using the usual combination of Extender, and then the Rotate, Stretch, and Move functions, build out the skull polygons using the background image to guide you. You should be doing most of the shaping in the Side viewport. Create eight bands of polygons altogether.

4. Delete the extra back polygons that Extender created, and align the remaining new geometry properly, making sure the polygons face forward. Then turn the shape into a SubPatch surface by pressing the Tab key. Figure 10.54 shows what you should end up with.

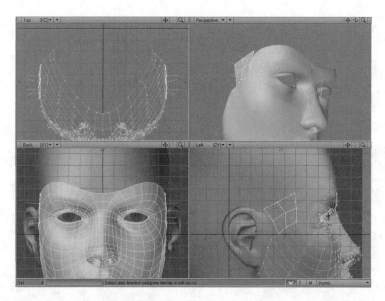

Figure 10.52   Extend four polygons from each brow edge to form the temples.

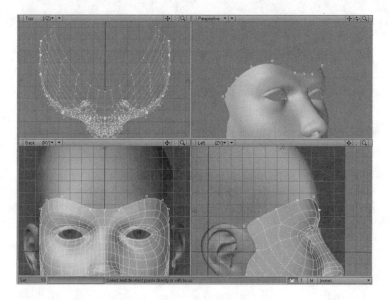

Figure 10.53   Use these points to extend the skull geometry.

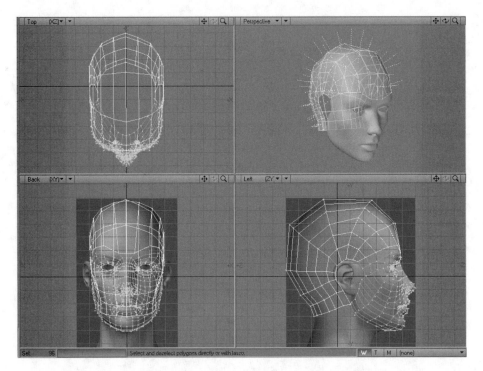

Figure 10.54   Here are the newly extended skull polygons. Note the change in profile as the neck joins the skull.

Note

In terms of shape, the skull is basically a fairly simple, elongated sphere, widening slightly in the front profile as it curves back from the face, and then tapering in again at the base where it meets the neck muscles. There is usually a light indentation at each temple, just behind the eye socket. Also there are some marked differences between the female skull, which you are modeling now, and the male skull. The female head tends to have a higher, more rounded forehead that blends quite smoothly into the brow. The male forehead tends to have more of a slope and a pronounced eyebrow ridge that protrudes from the skull.

Now it's time to join the skull to the edge of the jaw line:

5. Weld (Ctrl+w) the edges of the two polygons, as shown in Figure 10.55, on each side of the face. Save your work.

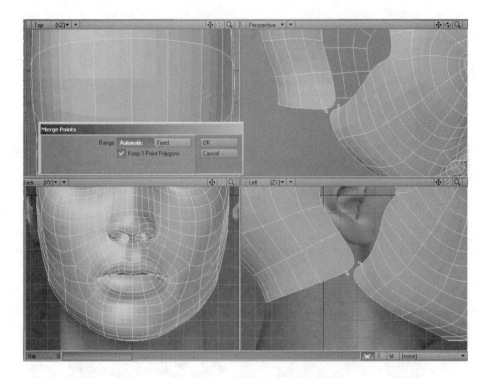

Figure 10.55   Join the jaw and the skull surfaces at the points shown here.

Exercise 10.18   Sculpting the Neck Area

Creating the neck geometry is a simple matter of extending the points around the lower edge of the skull and jaw.

1. Select the points around the lower edge of the skull and jaw in clockwise order. Use the Perspective window for this, as shown in Figure 10.56. Remember that you can hold the Alt key and left-click and drag in the viewports to precisely rotate the view.

2. Press p to make a polygon and, using either Extender or Bevel, create three new bands of polygons. If you use Extender, make sure you clean up the polygon alignment afterward.

3. Roughly shape the new bands of polygons as you use the Stretch and Move tools. Use the background images to guide the profile. Figure 10.57 shows the new surface after two bevels.

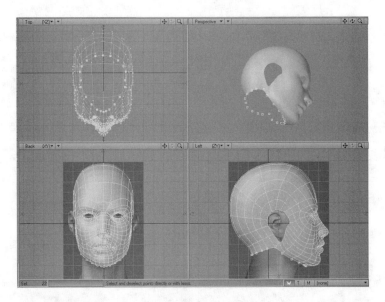

Figure 10.56   Select these points around the bottom edge of the head before extending the neck.

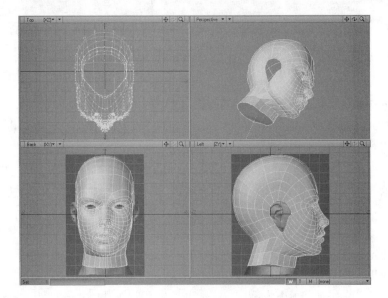

Figure 10.57   Bevel or extend out the neck as shown.

4. After you've got the three rows roughed out, start sculpting the neck into a more refined shape. You can use the Drag, Move, or Rotate tool to define the proper shape.

The fleshy part of the neck under the chin starts out quite thick and then narrows as it descends down to the collarbone. Two major tendons run along either side of the neck. You can usually see them right where they join the skull behind the ear. You should have enough geometry to easily sculpt both of these features. Refer to Figure 10.58 if you need some help.

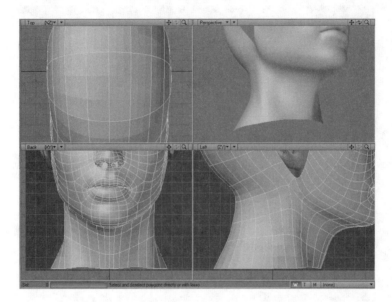

Figure 10.58   Here is the refined neck area after sculpting.

Now all you have left to do are the ears.

Note

The ears are probably the hardest bit of modeling you'll have to do on the entire head. The problem is that the ear surface is convoluted. That is to say, it's easy to get lost in Modeler when you're trying to sculpt the surface. There are so many tight turns and overlapping polygons that selecting the points you want to work on can be a time-consuming task in itself. Try to use the Perspective window, turning it a bit to get a clearer view each time you need to select points, and particularly, when you reach the inner ear stages. You will need to regularly hide geometry to get a clearer view of things.

Luckily the ear doesn't ever have to do much, certainly in terms of deformation. People don't tend to pay too close attention to them either. This means that you can get away with slightly "rough-and-ready" polygon structures when building the ear that might cause problems in other, more prominent parts of the face. In addition, after you build an ear, save it and use it over and over again for future characters.

5. To create the ear, go to an empty layer and build a set of profile points, as in Figure 10.59.

6. Use the profile points, and use the Extender tool to duplicate the outer ear surface, first going around the back of the ear toward the ear lobe. Make eight bands
   of polygons altogether, as in Figure 10.60. Clean up the alignment when you're
   done. Don't worry about back polygons just yet.

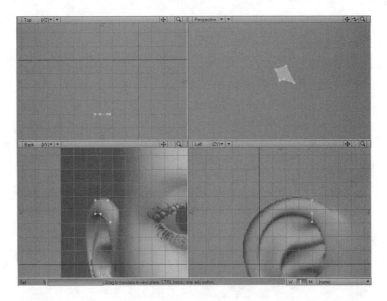

Figure 10.59   Here is the profile for the outer ear. The polygon shown here is just to make
the order of the points clearer.

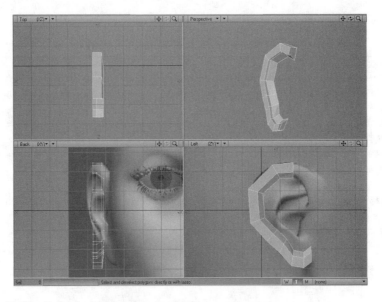

Figure 10.60   Build the back of the outer ear first.

7. Now reselect the original profile points in order again and extend the ear forward. This time create five bands of polygons going around the top corner of the ear and down where it would join the cheek. Select the band of polygons that runs around the inside edge. The easiest way to do this is to select two of them in the Perspective view and then run the Band Saw plug-in, found under the Construct tab. Leave the options for Band Saw as they are (that is, you don't want to split anything), and it will select the rest of the band of polygons for you. Then delete those polygons. Figure 10.61 shows the correct row of polygons to select.

Note

The Band Saw plug-in might easily become your new best friend in Modeler. As you can see in the preceding example, you can use Band Saw to select a region of intricate polygons. But what it is really good for is splitting polygons. By selecting a polygon, you can run Band Saw to instantly slice or divide the geometry.

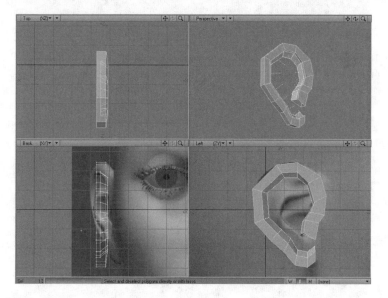

Figure 10.61 After creating the front part of the outer ear, select these polygons and delete them.

8. Now select the eight polygons at the back and side edge of the front part of the ear. Figure 10.62 shows the ones you want. Then delete these as well.

9. Press Tab to activate SubPatch mode, and adjust the outer edge profile of the surface along its length, as in Figure 10.63. It should be thin at the top-rear edge and fairly flat and thick at the lobe.

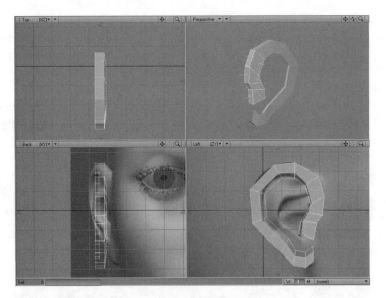

Figure 10.62   Delete the highlighted polygons at the front of the ear. Note that the Perspective view shows the back of the ear.

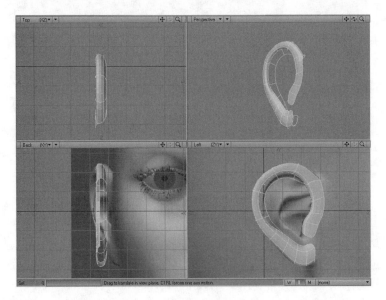

Figure 10.63   Refine the ear surface along the outer edge.

Next you're going to build the middle ear out of the inner edge of the existing geometry. Deselect any polygons at this point.

10. In the Perspective viewport, select the first nine vertices on the inner-front edge of the ear going from the lobe around. See Figure 10.64 to see which points to select.

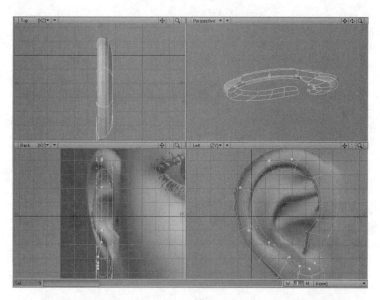

Figure 10.64   These points at the edge of the inner ear surface will form the basis of the middle ear.

11. Using Extender, create three new rows of polygons, scaling them in toward the middle of the ear (each time in the Side viewport).

12. Add one additional row with Extender, this time moving the points in toward the skull in the Front viewport.

13. Cut the extra back polygons (the big, long, thin ones) and align the remaining surface. You should now have something similar to Figure 10.65.

   You now need to attach this new middle ear surface to the two cheek side rows of the outer ear:

14. Using the Drag tool (Ctrl+t), rearrange the bottom couple of rows of the middle ear so that they smoothly flow into the edge of the outer ear, as shown in Figure 10.66. It's probably best to switch all the ear geometry back to Polygon mode to do this. Press the Tab key to turn off SubPatch mode. Select the border vertices where they meet (also highlighted in Figure 10.66) and weld (Ctrl+w) the corresponding pairs together.

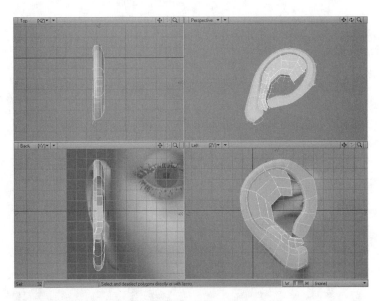

Figure 10.65   Here are the extended middle ear polygons.

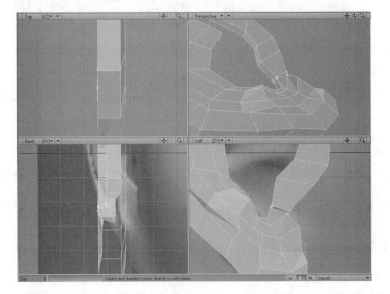

Figure 10.66   To complete the circular ear structure, join the middle surface to the outer edge in the area shown.

Return to the front-top edge of the ear, as you need to add a couple of polygons to smoothly integrate the two ear parts in this area.

15. Drag the three vertices selected at the edge of the middle ear, as shown in Figure 10.67, so that they are more closely aligned with the nearby outer ear points (also highlighted). Create two new polygons to connect the two surfaces between these points. Then create a third, three-sided polygon (or tri, as it's known in the trade) to join the last innermost row of the middle ear to the edge of the outer ear.

16. Press Tab to make the whole ear a SubPatch surface.

17. Using the Drag (Ctrl+t) tool, raise the rear-inner edge of the middle ear out from the head a bit so that it forms a distinct ridge.

This ridge continues around toward the earlobe where it kinks slightly and then blends smoothly into the lobe itself. The ridge on the outer ear also starts to blend smoothly into the lobe here.

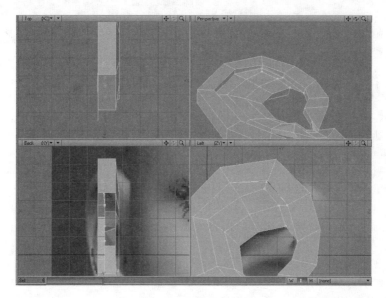

Figure 10.67   Build polygons between the highlighted points to join the top corner pieces together.

18. Weld (Ctrl+w) together the row of polygons that form the indent on the outer ridge over the lobe area. Delete the last four polygons on this row. Then weld the vertices on either side of the resulting hole, as in Figure 10.68.

Before going any further on the interior folds of the ear, it's a good idea to attach the ear to the skull while it's still relatively easy to see what's going where in all the viewports. It's also a good idea to save your work at this point.

19. First, angle the ear in toward the skull by rotating it 20 degrees counterclockwise in the Top viewport. Then rotate it another 10 degrees or so in the Back viewport so that the bottom moves closer to the jaw area.

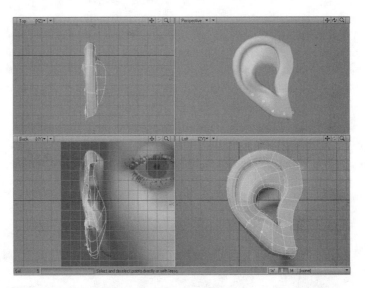

Figure 10.68   Welding the four polygons around the lobe gives you these results.

Next you'll use the Extender tool to create another row of polygons off the inner edge of the back part of the outer ear (that is, the polygons that face in toward the skull).

20. Select eight vertices on the back edge in order. Use the Perspective window to do this. You want only the middle eight points. Leave one unselected at either end of the row.

21. Using Extender, move the new points in toward the skull by about 15mm or so. Delete the one back polygon, and make sure the new polygons are facing outward, as in Figure 10.69.

22. Unhide the rest of the head and delete any geometry on the positive side of the x-axis.

   This should leave half a head and the unfinished ear on the left side. You'll do one side of the head and later mirror the whole thing across.

23. Cut the ear from its layer and paste it into Layer 1. Hide everything except the connecting ear polygons of the ear that you made a few moments ago, as well as the innermost band of skull polygons. It's important here to hide as much geometry as you can to leave yourself a clear view of the join area.

24. Weld (Ctrl+w) the border vertices between the ear and the side of the skull, as shown in Figure 10.70. Start from the bottom, near the lobe, and work your way around. Don't go farther than the sixth skull polygon. You'll have to weld three ear points to one skull point at some point around the seam, due to the differing number of polygons in each part. Merge (Shift+z) the two resulting three-sided polygons into one quad polygon afterward. (Nobody is ever going to really see around here anyway, so a little structural sloppiness doesn't matter.)

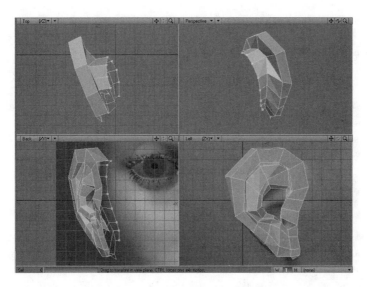

Figure 10.69   Create a row of polygons to connect the outer ear to the back of the skull.

25. Next repeat steps 23 and 24 for the front part of the skull. This time, build connecting polygons to fill in the seam between the front edge of the ear and the cheek. Figure 10.71 shows where. Note that again there are a differing number of head and ear polygons to join at the border edge. The triangular-shaped polygon (it is, in fact, a quad) you see near the bottom of the join in Figure 10.71 takes care of that.

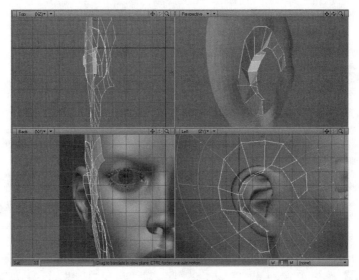

Figure 10.70   Weld the seam between the ear and skull. Note the three ear-piece polygons joined to one skull vertex just up from the lobe.

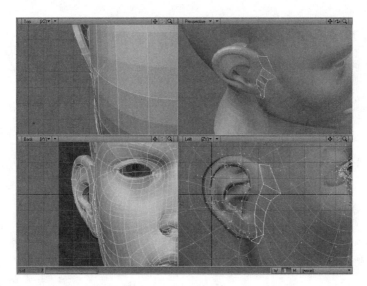

Figure 10.71   Build connecting polygons to join the seam at the front.

Note

It's probably becoming apparent that this final stage is a little messier than earlier stages. This is a side effect of the detail-out approach. This will happen with a human head model, a body, a crazy character, or even an animal. But don't think you've done something wrong. This is all perfectly normal and part of the modeling process.

Unless you have amazing foresight, the last few parts you join to complete the overall mesh tend to mismatch slightly. Here, for example, the ear has more rows of polygons that need joining than the head does.

Although this is hard to avoid, the trick is to arrange for this to happen in an area of your model where a few untidy seams won't make a big difference. In this case, around the back of the ear where it joins the head is pretty much perfect because the seam will be mostly hidden or lost in a natural crease line and this area hardly needs deforming at all. In addition, if you add hair to the model with LightWave's SasLite plug-in, or third-party plug-ins such as Worley Laboratories' Sasquatch and Joe Alter's Shave and a Haircut, this area will be covered up from view as well.

To finish joining the ear to the head, you have to fill in the two gaps at the top and bottom of the seam. At this stage, it's a case of just trying to get the holes patched up any way you can. Do try to avoid tri polygons as much as possible. If you patch it one way and it creates a visible pinch or ridge in the mesh that you can't get rid of, just try splitting a few polygons in the offending area and merging them in a different configuration. It usually takes only a couple of attempts, at most, to get it looking okay.

The following two figures show the gaps filled in. The bottom join in Figure 10.72 is a bit messy but does the job. The top join in Figure 10.73 is actually fairly neat. Don't worry about these joins being perfect. Do the best you can. If it looks right, it is right. (Conversely, if you see nasty tears or pinches, try again.)

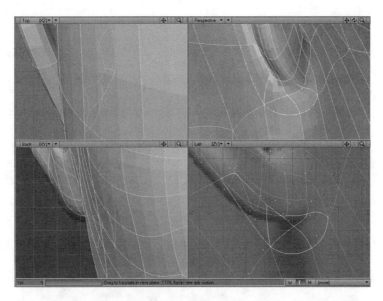

Figure 10.72   The bottom gap patched up—not too neatly, but it works. Sorting it out further would require fairly extensive re-editing of the surrounding surfaces.

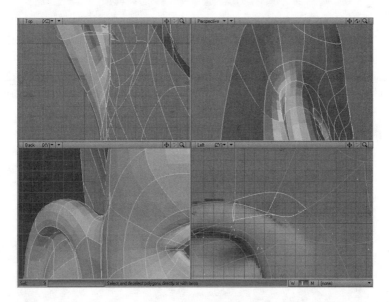

Figure 10.73   Luckily, the top gap is actually much easier to fill, requiring just three polygons to complete the join.

To finish the head model, all that's required now is to go back in and add the inner ear.

26. Select the inward-facing edge polygon halfway down the front edge of the ear hole. Bevel this polygon out three times to create the small ridge that runs into the inner ear, as in Figure 10.74.

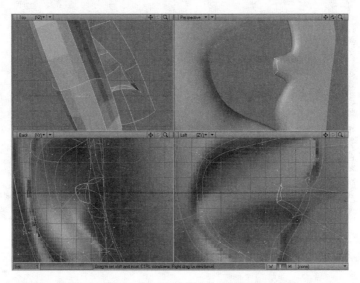

Figure 10.74   Bevel out the highlighted polygon from the forward ear edge.

27. Delete the polygon with which you have been beveling. Also delete the three back polygons created by the bevels that face into the skull. Using the Drag tool (Ctrl+t), reshape the ridge to smooth it out toward its end, as in Figure 10.75.

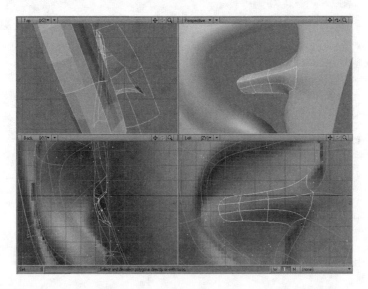

Figure 10.75   Here is the ridge after a bit of reshaping.

28. Using Figure 10.76 as a guide, build a semicircular band of polygons to fill in the remaining gap in the ear between the ridge you just built and the rest of the inner edge. Selecting the correct points to build polygons from can be quite tricky, so take your time. Try hiding as much extraneous geometry as possible to make your job easier. After you've built them, use the Smooth tool (Modify tab) a couple of times to iron out any kinks.

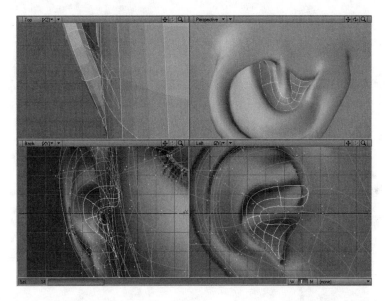

Figure 10.76   The highlighted polygons fill in the remaining gap. Watch that they join to the surrounding geometry without leaving holes in the recessed area behind the front ear.

29. Select the bottom four polygons you just made and smooth-shift them into the ear. You might have to numerically set the Smooth Shift angle to 179 degrees for the tool to behave correctly. Move them down and forward a bit in the Side view as well, as in Figure 10.77.

30. Zoom out a bit from the ear and make sure that it blends smoothly into the head, particularly at the front, where it joins the cheekbone and cheek. Again, use the Smooth tool to get rid of any kinks you find. The points highlighted in Figure 10.78 will probably need some attention.

31. To finish, just mirror the half head over x. Save your work.

Note

Modeling the ear can be the hardest part of your human head-modeling career—but ears don't vary much. Taking the time to do this ear correctly will pay off—save this ear object, and reuse it on future models!

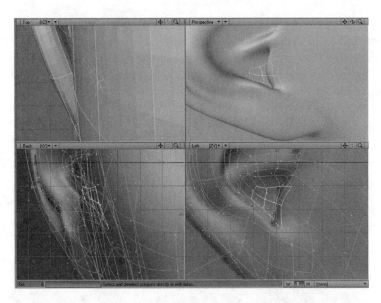

Figure 10.77   Move these four polygons in, down, and forward slightly to finish off the inner ear.

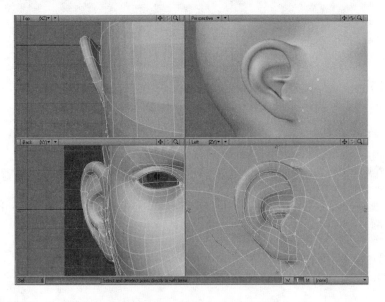

Figure 10.78   Smooth any small bumps or kinks in the front join area.

Finishing Touches

Believe it or not, the head modeling is complete! You have successfully created a young woman's face. Get ready to apply textures to the face to bring her to life. First, make some final tweaks to the model.

Final Tweaks and Asymmetry

Have another look at the whole head and refine any areas you still think aren't quite right with the Smooth and Drag tools. You can spend a lot of time at this stage changing little bits here and there. When you're happy with the model, save it!

It's also a good idea to add in a little asymmetry at this point too. Although it's convenient to build a computer-generated head as two symmetrical halves, heads and faces in real life are never perfectly symmetrical. Giving your model a few tweaks to knock it out of perfect balance will give that extra hint of believability and get away from the "too-perfect" look typical of computer-generated imagery.

The following are some examples of what you might do:

- A lopsided nose
- One eyebrow higher or at a different angle than the other (a la Sean Connery)
- One of the eyes a different shape than the other
- One ear that sticks out more
- A light twist in the lips to one side or the other

Unless you are deliberately modeling some poor, misshapen soul, don't go overboard. Subtle changes to one side of the face or the other will usually suffice.

Tip

To really see how different two sides of a face are, take a photograph of your own face. With two copies, cut the pictures in half. Put the two left halves together, and then put the two right halves together. It will look more like a relative of yours than your actual face. Think of this when creating computer-generated people in LightWave.

Eyelashes

Just to add that all-important final detail, you also need some eyelashes.

There are several approaches to eyelashes, depending on the task at hand:

- Use clip or transparency mapped polygons.

- Use two-point polygons.

- Build them from 3D tubes.

Exercise 10.19   Building Eyelashes

Because this tutorial is about realistic heads, you're going to build your model's eyelashes from 3D tubes. If you don't care to use a hair generation program, such as SasLite, eyelashes can take a little while to make, and they're not good as morph targets either; however for close-up renders, the results are worth the effort.

1. To start, go to an empty layer and build a long, thin cone. It should have three segments and four sides, be about 10mm long and .4mm in diameter, and have a thin end pointing into negative z. You can use the Numeric panel for adding specific values.

2. Bend it up at the thin end and delete the cap polygon at the other side. You should have something similar to Figure 10.79.

3. Change the surface name (q) to Lashes and move (t) it into place against the inner-corner end of the left-upper eyelid on the head. You'll need to place the head model in a background layer for visibility. The eyelash should be right against the lip of the eyelid. Rotate (y) it around its base slightly until you feel it's pointing the right way. (The background images should help here.)

4. Select the lash if it's not already selected and do a quick copy and paste. Rotate the new eyelash slightly and size or stretch it a bit along its length. Then move it along the length of the eyelid 1mm or so.

5. Copy and paste again and repeat the Rotation, Scale, and Move operations.

6. Repeat these steps several more times until you have a small clump of lashes, as in Figure 10.80. Around 10 lashes should be fine.

7. Select the whole clump, copy and paste it, and move the selected clump along the eyelid edge just enough so that it butts up against the pasted clump. Rotate it slightly to account for the change in curvature of the eyelid, and stretch (h) it slightly outward on the z-axis.

8. Repeat this copy and paste process along the whole length of the lid. It should take about 15 or so clumps to complete the row of eyelashes. When you're past the center of the lid, start sizing (Shift+h) the clumps in slightly on z rather than out. This way, they will be longest in the middle and shorter at both ends.

9. When you're finished, go along the row using the Drag tool, and tweak the odd individual lashes a bit. (That is, move, rotate, and size them slightly, just to add a bit more randomness.)

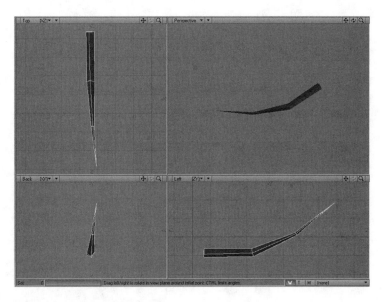

Figure 10.79   Start with a single eyelash.

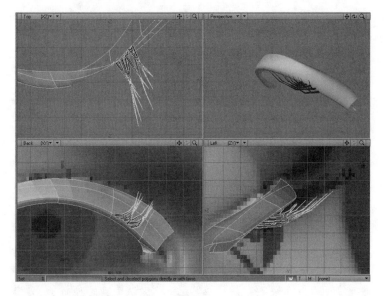

Figure 10.80   Ten lashes pasted in make a clump.

10. Select the entire lash and mirror it on y just at eye level to create the bottom set of lashes. Use the Modify tools—Magnet, Stretch, Move, Bend—to adjust the lashes' shape to fit the bottom lid. The bottom lashes are slightly sparser and shorter than the top ones, so drag out a couple of the longer lashes from the bottom set. Mirror the whole lot over x. Figure 10.81 shows the finished lashes.

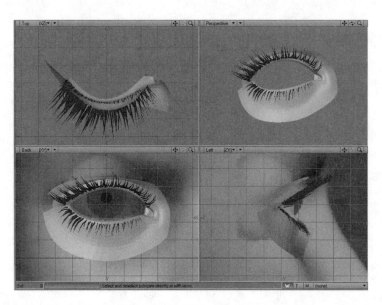

Figure 10.81   The finished lashes should look like this.

11. Use Smooth Scale to adjust the lashes if you think they're too thin or thick. Save your work. Figure 10.82 shows the finished model.

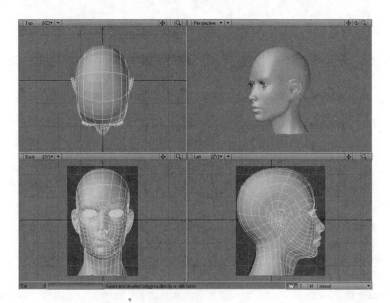

Figure 10.82   Here is the finished head model.

Modeling Summary

Now that you've finished modeling the head, here's a brief recap of the major points of this section:

- SubPatch surfaces are great for modeling freeform organic surfaces such as heads. To get the best out of them, however, give some thought to the underlying structure of the control cage. An easily editable cage relies on the following:

    Get the grid-like structure of the control cage to flow with the natural contours of the model. Your model will be easier to read in Wireframe, and it makes shaping the surface predictable and straightforward.

    Get the right number of control polygons to achieve the appropriate curvature in various parts of the model. Too many and the surface will be hard to shape, too few and you won't get the definition you need.

- To tackle complex subjects such as heads, break them down first into smaller, more manageable parts.

- Prioritize which parts are the most important in the model and start with them. On a face, these are the mouth and eye areas.

- Use background templates or images so that you don't lose track of the bigger picture. This helps keep the head's proper proportions.

- Model each part independently, concentrating on achieving the optimum polygon structure.

- Quickly lay down the control cage geometry—a row of points. Spend the time on actually sculpting the SubPatch surfaces into shape. Select individual bands of points or polygons at a time to work on if you're having trouble.

- "Grow" new geometry out of the existing mesh—using the Extender tool or any other means—when you can. This helps keep your polygon structure consistent (and it's generally quicker).

- Where the separate areas eventually meet, try to find elegant ways of joining them together by doing the following:

    Use five- (and three-) patch intersections of quad polygons rather than triangles.

    Plan ahead and try to get areas that will join up to have a similar number of polygons at the border edges.

    Have the seams occur in the natural creases of the model.

    If the final parts of the model are tricky to join, hide any untidy seams in places where they won't matter.

Rendering the Head

Although your model is complete, the key to creating the final render is surfacing and rendering. The next part of this chapter takes you through some quick surfacing and texture-mapping techniques for heads and faces. You don't have to be a genius with a graphics tablet to use these techniques. They will just give you a rough guide on how to best use LightWave's lighting features when rendering your head model.

Texture Mapping

When surfacing any object, the first step is usually to decide on how to map it. There are several ways you could map your head object in LightWave—for example, cylindrical, spherical, planar, UV—each with its own advantages and disadvantages. The following techniques make use of a compound approach, using different mapping types layered on top of each other and blended with alpha matte images. You'll use a cylindrical map for the base layer, as it's easy to wrap around the whole head and is well-suited to creating broad areas of texture, and then specific planar maps for the eyes and mouth (areas that require much more accurate placement of specific detail). The technique described here is often better than UV mapping, but as always the choice is up to you.

Exercise 10.20   Preparing the Surfaces

The easiest way to isolate the various areas for mapping purposes is just to give them a different surface. That way, you can just use auto-size to make sure that your texture map will fit properly. (Before beginning this exercise, make sure you have an image-editing program, such as Adobe Photoshop, installed on your computer.)

1. Select the entire skin surface of the head and assign it to a new surface (q). Call it Skin Head. You can do this through the Polygon Statistics panel.

2. Select the polygons that make up the left eye area (see Figure 10.83) and assign them to another new surface. Call it Skin Left Eye.

3. Repeat steps 1 and 2 for the right eye area. Select the same polygons on the right eye that you did for the left eye. Assign the right eye polygons to their own surface: Skin Right Eye.

4. Select the mouth area polygons and assign them to their own surface as well. Call them Skin Lips. You can see the eye and mouth areas with their newly assigned surfaces in Figure 10.83.

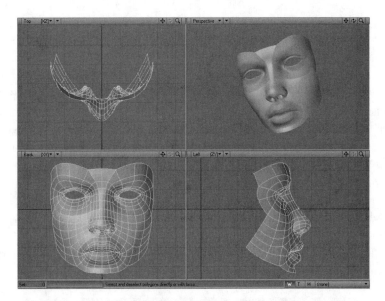

Figure 10.83   Give the eye and mouth areas their own specific surfaces, shown in the darker areas.

Note

Each of the four main mapping areas on the face—the head in general, the two eyes, and the mouth—will require a template image to guide you when painting the texture maps in Photoshop. You need to make these templates in the same manner they will be mapped in LightWave—that is, a cylindrical template for the general head base layer and z-axis planar templates for each eye and the mouth.

The three planar map templates are easy to create because Modeler provides you with the needed projection in the Back viewport. For each surface—Skin Left Eye, Skin Right Eye, and Skin Lips—perform the following steps:

5. Select the relevant surface and make everything else invisible by hiding (Display tab) the selected polygons. Expand out the Back viewport so that it fills the Modeler viewing area. Do this by moving the mouse over the viewport and pressing 0 on the numeric keypad. Pressing it again will return the view to the preceding view configuration. Then use the Fit All command (Ctrl+a) to zoom instantly to selected polygons. Also set this viewport to Wireframe Shade if it's not already, because it gives the clearest view of the geometry for painting over.

6. Press the Print Screen button on your keyboard, or use a screen capture program to grab a view of the Modeler interface.

    This will write a copy of everything you see on your monitor screen into your system's Clipboard.

7. Open Adobe Photoshop (or similar) and make a new image. The default parameters should already be set properly to match the Clipboard, so leave everything as is and click OK.

8. Paste in the screenshot you took. You should now be looking at a copy of your Modeler screen in the Image window.

9. Flatten all layers and then crop the image to the extents of the visible geometry in the Front view. Save the template image as a PSD (Photoshop) file. Figure 10.84 shows the completed template for the left eye. Treat the right eye and mouth areas in the same way.

   The cylindrical map for the head surface requires the use of a small LightWave Modeler plug-in called Unwrap, helpfully provided by Ernie Wright. If you don't already have it installed, you will find a plug-in with the filename unwrap.p on the CD that accompanies this book.

   After installing unwrap.p into LightWave Modeler, use it to create a cylindrical template for the head.

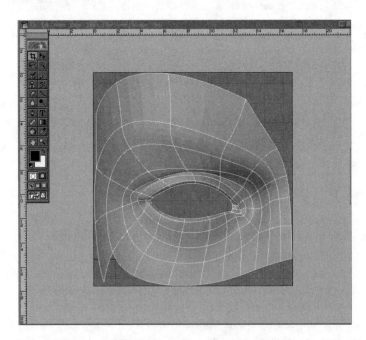

Figure 10.84   Here is the left eye template. Crop your image so that the borders just meet the outer extents of the visible surface on all four sides.

10. Back in Modeler, select the whole head object (complete with the eye and lip surfaces) and copy this to a new layer. Press the Tab key to turn the SubPatch geometry on this new copy back to polygons and then center (F2) it on all three axes. (For Texture Auto-Size to work properly later, the geometry needs to be absolutely centered in Modeler's coordinate system.)

11. Select Unwrap from the Additional Tools tab and enter the following into the dialog box that will appear:

- Texture type   Cylindrical
- Axis   Y
- Image width   2000
- Image height   1000

12. Click OK and Unwrap will ask you for the name and location of the 2-bit (black-and-white) IFF file it will save.

If you look at this IFF file in Photoshop now, you can see that it consists of a perfectly "unwrapped" cylindrical projection of the polygons that make up the head—hopefully just like the example shown in Figure 10.85. The image needs to be quite large to hold the textural detail for such a relatively large surface area.

13. Convert the image first to grayscale, and then to RGB color, and save it as a Photoshop file. Call it head_base.psd.

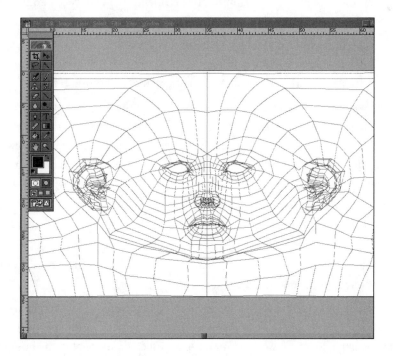

Figure 10.85   The unwrapped head template image looks like this.

Exercise 10.21   Creating the Base Texture Maps

Although it is often desirable to spend a lot of time intricately painting detailed maps for the whole face—an old man's head, for instance, would require a lot of time painting wrinkles, pores, blemishes, warts, and so on—it is not necessary for the young woman's head you have created for this tutorial. All that's really needed are some relatively simplistic textures that break up the surface—giving the impression that the character's virtual skin is organic and imperfect, as it would be in real life—with the addition of some basic makeup techniques to bring out the eyes and lips. Remember, this is the "organic modeling" chapter after all!

The base cylindrical mapping will be used on all four surfaces—the left eye, right eye, lip area, and head—to create subtle but appropriate variations in color as well as the other texture channels across the skin. Achieving this in Photoshop is a fairly simple task. Only the eye and lip area planar maps—the detail maps—that will be applied over this base layer will require any painting work that might require a steady hand.

Here are a few quick tips on using Photoshop layers when creating texture maps in general:

- Try as much as possible to paint discrete elements of any surface into their own separate layers. This enables you to make changes quickly and easily.

- You can then create all the various types of maps needed—that is, color, specular, bump, and so on—by recombining, duplicating, and altering the Visibility, Opacity, And Overlay mode of selected layers in one Photoshop file.

- Often you will need a feature dark in one kind of the map and light in another—for example, an eyebrow or a beauty spot would generally need to be dark in the color map and light in the bump channel because it is a raised feature. To achieve this, just paint it once in its own layer, and then duplicate this layer and invert it.

- Working this way also allows a lot of flexibility when altering or changing things. Going back to the previous example, the beauty spot is easy to get rid of if you don't like it and without changing anything else. Just switch off or delete the relevant layers. This would be much harder to do if you had painted the beauty spot directly onto an underlying texture.

- Similarly, by using Photoshop layers as much as possible, it is a simple matter to adjust the positioning of one feature or several together on the map without damaging underlying work—for example, you could move both the bump and color versions of an eyebrow over the face as one unit just by linking them in the Layers palette and moving them as one layer. (Click the small box next to the Visibility icon on any layer to link it to the active one. You should see a small chain symbol to denote its linked state.)

Back to the specific task at hand. If you need to see clear color examples, look at the PSD files on the CD for reference. Texturing is definitely an area where it's good to experiment a lot with combinations of various techniques—for example, photographic close-ups of skin, different combinations of noise types and filters, or, for the more artistically inclined, painting in the detail by hand. Finding your own unique methods for texture mapping is, together with lighting, the main opportunity you have for defining your own particular look and style.

1. In Photoshop, open the cylindrical head_base.psd you saved previously and add a new layer. Call it Color Base.

    This layer will be used to give the skin color a slightly mottled look, suggestive of the way blood vessels just below the skin vary the color over its surface. You can do this any way you like, but the following steps will give you a good, quick result.

2. Select a foreground color approximate to a neutral skin tone. Somewhere around R 254, G 195, B 165 gives a good, light-skinned look (although you may prefer something else). Select Fill to flood the entire layer with this color.

3. Use the Add Noise filter on the layer, set to Gaussian. A low amount, around 10 to 20, should be fine. Now apply a gaussian blur to the layer. A radius of around 2 should smooth out the noise nicely.

4. Next apply some grain (Texture submenu). Set the grain type to Clumped, but don't put the intensity up too high—don't make the image too grainy. You only want to add skin variations.

5. Finally, select the Paint Daubs filter from the Artistic Filter menu. Set it to Simple, brush size around 8, sharpness quite low—around 3 or so—and apply that.

    Feel free to repeat the last couple of steps a few times. The Fade Filter tool is also useful for altering the results of a filter after you've applied it. In any case, you want to end up with a subtle textured effect, with hues ranging from yellowish to reddish pink. The colors should blend to a nice, uniform skin tone if you squint at the image.

6. Now add another layer. Call this one Blush. You're going to use this one to add some pinker hues to the underlying base, simulating areas where the face would be naturally redder (nose, ears, cheeks) or even where blusher might be applied as makeup (generally just under the cheekbones and around the outer corners of the eyes). Using a separate layer makes it easy to adjust the strength of the effect by altering the layer opacity.

7. Swap the foreground and background colors and change the foreground swatch to a shade slightly darker and pinker than the preceding one (for instance, R 240, G 170, B 140).

8. Choose the Airbrush tool with a large brush—100 or above—but with a low pressure setting. Set the opacity for the previous color base layer at around 80 percent.

    This should enable you to see the unwrapped polygon template below the new layers.

9. Make sure the top blush layer is selected and paint on some blusher using the background template layer as a guide to where you lay down the color. Some soft strokes around the cheeks and over the tip of the nose and earlobes should be fine.

    Don't worry if you overdo it a bit. You can always lower the opacity of the blush layer to compensate. In fact, you will almost definitely need to tweak it up or down after doing the first test renders later.

10. Use the Eraser tool to remove any unwanted blusher.

    As a final touch for the color layers, and because the model is bald anyway, add a bit of stubble around the skull area for a newly shaved look.

11. Once again, add a new layer. This time call it Stubble.

12. Set the foreground color to a slightly bluish dark gray—for example, R 105, G 115, B 125. Fill the stubble layer with this color.

13. Press the Quick Mask Mode button at the bottom of the toolbar. Use the Airbrush with intensity set to 100 percent to paint in a mask over the shaved area at the top of the head, stopping where the hairline would be. (Remember to go around the ears!)

14. Apply a lot of noise to the quick mask. An amount of about 500 should be fine.

15. Use the Fade Filter option set at 100 percent Screen mode to remove the noise from the original unmasked area.

16. Press the Standard Mode button to make the quick mask into a selection. Select Cut from the Edit menu.

    This will remove most of the gray, leaving behind a layer of stubble-like grain sitting on top of the base color. Again use the layer opacity to control the strength of the effect to suit and, perhaps, a small amount of gaussian blur to smooth it out a little. Your Photoshop file should now look like Figure 10.86.

    These three layers together will form the color map.

17. Make sure all the new layers are visible and that the base color's layer opacity is back at 100 percent, and then choose Select, and then All (Ctrl+a).

18. Choose Copy Merged from the Edit menu to copy the combined layers to the Clipboard.

19. Make a new image (again, Photoshop should have altered the default image sizes to suit the Clipboard image) and paste the combined layers you copied in step 18.

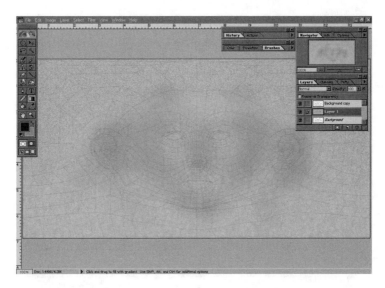

Figure 10.86   The first layers form the head color texture. Here the base layer has been reduced in opacity to see the template layer below it.

20. Finally, select Flatten Image from the Layer menu for the new image and save it as head_colour.png. The image format is up to you. The PNG format has good loss-less compression. Conversely, you also can choose Image, and then Duplicate.

Next, you need to add some more layers for the bump and specular features for the 3D model.

> **Note**
>
> To get a good skin-like surface, you need to somehow simulate the fine pores, pits, and creases that naturally occur in the skin. For young faces in particular, where these features are extremely subtle, painting them in by hand would be a painstaking process. But you need some method to suggest them. Specularity especially tends to pick out all the minute crevices in the skin, giving quite a distinctively grainy highlight.

One way to do this is to combine several layers, each containing a different sort of detail. Figure 10.87 shows two examples that are used in the example texture maps on the CD.

> **Note**
>
> The image on the left in Figure 10.87 is an adapted scan of some fine-detail leather grain. This has the familiar cellular look of tiny crisscrossed creases representing the fine wrinkles in the skin surface. The image on the right was made using repeated applications of the Noise, Gaussian Blur, and Grain tools, with Fade Filter frequently used with either the Screen or Multiply apply modes to modulate the effects of the filters. Both images are supplied for you on the CD in the Projects/Images/Chapter10/maps/templates folder: skin_tex.png and skin_pores.png.

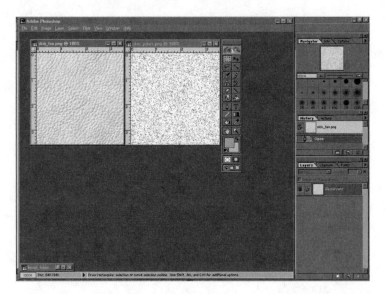

Figure 10.87   Here are two examples of fine detail textures used to create the skin bump map.

To combine these elements into the bump map, follow these steps:

21. In the head_base.psd image, duplicate the base color layer. Call this copy Texture Base and desaturate it because you need grayscale values only for the other texture channels. This layer will be used as the base texture for both the specular and bump maps.

22. Adjust the tonal levels slightly so that the image is a bit darker. It's good for the base to approach a mid-gray so that you can both darken and lighten bits for the bump map. Move this new layer to the top and hide the other color layers for now.

23. Open skin_tex.png and reduce it to 200×200 pixels.

    This will bring it down to a more appropriate scale relative to the head map.

24. Using Photoshop's level adjustment (accessed by clicking Image, then Adjust, and then Levels) move the white point in slightly, compressing the tones toward white.

25. Choose Select All (Ctrl+a) and choose Define Pattern in the Edit menu.

    This copies the selection to Photoshop's pattern buffer.

26. Go back to the head base image and make a new layer. Call it Wrinkle Bump and set its Apply mode to Multiply.

27. Choose Fill from the Edit menu and select Pattern in the Use drop-down menu. Click OK. (You might need to select the pattern in the Custom Pattern pop-up menu.) The layer should now be filled with the crease texture, which will selectively darken the underlying base texture.

Now do the same for the pores.

28. Make a new layer for the pores. Call it Pore Bump and again set it to Multiply.

29. Open skin_pores.png, select all, and then choose Define Pattern.

30. Go back to the head base PSD image and fill the newly made layer with the pores pattern.

Finally, you need a bump layer for the stubble:

31. Duplicate the color stubble layer, invert (Ctrl+i) the layer and move it to the top of the Layers list. Rename it Stubble Bump.

32. Hide all the color layers (by selecting the small eye icon in the Layers list), and then save a bump map by selecting the whole image and doing a copy-merge from the Edit menu. You must be in an active visible layer for copy-merge to work. Paste this into a new (grayscale) image.

33. Make sure the texture base, wrinkle bump, pores bump, and stubble bump layers are visible. Click the small eye icon beside each layer to switch visibility.

34. Save the new bump map as head_bump.png.

It's good to have a way to control how much these maps affect the rendered skin in LightWave over the various surfaces—for example, the tip of the nose and earlobes, where the skin is pulled tight over underlying cartilage, tend to have much smoother skin than, say, the cheeks or forehead, where the skin has to move and crease a lot.

The simplest way to do this is to create a grayscale layer that you can use as an alpha map to modulate the effects of the fine-detail bumps. Figure 10.88 shows an example.

It's usually not necessary to paint the alpha map with any great finesse. A quick five-minute job with the airbrush should be fine. Remember to make a new layer and switch off all the layers below so that you get a good view of the template background layer for reference.

Use blacks and dark shades where you want to lessen the effects of the bump map (make the surface smoother) and lighten areas where you want it to be at full effect. Everyone's face is different, of course, but as a rule of thumb, the ears, nose, and chin areas should be reasonably free of wrinkles while the forehead, cheeks, and, especially, under the eyes should be at full strength.

To save the map, just duplicate the layer to a new image, and then convert this new file to Grayscale mode (by clicking Image, then Mode, and then Grayscale).

Figure 10.88   This is the grayscale alpha image used to modulate the bump map.

To save memory later on, reduce the image size (say, to 25 percent of the original size) as well. There's no particular need for the alpha map to be at a high resolution because it doesn't contain that much detail.

Last but not least, you need a specular map.

The specular layer should be painted in the same manner as the bump alpha image. The only big difference should be around the ears where the image needs to be fairly light. Due to their waxy nature, the ears tend to be reasonably shiny (relative to the drier skin around them). The white or brighter areas of a specularity map will tell LightWave to apply more shininess where dark areas are duller.

Mix in a bit of the bump layers to break the specular map up as well. Figure 10.89 shows an example specular layer.

Save the specular layer on its own by using the Duplicate/Layer/New command (right-click on the layer). Remember to change the image to grayscale before saving.

This map also can be used in the glossiness texture channel to help vary the sharpness of the specular highlight across the skin. (The purists among you might want to go as far as painting a separate custom map for this too.)

Remember to save the final head template PSD file as well, just in case you want to change anything after you start doing renders. In general, you will want to make changes to the PSD file and then save these to the specific maps that will be used in LightWave.

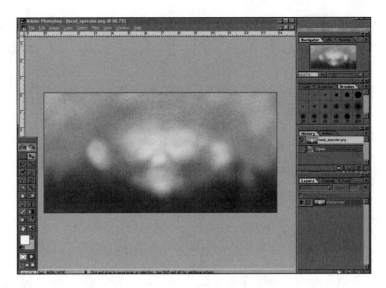

Figure 10.89   Treat the specular map shown here in a similar manner to the two bump alpha mattes.

Exercise 10.22   Creating the Detail Maps

With the base layer textures done, move on to the smaller, more specific maps for the eyes and mouth areas.

Start with the lips.

1. Open the mouth template PSD and create a new layer. Call it Lip Alpha.

2. Fill the new layer with pure black, and then lower the layer opacity so that you can clearly see the underlying template. Using the Pen tool, draw a shape representing the outer edge of the lips. It should encompass the area where lipstick would be applied on a real pair of lips. Make this path a selection, with a Feather radius of 2 and antialiased.

3. Fill the selection with pure white. Deselect and blur the black/white border a bit at the outer lower edges of the bottom lip.

   You have created the alpha matte that you will use later to blend the lip textures over the base layers on the head—the skin texture. The upper-left image in Figure 10.90 shows the finished alpha map.

4. The color map is easy to create. Just choose a suitable lip or lipstick color and fill a new layer with it. The alpha matte will take care of applying this color to the lips only when all images are applied in LightWave.

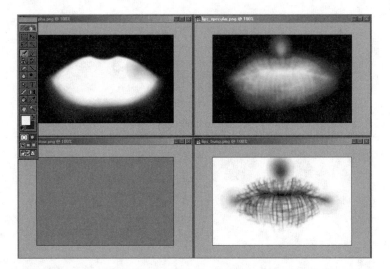

Figure 10.90   Here are all four planar maps for the mouth area, clockwise from the top left: the alpha matte, the specular map, the bump map, and the color map.

The bump layer requires a bit more work. As you can see in Figure 10.90, you need to paint in a few cracks and ridge lines going from the center outward and following the natural curvature of the lips. Although this is a tedious task, this is one area that adds great realism to the final render.

5. For the bump layer, make a new layer and call it Lip Bump. Fill it with white. Using a black foreground color and a fine airbrush set at a low pressure, make short strokes from the mouth center out along each lip. A pressure-sensitive graphics tablet will really make your life easier here. Again refer to Figure 10.90.

6. Blur the cracks a bit with the Gaussian Blur filter. Go over them again, this time with an even finer brush set on Multiply mode (from the drop-down selection in the Photoshop Layers panel).

7. Repeat step 6 until you are happy with the results.

8. Adjust the levels for this layer slightly, pushing the mid-gray arrow in the level graph toward white, compressing the layer. This helps make the strokes more crack-like in appearance.

9. To add the finishing touch, apply the Paint Daubs filter set on Simple with a brush size of about 3 or 4 and sharpness set to 2 or 3. This helps thin out your brushwork and makes the effect look a bit more organic.

    To create the specular layer, just recombine the alpha matte layer and the bump layer.

10. Duplicate the alpha matte layer, call it Spec Base, and move it to the top of the layers list. Do the same for the bump layer, this time calling it Spec Cracks. Make sure this layer is above spec base.

11. Using the bottom graph in the Levels dialog, cap the upper-white level for the spec base layer at around 150.

This will have the effect of leaving the lightest parts a mid-gray.

12. Blur this layer to smooth out the lip edge border. Invert the spec cracks layer and set its Apply mode to Screen.

13. Merge this layer down over its spec base. You should now have something similar to the upper-right image in Figure 10.90 that will create a nice, bright highlight on the lips.

14. Save the combined PSD file, and then save the four maps from the various layers as separate PNG files. Remember to change the alpha matte, specular, and bump maps to Grayscale mode before saving, because it will save memory later.

The eye maps are done in exactly the same sort of way as the lips. However, they will require more work.

15. Open the skin_eye.psd template.

You need to borrow some of the base color layer from the head map.

16. Open the skin_head.psd file and duplicate the base color layer into the eye template image.

This will give you a similar color base to work on, and avoid any mismatches between the color around the eyes and the rest of the face. The eye maps will blend in LightWave to reveal the skin map for the head, so the color needs to be a perfect match.

17. Create a new layer above this color base and call it Eyebrow.

18. Lower the opacity on the color base layer so that you can clearly see the eye geometry underneath. Using a fine airbrush set to Multiply, paint in individual eyebrow hairs over the appropriate area of the image—that is, along the eyebrow ridge. Start at the inner edge of the eyebrow and paint each hair outward. Use a low pressure, and build the eyebrow mass gradually. Again, a graphics tablet is far superior to using the mouse. When you've finished, you should have something like Figure 10.91.

You'll be duplicating and adjusting the eyebrow layer for each mapping type later, but for now keep concentrating on the color layers by adding some makeup around the eye.

It's not strictly necessary to add makeup, of course, but it helps blend the tricky border between eyelid, eyeball, and eyelashes, which tends to look a bit unconvincing otherwise. Even adding some dark shading will help bring the eyes out when rendered.

Note

Throughout this book, reference has been a theme. You can pick up a book on basic makeup techniques and apply that information to your Photoshop image map creations.

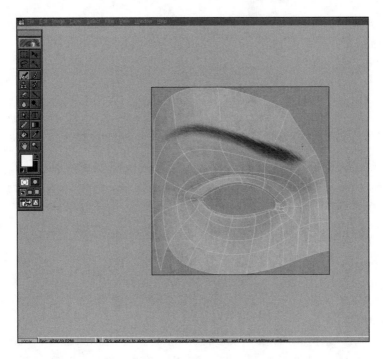

Figure 10.91   Your completed eyebrow layer should look like this.

If you don't use makeup on your own face it's probably best to get some reference for this. In today's society you are literally surrounded by images of artfully made-up women, so this shouldn't represent much of a problem.

19. Hide the Eyebrow layer for now and add another new layer. Call it Eye Shadow.

20. Choose a suitably fashionable shade, such as slate gray, and blend a bit of color from the edge of the top lid, toward the outer corner of the eyebrow. Try to get a smooth blend into the skin color as you move away from the eye. Don't worry about the eye-socket edge of the lid.

21. Bring a small amount around the edge of the bottom lid as well, and add another layer on top of the Eye Shadow layer. Call it Eyeliner.

22. Paint in some dark gray using a medium to fine airbrush, being extra careful to follow the edge of the eyelids in the background. Be fairly light in the inner corner of the eye, gradually building more tone as you reach the outer corner. The idea is to accentuate the outer edges of the eyelids. The top lid also should be denser than the bottom lid. Again, try to smoothly blend the color into the base.

23. Paint in some pink over the tear duct in the inner eye corner on a separate layer as well, just to get rid of any makeup there. Figure 10.92 shows the eye Photoshop file at this stage.

That pretty much does it for the color layers. You can see that having the screen grab reference of the texture area of the model is ideal for creating image maps. You'll see that these maps also line up perfectly when applied in LightWave.

24. To save them as one map, make sure all the layers are visible and that none of the background template geometry is showing through. Then copy-merge the combined layers to a new image. Call it eye_L_colour.png.

   For the other attributes, you need to duplicate and reuse these color layers, sometimes altering or inverting them. You also will need to add a few more elements, mainly some fine lines around the bottom lid and outer eye corner for the bump map.

25. Again, borrow a base layer from the head PSD file. Copy-merge all the bump layers (except the stubble layer) and paste this into a new layer—call it Texture Base—in the eye template file.

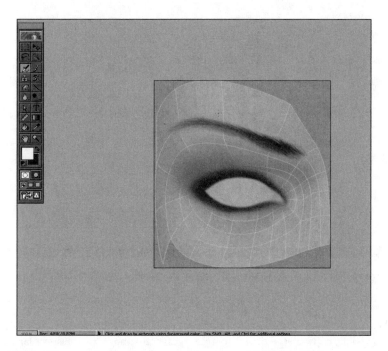

Figure 10.92   The completed color elements are arranged in separate layers.

26. Duplicate the eyebrow layer, invert the copy, and change its Apply mode to Screen (because it will be raised in the bump map). Place this above the texture base and name it Eyebrow Bump.

27. Repeat step 26 for the Eyeliner and Eye Shadow layers. Add some noise to these too. (Makeup tends to have a slightly grainy consistency.)

28. Add a new layer set to Multiply and paint in some wrinkles around the bottom lid and outer corner. Use the same techniques you used to paint the lip wrinkles. Paint in just enough to give the suggestion of extra creases and bumps around the eyes. You can see some finished wrinkles in the bump map in Figure 10.93.

29. Again, select Copy Merged on these bump layers and save to a new grayscale file. Call it eye_L_bump.png.

    For the specular map, you can reuse most of the bump map layers. The one major change is to make the eyebrows dark rather than light, as making them specular tends to enhance their texture-mapped nature.

30. Hide the eyebrow bump layer and then duplicate the eyebrows again, this time naming them Eyebrow Spec. Set Apply mode to Multiply this time. Also, paint in some lighter tones on another layer around the bottom of the eyelids and nose bridge to give a bit more specularity in these areas.

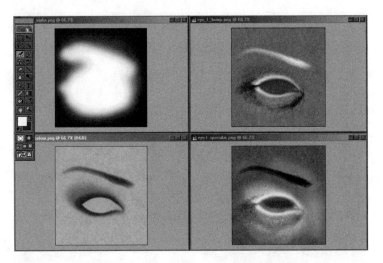

Figure 10.93   The four finished eye maps, clockwise from top left, are alpha, bump, specular, and color.

31. With these layers and the texture base, eye shadow bump, and wrinkle bump layers visible, copy-merge the lot to a new grayscale image for the specular map. Call it eye_L_specular.png.

32. Finally for the alpha matte, make one last layer. Fill it with black, and then lower the opacity slightly so that you can see the layers underneath.

33. Using a pure white airbrush, paint in the matte so that it covers all the underlying eye elements. Be careful to maintain a completely black border on all sides. Figure 10.93 makes this clearer. The alpha matte is at the upper left.

34. Make this layer fully opaque when you have finished, and then save it in a new file called eye_L_alpha.png.

35. For the right eye, either duplicate the procedures for the left eye, or if your geometry is symmetrical enough to allow it, you can apply the image with a negative x scale and invert the image.

Figure 10.94 shows the maps for the eyeballs. These are fairly straightforward, so this tutorial won't go into any detail. The figure shows the following from top left to right:

- A cylindrical color map with some blood vessels for the eyeballs (they don't require any other map types).

- Color and specular maps for the iris surface. The color map was made by painting in some rough color, adding noise and grain, and using the Radial Zoom Blur filter. The specular map was adapted from the color version by desaturating and altering levels.

- The last map is a transparency map for the inner edge of the iris—just to soften off the inner iris edge a bit. It tends to look a bit sharp otherwise.

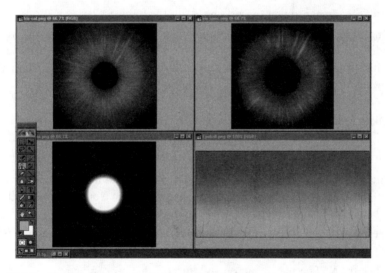

Figure 10.94   The texture maps for the eye objects look like this.

Surfacing and Lighting the Model

Surfacing and lighting cannot really be separated from one another. They both have a more or less equal role in how your rendered object will look. Because lights can have such a dramatic effect, it's important to have a decent lighting setup before you start surfacing. LightWave's default lighting is not a desired setup. This is because the default lighting is nothing more than a single distant light, with a high ambient intensity. This next exercise will teach you how to set up a basic lighting situation.

Exercise 10.23   A Basic Lighting Rig

1. Open Layout and load the layered LW_Head object.

   It should bring in the SubPatch skin mesh, the eyeballs, the corneas, and the eyelashes as separate objects.

2. Parent the corneas to the eyeballs, and then parent both the eyeballs and the eyelashes to the head. You can do this in the Scene Editor, or through the Motion Options panel (press m for the selected object).

3. Go under the Item Properties tab for the cornea objects (press p with the object selected) and make sure the Shadow Casting options are turned off. Do this for both cornea objects. Although these are transparent objects, LightWave still sees their geometry and calculates shadows, making the eyeballs below the corneas dark.

4. In the Render panel, turn on all the Raytracing options: Ray Trace Shadows, Ray Trace Reflection, and Ray Trace Refraction.

5. Aim the camera so that the girl's head fills the frame well.

   Try tilting the camera up at the subject slightly and just off to one side. Try adding a couple of bones and twisting the head around the neck slightly as well. This will give a bit of tension to the character and make the composition a bit more interesting. Chapter 11, "Character Construction," contains more information on bones.

   Okay, time to sort out the lighting.

6. Change the default light to a spotlight and change the shadow casting options to Shadow Map. Rename this light Key Light.

7. Increase the Light Intensity to around 130 percent and make it slightly yellow or off-white. Clone this light two times. Change the first clone's name to Fill Light. Change the second clone's name to Rim Light.

8. Decrease the Fill light's intensity to around 50 percent and tint the color with a bit of blue.

9. Click the No Specularity button and turn off shadow casting.

10. Increase the Rim light's intensity to 250 percent, and decrease the ambient light level to 0 percent.

11. Place the key light above and to the left of the head, just behind the camera. Use the Light view to make sure the head is centered and fills the shadow map area (the light cone angle). Narrow the cone angle if it doesn't.

Note

You now have the basis for a classic three-light rig. Most lighting setups in cinema and still photography are based on these three types of light:

- Key light is the primary light source and will usually provide most of the direct illumination. It's the dominant source of light in the scene.

- Fill light is used to lighten and, hence, soften the areas in the subject that are shadowed by the key light, playing an important part in how much contrast there is in the lighting.

- Rim light generally means light coming from the backside of the subject toward the camera at an oblique angle (usually creating a bright rim around one edge of the subject). It is used to counterpoint the key light, adding interest and drama as well as controlling how much the subject stands out from a dark background.

How you use these three kinds of light (their direction, intensity, softness, and color) together with the choice of camera angle and lens can have a dramatic effect on the mood of a scene. In general, try to come up with interesting lighting schemes. Don't be afraid to drop half the face in shadow, for instance, if it will lend your image a nice dramatic air. A common mistake, particularly when someone has spent a lot of time modeling something, is to bathe every nook and cranny in a broad, flat light from the front with little contrast.

The simplistic setup in Figure 10.95 (three spots) can be surprisingly versatile and effective in achieving a wide variety of looks and moods. For now, however, you just want a nicely lit view of the head with a reasonable amount of contrast so that you can see how the textures react across a range of light and shade. (More lighting information is found in Chapter 7, "Lighting and Atmospheres.")

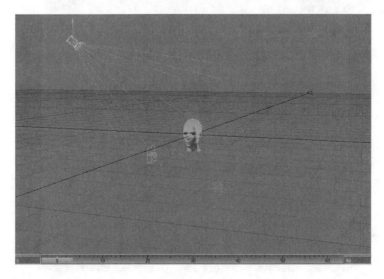

Figure 10.95   The basic three-light setup looks like this.

> **Tip**
>
> You can switch Layout to Light view (5 on the Numeric keypad) to help properly aim the lights. You also can change your viewport layout to a multiple view (through the Display Options panel) to keep an eye on placement and effect.

12. Place the fill light to the right and below the subject, again just behind the camera, making sure that it's lined up by using the Light view.

13. Finally, place the rim light behind, above, and to the left of the subject, looking back toward the camera and the back of the head.

14. Activate VIPER from the toolbar and make a quick test render (F9) to make sure you're happy with the lights' positioning and their relative intensities. Adjust them if necessary. You might want to experiment with alternative light positions, but this setup works reasonably well for texturing purposes. (That is, the figure is well lit without looking boring.) Figure 10.96 shows the result. Save your work.

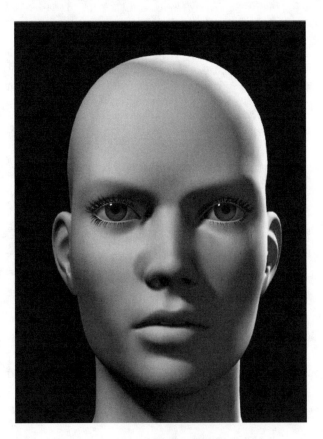

Figure 10.96   Here is the untextured object after an initial test render.

Exercise 10.24   Adding the Maps to the Texture Channels

Now that you have a complementary lighting rig in place, setting up your surfaces in Layout will be much easier.

1. Bring up the Image Editor and load in all the maps for the face (you can find them on the book's CD). You should have the following images loaded into Layout when you're finished:

   - Head color
   - Head specular
   - Head bump pores
   - Head bump pores alpha
   - Head bump wrinkles
   - Head bump wrinkles alpha
   - Lips color
   - Lips specular
   - Lips bump
   - Lips alpha
   - Eye left color
   - Eye left specular
   - Eye left bump
   - Eye left alpha
   - Eye right color
   - Eye right specular
   - Eye right bump
   - Eye right alpha
   - Eyeball color
   - Iris color
   - Iris specular
   - Iris transparency

2. Open the Surface Editor and make sure VIPER is turned on from the toolbar. As you make changes to the surfaces, they will show up in the VIPER preview immediately, saving you from having to do test renders all the time. Note that you need to render a frame first to get information into LightWave's buffer (by pressing F9).

3. Select the skin head surface for editing.

   You're going to set up the head cylindrical textures first because they will be used as a base layer for the other three surfaces.

4. Add a cylindrical map (y-axis, auto-sized) to the color channel and choose the head_color image. Do the same thing for the specular and glossiness channels, this time using the head_specular image.

5. Again, add a cylindrical map on the bump channel (y-axis, auto-sized) and select head_bump as the image. Copy and paste this layer using the Add to Layers option.

6. Change the Blend mode on the copy to alpha and change the image to head_bump_Alpha. This will make this map into an alpha channel for the bump below.

7. Double-click the sample sphere.

    This will put a copy of this surface into the preset shelf. You can open the Preset Shelf from the toolbar in Layout.

8. Right-click the preset shelf swatch and name the shelf copy Head Base.

9. Select the skin lips surface and double-click the Head Base swatch.

    This will paste the swatch settings into the current surface.

10. Repeat step 3 for both skin eye surfaces. Make all the skin surfaces double-sided to avoid any shadow errors (otherwise, light can creep in on the backside of the eyeballs).

    For the eyeball surfaces, do the following:

11. Apply the color map as a z-axis cylindrical map to the color channel on each eye-ball. (Remember to auto-size.)

12. Map the iris color, transparency, and specular files as z-axis planar maps to each iris. (Again, auto-size them.)

13. Make the cornea surface 100 percent transparent, set the cornea specularity to 200 percent, and set its glossiness high—around 70 percent.

    This will give a nice, strong highlight in each eye, which is important in creating a feeling that the character has some life.

    The cornea needs to refract the iris as well. The effects of this are particularly noticeable if you look at the eyes from the side.

14. Give the cornea a refraction index of around 1.3, which is approximately a glass refraction setting. Make the aqueous surface completely transparent. All other channels can be set to 0 percent. (Its only purpose is to set a thickness for the cornea for refraction purposes.)

    And for the eyelashes, do the following:

15. Color the eyelashes a dark gray. Give them a low specularity setting—around 25 percent—and set the glossiness to around 25 percent as well.

16. Under the Advanced tab, add the Transparent Edges plug-in and set the edges at .25 transparent to soften them a bit. Turn Double Sided on for these too. Save your work. That's all for the base skin surfaces setup. Check the VIPER preview to make sure everything's okay, as in Figure 10.97. (Obviously, the eye and lip maps will not be present because you haven't set those up yet.)

Note

VIPER does have a few limitations. Note that due to the cornea refraction, you won't be able to see the eyeballs behind them without doing a test render.

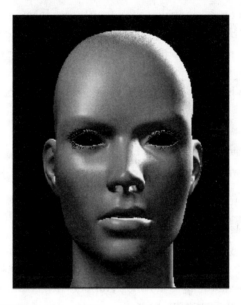

Figure 10.97   The VIPER preview panel is particularly useful when you make fine adjustments.

You might want to tweak some of the surface values at this stage. You can alter the relative strength of effect the maps have on the surfaces by changing the texture layer opacities on the map layers. This works in an almost identical fashion to the way it does in Photoshop. Play these off against the numeric values for each attribute channel. Most importantly, tweak only the values on the head surface and update the mouth and eye area surfaces afterward by using the Preset Shelf. This ensures that all the surfaces have the same values for the base layers. You don't want a mismatch between the surfaces.

Here are some sample values after making careful adjustments to the surface:

Color:	N/A	Texture opacity:	100%
Luminosity:	0%		

Diffuse:	105%		
Specular:	0%	Texture opacity:	25%
Glossiness:	0%	Texture opacity:	30%
Transparency:	0%		
Translucency:	0%		
Bump:	100%	Texture opacity:	50%
Alpha opacity:	85%		

You might also want to make tweaks to the actual maps themselves, in which case you can use LightWave's built-in editing capabilities in the Image Editor, which are useful for making quick adjustments to things such as map gamma or contrast. If you want to make any changes to the placement or strength of a particular element within one map, however, you'll have to re-edit the original PSD file in Photoshop and resave the texture map.

Exercise 10.25   Adding Details to the Eyes and Mouth

After you are happy with the base textures, it's time to add in the details you painted for the eyes and mouth.

1. Select the mouth surface. The base texture layers from the rest of the head should already be in place.

2. Go into the color channel and add a new layer on top of the existing head color cylindrical map. Make this layer a planar map on the z-axis and auto-size it.

3. Choose the lip color map as the image, turn off Height and Width Repeat for this map, and copy and paste this layer.

4. Change the image in the copy to Lip Alpha and change the Layer mode to Alpha. This layer will now effectively blend the lip color into the head color texture.

    It's the same for the specular, glossiness, and bump channels.

5. Add a new planar map to each channel using the appropriate image file on top of the existing head maps. Make sure the new layers are planar maps on the z-axis and are auto-sized.

6. Copy and paste this, changing the copy to an alpha map using the lip alpha image. (Make sure that the lip alpha map is the top layer.) Save your work.

Again, the alpha map will guarantee that the top lip maps blend smoothly into the base texture below, ensuring that there are no sudden changes in surface values.

With VIPER active, you can make any necessary changes to the new texture layer's opacity levels. Make sure that the specular and glossiness values are giving a nice sheen to the lips in particular. This will mean playing with the glossiness map opacity a bit on the lips. Try about 50 percent.

Applying the eye maps to their respective surfaces is an identical procedure. For each mapped channel, add a planar map with the appropriate image and an alpha layer to blend it in over the existing head maps using the eye alpha maps.

Reduce the layer opacities for the specular and glossiness maps to similar levels to the base head maps—around the 20 to 35 percent range.

Do a full-size test render (F9) after you've finished making adjustments, just to make sure everything is okay. Figure 10.98 shows the final texture layers applied and set.

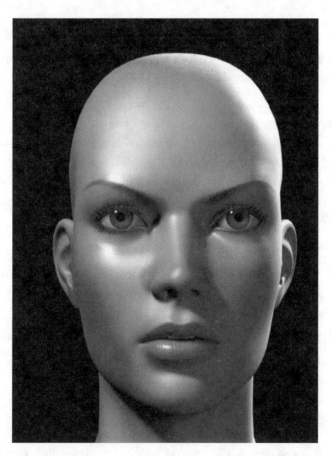

Figure 10.98   A bit of adjustment to the relative strengths of the texture maps is usually required. This test render shows the results afterward.

Realistic Shading Techniques

Although the basic spotlights you have used so far produce reasonable results, things could be better. For one thing, it's hard to get a realistic skin surface just by using standard spot, distant, and point lights. Skin, perhaps more than any other surface, is hard to simulate digitally. The way it responds to light in the real world is complex, compared to the relatively simplistic algorithms used to simulate light and surface interactions in 3D packages, which are more suited to reproducing hard plastic and metallic surfaces. The results often look distinctly less than realistic.

Luckily, LightWave has a few advanced lighting options to enable more realistic shading. Some of these techniques can lead to long render times, but the results are often worth it, generating images that have a quality of light that can look stunningly real.

Area Lights

One of the problems with conventional lights is that the source of illumination is an infinitely small point, something that never happens in the real world. Even the tightest spotlight beam emanates from its source with some volume or area.

The size of this area actually defines the major character of the light, in fact. A small area gives a tight, hard shadow, whereas a large area will give off a soft light that creates diffuse shadows. In real life, you are rarely lit by hard sources of light. Even in direct sunlight, there is enough reflected light from the atmosphere to soften shadows a bit. Photographers and cinematographers often go to some lengths to soften the light falling on their subjects (unless some dramatic effect is called for). Soft light tends to flatter the human face.

LightWave's area lights can be used to give a much softer illumination. To use LightWave's area lights, do the following:

- Switch the key and fill lights from spots to area lights in the Item Properties panel.
- Area lights tend to be a bit brighter than their standard counterparts, so set the light falloff options to compensate. This also will add a bit more realism.
- For each light, set the falloff to inverse distance squared and the nominal range to 1 meter. Lower the intensities by about 25 percent.

With area lights, you also have to consider the size of the illumination surface. As in reality, a large area light will give much softer shading than a small one. Try experimenting with various sizes and note the different feel it gives to the image. Figure 10.99 shows two examples at either extreme. (Also note the difference to the eyes when there is no longer a highlight, as in the left render.)

Be prepared to wait a while for LightWave to finish rendering. Area lights take much longer to render than shadow-mapped spots. Realism takes time.

Area lights are expensive on render time, but a big improvement over the spotlights. The skin in particular looks much more realistic now.

Because of the way they are calculated, area lights tend to produce slightly grainy shading. You will notice this especially with large light areas. You can control this to some degree with the light quality setting in the Item Properties panel; but even with a high-quality setting of 4, you will get some grain. Turning Motion Blur on and increasing the antialiasing level will help smooth it out.

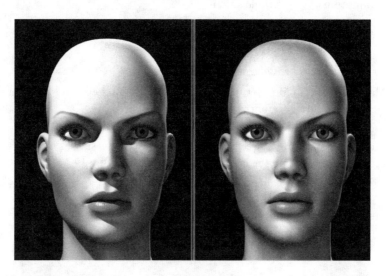

Figure 10.99   Here are the effects of area lighting. The render on the left has the key set to .1 meter, whereas the one on the right is set at around .8 meter.

Global Illumination

Large area lights (that is, soft lights) pose a bit of a dilemma. The grain just becomes too much of a problem. At this point it's time to use another great feature in LightWave's rendering arsenal: radiosity.

Traditionally, radiosity has been mainly associated with architectural visualization where accurate simulation of the diffuse qualities of light is necessary when designing building interiors. But it also can do wonders for realistic depiction of human subjects, bringing a subtlety to lighting faces (or anything else, for that matter) that is almost impossible to get any other way.

Briefly, it is a technique that models the way diffused light bounces off one surface onto another. Rather than a light ray just stopping when it hits a surface (which is pretty much what happens with normal lighting), radiosity takes into account the fact that some of this light will be reflected by the surface onto the objects around it.

Radiosity also opens a host of new options in terms of what you can use as a light source. Anything luminous, including geometry, backgrounds, and even image environments, can create light in the scene. This means that you can now re-create almost any real-world lighting effect using bounce cards to fill in shadows, a luminous box as a soft-box light, or a high dynamic range image-mapped environment to re-create the exact global illumination from a real-world location.

Try the following exercise to sample some of LightWave's radiosity features.

Exercise 10.26   Applying Radiosity

1. Make a flat box in Modeler that is 1-meter square on the x- and z-axes and assign it the surface bounce card.

2. Save it and load three copies into Layout. Place them so that they occupy the rough positions of the three lights and orient them in a similar manner so that the surfaced sides face the head in the center, as in Figure 10.100.

Figure 10.100   These three luminous squares will be used to provide all the diffused light for the radiosity render.

3. Make the bounce card surface about 500 percent luminous.

4. Turn off the fill and rim lights completely.

5. For the key light, turn off Affect Diffuse and turn it back to a spotlight.

   The key will now only cast specular light and will have no effect on diffuse shading. (Radiosity does not take specularity into account, so you still need this one light to create specular highlights.)

6. Go into the Global Illumination panel and activate radiosity. Lower the tolerance to 1.5, increase the sample rate slightly, and lower the minimum evaluation spacing parameter to 5mm.

7. Press F9 to render this. (Make sure antialiasing is at least set at Enhanced Low and that Motion Blur is on.) It might take a while to finish.

   When it's done, have a good look at the results. The subtle variations in the shading make all the difference. In general terms, the image is a big improvement.

   There will be some problems, however. The radiosity technique that LightWave uses tends to produce slightly smeary artifacts and you will notice the odd shading discrepancy here and there. You can get rid of these, however. In general, lowering the tolerance and minimum evaluation spacing and increasing the sample rate will produce more accurate results, though unfortunately at the expense of rapidly increasing render times. Using radiosity for all the lighting in a scene like this tends to be prohibitively expensive in terms of the time it takes.

   The best solution is to combine some direct illumination from standard lights with radiosity fill light.

8. Clear the bounce card next to the key light and reactivate Affect Diffuse for the key.

9. Press F9 to re-render the scene. Save your work.

The results this time should be much more acceptable. The artifacts from the radiosity are, in fact, still present, but they are much less noticeable when mixed in with some direct illumination from a standard light. You can even lower the radiosity quality a bit (lower the sample rate and put tolerance up to 2 or 3) without much noticeable difference.

Figure 10.101 shows a comparison between a fully radiosity-illuminated head (on the left) and one lit by the key with radiosity fill and rim light (on the right). The render on the right took about one-third the time as the one on the left and has fewer radiosity artifacts, especially around the eyes.

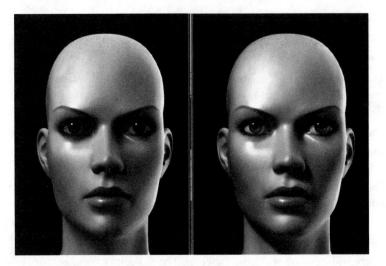

Figure 10.101   For the optimum balance between image quality and speed, mix radiosity fill lighting with shadow-mapped spots or area lights for the key.

Post Processing: Finishing Touches

No matter how good a rendering engine is (and LightWave has one of the best), you can almost always get a bit more out of an image by using a few post-processing techniques. This is not cheating. All that matters is the final image, not how you get there, and 2D post processing is just as valid as modeling, lighting, or surfacing. In fact, try to think of it as the natural final step in the entire 3D process.

Some things are just easier to do in post. Things such as altering the final tonal and color qualities of an image are much quicker to do in a 2D image application than by constantly tweaking things in LightWave. Plus you have the advantage of being able to change your mind or try a variety of options quickly without having to go back and spend a long time re-rendering a sequence.

Most rendered output also tends to look quite hard-edged—even with radiosity. By adding subtle blooms and glows to bright parts of the image after rendering and even faking a bit of depth of field, you can get a much softer, more photographic feel.

Finally, post processing is a great way to make your images more distinctive. It can be hard sometimes to get away from the signature that rendering engines tend to impose. Post processing opens a whole new set of tools to enable you to give a unique look to what you do.

For an example, have a look at Figure 10.102 and compare it with the final rendered result in Figure 10.98. The changes are subtle (less so in color), but they do make a difference.

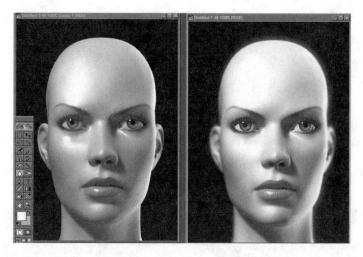

Figure 10.102   A few minutes in Photoshop can transform the final rendered output. The image on the left is the original, whereas the image on the right is processed, and much softer—easier on the eyes, as they say.

Save the last render and try the following in Photoshop, but remember that this process is fairly subjective. Find settings that suit your personal tastes.

Exercise 10.27   Applying Post-Process Effects

Add some "bloom" to the highlights. This also tends to give your images more of a feeling of atmosphere about them.

1. Copy the whole image and then paste it into a new layer.
2. Set this layer's Apply mode to Screen and reduce the opacity to around 50 percent.
3. Apply a gaussian blur at around 10 pixels.

   You should now have a subtle glow over the whole image. (The size of the glow is controlled by the blur radius.)
4. To control the effect, play about with the Curves command. Generally you want to push up the blacks so that the bloom concentrates around the bright parts of the image.

   Merge down the bloom layer once you're happy.

Next try playing with the tonal contrast of the whole image. There are several ways to do this:

- Use the contrast and brightness controls.
- Use the Levels panel.
- Use the Curves panel.

Generally, the Curves graph gives you the most control. Most images can benefit by compressing the tonal range slightly. Have a look at the Curve graph in Figure 10.103. Push both the extreme black and white points in slightly by making the curve into an "s" shape.

Tip

Although Adobe Photoshop was used to post process this single image, you can use Eyeon Software's Digital Fusion to produce the same effects on a complete animation. Other packages, such as NewTek's Aura and Adobe's After Effects, also can provide post-process techniques.

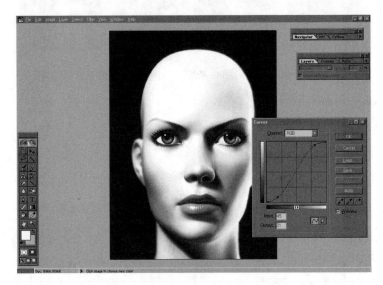

Figure 10.103   Adjust the Curve graph to compress the tonal range in the image.

Do the same for the color values; again, you have more than one option:

- Hue and saturation controls.
- Color balance.
- Use the RGB channel options in either Levels or Curves.

Using the Color Balance panel is a good way to work because it enables you to affect the color on specific tonal ranges differently, which can often give some nice effects. Play around with this (for example, push the shadows toward red/yellow and the highlights toward blue/cyan). Try to find settings that create a distinct mood.

Finally, use the Blur tool to simulate depth of field. Soften the outer extremes of the head—around the ears, back of the skull, and lower neck. Although probably not a good idea on an image sequence where you would want to use proper 3D depth of field for consistency, this can give a nice effect on a still, making the center of the face leap out at the viewer.

> **Note**
>
> Appendix C, "Reference Materials and Tools," discusses third-party plug-ins for use with LightWave 7. One of the plug-in sets covered in that appendix is Worley Laboratories' Polk plug-ins, and one of the Polk plug-ins is called Confusion. Confusion enables you to set depth-of-field effects in your animation based on the position of a null object. You could use it on the face model to make the eyes the focal point, while slightly blurring the back of the head. Also try using the Digital Confusion plug-in that comes with LightWave for cool depth-of-field effects. Learn more about Digital Confusion in Appendix B, "LightWave 7 Plug-in, Tool, and Technical List."

Rendering Summary

A quick recap on the main points of this section:

- Choose your mapping types carefully. Layer different kinds of maps to suit different areas and blend them using alpha layers.

- Texture mapping does not require amazing painting skills (although they certainly help). Carefully modulated but reasonably simple structured textures will often suffice.

- Always try to use geometry templates to guide you when making the maps. Crop the images to suit the templates. That way, you can quickly auto-size textures to fit.

- Use the Photoshop Layers feature. Making changes and mixing elements to create multiple map types becomes a lot easier.

- Use VIPER to quickly view changes to surfaces.

- Make your lighting interesting by using a careful balance of key, fill, and rim lights. Try to maintain some contrast in your images.

- Control how soft your lighting is by changing light types. Generally, area lights are superior if you can afford the rendering time.

- Radiosity opens a whole new raft of lighting options and can create wonderfully realistic illumination. But watch out for the down sides: shading artifacts and huge render times. Try to use a variety of lighting techniques and settings to get the right balance between realism and speed.

- Treat post processing as part of the whole 3D process. Final tweaks are often much easier to do after rendering and can give you that extra 5 percent.

Further Reading

Here is a list of recommended books that deal in-depth with many of the more general issues dealt with in this chapter:

- *The Artist's Complete Guide to Facial Expression*, Gary Faigin, published by Watson-Guptill Publications (ISBN: 0823016285, October 1990).

  Utterly indispensable. If you have the slightest interest in representing the human face in any medium, you need this book.

- *Drawing the Human Head*, Burne Hogarth, published by Watson-Guptill Publications (ISBN: 0823013766, March 1989).

  Although aimed at traditional artists, any digital sculptor will find a wealth of good material to help him understand the human head here.

- *Painting with Light*, John Alton, published by University of California Press (ISBN: 0520089499, November 1994).

  Classic text on cinematography and lighting.

- *Digital Lighting & Rendering*, Jeremy Birn, published by New Riders (ISBN: 1562059548, July 2000).

- *Digital Texturing & Painting*, Owen Demers, published by New Riders (ISBN: 0735709181, August 2001).

The Next Step

Make more fantastic models and try your luck at using the techniques in this chapter to create animals, aliens, and more. Study the people around you anytime you can. Notice their differences and their similarities. Take a look at different eye shapes, facial tones for texturing, and anything else that might stand out to you. Through keen observation and practice in LightWave Modeler, you can build anything you want.

Summary

This chapter instructed you on just how powerful the SubPatch feature is in LightWave. You followed this real-world project to learn about proper modeling, texturing, and image mapping. You also learned how important lighting is to your final work. It's up to you to experiment and take the information listed here even further. For now, turn the page and learn how to make the beauty you modeled come to life.

Chapter 11

Character
Construction

You might be the type to dive right into

character animation in LightWave, or you

might be the type who thinks you'd never

use the character animation tools in this

software. But the reality is that the Bones and Skelegon tools available in LightWave 7 for creating movable characters can be used for animations other than those involving characters.

For example, say you want to create a street scene and you'd like some blowing newspapers flying by the camera. By using a couple of bones in the newspaper, you can bend and deform it. Or, say you need to create a beating heart for a medical animation. By adding a few simple bones and skelegons into the heart model, you can make it pulse, grow, and beat as you need.

So, whatever your situation might be, you should read through this chapter, because it will provide you with a solid understanding of these new tools and show you how to use them in your animations.

Project Overview

The focus of this chapter is bones, Skelegons (which are like bones but act as polygons that can be adjusted, split, mirrored, and so on), and proper character setup for animation. Now, rather than bore you with technical babble about offsets and muscle structures, this chapter discusses the following:

- Bones
- Skelegons
- Bone weights
- Placing skelegons in a bat
- Character weighting
- Bone up tags

Specifically in this chapter, you'll see a basic bone setup and get a glimpse of how problematic bones used to be in LightWave. You'll see how a few bones have more control than you can imagine, due to LightWave 7's Weight Map tool. In the exercises, you'll set up a bone structure for a full human character using the Skelegon tools in Modeler, and then you'll take that model into Layout and give the character motion.

Bones

Before you begin the first exercise, take a quick look at the following examples to help you better understand the concept of bones. Bones are a deformation tool. Represented by a tie-shaped outline in Layout, a bone can deform the points of an object. Because points make up polygons, the polygons are, in essence, manipulated. The purpose of bones is to create a skeletal deformation of a solid object to give it movement and life. Without the use of bones, objects would need separate limbs to move independently of each other. A human, for example, does not have any joints at the elbows, wrists, knees, and so on. For the arms and legs to bend, a bone structure must be set up to deform the polygonal mesh. Because a robot would have joints at the elbows, wrists, and knees, bones are not needed. Figure 11.1 shows a bone in Layout.

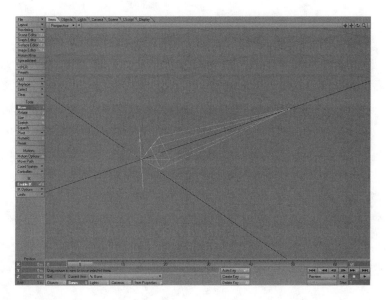

Figure 11.1   This is a bone.

Bones are much simpler to work with than you might imagine. You must follow some rules, however, to make them work properly. First, bones must be associated with an object. The following exercise provides the steps to do just that.

Exercise 11.1   Creating Bones in Layout

Bones must be associated with an object because their purpose is to deform an object. Given that, bones have no purpose by themselves other than as a representation in Layout. Even then, an object needs to be added to create bones.

1. Start Layout, select Add from the Items tab, Objects, and then Add Null. Rename the null if you like, but the default name "Null" is fine.

   This null object is your base, or root object. Even though bones need to be associated with an object, the object can be just a null object.

2. With the null object selected, click Add, then Bones, and Add Bone. LightWave asks you to rename the bone. Just click OK for now.

   You'll see a 1m bone, like the one in Figure 11.1, but sticking out down the z-axis from the null object at the 0, 0, 0 axis. Figure 11.2 shows the example.

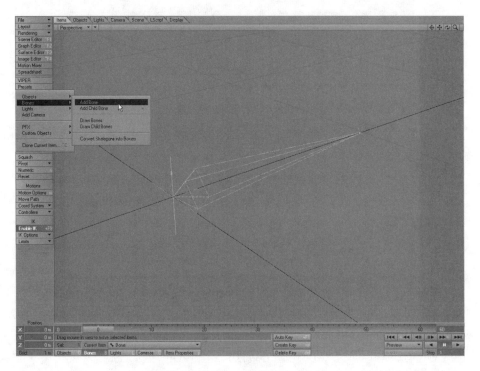

Figure 11.2   Adding a bone to a null object creates a 1m bone heading down the z-axis.

   Next you will set up a chain of bones using child bones.

3. With the first bone selected, choose Add, then Bones, and Add Child Bone. Click OK because you don't need to set a name when the requester asks you to.

   You'll see a bone attached to the end of the previous bone. Figure 11.3 shows the additional bone.

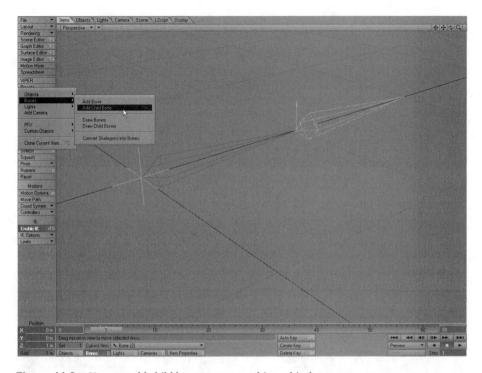

Figure 11.3   You can add child bones to create a hierarchical structure.

4. Add one more child bone as you did in step 3. After it is added, select the first bone and rotate it.

You'll see the child bones rotate as well. If you select and rotate the second bone, the child of that bone rotates.

This hierarchical structure is explained in detail in Chapter 13, "Inverse Kinematics." For now, you can think of this structure as similar to your own arm. The shoulder is connected to the upper arm, which is connected to the forearm, which is connected to the hand, and so on. If you move the shoulder, the other parts of your arm move too.

> **Note**
>
> Using the Scene Editor, you can recolor the bones for easier visibility and better organization in Layout. The color change affects only the bone's visibility, not its influence.

This example showed you how to create bones in Layout. The null object to which you assigned bones can be anything you want, from a character, to a snake, to a piece of paper. You can add bones to anything you want to deform.

Note

For bones to deform an object, the object must be made up of multiple polygons. A solid object, such as a box that has a minimum of six sides, will not deform well with bones. If the box were subpatched or subdivided into multiple segments, it would be more malleable and, therefore, could be deformed by bones.

Exercise 11.2   Adding Bones to an Object

Although you could read about bones for pages on end, the best way to learn about them is to use them. This exercise uses the same techniques introduced in Exercise 11.1 to add bones in Layout. This time, however, you'll add bones to a human hand and see the effects.

1. Select Clear Scene from the File drop-down list in Layout. Load the hand object from the book's CD-ROM. Bones need to be added to move each individual finger.

2. Go to the Top view in Layout (press 2 on the numeric keypad). At the top of the Layout window, change the Maximum Render Level to Vertices. You can find this on the small drop-down list, as pictured in Figure 11.4.

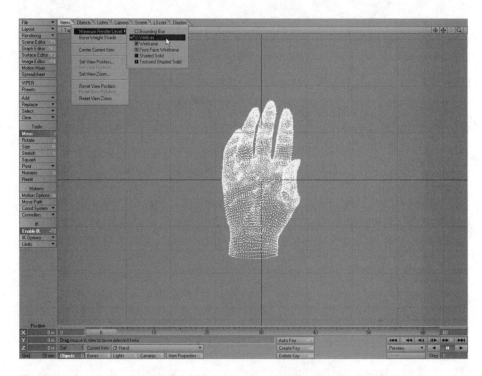

Figure 11.4   Change the visibility of the object from Solid to Wireframe directly in Layout by using the Maximum Render Level settings.

Changing the view to Wireframe helps give you better visibility when you are setting up bones. LightWave enables you to see the bones, regardless of whether the object is solid. You'll work with the solid object in a moment.

3. For now, with the hand object selected, choose the Add drop-down list, then Bones, and then Add Bone. Name the bone Base when prompted. This is the first bone in the hand structure.

4. Press the comma key (,) to zoom out to make sure the object and the bones are all in view.

You'll see that the bone is huge in comparison to the hand, as shown in Figure 11.5. This is because bones by default are 1m in length. The hand object is roughly 65mm in size. Not a problem, though. The bone is not yet active and can be changed.

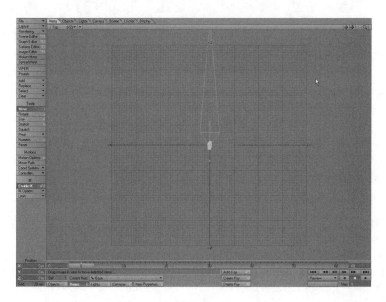

Figure 11.5   Bones by default are 1m in length—much larger than the hand object!

To adjust the bone to the proper length, you must change the rest length, not the size. This can't be stressed enough. The rest length is the final length of the bone before it is made active—in other words, its resting position. The number-one mistake LightWave animators make with bones is changing the size to set up a bone, instead of the rest length. If you change the size of the bone now, after it is activated, the action will change the size of the object with which it is associated.

5. Select Rest Length from the Objects tab, and click and drag the bone down to 0.020. Press the period key a few times to zoom in.

You can see the rest length value changing in the bottom-left corner of the information window. Figure 11.6 shows the bone's new rest length.

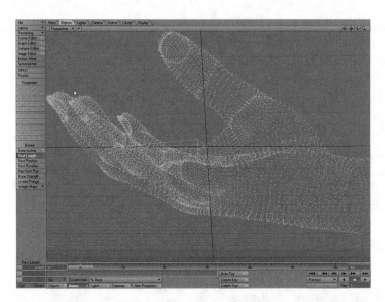

Figure 11.6   The rest length is changed to make the bone the appropriate length for influence. The Rest Length tool, not the Size tool, is used to do this. Here, Perspective view is used to rotate the view so that the palm and bone are more visible.

Note

Figure 11.6 is shown in Perspective view so that you can see the bone's new Rest Length. For now, you can remain working in Top view.

Now it's time to position the bone in the wrist area because this is the area you want this bone to affect.

6. Select Move (t) and move the bone down toward the base of the hand on the z-axis. You can grab the blue handle if you have Show Handles enabled from the Display Options tab (Preferences panel). Move the bone over to the left to center it in the wrist area, as shown in Figure 11.7.

7. Press 3 on the numeric keypad to switch to a side view. Notice that the bone is below the hand. This is not ideal, so move the bone up so that it is centered on the Y in the hand, and create a keyframe at frame 0 to lock it in place. Figure 11.8 shows the bone in position.

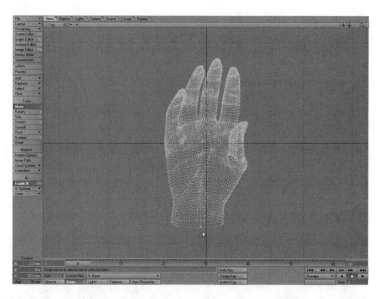

Figure 11.7   After the rest length has been changed, the bone is positioned and moved to the back center of the hand.

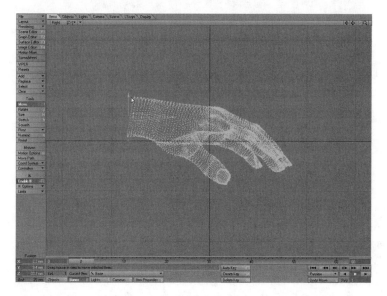

Figure 11.8   From a side view, the base bone is moved up into the relative center wrist area of the hand. Always remember to look at all views.

8. Lastly, rotate the base bone by selecting it and pressing y on the keyboard. Rotate on the Pitch just about 7 degrees. You can grab the green rotational handles to do this. Be sure to create a keyframe at frame 0 to lock the new position. Or, use the Auto Key feature. This rotation points the bone down the slope of the hand. Figure 11.9 shows the final base bone position.

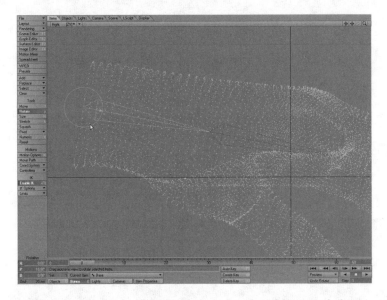

Figure 11.9   From Side view, the base bone is rotated on the pitch to match the orientation of the hand.

Setting up that first bone is the hardest part. Now that it is in place, you can set child bones. And because they will be "children" of the base bone, they will not be so out of scale to the hand when added, like the first bone was.

9. The hand bone is a child of the base bone. Make sure the hand bone is selected and press the shortcut equal sign (=) key to add a child bone. Name the bone hand_bone when prompted.

You'll see a bone added to the top (or end) of the base bone, as shown in Figure 11.10. Notice that this bone's rest length matches the base bone, as does its rotation.

10. Because the entire hand area needs more influence from other bones, you need to adjust the Rest Length of the hand bone to fit the area. Select the hand bone and change the Rest Length (Objects tab) to 0.023m.

11. Now add a child bone for the hand bone and name it "middle finger bone." Notice that the newly added bone took on the Rest Length and rotation of the parent hand bone. The bone still needs to be adjusted to fit the hand, however (see Figure 11.11).

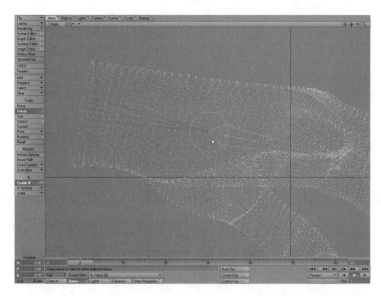

Figure 11.10   After a child bone is added, it takes on the rest length and rotation of the parent bone.

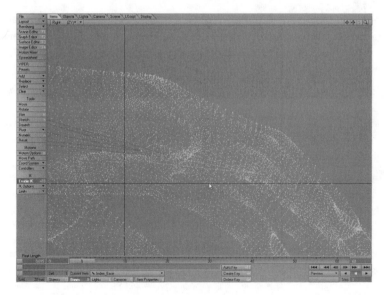

Figure 11.11   When a child bone has been added, it takes on the rotation and rest length of the parent.

12. Rotate the hand bone about 6 or 7 degrees to the right on its heading. This will make the bone point toward the middle finger of the hand, and the new middle finger child bone will follow, as shown in Figure 11.12.

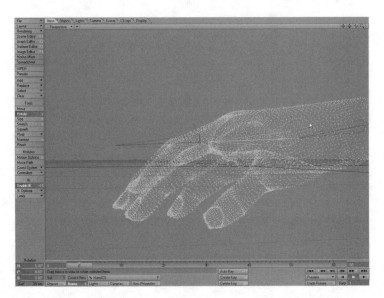

Figure 11.12   The child bone takes on the rotation and rest length of the parent. This is good because when the hand bone is rotated up slightly, the child follows.

13. Press 4 on the keyboard to switch to Perspective view, and rotate the hand and bone setup. You'll see that because the hand object is not perfectly flat, the bones start to stick out between the fingers. Select the hand bone and rotate it up on its pitch about –8 degrees. As you're setting this, be sure to rotate Perspective view to look at the bone's position. Make sure the bone is centered in the finger, as shown in Figure 11.13.

14. Switch back to the Top view (2) and set the Rest Length of the middle finger bone to roughly 0.010m. The end of this bone should point to the middle knuckle, as shown in Figure 11.14. Feel free to rotate the middle finger bone as well.

   You're doing this because when you add a new bone, it will rotate and deform the object, right? Well, when a finger bends, it bends at the knuckles. If you create a bone between each knuckle, when those bones are bent, the fingers will bend properly. Just like your own hand bone structure.

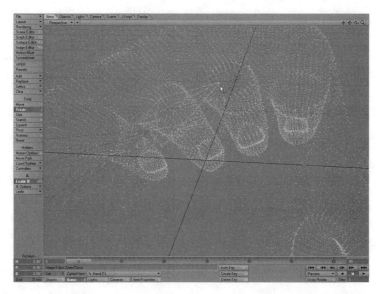

Figure 11.13   The hand bone is rotated to point toward the center of the middle finger for proper bone deformation. Although it's hard to see, you should rotate the setup using Perspective view.

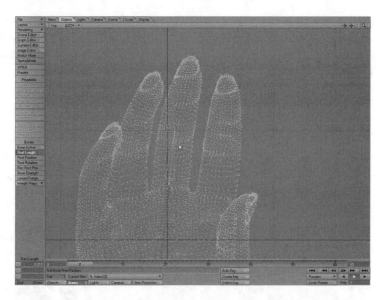

Figure 11.14   The middle finger bone is adjusted using Rest length to point to the middle knuckle so that the child bone rotates properly.

15. Switch to a Right view, and rotate the bone down on its pitch to match the orientation of the hand object, as shown in Figure 11.15.

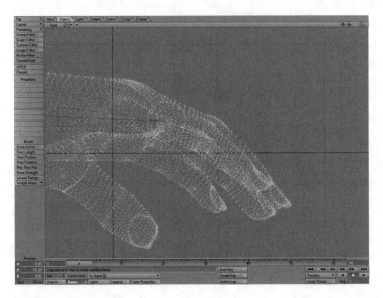

Figure 11.15   Always remember that even though one view looks correct when you are setting up a bone structure, you need to check it in another view. Here a side view is used to rotate the bone down on the pitch.

16. Add two more child bones, one after the other, and position them as you've done here using Rest Length and rotation. Figure 11.16 shows the final bone setup for the middle finger.

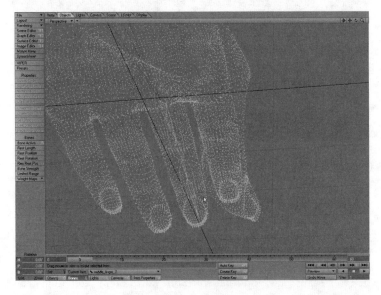

Figure 11.16   Three bones are shown for the middle finger, each being a child of the one before it.

Now the bones are in place, but they are not yet influencing the model because they are not active.

17. Activating the bones tells LightWave this is where you want the bones to rest and begin working.

Because middle_finger_bone(3) was the last bone you created, it should still be selected. If not, select it.

18. Press the r key.

Do you see what happened? The hand object went crazy! This is not a problem. Many animators stop here and freak out, usually emailing the author of this book. But wait! Read on. You did nothing wrong.

What's happening at this point is that the bone you've set into position is now active and influencing the model. But, it is the only bone influencing it, so the model is deforming based on the position of this bone only. When you activate the other bones, the model will return to its proper shape and position. What you can do is start activating the bones beginning from the base bone. Your object will not distort this way.

 Tip

Press Ctrl+r to deactivate a bone. Press r again to toggle back to activate mode.

19. Use the up arrow to select the next bone and press r to activate it. Repeat the bone activation by pressing r for each bone.

When you activate base bone(1), the hand bone, and the middle finger bones, the model will return to its original shape. This is because all bones are now active and properly influencing the deformation of the model. When only one bone was active, such as the last bone for the finger, the entire hand was being influenced by only one bone.

Note

You can see the difference between an inactive bone and an active bone. Dashed lines represent an inactive bone. When the bone is active, solid lines represent it. And remember, you can change the color of these lines with the Visibility commands in the Scene Editor.

20. Go back to Camera view and change the Maximum Render Level in the scene to Shaded Solid. Select the hand bone, and press the y key to rotate the bone. You'll see the hand deform, as shown in Figure 11.17.

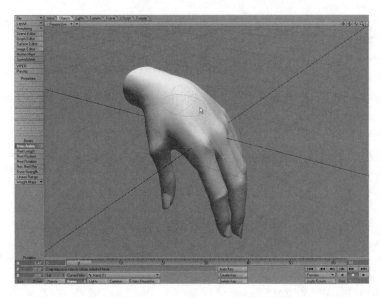

Figure 11.17   When the bones are in place and active, rotating deforms the object.

21. Select the middle finger bone and rotate on the pitch. What happens? All the fingers bend, as you see in Figure 11.18. And the fingers pinch as well.

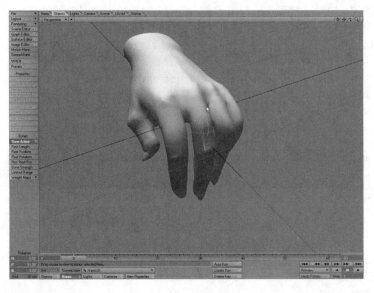

Figure 11.18   Although the bones are set properly, the influence of the middle finger bone is too much for the hand model. Just rotating the bone a small amount deforms the hand and fingers, which is not desired.

Often, adding bones in Layout for skeletal deformation is all you need for things such as cloth, breathing creatures, or exaggerated movements. In objects such as this simple hand, however, the deformation is not right. To correct this unwanted deforming, you would place more bones as "anchor" bones to hold the hand in place. You also could increase the falloff of the bone influence, or set a limited range. Essentially, the normal bone controls don't allow you a precise way to confine their influence. Although these techniques work just fine, they can be labor intensive. They also increase the complexity of your hierarchy. LightWave however, can solve all your problems with bone weights.

Bone Weights

Bone weights help you set up a limited range of influence on the bones you create in LightWave. The bone weights feature, which you'll find in Modeler, automates the process of creating weight maps that approximate what the normal bone influence would be. Before you can use bone weights, however, you must have Skelegons already in place. Skelegons are discussed in greater detail later in this chapter. After a weight map is created, you can adjust the maps to suit your needs through the Bone Weights feature. Figure 11.19 shows the Make Bone Weight Map panel in Modeler, found under the Map tab list of tools.

The reason this is mentioned here is to make you aware of the tools available to you when setting up bones for object deformation. Bone weights are just one option of weighting in LightWave; you also can create weights for bones without bone weights or Skelegons. As you work through the rest of this chapter and other Modeler functions in the book, you'll see how useful and diverse weights really are.

The first step in understanding the use of bone weights is to explore LightWave's weights in Modeler. Weight maps were demonstrated earlier in the book in Chapter 3, "LightWave 7 Modeler;" they enable you to scale the falloff of various tools in LightWave. With a weight map, a bone affects points according to the weight you set. The result is a controlled influence that eliminates the problem you saw in Exercise 11.2 and in Figure 11.18.

Falloff

The Falloff selections within the Bone Weights panel determine how the influences of bones fade with distance. The settings work mathematically, and the default is Inverse Distance^4. This exponential value of ^{4} sets a fair amount of falloff for a bone, whereas a higher value of ^{16} will have a greater (or faster) falloff. Layout's Bones Falloff Type ranges from ^{2} to ^{128}. Exercise 11.3 uses a falloff setting so that you can see the effects.

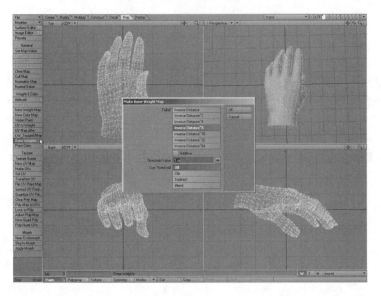

Figure 11.19   With the Make Bone Weights Map panel in Modeler, you can control falloff and influence of your bones.

Additive

The Additive selection within the bone weights panel tells LightWave to add weight to any existing value. Therefore, in the case of the simple hand object in the previous exercises, the finger bones were not named the same. If their names were the same, LightWave would have added the weight values to each. Using Additive quickly sets up bone weights without renaming every bone.

Threshold Value

The Threshold Value is similar to Limited Region for bones in Layout. It is an encapsulated region around a bone, and the value set (such as 1m) determines the size of the region.

Using Threshold

This setting takes the weight value of the set threshold distance as Off, Clip, Subtract, or Blend. Off ignores the Threshold Value set. Clip simply cuts the weight when outside the threshold to 0. Subtract subtracts the weight from all values, making the weights run smoothly at 0 and negative at the threshold. Finally, Blend subtracts the Threshold Value, and then clips the negative weights to 0. This setting often is the most useful.

More information and specific details are highlighted in the LightWave Reference manuals that came with your LightWave 7 software. For now, this next exercise guides you through the use of setting up bone weights in Modeler and then applying them in Layout. The result is perfect deformations, unlike the bone setup outlined in Exercise 11.2.

Exercise 11.3   Applying Bone Weights

Bone weights enable you to specify regions of influence. Much of the time when creating character animation, you'll build your model from the ground up. You can assign weight maps as you go. You also can use existing models, either from a previous project, by another artist, or perhaps from this book's CD.

1. Open Modeler, and load the Hand_2.lwo object from the book's CD. This is the same simple hand object you used in the previous exercises, but it has been renamed for clarity. Figure 11.20 shows the model loaded. Press the a key to fit the model in view to match the figure.

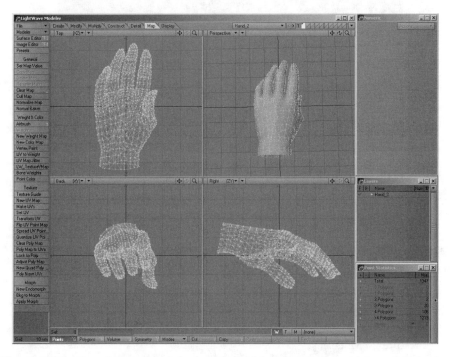

Figure 11.20   An existing model is loaded into Modeler, ready to have weights assigned to it.

Note

Figure 11.20 shows the Modeler interface sized to the left a bit, with the Numeric (n), Layers (Display tab), and Point Statistics (w) panels left open on the right. You can set up your view like this if you want.

In Exercise 11.2, you created five bones: one bone for the base of the hand, one bone for the hand (palm area), and three bones for the fingers. You need only to set up some weight maps for these areas, and your model will deform properly in Layout.

2. Choose Polygon Selection mode by clicking the Polygon button at the bottom of the Modeler interface.

3. In the Top view (top-left quadrant), click once on the tip of the middle finger to select a few polygons, as shown in Figure 11.21.

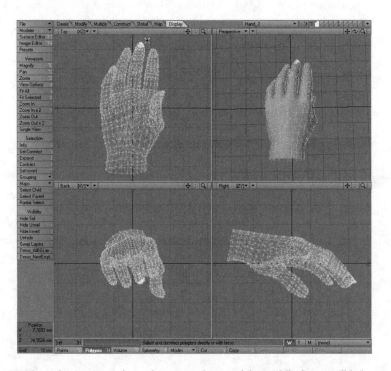

Figure 11.21   Selecting just a few polygons on the tip of the middle finger will help you select the isolated finger.

You could have told Modeler where to apply weight maps by going to the Statistics panel and selecting the polygons of the middle finger. Because the entire hand is one surface, however, you can simply use the Select Connected features in Modeler.

4. With the few polygons selected at the tip of the finger, hold the Shift key and press the right bracket key (]).

Pressing only the right bracket applies the Select Connected command found under the Display tab. Holding the Shift key while pressing the bracket key activates the Expand Select option. You can continually press the Shift +] to expand the polygon selection. Note that pressing Shift+] deselect in the same manner.

5. Press Shift+] five times to select the front part of the middle finger up through the knuckle, as shown in Figure 11.22. Note that the Top view has been expanded to full screen for visibility. Note that you also can use the Lasso select command with the right mouse button to select the polygons.

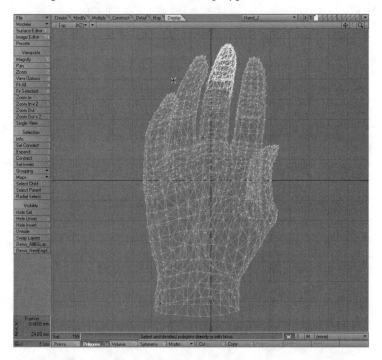

Figure 11.22   Pressing Shift+] five times selects just the front polygons of the middle finger.

6. With the polygons of the tip of the middle finger selected, select the W at the bottom of the Modeler interface (next to T and M) to choose Weight mode. In the drop-down list next to these choices where it reads [none], select [new]. Figure 11.23 shows the selection.

The Create Weight Map panel comes up. You now can assign a weight map to the selected polygons. Remember, the selected polygons are for the fingertip.

7. Change the Name to FingerTip_weight. You don't need to call it "weight," but it helps to keep things clear when many weights and surfaces are similarly named. Keep Initial Value checked, and leave 100 percent applied, as shown in Figure 11.24.

Figure 11.23
You assign a weight map to selected polygons by selecting [new] from the W drop-down list.

Figure 11.24   When you assign a weight map, you also can set the name of the weight. This is a good habit to get into for organization.

You've now set a weight map for the fingertip, but, as you might remember, there are three bones in the finger. This is a good time to change your Perspective view (or any view) to Weight Shade Render View mode.

8. Before you deselect all the fingertip polygons, deselect just up to the knuckle and leave a portion selected, as shown in Figure 11.25.

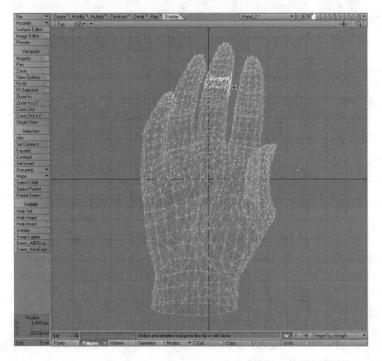

Figure 11.25   Weight maps can overlap, which means that you can leave a portion of the fingertip polygons selected when choosing the next portion of the finger.

9. Hold the Shift key and select the polygons making up the middle portion of the finger—basically from knuckle to knuckle—including the extra few polygons left over from the previous step. Figure 11.26 shows the selection.

You can use the Expand Select command again, deselecting any unnecessary polygons; or better, use the Lasso Select function for the desired polygons. Simply drag using the right mouse button.

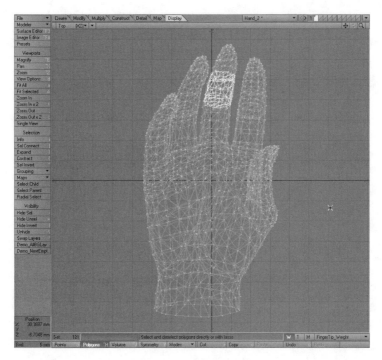

Figure 11.26   The middle portion polygons of the finger are selected so that a weight map can be applied.

   10. Select [new] again from the W command to Create Weight Map for this selection. Name the new weight map MiddleFinger_Weight, as shown in Figure 11.27.

Figure 11.27   Another weight map is added to the middle portion of the finger.

You can assign weight maps to selected polygons or points. But if you apply a weight map to selected polygons, you really are applying the weight to the points of the selected polygons.

   11. So, switch over to Point mode by selecting the Point button at the bottom of the Modeler interface, or by pressing the Ctrl+g key combination. This tells Modeler you're now working with points.

   12. Using the right mouse button in Top view, lasso the points of the finger, from the middle knuckle up to the base of the finger. Figure 11.28 shows the selection.

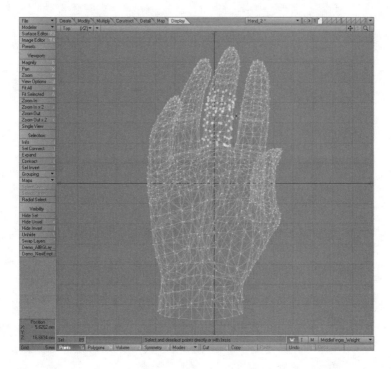

Figure 11.28   You can assign weight maps to points as well as polygons. Here, the points of the finger base are selected for a weight map to be applied.

Note

The decision about selecting polygons or points (or vice versa) for weight maps is up to you. You've been shown both options here so that you can understand how it all works. Polygons are sometimes a better choice for weight map polygon selection, however, because when you use polygons it is much easier to see what is—and more importantly, what is not—selected.

13. From the same drop-down list next to the W, choose [new], and select Create Weight Map. Set the Name to BaseFinger_Weight.

14. Set up one more weight map. Deselect the points of the base finger and select all the points that make up the palm of the hand. You can do this by lasso-selecting in Top view, and then lasso de-selecting the thumb points in Side view, as shown in Figure 11.29.

15. After the palm points are selected, create a weight map for them and name them Palm_Weight. When completed, save your object as PalmWeight or something similar.

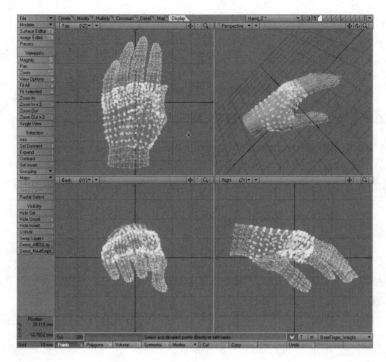

Figure 11.29   Select the points of the palm of the hand to set one more weight map.

16. Go to Layout and load the HandBoneActive scene from the book's CD. This is the scene from Exercise 11.2. If you remember, rotating only the base finger bone deformed the entire hand.

17. Select the hand object, and then select Replace from the Items tab, then choose Replace With Object File, as shown in Figure 11.30.

18. Select the PalmWeight object when prompted. This is the hand object with weight maps assigned.

    By replacing the existing hand, the bones will now be assigned to the weighted head. All you need to do is tell the bones to use the weight maps.

19. Be sure that the PalmWeight object is selected, and then press the Bones button at the bottom of the Layout interface (or press Shift+b). You're now working with the bones of the hand object. The hand bone (1) should be selected; if it is not, select it. Press the p key to go to the Item Properties panel for Bones.

20. In the middle of the panel, select Palm_Weight for Bone Weight Map, as shown in Figure 11.31.

Figure 11.30
Updating an object is easy to do by using the Replace With Object File command in Layout.

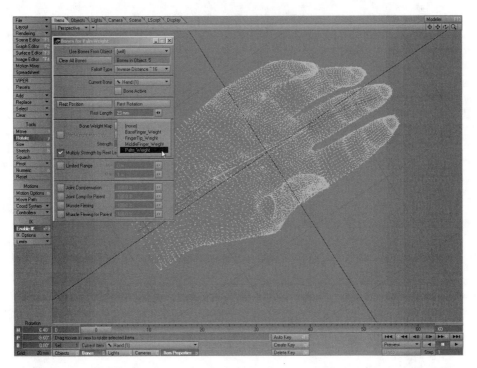

Figure 11.31   The weight maps created in Modeler can be assigned to bones through the Bones Properties panel in Layout.

21. While still in the Item Properties panel for bones, press the down-arrow key on the keyboard to select the Hand(2) Bone. To verify your selection, you can move the Properties panel aside to view both the panel and Layout. Set the Bone Weight Map to BaseFinger_Weight. Can you now see why appropriately naming the bones and the weights is important? The Current Bone property panel also shows the selected bone.

22. Assign the rest of the bone weight maps to the finger bones.

    Figure 11.32 shows the Middle_Finger bone rotated in one direction on the pitch, while the parent bones remain in place. Notice that the hand object no longer gets squashed or deforms oddly. When the finger bones are moved, only the appropriately weighted area moves, not the polygons nearby, as was the case in Exercise 11.2. Welcome to bone weights!

You might have noticed that some other selections were available in the Bones Properties panel, such as Use Weight Map Only and Weight Normalization. If you want your weight maps to be the only control over influence, you can activate Use Weight Map Only. When you do, the Weight Normalization simply "normalizes" the weight values, which is useful for bone weighting. Otherwise, you have to be very careful about the weight values.

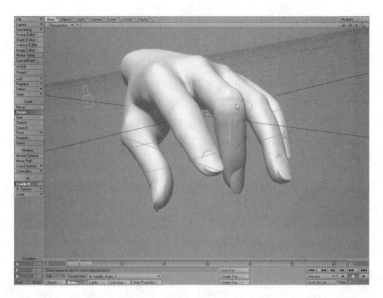

Figure 11.32   Bone weights applied to the model allow much greater control over bone influences.

> **Note**
>
> There's a little trick in LightWave you can try when setting up additional bones and weights. If the weight map created in Modeler is named exactly the same (capitalization included) as the bone, the weight map in Layout will be automatically applied.

The subtlety of using weight maps with bones is that you can define the falloff influence of a bone. This exercise created all weight maps with 100 percent initial value, which tells the models to rely on the bone falloff with this value only. You can have even more power over your models with weight maps because you can control the bone influence absolutely. For example, you can use one of the weight tools to drop off the weighted influence from 100 percent to 0 toward the top. Try experimenting with the scenes on the book's CD and change the influences to see what sort of results you can create.

Skelegons

As you worked through the setup of just five bones for the hand and middle finger earlier in this chapter, you probably realized that applying bones can be a tedious process. And it can! However, Skelegons give you a much better method for setting up bone structures. You do this in Modeler.

You'll grow fond of the term Skelegons as you work through this next section because Skelegons are polygons that resemble bones. In Modeler, you can create and modify Skelegons as though they were polygons and then convert them to bones in Layout. The benefit of this is the ability to set up bones for a character in Perspective view with modeling tools such as Drag and Rotate. Even better, the skeletal structure you create for a character is saved with the object! All the skeletal information is saved with the object. This means you can set up full bone structures for characters and load them individually into a single scene.

When you create a character with Skelegons, you can change the model at any time and adjust its skeletal structure. In addition, you can create one base skeletal structure and use it over and over again for future characters. The next exercise gets you right into it by setting up Skelegons for a full figure.

> **Note**
>
> Be sure that you always save a copy of your model with Skelegons. When you convert Skelegons to bones, they can't be changed back to Skelegons.

Creating Skelegons in Modeler

You can create Skelegons in Modeler a couple of different ways. You can build them point-by-point and convert single-line polygons to Skelegons, such as two points connected with a line polygon or a curve. This is useful for creating Skelegons from existing models. The Draw Skelegons feature is fast and easy, and it is the focus of this next exercise.

Exercise 11.4   Creating Skelegons in Humans

This exercise uses an existing model to demonstrate how quick and easy it is to set up a full hierarchy for a human character. Using the bone weight information from the previous exercises and the Skelegons information provided here, you'll be animating a fully articulated character in no time. You're going to use an automatic feature in LightWave to automatically apply weights to the character. The trick is building the Skelegons in the same layer as the geometry. However, for visual examples, this tutorial will show you the Skelegons in a separate layer. You, however, should build the Skelegons in the same layer as the geometry.

    1. In Modeler, clear any work after you've saved it by selecting Close All Objects from the File menu. Press the a key to reset your views. Load the snowman object from the book's CD. This is a full-figure abominable-snowman-Bigfoot-type character. Figure 11.33 shows the model loaded with the Layers (Ctrl+F5), Numeric (n), and Statistics (w) panels open.

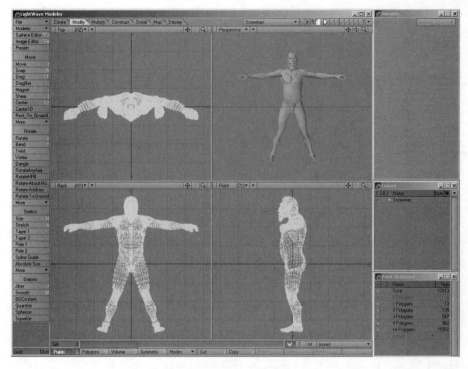

Figure 11.33   The full-figure object loaded into Modeler.

2. Select a new layer, making the figure a background layer. From the Create tab, select Skelegons, as shown in Figure 11.34.

Note

If you like, you can use the Edit Menu Layout command to set up a group of Skelegon tools that you use often. Refer to Chapter 1, "Introducing LightWave 7," for more information on customizing buttons and menus.

3. Move the mouse over the Back view (Viewport 3) at the bottom left of Modeler, and press the 0 key on the numeric keypad to make the view full-screen. Use the period key (.) to zoom in. Now, click and drag up, just above the creature's waist, as shown in Figure 11.35.

Figure 11.34
The Skelegons command is under the Create tab.

Note

Be careful to click and drag just once. It's very common to click, then let go of the mouse, and then click and drag again. Although you can't see it, doing that made a tiny little bone that will haunt you later in Layout.

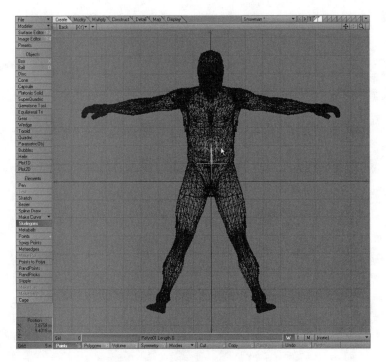

Figure 11.35   Drawing Skelegons is as easy as clicking and dragging.

4. Name the first bone Pelvis and uncheck the Fill Weight Map button, as shown in Figure 11.36.

Tip

With the Numeric window open (n), you can set a name for the Skelegon and add a weight map assignment at the same time. To do this, you must draw your Skelegons into the same layer as the geometry. This can be very hard to do, however, because of visibility. Instead, you'll add the weights after you create the Skelegons.

Note

The Digits selection in the numeric panel for Skelegons tells Modeler to name the Skelegons as you create them. Sometimes, you might not set a name for each Skelegon, so Modeler will name them Bone.00, Bone.01, Bone.02, and so on. In addition, these settings determine how the weight map is applied to the geometry based on the Skelegon (in the same layer). If you are using this auto-weight map feature, you need to draw Skelegons in the same layer as the geometry. This is a real-time implementation of the Bone Weights function.

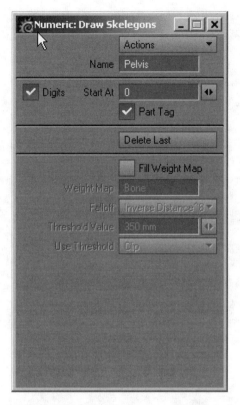

Figure 11.36 The numeric panel for Skelegons enables you to set a Name for the current Skelegon.

5. Click in the middle of the chest of the snowman object.

You'll see the Skelegons draw automatically, creating a child bone, as shown in Figure 11.37.

The small circles around the ends of the Skelegons are the controls for that bone. If you are in DrawSkelegons mode, clicking outside this circle will draw a Skelegon attached to the one before it. If you need to adjust the Skelegon, be sure to click within the circles.

6. Click the right shoulder, on the elbow, on the wrist, and once more on the middle of the hand. Press the spacebar when finished to turn off the Skelegons tool and to keep the bones. You can set names and weights later for individual bones with the Skelegon Tree. Figure 11.38 shows the Skelegons down the right arm.

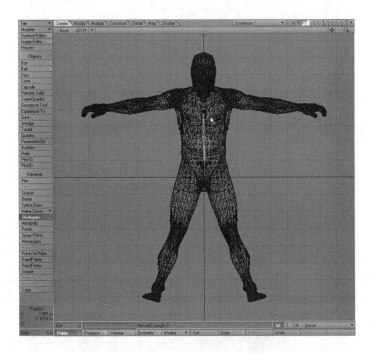

Figure 11.37   You can quickly add Skelegons by clicking in the desired locations.

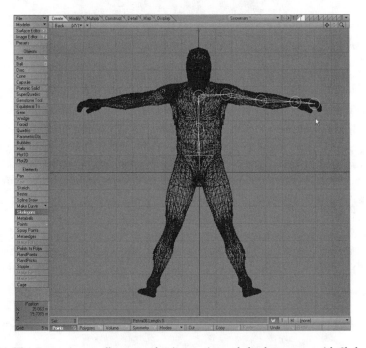

Figure 11.38   In no time at all, you can begin creating a skeletal structure with Skelegons.

Note

If you mess up while creating Skelegons—for example, you might create too many acci-dentally—don't worry! It's a common mistake. Just press the spacebar to turn off the Skelegons command. Then press the Delete key to get rid of them. Select Skelegons, and draw them again, remembering to name them and set the weights in the Numeric panel. You also can select one Skelegon as you would a polygon, and then simply delete it. To continue, select the last polygon in the chain, then choose Draw Skelegons, and continue. The next Skelegon you create will be properly added into the hierarchy.

7. From the Detail tab, select Skelegon Tree. When the panel comes up, drag the corner to expand the size of the panel slightly if you need to.

You'll see a hierarchy of bones named Pelvis (the first Skelegon you drew) with weight maps. Figure 11.39 shows the Skelegon Tree.

You know that the first bone is the pelvis bone, so you don't need to rename it.

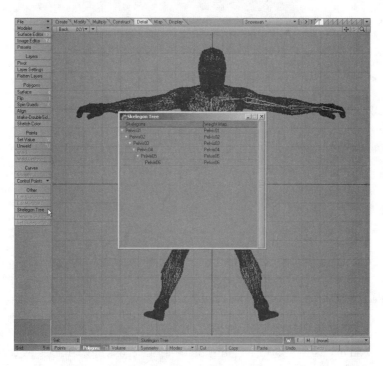

Figure 11.39   The Skelegon Tree helps you manage your Skelegon structures. Because only one name was applied for the first Skelegon, every Skelegon thereafter uses the same name. Remember to name each Skelegon as you create it from the numeric panel.

8. Double-click the second bone indented in the list, under the Skelegon heading in the Skelegon panel. This calls up the Rename Skelegon command. Rename this bone Chest, because it was created in the chest area of the object.

9. Double-click the second bone in the list under weight map to rename it. This is the weight map for the chest.

10. Continue renaming the Skelegon and the weight map accordingly. Figure 11.40 shows the Skelegon Tree with the bones and weights renamed.

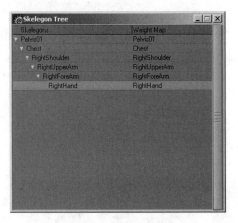

Figure 11.40   You can rename all bones and weight maps in the Skelegon Tree.

11. Save your object. Saving the object also saves the bone structure.

From here, you can create the Skelegons for the legs. The upper-body bones are children of the pelvis bone, but don't worry—this is a straightforward process.

Tip

If you name the Skelegon and the weight map identically, the weight maps will automatically be applied in Layout when the Skelegons are converted to bones. Note that this is case-sensitive.

12. Select the Skelegons button from the Create tab, and draw out a bone for the right hip, as shown in Figure 11.41.

Keep this Skelegon orthogonal on the x-axis. Doing so will allow better control in Layout. If you draw this bone diagonally, rotational movement in Layout is more difficult.

13. As you did with the arm, continue drawing Skelegons down the leg by clicking on the knee, ankle, and foot. Press the spacebar to turn off the Skelegons tool. Figure 11.42 shows the Skelegon structure down the leg.

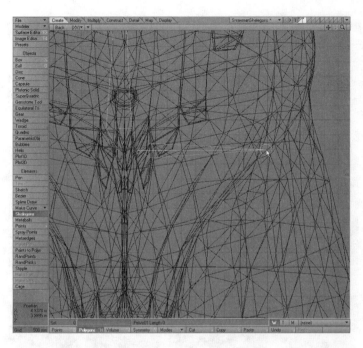

Figure 11.41   A new hierarchy of Skelegons is created for the leg.

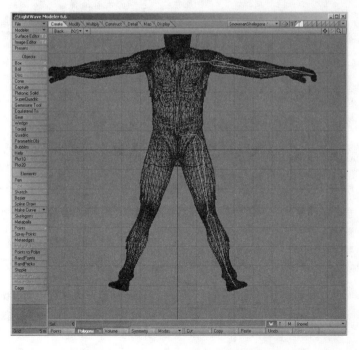

Figure 11.42   Continue creating Skelegons down the leg of the character.

In the real world, moving the pelvis of a person would influence the thighs. Because you have a main pelvis bone in the middle of the character, you need to attach the right thighbone to it.

14. Go to Point mode by selecting the Points button at the bottom of the Modeler interface, and select the point on the left side of the thighbone, at the fat end, and then select the point at the fat end of the pelvis bone, as shown in Figure 11.43.

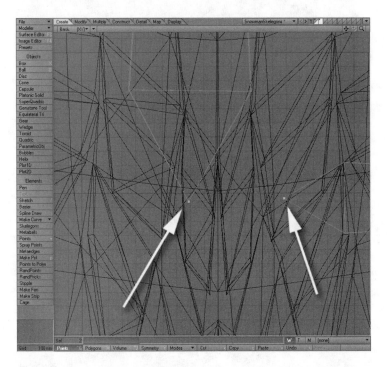

Figure 11.43   The two points at the end of the bones are selected to be joined.

15. Weld these together by pressing Ctrl+w. Now the thighbone and its children are a child of the pelvis bone. Save the object.

It's very important to select and weld these points in order. By selecting the top point of the leg hierarchy, and then selecting the top point of the upper body hierarchy, you're telling Modeler to parent the first point to the second. The right leg hierarchy is now a parent of the upper body.

The process you've just completed puts you on your way to successfully creating a bone structure for a human character. You'll need to select the points of the Skelegons in the Right view to properly position them into the feet and arms. But what about the other half of the body? It's not complete, you say? No problem. You don't have to draw Skelegons again because Skelegons are a polygon type. In the next exercise, you can apply Modeler tools to them and adjust their position, size, and so on.

Exercise 11.5   Adjusting and Positioning Skelegons

This exercise shows you how to take an existing Skelegon structure and adjust the position and size of each Skelegon. In Exercise 11.4, you created the Skelegons from only one view, and if you remember, this is 3D animation, which means you have two other axes to worry about.

1. In Modeler, select Close All Objects from the File menu to create a clean workspace. From the book's CD, load the halfman object into Modeler. This is the snowman figure with Skelegons in another layer. The Skelegons cover only half of the creature's body.

2. Move the mouse over Perspective view (Viewport 2) and press the 0 key on the numeric keypad to bring this view to full frame. Select layer 2 (the bones) as the foreground, and layer 1 (the snowman object) as the background. Figure 11.44 shows the setup.

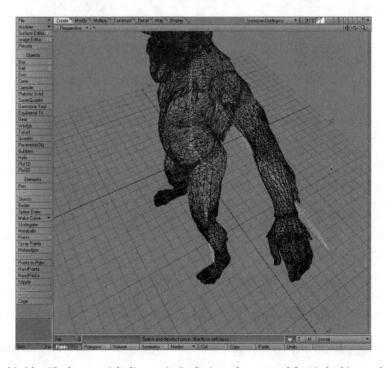

Figure 11.44   The bones might line up in Back view when created, but in looking at the setup from Perspective view, they need some adjustment.

3. Select the Drag tool (Ctrl+t) to start adjusting the bones. Do this by clicking and dragging on the points that make up the Skelegons.

   Rotate Perspective view so that you have more of a top-down view. Click and drag on the end of the bone near the hand. Drag until the bone is lined up inside the hand. Do the same for the elbow, dragging the end point to the elbow joint. Figure 11.45 shows the two bones adjusted.

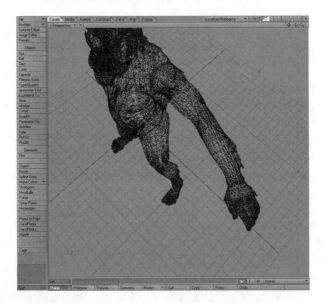

Figure 11.45   The Drag tool can be used to adjust the position of the Skelegons. Take a close look at the position of the Skelegons in the arm, and compare them to Figure 11.44. You'll see that this image shows them lined up with the geometry.

4. Go back to the Quad view by pressing 0 on the numeric keypad. Depending on your skill, you might have an easier time adjusting the Skelegons from orthogonal views. Adjust the remainder of the Skelegons in the upper body—for example, the shoulder bone and upper arm bone—so that they fit appropriately.

5. In Right view, drag the bones to fit the knee and feet more accurately, as shown in Figure 11.46.

6. For the foot bone, drag the end point on the last bone to the tip of the foot. There's no need to rotate or redraw the Skelegons.

7. Save the object when all the bones are centered within the object and adjusted to your liking.

8. In Back view (bottom left), switch to Point mode, and select the three points that are in the center of the snowman. Press Ctrl+v to call up the Set Value command (Detail tab), and set the selected points to an equal location, 0 on the x-axis. Figure 11.47 shows the selection.

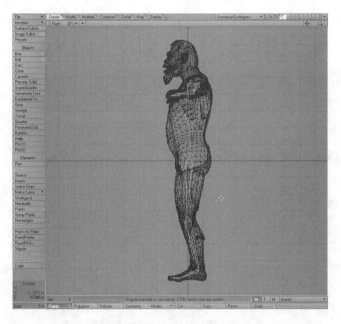

Figure 11.46   In Right view, you can adjust bones easily with the Drag tool.

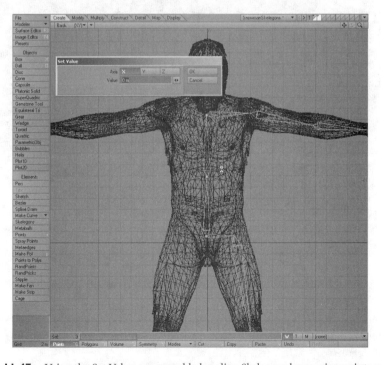

Figure 11.47   Using the Set Value command helps align Skelegons by moving points equally.

9. Select all the Skelegons in Polygon mode except for the pelvis and chest bones. Figure 11.48 shows the selection.

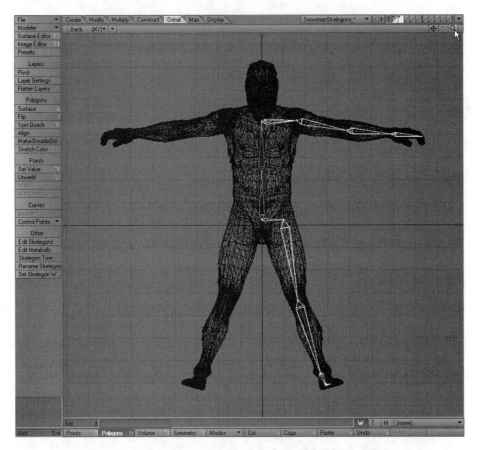

Figure 11.48   The right half of the snowman's Skelegons (except for the pelvis and chest) are selected and are ready to be mirrored.

10. With all the Skelegons selected except for the pelvis and chest, open the Mirror tool from the Multiply tab, and click the y-axis in either the Top or Back views to Mirror the bones over the Y, duplicating them for the x-axis.

   You can adjust the Mirror tool through its numeric panel for more precise control. Feel free to add the background layer as reference for mirroring. Figure 11.49 shows the mirrored bones.

   You now have a bone structure for the left side of the character that's close to being complete. From here, you can add detail to the hands by setting up Skelegons for the fingers.

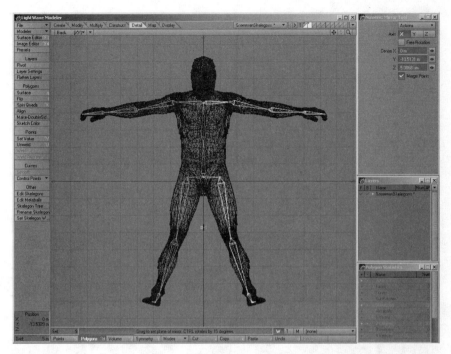

Figure 11.49   The bones for the arms and legs of the character are easily copied using the Mirror tool.

11. In step 8, when you used the Set Value command to set the points of the center Skelegons to 0 X, you also saved yourself a step. When you mirrored directly across the x-axis, you placed the new Skelegons in the exact same place on the negative x. There is a Merge Points function that is turned on by default in the Numeric Requester for Mirror. This function automatically merged the duplicate points that occupied the same space, essentially completing your hierarchy for you. The base of the left arm hierarchy is already parented to the chest Skelegon. Figure 11.50 shows the selection of the chest and shoulder bones welded.

12. Save the object.

Beyond this, you can add additional Skelegons for the character's neck and head. In addition, you can add single Skelegons in the chest for breathing. Set the Oscillater motion plug-in in Layout and you have a breathing, deforming chest.

Note

Depending on how perfect your model is, you might need to use the Drag tool on the mirrored bones for fine-tuning their positioning.

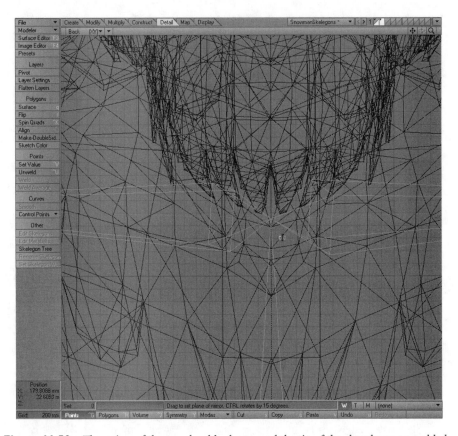

Figure 11.50   The points of the two shoulder bones and the tip of the chest bone are welded automatically with the Mirror tool to become one hierarchy from the chest and pelvis.

Here are a few extra tips about Skelegons:

- You can use them like polygons, adjusting the points and varying the size.
- Once an object has a Skelegon structure, it can be loaded back into Modeler and adjusted or added to at any time without affecting the model.
- If you have created a full structure for a creature but then realize that you need more control, you can split a Skelegon.
- You can define a weight map for a Skelegon (Detail tab).
- If you need to separate a hierarchy, you can use the UnWeld command (Detail tab).
- You can split a Skelegon by selecting Split Skelegon from the Construct tab.
- You can create Skelegons instantly for points of an object by clicking the Make Skelegon option under the Construct tab.

Using Skelegons in Layout

The final part of this chapter takes you back into Layout, where you convert these Skelegons to actual bones and make them control your model. You also assign the weight maps created to each Skelegon. It's not necessary to move the Skelegons to the Modeler layer that contains the object that will be influenced. The Skelegons can keep their own layer, thanks to LightWave's MultiMesh object format.

For a full body character with full weight maps, however, it's good to take advantage of the automatic weight map feature. Once your Skelegons are created and in place, you can cut and paste them into the object layer. If your weights are named identically as your Skelegons, when you convert the Skelegons to bones in Layout, the weights will automatically be applied. You can load the Snowman_Weighted object into Modeler and look at the weights assigned. Create Skelegons as you did in this chapter and name them exactly the same as the weights.

Beyond this exercise, you can select portions of the model to assign weight maps just as you did with the hand and fingers earlier in this chapter; then apply the bones in Layout. You also can go further with the techniques you started in Exercise 11.2 and select the regions of points on the full snowman object, assign a weight map, and apply the bone weights. If you remember, applying bone weights to the fingers of the hand object enabled you to control the influence of bones—you can do the same throughout the body. Remember that the Skelegon Tree in Modeler shows the name of the weight map that will be used, if you've created one. If you've assigned weights in the numeric panel along with a bone name, your weights should automatically be assigned to the appropriate bone in Layout.

Exercise 11.6   Converting Skelegons to Bones in Layout

You'll find that the more you practice creating Skelegons, the less likely you'll be to set up bones directly in Layout. The functionality of Skelegons far exceeds that of just ordinary bones. It is those ordinary bones that deform the objects, however, and you need to convert the functional Skelegons to bones before you can see the results.

1. Open Layout, and load the SnowmanSkelegons object from the book's CD. This is the snowman object with a separate layer of Skelegons.

2. From the Current Item list at the bottom of the Layout interface, select the SnowmanSkelegons:Layer1 object, not Layer 2. Select the Bones button at the bottom of the Layout interface. The Current Item list will show *none,* meaning that there are no bones associated with this object. Press the p key to enter the Bones Item Properties panel.

3. At the top of the Bones Item Properties panel, change the Use Bones From Object selection to SnowmanSkelegons:Layer2, as shown in Figure 11.51.

Figure 11.51   Because the bones are in a separate layer of the object, you need to tell Layout where the bones are.

> ![icon] **Note**
>
> You don't always have to tell the object which bones to use in Layout. Often in Modeler, cutting and pasting the Skelegon structure into the object layer works better, eliminating the need to set the Use Bones From Object command. If you bring this model back into Modeler at some point, however, your Skelegons will already be on their own layer, ready for editing. If they are in the same layer as the object, you need to open the Statistics panel for polygons, select the Skelegon listing, and cut and paste into a new layer. The choice is yours.

4. Move the Bone Properties panel out of the way and return to Layout. Select the SnowmanSkelegons:Layer2 object. From the Item tab, select the Add button, then Bones, and then Convert Skelegons into Bones. Layout will convert the Skelegons to bones and let you know how many bones were created. Figure 11.52 shows the command.

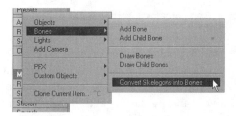

Figure 11.52   Before you can use the Skelegon you created in Modeler in Layout, you need to convert them to bones by using the Convert Skelegons to Bones command.

Note

If your Layout has Expert mode set from the General Options tab in the Preferences panel, you won't see a Skelegons to Bones conversion message. Instead, the message will be highlighted in the status bar below the timeline at the bottom of the interface.

5. With Bones selected at the bottom of the interface, select the Pelvis bone. Press y to rotate, and rotate the bone. Select a few others and rotate them as well.

   The object moves with the chest and arms accordingly.

The exercise here is basic and straightforward. However, much of your character work does not need to be more complex than this. You can go further by adding Skelegons for the fingers in the hands and perhaps in the toes as well. At any time, LightWave enables you to bring this model back to Modeler, make adjustments, and add more Skelegons or weight maps. Figure 11.53 shows the object with a few bones rotated.

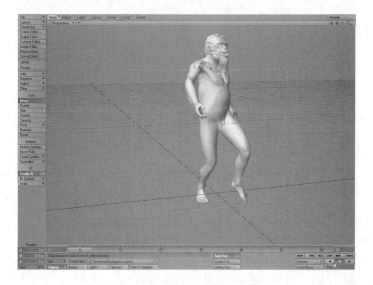

Figure 11.53   With Skelegons now converted to bones, the character can have motion.

Exercise 11.7   Creating Skelegons for a Vampire Bat

To give you the most complete coverage of bones, this last exercise will take what you've learned in this chapter and apply it to a non-human type object. You'll learn how to properly set up a skeletal structure for a vampire bat. Then, in Chapter 12, "Deformations and Movement," you'll bring this bat to life. Later in the book, you'll use LightWave's particle engine to make a flock of bats. But first, begin by entering Modeler.

1. Create a new object, either from the File drop-down menu or by pressing Shift+n. This will clear the workspace. Press a to fit and reset all views.

2. Load the NastyBat object from the book's CD. Again, press a to fit all views. Figure 11.54 shows the bat loaded.

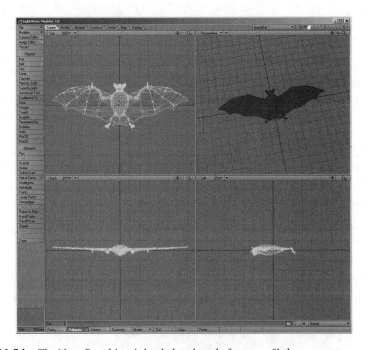

Figure 11.54   The NastyBat object is loaded and ready for some Skelegons.

3. This bat is a great object to use for a Skelegon lesson because Modeler's weight maps can be used for greater control. Go to a new Layer, and place the NastyBat in a background layer.

4. Select the Skelegon tool from the Create tab. In Top view, draw out a Skelegon from the lower midsection of the bat's body to just below the shoulder blade, as shown in Figure 11.55.

5. Create three more Skelegons: one continuing from the first Skelegon up to the shoulder blade area, another for the neck, and one more for the head. Figure 11.56 shows the creation.

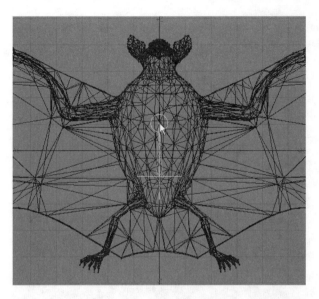

Figure 11.55 The first Skelegon is created in Top view, starting at the lower midsection of the bat.

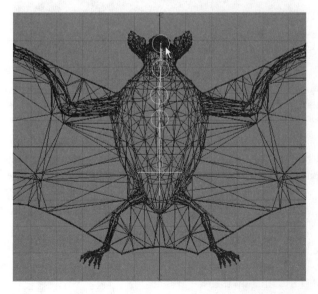

Figure 11.56 Three more Skelegons are created up the back of the bat, to the neck and head.

6. Turn off the Skelegon tool under the Create tab to keep the Skelegons you've just created. Make sure that you're in Polygon Edit mode by clicking the Polygon button at the bottom of the Modeler screen. Now select the second Skelegon that you created, and turn on the Skelegon tool.

7. Add four more Skelegons down the right side of the bat and across the wing, as shown in Figure 11.57. Because you'll be adding weight maps, the Skelegons can be centered down the wing.

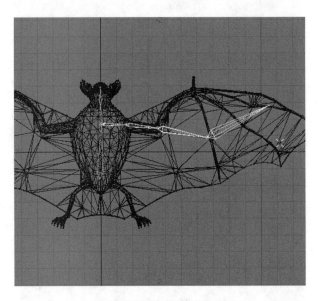

Figure 11.57   Four more Skelegons off of the spine Skelegons create the structure for the right wing.

8. Turn off the Skelegon tool to keep the new Skelegons you've created. Now create four more Skelegons down the right leg, starting from the body, as shown in Figure 11.58.

9. Turn off the Skelegon tool to keep the leg Skelegons. Use the Drag tool from the Modify tab, and align the Skelegons using the other views. Make sure that the Skelegons are centered within the body, neck, and head (see Figure 11.59).

10. Finally, select all the Skelegons of the leg and wing and mirror them over the x-axis for the left side of the bat. Figure 11.60 shows the full structure.

11. Press the single quote key (') to reverse layers, putting the bat in the foreground and the Skelegons in the background. Similar to the way in which you used the bat as a template for aligning the Skelegons, you'll now use the Skelegons as a template for setting up the weight maps.

12. Switch to Polygon mode at the bottom of Modeler. Select the polygons that make up the head of the bat. Then, in the bottom-right corner of Modeler, select the W button, for Weight. In the drop-down list to the right, select New, and name the selected polygons Head. Make sure that Initial Value is checked and that the value is 100 percent. In Perspective view, switch to Weight Shade view. Figure 11.61 shows the weighted head.

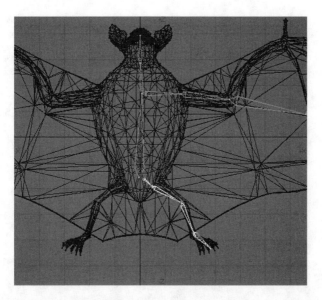

Figure 11.58   Create four more Skelegons from the body for the back-right leg.

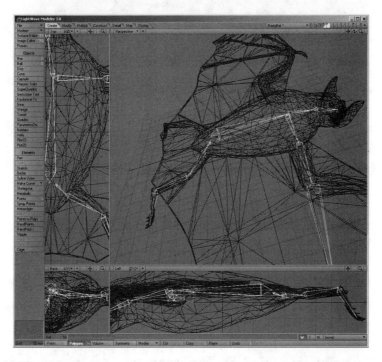

Figure 11.59   Using the Drag tool and in the Perspective window, align the Skelegons so they are positioned properly in the bat.

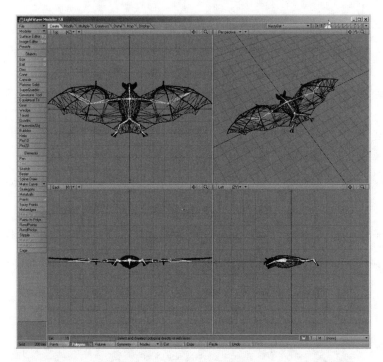

Figure 11.60   The Skelegons of the right side of the bat are mirrored to the left.

Figure 11.61   The head of the bat has a weight map set.

13. Deselect the head polygons, and select the polygons that make up the left wing, making sure not to select any polygons of the body. Create a weight map for the left wing. Figure 11.62 shows the weight.

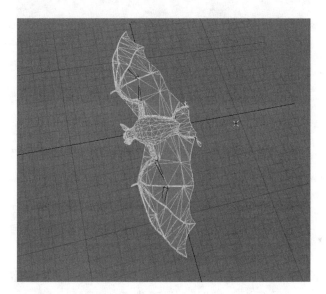

Figure 11.62   A weight map is created for the left wing.

14. Repeat step 13 and create a weight map for the right wing, and save your object.

From this point, you can load the bat into Layout, convert the Skelegons to bones, and assign the weight maps in the Bones properties panel, as you did with the hand and finger bones at the start of this chapter. The benefit of creating weights for the bat is that the wings are so large in comparison to the body, the size of the bone to move the wing would deform the body. Using a weight constrains the bone control to the specific area. Load up the BatBone scene from the Chapter 11 project directory to see the final bat with weights and Skelegons applied. This scene shows the bat flapping his wings, which you can learn to do yourself in Chapter 12.

Bone Up Tags

There's another control you should know about when setting up a Skelegon structure in Modeler. Bone Up Tags are small controls that most people aren't aware of. Often, after you create a Skelegon in Modeler and convert it to a bone in Layout, as you've done in this chapter, the rotational control is off. For example, support that you begin creating a Skelegon structure in Right view (bottom right). You begin creating a hierarchy, and then you decide to continue the hierarchy in Top view (upper left). Figure 11.63 shows three Skelegons created this way.

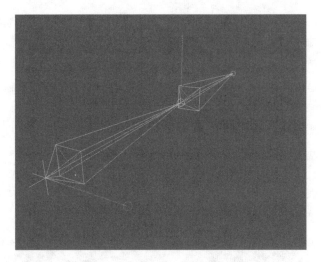

Figure 11.63   A Skelegon is drawn in succession in Right view. Then, the second Skelegon is drawn in Top view. This creates a rotation problem in Layout.

Note

Bone Up Tag suggestion is credited to Lee Stranahan. For more about Lee and his character animation classes, be sure to visit *www.learnlightwave.com*.

Take a close look at the small tags sticking out from the Skelegons in Figure 11.63. One points to the side (this is the Skelegon created in Right view) and one points up (this is the Skelegon created in Top view). What this relates to is the initial rotation of the Skelegon when it becomes a bone in Layout.

So, here's the problem: Take a look at Figure 11.64. This illustration shows the same two Skelegons converted to bones in Layout. Both bones are selected, and the Rotate tool is selected. Look closely at the rotational handles. The heading for the first bone is correct, laying flat on the y-a-axis. But the heading (red rotational handle) on the second bone is rotated, on the x-axis. Therefore, rotating the second bone on its heading would look more like a pitch rotation. Pitch acts more like heading, and so on. It can get very confusing with even the simplest of setups.

The reason this happens is that when you created the first Skelegon in Right view, the Skelegon was created in its proper origin, down the z-axis. If you created a bone in Layout, it would be created down the z- axis. Therefore, creating a Skelegon in this origin in Modeler creates the proper rotational setup. By creating a Skelegon in Top view, you rotate the origin of the bone that will be created.

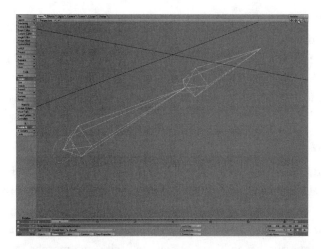

Figure 11.64   Skelegons converted to bones in Layout show the rotational differences when the Show Handles option is turned on from the Display Options tab (d). Remember that full-color versions of the book's figures can be found on the accompanying CD for better visibility.

To fix this, you can change the Coordinate system in Layout to World. However, you also can fix this right in Modeler when creating your Skelegons. Simply grab those small tags sticking out from the Skelegons. While in Skelegon mode (as you're still creating them), simply grab each of these tags and drag them in the same direction.

You might have never even come across this problem. If that's the case, you've been creating your Skelegons properly. For example, creating the Skelegons in Top view for the bat in the previous exercise yields proper rotations when the Skelegons are converted to bones in Layout. If you built some of the Skelegons in Back view, you would need to adjust the Bone Up Tags.

The Next Step

This chapter introduced you to bones and Skelegons and showed you how to create both. You also learned how to set bone weights to control the influences of bones. In addition, you applied weights to a human hand for precise control. The weighting applies to many areas of LightWave, especially for character animation. Take the snowman Skelegon tutorial a step further and set up weights throughout the character for the hands, forearms, upper arms, legs, and so on. Load up the Poser demo and learn how you can build characters in the program and export them right to LightWave with the Poser Pro Pack.

With the basic knowledge presented here, practice setting up full characters whether they're full humans, simple characters, or even inanimate objects like a chrome toaster—the bone and Skelegon information covered here still applies. Position bones using the Drag tool, and use the Mirror tool to copy the Skelegons. See what kind of other uses you find for these tools, creating animals, aliens, or your own fascinating creatures.

Summary

Skelegons and Bones are powerful animation tools in LightWave. Of course, one chapter can't present all the different possibilities of these tools. With the right project and a little time, however, you'll be setting up skeletal structures faster than you could have imagined. But where can you go beyond this? You can turn to Chapter 12 and make your characters not only move with bones, but also talk with endomorphs.

Part III

A Project-Based Approach to Animating Scenes

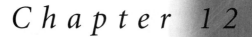

Chapter 12

Deformations and Movement

Throughout *Inside LightWave 7*, you've

learned different techniques, tips, and

tricks. You've learned about keyframing

and the Graph Editor. You've learned about

organic modeling and lighting. This chapter takes you a step further into organic animation. Organic animation in LightWave is more than just moving a ball from point A to point B. It is the blending of points and the changing of shapes. It is movement and timing. You'll use tools within Modeler and LightWave to deform objects into different shapes.

Project Overview

The goal of this chapter is to help you create talking characters and put a creature in motion using bones. The endomorph technology in LightWave that you'll learn about in this chapter has many uses, but its primary function is for character animation. You learned how to make a human head in Chapter 10, "Organic Modeling." This chapter (originally written by Stuart Aitken) has been updated for LightWave 7 from the popular *Inside LightWave [6]* book. You'll use the head model from the book's CD and learn how to give that face motion. In addition, you'll learn what the next step is after setting up Skelegons and converting them to bones. Specifically, this chapter covers the following:

- Creating endomorphs
- Grouping points and polygons
- Vertex Map (VMap) tools
- MorphMixer for lip sync
- Using SockMonkey
- Facial bones for animation
- Movement for a bat

Preparing for Facial Animation

Although there is not enough room in this book to describe the entire process of creating facial expressions, movement, timing, and the art of character animation, there is enough space to stress the preparation you can take before you embark on such endeavors. Facial animation is one of the most difficult aspects of 3D animation. Human facial expression has so many nuances that we take for granted. If you stop to look, really look, however, you'll find that with a few key facial expressions, you can make a character come to life in LightWave.

A number of books on the market deal specifically with character animation and the human form. Many of these books discuss facial muscle structure and illustrate various facial positions. This chapter takes a different approach and uses a simple method—do it until it looks right. Although most of your preparation requires manipulating the 3D model, you should take some time and visit your local library or bookstore to study the human form. This, along with just watching people's movements and expressions, is the best way to prepare yourself. From there, it's up to you to create facial animation.

Endomorph Technology

The endomorph technology in LightWave is not only smart, it's also helpful and user-friendly. Endomorphs enable you to create a 3D object in Modeler and build an unlimited number of morph targets into the object. A *morph target* is a change in the position of the points or polygons of an object. You can use morphs to change a straight road into a curved road, or a car into a boat, and so on. Although you'll be using morph targets for animating faces, you'll see that they are useful for many other types of animations.

In versions of LightWave earlier than 6, to create a morph you needed separate objects. The endomorph technology in today's LightWave software enables you to create all your morph targets with one single object. You can change the base model and add polygons to it. Adding polygons to a morph previous to the endomorph technology resulted in crazy morphing results. Endomorphs solve many of the production headaches of morph targets, as you'll discover in this chapter. Endomorphs are an extension of LightWave's VMap capabilities. Weight and UV maps generally use the same feature. The difference is in how the information is interpreted. With endomorphs, different point position sets are defined.

Note

Although you can edit your model with endomorphs, you still need the same number of points and polygons to properly morph between targets.

Animating Faces

Facial animation is the number one reason endomorph technology exists. If you remember the Morph Gizmo plug-in in earlier versions of LightWave, you'll understand what the new technology of endomorphs and MorphMixer can accomplish. Animating faces can be a complex, arduous task. You need to understand the timing of eye movements, phonetics of speech, and everyday expressions. However, you can easily set up facial animation in LightWave by sometimes just looking in the mirror. It's often difficult to picture, say, the facial expression when someone says the word "trumpet." If you look into a mirror and say it, however, you have your animation reference. Animators who keep mirrors at their desks are not usually that vain. By keeping a mirror at your desk, you have an encyclopedia of facial expression animation references.

Full Bodies and Endomorphs

Because many of the demonstrations of the endomorph technology depict a face, it shouldn't go unmentioned that a body can be attached to the face as well. The process of setting up bones for a character is only enhanced by the animation created with endomorphs for a face, and muscles. Using full bodies with endomorphs is easy. In another layer, the body can have a full bone structure set up with Skelegons. By bringing the object into Layout, you have a full character, bone structure, and morph targets all in one model. You can animate to your heart's content. Add to that endomorph targets for bulging muscles and breathing, and you're on your way.

Creating Endomorphs

Creating endomorphs is easier than you might think. By using some of LightWave's grouping technology in the next exercise, you'll be able to adjust and manipulate your model into just about any expression you like.

Exercise 12.1   Creating Selection Sets

In Chapter 10, you learned how to create a female head. This chapter takes that model even further by creating blinking eyes, facial expressions, and a few mouth phonetics. The first step is to create a Selection Set. Selection Sets define a group of points. They are not always needed to create endomorphs, but they can be very helpful for this project, or any project you come across.

1. Open Modeler and load the LW7_Head object. This is a copy of the head model from Chapter 10, "Organic Modeling." When loaded, press the a key to fit all views.

2. Be sure you have a default quad view in Modeler to match this exercise. You can see from Figure 12.1 that the model has multiple layers. The layers contain eyes, teeth, a tongue, and the head itself. Select the first layer, the head.

   The first step in creating endomorphs for this model is the setup of Selection Sets. Selection Sets enable you to select a range of points and give them a group name. To select a particular polygonal region in previous versions of LightWave, you needed to create a separate surface name, even if the surface attributes were the same. Now you can group selections within one surface. ("Parts" are used in place of different surface names because they work at the polygon level. Point groups are really like nothing that existed prior to version 6.)

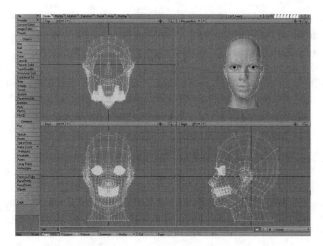

Figure 12.1   A copy of the head model created in Chapter 10 is loaded and ready for some endomorphs.

3. Select just layer one of the head object. Zoom into the lips of the head object by pressing the period key (.). You can move the mouse pointer over a specific area in a viewport, and press the g key. This instantly brings to the center the area where the mouse is. Use this while zooming in to get the lips to full view.

4. Switch to Point mode at the bottom of the Modeler interface. Selection Sets work with points, and although you can select polygons and create a Selection Set just as easily, point selection can be more precise for this exercise.

5. Click and select a point or two on the bottom lip. If you work in a Shaded mode (such as Texture), it's a bit easier to see the selection. Also if you decide to hide points for easier visibility, you won't be able to select them. Figure 12.2 shows the selection.

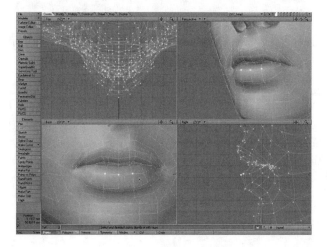

Figure 12.2   Selecting a couple of points on the bottom lip is all you need to do to get started.

6. Because the original model's lips are close together, selecting just the bottom lip is difficult and time-consuming. To make sure you selected what you wanted, use the Expand Select command, found under the Tools tab or by pressing Shift+]. (That's the right bracket key, two keys over from the p key.) Expand Select one time and notice that points are being selected outward from the initial few first selected.

> **Note**
>
> The points in Figure 12.2 might seem a bit large to you. This is because the Simple Wireframe Points option is on in the Display Options panel under the Interface tab. This enables you to change the visible size of the points in Modeler. You also can turn on the Simple Wireframe Edges option. Figure 12.3 shows the Simple Wireframe Points option.

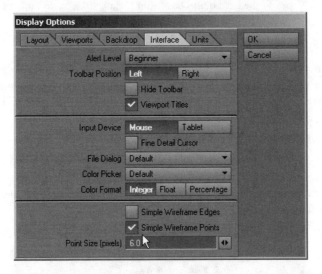

Figure 12.3   Simple Wireframe Points is on to make the points more visible in Modeler's views.

7. Continue using Expand Select until the entire bottom lip is selected, as in Figure 12.4.

8. Zoom out slightly using the comma key (,) to fit the jaw into view. In the right view, while holding down the Shift key, select the points that make up the jaw area of the head object. If you're working in Shaded mode for this view, switch to Wireframe to be sure you select the points on both sides of the head. Figure 12.5 shows the selection.

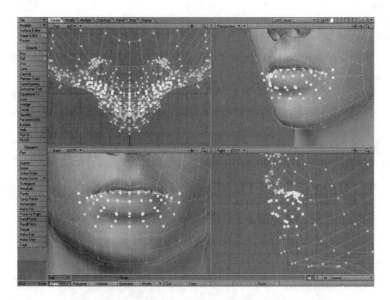

Figure 12.4   Using Expand Select, the points in just the lower lip are easily selected.

 Tip

If you're working in a Wireframe mode in the Right viewport (bottom right), you can right-lasso around the wanted points. Using Wireframe mode while selecting points or polygons selects "through" the object, selecting both sides of the jaw.

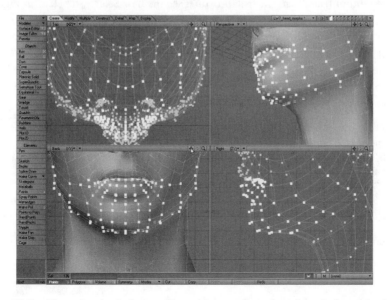

Figure 12.5   The points in the bottom lip and jaw are now selected, ready for a Selection Set assignment.

9. This group of points can now become a Selection Set. While the points are still selected, choose the Point Selection Sets command from the Display tab.

You'll find the command under the Grouping drop-down list, which is located under the Selection heading of tools on the left side of the interface.

Enter the name Jaw for the Point Set, as in Figure 12.6. You do not want to remove points. Click OK and the Selection Set is created. Deselect the points. You can quickly deselect points by pressing the / key, or clicking the blank area on the toolbar. If a tool is selected, such as Rotate, press the spacebar first to turn off the tool.

Remember to work with just the first layer, which contains only the head model.

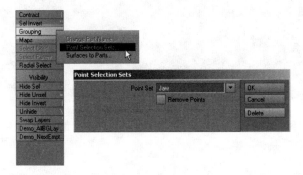

Figure 12.6   After points are selected, the Selection Set tool enables you to name the group.

10. While in Point mode, press the w key to call up Point Statistics. Click and hold the bottom triangle in the list and you'll see the new Selection Set, as in Figure 12.7. Choose the Jaw selection set. Click the plus sign (+) next to the name on the left of the Statistics panel to select the points defined by the Jaw Selection Set. (Clicking the minus sign [–] deselects it.) As you create more point Selection Sets, the names you assign to them will be here in this list as well.

Note

If you have older LightWave objects that use different surfaces to control selections, you can use the Surface to Parts command. You can find it under Additional List of Tools. It assigns a selection of polygons to a specific surface. This "parts" list is available in the Polygon Statistics panel, similar to the Selection Sets for points.

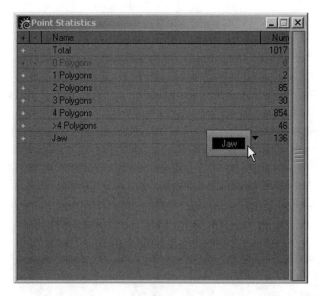

Figure 12.7   The created Selection Set is now accessible through the Point Statistics panel (w).

11. Create additional Selection Sets, such as for the eyelids, nose, and so on. Create these sets for areas that you want to easily select later. It doesn't affect your model in any way, but rather, defines areas of points for easy selection.

Remember that using Selection Sets isn't just for characters. You can create them for any model you build. Perhaps you have a model of an aircraft. At times, your client wants to see the model with the door open to make modeling adjustments. Because the door would have the same surface name as the aircraft itself, you would have to manually select the necessary points or polygons to move them. Instead, just define a Selection Set as shown here. This will enable you to quickly select the points of the aircraft's door and make necessary adjustments.

Note

The biggest difference between a Selection Set (points) and a part (polygons) is that a point can be in more than one Selection Set, but a polygon cannot.

For the next exercise, you will work with a model from the book's CD. This is the same model you were working with in Exercise 12.1, but it has a few Selection Sets already applied.

Exercise 12.2   Building an Endomorph Character

Using a version of the same head object as in the previous exercise, this exercise shows you how to create the various endomorphs for facial animation in Layout. Using the Selection Sets from Exercise 12.1 will help you get started.

1. Select Close All Objects from the File menu in Modeler to start clean, and then load the Head_Sets object.

   This is the head object you loaded in Exercise 12.1, but with Selection Sets applied to the eyes, upper lip, and lower lip. These areas are normally hard to select, and because the specific surfaces cover more area than is needed to adjust their position, a Selection Set is appropriate.

2. Open the Point Statistics panel, and click the bottom triangle to view the Selection Sets, as in Figure 12.8.

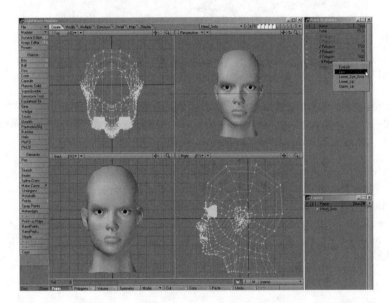

Figure 12.8   The Selection Sets for the head model are ready to be selected and used to create endomorphs. Here, the Statistics panel is left open, and the Modeler interface is squeezed to the left for a controlled working environment. The Layers panel (Ctrl+F5) also is open.

   At the bottom right of the Modeler interface are the W, T, and M buttons, for Weight, UV Texture, and Morph.

3. Select M for Morph. The drop-down list next to it says Base. The model you're viewing in this neutral position is the base model. Click and hold on this list and select New. The Create Morph Map panel opens.

4. Type in the name Mouth.Open.

   It's important to add the dot (.) between Mouth and Open. This creates a group and a slider for the MorphMixer plug-in in Layout. The Mouth becomes a group tab, and the Open becomes a control. You'll see these results later when the model is animated in Layout.

5. For now, keep the type at Relative and click OK. Figure 12.9 shows the Create Morph Map panel.

Figure 12.9   Selecting New from the M list creates a new morph map, or endomorph.

6. In the Point Statistics panel, select the Jaw Selection Set. Click the white plus sign (+) to the left of its name.

   The points of the jaw are highlighted.

7. Press the y key to select the Rotate tool, and from where the joint of the jaw would be—in the Right viewport, in front of the ear—click and drag slightly to the left, to rotate the jaw, opening the mouth. You just created an endomorph!

   Figure 12.10 shows Modeler, with the Point Statistics panel open, and the Rotate Numeric tool. These are moved to the side so that all tools and the interface are visible.

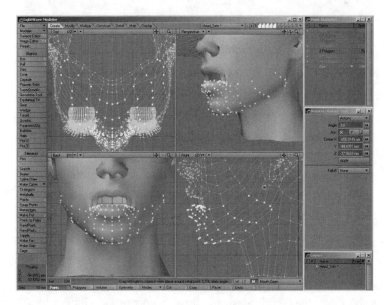

Figure 12.10   Use the Selection Set and the Rotate tool to easily open the character's mouth in preparation for setting up an endomorph.

8. From the M drop-down list, select Base, and the mouth should return to its original position, closed. Then from the list, select the newly created endomorph, Mouth.Open.

   You'll see the mouth open.

9. Deselect the jaw points by clicking in a blank area of the screen, or by pressing the minus sign (–) next to the Selection Set name in the Point Statistics panel. Turn off the Rotate tool by pressing the spacebar.

10. From the M (Morph) list at the bottom right of the Modeler interface where you created your first endomorph, select New again.

11. Name this new morph map Eyes.Blink and click OK.

12. Select the Eyelids Selection Set from the Point Statistics panel. When the name is added to the list, press the white plus sign (+) next to the name to select the eyelid set on the left.

13. Again, select the Rotate tool (y) and from the corner of the eye in the Right view, click and drag to the left to close the eyelids. You might need to move (t) them forward slightly on the negative z-axis to completely cover the eyeballs. Figure 12.11 shows the change.

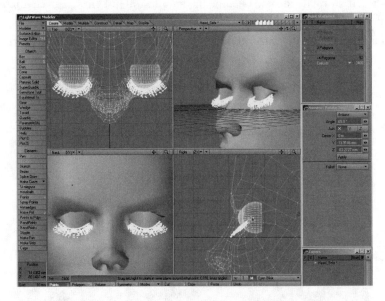

Figure 12.11   The Eyelids Selection Set is used to close the eyelids and create another endomorph.

14. Turn off the Rotate tool, and deselect the eyelid points. Choose the base endomorph to view the eyelids open, and then choose the Eyes.Blink endomorph you just created. You'll see the eyes open and close.

From this point on, you need to create the phonetics of speech. Doing so is easy with reference and Selection Sets. The model you've loaded for the previous exercise has the Selection Sets you need to begin shaping the mouth into proper phonetics. A model with many endomorphs already made is on the CD. The file is labeled Head_Morphs. This model has Selection Sets as well as a full set of endomorphs. When you get a chance, load this model into Modeler and look at the different endomorph positions.

Before moving on to the next section, make a note of the following things to remember when creating endomorphs:

- Always select New from the M list before creating an endomorph. If you don't, you will end up making adjustments to an already set morph target.

- Use the something-dot-something naming convention to properly set up group assignments for the MorphMixer in Layout (for example, Mouth.Open and Mouth.Closed). The Mouth becomes a group, and Open and Closed become slider controls. You can of course create endomorphs without this convention to have one list of slider controls in Layout. The choice is yours.

- Although phonetic speech is complex, you can convincingly get away with making only vowel sounds and facial expressions. For example, A, E, I, O, and U, along with a smile, open mouth, frown, and grin, can create enough combinations of morphs for lip-syncing.

- Try using the Bkd-to-Morf command from the Map tab to create a morph map from a background object. For example, if you have multiple morph target objects—say, from a previous version of LightWave—you can combine these targets into one target with Bkd-to-Morf. With the LightWave 7 endomorph in the foreground and the morph target in a background, you can apply the tool to create a new morph map.

- Use the Copy Map command from the Map tab to copy one endomorph to another. For example, you've created an endomorph of a great smile. It took some time to get it just right. The next endomorph you need to create is similar to this smile but needs to be slightly different. If you select New to create a new endomorph, your model will jump back to the base model.

  Instead, run Copy Map, as seen in Figure 12.12. First, select the endomorph you want to copy. Run Copy Map and type in a new name. Back in the Endomorph list at the bottom right of the screen, you'll see the new endomorph. Select it and make any necessary adjustments. Copy Map enables you to take a preexisting endomorph and create a new endomorph from it.

- You can clear a map, morph or otherwise, by selecting the Clear Map command, also found under the Map tab. Select the morph map you want to clear, and then run the command, or press the underscore key (_). Clear removes the current VMap from the points. In other words it resets the map values to nil (that is, not zero). Right after you clear, you can edit the map. If you don't edit, it will soon disappear because the map is empty. This is different from Delete map. Delete kills the map immediately.

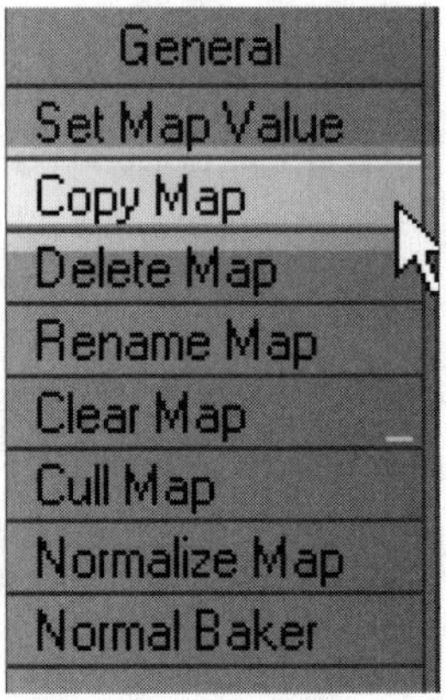

- When creating phonetics for speech, don't just move the lips. Too often, animators forget about the rest of the face, making their characters look stiff and unnatural. By the same token, don't just close the eyelids during a morph. Bring the bottom area of the eye up, and bring the brows down a bit, in addition to closing the lids. Take a look at the Head_Morphs object's Eyes.Blink endomorph. You'll see more movement in the eye area when applying the morph.

Figure 12.12 The Copy Map tool enables you to copy any of your morph maps.

Figures 12.13, 12.14, 12.15, and 12.16 show different facial expressions you can use as references.

These figures and letter references are not rules, just guidelines. Remember that you can use just a percentage of a morph target, or you can blend targets to create different facial expressions. The examples here are good for many situations; if you are creating a larger production, or something that is higher profile (such as a network television show), however, you should consider modeling many morph targets. Although the vowel sounds can suffice for most everyday projects, taking the time up front to create morph targets of the full alphabet (a, b, c, d, and so on) will pay off in the long run. With all 26 letters of the alphabet created as morph targets, as well as many expressions (sad, happy, angry), you will never be at a loss for achieving the right look.

From this point on, take some time and make many endomorph targets with different vowel sounds. Along with applying Selection Sets to points, the best way to shape the face of a character is to do it a few points at a time. It is situations such as this when modifying detailed areas of a character benefit from good modeling. Overbuilt models will give you more headaches than you can imagine. Making morph targets and phonetics for faces is exceedingly easy when the character is built with simple geometry, and subdivided later.

Figure 12.13   A look of pleasure. Notice how the lower lids of the eyes ride up, as do the cheeks, even though the eyes are closed. The facial expression is more than just a change to the mouth.

Figure 12.14   A pucker. This expression is a morph target used for the letters P, B, U, Q, G, and O.

Figure 12.15   The same face making the E sound. This can be a morph target for E, I, C, S, T, Z, and D.

Figure 12.16   An open mouth. This can be used as a morph target for A, H, J, K, R, and Y.

Endomorphs in Layout

As much fun as you had creating different expressions for your character, when it comes to facial animation, the real fun is in Layout. LightWave's Layout gives you the tools you need to create talking characters. In the next exercise, you will load an audio track from the book's CD-ROM directly into Layout and animate the cover model of this book to the sound track. You'll use a displacement plug-in called MorphMixer, as well as the Graph Editor.

LightWave has some features that can make your life much easier when it comes to bones, characters, and parented objects. It has always been a challenge for animators to parent eyeballs attached to a character head whose motions are controlled by bones. LightWave enables you to parent anything you want to bones. When you bring in a MultiMesh object, such as the head for this tutorial, there are separate layers with the head, eyeballs, teeth, and tongue. These layers can be parented to the head; but if the head has bones deforming it, the parented objects will not be deformed. Instead, you can parent the eyeballs directly to the controlling bone. To do this, select the item you want to parent, such as the eyeball, and press m on the keyboard to open the Motion Options panel. At the top for Parent Item, select the appropriate bone. After it is parented, the eyeball will follow the bone movement. The bone won't deform the item parented to it unless you tell the object to Use Bones From in the Bone Options panel.

Another way to associate parented items with a boned layer is to use the same bones for every layer. For example, the head in the scene you'll load has two bones in it, just like the examples in Chapter 11, "Character Construction." The bones are associated with the hand object in that chapter. The other layers, such as the eyes, tongue, and teeth, have no bones. Essentially, every layer from Modeler is treated as an independent object. You can associate any layer of the object, such as the eyeballs, to the bones of the head. If you select the eyeball layer of the object and then switch to Bones mode, for example, you'll see that the current item listing for bones reads [none]. Even so, pressing the p key brings you into the Bones Properties for the eyeball layer. At the top of the interface, you can specify to Use Bones From Object, such as the head. Figure 12.17 shows the panel.

 Note

Applying the Use Bones from Object method is great, but you will not be able to independently animate these associated objects. The bones from the selected object will solely influence them.

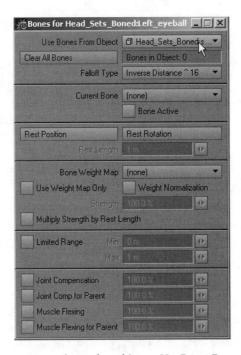

Figure 12.17   You can assign any layer of an object to Use Bones From Object.

Exercise 12.3   Creating Talking Characters

For this exercise, be sure to save any work you've done, and then select Clear Layout from the File drop-down list. Also save any work you might have back in Modeler and close Modeler. Using audio in Layout requires more system resources than normal, and because you won't need any program other than LightWave Layout, close them all now.

1. In Layout, load the LW7_head_morphs scene from the book's CD-ROM. This is a version of the cover head that you can use for setting up lip sync. The eyeballs, tongue, and teeth are parented to the head. Figure 12.18 shows the scene. Note that the camera is cheated over to the left to leave room for use of the MorphMixer panel.

2. Select the Objects button at the bottom of Layout.

3. Press the p key to enter the Object Properties panel.

   You'll see under the Geometry tab that the Display SubPatch Level is set to 1 for faster display in Layout, but the Render SubPatch Level is set to 4, creating a high-quality model when rendering.

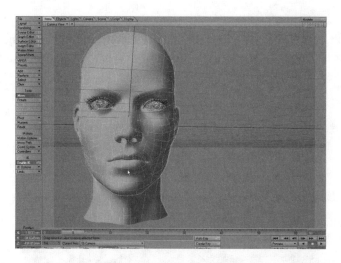

Figure 12.18   Here is the LW7_head_morphs scene when loaded. The Display SubPatch Level is set to 1 for faster updates in Layout. Show SubPatch Cages also is turned on from the Display Options tab (d) in the Preferences panel. You can turn this display off if you want.

Note

Remember that the SubPatch level is set independently for each object in the Object Properties panel.

Also under the Geometry tab of the Item Properties panel for the head, you'll find the Subdivision Order drop-down list. This is important for SubPatched objects in Layout. Figure 12.19 shows the list.

Figure 12.19   This is the Subdivision Order list within the Geometry tab of the Item Properties for an object.

These settings tell LightWave when you want the SubPatch data calculated. By default, the value is set to First, meaning LightWave will subdivide the object before applying effects such as displacement. Figure 12.20 shows the head model morphed with the Subdivision Order set to First.

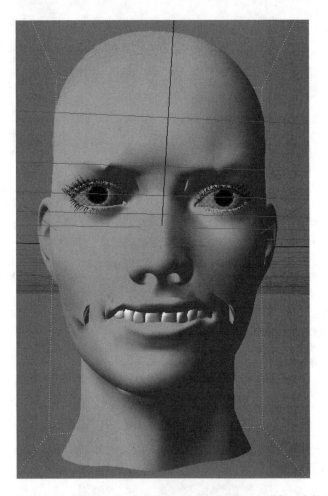

Figure 12.20   With the Subdivision Order set to First, your object will be subdivided and then morphed (for lip-syncing). With this order, your morph is stretching the final model, resulting in a cracked surface. Note the corners of the mouth and the brow area in this image.

With Subdivision Order, you can choose from First, After Morphing, After Displacement, After Bones, After Motion, and Last. Figure 12.21 shows how the same model looks in Layout with Subdivision Order set to Last.

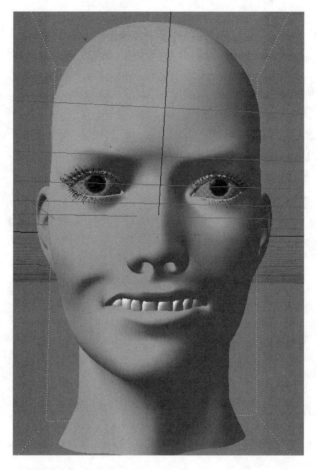

Figure 12.21   With Subdivision Order set to Last, the cracked surface at the corner of the lips is no longer there, and the brow area is smooth.

As you can see, changing (or setting) the Subdivision Order is important to your projects.

4. For this exercise, set the Subdivision Order to Last for best results. Because you're working only with the head, you don't need to change the subdivision order for the objects in other layers. Do change them, however, if you are applying morphs to them.

Note

Using Subdivision Order set to Last, your system performance will suffer slightly. Be patient. Also you'll need to be aware of the Subdivision Order setting for other areas within LightWave (such as Motion Designer for soft body dynamics, explained in Chapter 21, "Motion Designer Creations").

5. Set your Current Object to Head_Morphs:Head from the top of the Object Properties panel, and then select the Deformations tab. From the Add Displacement list, select MorphMixer. Figure 12.22 shows the selection.

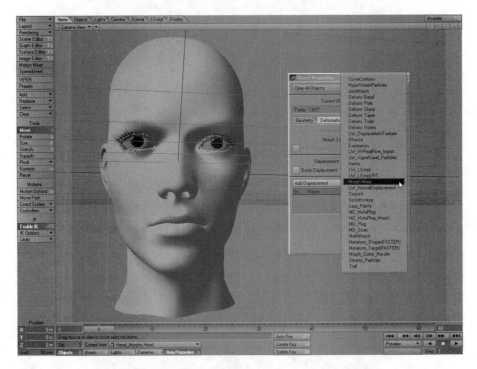

Figure 12.22   Selecting the displacement plug-in MorphMixer applies the MorphMixer to your object.

You should see the words Mixing 12 MORFs in three Groups under the Name column.

6. Double-click this selection listing to open the MorphMixer panel. Figure 12.23 shows the MorphMixer interface.

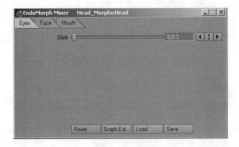

Figure 12.23   The MorphMixer interface shows all the endomorphs created in Modeler.

You can see in the image that there are three groups across the top. As discussed earlier, if you create new endomorphs with the Mouth.Open (or Eyes.Blink) style, the Mouth portion of the name is now a tab or group. You can see that sliders have been created for the second part of the name. Here, the Eyes are a group, and Blink is a control slider.

7. Close the Object Properties panel, leaving only the MorphMixer panel open. Move the panel down to the right so that the model in Layout is in view, as in Figure 12.24.

> **Note**
> If you have a dual-monitor setup, now is the time to use it.

8. Click in the Layout window, and then press the d key to call up the Display Options tab. Be sure to set the Bounding Box Threshold to 6000 or higher. If you want to see the teeth, eyes, and other objects as well, you'll need to set the threshold higher than 11,000. Make sure your system can handle it.

   With a Display SubPatch level of 1 for the head object, and a threshold of 6000, the head object will remain solid while using MorphMixer.

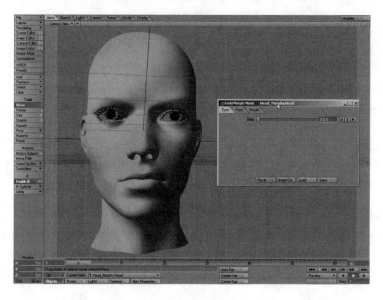

Figure 12.24   LightWave's non-modal panels enable you to keep the MorphMixer window open and move it aside while working.

9. Back in the MorphMixer panel, click and drag the slider labeled Open from the Mouth group.

Watch the mouth open on the character. You'll also notice that a small key mark has been added to the end of the slider, telling you a keyframe has been made. Figure 12.25 shows the mark.

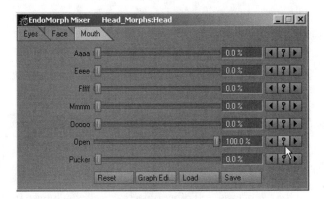

Figure 12.25   Clicking a slider button and either sliding it or not creates a keyframe, which is represented by the small key mark in the MorphMixer window.

The timeline slider in Layout was at frame 0. By moving the slider for Open in the MorphMixer window, you instantly created a keyframe of an open mouth at frame 0.

10. Now, move the timeline slider in Layout to frame 10. Back in the MorphMixer panel, click the Face tab.

   You'll see four sliders for the face: Frustrated, Grin, Happy, and Sad.

11. Drag the Frustrated slider to 100 percent.

   You'll see the model update in Layout. You now have made a combination of Mouth.Open and Face.Frustrated endomorphs. If you make a small preview in Layout, you can see the face with an open mouth at frame 0 and a frustrated look at frame 10.

Some basics apply to setting up MorphMixer with an endomorph character. Try different settings, different timings, and different combinations of morphs to see what you can come up with. Also take your time to get a feel for how the sliders work in combination with other groups in the model.

Exercise 12.4   Animating with Audio

This exercise uses LightWave's audio feature to do more with endomorphs and the MorphMixer plug-in. What good is a cool morphing plug-in without audio to sync it up to?

1. With the LW7_head_morphs scene from Exercise 12.3 loaded, open Layout's Scene Editor. From the Audio drop-down list at the top of the interface, select Load Audio, as in Figure 12.26. Load the wouldnt.wav audio file from the book's CD-ROM.

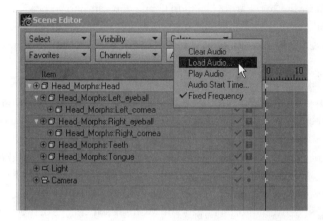

Figure 12.26   You can load a WAV file into Layout to time your animations, or to lip-sync characters to it.

2. Click the Fixed Frequency option in the Audio drop-down list to keep the audio playing at the right pitch in Layout. Also from the Audio drop-down list, select Play Audio.

   You should hear "wouldn't you like to know." This is the audio file to which you'll animate.

3. Close the Scene Editor.

   If you look at the timeline in Layout, you'll see a visual representation of your audio, as in Figure 12.27. This is a helpful guide when lip-syncing characters.

Figure 12.27   Adding audio to Layout is represented by a visual graph in the timeline.

4. Open the MorphMixer panel to animate the face of the character.

5. Move the panel to the side but above the Layout timeline so that everything is visible. You'll be using both the Layout timeline and the MorphMixer panel. Drag the Layout timeline back and forth and you'll hear the loaded audio. Listen carefully. What is being said and at what frame? Repeat the words and pay attention to the shape of your mouth.

   To say the first word of the audio ("wouldn't"), the mouth starts to open and then closes just five frames later.

6. At frame 0, slide the Mouth.Open slider to 0 percent. You can just type 0% percent into the MorphMixer panel as well. This closes the mouth. At frame 2, slide the Mouth.Pucker to 30 percent and Mouth.Open to 60 percent.

7. Now move the Layout timeline to 5.

   You'll hear the "n't" part of "wouldn't," and you can start to hear the "y" sound of "you," the next word in the audio track.

8. At frame 5, bring the Mouth.Pucker slider back to 25 percent. Bring the Mouth.Oooo slider to 25 percent as well.

   A keyframe is automatically created for you.

   Now, around frames 7 to 11, the "you" sound is happening. Here you can accentuate the "y" part of "you" before the character opens her mouth again to say the "ou" part of the word.

9. At frame 8, move the Mouth.Oooo slider to about 80 percent and the Open slider to 15 percent.

   You'll see that the mouth of the character changes slightly. This adds a nice, soft transition between morph targets and avoids linear change between keyframes.

10. At frame 11, bring all the sliders back to 0 percent and bring the Eeee slider to 60 percent for the "l" in "like."

11. Move the Layout timeline to frame 13 and you'll hear the "i" part of the "like to know" phrase. Drag the Open slider to about 42 percent.

    As you can see, you can get away with making a character talk without many phonetic morph targets. If you create the vowel sounds, you can re-create most speech patterns. Of course, a full endomorph with proper phonetics is always best if you have the time (or better, the client is paying for it).

12. At frame 16, the audio finishes the word "like" and begins to say "to know," so set a keyframe at 16 with the muth closed (all sliders at 0 percent) and then opened slightly at frame 18 or 19.

    This will keep the mouth closed right until the time it should speak and then close slightly after frame 18.

13. From here, move the Oooo slider to 50 percent and the Open slider to 30 percent to shape the character's lips to the "to."

    This is the next syllable the character will say at about frame 22 or so. This is where you'll hear the "know" part of "wouldn't you like to know."

14. Bring the Mmmm slider up to 45 percent and the Pucker slider to 70 percent, for the "n" part of "know" At frame 24.

15. Finally, at frame 29, bring the Pucker slider to 0 pecent. At frame 32, bring the Oooo slider to 0 percent. The offset of these two values closing makes the mouth less stiff when closing. One morph happens, and then the next.

Another thing you can do is copy and paste the Morph Mixer settings to other object layers, such as the teeth. In the Object Properties panel where you added the Morph Mixer plug-in, you can select Copy from the Edit drop-down list. Then select the Teeth object layer and select Paste. The morphs you've set up for the face are now applied to the teeth, and they'll animate in conjunction with the face.

From this point on, you can drag the Layout timeline, listen to the audio, adjust the endomorph, and continue making the character talk. Here's a rule to work by: Do it until it looks right! There's no set formula for creating the perfect endomorph character. Use your morph targets together to make your character look and act the way you want. After you have the mouth positions set, you can go back to frame 0 in the Layout timeline and then start adding other endomorph groups. As the character begins talking, for example, choose the Eyes.Blink endomorph and make her blink. Move through the timeline listening to the audio, and when you feel that the character should blink, set the endomorph.

At the end of the audio file, she giggles. Go to the Face tab and where you hear the laugh begin (about frame 37), click the Happy slider handle once. Just click it, don't move it. This will create a keyframe for it at that position and you'll see the small key symbol appear to the right. Then a few frames later at about frame 44, bring the slider to 100 percent. From there, bring it back to 0 percent at frame 53 or so. This tells LightWave not to start the smile until frame 37. Otherwise, the morph would begin at frame 0 through 44!

Remember that you need to set a keyframe to keep the eyes open until the blink occurs. If not, the blink will begin from the last keyframe, which could result in a blink taking many seconds! Most blinks happen in about three frames—three frames to close, three frames to open. If you set up endomorphs for the eyelids individually, you can offset the blinks. This is great for expressive character animation.

Continue just like you have in these steps. Drag the Layout timeline slider, listen to the audio, and then adjust your morph target. You'll be doing this over and over to make sure your audio is in sync with the character's face. It becomes quite repetitive, and sometimes confusing, when you hear the same audio track over and over. When this happens, take a break and come back to the animation. You'll be better for it. You also can make a preview of the animation for better playback. Do this by selecting Make Preview from the Preview drop-down list at the bottom right of the Layout interface.

Note

You can load the LW7_head_lipsync scene from the book's CD-ROM to see the scene described here. However, audio files do not load even if they are in a scene when saved. You'll need to load the audio file as described in step 1 of Exercise 12.4. Be aware that this audio will not render with your animation. It must be added in a third-party editing software package such as Adobe Premiere, Final Cut Pro, Speed Razor, Video Toaster 2, or any other video editing application that handles WAV files.

Endomorphs and the Graph Editor

At times, the MorphMixer panel may just not be enough. This is when you could use LightWave's Graph Editor. At the bottom of the MorphMixer interface is a button labeled Graph Editor. Entering the Graph Editor through the MorphMixer panel automatically loads the channels of the endomorphs. This enables you to see and grab the keyframes and adjust the values in real time. Figure 12.28 shows the Graph Editor, as accessed through the MorphMixer.

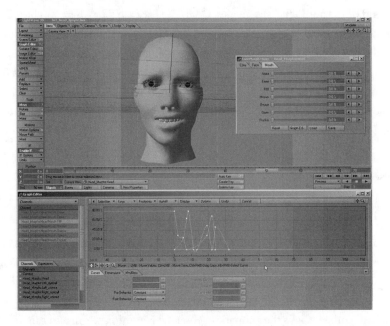

Figure 12.28   The Graph Editor might be your choice for better control or just timing adjustments for your morphs. Here, LightWave Layout has been sized down, the MorphMixer panel moved to the right, and the Graph Editor moved to the bottom. This configuration enables you to see all your controls simultaneously.

You don't always need to use the MorphMixer interface for editing endomorphs. Using the Graph Editor can be superior because you can delete and move keys. MorphMixer is very limited because you can create and adjust existing keys only, however you still need to access the channels in Graph Editor through the MorphMixer panel. By accessing the Graph Editor through the MorphMixer window, the channels will be entered into the Graph Editor. Any time you open the Graph Editor after that, you will see each endomorph channel of motion. You also will see the keyframes created by MorphMixer. Using the Graph Editor for endomorphs enables you to precisely control keyframes by adding them, deleting them, or adjusting values. Of course, you'll have real-time feedback in Layout. Using the Graph Editor to tweak your lip-syncing projects is highly recommended, because you can cross-reference channels with others. In Figure 12.28, for example, the Mouth.Ffff channel is selected as well as two others, and you can see the curve with keyframes in the Curve Window. The other channels are visible in the background. This is beneficial because you can see whether a facial expression is overriding a mouth position, or perhaps an eyeblink is drifting over too many frames.

Note

If you've set up groups for the MorphMixer in Modeler, such as Mouth.Open, clicking the Graph Editor button from a specific tab in the Morph Mixer panel adds those channels to the Channel Bin in the Graph Editor. But what if you need to add the channels from the Eye tab or another morph group you've created? If you take a look at the Scene Display portion of the Graph Editor in the lower-left corner, you'll see all of your object's motion channels, as well as its morph channels. Just add a channel as necessary. Chapter 5, "LightWave 7 Graph Editor," describes the Graph Editor in detail.

In addition to using the Graph Editor to edit and create keyframes for your endomorph character, you can use modifiers to automate endomorphs. The following exercise shows you how to add modifiers to endomorphs.

Exercise 12.5   Adding Endomorph Modifiers

1. Load the LW7_head_graph scene into Layout. Go to the Objects Properties panel and select the HeadMorphs:Head object. Add and open the MorphMixer plug-in (Deformations tab, Add Displacement).

2. Select the Eyes group, and click the Graph Editor button from within the MorphMixer panel.

   The Graph Editor opens and the Eyes.Blink channel is in the Curve Bin.

3. Click the Modifiers tab in the Graph Editor and from the Add Modifier list select Oscillator. After it's loaded, double-click the oscillator listing to open its control panel.

4. In the Oscillator panel, change the Cycle time to .5, making the blinks occur every half-second. All the other settings are okay at their defaults. You can, however, change the Damping to 25 percent or so, to make the oscillator modifier fade off toward the last frame of the animation. If you set a value for Damping, you'll see the change reflected in the curve line in the Oscillator panel.

5. Close the Oscillator panel, and press the Play button in Layout.

You'll see the character blink repeatedly, and you didn't set up keyframes. You can do this for objects, envelopes, morphs, and so on.

Note

The only way to clear endomorph keyframes is through the Graph Editor.

Using modifiers with endomorphs is much more powerful than the basics in this exercise. You can easily create repeating motions with offsets. You can modify an endomorph in Modeler and assign the change to the modified channel. Suppose, for example, that you've set up the Oscillator plug-in for the eyes. Perhaps your client wants you to make the ears wiggle while the eyes blink. Instead of adding another channel to the ears, you can assign the Ear selection to the Eyes.Blink endomorph in Modeler. Saving the changed object updates Layout, in turn updating the channels the oscillator modifies. You must have the LightWave Hub running for updates between Modeler and Layout.

Note

You need to remember that a keyframe will drift if it is not locked down. If you want the character to blink 16 frames into the animation, for example, setting only a keyframe at frame 16 will make a blink that's 16 frames long—very slow. Instead, remember to create a keyframe a few frames before the blink so that the eyes stay open until it's time for them to blink.

Experiment with other modifiers, such as the AudioChannel modifier. This modifier enables you to load an audio clip and assign it to a channel. If you selected the Mouth.Open channel and applied the AudioChannel modifier, LightWave would move the endomorph based on the strength and weakness of the audio waveform. You might need to adjust the values to get the right effect.

You might think, why not use this for making the character talk! The AudioChannel modifier is really useful for things such as animated VU meters (VU is short for "volume units," a measure of average audio power). It also is useful for any movement that needs to be modified to match a sound. You can load a music file with the AudioChannel (double-click to open the controls) and assign the modifier to a channel.

Additional Lip-Sync Tools

LightWave has just about everything you need for quality character animation work. Its methods, however, might not be suited for you. If that's the case, there is another program that works with LightWave, but it is a standalone application. Magpie Pro, from Third Wish Software, offers the user an integrated set of tools for lip-syncing characters. It uses prerendered thumbnail images and also can reference an AVI file. You can even load 3D objects into Magpie Pro as well. Figure 12.29 shows the Magpie Pro interface.

Magpie Pro can be used to scrub the audio track and manually fill the exposure sheet frame by frame to obtain a highly detailed animation, or it can automatically analyze the audio and fill the exposure sheet. Magpie Pro's audio support is excellent, providing real-time feedback of your character lip-syncing.

Besides syncing character mouths to audio tracks, you can use Magpie Pro to sync almost anything to the audio. It also can be used as a timing tool without the need for an audio track. Magpie Pro provides export options to many 3D animation programs, generating animation files with the preview contents. Another cool feature of Magpie Pro is that you can print the exposure sheet of your audio track as reference for setting up animations and timing. The software exports its information for LightWave. Check out Magpie Pro at *www.thirdwish.simplenet.com*.

Figure 12.29   Magpie Pro is a third-party software application that can enhance your lip-syncing capabilities.

Using SockMonkey

Earlier in this chapter you learned about Selection Sets. Although the information described earlier is simple, you can use Selection Sets for lip-syncing. What SockMonkey does is give you the power to control Selection Sets directly in Layout. It's easy, just follow along:

1. Clear Layout and load the Head_Sets object from the book's CD-ROM. This is a model with a number of Selection Sets applied.

2. Select the Head_Sets:Skin object and press p to open the Object Properties panel.

3. First, make sure the Subdivision Order is set to Last under the Geometry tab. Then under the Deformations tab, select SockMonkey from the Add Displacement drop-down list. When added, double-click the listing to open the plug-in interface. Figure 12.30 shows the panel.

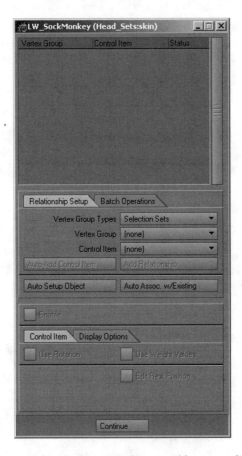

Figure 12.30   The SockMonkey displacement plug-in enables you to directly control Selection Sets in Layout.

4. In the SockMonkey panel, under the Relationship setup, choose the Vertex Group Type. By default this option shows Selection Sets; but if you click and drop down the list, you'll also see an option for Weight Maps. For now, choose Selection Sets.

5. Click and hold the Vertex Group drop-down list. Look what's in the list—all the Selection Sets created in Modeler. For now, leave this set to [none]. You would normally choose one of these for specific control. Instead, you're going to set up the entire object with SockMonkey.

6. The Control Item is useful for setting up a null object—for instance, to control a Selection Set. An easier way to set up SockMonkey is to click the Auto Setup Object option, as pictured in Figure 12.31. Click the Auto Setup Object button.

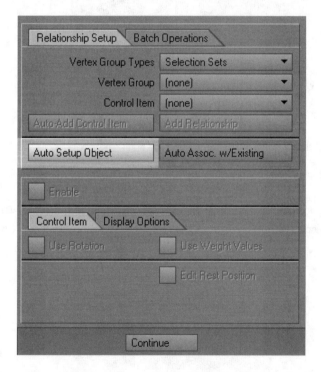

Figure 12.31   SockMonkey's Auto Setup Object option easily assigns the plug-in to selection sets.

7. When you click the Auto Setup Object button, you'll see all the relationships added in the SockMonkey display window, as in Figure 12.32. If you click any of these listings, you have controls available at the bottom of the interface for line pattern display, bounding box, color, and more.

Figure 12.32   Auto Setup Object sets up control items (nulls) for the Selection Sets.

8. Click Continue to close the panel. In Layout, click and hold the Current Item list for Objects (from the bottom of the Layout interface). You'll see your list of objects, but also your Selection Sets, as in Figure 12.33.

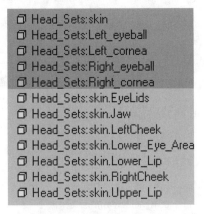

Figure 12.33   When you apply SockMonkey to an object and use the Auto Setup Object option, you'll have control over each Selection Set directly in Layout through the Current Item list.

9. In Layout, select Head_Sets:Skin_LowerLip and rotate (y) on the Pitch (green handle). Watch the lip move.

   Try moving some other Selection Set controls this way. You'll see how you can quickly and easily Control Items in Layout with Selection Sets applied.

Here are few things to remember when using SockMonkey:

- When using the Auto Object Setup, SockMonkey sets up control items for each Selection Set. Because each Control Item is seen as a separate object, they each need to have their Subdivision Order set to Last. Do this under the Geometry tab of the Objects panel.

- The control for each Selection Set will be located at the 0,0,0 axis. This location will most likely be in the middle of the main object.

- Knowing what SockMonkey can do with your Selection Sets, think ahead while working in Modeler and building objects. You can use SockMonkey for all kinds of objects instead of morphing, and it's good for lip-syncing.

Setting Up Skelegons for Facial Deformation

Creating endomorphs in Modeler for a face, and then using MorphMixer in Layout to animate those morph targets, is a great way to go. At times, however, using bones rather than, or even with MorphMixer is a good idea. Of course, the choice is up to you and your project at hand. This next exercise shows you how and where to place bones in a character's face for facial animation.

Exercise 12.6   Placing Bones for Facial Animation

1. In Modeler, load the BoneHead_Blank object from the book's CD.
2. Go to an empty layer, and place layer 1 (the head) in a background layer. Figure 12.34 shows the setup.
3. From the Create tab, select Skelegons. In the Right view, click and drag up in the center of the neck to create a Skelegon for the neck area.
4. Click above the initial Skelegon, creating another Skelegon to the back of the jaw, as in Figure 12.35. These two bones will act as anchors for the head, and give added control. Then add one larger bone for the head itself.

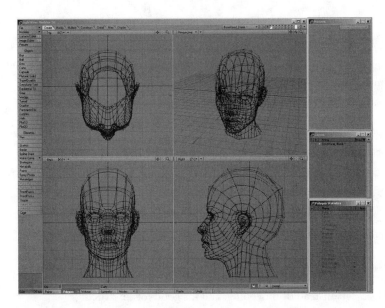

Figure 12.34   A new layer is brought to the foreground, and the head object layer is in the background.

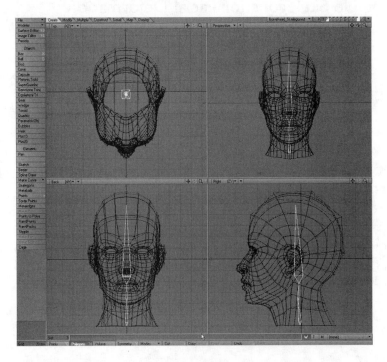

Figure 12.35   Create three Skelegons in a hierarchy, starting at the neck, up to the back of the jaw, to the head.

5. Press the spacebar to turn off the Skelegon tool. Now you'll create an additional hierarchy. This setup will control the lower jaw area of the face. From the Right view, starting at the bottom of the jaw, draw out a Skelegon about 30mm, to the front of the jaw. Create another Skelegon from there by clicking once under the lip, as in Figure 12.36.

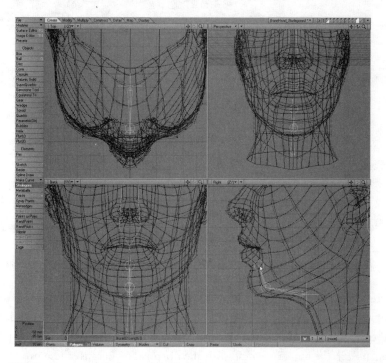

Figure 12.36   Starting at the base of the jaw, start a Skelegon chain. Create two Skelegons for the chin area.

Note

You can use the Skelegon Tree from the Detail tab to see your Skelegon hierarchy and rename the Skelegons for clarity.

6. Make sure the last Skelegon you created is selected (front of the chin) and continue and create three more Skelegons by clicking up toward the lower lip in the Back view, looking at the front of the face. Click once to the right of the lower lip about half way to the corner of the mouth, about 10mm, and click again at the corner of the mouth. Figure 12.37 shows the three new Skelegons.

Remember to adjust your Skelegons by clicking and dragging within the small circles at the end of each Skelegon. Clicking outside the circles will create additional child Skelegons, so be careful.

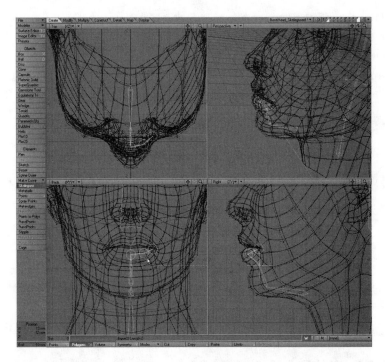

Figure 12.37   Continue creating three more Skelegons for the jaw area up through the lip.

7. Press the spacebar to turn off the Skelegon tool. Select the two bones to the right of center, and using the Mirror tool (Ctrl+v), mirror the selected Skelegons to the left side of the lip, as in Figure 12.38. Be sure that the Merge Points option is enabled in the numeric window for the Mirror tool. Because these two Skelegons were child Skelegons of the center lower lip bone, the mirrored bones are children of that Skelegon as well. To see the hierarchy, open the Skelegon Tree from the Detail tab.

 Note

When you create the Skelegons, before you press the spacebar to turn off the Skelegon tool, you can click and drag directly within the small circles at the end of each Skelegon to position them. Carefully position the Skelegons using all views so that they line up within the upper lip area.

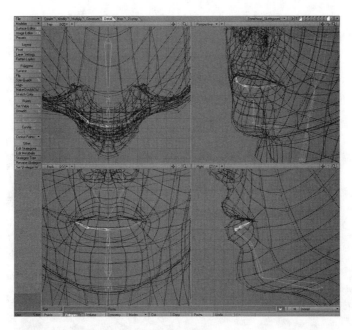

Figure 12.38   After the right side of the lip's Skelegons have been created and positioned using the Drag tool, you can mirror them to the left side.

8. Select the five Skelegons that make up the lower lip, and in the Right view, mirror them to the upper lip, as in Figure 12.39.

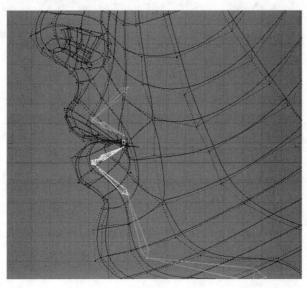

Figure 12.39   Because the upper lip resembles the lower, you can just mirror the Skelegons rather than rebuild them.

9. Use the Drag tool to position the upper lip Skelegons so that they are centered within the lip area. You also might use the Move tool to move the Skelegons into place and then use the Drag tool for added detailed placement.

10. Press the spacebar to turn off any tool that you've been using. You're going to want more control over the mouth area, so draw two separate Skelegons on either side of the nose, as in Figure 12.40.

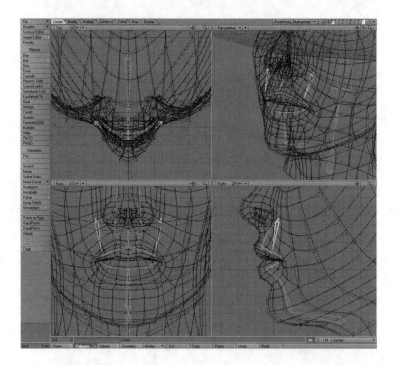

Figure 12.40   Add more control for the mouth area by adding two separate Skelegons on each side of the nose.

11. Now add some control in the jaw. From the Right view, click and draw out a Skelegon starting at the base of the ear, down toward the chin. Create three Skelegons.

12. Position the hierarchy using the Move and Drag tools, paying attention to their positioning in all views. Figure 12.41 shows the new Skelegons.

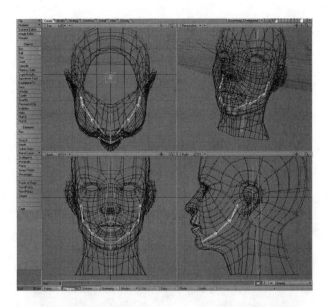

Figure 12.41   A hierarchy of Skelegons is created on one side of the face for the jaw area, down to the chin, and mirrored to the other side of the face.

13. You can add even more control in the face by creating a couple of Skelegons for the cheeks. Draw out one Skelegon, remembering to position it using the Move and Drag tools as needed, paying attention to all views. Once in place, mirror it to the other side of the face. Figure 12.42 shows the cheek Skelegons.

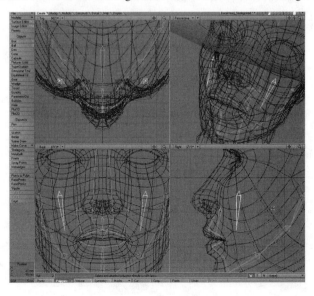

Figure 12.42   Cheek Skelegons are set in place for added control.

14. Press the spacebar to turn off any tools you might have been using. Now you can create the Skelegons for the eye area. Similar to the lower lip, start below the right eye and create three Skelegons—one up, and then two to the right. Use the Drag tool to position the Skelegons. Figure 12.43 shows the Skelegons.

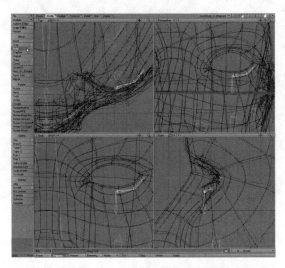

Figure 12.43   The lower eye hierarchy is started, beginning below the eye.

15. To make things easy, select the two Skelegons to the right of the lower eye. Then select the Mirror tool (Ctrl+v) from the Multiply tab and mirror them on the y-axis. Figure 12.44 shows the action.

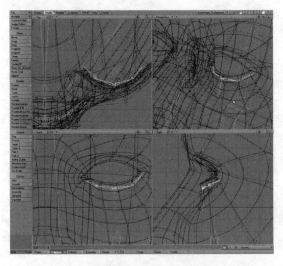

Figure 12.44   The two Skelegons of the lower eye are mirrored, finishing the hierarchy for the lower eye. You can use the Drag tool if needed to adjust and position the mirrored Skelegons.

16. Mirror the entire lower eye hierarchy to the upper eye, and then mirror those eye Skelegons to the other side of the face. Adjust with the Drag tool as needed. Figure 12.45 shows the final structure for the eyes.

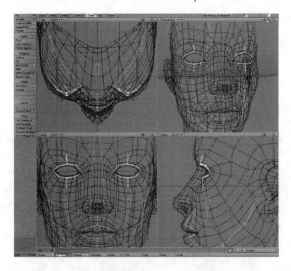

Figure 12.45   The lower-right eye Skelegons have been mirrored to the upper-right eye. That entire structure has been mirrored to the other side of the face.

17. Save your object if you haven't already. Now add just a few control bones for the eyebrow area and nose. Figure 12.46 shows the selection.

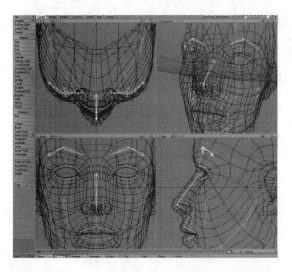

Figure 12.46   A few more Skelegons complete the Skelegon structure for the face. Two Skelegons are added for the eyebrows, and three Skelegons are built down the nose. The full facial Skelegon structure has been created.

18. Save your object. Figure 12.46 shows the full Skelegon structure. Send the object to Layout.

19. With the object loaded in Layout, convert the Skelegons to bones (Item tab, Add, Bones, Convert Skelegons to Bones).

20. Select the Bonehead:skin object layer and click the Bones button. Then click the Item Properties button. In the Properties panel, for Use Bones From Object selection, choose the layer with your Skelegons. Figure 12.47 shows the selection.

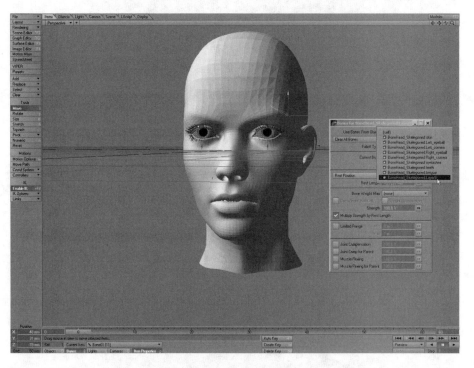

Figure 12.47   Because the Skelegons were created in their own layer in Modeler, you need to tell the head object to use those Skelegons with the Use Bones From Object option.

21. Select the first bone you created for the base of the chin. This bone is located below the chin, lying flat on the z-axis. Press y to rotate, and click and drag on the green rotational handle to rotate the pitch. Note that Show Handles should be On from the Display Options tab (d).

22. Rotate the mouth open a bit. Select a bone in the upper eye and move it down slightly. You'll see the eyelid begin to close.

Note

Changing your model so that the mouth is wide open can help make lip motions easier.

From here, adjust the bones and set keyframes to animate the face. Although this setup is just a basic overview, the process had been started for you to continue and add additional control bones, and perhaps weight the face for added animation control.

Animating a Bat with Bones

Timing and movement are so important to animation that they're something you'll always perfect. Keep your eyes open. Motion information that you can use in your animations is all around you. Suppose, for example, that you want to animate a human walk cycle. You can get relative information just by watching your coworker move across the room. Other motions are often hard to reference, however, such as motions of animals or birds.

Exercise 12.7   Flapping Bat Wings with Bones

In this exercise, you're going to rotate the bones of a bat to make the wings flat. A slight offset on the outer bones will provide for a less rigid movement. You also will move the bones in the body so that more than just the wings are moving. The scene you'll use is a bat with bones already in place, which were created with Skelegons. It also has weights set on the arms for added control.

1. Load the BatBoneKeyMe scene from the accompanying CD. Select Bone02(3). Press y to rotate. Note the rotational position for the Pitch—it's at –45 degrees. This is your first frame. You'll want the last frame to be at this exact position as well so that the wing can loop. So, with the bone in this position, create a keyframe at 15. Now rotate the bone on its pitch about 43 degrees (downward). Create a keyframe at frame 7.

2. Press the down arrow to select the next bone, Bone03(2). Its keyframe at 0 shows the bone rotated at –55.0 degrees on the Pitch. Create a keyframe for this bone's position at 15. Rotate it downward to 30.0 degrees and create a keyframe at frame 7. Also create a keyframe in this same position at frame 9.

   This bone will lag behind the first bone, creating a slight extra motion so that the wing sort of sweeps down, instead of just rotating.

3. Select the next Bone04(2) and note its initial position at frame 0 to 45 degrees. Create a keyframe for it at this position for frame 15. Rotate it on the Pitch to –37.00 and create a keyframe at 7. Then rotate it to 70.00 and create a keyframe at 9. Figure 12.48 shows the first wing in position.

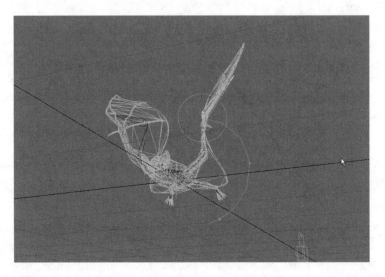

Figure 12.48   The bat's right wing is put into motion after movement of just a few bones.

4. With the same bone selected (Bone04(2)), open the Graph Editor. Select the Position P (pitch) channel, and set the Post Behavior to Repeat. Do the same for the other two bones in the wing.

5. You can set the exact motions for the bones on the bat's left wing, making sure to set the Post Behavior to Repeat as well. When you keyframe the bones on the left side of the bat, however, offset the timing by a frame or two. Also don't use the exact rotations for the bones—vary them a bit for added realism.

6. Select the bat's body bone, Bone01(1). At frame 0, you'll see the Pitch is set to −3.03. Create a keyframe for this position at frame 15. Then rotate it to 5.0 degrees on the pitch and create a keyframe at 6. Also repeat its Post Behavior in the Graph Editor.

   Drag through the timeline and you'll see the bat flapping its wings, while its body is slightly moving.

   From this point, use the same formula to animate other bones of the bat, such as the feet, neck, and head. If the wings swoop downward, the neck and head would raise up a bit, and vice versa. Here are a few things to remember:

   - Make sure the first and last frames are the same for looping motions.
   - Add secondary motion to the object's body.
   - Don't forget to animate the feet and/or legs as well.

- When rotating the bones in the wing, add a slight offset by adding extra keyframes for child bones so that the wings are fluid and not as stiff.

This technique is very useful for bats, birds, and even dragons.

The Next Step

On the accompanying CD, you will find 10 various WAV audio clips. These are here for you to use to animate your characters. Use the models on the CD to make endomorphs and try to animate them to the audio provided. The details in this chapter have given you enough references and examples so that you can build your own characters with expression and personality and make them come to life. Remember that you can use the Audio feature in Layout for more than just lip-syncing. You can use the Audio feature to time your animations. By listening to the audio track, you can quickly determine what position a character should take. More importantly, you'll know exactly when to change the character's position (because the change will be based on the timing of the audio). Use the bones in the sample animation to move the character's head around after you assign morph targets for speech. When the animation is timed up, you can render it and, in your favorite editing solution, such as the Video Toaster, attach the audio clip you've been using as a reference to the final animation. They will time up perfectly.

Summary

You can read all the chapters in all the books you want, but the real magic of being an animator comes from practice. Experiment, practice, and always keep learning. No matter where you are in your career, whether a student, hobbyist, or professional, learning character animation takes patience and time. Throughout this chapter, tips and tricks were mentioned to help you along your way. It's up to you to take this knowledge of endomorphs, SubPatches, MorphMixer, and SockMonkey and put it all together to create the type of characters and animations you've always wanted.

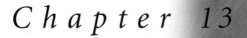

Chapter 13

Inverse Kinematics

Character animation has long been the veritable Holy Grail of 3D animation. Until recently, only an elite few could do it, and those who were good at it were often of the programmer-type personality and in high demand.

Reaching a competitive level of character animation required expensive software running on even more expensive workstations. With today's advances in technology, however, more and more of these high-end tools are becoming available to the general public. LightWave offers character animation tools that not only rival those of the big boys, but also surpass them on many levels. One such tool is the hybrid kinematics engine for character setup and animation. Figure 13.1 is a character rigged with LightWave's hybrid kinematics. You'll set up the rigging for this character later in this chapter.

Figure 13.1   This character was set up with a mixture of kinematics systems in LightWave 7.

The basic method for manipulating a character is with Forward Kinematics (FK). FK systems have been around for awhile, and since the early days of animation they have been the main technique for character manipulation. Many systems today, including LightWave, now offer a more powerful and easy-to-use kinematics system: Inverse Kinematics (IK).

Although IK has many benefits over FK, due to its lack of proper integration into animation software, many animators still prefer using FK. Several animation packages limit the amount of control available to IK setups. Some software even gives preferential treatment to one kinematics system over the other. Obviously, limiting the power of one system in favor of another is not the best solution. LightWave is built around a hybrid IK/FK engine that seamlessly integrates IK and FK systems in a user-friendly environment. This hybrid system is one of the fastest and most powerful systems available.

This chapter introduces you to the world of IK, and through the use of exercises it teaches you the techniques involved in using IK in character animation. Specifically, this chapter discusses the following:

- Basic IK usage
- Character setup
- Rigging a character
- Configuring IK chains

Understanding Kinematics

Kinematics is the study of motion without consideration of the forces acting upon it. Essentially, it is the study of raw motion—motion in its most basic form. Kinematics in 3D animation is not too different from kinematics in the real world. In 3D animation, kinematics refers to the basic technique of manipulating items or placing items into motion. The actual method used to manipulate the item is called a *kinematics system*.

Kinematics systems come in two basic flavors: forward and inverse. Each system is unique and can be used for your benefit. Because LightWave enables the use of both FK and IK, you should familiarize yourself with each system.

Forward Kinematics

FK, a technique more commonly known as *keyframe animation*, is the default method of motion in LightWave. The actual term "Forward Kinematics" is rarely mentioned unless it's being referred to in hierarchical or character animation. The main advantage of FK is its accuracy. In FK, you place the items exactly where you want them placed. FK doesn't require any additional setup to begin using it. You are animating with FK when you begin directly keyframing objects. FK also has a huge disadvantage; it is time consuming. After all, it is basically the technique of hand-positioning each object in a hierarchy—starting with the root object and then moving forward through the chain, rotating and keyframing each item to form the desired pose. Every time you need to change something you must re-keyframe all the items in the chain.

If you were to animate a character's arm with FK, you would first create the arm in a hierarchical form. This arm would consist of fingers parented to a hand, the hand parented to a forearm, and the forearm parented to an upper arm. The pivot point for each item would be located at the joint between the child and its parent, resulting in rotation that is similar to that of a real arm. Due to the nature of parent/child relationships, any time a parent item is manipulated, its movement is directly translated to its children. To animate this arm, you would start by rotating the upper arm into position, followed by the forearm, the hand, and finally the fingers. Figure 13.2 shows the technique of using FK to animate such an arm.

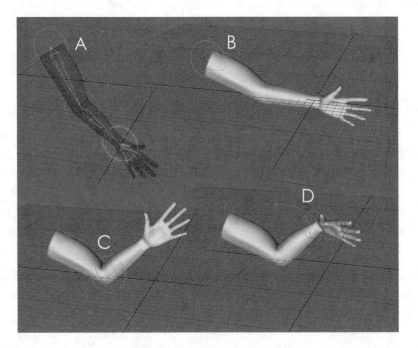

Figure 13.2 When positioning this bone structure (A) with FK, the upper-arm bone is first rotated into position (B), followed by the forearm (C), and finally by the hand bone (D).

With FK, a keyframe must be created for each item in the hierarchy every time you change something. Imagine animating a complex character with nothing but FK. Obviously this is not the ideal way to animate. A faster, easier-to-use, and much more flexible kinematics system exists: IK.

Inverse Kinematics

IK—or, as it is more descriptively called, *goal-driven animation*—operates on the principle of manipulating a single "goal object" to position an entire object hierarchy. In essence, it is the opposite of FK. Rather than working from the root item forward through the hierarchy, you use a goal object to manipulate the hierarchy from the end, through the root item.

Where FK requires the keyframing of multiple items, IK requires you to keyframe only a goal object to control the entire hierarchy. The obvious advantage of this is the amount of time saved during animation. You now have free time to focus on much more important things, such as timing. A few more initial steps are involved in setting up an IK system, but the time saved in keyframing outweighs the extra expense of setup.

To animate the aforementioned arm with IK, you would need to add only a goal object, and then set up controllers for each joint. After the joints are set up, you can control the entire arm by simply moving the goal object (see Figure 13.3).

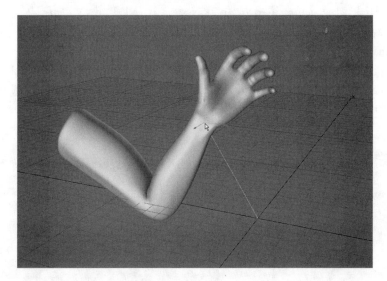

Figure 13.3   IK is controlling the arm. The null object at the joint between the hand and the forearm serves as the goal object.

The easiest way to understand each kinematics system is through the following analogy: If you were to pull on someone's finger, his or her arm would follow wherever you moved the finger. Every joint in the arm would automatically rotate to allow the finger to reach its goal. This type of movement is basically real-world IK. However, if a person were to reach out for a glass of water, their brain would tell their upper arm to rotate a certain amount, followed by the rotation of the forearm and of each joint thereafter, until it reaches the glass. This movement is FK.

Note

Think of FK as an "internal force" driving the movement of the hierarchy to the desired position, and IK as an "external force" pulling the hierarchy into position.

As you can see, both techniques are quite useful and each offers its own set of advantages and disadvantages. The benefits of each system are far too great to consider throwing one out in favor of the other. FK will definitely work better than IK in certain situations, and vice versa. In a perfect world, you could use both at the same time. LightWave brings you as close to a perfect world as you can get with its hybrid IK/FK engine, which enables you to mix IK and FK in the same character, chain, or even bone!

Basic IK Usage

The hierarchical structure used in an IK system is called an *IK chain*. IK chains in LightWave can be composed of any item capable of existing in a hierarchy. When using an IK chain, LightWave internally computes the rotations of each item in the chain based on the position of a goal object (see Figure 13.4). The result of this internal calculation is called a *solution*. The process of reaching the solution is referred to as *solving*, or *being solved for*.

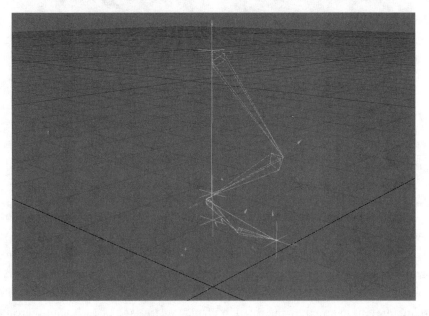

Figure 13.4   Manipulating the goal object in this IK chain automatically creates the rotations for each bone.

Unfortunately, an IK chain often can have more than one solution, which could result in errors. To help avoid these errors, the chain must be cheated slightly using "preferred angles." A slight bend at the joints in a chain tells LightWave this is the "preferred angle" of rotation (see Figure 13.5). LightWave will then try to rotate the items based on that angle. Even with preferred angles, solutions can still get messy and sometimes require the setup of angle limits.

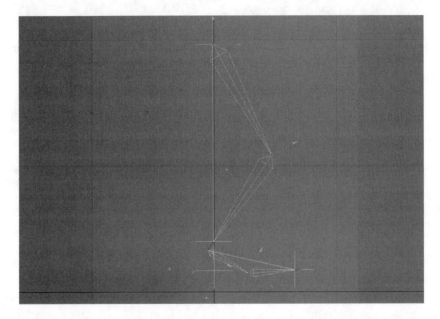

Figure 13.5   The slight rotation of the two highlighted joints in this chain tells LightWave to rotate the chain based on this "preferred angle."

LightWave has the ability to use multiple IK chains in the same structure. This enables the creation of complex systems. Multiple IK systems in the same skeletal structure offer a greater level of control over an object. For instance, a biped character commonly will have separate IK chains for each leg and arm (see Figure 13.6). You could then animate the entire character simply by moving the goal objects.

Figure 13.6   This character contains four IK systems, all in one complete structure. The arms and legs are all controlled by IK.

Constraining Rotations with Angle Limits

Many times when you are setting up a character, you will want to limit the range of motion a joint can rotate. Some classic examples of this are the human knee, elbow, or joint. If you were to set up an IK chain similar to a human leg, you wouldn't want the lower leg to overextend itself beyond the normal range of motion. Without angle limits, the results could look quite painful. Figure 13.7 demonstrates the benefits of using angle limits in an IK chain.

You can set up angle limits interactively for each joint with the Record Angle Limits button under the Items tab (from the Limits drop-down list). When recording angle limits, you can control which rotation channels receive the limits through the use of local constraints. If only the pitch is activated, the recorded limit will affect only the pitch channel.

You also can set up angle limits in the Controllers and Limits section of the Motion Options panel. Setting up limits in the Motion Options panel is the most precise method because you can directly input the minimum and maximum rotational limits for each channel (see Figure 13.8). Setting rotational limits applies to both IK and FK.

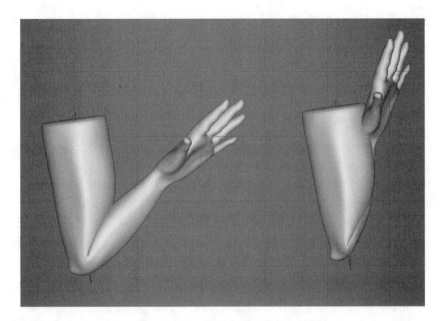

Figure 13.7   The arm on the left uses angle limits to prevent rotation beyond its fully extended position. A limit has been set so that the elbow doesn't crack off (figuratively) during the animation. The forearm rotation stops when it touches the biceps. The arm on the right has no limits set. Ouch!

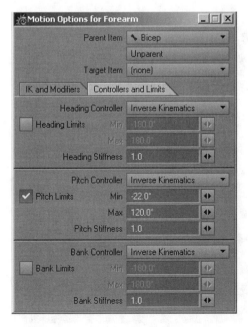

Figure 13.8   You can directly input values for the angle limits in the Motion Options panel. Here, you can see that minimum and maximum values have been set for the Pitch Controller.

The Motion Options Panel

LightWave offers the most powerful IK engines on the market, and you harness most of this power in the Motion Options panel. The Motion Options panel is the centerpiece of IK setup. Here you will find most of the controls you'll use to set up, control, and activate IK chains. Like all other panels in LightWave, the Motion Options panel is laid out in an easy-to-understand format.

The first tab is the IK and Modifiers tab (see Figure 13.9). This is where you set up the basic functionality of your chain. Here you select goal objects, activate full-time IK, and set the goal strength for IK chains. *Full-time IK* means that when IK is applied to elements in your scene, LightWave will always be calculating. When full-time IK is off, IK is calculated only when you are manipulating the goal object. You would turn this off for extremely complex kinematics setups that require large amounts of processing information. Most IK solutions work just fine with full-time IK active.

The second is the Controllers and Limits tab (see Figure 13.10). The controllers determine what will control the rotation channels of each item. Each item has three controllers: a Heading Controller, a Pitch Controller, and a Bank Controller. Using the pop-up menu, you can configure each controller to use FK or IK independently. You also can set Align to Path under the IK and Modifiers tab to keep things aligned to a set motion path.

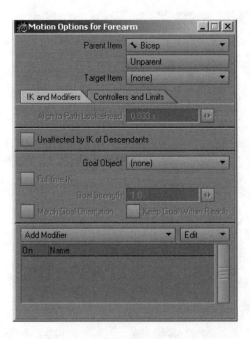

Figure 13.9   The IK and Modifiers tab is where you set up basic IK information.

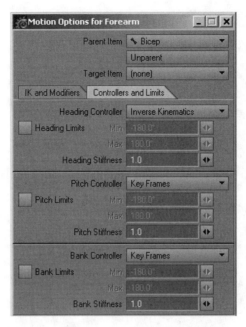

Figure 13.10   The Controllers and Limits tab is where you set up rotation controllers. Here, only the Heading Controller has IK applied. The Pitch and Bank Controllers are set to use keyframes.

Goaled Items

Before an IK chain will function, LightWave needs an item in the chain that will point to a goal object and position the items farther up the chain. This "pointer" is nothing more than a control item. The control item can be any item as long as it resides in the hierarchy to be controlled by IK. You can configure a pointer item in the Motion Options panel by specifying a goal object for it. When given a goal object, LightWave automatically understands that this item will point to the rest of the chain. These pointers are often called *goaled items* because they have a goal to follow. Figure 13.11 shows proper setup of a goaled item. Generally, a null object is perfect as a goal object.

Figure 13.11   Goaled items are configured in the Motion Options panel by specifying a goal object to follow.

Under normal circumstances, the pointer item usually is the last item in the chain; however, this is not always the case. LightWave allows the use of multiple goals in the same chain, so one pointer might be at the end of a hierarchy pointing to one of the goals, while another pointer is in the middle of the hierarchy pointing to a different goal. The location of the pointer is determined by the design of your IK chain and will vary with different setups. For example, the setup you'll create in this chapter uses goal objects in the middle of a chain to control the knees and elbows of the motorcross dude.

Exercise 13.1   Creating a Basic IK Chain

As always, the best way to learn something is to sit down and try it, so fire up LightWave and get to it! You'll find that many 3D applications tend to make IK as confusing as possible. IK in LightWave is simple, easy to understand, and straightforward.

It might seem like many steps are involved with setting up a simple IK chain. You will soon realize that many of these steps are there because of the flexible choices LightWave offers. This exercise shows you how to set up IK with a chain of bones in Layout. Note that this is only one example, and this IK information can apply to your objects as well, not only to bones. To see just how simple it is to set up an IK chain in LightWave, follow these steps:

1. Start Layout, or if you were already running Layout, clear the scene by choosing Clear Scene from the File drop-down menu.

2. Select Add, then Objects, and then Add Null from the Items tab. When prompted for a name, type Root.

   This creates a null object named Root that will serve as the root or base object of the hierarchy.

   In LightWave, bones require an object to reside in; therefore, an object must be created before any bones can be added. Under normal circumstances your bone structure will exist inside a seamless object like a model of a human arm. The seamless object would serve the same purpose as the null does in this example. For this example, a set of five bones will be used. The number of bones is irrelevant and is just an arbitrary number for demonstration purposes. You should try this exercise again on your own with more than five bones.

Note

Bones are used here for a simple example. It is not necessary to use bones for IK setups. You'll use IK with and without bones in exercises in this chapter.

3. Create five bones by pressing the equals (=) key, and then pressing Enter or Return five times. Accept the default bone name (which will be named bone) each time you are prompted to enter a name.

   Using the equals (=) key, bones are automatically created in a hierarchical format, as shown in Figure 13.12. Each bone is parented to the bone before it. By default, each bone's rest length is set to 1.000, and the bones are drawn pointing down the z-axis.

4. Create another null by selecting Add, then Objects, and then Add Null from the Items tab. Give this null the name Goal. This null object will function as the goal object of the IK chain.

Note

Naming the null object Goal has no effect on the IK chain. It could be given any name; however, using descriptive names makes setup a little easier. You should get into the habit of giving everything a descriptive name when setting up IK chains, or anything else in LightWave.

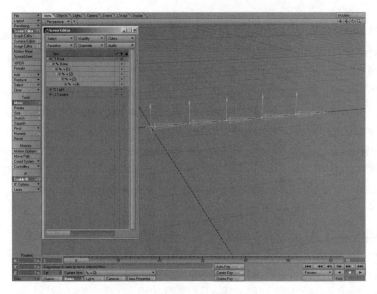

Figure 13.12   A parent/child relationship was established between each bone in the scene. This relationship is what forms the hierarchy. The first bone is parented to the Null (root object), the second bone is parented to the first bone, and so on.

5. Move the goal null 4m on the z-axis. Press the n key to activate the numeric input fields. Enter 4m for the Z value. Moving this null is not necessary for IK to work; however, doing so prevents the bone chain from jumping to attach to the goal when the IK is activated.

   The goal null will now jump to 4m on the z-axis. Your scene should now resemble Figure 13.13.

Note

Notice that the goal was placed at the pivot point of the last bone rather than at the end of the hierarchy. LightWave uses the pivot point of the bone to reach for the goal. Just like parenting or targeting in LightWave, IK goals point to the pivot point of Layout items such as bones.

In the next few steps, you will configure the IK for the bone hierarchy.

6. Select the last bone in the hierarchy (Bone 5). This bone will be the item that points to the rest of the IK chain.

7. With the last bone still selected, display the Motion Options panel by pressing the m key. The Motion Options panel is where you set up most of the controls for the IK chain.

8. Choose the null object named Goal from the Goal Object pop-up menu.

   This will tell LightWave to use the goal as the goal object for the IK solution.

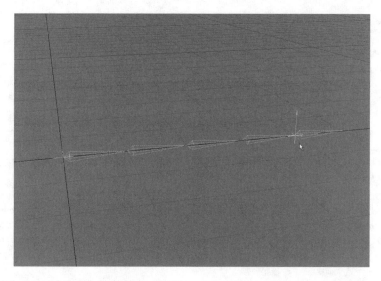

Figure 13.13   Properly laid out, the chain is now ready to be configured for IK.

9. You'll notice the Full-time IK option in the Motion Options panel. You'll see a line drawn in Layout from the root to the goal object if you turn it on, as shown in Figure 13.14.

Full-time IK forces LightWave to continuously solve for an IK solution. For now, keep this turned off.

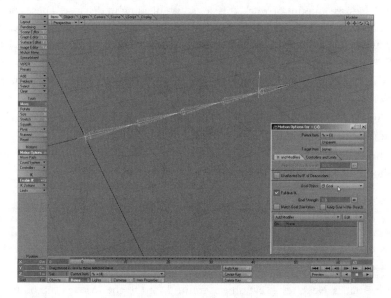

Figure 13.14   The bone has been given a goal object, and Full-time IK has been activated.

Note

LightWave's default IK mode is with Full-time IK deactivated. In the default mode, LightWave calculates IK only while you are physically moving the goal object. If you advance a frame without keyframing the items in the chain, the chain jumps back to its previous pose. The default IK mode is designed to let you pose your character with IK while you use FK to create keyframes. This is useful for quickly posing a character and works much like a puppeteer.

When using Full-time IK, LightWave will continuously solve for an IK solution. It enables you to animate the goal object. You move a goal and the chain follows, and that's all there is to it. If AutoKey is activated, you won't even need to create keyframes; just move the goal around. You will find that you use Full-time IK more often than not.

The benefit of turning Full-time IK on and off is to control system resources. There might be times when too many complex hierarchies in a scene, all set up with IK, might bring your system to a halt. It's rare, but possible. Turning this feature off gives LightWave some breathing room during larger scenes. IK also might not give you desirable solutions all the time, so keyframes often are needed.

You now have a completed IK chain. The solid blue line extending from the root object to the goal object indicates the completed IK chain. This IK chain in its current state is worthless, however. Before the IK solution will actually control the bones, each bone needs to have a controller set to use IK. You set up these controllers in the Controllers & Limits tab of the Motion Options panel.

Controllers enable you to set up each channel of the current item to be controlled by FK or IK. Although the setup of the controllers at first might seem like an excessive amount of work, it is actually a blessing in disguise. These controllers are one of LightWave's great strengths in character animation because you can mix and match FK and IK in the same item. To set up the controllers for the bones, follow these steps:

10. With the Motion Options panel still open, select the next bone up the chain. Switch to the Controllers & Limits tab.

    Three pop-up menus will appear. These enable you to specify what controls each of the current items' rotation channels.

11. Choose Inverse Kinematics under the Pitch Controllers pop-up. Your setup should look like Figure 13.15.

Note

You can leave the Motion Options panel open, and use the up- or down-arrow keys to select the different bones.

12. Set the Pitch Controller for all the other bones in the chain to Inverse Kinematics. Next, set a keyframe at frame 0 for the goal. Move it up on the Y, and create a keyframe at 30. Play the scene.

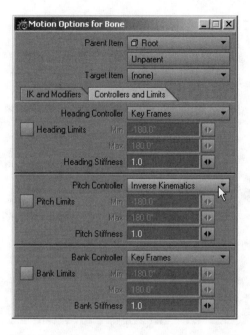

Figure 13.15   The Pitch Controller for each bone is set to Inverse Kinematics.

13. You'll see that nothing happens! The chain does not follow the goal. Back in the Motion Options panel, turn on Full-time IK (refer to Step 9), and play the scene again. The chain now follows. Save your scene!

The IK chain is now completely functional. Select the goal object in Layout and move it around in the scene. The bones will now follow the goal, similar to Figure 13.16. Notice that regardless of the goal's X position, the chain only follows on the yz-axis. This is because the chain is planar or 2D. It's planar because you set IK to control the pitch.

Experiment with the basic IK chain by activating IK on different rotation controllers, such as heading. Apply IK to the heading or bank controllers for each item in the scene. Does the IK chain move differently with the other controllers activated? Experimenting with different configurations will give you more insight into how IK works. You'll also find that the most common IK controls are heading and pitch.

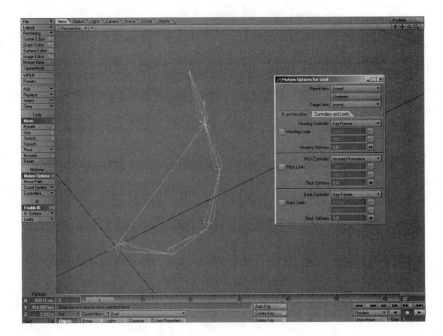

Figure 13.16   IK is being used to manipulate these bones' pitch axis.

Joint and Chain Types

IK consists of two basic joint types: 3D and planar (2D). Joint types in LightWave are determined by their controller's setup. An IK chain can consist of multiple joint types throughout. With the two basic joint types alone, almost any naturally occurring joint can be replicated in LightWave.

Planar Chains

A chain composed of 2D joints is called a *planar IK chain*. 2D joints are probably the most commonly used types of joints in character animation. Planar joints are often referred to as *hinge joints* because they rotate much like a hinge. The elbow and knee joints in human skeletal structures are planar joints. Planar chains are the easiest types to work with because they are limited to one axis around which to rotate. Figure 13.17 shows a planar joint in action.

To create a planar joint in LightWave, activate IK for only one rotation controller. This will limit the rotation to one axis controlled by IK.

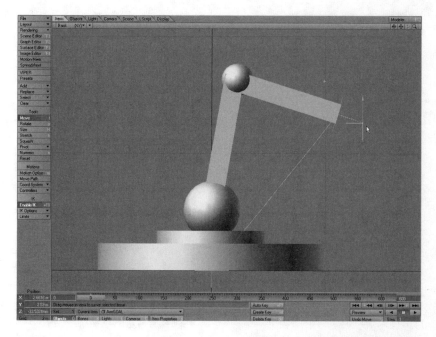

Figure 13.17   A planar joint is limited to rotate around one axis and is often referred to as a hinge joint.

3D Chains

A 3D chain occurs when all the joints of the chain are set to rotate on more than one axis (see Figure 13.18). The joints of a 3D chain are sometimes called *ball joints*. A 3D joint will have two or more controllers set to Inverse Kinematics. 3D joints occur everywhere in nature, and you will use them often when setting up characters. The human shoulder is considered to be a 3D joint. Due to the rotational freedom of 3D chains, they also are the most difficult to use.

Rigid IK Structures

Until now, you used IK exclusively with bones. The nice thing about IK in LightWave is that it will function with any hierarchical structure, not just with bones. In LightWave, items capable of being parented to other items (except for lights) can participate in an IK chain. IK systems composed of objects rather than bones are referred to as *rigid*.

A rigid IK system physically rotates the objects rather than deforming them with bones. Rigid IK systems are great for creating mechanical movement such as that of a robot or a hydraulic actuator. You create a rigid IK system in the same manner as you would an IK system for bones, except that you use a hierarchical structure of objects instead of bones.

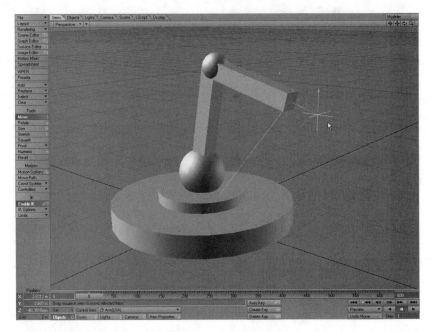

Figure 13.18   3D chains are useful for manipulating objects such as a crane or robot arm.

Exercise 13.2   Creating a Rigid IK System

To better understand how to use a rigid IK system, follow the steps in this exercise. This exercise will help you set up a rigid IK system to simulate a robotic arm.

1. Clear the scene and load the RobotArm.lwo object from the content CD. RobotArm is five separate objects within the same file. Press the 3 key to switch to Right view mode. The default position of the arm when the object is loaded is shown in Figure 13.19.

    The RobotArm object consists of five separate objects saved as one object file. Each object has its own pivot point positioned in Modeler to give proper rotations for each joint. The object structure for the robot arm is as follows:

    - **RobotArm:Base.** The Base is the platform on which the robot arm rests. It is not controlled by IK but can be manipulated through regular keyframe animation. It is the root object in the hierarchy.

    - **RobotArm:Stand.** The Stand is the portion of the robot arm that holds the actual arm in place. In the real world, the stand has a motor at its base to rotate its heading, and it has a motor at the top that rotates the Primary Arm. The robot arm's Stand should have its heading controlled by IK.

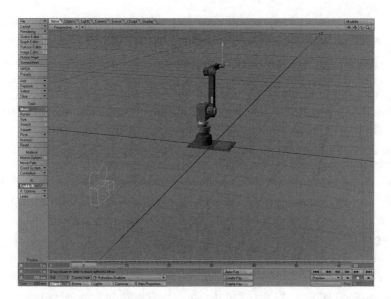

Figure 13.19   The RobotArm is ready to be animated with IK.

- **RobotArm:Primary.** The Primary Arm is connected to the motor on the stand. As such, it can be rotated only up and down. You will need to configure the pitch controller of the Primary Arm to use IK.

- **RobotArm:Secondary.** The Secondary Arm is attached to a motor located at the end of the Primary Arm. It is also rotated only on its pitch and should be controlled with IK.

- **RobotArm:Grabber.** The Grabber is the hand of the robot arm. In this case, it contains a tool used for soldering rather than a physical hand. The Grabber can be rotated only on its pitch axis, but it will be the goaled item in the hierarchy and won't need IK controllers.

You should configure the joints of the robot arm according to the information in the preceding list. Before configuring the joints, you will need to add a goal object for the arm to follow.

2. Select Add, then Objects, and then Add Null to add a null to the scene. When prompted to enter a name for the null, enter Goal. This null object will serve as the goal object of the robot arm. To manipulate the robot arm, you will just drag the goal around. Select the RobotArm:Grabber and press the m key to open the Motion Options panel.

3. Select Goal (the null object you just added) as the Goal Object. Click the Keep Goal Within Reach option. This will tell LightWave to follow the goal with the RobotArm:Grabber object and that the grabber is at the end of the IK chain.

   The exact positioning isn't all that important, but this option will keep the goal object attached to the IK chain, which helps keep your scene organized.

You need to configure the joints for the arm segments. After they are configured, you can animate the entire arm by dragging the goal object around. The next steps will show how to configure the joints.

4. In Layout, select the RobotArm:Stand object. In the Motion Options panel (m), switch to the Controllers & Limits tab. Using the Heading Controller's pop-up list, choose Inverse Kinematics. Leave all the other settings unchanged. The stand will now rotate around its heading when the goal object is moved.

5. Keep the Motion Options panel open, move it off to the side, and select the RobotArm:Primary object in the Layout interface. Conversely, you can use the down arrow to cycle through the objects. Use Inverse Kinematics to control the pitch of the primary arm by choosing it from the pitch controller pop-up.

6. Like the primary arm, the secondary arm can be rotated only on its pitch. Select the RobotArm:Secondary object and set the pitch controller to use IK.

7. Switch back to the Inverse Kinematics and the Modifiers tab of the Motion Options panel. Select the RobotArm:Grabber.

   This object will point the rest of the chain by following the goal object.

Note

Because the RobotArm:Grabber object is a rotatable part of the structure, you also can parent a null object at the very tip, and goal that item instead. The benefit is that you will have more control over movements.

8. Finally, activate Full-time IK for the grabber. Make sure that Show IK Chains from the Display Options tab (d) is active, and you'll notice the light-blue line drawn from the RobotArm:Base to the goal object indicating a complete IK chain. Switch to Perspective view, and select the Goal in Layout and move it around (see Figure 13.20).

A rigid IK chain now controls the RobotArm. Manipulating the goal will move the RobotArm. Notice that the arm moves like a real robot arm. This is due to the rigid IK solution. Although a similar setup could be achieved with bones, it isn't necessary and wouldn't give the rigid-looking results—the objects would be improperly deformed.

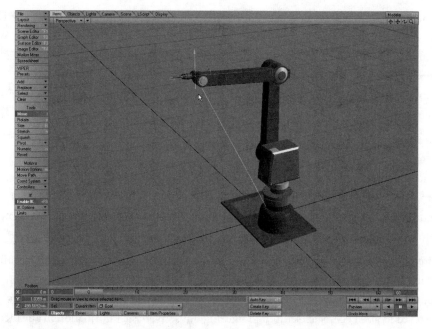

Figure 13.20 Indicated by the line from the base to the goal object, an IK chain is set to control the RobotArm.

Introduction to Character Setup

The proper setup of a character is the most important step to an enjoyable experience in character animation. If you overlook something in the initial stages of setup, you might have hell to pay later when animating the character.

Setting up a character is often called *rigging*. Rigging is basically the process of configuring a character with animation controls. These controls can be based on FK, IK, or a combination of both. The next few sections of this chapter focus on the rigging of a human-like skeletal structure and guide you through the process of setting up the animation controls.

The Importance of Preplanning

Character setup can be complicated and, like other aspects of 3D animation, is greatly simplified through some preplanning. Whether you are rigging a simple biped character or a multi-legged centipede, preplanning will be your most important resource.

When planning, gather as much information about your character as possible. The amount of preplanning you need to do varies depending on the type of character you want to animate. Research the type of character that you are going to animate to determine how it moves, what range of motion it has, how its joints work, and what traits you want to integrate. The more research you do up front, the more time you will have available to animate.

After you've done your research, it's time to figure out the best setup to use for your character. If your character has a seamless skin, you will more than likely be animating it with bones. A segmented character will probably best be animated with a rigid kinematics system, but you might want to use bones with it as well. If you are using bones, you need to figure out the best placement of the bones to give you the best deformation. For more information on bone setup, see Chapter 12, "Deformations and Movement."

After you have a basic setup, be it with bones or object segments, you need to determine which joints will be 3D and which need to be planar. Also think about which portions of your character are going to be controlled by what kinematics system. Many factors are involved in good character setup, and figuring out some basic information in advance is essential.

Schematics, like blueprints, can be useful tools during both the preplanning and rigging stages. Using LightWave's Schematic view will help you determine parent/child setup, joint types, and goal placement, as well as many other important factors.

For the purpose of the next exercise, you will set up a simple biped skeleton. Because this chapter focuses on the actual kinematics setup, the bone structure has already been created for you. Examine the skeletal structure closely and determine which animation controls need to be set up. Figure 13.21 shows the skeletal structure in its default pose.

While looking at the skeleton, ask yourself:

- What types of joints need to be set up?
- Is IK the ideal system for this character, or should FK be used? Maybe both systems should be used?
- Where is the best position for the goal objects?
- What range of motion does the character need?

This character was designed to offer a generic range of humanlike motion. After the character is rigged, you can make it walk, run, sit, wave, dance, or perform any other basic primary motion. The skeletal structure also could be modified to offer a precise range of motion for specific tasks.

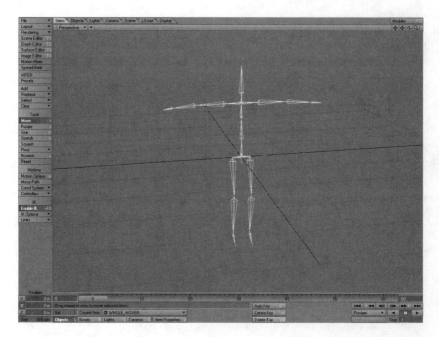

Figure 13.21   The bone structure has been created in an "arms wide open" pose to aid in the setup of the animation controls.

In 3D animation, it often can be helpful to make different variations of an object designed with different types of motion in mind. If you wanted to make a generic walk cycle, a simple skeleton with basic kinematics control would be more than adequate. However, if you wanted to animate a character with complex motion (such as falling down stairs or washing a car), you would need to design the rig accordingly.

Preparing the Object

After planning the character's setup, the next step is to set up basic controls. The character you will be working with is a basic skeletal structure designed to exploit the setup of IK in LightWave. The actual bone structure is not necessarily the best layout for all characters, but the techniques used in rigging the structure are essential to every character.

Note

One thing you should be aware of is LightWave's alert levels. If you press o on the keyboard to open the General Options tab of the Preferences panel, you can set the Alert level to Beginner, Intermediate, or Expert. Setting it to Beginner will display a panel in the middle of Layout when you need to be alerted of an error or change based on an operation you perform. If you set the Alert Level to Intermediate or Expert, you'll see the alert in a small window below the timeline at the bottom of Layout. Setting the Alert level to Intermediate or Expert will not disturb your workflow.

Exercise 13.3   Setting Up Basic Controls

1. Clear the scene and add a null object from the Items tab by selecting Add, then Objects, and then Add Null. Give this null the name WHOLE_MOVER, and press Enter to accept the name. Load in the IKSkeleton object from the book's CD. Notice that the object is an empty bounding box. The object actually is a group of skelegons that will need to be converted into usable bones.

> **Note**
>
> The IKSkeleton object is a group of skelegons arranged in a biped skeletal structure. It consists of 30 skelegons ready to be rigged with animation controls. After you feel comfortable with the setup of this structure, with only a few minor modifications, you can use it as the skeleton for any of your characters.

2. From the Items tab, select Add, then Bones, and then Convert Skelegons to Bones. This will convert the skelegons in the object to regular bones so that they are usable in Layout. After converting the skelegons, you will be told that 30 bones were created. The converted skelegons should look like Figure 13.22. Note that this is an adjusted Perspective view.

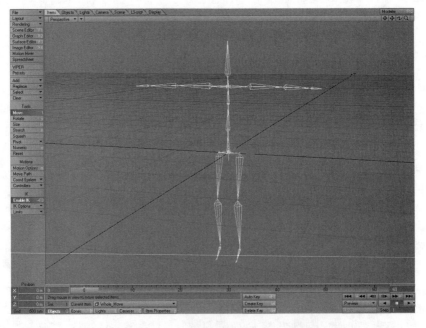

Figure 13.22   This is the IKSkeleton after the skelegons have been converted to regular bones.

Note

Depending on which Alert level you've chosen for Layout (General Options tab of the Preferences panel, which you display by pressing o), the message telling you how many bones were converted from skelegons might appear either in the lower portion of the interface or as a pop-up display. The Beginner Alert level will show a pop-up display. Intermediate and Advanced will be displayed at the bottom of the interface.

3. Due to the nature of parenting skelegons in Modeler and LightWave's use of pivot points, a few bones need to be tweaked before setting up the animation controls.

4. Click the Bones button at the bottom of the Layout interface, and then look closely at the Left.Arm.Upper bone. It isn't properly aligned with the collarbone; instead, it is located at the tip of the shoulder's control bone. This is a result of parenting skelegons in Modeler.

   When you parent a skelegon to another in Modeler, it will be shifted to the tip of the parent skelegon. Usually, this would be perfectly acceptable, but because the Left.Arm.Upper bone needs to be aligned with the collarbone and yet remain the child of the shoulder's control bone, you will have to correct it in Layout. Correcting this is as simple as zeroing out the position values of the shifted bones.

Tip

If you use the middle mouse button (if you have one) to select objects or bones in Layout, you do not need to be as precise selecting Layout items. You can select items easily by clicking near them. To use this feature, deactivate the Left Mouse Button Item Select feature in the General Options tab (press o), which helps keep your selections deliberate. Often, when you have enabled the Left Mouse Button Item Select feature, you inadvertently select different Layout items while trying to move or rotate; now you can instead use the middle mouse button (if you have one). You'll be so cool!

5. Select the Left.Arm.Upper bone, either by middle-clicking the bone itself or by choosing it from the Scene Editor. Press the n key to activate the numeric input fields. Enter 0 for all the fields so that the bone's position is indicated as

$$X \quad 0$$
$$Y \quad 0$$
$$Z \quad 0$$

   The bone will jump back to its proper place and remain parented to the appropriate bone.

6. Repeat this procedure for all the misplaced bones, create keyframes at frame 0 to lock the position in place, and be sure to save your scene. The bones that need to be fixed are

Left.Arm.Upper

Left.Leg.Upper

Right.Arm.Upper

Right.Leg.Upper

After you finish zeroing out the shifted bones, the skeleton will be ready for setup. The actual rigging process will take a little while to complete, so sit back and enjoy the ride.

Placing Goal Objects

Goal objects are the manipulators for IK chains. They technically can be any objects, but null objects are commonly used because they don't render and are easy to manage. The IKSkeleton will consist of four independent IK chains. It will have a chain for each arm and one for each leg. You will need to create goal objects for each IK chain.

Exercise 13.4   Creating Goal Objects

1. Choose Add, then Objects, and then Add Null from the Items tab. When prompted for a name, enter LeftARM.GOAL. This null object will serve as the goal object for the left arm IK chain.

   Rather than adding all the nulls at the same time, it is best to configure one side of the character first and then clone the nulls for use on the other side. This will ensure exact goal placement for a symmetrical character.

2. Select the LeftARM.GOAL. This goal needs to be placed into position at the joint between the Left.Arm.Hand and the Left.LowerArm bones. Move the goal into position by either dragging it into a rough position or by entering the following values in the numeric field:

X	760mm
Y	600mm
Z	−121mm

> **Note**
>
> It isn't always necessary to place the goal in an exact position because the IK chain will jump to the goal when activated. However, keeping your scene clean and precise will make animating much more enjoyable.

3. Clone the LeftARM.GOAL by first selecting the LeftARM.GOAL, choosing Add, and then Clone Current Item. Set Number of Clones to 1 in the dialog that appears, and then click OK or press Enter.

   Doing so will create an exact copy of the LeftARM.GOAL. The clone will be used as the goal object for the right arm.

4. Choose Replace, and then Rename Current Item from the Items tab. Rename the currently selected null RightARM.GOAL.

5. With the RightARM.GOAL still selected, position it on the opposite side of the character between the Right.Hand and the Right.Forearm bones. The easiest way to do this is to add a negative (–) sign to the X value. The positional values for the RightARM.GOAL should be as follows:

X	–760mm
Y	600mm
Z	–121mm

You now have the two goals for the arm IK chains in position. When the setup is complete, moving these two goals will give you a full range of motion for the arms. Although all the other goals will be parented to the WHOLE_MOVER null, it is essential that you do not parent the arm goals because they will be controlled by the Keep Goal Within Reach command discussed in the next exercise. If you've followed along exactly, your scene will look like Figure 13.23.

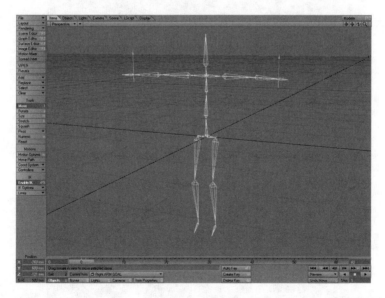

Figure 13.23   The IKSkeleton's arm goals have been placed in the proper positions.

Now you are ready to create the goals for the legs. The legs will be a little more complicated than the arms because of the need for two extra goal objects. The extra goals will help keep the feet planted on the floor and give a broader range of motion for the legs. Again, creating the goals for one side and then cloning them for the other side will make things a little easier on you.

6. Add a null object and name it LeftLEG.MASTER. This null will be the main goal you use to manipulate the left leg. Parent this goal to the WHOLE_MOVER null.

7. Add another null object, but this time give it the name LeftLEG.GOAL. The LeftLEG.GOAL will be a descendent of the LeftLEG.MASTER and as such will inherit its rotations to give a greater level of control for the feet.

8. Using the Scene Editor, drag the LeftLEG.GOAL under and to the right of the LeftLEG.MASTER so that it becomes a child of the LeftLEG.MASTER. When dragging an item in the Scene Editor, you will see a small yellow line directly under the selected item. This line helps you parent items to each other. When the line is slightly offset from the item you want to be the parent, release the mouse button (see Figure 13.24).

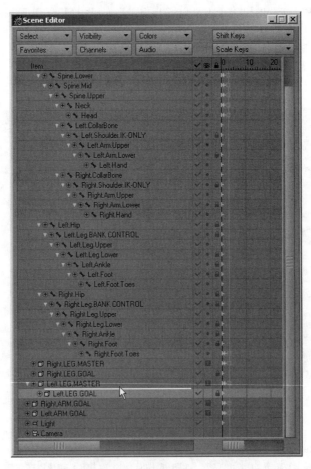

Figure 13.24   The Scene Editor enables you to parent an item to another simply by dragging it on top of the other item.

9. Select the LeftLEG.MASTER object. Move this object to the joint between the Left.Foot and Left.Toes bones. If you choose, you can enter the following values in the numeric field:

X	100mm
Y	−1m
Z	−108mm

Note

The LeftLEG.MASTER is the main item you will use to manipulate the left leg. It is essentially the ball of the foot. Using the goal in this position gives you greater flexibility when posing the feet. Things like heel and toe control are gained using this setup.

Now you will position the LeftLEG.GOAL object at the ankle.

10. Select LeftLEG.GOAL and move it 100mm on the y- and 108mm on the z-axes.

This will place it at the joint between the Left.LowerLeg bone and the Left.Ankle bone. The values for the LeftLEG.GOAL's position should look like this:

X	0m
Y	100mm
Z	108mm

That wraps up the goal positioning for the left leg. To create the goal objects for the right leg, follow these steps:

11. Select the LeftLEG.MASTER object and clone it by choosing Add and then selecting Clone Current Item. Cloning does not clone descendents, which means that you will need to clone the LeftLEG.GOAL separately.

12. With the LeftLEG.MASTER selected, choose Replace and then select Rename Current Item from the Items tab. Name this object RightLEG.MASTER.

13. As you did with the arm goals, give the RightLEG.MASTER a negative (−) value on its X channel.

The negative value will move it across the median into the exact same position on the opposite side of the character. The position values for RightLEG.MASTER should be as follows:

X	−100mm
Y	−1m
Z	−108mm

14. Now select the LeftLEG.GOAL object and clone it. Rename it RightLEG.GOAL and, using the Scene Editor, parent it to the RightLEG.MASTER object. Save your work.

You also can parent an item using the Motion Options panel (press the m key) by choosing the desired parent object from the panel's Parent Object pop-up list. Notice that it jumps into the proper position on the right side of the object.

That concludes the goal creation and positioning portion of this project. You did it! Figure 13.25 shows what the scene should look like if you are following along exactly.

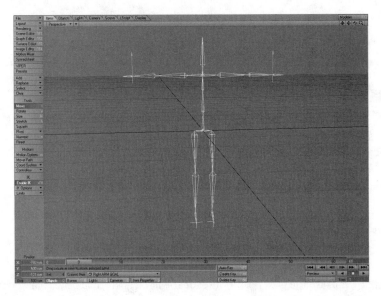

Figure 13.25   This is the complete IKSkeleton with goal objects positioned and ready to be rigged with animation controls.

Configuring the Joints

The only thing left to do is configure the joints and activate the goal objects.

If you closely examine the skeleton, you will notice some awkwardly placed bones at the shoulder and hip joints. These are the control bones mentioned earlier in this chapter. In certain instances, a bone's rotation channels won't allow the desired range of rotation for a specific joint. An example of this would be a bone that is slightly rotated on its pitch. The heading and bank channels would then be based on the angle that the bone is pitched. If you wanted to rotate the bank of the bone in a planar fashion around the z-axis, you'd be out of luck. This is where control bones come into play. Parenting the pitched bone to a control bone (which is lying flat on the xz-axis) will enable you to control the bank angle of the pitched bone in the desired manner by rotating the control bone on its bank channel.

You also can go one step further and change the Coordinate system to Local for the odd bone. This will change the bone's rotational handles to its own local origin, making movements much easier and often eliminating the need for control bones. You also can use the Record Pivot Point tool found under the Pivot list in the Items tab to accomplish this task.

> **Note**
>
> You can bypass the need for control bones by using the Record Pivot Point feature found under the Items tab in Layout. Clicking it for a selected item, such as a bone, records the current pivot point, which saves time by eliminating the control bones.

Figure 13.26 shows a control bone in action. Control bones can be an invaluable resource when used properly. Always remember that with LightWave nothing is set in stone, and you should experiment with different techniques to get the results you want.

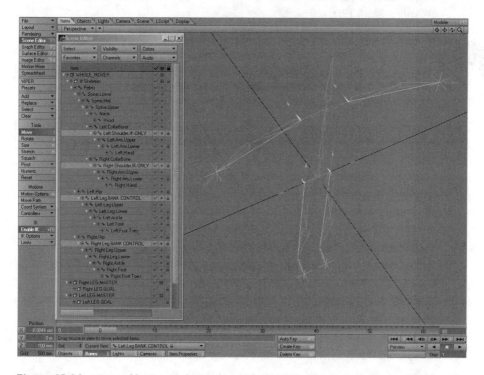

Figure 13.26   Control bones can be used to give a third degree of rotation to a planar joint when desired.

Keeping the types of joints found in the human skeleton in mind, it's time to set up the joints of your character, starting with the arms. The shoulder is usually a 3D or ball joint and can rotate into almost any position. The next joint in the arm is the elbow. The elbow is a planar (2D) joint, also referred to as a *hinge joint* because, like a hinge, it can only open or close on one axis. With the exception of the fingers, the last joint in the arm is the wrist, which is also a 3D joint. Following along with the next few steps will assist you in configuring the joints.

Exercise 13.5   Setting Up Joints

1. Select the Left.CollarBone and press the m key to bring up the Motion Options panel. This bone will be controlled by FK, so you don't need to set up any controllers for it. This bone also will serve as the terminator for the IK in the left arm, so activate Unaffected by IK of Descendents.

2. With the Motion Options panel still open, advance to the next bone by pressing the down-arrow key. This bone is the Left.Shoulder.IK-ONLY bone. Select Controllers and Limits in the Motion Options panel.

    This shoulder bone is a control bone for the rest of the arm. It will be controlled exclusively with IK.

> **Note**
>
> You can make extensive use of non-modal panels such as the Motion Options panel. These panels can remain open while you work. It is recommended that you keep the Motion Options panel open while rigging your characters. You should place the panel so that you can see your scene while you set up all your bones. Not all panels are non-modal, but the Motion Options panel is. Non-modal means a panel that is not tied to a specific mode, and can therefore stay open while you work.

3. Choose Inverse Kinematics from the Heading Controller pop-up menu. Leave the Pitch and Bank Controllers set to Key Frames.

4. Once again, select the next bone, which should be the Left.Arm.Upper bone. Select Inverse Kinematics for the Heading Controller.

    The upper arm bone functions like that of a 3D or ball joint. Rather than using IK for all its controllers, the bone will share rotations with the shoulder control bone to simulate a 3D joint (see Figure 13.27).

    The next bone is the Left.Arm.Lower bone. This bone represents a humanlike forearm. The joint between it and the Left.Arm.Upper bone simulates an elbow. Because an elbow is a planar (2D) joint, it will be rotated only on one axis.

5. Choose Inverse Kinematics for the Heading Controller.

    Moving right along, you should now be at the final bone of the arm—the hand bone. The hand bone will be rotated exclusively with FK. It also will serve as the "pointer" bone for the IK chain.

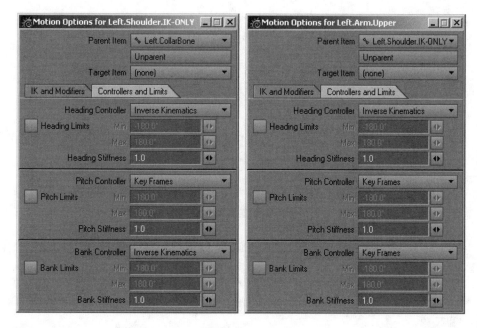

Figure 13.27   Inverse kinematics is controlling the heading and bank of the shoulder control bone (left) and the heading of the Left.Arm.Upper bone (right) to form a simulated 3D joint.

6. To set up the Left.Hand bone as the pointer bone, switch back to the IK and select the Modifiers tab of the Motion Options panel. Under the Goal Object pop-up menu, choose LeftARM.GOAL.

   This tells LightWave to use the LeftARM.GOAL as the goal object for this IK chain.

7. Activate Full-time IK for the hand bone by pressing the Full-time IK button under the IK and Modifiers tab of the Motion Options panel. This forces LightWave to continuously calculate a solution for this IK chain.

8. Select Keep Goal Within Reach under the IK and Modifiers tab to lock the goal to the IK chain.

Note

Keep Goal Within Reach is a LightWave feature that locks the goal to the IK chain. With this feature activated, LightWave works to keep the goal object from being moved beyond the reach of the IK chain. This is a wonderful feature that is used primarily in single-goal IK chains.

9. The left arm is now complete. Repeat steps 1 through 8 for the items on the right side of the character, and save your work when you're done. The upper body should now be ready to animate. Figure 13.28 shows the scene in its current state.

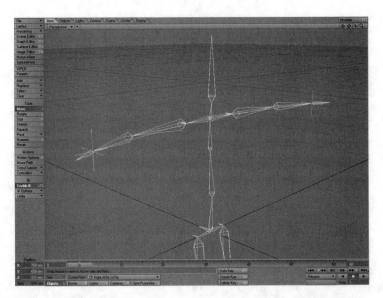

Figure 13.28   All the joints in the upper body have been configured and are ready to be animated.

You are now ready to set up the legs. Once again, look at the real-world equivalent of the leg joints and determine the type of joint needed in the IKSkeleton. The joint between the hip and the upper leg is a 3D joint. The IKSkeleton will use a planar joint for the upper leg in combination with a bank control bone to create a 3D joint. The next joint in the leg is the knee, which is a planar joint. Although the ankle is slightly limited in range of motion, it also is a 3D joint. Knowing this information, follow the next few steps to complete the leg setup.

Exercise 13.6   Applying IK to Legs

1. Select the Left.Hip bone. The hipbones are not controlled by IK. Activate the Unaffected by IK of Descendents function found in the Motion Options panel (m) to terminate the IK chain at the end of the hipbones.

2. Select the Left.Leg.BANK CONTROL bone. You can use the up- and down-arrow keys to move through the bone hierarchy. Select Inverse Kinematics as the Bank Controller for this bone. Controlling only the bank of this bone will give you good results when moving the leg side to side.

3. Press the down-arrow key to select the next bone, which is the Left.Leg.Upper bone. This bone is the equivalent of the human thigh. Set it to be controlled only by IK on its pitch. Leaving the heading controlled by FK will give you the ability to point the knee. Although it isn't necessary for this bone right now, you could set up the pitch angle limits to constrain the rotation of the upper leg.

4. Select the Left.Leg.Lower bone and activate Inverse Kinematics for the pitch controller. Leave all the other controllers set to Key Frames.

5. With the Left.LowerLeg bone still selected, activate Pitch Limits under the Controllers and Limits tab of the Motion Options panel. Enter 5.0 in the Min field, and enter 145.0 in the Max field.

Note

Applying pitch limits to this bone will prevent the bone from rotating beyond its natural range of motion. You don't want your knee to rotate backward, do you? Ouch! Remember that IK is not perfect and can occasionally come up with multiple solutions for a chain, even though it was created using a preferred angle. Setting angle limits will help reduce strange IK solutions.

6. Select the Left.Ankle bone. The anklebone will point to a goal object and terminate an IK chain that will exist in the foot. Switch to IK and Modifiers in the Motion Options panel and activate Unaffected by IK of Descendents. Choose LeftLEG.GOAL from the Goal Object pop-up menu, and finally activate Full-time IK for this bone.

   You should see a blue line indicating a complete IK chain appearing between the hipbone and the anklebone.

7. Look directly under the Goal Object pop-up menu, and you will see a Goal Strength field. Enter a value of 50.0 into the field. Turn on Keep Goal Within Reach.

Note

The Goal Strength field enables you to input the strength that an IK chain reaches for its goal. Imagine the goal strength setting as a magnet between the goaled bone and the goal. As the value increases, so does the strength of the bond between the two items. Goal strength's main purpose is apparent when you have multiple goals in the same chain; in this situation, you can give one goal preference by increasing its relative goal strength. Multiple goals in the same chain with the same strength can result in erratic responses as the IK tries to calculate them both. Experiment with different goal strengths for each pointer bone to come up with different results.

The LeftLEG.GOAL will control all the items in the leg, from the hip to the ankle. The LeftLEG.GOAL is parented to the LeftLEG.MASTER, so you won't ever directly control the LeftLEG.GOAL. The LeftLEG.MASTER also will be the goal object for a small IK chain in the foot section of the leg. To finish setting up the legs, continue on to the next steps.

8. Select the Left.Foot bone. Open the Motion Options panel and switch to the Controllers and Limits tab to configure the controllers for the foot. Activate Inverse Kinematics for the pitch controller only. Leave everything else as it is.

9. Now select the Left.Foot.Toes bone. It is a pointer bone and doesn't need any controller adjustment, so switch to the IK and Modifiers tab. From the Goal Object pop-up menu, choose LeftLEG.MASTER. Make sure that Keep Goal Within Reach is turned on.

10. Enter 200.0 in the Goal Strength field of the Left.Toes bone.

   That completes the setup of the IKSkeleton's left leg IK chain. The setup of the IKSkeleton is almost complete. The only thing left to set up is the right leg. The right leg uses an almost identical setup as the left leg.

11. Select the Right.Hip bone. Activate Unaffected by IK of Descendents (located in the Motion Options panel) to terminate the IK chain at the end of the hipbones.

12. Select the Right.Leg.BANK CONTROL bone. Select Inverse Kinematics as the bank controller for this bone.

13. Select the Right.Leg.Upper bone. This bone will function as the thighbone. Set it to be controlled by IK on its pitch. This setup enables you to point the knee using FK by rotating the heading.

14. Select the Right.Leg.Lower bone and activate Inverse Kinematics for the pitch controller. Leave all the other controllers set to Key Frames.

15. With the Right.Leg.Lower bone still selected, activate Pitch Limits under the Controllers and Limits tab of the Motion Options panel. Enter 5.0 in the Min field, and enter 145.0 in the Max field.

16. Select the Right.Ankle bone. Switch to IK and Modifiers in the Motion Options panel and activate Unaffected by IK of Descendents.

17. Choose RightLEG.GOAL from the Goal Object pop-up. Set a value of 50.0 in the Goal Strength field and make sure that Keep Goal Within Reach is turned on.

18. Select the Right.Foot bone. Open the Motion Options panel and switch to the Controllers and Limits tab to configure the controllers for the foot. Activate Inverse Kinematics for the pitch controller. Leave everything else as it is.

19. Now select the Right.Foot.Toes bone. This is a pointer bone and doesn't need any controller adjustment, so switch to the IK and Modifiers tab. From the Goal Object pop-up menu, choose RightLEG.MASTER. Again, make sure that Keep Goal Within Reach is turned on.

20. Enter 200.0 into the Goal Strength field of the Right.Toes bone.

21. From here, select a goal and move it around. You'll see the limb move! Now all you need to do is keyframe the motion of the goal to animate the chain of bones. When an object is attached to these bones, the object would be deformed.

   Pretty cool, isn't it? Moving just one simple null object to bend a leg or an arm—this is the beauty of IK.

That's all there is to it. You now have a completely set-up kinematics skeletal structure. If you followed along step by step with the exercise, your scene should look like Figure 13.29.

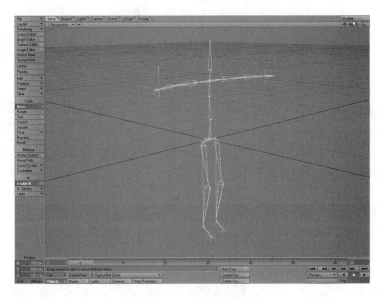

Figure 13.29   This is the completed IKSkeleton skeletal structure.

Enhancing the Setup

You can take this setup to the next level with some minor adjustments to the scene. To further enhance the IKSkeleton setup, try the following:

- Lock some of the bones with the Scene Editor to prevent accidental selection. You can do this by clicking next to the desired bone in the Scene Editor under the Lock column. A small padlock icon identifies this column.

- Deactivate the motion channels for all the bones in the scene. This will keep you from accidentally moving a bone. You can do this by clicking the X, Y, or Z buttons in the bottom-left corner of the Layout interface, next to the numeric information panel.

- Deactivate all the rotation channels for the bones that you aren't manipulating with FK. You can do this by clicking the H, P, or B buttons in the bottom left corner of the Layout interface, next to the numeric information panel.

- Set up angle limits for joints in the skeleton. Properly set-up angle limits will prevent unwanted rotations. You can do this in the Motion Options panel, under the Controllers and Limits tab.

- Turn AutoKey on! With AutoKey on, you can animate the character without manually creating a single keyframe. To use AutoKey in this situation, remember that AutoKey Create must be set to Modified Channels in the General Options tab (o). Then, click the AutoKey button on the Layout interface to activate and deactivate the tool—this action functions as a kind of on/off switch.

Rigging a Real Character for Full Inverse Kinematics

Now that you have a firm grasp of the basic techniques involved in character setup, it's time to put your knowledge to work by rigging a usable character. As you will soon see, properly setting up a character will give you a pleasurable animation experience. After all, animation is supposed to be fun, isn't it?

The character you will be rigging requires the same techniques you just used for setting an IK structure for bones. However, you can perform these steps directly to objects as well. In the next exercise, you'll be setting up a complex hierarchy for a motorcross racer. When complete, you can move the motorcycle and have the racer sitting on the bike stay parented. While the bike is moving, the racer character can move around while his hands and feet remain attached to the bike. His head can rotate independently while staying attached to the body (which is a good thing) and the individual arms and legs can be raised at any time with the movement of one null object. Sound confusing? It's not. Figure 13.30 shows the motorcross racer in action.

Although you'll add multiple goal objects to this character, the setup is still relatively simple. Using LightWave's mirror tool, setup is made even easier. Follow along!

Exercise 13.7   Hierarchy Setup of the Motorcross Racer

The racer's rigging is based on the same principles of IK that you learned in the previous exercises. For this scene, the racer needs to be placed in a variety of poses, so creating multiple versions of the character for different ranges of motion was out of the question. The hybrid IK/FK engine in LightWave will enable you to create a single character with a relatively simple rig to accomplish every shot, such as a jump with hands in the air, while the wheels of the bike remain rotating. Follow these steps to rig up your own motorcross racer.

1. Start with a fresh scene by choosing Clear Scene from the File pop-up menu. The scene you'll end up with after you finish setting up this character can easily be integrated into other scenes with the Load Items From Scene command.

Figure 13.30   Here is a sample shot of the motorcross racer. This is a complex setup in which you have complete control over all motions using IK. Here, the Spreadsheet Scene Manager is opened and configured to see the hierarchy of the full setup, as well as any IK properties.

2. Select Add, then Objects, and then Add Null to add the most important object in the scene, the root null. Name it Root.

   This null will be the root object of the racer and will enable you to move the entire character anywhere in the scene, maintaining any walk cycles or positioning information you've created.

Note

It really isn't necessary for this null to be added as the first item in the scene, but doing so will keep things tidy. A good habit to get into is adding items to a scene in a logical order. This will make it easier to select items using the up- and down-arrow keys as well as make for a clean setup. Keeping your scene clean will add years to your life of animating.

   Now it's time to bring in the actual racer object.

3. Select Add, then Objects, and Load Object. When the load requester pops up, navigate to the book's CD and load the MotorCrossDude object. Objects also can be loaded by pressing the (+) on the numeric keypad.

Note

The MotorCrossDude object is a layered object that makes use of LightWave's powerful layered object format. The object consists of the helmet, upper and lower legs, separate chest and neck, upper and lower arms, hands, and boots. Each is set up on its own pivot points, and each is a separate object to be used as a rigid IK chain. The hierarchical structure of all the objects was established in Modeler through the use of the Layers panel. All the individual objects are contained in one object file.

If you click the Current Item list for Objects, or open the Scene Editor or Spreadsheet, you'll see the following:

- MotorCrossDude:Helmet
- MotorCrossDude:Chest
- MotorCrossDude:MidSection
- MotorCrossDude:RightUpperLeg
- MotorCrossDude:RightLowerLeg
- MotorCrossDude:RightBoot
- MotorCrossDude:LeftUpperLeg
- MotorCrossDude:LeftLowerLeg
- MotorCrossDude:LeftBoot
- MotorCrossDude:RightUpperArm
- MotorCrossDude:RightForeArm
- MotorCrossDude:RightHand
- MotorCrossDude:LeftUpperArm
- MotorCrossDude:LeftLowerArm
- MotorCrossDude:LeftHand
- MotorCrossDude:Neck

4. You'll need to set up the proper parenting structure first, before any IK work can begin. Open the Scene Editor, and you'll see a straight list of the objects. You instantly can tell that there is no hierarchy setup because no listing is indented.

5. Select the first listing, MotorCrossDude:Helmet. Hold the Shift key, and select the 4th from the last MotorCrossDude listing, MotorCrossDude:Neck.

6. With those elements selected, drag them under and to the left of the Root null object to parent them to the Root.

To set up a proper IK chain, the individual objects need to be parented to the objects preceding them. Figure 13.31 shows the Scene Editor at this point.

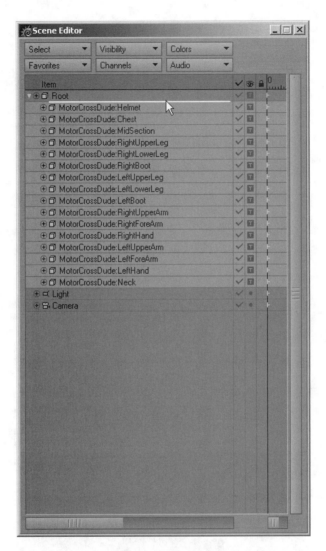

Figure 13.31   The object parts of the MotorCrossDude are selected at once in the Scene Editor and parented to the Root.

Now you can begin setup of the necessary hierarchy. You parented everything to the Root to begin the hierarchy from the top down. Once again, you can see that organization is key.

You're going to base everything on the chest for this character. When you move the chest with IK on the hands, the shoulders and arms will move naturally. The effect is that the character can change from a sitting position to a standing position while still driving the motorcycle.

7. Select the MotorCrossDude:Neck object in the Scene Editor. Drag it under and to the right of the MotorCrossDude:Chest object. The neck object layer is now parented to the chest, as shown in Figure 13.32.

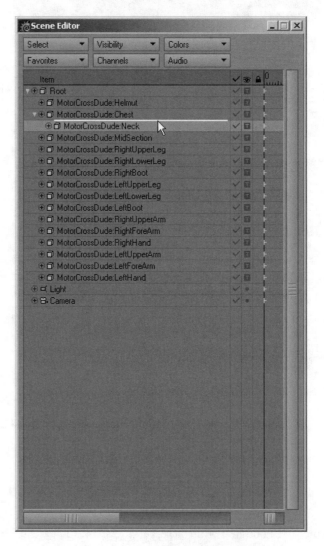

Figure 13.32 Dragging the MotorCrossDude:Neck object under and to the right of the Chest indents and parents the object.

8. Now you'll parent the helmet to the neck by dragging the MotorCrossDude: Helmet object under and to the right of the neck. Now the helmet is parented to the neck, which is parented to the chest. Figure 13.33 shows the hierarchy.

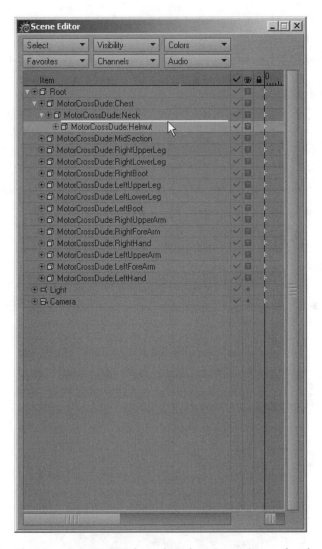

Figure 13.33   The MotorCrossDude:Helmet object layer is now parented to the neck, which is parented to the chest.

9. Continue parenting the rest of the objects as follows:

- Parent the MotorCrossDude:RightHand to the MotorCrossDude: RightForeArm.
- Parent the MotorCrossDude:RightForeArm to the MotorCrossDude: RightUpperArm.
- Parent the MotorCrossDude:RightUpperArm to the MotorCrossDude:Chest.
- Parent the MotorCrossDude:LeftHand to the MotorCrossDude:LeftForeArm.

- Parent the MotorCrossDude:LeftForeArm to the MotorCrossDude: LeftUpperArm.

- Parent the MotorCrossDude:LeftUpperArm to the MotorCrossDude:Chest.

- Parent the MotorCrossDude:RightBoot to the MotorCrossDude: RightLowerLeg.

- Parent the MotorCrossDude:RightLowerLeg to the MotorCrossDude: RightUpperLeg.

- Parent the MotorCrossDude:RightUpperLeg to the MotorCrossDude: MidSection.

- Parent the MotorCrossDude:LeftBoot to the MotorCrossDude:LeftLowerLeg.

- Parent the MotorCrossDude:LeftLowerLeg to the MotorCrossDude: LeftUpperLeg.

- Parent the MotorCrossDude:LeftUpperLeg to the MotorCrossDude: MidSection.

Figure 13.34 shows the final hierarchy as seen in the Scene Editor. Note that your order of objects might not be exactly the same, and that's okay. Just make sure the hierarchy is correct.

Figure 13.34   Here is the final hierarchy for the motorcross dude.

10. In Layout, select the chest object layer and press y on the keyboard to rotate. Click and drag the green rotation handle and watch what happens. Make sure that Show Handles is on in the Display Options tab (d).

The hierarchy is correct, because the arms, neck, and head follow the movement of the chest while the lower half of the body is stationary. That's fine. However, the chest separates from the midsection (see Figure 13.35).

Figure 13.35   Because the pivot point of the chest is centered, the rotation happens incorrectly.

This improper rotation is happening simply because all movements, targeting, parenting, and so on, are done from an object's pivot point. If you're setting up a magic trick here, this is fine. If not, fix it like this:

11. Go to the Back view (XY) by pressing 1 on the numeric keypad or selecting it from the drop-down list at the top of your Layout view. From the Items tab, click the Pivot drop-down list and choose the Move Pivot Point Tool, as shown in Figure 13.36.

12. Once the Move Pivot Point Tool is selected, simply grab the green arrow (make sure that the Show Handles feature is on) and bring the pivot down to the waist of the character. Figure 13.37 shows the new pivot position on a bounding box display of the character.

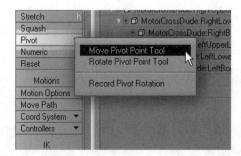

Figure 13.36   You can move pivots quickly in Layout for proper rotations with the Move Pivot Point Tool.

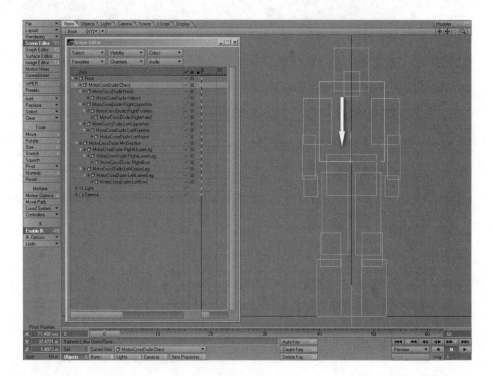

Figure 13.37   The new pivot in position will make the chest of the motorcross dude rotate without his body separating. That's much better.

13. Turn the Move Pivot Point Tool off by selecting another function, such as Move or Rotate. Save the scene!

What you've just done here is set up the proper hierarchy for animating the motorcross dude with IK. Now all you need to do is set up the goal objects.

Exercise 13.8   Adding Goal Objects to the Motorcross Racer

There are three basic steps to setting up any character for IK animation. First, you set up the parenting hierarchy structure, which you did in Exercise 13.6. Then you add goal objects as IK controls—usually a null object—which you'll do in this exercise. Finally, you configure the IK chains for proper motions. That part is coming up shortly.

1. With the setup you've just created in Exercise 13.7 still loaded in Layout, add a null object from the Items tab. Name this LeftHand_Goal.

2. Add another null and name it LeftFoot_Goal.

3. Add two null objects and name one RightHand_Goal and the other RightFoot_Goal.

4. Select the MotorCrossDude:LeftHand object layer, and press the m key to open the Motion Options panel. Move it aside to see your object. Select the LeftHand_Goal as the goal object. Click Full Time IK, and also select Keep Goal Within Reach. You'll see a blue line connect the hand to the null object, as shown in Figure 13.38.

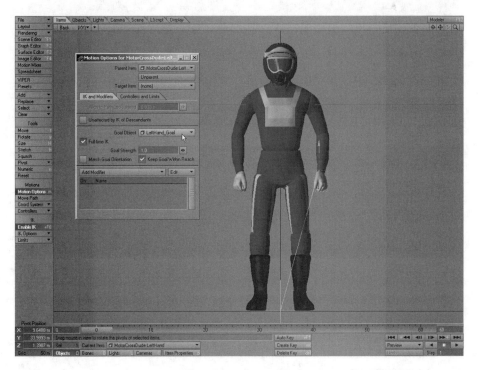

Figure 13.38   The null object added in step 1 is used as the goal object for the left hand. This will be the control for the left arm of the motorcross dude.

5. Leave the Motion Options panel open, but in Layout, select the MotorCrossDude: RightHand object layer. Set its goal to RightHand_Goal, and also turn on Full-time IK and Keep Goal Within Reach. Figure 13.39 shows the panel.

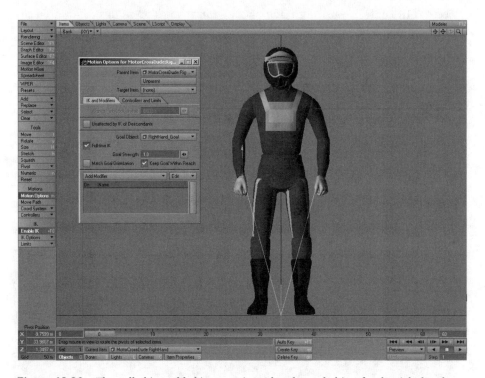

Figure 13.39 The null object added in step 3 is used as the goal object for the right hand. This will be the control for the right arm of the motorcross dude.

6. Now attach the two foot goals to the legs accordingly, as you just did for the left and right hands in steps 4 and 5. These goals should be attached to the boots of the character.

7. After you've set up the two leg goals, open the Spreadsheet (top-left side of Layout). You'll see all of the MotorcrossDude object layers listed. From the top left of the Spreadsheet view, click the first drop-down list, and select Hierarchy instead of All Items. This will display the parenting structure setup for your objects.

8. Two drop-down lists to the right, click and select Motion Options:IK. This will show the objects in the hierarchy and the goals attached to them. Figure 13.40 shows the panel.

Figure 13.40   The Spreadsheet Scene Manager comes in handy while setting up IK rigs. You can use it to see which objects are attached to goals, what the goal strength is, whether Full-time IK is enabled, and more. Here, the four goals' setups are selected.

Configuring the IK Chains

After you've created and placed the goal objects, you need to set up the IK chains. The motorcross racer makes full use of LightWave's hybrid IK engine, and because of this you can pose the legs with both IK and FK. Even with this basic IK setup in the legs, you are given much control over the character.

The process of configuring a character for IK is made easier by leaving the Motion Options Panel and Spreadsheet open. By keeping either of them open, you can work with various parts of the character, and set up the IK accordingly without constantly opening and closing the Motion Options panel. Seeing which objects and/or bones you're working with while assigning IK and seeing the IK effect while you work is essential to your productivity.

Exercise 13.9   Controlling the Legs and Arms

You can control the legs and arms of the character by using the same methods described earlier using bones. In this exercise, you'll tell LightWave which objects' channel positions should be controlled by IK.

1. Select the MotorCrossDude:RightUpperLeg and press m to open the Motion Options panel. Click the Controllers and Limits tab and set Pitch Controller to Inverse Kinematics, as shown in Figure 13.41.

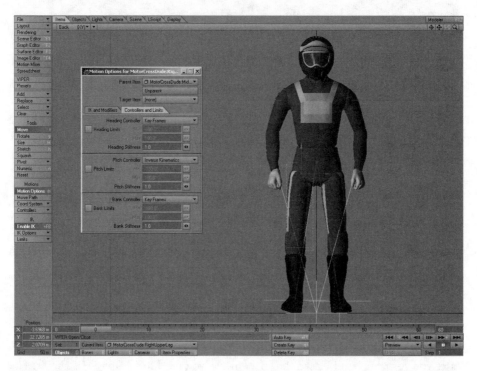

Figure 13.41   In the Motion Options panel, you tell LightWave to apply IK to the Pitch of the right upper leg.

2. Select the MotorCrossDude:RightLowerLeg and set its Pitch Controller to Inverse Kinematics as well. Do the same for the MotorCrossDude:RightBoot.

3. Back in Layout, grab the RightFoot_Goal, press t to Move, and then move the goal to move the leg. The whole leg moves, but rotates sort of strangely—it flips back and forth. You need to set up some rotational limits.

4. In the Motion Options panel for the MotorCrossDude:RightUpperLeg, click Pitch Limits under the Controllers and Limits tab. Set the Min value to 0 and the Max value to 95. This will ensure that the upper leg bends only from straight up and down (0) to about waist height (95).

5. Set a Pitch Limit for the MotorCrossDude:RightLowerLeg to Min –110, and Max –15.

6. Back in Layout, drag the RightFoot_Goal again, and the leg's odd flipping rotations are gone.

    From this point, you can turn on Inverse Kinematics for the other objects in the model that are part of the IK chain. This would be the LeftUpperLeg, LeftLowerLeg, RightHand, RightForeArm, RightUpperArm, LeftHand, LeftForeArm, and LeftUpperArm. The arms also will need the Heading Controller set to Inverse Kinematics so that they can move left and right, and you'll need to set any rotational limits so that the arms don't bend into the body. Rotational limits help with control, but are not necessary for IK to work.

    You can do this quickly by leaving the Motion Options panel open, and using the up arrow on your keyboard to select the different object layers of the model. Click the Motion Options panel, set the control, press the up arrow, and repeat.

7. Lastly, select the Chest, and turn on Inverse Kinematics for the Pitch and Heading Controllers. Watch what happens—the motorcross dude takes a major bow! That's because the goal objects on the chain are at the bottom of the character and the chest moved to meet them. If you pick up a goal object for either arm, you'll see the chest follow.

8. For this setup, the chest doesn't need to follow the chain, but does need to be attached to it for proper control. So, with the chest object selected, in the IK and Modifiers tab of the Motion Options panel, click Unaffected by IK of Descendants. The chest will jump back to its original position.

    What you just did was tell the IK chain, in this case the arms, not to affect the chest. But, because the chain of objects up the arm is parented to the chest, moving the chest moves the arms slightly. When the character is attached to the motorcycle, you'll see why this is important.

 Note

When you activate the Heading Controller for Inverse Kinematics for the arms, you'll see them jump out of position like the chest did. Don't worry—they're just moving because of the position of the goal object. Simply select the appropriate goal object and move it up and over to meet the base of the arm.

Adding the Motorcycle

Here comes the good stuff. The motorcross dude is using a complex IK structure. Although the setup is considered complex, it is still extremely easy to set up in LightWave.

The actual body was designed to be a rigid IK structure so that it would rotate in segments, much like that of a real person. Unfortunately, a simple rigid IK system wouldn't affect an additional object at all, and everyone knows that the body would move a little to compensate for the motion of the motorcycle it's sitting on. The solution to this is to actually connect the motorcycle into the skeletal structure of the motorcross dude's body. After it is configured, you can use the single goal objects to manipulate the arms and legs while still being able to move the motorcycle accordingly.

In addition, the motorcycle will have its own simple hierarchy for the wheels. These two separate object layers need to rotate but remain parented to the motorcycle.

Exercise 13.10   Configuring the Motorcycle with IK

1. With your rig still loaded in Layout, load the Motorcycle object from the book's CD.

   You'll see the motorcycle load into position below the motorcross dude.

2. Select the MotorCrossDude:Chest, and parent it to the motorcycle object. It was originally parented to the Root null. Now parent the motorcycle to the Root.

3. While the motorcross dude was standing, the figure's upper body could be moved or rotated separately from the lower body. That was good for standing or walking. But now that the character needs to sit on the motorcycle, it should move as one. Given that, parent the MotorCrossDude:MidSection to the chest.

4. Now select each goal object, and parent them to the motorcycle. You can do this in one shot using the Scene Editor. Pressing and holding the Ctrl key, select the LeftHand_Goal, RightHand_Goal, LeftFoot_Goal, and RightFoot_Goal, and then drag the objects up and under the motorcycle listing, as shown in Figure 13.42. Remember that when you drag your selection to parent, the yellow line should become indented, signifying the parent/child relationship, before you let go of the mouse.

5. Be sure to save your scene at this point! Now, select the LeftHand_Goal and in Right (or Left) view using a wireframe visibility, move the goal (which moves the arm) up to the handlebars. You'll need to switch between Front, Right, or Perspective views to make sure you get proper positioning. Create a keyframe at 0 to lock the position in place. Figure 13.43 shows the goal in position.

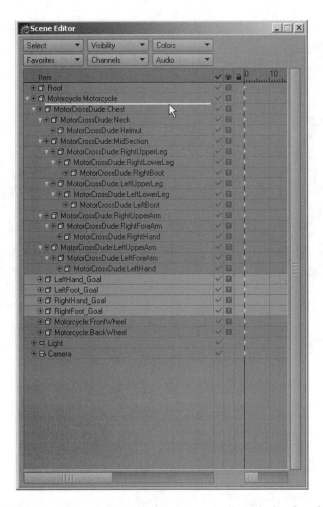

Figure 13.42   Parenting the goal objects to the motorcycle allows the hands and feet to "stick" to the bike.

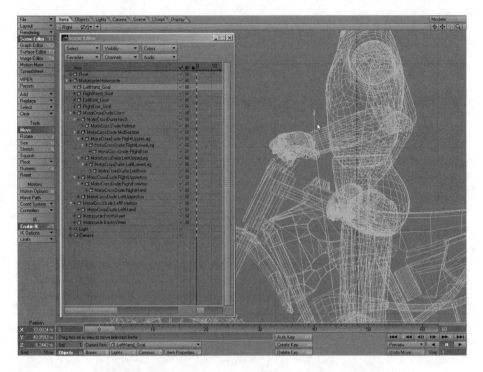

Figure 13.43 Moving the LeftHand_Goal into position on the handlebar of the motorcycle attaches the arm to the bike.

   6. Move the RightHand_Goal up to the handlebars as well. Create a keyframe at 0 to lock the position in place.

   7. You're going to need to do the same thing for the legs, but first, select the chest and move it up and back in Right view. Watch what happens—the hands stay positioned on the handlebars as though the rider is holding on (see Figure 13.44).

   Move the chest up and back so that the rider is sitting, and then adjust the positioning of the hands and feet for precise placement. A combination of all these movements helps you set everything in place.

There are a few more things you can do to make the animation of this motorcross dude easier. You can add additional goals to the knees and elbows. This would allow even more control over the character's motion while riding the motorcycle.

Additionally, you can add more precise control by putting a null object at the front of the boots and then attaching another "toe" goal. This will allow you to rotate the foot, while the existing goal is used to move the entire leg. You also might want to experiment with constraints as described in the next section.

Load the motorcross scene from the book's CD to see the final setup, and view the bike in motion.

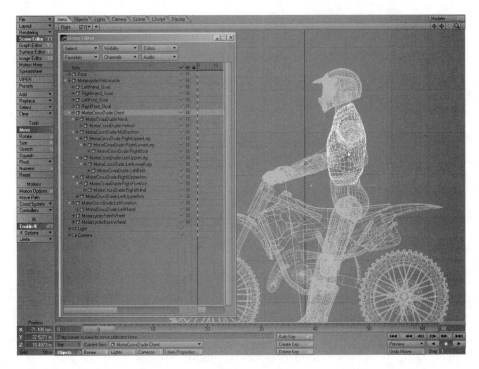

Figure 13.44   Now the beauty of this entire process can be seen. By moving the chest of the motorcross dude, his IK-enabled arms and legs—which are parented to the motorcycle—stay in place.

Constraints

A complex character such as the motorcross dude can be confusing to work with after it has been set up. So many individual parts can be selected and manipulated easily, which could cause disastrous results to your scene. To prevent this from happening, you can set up local constraints as well as lock items in the Scene Editor.

Local constraints are the little buttons in the lower left corner of Layout next to the numeric input fields (see Figure 13.45). They are indicated by an X, Y, or Z or by an H, P, or B, depending upon which tool you have activated (move, rotate, scale, and so on). These constraints can function in two modes. The first is *activated*, which enables the item to be manipulated for that channel. The second mode is *deactivated*, which locks the item from being manipulated on that channel.

If an object's local constraint is on for the X channel and off for all the other channels, your ability to manipulate that object is constrained to the X channel.

It is recommended that you save the scene before manipulating anything. With the scene saved in this current state, you easily can bring the motorcross dude into any other scene using the Load Items From Scene command. For example, you set up the rider in this chapter. Chapter 8, "Architectural Environments," shows you how to build a realistic skyscraper. Perhaps you'd like to set up a race of riders on the street in front of the building. Just use Load Items From Scene to import an existing scene into your current scene.

You still can do a few other things to the scene to make a more user-friendly animation environment. Using the Scene Editor, you can lock items so that they can't be selected. This will make it easier to select the goal objects without inadvertently selecting something else. You also can color-coordinate all the items in your scene. Setting up the display colors in the Scene Editor will make it easier to understand the scene. You also can set up angle limit constraints to the segments on the motorcycle to prevent it from going through the ground plane. If you're feeling really lucky and have a good understanding of the expressions engine in LightWave, you can rig some expressions into the character to automate some of the animation tasks.

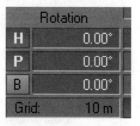

Figure 13.45
Motion channels can be activated or deactivated with these buttons.

The Next Step

LightWave gives you flexibility for experimenting and trying new techniques. Use this flexibility to your advantage. The information covered in this chapter is not the only way to complete a kinematics setup. Take this basic information and build on it. Mix techniques together or create your own. LightWave gives you the freedom to create. The information in this chapter can be used for a countless number of projects, from animated ropes to slithering snakes, crazy aliens, or even animals. IK is useful for robotic movements, characters, and even everyday occurrences such as blowing curtains. You can use IK with bones to animate things such as water surfaces or with image-mapped tubes to simulate a twisting tornado. The ideas are endless, but with the right information, you can create anything!

Summary

IK often seems overwhelming. But after reading through this chapter, you can see that in a matter of steps, you've broken through the barrier and set up simple objects such as a robotic arm, as well as the complex setup of a human riding a motorcycle. Bones and objects both can be set up to work with IK, and it's now up to you to go to the next level and set up IK on one of your own creations. The following chapters help you use expressions and compositing for your characters, so read on!

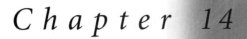

Chapter 14

Expression
Applications

Expressions are a high-school math teacher's

ultimate vindication: proof that you *will*

use math outside of the classroom. But

beyond being an incentive to pay attention

in geometry and trigonometry classes, expressions are tools that will allow you to do things with animation that you've never done before.

The truth, as you might have guessed by now, is that expressions are about math. Math, and a little bit of programming. But before you let your eyes glaze over and roll back, be assured that this is *fun* math and *fun* programming. It's probably the only time you'll ever enjoy math, so take advantage!

An Introduction to Expressions

Expressions are the essential component of a special kind of animation known as *procedural animation.* (You'll see this same sentiment expressed again in Chapter 15, "Animation with Expressions;" as they say, repetition is the key to comprehension.) As the name suggests, this method of animation uses mathematical procedures to produce the motion, rotation, and all other applicable parameters of modification to your objects.

At first glance, expressions can seem quite daunting. Because they give you the freedom to do almost anything, there are usually several ways to accomplish any one goal. Consequently, learning to use expressions can get a little overwhelming. What you will find with experience, though, is that certain patterns often recur in your use of expressions that will help you to break them down into more manageable chunks.

This chapter introduces you to the basic functions and uses of expressions in LightWave. You'll also be shown some of the "building blocks" of expressions, which you can then incorporate into your own work.

In this chapter, you learn about the following:

- Basic expression syntax
- Using channels, operators, and functions
- Centering and following with expressions
- Subexpressions
- Dynamic parenting with expressions

A Word about Channels

All the position, rotation, scale, and many, many other parameters in your LightWave scene are accomplished by changing values over time. Your object, for instance, might travel from X = 1m at frame 1 to X = 30m at frame 15. LightWave takes the information that tells where the object will be in the x-axis at each keyframe, stores it, and interpolates the values between frames. This makes up a channel: the collection of values of a parameter over time.

The combination of three parameters—X position, Y position, and Z position—gives your object its overall position. LightWave knows the value of each parameter at each frame, and by looking at the changing values over a series of frames, an illusion of motion is produced. This is the essence of animation.

Beyond just the three position parameters, each object also has three rotation parameters—heading, pitch, and bank—as well as three scale values—X, Y, and Z. The combination of these nine values tells LightWave, at each frame, where the object is, which direction it is facing, and how big it is. These are channels that every LightWave object has, no matter what. But other channels can be added to further describe the situation of the object at each frame. These channels are called *envelopes*, and they are added as needed in areas where they are available. It is important, though, to realize that an envelope is just another channel of data...just a collection of values changing over time.

Dissolve, for instance, describes how opaque or transparent your object will appear when rendered. It can have a static value, such as 50 percent, or if you click the E button beside the value, it can be controlled by an envelope. This envelope channel simply tells LightWave what dissolve value to use at each frame. At frame 50, then, LightWave will take a look at the Dissolve channel and see what value is stored there. If a keyframe exists there, then the value is the keyframed value. If not, LightWave calculates the value according to the curve type, be it a TCB (Tension, Continuity, Bias), Hermite, or Bezier curve.

In addition to the keyframed or curve-calculated value, LightWave also gives you the option of adding modifiers. A modifier is a plug-in that reads in the channel's value at each frame, modifies it, and then returns the value back to LightWave. Once you've added a modifier to a channel, the raw channel data is no longer being used—the data is processed through the modifier, and that result is what LightWave uses in the scene. For instance, if you used the Noisy Channel modifier, then a semi-random value would be added to or subtracted from the normal keyframed value and reported back to LightWave.

Expressions are another type of modifier. The value of a channel—or several channels—is run through a mathematical operation and the result is returned to LightWave. In this way, a channel's value can be modified or even completely replaced.

> **Note**
>
> LightWave actually comes with three different ways to apply expressions: the item modifier, channel modifier, and built-in expressions. In this chapter, you will use LightWave's built-in expressions.

Expression Syntax

To use expressions, you must use their "language." The language is made up of channel references, mathematical operators, and built-in functions.

Channels

Channels are the different parameters mentioned before, such as position, rotation, scale, as well as envelopes such as dissolve. In an expression, channels are usually referenced using this notation:

[Object.Channel]

For example, the dissolve value of an object would be referenced as

[Object.Dissolve]

In the cases of channels such as position, rotation, and scale, and certain other channels, there are actually three parts to the notation:

[Object.Channel.Axis]

For example, an object's Z position would be referenced as

[Object.Position.Z]

For a channel, such as the luminosity of an object's surface, the notation would be

[Surfaces.Object.SurfaceName.Luminosity]

When these references are placed in an expression, they report the value of their channel at the current time and current frame. These are the variables in the equation. There are also three other special variables that are always available to you: Value, Time, and Frame. Value will return the keyframed value of whatever channel it is applied to at the current time. Time will return the time, in seconds. And Frame will return the current frame number. These are things you might need to access for certain calculations, or you might need to access the value of a channel at a frame other than the current frame. If you need to do that, you can add that into your channel reference. For example:

[Object.Position.X, Frame + 5]

would return the X position of the object 5 frames ahead of the current frame.

[Object.Position.X, 5]

would return the X position of the object at frame 5.

[Object.Position.X, Time + 1]

would return the X position of the object 1 second into the future. It's easier to show than
to tell, so here's a hands-on exercise to explain better.

Exercise 14.1   Channels in Expressions

Your work with expressions will take place in the Graph Editor. Here, expressions are
created, modified, deleted, and saved. This exercise takes you through the steps of creating a few simple expressions.

1. Load the objects Needle1.lwo and Needle2.lwo from the accompanying CD-ROM.
   These objects are speedometer-type "needles" that will be used to show the
   results of your expressions.

2. Select the object Needle1.

3. Go to frame 60.

4. Rotate the object to –180 degrees on its bank, and create a keyframe. This will
   rotate the needle from left to right over 60 frames (see Figure 14.1).

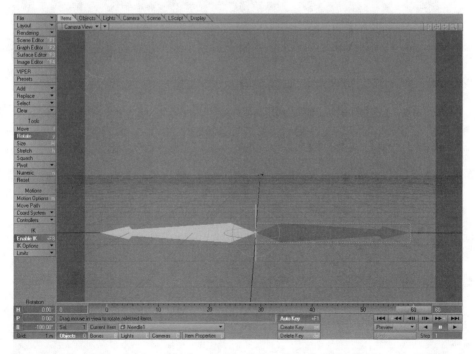

Figure 14.1   The Layout interface showing Needle1 and Needle2. Needle1 is on the right,
rotated to –180 degrees.

5. Select the Needle2 object.

6. Open the Graph Editor.

7. Click the Expressions tab.

8. Also click the Expressions tab in the Scene Display window. This will show the Expression Tree, which at the moment will be empty (see Figure 14.2).

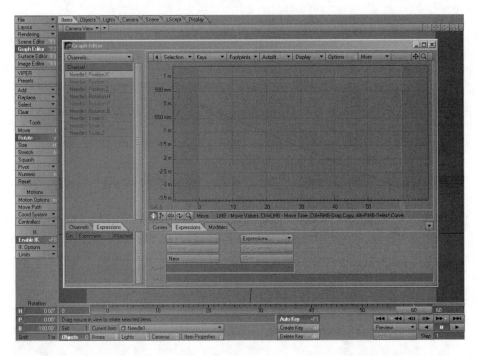

Figure 14.2   Here is the Graph Editor, showing the Expressions tab and the Expressions Tree (lower left corner).

9. In the Expressions window, click New to create a new expression.

10. In the Name field, rename the expression Matcher.

In the Value field, you can see that Value is already entered. This variable stands for the pre-expression value of the channel. Using this variable, you can incorporate the original keyframed value into your expression.

11. In this case, because we're not going to use the keyframed value at all, delete Value from the field.

12. In the Value field, type [Needle1.Rotation.B].

13. In the Curve Bin, click Needle2.Rotation.B.

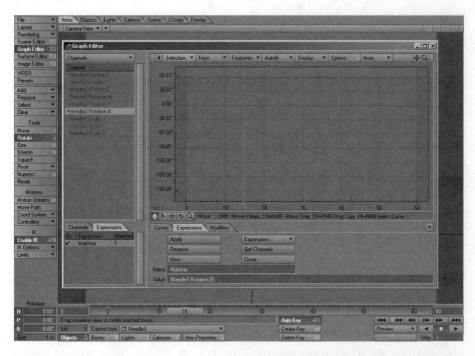

Figure 14.3   In the Expression Tree, all the available expressions are shown, along with how many channels to which they're currently being applied. The check mark shows whether they are on or not. The Matcher expression here is applied to one channel.

14. Under the Expressions tab, click Apply.

Clicking Apply applies the selected expression to any channels you have selected in the Curve Bin. LightWave then places a small dot beside the channel, to alert you that there is a modifier on that channel. The same dot would appear if you used a modifier plug-in (see Figure 14.3).

15. Minimize the Graph Editor and scrub through the animation.

Now Needle2 rotates exactly like Needle1. The expression simply reads Needle1's bank value at each frame, and makes Needle2's bank the same value. What would happen if the expression were to read Needle1's bank value at a different time?

16. Re-open the Graph Editor.

17. Change the Value field to [Needle1.Rotation.B, Frame + 5].

18. Minimize the Graph Editor and scrub through the animation.

Now Needle2 rotates before Needle1. This is because the expression actually is reading Needle1's position 5 frames from the current frame, giving it a 5-frame headstart on Needle1. You also could use Time as an offset, rather than Frame.

19. Re-open the Graph Editor.

20. Change the Value field to [Needle1.Rotation.B, Time + 1].

21. Minimize the Graph Editor and scrub through the animation.

Now Needle2 rotates a full second ahead of Needle1. The flexibility to use either Frame or Time units allows you to work in whatever units are most appropriate for your scene. Incidentally, this technique creates the same effect as LightWave's Follower and Channel Follower plug-ins—but without a plug-in!

> **Note**
>
> LightWave internally uses time as the basis for its calculations. Frame references are determined by multiplying the time (in seconds) by the Frames Per Second value (in the Options panel). For the most part, you won't have to concern yourself with this because expressions allow you to work with either Time or Frame interchangeably, but it's something to be aware of.

The next degree of complexity in expressions begins when you start using operators in your expressions.

Operators

Operators are the standard mathematical functions that you've been used to hearing about since grade school. Addition, subtraction, multiplication, and division are the stars here, along with the special guest, parentheses. And, just like eighth grade algebra, expression language follows the standard order of operations: parentheses are executed first, followed by exponents (which are a function and will be covered later), multiply, divide, add, and subtract. Often, a mnemonic is used to help you remember the order. This book suggests the use of this mnemonic: Perfect Expressions Make Dan Ablan Smile.

You've already seen how the addition operator works (as you added 5 frames and 1 second to the previous expression). To further demonstrate, we'll start by building some simple expressions, and move to ones of higher complexity.

Exercise 14.2   Using Operators in Expressions

1. Re-open the Graph Editor.

2. Make sure that the Needle2.Rotation.B channel is selected in the Curve Bin and that the Matcher expression is showing under the Expressions tab.

3. Click the Remove button. This will remove the expression from the Channel. It does not, however, delete the expression. If you wanted to apply this expression to another channel, you still could. The expression will be stored with the scene, even if it's not applied to anything (see Figure 14.4).

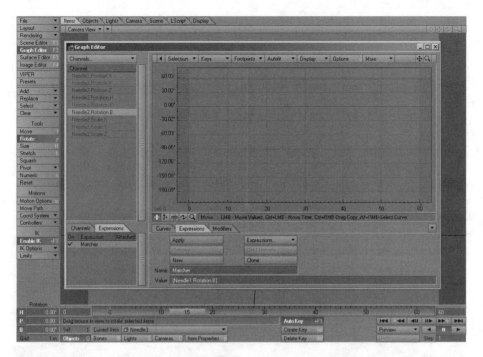

Figure 14.4   Now that Matcher has been removed from the channel, the Expression Tree reflects that fact.

4. Click New to create a new expression. Name it Multiplier.

5. In the Value field, enter [Needle1.Rotation.B] * 2.

6. Click Apply to apply the expression to the channel.

7. Minimize the Graph Editor and scrub through your animation to see the results.

   Needle2 should rotate a full revolution, ending up where it started, while Needle1 rotates only half a revolution. Because the expression multiplies Needle1's bank by 2, Needle2 rotates 2 degrees for every 1 of Needle1.

   But you can do more than simply apply operations to numbers. You can also operate channels by other channels.

8. Re-open the Graph Editor, and remove the Multiplier expression from Needle2.

9. Load the object Needle3.lwo from the CD.

10. Create a new expression, and name it Center.

11. Change the Value field to ([Needle1.Rotation.B] + [Needle3.Rotation.B]) / 2.

12. Apply this expression to Needle2.Rotation.B.

13. Minimize the Graph Editor window and scrub through your animation to see the results (see Figure 14.5).

14. Save your scene.

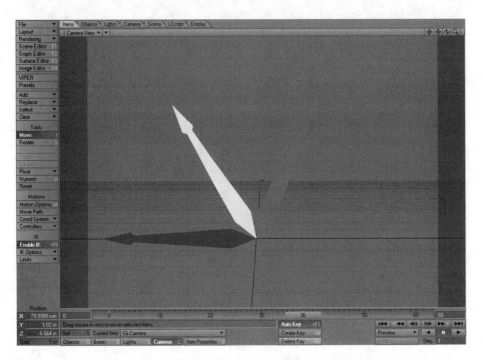

Figure 14.5   With the averaging expression applied, Needle2 will always stay centered between Needle1 and Needle3.

Now you can see that Needle1 rotates as usual, Needle3 remains still, and Needle2 stays directly in the middle of them. This is because your expression is an average of the two rotations. By adding the rotation values together and dividing by two, you are able to find the exact middle of the two objects and place Needle2 there. This is the basis for a centering expression, and it can be quite useful. Let's take a look at a more fun and practical example.

Exercise 14.3   Centering a Character's Hips

1. Load the scene Robot.lws from the book's CD.

2. Once loaded, play the animation. You'll see the hips and legs of a little robot, already set up with Inverse Kinematic's (IK), and trying to walk. Problem is, the hips aren't moving! You will use expressions to put the hips in the proper position (see Figure 14.6).

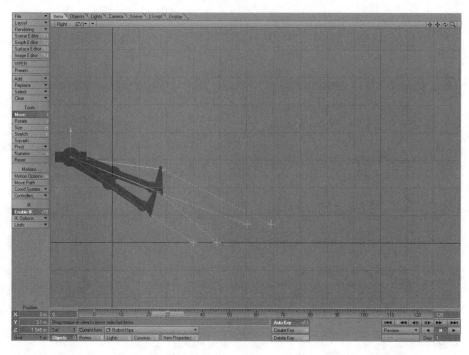

Figure 14.6   Try as they might, the feet just can't reach their IK goals…but it's not their fault. The hips aren't doing their job, so you'll have to do it for them!

3. Select the object Robot:Hips and open the Graph Editor.

4. Under the Expressions tab, click New to create a new expression. Name it ZCenter.

5. Under the Value field, enter the following:
([Left_Heel_Goal.Position.Z] + [Right_Heel_Goal.Position.Z])/2

   This expression does basically the same thing as the averaging expression you made for the needles earlier. It adds the Z position of the left and right heels, and then divides that value by two. The result is the exact middle of the two objects.

6. Select the Robot:Hips.Position.Z channel from the Curve Bin and click Apply.

7. Minimize the Graph Editor and play through the animation.

   Now you'll see that as the robot's feet walk along, the hips always stay centered between them! Automatically—no keyframing! (See Figure 14.7.)

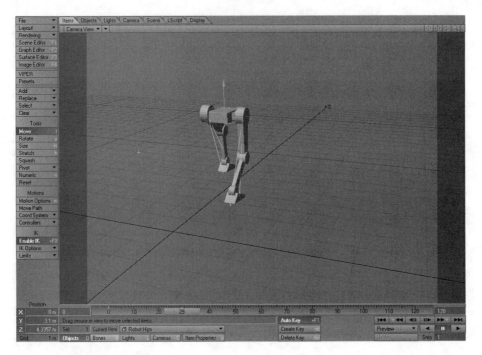

Figure 14.7   That's more like it. The expression keeps the hips centered between the feet, ensuring that the robot keeps its feet on the ground.

Unfortunately, the walk looks a little, well, robotic. The hips don't bounce up and down, as they would if a real person were walking. Would you believe that an expression could help here?

8. Save your scene before continuing.

9. Re-open the Graph Editor.

10. Click New to create a new expression. Call this one YCenter.

11. In the Value field, enter the following:

    Value + ([Left_Heel_Goal.Position.Y] + [Right_Heel_Goal.Position.Y]) / 2

12. Select the Robot:Hips.Position.Y channel from the Curve Bin and click Apply.

13. Minimize the Graph Editor and play through the animation.

Let's break this expression down. You'll recognize the averaging expression here—the two heel positions added together and divided by two—but now Value has been added. What this does is take the middle of the feet—this time on the y-axis—and add that to the keyframed value of the hips. This ensures that the hips are always a certain height above the ground. The addition of the Y center position just gives the hips that little bounce that makes the walk look more natural.

One of the biggest virtues of expressions is that, if they are set up correctly, they can be incredibly flexible. Take the centering expressions you just made, for example. They seem really simple—and they are! But they also are very versatile. Because of the way they were set up, they can react to almost any change in the animation you may want to make. To demonstrate, you'll now change the robot's walking from walking on flat ground to climbing stairs—and see the expressions go right along with you.

14. Select the Robot:Hips object.

15. At frame 0, set the height to 2 meters and set a keyframe.

16. Select the Left_Heel_Goal object.

17. Go to frame 23, and move the object to 3 meters in the y-axis.

18. Go to frame 30, and move the object to 2 meters in the y-axis.

19. Select Right_Heel_Goal.

20. Go to frame 0, and move the object to –1 meter on the y-axis.

21. Go to frame 8, and move the object to 2 meters on the y-axis.

22. Go to frame 15, and move the object to 1 meter on the y-axis.

23. Play the animation.

24. When you're finished looking, save your scene.

Now as the robot walks forward, it also walks upward—and the hips automatically adjust! (See Figure 14.8.) Because the keyframed value of the hips is always added to the center of the feet, whenever they go up, the hips go up to adjust. Try moving around in the Perspective view as your robot walks!

Of course this example is the simplest scenario—a single character walking in a single direction, and with a fairly mechanical walking motion. However, expressions could be made to react to other circumstances, such as sidestepping, turning around, walking in circles, and so forth. You might also modify the expression to give a little more spring to the robot's step (hint: use a time offset).

You've seen now how channels and operators work and how they work together. For a majority of the things you'll commonly want to do with expressions, using only math operators with channels will get you there. But for higher math operations and more advanced programmatic procedures, you'll need to make use of LightWave's built-in functions.

Functions

A *function* is an operation, or set of operations, that performs a calculation or manipulates data in some way other than basic math operators. A function takes in an input value, does its processing, and returns the new value.

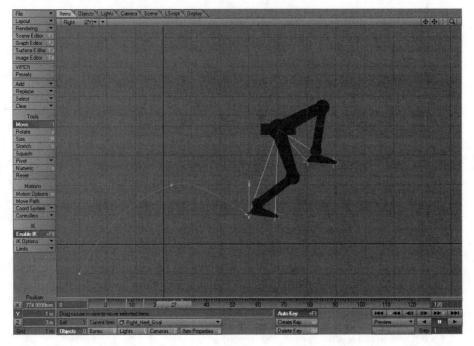

Figure 14.8   By adjusting a few keyframes, you can make the feet seem to walk up stairs, but the real magic is that no change is required to the hip expressions. They'll simply keep on working, no matter where the feet go.

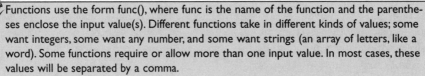

Note

Functions use the form func(), where func is the name of the function and the parentheses enclose the input value(s). Different functions take in different kinds of values; some want integers, some want any number, and some want strings (an array of letters, like a word). Some functions require or allow more than one input value. In most cases, these values will be separated by a comma.

Some functions that are available are square root, log, and factorial, as well as the entire range of circular trigonometric functions (sine, cosine, tangent, secant, cosecant, cotangent, and so forth). Pretty much any trigonometric or geometric function you might need is available. Other functions allow you to calculate the absolute value of a number, convert from degrees to radians and back, and get random values. There are even functions that will allow your expressions to make simple decisions. Functions round out the capabilities of expressions, making possible almost anything you can think to do.

> **Note**
>
> Two notes about the math functions available in LightWave:
>
> - LightWave's trigonometric functions work in radians, not degrees. One radian is equal to 57.3 degrees. The rad() function will convert from degrees to radians for you. The deg() function will convert back from radians to degrees.
>
> - By their very nature, some trigonometric functions have limitations on the input they can receive without returning a nonsensical result. Make sure that whatever value you "feed" the expression will return a useful value.

You can use expressions not only to modify existing animation, but also to create the entire animation—no keyframes necessary. An example is warranted.

To begin, you'll start by building a simple trigonometric expression and flesh it out to examine some of the more advanced functions LightWave offers.

Exercise 14.4   Bouncing a Ball

1. Clear the scene.
2. Load the object Ball.lwo from the accompanying CD.
3. Open the Graph Editor.
4. Under the Expressions tab, create a new expression and call it Bouncer.
5. In the Value field, enter sin(Time * 5).

   This will move the ball up and down in a sinusoidal pattern, using Time as the input value.

> **Note**
>
> Time, Frame, and Value—LightWave's three special variables—must always be capitalized.

Now might be a good time to talk about Always Show Modified. LightWave's Graph Editor has the ability to show not just the graph of the keyframed motion you create, but also the graph as modified by any modifier plug-ins or expressions. (Understanding the curves in the Graph Editor is outside the scope of this chapter; it is assumed that you are at least basically familiar with them.) This is a great help in creating and adjusting expressions, as you are able to see quickly the results of the expression without even leaving the Graph Editor.

Normally the Display option is enabled by default, but just in case, check the Display option now by clicking the Options button, and looking under the Display tab (the default hotkey is d). Always Show Modified should be checked on; if it's not, do so now.

6. Select the Ball.Position.Y channel in the Curve Bin, and click Apply.

Instantly, you should see the oscillating sine pattern appear as a dotted line around the flat keyframe graph (see Figure 14.9).

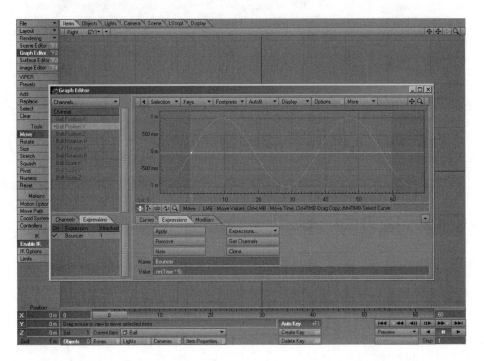

Figure 14.9   Once the Bouncer expression has been applied, you will see the sinusoidal patten appear in the Curve window.

7. Minimize the Graph Editor and play through the animation to see the results.

8. Save your scene.

The value of a sine expression such as this may not be readily apparent, but actually, there are quite a few things in nature that move in patterns such as this. A boat on a wavy lake, for instance, or an antenna waving in a gentle breeze, or even one of those silly drinking bird things.

Or, with a slight modification, it can even make a ball bounce.

9. Re-open the Graph Editor.

10. Change the Value field to abs(sin(Time * 5).

Abs() is the absolute value function. For those who've slept since high school, the absolute value is simply the positive version of any number. You should be able to see in the Graph Editor that the oscillating pattern has changed to a pattern that looks like a ball bouncing. Absolute value has taken any place where the ball's Y value is negative and made it positive (see Figure 14.10).

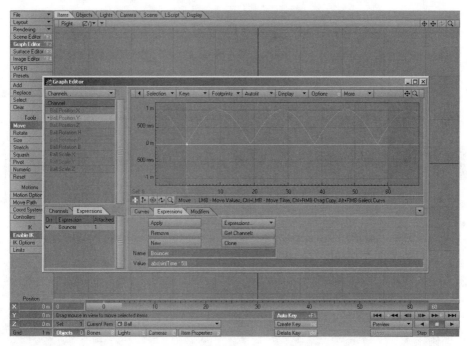

Figure 14.10 With the abs() function applied, the sine pattern can no longer have negative values. Where the values would have gone negative, they are made positive, giving the "bouncing" pattern shown here.

11. Minimize the Graph Editor and play through the animation to see the results.

    Now you have a nice bouncing action for the ball. But really, the ball should stretch and squash when it bounces. And would you believe that an expression can take care of that for you?

12. Save your scene before continuing.

13. Next, the pivot point of the ball needs to be moved to the bottom of the ball so that the ball stretches from the bottom, rather than the center. Change the Pivot Position of the ball to −500mm.

14. Re-open the Graph Editor.

15. Create a new expression and call it Squash.

16. In the Value field, enter [Bouncer].

17. Select the Scale.Y channel from the Curve Bin, and click Apply to apply the expression.

18. Minimize the Graph Editor and play through the animation.

    Notice what you just did—for the value of the expression, you used the name of another expression. In LightWave's expressions, you can use the results of another expression just like you would use a channel reference (including Time and Frame offsets). This is called using a subexpression. In this case, you're using the Bouncer expression as the input for the Squash expression. The Bouncer expression is evaluated, and those results are fed not only to LightWave, but also to Squash.

This creates a chain of dependency that is wonderfully flexible because any change you make to the Bouncer expression is automatically reflected in the Squash expression.

Note

Subexpressions can have only one level of dependency; an expression that uses a subexpression cannot then be used as a subexpression in another expression. If you try it, the value of the subexpression will be reported as 0.

Now, regardless of how cool it is, you're not getting exactly the results you want. The basic motion is right, but ball needs some tweaking.

19. Re-open the Graph Editor.

20. Change the expression to [Bouncer] + .4.

This prevents the ball from ever squashing all the way to 0 and also allows it to stretch higher than its normal height (see Figure 14.11).

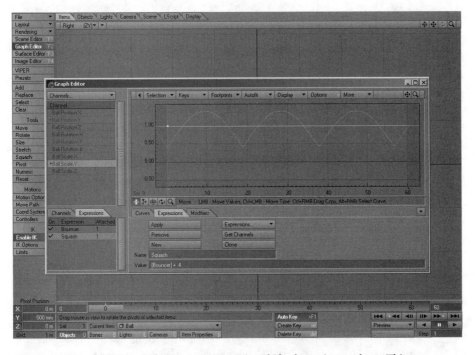

Figure 14.11 Adding .4 to the Bouncer expression shifts the entire graph up. This ensures that the smallest scale possible is .4—thus keeping the ball from squashing down to nothing as it did before.

21. Minimize the Graph Editor and play through the animation to see the motion.

    That's better. Not exactly a perfect bouncing motion, but good enough for government work. (Creating a better bouncing motion would be a great way to expand upon the things you've learned in this chapter.)

    Now, you have a ball that's bouncing up and down, and the motion is entirely generated through expressions. Neat, but it could be more interesting. A simple expression can help us out there.

22. Save your scene before continuing.

23. Re-open the Graph Editor.

24. Make a new expression and call it Xmover.

25. In the Value field, enter Time * 4.

26. Select the Ball.Position.X channel, and click Apply to apply the expression to the channel.

    Now you should see the dotted line angle up to the right toward infinity. The expression simply takes the current time, multiplies it by 4, and uses that as the X position. And because Time will always increase in the scene, so will the X position (see Figure 14.12).

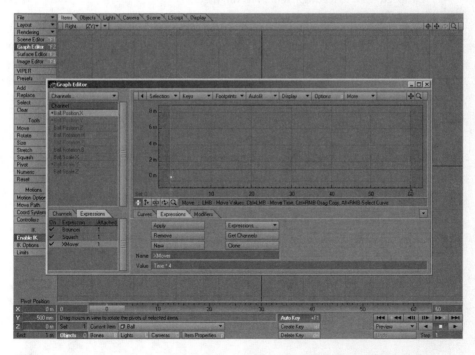

Figure 14.12   Using a constantly increasing variable such as Time gives a linear result, as shown. The ball will always move at a constant speed in the X direction.

27. Minimize the Graph Editor and play through the animation to see the results. Now the ball bounces up and down, and also bounces to the side, adding something a little more interesting.

Now, it was mentioned before that LightWave's expressions are capable of making simple decisions. This is accomplished by the use of the if-then function. An if-then looks at an input value, compares it to another value, and then takes some action according to what it finds. They take this format:

(Value1 {comparator} Value2 ? Result1 : Result2)

As an example, say you had a car that had brakelights, and you wanted the brakelights to switch on every time the car fell below a certain speed. In English, we would write a sentence something like this:

If the speed of the car drops below 50 mph, then the brakelights are on; otherwise, they are off.

In Lightwave's language, it would look like this:

(Speed < 50 ? HeadlightsOn : HeadlightsOff)

A more concrete example would help. What you're going to do is set up an if-then statement that will make the ball flash on and off. You'll do this by applying this statement to the Luminosity channel.

Exercise 14.5   Using If-Then Statements

1. Save your scene before continuing.

2. Open the Surface Editor, and select the Ball surface in the Ball object.

3. Click the E beside Luminosity to add an envelope. This will bring you into the Graph Editor, and the Luminosity channel will be the only channel in the Curve Bin.

4. Create a new expression and call it Switcher.

5. In the Value field, enter ([Ball.Position.Y] > .5 ? 4 : 0).

6. Select the Luminosity channel from the Curve Bin, and click Apply to apply the expression.

What this expression does is say, if the ball is above 500mm, set its Luminosity to 400 percent. If it's not above 500mm, then leave its Luminosity at 0 percent (see Figure 14.13).

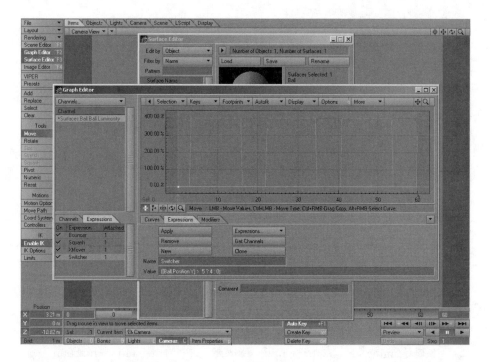

Figure 14.13   The Graph Editor shows the results of the expression: when the ball goes above 500mm, the Luminosity increases to 400 percent. When the ball goes below, it decreases to 0 percent.

Now because this is an either-or thing, there are no in-betweens. The Luminosity does not ramp up; it simply jumps from 0 to 400 and back. You can see this reflected in the dotted line of the graph.

7. Minimize the Graph Editor and play through the animation to see the results.

Now you can see that as the ball bounces along, once it gets halfway up, it brightens up, and dims back down as it falls below the halfway point.

Changing the luminosity of the ball is just one of many possibilities. Any surface parameter that is envelopable—indeed, any channel anywhere that's envelopable—could be affected by this expression.

One of the other functions available to you is random(), which generates random values. You may specify the upper and lower boundaries for these numbers. Random's usage looks like this:

    random (lowvalue, highvalue)

Random's results include the low and high values, so if you specified 6 and 10, you could get back 6, 7, 8, 9, or 10. Also of note, random accepts and returns only integer values—that is, numbers that have no decimals.

The fact that you can specify the upper and lower boundaries of the results make this a good function to use with color, because red, green, and blue values are generally between 0 and 255 (even though LightWave does support values above 255).

Inside an envelope, however, LightWave doesn't use values between 0 and 255. It uses percentages, 0 to 100 percent for each color. Therefore, a little calculation will be necessary.

Exercise 14.6   Using the Random Function to Color the Ball

1. Save your scene before continuing.

2. Open the Surface Editor, and click the E beside Color. This will bring you into the Graph Editor, where you will have three channels in the Curve Bin. These are the R, G, and B values of the color of the ball.

3. Create a new expression, and call it RandColor.

4. In the Value field, enter (random (0, 255)) / 255.

   Let's examine what happens in this expression. First, the random function is called and given the upper and lower boundaries of 0 and 255, respectively. Therefore, it will return a value between 0 and 255. Then, that result is divided by 255. And that's no accident—255 is the maximum value specified for the random function. So, if the function were to return a value of 255, it would be divided by 255 to give a result of 1.0, or 100 percent. Anything lower than 255 would be given a decimal value between 0 and 1, which is the proper range for a color triplet in an envelope.

Note

This kind of adjustment is often called *normalizing*. Normalizing means taking a range of values and fitting it into another range of values (usually 0—1). This is something you could encounter with some regularity, so it's worth taking a moment to examine.

For a variable that has a range of values that you want to normalize between 0 and 1, it's a fairly simple process. You simply add or subtract to make the lowest value 0, and then divide by the highest value plus the number you added or subtracted.

For example, say you had a channel [Null.Position.Y] thats lowest value was –6.934 meters, and whose highest value was 22.689 meters. To normalize this between 0 and one, the expression would be the following:

([Null.Position.Y] + 6.934) / (22.689 + 6.934)

This works for just about any situation. In the case of the color channels, it was very simple, because the lowest value was already 0. All that was necessary was to divide by the highest value, 255.

5. Make sure that all three channels are selected, and then click Apply to apply the expression to them. There's no need to make different expressions for each channel—you want a random value for each, anyway.

Now you should see the curves for each color go completely crazy, and the color bar at the bottom of the curve window should be a complete jumble of every color imaginable (see Figure 14.14).

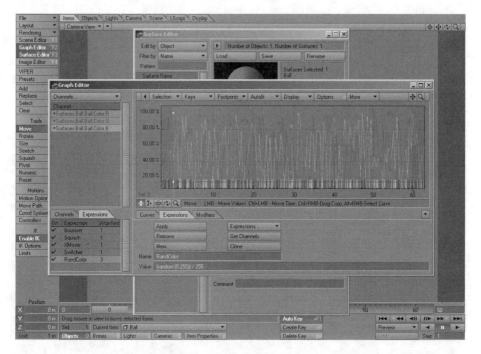

Figure 14.14   With the random() function applied, the R, G, and B values of the ball go all over the place, causing a psychedelic mix of colors.

6. Minimize the Graph Editor and play through the animation to see the results.

7. Save your scene and object.

Now you should see a veritable kaleidoscope of colors washing over your ball as it bounces through your scene. This is a vivid example of the use of the random function.

However, what if you wanted more precise control over the animation of the color?

Exercise 14.7   Using Expressions to Precisely Control the Color

1. Re-open the Graph Editor.

2. First, select the Switcher expression in the Expression Tree.

3. In the Value field, change it from ([Ball.Position.Y] > .5 ? 4 : 0) to ([Ball.Position.Y] > .5 ? 1 : 0). This will keep the Luminosity at a reasonable level, ensuring that it won't go all the way to white.

4. Making sure the R, G, and B channels are all selected, click the Remove button to remove the RandColor expression.

5. Make a new expression and call it RedRamp.

6. In the Value field, enter [Ball.Position.Y].

   It seems overly simple, but because we know the ball never goes over 1m or below 0m, it's in the perfect range for color. At the ball's highest point, the red value will be its highest, and vice versa.

7. Click the Color.R channel, and click Apply to apply the expression to the channel (see Figure 14.15).

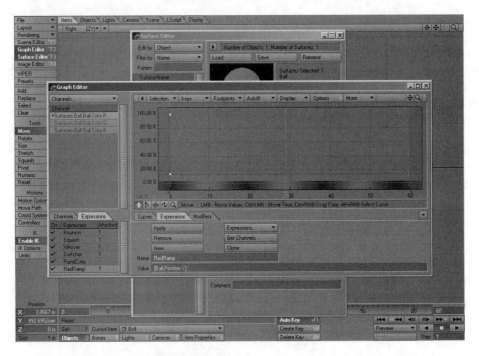

Figure 14.15   With the RedRamp expression applied—and no other color channels affecting it—the color bar at the bottom varies between red and black.

8. Click the Clone button to clone the expression, and rename it BlueRamp.

9. Change the value field to 1 − [Ball.Position.Y]. (Cloning saves you from having to retype the entire expression—all you have to do is add the "1 −". This is especially useful for lengthy expressions.)

10. Click the Color.B channel, and click Apply to apply the expression to the channel.

This will make it so that when the ball is at its lowest point, the Color.B channel will be at its highest (see Figure 14.16).

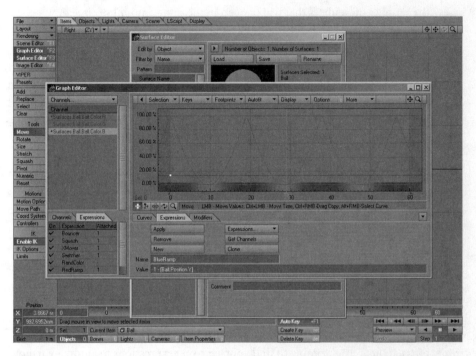

Figure 14.16   Now with the BlueRamp expression also applied, you can see the ball's color vary between blue (when the ball is lowest) and red (when the ball is highest).

11. Minimize the Graph Editor and Surface Editor, and play through the animation to see the results.

Now that's all fine and dandy. Your ball is bouncing around like a Broadway performer, changing colors and flashing like an insane roadsign. But what does it all mean, and more importantly, why was it better to do this animation with expressions instead of keyframes?

To see for yourself, follow the few steps of the next exercise.

Exercise 14.8   Changing It All with One Number

1. Re-open the Graph Editor.

2. Select the Bouncer expression from the Expression Tree. This expression is the core of the animation; everything else depends, in some way, on this expression.

3. Change the Value field from abs(sin(Time * 5)) to abs(sin(Time * 10)).

4. Minimize the Graph Editor and play through the animation to see the results.

5. Save your scene when you are finished.

   By doubling the amount Time was multiplied in the sin() function, you double the number of bounces that will happen in the same amount of time. And because both the Luminosity and the Color of the ball were determined by expressions, they automatically adjust. They react to the position of the ball, regardless of what method of animation put the ball into that position.

So, like the robot legs in the example earlier, you've created an animation with a set of expressions that will automatically react to any changes you might have to the scene further down the road. This is invaluable when you've got that client that just keeps changing everything.

What must be stressed here is that careful planning is key to making good expression-driven animations, or even animations that are only partially driven by expressions. It's important to know not necessarily exactly what all the items in your scene are going to do, but what they might do. In our example, it's mostly coincidence that made all the boundaries line up so nicely, but had they not, the appropriate steps would have been taken. Know your items' boundaries, and plan for them. "Pushing the envelope" is a great marketing phrase, but it makes for lousy results when you're using expressions.

Using expressions to build entire animations, as in the previous example, certainly has its place in the 3D animation world; indeed, some software packages are built around it. More often, though, you're going to find yourself using expressions to automate tedious tasks or to let the computer keep track of things you don't have the ability (or the inclination) to do—or to do things that just aren't possible to do in any other way.

Take dynamic parenting, for example. This much sought-after tool would give animators the ability to have an object switch parents mid-animation. Some plug-ins such as Dynamic Realities' Lock and Key and Steve Worley's Polk Parent have this ability, but it's an on/off switch; the object is parented to either object A or object B—there is no in-between.

But with an expression, dynamic parenting with an in-between is possible. And it turns out that the expression has more uses than just dynamic parenting. It is one of the "building block" techniques mentioned earlier. You will be able to adapt and modify this technique to suit a variety of needs.

To meet the basic functionality of dynamic parenting, the expression must make an item follow another item (using channels as before, to emulate the ChannelFollower plug-in).

Then, under the control of a specified object, the expression must, over time, stop following the first item and start following the second.

Like many things, it's a lot simpler than it sounds.

Exercise 14.9   Using Expressions for Dynamic Parenting

1. Load the scene BowSetup.lws from the accompanying CD.

   BowSetup.lws is a scene made up of three objects: a bow, an arrow, and a target (see Figure 14.17).

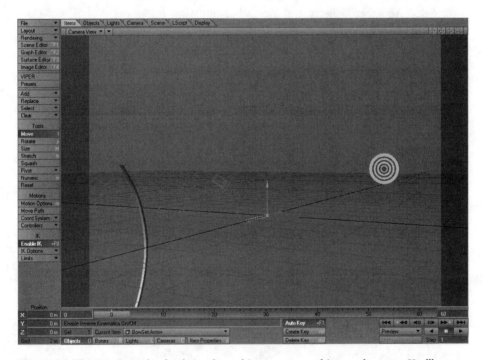

Figure 14.17   BowSetup.lws loads in a bow object, an arrow object, and a target. You'll use dynamic parenting to make the arrow fly unerringly to the target.

2. Select the BowSet:Arrow object and open the Graph Editor.

3. Click the Expressions tab.

4. Click New to make a new expression and call it ZParent.

5. In the Value field, enter [BowSet:Bow.Position.Z].

6. Click the BowSet:Arrow.Position.Z channel, and then click Apply to apply the expression.

7. Minimize the Graph Editor and see the results.

Now the arrow's Z position follows that of the bow object, effectively making it "parented" to that object.

8. Re-open the Graph Editor.

9. Change the Value field to [BowSet:Bow.Position.Z] + [BowSet:Target.Position.Z].

Obviously, simply adding the channels does not give the results you want. What needs to happen is that at some point, the arrow begins to be less and less affected by the bow object, and more and more affected by the target object, until it's completely controlled by the target object.

10. Select Add, then Objects, and then Add Null. Name it Ramper.

This object will be the control object. Ramping it from 0 to 1 in the Y position will change the parent from the bow to the target.

11. Go to frame 10, and set a keyframe.

12. Delete the key at frame 0.

13. Go to frame 40.

14. Move Ramper to 1m in the y-axis, and set a keyframe.

15. Re-open the Graph Editor.

16. Change the Value field to ((1 − [Ramper.Position.Y]) * [BowSet:Bow.Position.Z]).

17. Minimize the Graph Editor and scrub through the animation to see the results.

The basis of our dynamic parenting expression is the fact that anything multiplied by 1 is itself, and anything multiplied by 0 is 0.

What's happening is that the value of (1 − [Ramper.Position.Y]) is going from 1 to 0 as Ramper moves from 0 to 1 on the y-axis. This value is being multiplied by [Bow.Position.Z]. The end result is that when ramper goes all the way to 1 in the y-axis, the bow object no longer has any influence at all, returning the arrow to its default position.

The next step is to make it so that instead of returning to 0, the arrow goes to the target object.

18. Change the Value field to ([Ramper.Position.Y] * [BowSet:Target.Position.Z]).

19. Minimize the Graph Editor and scrub through the animation to see these results.

Now you've made the second half of the animation. The arrow starts in its default position, and as ramper rises in the y-axis, the arrow is more and more influenced by the target object.

With both halves of the expression done, all that remains is to add the two together.

20. Re-open the Graph Editor.

21. Change the Value field to ((1 - [Ramper.Position.Y]) * [BowSet:Bow.Position.Z]) + ([Ramper.Position.Y] * [BowSet:Target.Position.Z]).

22. Minimize the Graph Editor and scrub through the animation to see the results.

    Now the arrow flies unerringly toward the target, striking it—well, there's a problem. It hits well below the bullseye. This happens because so far, we've done dynamic parenting only in the Z channel. That's easy enough to fix.

23. Re-open the Graph Editor.

24. Clone the ZParent expression, and rename the clone to YParent.

25. Change the Value field to ((1 – [Ramper.Position.Y]) * [BowSet:Bow.Position.Y]) + ([Ramper.Position.Y] * [BowSet:Target.Position.Y]).

26. Select the Position.Y channel from the Curve Bin and click Apply to apply the expression.

27. While we're here, we might as well do the same in the X channel. Clone the expression and rename it XParent.

28. Change the value field to ((1 – [Ramper.Position.Y]) * [BowSet:Bow.Position.X]) + ([Ramper.Position.Y] * [BowSet:Target.Position.X]).

29. Select the Position.X channel from the Curve Bin and click Apply to apply the expression.

30. Minimize the Graph Editor and scrub through the animation to see the results.

    Now the arrow really does fly unerringly to the bullseye! (See Figure 14.18.)

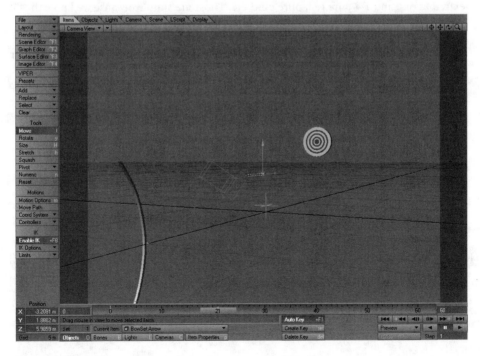

Figure 14.18   The arrow on an intercept course with the bullseye.

This setup seems overly complicated for something as simple as an arrow shot to a target. But what if it were a *moving* target?

31. Go to frame 60.

32. Move the BowSet:Target object to X: –25 m, Y: 11 m, Z: 31 m, and make a keyframe.

33. Play through the animation to see the results.

34. When you're done, save your scene.

Now, even though the target is moving, the arrow moves to follow it. No matter where you might move either the target object or the bow object, the arrow will go from one to the other without error.

The uses for this are endless—one character handing an object to another character, for example: a homing missile tracking its target. Any instance, really, when an object must be attached to one object for a certain amount of time, and then switched to be attached to another object.

But this "switching" technique is useful for more than just dynamic parenting. Any time you might need to switch from one value to another, it can be used.

Take color, for example. So far, when we used expressions with color, it was at the extremes of 0 and 1—pure red, pure blue, etc. Those are simple because we know they'll either start at or end at 1 or 0, which simplifies expressions tremendously.

But suppose that you had a specific color you needed to switch from, and a specific color you needed to switch to? You can use the same techniques you just used for X, Y, and Z to control R, G, and B.

Exercise 14.10   Switching Color Values

1. Open the Surface Editor.

2. Select the Stripes surface from the BowSet object.

3. Change the color of the stripes to R: 213 G: 153 B: 187.

4. As for the color we'll switch to, that will be R: 001 G: 219 B: 173.

Tip

Click with the left mouse button and drag on the R, G, and B numbers to change the values quickly.

5. Click the E beside Color to activate its color envelope. You'll pop into the Graph Editor.

6. Click New to create a new expression, and name it Rswitcher.

7. Change the value field to ((213/255) * (1 – [Ramper.Position.Y])) + ((1/255) * [Ramper.Position.Y]).

   Because color envelopes work in the 0 to 1 range, it's necessary to divide our RGB numbers by 255. You could divide the numbers in a calculator or some other place, but because there's already so much math being done here, why not let the computer do the work for you?

8. Select the Color.R channel from the Curve Bin, and click Apply to apply the expression (see Figure 14.19).

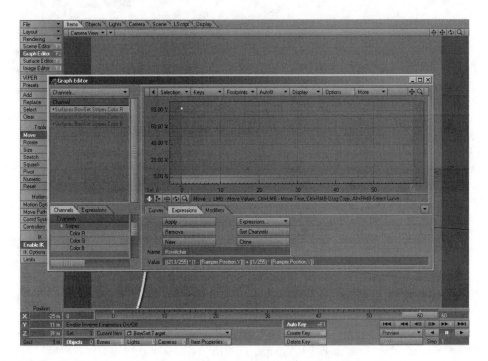

Figure 14.19   Here we have applied the expression to the Red channel.

9. Clone the expression and rename it Gswitcher.

10. Change the value field to ((153/255) * (1 – [Ramper.Position.Y])) + ((219/255) * [Ramper.Position.Y]).

11. Select the Color.G channel from the Curve Bin, and click Apply to apply the expression (see Figure 14.20).

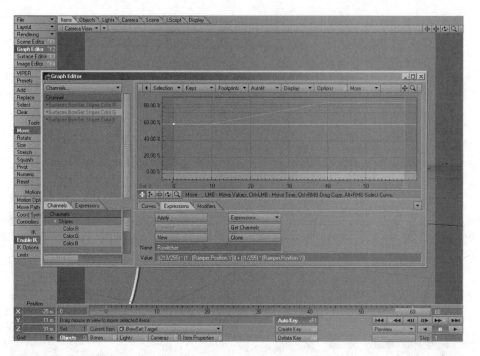

Figure 14.20 Here we have applied the expressions to the Red and Green channels.

12. Clone the expression and rename it Bswitcher.

13. Change the value field to ((173/255) * (1 – [Ramper.Position.Y])) + ((1187/255) * [Ramper.Position.Y]).

14. Select the Color.B channel from the Curve Bin, and click Apply to apply the expression (see Figure 14.21).

15. Minimize the Graph Editor, and play through the animation to see the results.

   Now the stripes of your target change from a lovely mauve, to a delicate sea foam green (never fear, there will *not* be a quiz on those colors).

It's interesting, isn't it, that the same formulas would work to achieve such widely different goals? That's the power of this expression. Over time, you'll learn to recognize where it might be useful, and you'll already know what to do when you see that it's needed.

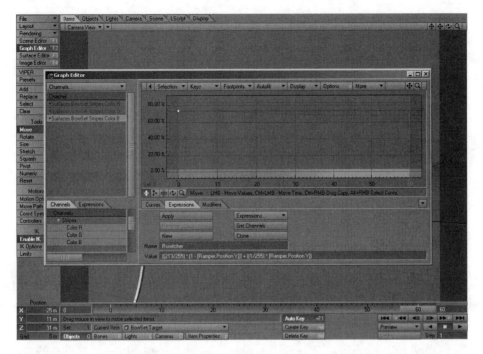

Figure 14.21   Here we have applied the expressions to all three of the color channels. The switch from one color to another is now complete and visible in the color bar at the bottom of the Curve Window.

The Next Step

The projects in this chapter were, for the most part, created specifically to illustrate how to use expressions in your work. They're not scenarios you're likely to run into in the normal course of your work (though the dynamic parenting/color switch expression is the most real-world of all, and probably the technique you will get the most mileage out of when it's all said and done). The intention in this chapter was to plant the seed in your brain, and give it some water and fertilizer. The next step is yours to choose.

Some suggestions to get you on your way:

- Complete the rest of the body of the robot. Make two robots walk past each other, and have one hand an object to the other.

- Add an X component to the robot's hips and animate it walking in different directions.

- Apply the random function to the color of lights for that big city nightclub feel. Maybe even bring your newly completed robot in for a dance or two.

- Use the switching expressions to change one surface to another, say molten rock to smooth black glass. You can apply the expression to every surface parameter.

There are more ways to use expressions than can ever be taught. Ninety-nine percent of the time, they're just thought up on the spot, when an animator realizes that an expression would probably make his or her life easier.

Summary

In this chapter, you learned the basic form of expressions. You learned how to reference channels in an expression, use math operators with them, and use functions on them. You learned how to use Time, Frame, and Value. And you learned some of the building-block expressions, pieces that you will use to build expressions in the future. You learned how to normalize a value that has an arbitrary range and how to use the random function to get a little wacky.

At the end of the day, there's no way to predict what you might need expressions for, because the truth is that they can be used for almost anything. From tank treads to bee wings, from apples falling to zebras running, the possibilities are truly endless, and limited only by your imagination and skills. What's important is that you learn to recognize when and where expressions are appropriate, and the basic forms you can start with to get you going. A huge percentage of research and development time consists of the animator staring blankly at the monitor, thinking "How am I going to do this?" If the knowledge you've gained in this chapter can shave some time off of that think time, then it has done its job.

Expressions might not be the end-all, be-all of animation, but their value is immeasurable. Learn to use them well, and you will be rewarded.

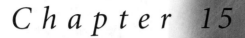

Chapter 15

Animation with Expressions

In this chapter you will learn how to use

expressions to enhance and simplify your

animations. *Expressions* are the individual

pieces that make up a special subset of

animation known as *procedural animation*. In its simplest form, an expression links one item's motion to that of another by using a mathematical formula. At its most complex, an expression could make virtual worlds rise and fall with the touch of a button.

In LightWave 7, there are several ways to harness the power of expressions. A true expression is a mathematical formula that defines the behavior of one item by the behavior of another item. In LightWave 7, working with expressions is available through either LightWave's built-in expressions or the Expression plug-in. In this chapter, you will use LightWave's built-in expressions to accomplish certain tasks for which they are uniquely suited. In fact, everything accomplished in this chapter could be done using this method, but this is not necessarily the fastest or easiest method to accomplish your goals.

A true expression requires you to define behaviors using formulas that could be quite lengthy and complex or involve an amount of programming knowledge. To free you from this burden, LightWave provides plug-ins that automatically handle these situations. Although technically not "true" expressions, these plug-ins are used to carry out the same duties of an expression, but in a simpler manner. Although true expressions are broad enough to deal with almost any situation, these plug-ins are made for specific jobs.

Although this chapter uses these expressive plug-ins, along with true expressions, you should realize that all these plug-ins are a form of expression and should be thought of as such. This chapter will instruct you on the following:

- Using Cycler
- Using ChannelFollower
- Using LightWave's built-in expressions

Using Expressions to Enhance and Simplify Animation

Animating with expressions is one of the truly unique experiences in 3D graphics. It has no parallel in any other form of animation. Being able to take advantage of the power of expressions can take your animation to a new level of realism and usability.

Expressions (like computers) are at their most useful when they are employed to automate repetitive or complex tasks. Animation of mechanical objects such as gears, pulleys, and wheels are often quite simple, yet when combined in large numbers and complex relationships, the task of animating each individual piece becomes tedious and inspiration-sapping. Linking these objects through expressions frees the animator from worrying about each individual piece, allowing the creative flow to continue uninterrupted.

Characters and other organic shapes can benefit from expressions, as well. Imagine being able to automatically keep the hips of a character centered between the feet. Or a character's eyes that automatically turn in the same direction as the head a split-second beforehand. All these things and more are possible through expressions.

LightWave 7 gives you the power of expressions in every channel of data, from position and rotation, to surface and light color, even to morph data. In this chapter, you will animate a fighter jet as it prepares for takeoff and leaps into the sky to perform a few maneuvers. You will use expressions to control or drive the following:

- Complex landing gear retraction
- Engine nozzle rotation
- Engine exhaust size and shape
- Aerodynamic control surface motion

Examining the Model's Parts

First of all, let's take a look at your model. Examine Figures 15.1 and 15.2 to familiarize yourself with the major parts of the model. These are

- Fuselage and wings
- Ailerons
- Elevons (a combination of aileron and elevator)
- Elevator
- Front landing gear and door
- Rear landing gear and doors
- VTOL (vertical takeoff and landing) engine nozzles

Figure 15.1   Here is the fighter at rest, with its landing gear down, engine nozzles vertical, and control surfaces in default positions.

Figure 15.2   Here is the fighter in flight mode. The engine nozzles are horizontal, and the landing gear is up. The control surfaces are moved out of rest position so that they can be seen more clearly.

The landing gear of an aircraft such as this is the perfect case for the use of expressions. Each of the three gear sets is made up of several separate parts, each of which must be animated to extend or retract the gear. This is not something you would want to do repeatedly, so you will use expressions to make the process nice and easy. For the rear gear set, you will use Cycler and ChannelFollower.

Using Cycler and ChannelFollower

Cycler works by using a control object to "cycle" another object through a defined range of keyframes. You define the start and end keys for the object and tell Cycler the low and high values that the control object will go through. As the control object goes from its low value to its high value, the controlled object cycles from its first defined keyframe to its last. For example, you can use Cycler to define the rotation of wheels on a car. With the plug-in set up, you can animate the car so that the wheels turn automatically.

ChannelFollower allows one motion channel of one object "follow" a motion channel of another object. An example application of this would be a character's eyes; one eye would be animated with keyframes, while the other would simply follow the exact rotation of the keyed eye, but from its own location.

In your case, you are going to animate the unfolding sequence for each part of the landing gear, and use Cycler to link their motion to a single control object. You will use ChannelFollower to duplicate the motion of the left side gear on the right side, eliminating the need for keyframes on that side completely. You will drive the animation of the front gear from the same control object using built-in expressions. From then on out, all you need to do to extend or retract the entire gear assembly is move one null.

> **Note**
>
> Procedural animation (that is, using expressions or other math to control object motion) has its own set of terms with which you should be familiar. An item that is procedurally animated could be *dependent* upon another object, which is often called the *control* object. It also could be *linked* to that object, although *link* most often means a very simple, direct relationship, as in one object exactly following another or mirroring its motion. Another way to express a mathematical relationship between two objects is to say that the *dependent* object is driven by the control object. Because this is the way you will encounter these terms in the real world, this chapter will use all of them interchangeably. This will help you begin to get used to using and thinking about them.

Before you start setting up your landing gear with Cycler, you need to bring in the objects and set them up properly. A scene has been included on the CD with the basic setup. However, before loading that file, there are a couple of techniques that are good to know and great to get in the habit of doing.

Exercise 15.1   Preparing Objects for Animation

1. First, add a null to the scene, and name it Fighter_Global.

2. Add another null to the scene. Name this one Fighter_Control. Parent this null to Fighter_Global.

Note

This two-extra-null setup is quite common in production environments. Having a Global null will allow to you move and rotate the entire motion path of the fighter at any time. The need for this might not be readily apparent, but should you ever need it, you will be glad you have it.

Also you will be animating the motion of the ship with the Fighter_Control null instead of the actual fuselage object. Animating in this way gives you more control, allowing you to easily rotate the fighter independently of its motion path. (Yes, this is possible with LightWave's motion channels, which allow independent position, rotation, and scale keyframes. However, it is not always the fastest way of accomplishing the same goal.)

Now, because you already know what items of the ship you will need to control, you can make control nulls for them. They could, of course, be created at any time, but making them now will put them at the top of the object list, making them easier to find and access. You will need to add two nulls, both of them parented to Fighter_Control. They are

- Landing_Gear_Cycle

- Throttle

Now you can bring in and prepare your scene.

3. From the File drop-down menu, first select Load, and then select Load Items From Scene from the ..\..\Scenes\Ch15_Fighter_Setup.lws file (*do* load the lights, when asked).

   When using the Load Items From Scene command, you are telling LightWave that you want to load another scene into the current scene. Say you have an animated bat setup in its own scene. Now you want to load the bat into the scene you're currently creating. Simply loading the object doesn't load all the motions you've applied. Load Items From Scene will.

4. Select the light named Light and delete it. To delete a selected item, simply press the minus (–) key.

5. Parent the Fighter:MainHull object to the Fighter_Control null. You can do this through the Motion Options panel for the object by pressing m. You also can drag and drop to parent in the Scene Editor.

Because the complete hierarchy and all rotations were set up in the scene you loaded, you don't have to do anything more to prepare the objects. Your scene is now ready to begin animation.

Exercise 15.2   Animating the Left Side Landing Gear

The landing gear loads into Layout in the extended position. For the left side gear, you'll need to move each piece in to the retracted position and set keyframes. You'll also need to make sure that everything happens in order so that the pieces don't collide.

Note

You will animate so that the gear is completely extended by frame 30. This is really an arbitrary number; any would do. However, animators generally have an easier time thinking in multiples of 30, because animations are often made at 30 frames per second (the frame rate of video; another popular frame rate is 24 frames per second—the rate for film). If multiples of 30 rack your brain, feel free to count in your head in seconds. Either way, the most important thing is that this will give sufficient time to get all the steps in order. For example, the doors must close only after the gear is retracted enough that they pass by without intersecting each other.

You'll start by animating the left side gear, and then use ChannelFollower to drive the right side gear.

1. Select the object Fighter:Rear_Left_Gear_Top.

2. Go to frame 10.

3. Rotate the object to –5 degrees on the Heading axis. Set a keyframe.

   This will rotate the gear leg under the gear well by frame 10, which is necessary for the wheel to clear the edge of the opening.

Note

You might need to increase the Bounding Box Threshold to have your objects remain drawn while moving. Do this through the Display Options tab in the Preferences panel.

4. Go to frame 20 and select Fighter:Rear_Left_Gear_Middle. Rotate the object to 0 degrees on both the Pitch and Bank axes. Set a keyframe.

5. Go back to frame 10, and select Fighter:Rear_Left_Gear_Bottom. Rotate the object to 0 degrees on the Pitch, and set a keyframe.

6. Select the object Fighter:Left_Rear_Door.

7. Create a keyframe in this position at frame 15.

8. Delete the keyframe at frame 0.

9. Go to frame 30, and set the Bank to 0. Set a keyframe.

10. Save your scene.

That completes the animation of the left side landing gear. In the next exercise, you will assign ChannelFollower to the right side landing gear, allowing them to mimic the movements of the left.

Exercise 15.3   Using ChannelFollower to Link the Right Side Gear Objects

1. Select Fighter:Right_Rear_Door.

2. Open the Graph Editor.

3. Because the gear doors open on the bank channel, select the Fighter:Right_Rear_Door.Rotation.B channel in the Curve Bin.

4. Click the Modifiers tab. Click Add Modifier and select ChannelFollower.

5. Double-click the ChannelFollower listing to bring up the interface (see Figure 15.3).

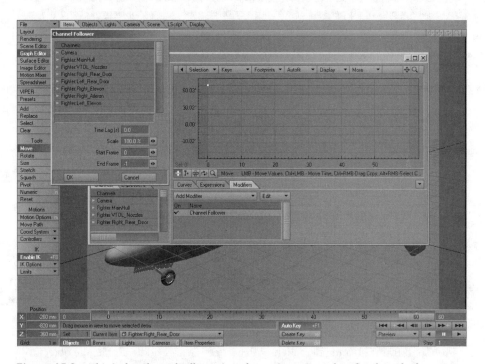

Figure 15.3   This is the ChannelFollower interface as it appears when first launched.

At this point, let's examine the ChannelFollower interface. Figure 15.3 shows the interface as it initially opens. The top of the interface is an expandable list of all the items in your scene. Clicking the triangle at the left of any item gives you the channels associated with that item. The channel you select here becomes the "driving" channel, the channel that the selected object will follow.

Below that is the Time Lag setting. This allows you to set a length of time, in seconds, for which the selected object will wait before following the driving channel.

Beneath Time Lag is the Scale value. The driving channel's value is multiplied by this value to determine the followed value. For instance, if you had a gear that turns once, 360 degrees, but the object you wished to drive needed to turn twice, your Scale would be set to 200 percent. This gets the job done, because 360 degrees * %200 = 720 degrees.

Below Scale are the Start Frame and End Frame values. These numbers set the range of keyframes in which ChannelFollower will be active. For instance, if you only need to have a ball follow a hand for the frames between 47 and 92, you would specify 47 as your Start Frame, and 92 as your End Frame. By default, the values are set to 0 and −1, which means that ChannelFollower will be active at all times throughout the scene.

6. What you're interested in is the opposite landing gear door. Scroll through the item list until you find Fighter:Left_Rear_Door. Click the triangle on the left side to reveal all the channels available for the object.

7. The Bank channel of Fighter:Rear_Left_Door (Rotation.B) is what you want, so double-click that. Notice as you do that the name of the channel is placed in the box beneath the item list.

8. You don't want any Time Lag, but you do need to alter the Scale. If you were to leave it like this, the door would rotate the wrong way, plunging into the fuselage instead of rotating out. So set the Scale to −100 percent. This will make the door rotate in the opposite direction. You want it to always be active, so you don't need to alter the Start and End frames; you're done. Click OK and close the Graph Editor.

Because this part is on the opposite side, remember that it needs to rotate inversely.

9. Now, because ChannelFollower is an *additive* plug-in (meaning it adds its effect to the already-keyframed motion rather than completely replacing it), you should reset the rotation of the Fighter:Rear_Right_Door object. Go to frame 0 and set the bank to 0. Make a keyframe.

10. Now scroll through your animation slowly and watch the second door move just exactly when and where it should, following its neighbor perfectly.

11. Continuing with the rest of the right gear object, select Fighter:Rear_Right_Gear_Top. Open the Graph Editor.

12. Click the Fighter:Rear_Right_Gear_Top.Rotation.H channel. Add ChannelFollower and double-click it.

13. This time, the control object is the Fighter:Rear_Left_Gear_Top object, and you want its Rotation.H channel. Double-click to set.

14. Set the Scale to −100% (so that it rotates in the opposite direction as the left gear), click OK, and either close the Graph Editor or move it out of the way. You don't need to close the Graph Editor if you have enough screen real estate or a dual monitor setup.

15. Set the Heading of this object to 0 and the keyframe to 0.

16. Next up is the middle segment of the right side landing gear: Fighter:Right_Gear_Middle. Select it and open the Graph Editor.

17. This object is animated along both its pitch and bank; we'll deal with each separately. First, add ChannelFollower to the Rotation.P channel and open the interface.

Note

You also could use the Follower motion modifier instead of the ChannelFollower here. This plug-in would allow you to follow both channels at once. The choice is yours. Motion modifiers are found by first selecting the particular object, and then pressing m on the keyboard. At the bottom of the Motion Options panel that opens, select Add Modifier.

18. The control object is Fighter:Rear_Left_Gear_Middle, and its channel is Rotation.P. Double-click to set. Because both objects pitch in the same direction, it is not necessary to set the Scale to –100 percent this time. Click OK.

19. Back in the Graph Editor now, select the Rotation.B channel and add ChannelFollower to it. Open the interface.

20. The control object is the same, but this time it's the Rotation.B channel. Double-click to set, and set the Scale to –100 percent. Click OK, and close the Graph Editor.

21. Set the Pitch and Bank rotations of the object to 0 and set a keyframe at frame 0.

22. The final piece is Fighter:Rear_Right_Gear_Bottom. Select this object and open the Graph Editor.

23. Select the Rotation.P channel, and add and open ChannelFollower.

24. The control object is Fighter:Rear_Left_Gear_Bottom, using the Rotation.P channel. Scale is –100 percent. Click OK and close the Graph Editor.

25. Set the pitch to 0 at frame 0 and make a keyframe.

Tip

You can save time by using the Copy and Paste functions for the modifiers, found in the Edit drop-down list next to the modifier area.

26. Save your scene.

That's it for the right side gear! Now when you scrub through your animation, both the left and right side gear should retract themselves at the same time.

Exercise 15.4   Setting Up Cycler on the Left Side Gear

In this exercise, you will add Cycler to the left gear objects so that you can control them with a single null. This, in turn, will also drive the right gear.

1. Select Fighter:Rear_Left_Gear_Top, and open the Graph Editor.

2. Select the Rotation.H channel.

3. Click Add Modifier, and select Cycler (see Figure 15.4). Double-click its name to open its control panel.

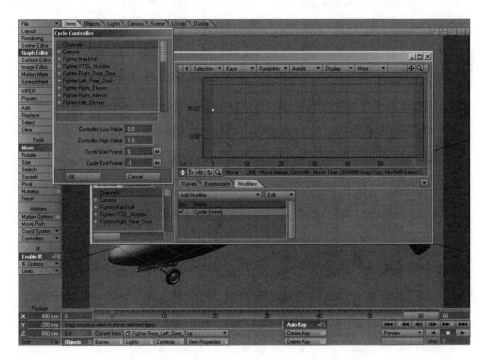

Figure 15.4   Here is the Cycler interface as it appears when first launched.

Controller Low/High Value defines the range of motion over which the controller object will move to cycle the dependent object. If you think of your control object as a "handle," this would define the starting and ending positions of the handle. Using the defaults 0 to 1 means Position.Y 0m to 1m.

The Start and End Frames define the range over which the plug-in will be active. Because we want it active for the entire shot, leave that at 0 and –1. Note that –1 means to use the entire animation.

4. Find and double-click Position.Y for Landing_Gear_Cycle, making it the active controller object. That's really all that's necessary here—all the other values are already exactly what we want them to be.

5. Click OK and close the Graph Editor.

> **Note**
>
> The controlling parameter here, Position.Y, is really completely arbitrary. Any channel would work, including Master Channels, or channels attached to regular objects. The Low and High values also are arbitrary. A range of 0 to 1 is just very simple, and there-fore, usually preferable.

6. Repeat steps 4 and 5 for the rest of the left gear objects, remembering that you still want Position.Y as the controller. Here, you can save some time using the Copy and Paste functions for the modifier because all the settings are identical:

   - Fighter:Rear_Left_Gear_Middle Rotation.P
   - Fighter:Rear_Left_Gear_Middle Rotation.B
   - Fighter:Rear_Left_Gear_Bottom Rotation.P
   - Fighter:Left_Rear_Door Rotation.B

7. Save your scene.

This completes the animation setup for the rear landing gear. Now it's time to work with the front gear, which we've ignored up until now. You will do a very similar setup with the front gear.

Exercise 15.5   Animating the Front Landing Gear

1. Select Fighter:Front_Gear_Bottom. Go to frame 10.
2. Rotate the object –55 degrees on its Pitch, and make a keyframe.
3. Select Fighter:Front_Gear_Top, and go to frame 20.
4. Move the object up to –700mm in the y-axis, and make a keyframe.
5. Select Fighter:Front_Gear_Door, and go to frame 30.
6. Set the Heading, Pitch, and Bank all to 0, and set a keyframe.

This completes the animation of the front gear retraction.

Exercise 15.6   Setting Up Cycler on the Front Gear

Now you will assign Cycler to the front gear, just like you did for the rear gear.

1. Select Fighter:Front_Gear_Bottom, and open the Graph Editor.
2. Select the Rotation.P channel, and add Cycler. Double-click to open Cycler.
3. Just as you did with the rear gear, double-click the control object and leave the rest of the settings at their defaults. Click OK and close the Graph Editor.
4. Repeat steps 1 through 3 for the last two objects or simply use the Copy and Paste from the Edit drop-down list next to modifiers:

- Fighter:Front_Gear_Top Position.Y
- Fighter:Front_Gear_Door Rotation.P
- Fighter:Front_Gear_Door Rotation.B

5. Save your scene.

Congratulations! You've now completed the entire setup! All that remains is to animate the control null. You will animate it from frames 10 to 40, to show that the gear is now really controlled with the null.

Exercise 15.7   Animating the Control Null

1. Select the Landing_Gear_Cycle null and make a keyframe at frame 10.
2. Go to frame 40. Move Landing_Gear_Cycle to 1.0 meters on the y-axis, and set a key. Now make a preview to see the fruits of your labors!
3. When you're done, delete the key at frames 10 and 40.

What remains of the project is to set up the engines and control surfaces. They'll be set up using LightWave's built-in expressions to respond automatically to the animation of the fighter. The main components to be set up are

- Ailerons
- Elevons
- Elevator
- Rudders
- Winglets
- Engine nozzles
- Engine flames

Each one of these parts will be set up in such a way as to make the fighter look like it's moving *because* of them, even though they're actually *responding* to the motion of the fighter. You'll use a lot of math, but don't worry; it's all pretty simple to understand.

The core of the setup is a simple formula that measures the change over time of the components of motion of the fighter. This is commonly known as *delta t*. You are going to work with five delta t's:

- Y delta t
- Z delta t
- H delta t
- P delta t
- B delta t

From these values, we will be able to set the control surfaces and engines to move properly. Begin in the y-axis.

Exercise 15.8   Calculating the P_delta_t

1. Select Fighter_Control.
2. Go to frame 0, and move the object to 1.96 meters on the y-axis. Set a keyframe.
3. Go to frame 30. Rotate the object to –30 degrees in Pitch. Set a keyframe.
4. Go to frame 60. Rotate the object to 45 degrees in Pitch. Set a keyframe.
5. Open the Graph Editor, and select the Rotation.P channel.
6. Select all three keyframes, and set their tension to 1.0.

   Now the Fighter_Control object has rotation in the P channel. Therefore, it has some delta t. We can use LightWave's built-in expressions to calculate that value (see Figure 15.5).

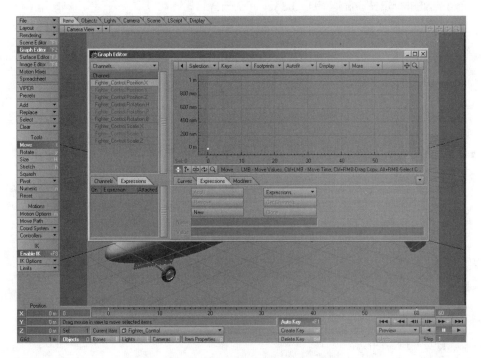

Figure 15.5   The Graph Editor, with the Expression tab selected.

7. Click the Expressions tab.
8. Click the New button to create a new expression.
9. In the Name field, name the expression P_delta_t.

10. Under the Value tab, enter the formula:

([Fighter_Control.Rotation.P, Frame +–3] – [Fighter_Control.Rotation.P])/3

11. Close the Graph Editor.

This formula takes the P rotation of the object three frames ahead of the current frame and subtracts the P value of the object at the current frame. This is the change over time—the delta t.

With only the subtraction, what you have is the value of the change over three frames. Then, that value is divided by three, giving us an average of the change over three frames; roughly equivalent to the value you would get if you subtracted the current frame from one frame ahead. Simply put, the value is the average per frame rotation over the next three frames.

Why sample three frames ahead if you're just going to divide by three? By averaging over three frames, the motion will be smoothed out a bit, keeping large, strange jumps out of the motion. (For you Quake/Half-Life fans, their setups allow this kind of averaging in mouse movements, to smooth out the jerky motions.) If you were to sample five frames ahead and divide by five, the motion would be even smoother. And the motion would continue to get smoother as you continued to widen the frame gap. However, as it got wider, the motions would grow less and less accurate. So you must balance the smoothness with accuracy.

So, why subtract the current frame from a future frame, instead of subtracting a past frame from the current frame? Because we want the fighter to act as though it's reacting to the control surfaces, the expression should look into the future. This way, the control surfaces will act just slightly before the fighter moves.

Now you have the expression, but it's not yet attached to anything. In fact, you won't be attaching this expression to any channels directly. This expression will be referenced as a sub-expression to drive other expressions. This is the "raw material" out of which you will construct the expressions for a couple of control surfaces.

Pitch was chosen as the first channel to add an expression to because pitch will control the elevator in a very straightforward, easy-to-see manner.

Exercise 15.9   Animating the Elevator with Expressions

1. Select Fighter:Elevator. Open the Graph Editor.

2. Under the Expressions tab, click New to create a new expression.

3. Name this expression Elevator_Pitch.

4. In the Value field, enter: [P_delta_t] * 15. This formula references our previously created expression "P_delta_t" and simply multiplies it by 15. This is necessary because the calculated value of P_delta_t is much too small by itself.

5. Select Rotation.P in the Curve Bin, and then click Apply.

6. Close the Graph Editor, and scrub through your animation in the Side view. Observe how the elevator now rotates on its pitch, seeming to drive the motion of the fighter (see Figure 15.6).

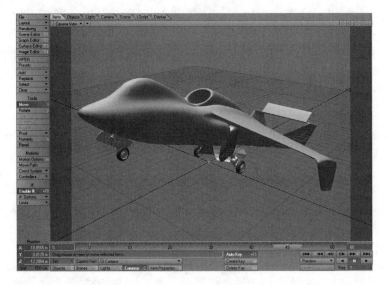

Figure 15.6   As the fighter pitches upward, the elevator reacts, rotating in the opposite direction.

It's really as simple as that. The plane pitches over, but just a few frames before it does, the elevator pitches in the opposite direction, making it appear as though the elevator caused the rotation. The link between the two doesn't follow any realistic, physics-based simulation. We're not really interested in reality, though—just results. This setup would be good enough for 99 percent of the situations you're likely to run into.

We've taken this detour and completed one of the control surface setups to illustrate the basic principles and show you the results. But now, we should get back and finish setting up the other four "raw material" expressions.

Exercise 15.10   Setting Up the Remaining delta t Expressions

1. Open the Graph Editor, and go to the Expressions tab.

2. Click New to create a new channel. Name it Y_delta_t.

   Because these channels won't be associated with any channels, it's not necessary to have any one channel selected while working here.

3. In the Value field, enter the following:

   ([Fighter_Control.Position.Y, Frame +−3] − [Fighter_Control.Position.Y])/3

4. Click Clone, which will create a copy of the expression. Rename the expression to Z_delta_t.

5. In the Value field, enter the following:

   ([Fighter_Control.Position.Z, Frame +−3] − [Fighter_Control.Position.Z])/3

6. Clone this expression, renaming it to H_delta_t.

7. In the Value field, enter the following:

   ([Fighter_Control.Rotation.H, Frame +−3] − [Fighter_Control.Rotation.H])/3

8. Clone this expression, renaming it to B_delta_t.

9. In the Value field, enter the following:

   ([Fighter_Control.Rotation.B, Frame +−3] − [Fighter_Control.Rotation.B])/3

   Now all the basic "sensing" expressions are done; these expressions will always hold the current delta t for their channels, and we can write other expressions that will draw from this information.

   Now the fighter must be rotated so that it affects all the rotation channels, enabling you to see the results of your expressions when they are completed.

10. Select the Fighter_Control object, and go to frame 30.

11. Set the Heading to −90 degrees, the Pitch to −35 degrees, and the Bank to 25 degrees. Create a keyframe.

12. Go to frame 60.

13. Set the Heading to 25 degrees, the Pitch to 30 degrees, and the Bank to −45 degrees. Create a keyframe.

14. Go back to frame 15.

15. Set the Bank to −30 degrees. Create a keyframe.

16. Go to frame 45.

17. Set the Bank to 25 degrees. Create a keyframe (see Figure 15.7).

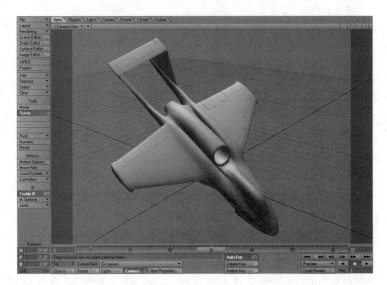

Figure 15.7   These are some strange rotations, to be sure, but useful in demonstrating your expressions.

If this animation seems a little wacky, it is. It's not intended to reflect reality, just to give nice large rotations to clearly demonstrate the operation of the control surfaces. Now you will begin creating expressions for the remaining control surfaces, beginning with the rudders.

Exercise 15.11   Animating the Rudders with Expressions

1. Select Fighter:Right Rudder. Open the Graph Editor.

2. Under the Expressions tab, click New to create a new expression. Name it Rudder_Heading.

> **Note**
>
> Notice that all of the expressions, and everything else in the scene for that matter, have been well labeled. This is probably the single best habit to get into. If you have to go back to a scene weeks, months, or even years later, you'll be better able to decipher what you originally did in the scene. Or if you're in a production environment and someone else will have to work with your scene, they will thank you profusely for good labeling practices.

3. In the Value field, enter the following:

    [H_delta_t] * 7

    Note that this multiplier was just figured out by trial and error, by seeing how the objects behave. It hasn't been tested under all conditions, and in fact, it wouldn't be hard to drive it past "normal" behavior. This is one of those times when you just have to feel things out and adjust the numbers as necessary to fit your scene. In this case, seven looked to give the rudders a nice amount of rotation. If you feel that they should have more, or less, feel free to increase or decrease the multiplier. "Season to taste," as they say.

4. Select the Rotation.H channel in the Curve Bin, and click Apply. You should see a curved dotted line appear in the Graph Editor, representing the calculated value of the expression. This is the new heading curve that your object will follow.

5. Without closing the Graph Editor, click back into Layout and select Fighter:Left_Rudder.

6. In the Selection menu, select Get Layout Selected. This will put all the channels from Fighter:Left_Rudder into the Curve Bin.

7. Select Rotation.H, and again click Apply. Because the right rudder moves exactly the same way as the left rudder, you can use the same expression for both. And LightWave lets you apply expressions to multiple channels very easily.

8. Minimize the Graph Editor, and scrub through your scene. Observe the rudders moving, just slightly before the ship, as did the elevator (see Figure 15.8).

9. Save your scene.

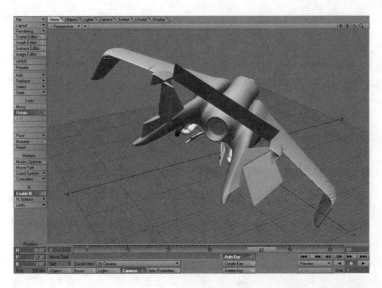

Figure 15.8   The rudders' headings are now controlled automatically by the expressions.

Now that you have the rudders operating properly, it's time to move onto the next segments. We might as well stay with the heading-controlled objects, the last two being the winglets.

Exercise 15.12   Animating the Winglets with Expressions

1. Re-open the Graph Editor.

2. Clone the Rudder_Heading expression and rename the clone to Winglet_Heading.

3. Change the Value to [H_delta_t] * 10. By increasing the multiplier value from 7 to 10, we'll increase the amount the winglets rotate when the fighter rotates.

4. Without closing the Graph Editor, click back into Layout and select both Fighter:Right_Winglet and Fighter:Left_Winglet. Using the Scene Editor or Schematic View to multi-select objects is usually the easiest way.

5. Use Get Layout Selected again to bring all the channels for both objects into the Curve Bin.

6. By holding Ctrl and clicking on each of the channels, select Rotation.H for both Fighter:Right_Winglet and Fighter:Left_Winglet.

7. Click Apply to put the expression on both channels.

8. Close the Graph Editor and observe the winglets now moving in concert with the rudders (see Figure 15.9).

9. Save your scene.

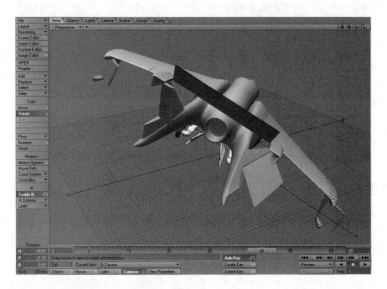

Figure 15.9   Now the winglets get in the game.

Now you have successfully used the same sub-expression to affect the heading on different objects in different ways. In a situation like this, you can think of the sub-expression like a "sensor." It reports to the other expressions what the fighter is doing, and the other expressions use that information to act accordingly.

In the case of the rudders and the winglets, there wasn't really much difference between them—only a difference in the multiplier. In the case of the ailerons and elevons, things are going to get a bit more complex.

Ailerons are the flaps on the back of the wings that cause the fighter to bank left and right. They pitch up and down, deflecting the air over the wings, causing the wings to rise and fall, and thereby, the fighter to roll. To do this, the left and right ailerons must have the opposite pitch (if they were to have the same pitch, they would just pitch the fighter up or down, same as the elevator).

Elevons are a combination of ailerons and the elevator. They, too, will pitch opposite from each other, but they also will respond to the overall pitch of the fighter. This will make for a more interesting expression, to be sure.

Exercise 15.13   Animating the Ailerons with Expressions

1. Select Fighter:Left_Aileron, and open the Graph Editor.
2. Under the Expressions tab, click New to create a new expression, and name it Left_Aileron.
3. In the Value field, enter [B_delta_t] * 15.
4. Select the Rotation.P channel from the Curve Bin, and click Apply. In the case of the ailerons, even though the rotation axis that you're measuring is the *bank*, it is the *pitch* of the ailerons that you'll be affecting with the expressions.
5. Minimize the Graph Editor, and scrub through your animation, observing the aileron.

   What you should see is that the aileron is moving at the proper time, but in the wrong direction. That's a simple enough fix.
6. Re-open the Graph Editor, and change the Value of Left_Aileron to be −[B_delta_t] * 15.
7. Minimize the Graph Editor and again look at the rotation of the left aileron. It should be rotating correctly now.
8. Back in the Graph Editor, clone the Left_Aileron expression, and rename the clone Right_Aileron.
9. Change the Value to [B_delta_t] * 15.
10. Without closing the Graph Editor, click back into Layout, and select Fighter:Right_Aileron.
11. Use Get Layout Selected to bring the Right Aileron's channels into the Curve Bin.
12. Select the Fighter:Right_Aileron.Rotation.P channel from the Curve Bin, and click Apply to apply the Right_Aileron expression to the channel.

13. Close the Graph Editor and scrub through your animation, observing the ailerons (see Figure 15.10).

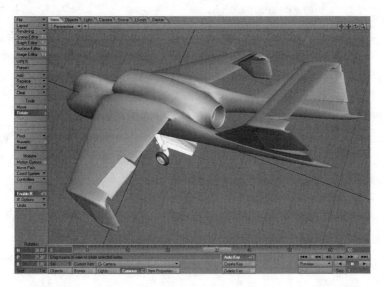

Figure 15.10   The ailerons are now under expression control, left and right moving opposite of each other.

The elevons are going to be a combination of the elevator pitch, which you set up earlier, and the ailerons, which you just completed.

Exercise 15.14   Animating the Elevons with Expressions

1. Select Fighter:Left_Elevon, and open the Graph Editor.

2. Click New to create a new expression, and name it Left_Elevon.

3. In the Value field, enter ((–[B_delta_t] * 15) + ([P_delta_t] * 15))/2.

The bulk of this formula is made up of two expressions you've already seen. The first part, involving B_delta_t, is the expression you used for bank just now. The second part you might recognize as the equation for the pitch of the elevator. What's happening here is that those two values are added together and then divided by two, giving the average of the two values.

> **Note**
>
> Adding the two values and dividing the sum by two is the equivalent of dividing each value by two and then adding them, or multiplying each value by .5 and then adding them, like so: ((–[B_delta_t] * 15)*.5) + (([P_delta_t] * 15)*.5)
>
> This gives you a weighted average. Or, a way to divide a whole amount into two or more smaller amounts. If, for example, you wanted the roll of the fighter to account for more of the elevons' motion than the pitch, you could alter those values like this:
>
> ((–[B_delta_t] * 15)*.75) + (([P_delta_t] * 15)*.25)
>
> This formula means that 75 percent of the elevons' pitch will come from the roll calculation, and 25 percent will come from the pitch. You can adjust these two multipliers to give you whatever effect you desire, as long as the percentages add up to 100 percent.

4. Select Rotation.P from the Curve Bin, and click Apply.

5. Minimize the Graph Editor and examine the rotation of the left elevon. Notice that although the elevon does move quite similarly to the aileron next to it, it doesn't mimic it exactly. Rather, you can see that it is influenced by both the bank and the pitch of the fighter.

6. In Layout, select Fighter:Right_Elevon, and re-open the Graph Editor.

7. Use Get Layout Selected to put the channels for the right elevon into the Curve Bin. Select Rotation.P.

8. Under the Expressions tab, clone Left_Elevon, and rename it to Right_Elevon.

9. Change the Value field to ((([B_delta_t] * 15) + ([P_delta_t] * 15))/2. (Note that the only change is taking off the "–", so that the elevon will rotate in the opposite direction.)

10. Click Apply to add the expression to the right elevon.

11. Close the Graph Editor and save your scene.

12. Make a preview (see Figure 15.11).

Now that all the wing control surfaces are complete, it's time to tackle the engines.

Though there is just one engine in this fighter, there are three exhaust nozzles: one in the back for forward thrust, and one on each side for VTOL capability. The nozzle on the back is fixed in place; it cannot rotate. The nozzles on the side can rotate from facing straight down to facing straight back. This will give the effect of the transition from vertical to horizontal flight. In addition, each engine will have an exhaust flame that will grow or shrink depending on the motion of the fighter.

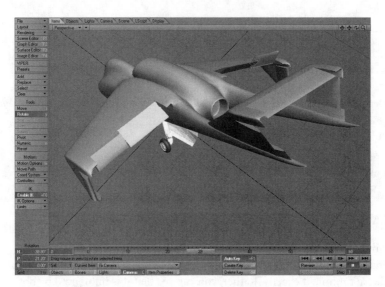

Figure 15.11   Now the elevons are set up, combining motion from both the ailerons and the elevator.

The automatic controls you will put in place will control the rotation of the VTOL engines and the size of each of the exhaust flames. There will be a Throttle control that will determine the overall strength of the exhaust flames. This value will then be divided proportionally between the side and back engines. The proportion will be determined by how much the fighter is moving forward versus how much it's moving up and down.

To see the effects of the expressions as you apply them, you'll need a new motion for the fighter. The current motion does not move, it only rotates, which means that it won't be at all useful for the upcoming set of expressions.

Though it seems premature to do so, at this point you will set up the basic motion for your final animation. No sense animating twice, right? You will finalize the animation later, adding the retraction of the landing gear. But for now, you'll animate just the fighter and the camera.

At this point, the animation process gets a bit subjective. Nothing says that you have to follow the instructions below. But if you do, you'll be assured a fairly good, dramatic animation, and a good view of the work you've accomplished up to this point.

In practical (real) filmmaking, the cinematographer or director generally frames the shot as he or she wants it to look at the beginning, and if the subject moves, the camera operator rotates the camera so that it keeps the subject in frame, even if it's not the original frame. He or she just keeps it looking nice throughout the shot.

In 3D, it's not quite as easy as just watching what happens and moving the camera. You don't have the benefit of real-time feedback, but you do have the added bonus of being able to control time, and go back and fix errors. Practical cinematographers would probably gladly trade with us for those abilities.

The trick is to *think* like a real camera person, to see the view through the virtual camera as they would through a real one. There are a couple of basic rules that will help guide you in deciding where and how to place and move the camera.

- Real camera people do not have the benefit of looking into the future to see where their subject is *going to be*. They can only focus on where it is *now*. They cannot anticipate the movement of their subject, so they cannot move the camera before the subject moves. They must respond to that motion. The camera anticipating a subject's motion is an obvious sign that what you are viewing is a CGI (computer-generated image) and is something to be avoided if possible, to help your animation look more realistic.

- Real cameras must obey the laws of physics. If your virtual camera does not at least try to act in the same way, it is another large telltale sign that could pull the viewer out of the illusion and ruin the effect. Now, if the subject matter is appropriate, by all means, throw physics out the window. There's no way to truly, realistically move a camera down a person's bloodstream, for example. Physics has no place in an animation like that.

An easy way to begin acting like a virtual cinematographer is to drag the time slider until your subject begins to move out of frame, and then adjust the camera to put it back in frame at that point. Usually, for slower-moving subjects, letting the subject get about halfway off screen will give a good effect, allowing the camera to seem to react to the subject, rather than the other way around. For faster movers, it might be better to let it go all the way off screen before adjusting.

And if, in the final animation, the subject does go off-screen a little, don't panic. It's not necessary to have the subject dead center at all times. Because you pour so much time and energy into the objects you animate, the natural reaction is to make sure that they get as much screen time as possible; but this isn't always the best course of action. Examine some of the better effects films of the past decade or so and see for yourself.

Exercise 15.15 Animating the Fighter and Camera

1. Select Fighter_Control, and delete all the keys except the key at frame 0.

2. Set the end frame of your timeline to 240.

3. Set keyframes for Fighter_Control at these positions and rotations at the listed frames:

   Frame: 0 Pos: 0m, 1.96m, 0 Rot: 0, 0, 0

   Frame: 60 Pos: 0m, 6.3m, 35 mm Rot: 22.5, 0, 7.5

   Frame: 90 Pos: −5.5m, 8.3m, −2.8m Rot: 144, 0, 42

   Frame: 120 Pos: −9.7m, 7.4m, 10.5m, Rot: 189, 10, 42

   Frame: 180 Pos: −8.6m, 11.9m, 53.8m, Rot: 177, 24.8, −28.3

   Frame: 240 Pos: −8.7m, 28.7m, 108.6m, Rot: 182, 18.8, 54

4. Go to frame 0. Set the position of the camera to X: −41m, Y: 2.3m, Z: −1.5m. Set a keyframe.

5. Set keyframes for the Camera at these rotations at the listed frame:

   Frame 0: Rot: 87, 0, 0

   Frame 60: Rot: 86, −7, 0

   Frame 90: Rot: 91, −10, 0

   Frame 120: Rot: 71, −8, 0

   Frame 180: Rot: 30, −5, 0

   Frame 240: 24, −10, 0

6. Open the Camera Properties panel, and change the camera zoom to 4.0.

This should give you an animation of the fighter taking off, turning around, and flying off in the opposite direction from which it started. You'll have a good view of the fighter's engines, which you are about to set up, as well as the control surfaces you set up previously.

The first step in setting up the engines is to set up the VTOL exhaust nozzles. These are the engine nozzles below the wings. They can rotate from pointing straight down to pointing straight back. They point straight down for vertical flight and rotate backward to thrust the fighter forward. You will automate this rotation with expressions so that if the fighter is moving forward, the jets will point back, and vice versa.

Exercise 15.16   Animating the VTOL Nozzles with Expressions

1. Select Fighter:VTOL_Nozzles, and open the Graph Editor.

2. Under the Expressions tab, click New to create a new expression, and name it VTOL_Nozzles.

3. In the Value field, enter the following:

(((([Z_delta_t]) * 120) + 90) < 0 ? 0 : (((([Z_delta_t]) * 120) + 90))

Now, this looks really complicated, but it's actually quite simple. Let's break it down into its components.

First, you'll notice a reference to [Z_delta_t]. So, obviously, we're using the delta t along the Z channel to drive something, and in this lies the biggest fault in this expression—for simplicity's sake, the expression reads only the change over time in the world Z direction, not the actual distance traveled. If there were to be any substantial movement along the x-axis, this expression would become useless. A far more complicated expression would be required to measure the combined X and Z motion.

Twice in the expression, you'll see ((([Z_delta_t] * 120) + 90). This can be thought of as a unit. And what does this unit do? To figure that out, look at the result of calculating this equation by substituting a number for Z_delta_t. Now, to guess randomly would be inefficient at best. So how do you figure out what range of numbers you're looking at here?

Simple. You look at the results of Z_delta_t.

4. Click Scale.Z in the Curve bin. From the Expressions tree, select Z_delta_t.

5. Click Apply to attach the expression to that curve.

Now, examine the dotted line curve of Z_delta_t. At a glance, you can see that it goes from just above zero to just above −1. Now you know that over the course of the animation, these are the values that Z_delta_t is going to be going through. And you can plan your expression accordingly.

If you plug −1 into the equation in place of Z_delta_t, you get

((−1 * 120) + 90), which equals −30.

If you plug 0 into the equation, you get

((0 * 120) + 90), which equals 90.

Now, 90 degrees is the proper rotation for the nozzles when they are pointing straight down. Therefore, this is a good expression: When the Z velocity is 0, the nozzles point straight down. Perfect.

So what's all the other junk for? LightWave's built-in expressions contain not only a way to use math to calculate values, but it can also do basic if:then decision making. And that's what's happening here.

The basic format for an if:then statement in LightWave is

(x < y ? z, −z)

What this statement says in English is, "If x is less than y, return the value of z; otherwise, return negative z." Using this function, then, you can have LightWave make simple decisions about what to do.

In this case, the if:then statement is saying, "If (our measuring unit result) is less than zero, make it zero; otherwise, leave it alone". This way, the nozzle can never be rotated past zero and cause all kinds of mayhem in your scene.

This kind of limiting expression can be used in almost any situation when you know the outer borders to which you can allow your expression to go. Let's get back to it.

6. Click Remove to remove the Z_delta_t expression from the Scale.Z channel.

7. Select the Rotation.P channel from the Curve Bin, and the VTOL_Nozzles expression from the Expression Tree.

8. Click Apply to apply the expression to that channel.

9. Close the Graph Editor.

10. Save your scene, and make a preview.

Now you'll see in your preview that, as the fighter starts to move forward, the engine nozzles smoothly rotate from vertical to horizontal, just like they would on a real VTOL jet (see Figure 15.12).

Figure 15.12   The fighter rises and begins to fly away, and the engine nozzles rotate backward as it accelerates forward.

The final step in your setup is to add the jet exhaust flames. These will be done with volumetric lights, which give a great effect and have a myriad number of controls to get the look you want.

Each of the flames will be more or less a clone of each other, so it's best to start with the back center flame, because it's the largest and easiest to see.

Exercise 15.17   Setting Up the Engine Exhaust Flames

1. Add a distant light, and name it Engine_Volumetric.
2. Parent this light to Fighter:MainHull.
3. Move the light to X: 0, Y: 85mm, Z: 4.215, and make a keyframe at frame 0.
4. Go to the Properties panel for the light, and check on Volumetric Lighting.
5. Turn the Light Intensity of the light to 100 percent.
6. Uncheck Affect Diffuse and Affect Specular, and set Shadow Type to Off.
7. If you look back in your Layout view, you'll see that when you checked Volumetric Lighting On, a cylinder appeared at the light, representing where the volumetric effect will appear. Because this is a distant light, you get a cylindrical effect (versus a cone for a spotlight, or a sphere for a point light). Click the Volumetric Light Options button to bring up the control panel for it (see Figure 15.13).

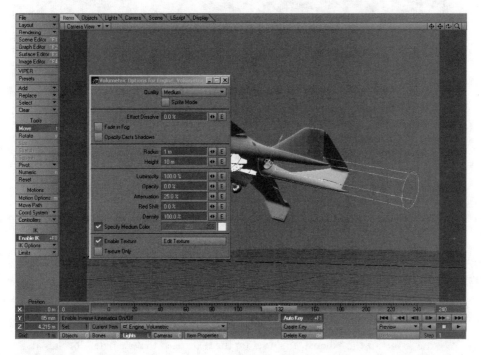

Figure 15.13   Here is the Volumetric Options panel, with all the default settings. Note the preview cylinder drawn around the light in the Layout window. This represents the height and radius of the volumetric effect.

8. In here you'll see all the controls for your volumetric light. The first thing to do is adjust the Height setting so that the exhaust flame is at the length you want it to be. Through trial and error, this turns out to be 3m.

9. The next step is to set the radius of the volumetric so that the light fits within the engine nozzle. Set the radius to 400mm.

10. Set the Attenuation to 0 percent.

11. Uncheck Specify Medium Color (see Figure 15.14).

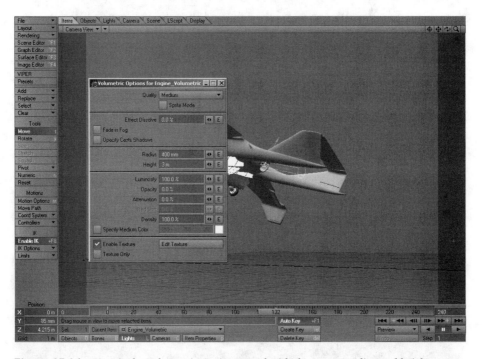

Figure 15.14   Here is the Volumetric Options panel with the proper radius and height settings. Notice the changed shape of the preview cylinder.

12. Make sure Enable Texture is on, and also check Texture Only.

13. Click Edit Texture to bring up the Texture Editing panel.

14. In the Texture Editor, set the Layer Type to Procedural Texture.

15. Set the Procedural Type to Dots. (Dots is a highly underrated texture, and far more useful than you might imagine. It can be used for anything from faking soft shadows to making rivets.) In this case, you're going to use dots to define the "cone" of the exhaust. You'll set up the texture so that a single "dot" lies at the center of the volumetric light, and stretches to the end (you will, of course, see only one half of the dot). The round shape and soft edge give a great look to the exhaust flame.

16. Under the Scale tab, leave X and Y at 1, but set Z to 6m (recall that the exhaust flame Height is 3m—if our dot is to sit at the center and stretch to the end, then it must stretch 3m in each direction—a total of 6m).

17. Set the Dot Diameter to .4 (400 mm). Recall that 400mm is the radius of the exhaust flame. Set the Fuzzy Edge Width to .4, as well. This will give the softest edge possible.

18. Set the Texture Color to R:255, G: 255, B: 255.

 Tip

You can easily change the value of your texture color by right-clicking and dragging on the color swatch. Dragging to the right increases the value; dragging to the left decreases it.

19. Now, the dots texture gives you exactly the shape you want, but it's also good to have a moving texture in the flame to help give it more of a sense of energy. To accomplish this, you're actually going to use the Dots texture above as an alpha for another texture. Click Add Layer, and select Procedural Texture.

20. Drag this layer below the Dots layer.

21. The Procedural Type should already be set to Turbulence; this is fine. Set the Texture Color to R: 55, G: 148, B: 255 (see Figure 15.15).

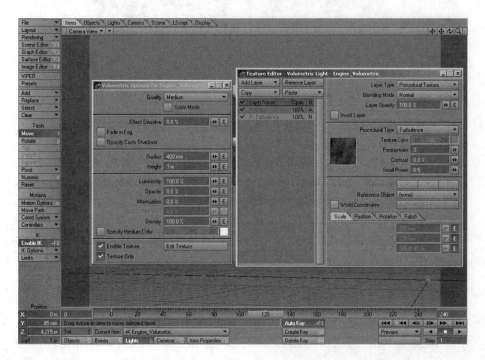

Figure 15.15   The Volumetric Texture panels, with the Turbulence texture showing.

22. Set the Scale to X: 200 mm, Y: 200 mm, Z: 2m.

23. Click the Position tab, and click the E beside the Z field to add an envelope in that channel. The Graph Editor will open.

24. In the Graph Editor, create a key at frame 15, with a value of 50m.

25. Set the Pre and Post behavior to Linear, thus assuring that the texture will always be moving in the z-axis.

26. Close the Graph Editor.

27. Select the Dots texture layer, and set its Blending Mode to Alpha.

28. Close all the open windows to get you back to Layout. Do a render at frame 120. You should be able to see the flame quite clearly (see Figure 15.16).

29. Save your scene.

Figure 15.16   Here is the render at frame 120. Note the exhaust flame coming out of the back.

The next step is to automate this flame so that it grows and shrinks properly as the fighter moves. It's a fairly straightforward setup, very similar to the one you just did with the VTOL nozzles. The process is complicated, however, because you must scale not only the height of the engine flame but also the Dot texture; otherwise, the flame will seem to cut off abruptly.

The way to do this is to make an expression so that the result is always between one and zero. In this way, it becomes like a switch. Multiplying anything by one gives itself; anything multiplied by zero is zero. If the expression results in values between one and zero, then you need only multiply that expression by the length of the flame and the length of the dots texture.

On top of all this automation, there will be a Throttle control that will allow you to force the engines off or force them beyond the maximums of the default setups. This will be yet another multiplier between one and zero, but fortunately, you will have complete control over the position of this null.

The first step to this setup is to determine precisely what the minimum and maximum values of Z_delta_t are. You saw this earlier, when you set up the VTOL nozzles. You'll go through the process a bit more precisely this time.

Exercise 15.18   Normalizing Z_delta_t

1. Select Throttle, and open the Graph Editor (Throttle was chosen here because as of yet, it has no function—therefore, nothing you're going to do with it will mess anything else up).

2. Select the Throttle.Position.Z channel in the Curve Bin, and select the Z_delta_t expression in the Expression Tree (see Figure 15.17).

3. Click Apply to apply the expression. You should see the dotted curve appear, showing the modified motion curve. (If it doesn't appear immediately, you might have to press a to autosize the window.)

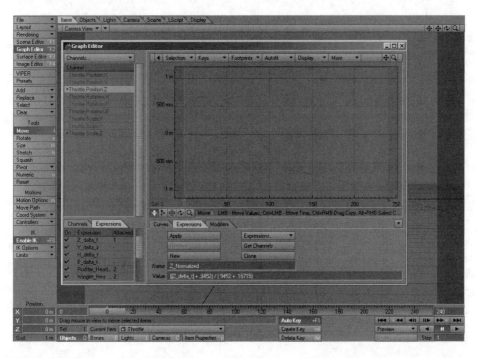

Figure 15.17 Here is the Z_delta_t expression before normalization.

4. Keeping the Graph Editor open, scrub the Layout time slider until the time marker inside the Graph Editor intersects with the tallest part of the dotted curve. Observe the values in the Numeric panel in Layout. Scrub until you see the highest value in that area, and make a note of that value.

   Certain variables such as frames per second and the units of measure you are using can affect this value, so it's impossible to predict what it will be. This book will refer to it as "HighCurve"—whenever you see "HighValue" in an equation, put the value you just noticed instead. There also will be an example provided, with sample numbers, which you can view in the Graph Editor. The sample number for "HighCurve" is 187.15 mm.

5. Now scrub over to the lowest part of the curve and examine those values. Note the lowest value, which will be referred to as "LowCurve." Its sample value is −945.2 mm.

6. Click New to add a new expression, and name it Z_Normalized.

7. Click Throttle.Scale.Z in the Curve Bin, and click Apply to add the expression to the channel. (There's nothing there yet, but it will be good to monitor the progress of the expression as it's built.)

8. Now, to ensure that your normalized expression's lowest value is zero, simply add the lowest value of Z_delta_t to itself, thus shifting the entire curve upward. In the Value field, enter the following:

   [Z_delta_t] + "LowCurve"

   Using the following sample values:

   [Z_delta_t] + .9452

   You should see the dotted line curve shift upward so that the very lowest part of the curve now reaches only to 0. Now, to complete the normalization and ensure that the maximum value is never greater than 1, divide the entire equation by the highest value—the highest value *after* addition. A number divided by itself is one, so it would be impossible for the expression to go above one.

9. In the Value field, change your expression to read as

   ([Z_delta_t] + "LowCurve") / ("HighCurve" + "LowCurve")

   Using the following example numbers:

   ([Z_delta_t] + .9452) / (.9452 + .18715)

   This completes the normalization of the expression, ensuring that it will never exceed one or go below zero (see Figure 15.18). However, there's one small problem—the point at which we know that the jet is moving slowly is the highest point. Therefore, the exhaust flame would be the longest at the point, which is not what we want.

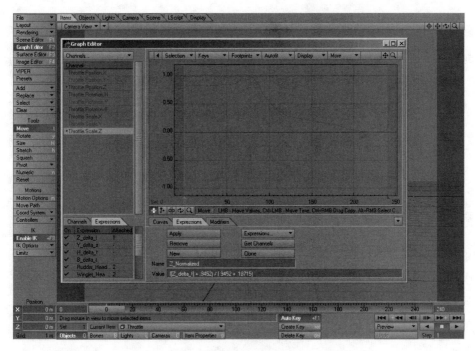

Figure 15.18 Here is the Z_Normalized expression after normalization.

10. The fix for this is relatively simple. All you have to do is subtract the expression from one. When the expression is one, the result will be zero, and when the expression is zero, the result will be one. Exactly what you want. Change your expression to read as

1 – (([Z_delta_t] + "LowCurve")/("HighCurve" + "LowCurve"))

Using the example numbers, the expression would be

1 – (([Z_delta_t] + .9452) / (.9452 + .18715))

After entering this new expression, your dotted curve should appear to flip vertically, giving you exactly the results desired (see Figure 15.19).

11. Up until this point, you have referenced Z_delta_t as a subexpression, and it has worked perfectly. However, LightWave will not allow an expression to reference a subexpression that contains another sub-expression; in other words, a sub-sub-expression. Because of this, it will be necessary to replace Z_delta_t with its actual expression syntax. Change your expression to read as follows:

1 – (((([Fighter_Control.Position.Z,Frame+ –3] – [Fighter_Control.Position.Z])/3) + "LowCurve")/"LowCurve" + "HighCurve")

Using the following example numbers:

1 – (((([Fighter_Control.Position.Z,Frame+ –3] – [Fighter_Control.Position.Z])/3) + .9452)/(.9452 + .18715)

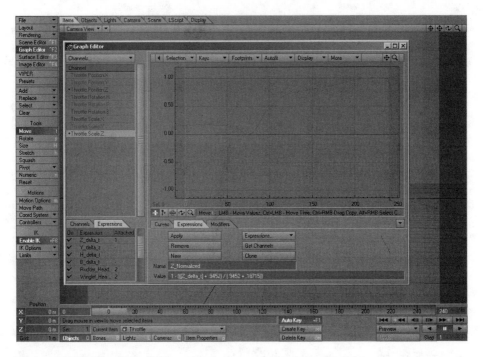

Figure 15.19   Here is the Z_Normalized expression after being flipped.

12. At this point, remove any expressions from all of the Throttle channels.

Now that Z_delta_t has been normalized, all that remains is to multiply this value by the engine volumetric's height, and the dot texture's scale.

Exercise 15.19   Applying the Expressions to the Center Exhaust Flame

1. Select the Engine_Volumetric light, and open its Properties panel. Click the Volumetric Light Options button to open its control panel.

2. Click the E beside Height to add an envelope. The Graph Editor will open.

3. Under the Expressions tab, click New to add a new expression. Name it Exhaust_Height.

4. In the Value field, enter:

Value * [Z_Normalized]

"Value" in an expression represents the normal keyframed value of that channel at that point. Because you have now multiplied our normalized Z value to the keyframed value, the exhaust flame will now reach a maximum height of 3 meters, and a minimum of 0 meters. Exactly what you want.

5. Click Apply to apply the expression to the channel.

6. Now, one more step remains. By multiplying the results of this expression by the Throttle multiplier, it will enable you to shut off the engine or ramp it past its maximum. Change your expression to read as

[Throttle.Position.Y] * (Value * [Z_Normalized])

You'll see the dotted curve flatten out at 0. That's because currently, the Throttle null is at 0,0,0.

7. In Layout, select Throttle.

8. Move it to X:0, Y:1, Z:0, and set a keyframe at frame 0.

Normally, you will want to leave the Throttle set at 1 (full blast, full automatic control). However, if you need to go beyond full blast, or below, simply move the Throttle up and down in the Y channel. Because it is a multiplier, whatever height you set the Throttle null will be multiplied by the length of the flame (see Figure 15.20). Like the control null for the landing gear, Position.Y was chosen as the control channel arbitrarily. Any channel would work.

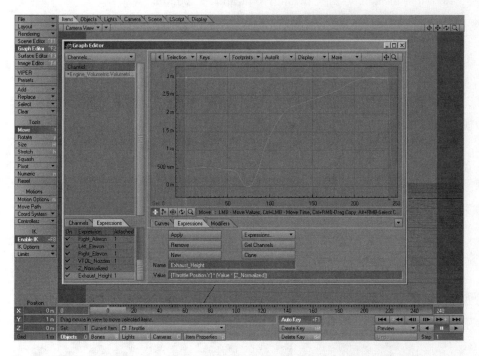

Figure 15.20   After the Throttle is set to "on"—1m in the Y channel—you will see the curve of the exhaust flame's height.

9. With the throttle set, re-open the Volumetric Options panel, and click Edit Texture.

10. Select the Dots texture from the texture list on the left.

11. Under the Scale tab, click the E button beside the Z field. This will open the Graph Editor.

12. Scale.Z should already be selected in the Curve Bin; if it is not, select it now.

13. From the Expression Tree, select Exhaust Height.

14. Under the Expressions tab, click Apply. Now the same multiplying expression you set up for the volumetric light height will scale the Dots texture as well, so that the texture always fits.

15. Close the Graph Editor, volumetric light options, and the light properties panel.

    With that completed, all that remains is to clone this light and attach it to the VTOL jets.

16. With Engine_Volumetric selected, select Add > Clone Current Item, and enter 1 for the number of clones.

17. Parent the clone light to Fighter:VTOL_Nozzles.

18. Move the light to X: 1.7525m, Y: 0 m, and Z: .100mm.

19. Create a keyframe at frame 0.

20. Open the Properties for this light. Click Volumetric Light options.

21. Change Radius to 200mm.

22. Now, clone this light.

23. Change the new cloned light's X position to −1.7525m and create a keyframe at zero (see Figure 15.21).

24. Save your scene.

Figure 15.21   Now all three engines have flames.

The final step is to animate the landing gear retraction.

Exercise 15.20   Animating the Landing Gear Retraction

1. Select the object Landing_Gear_Cycle.
2. Go to frame 40. Create a keyframe.
3. Delete the keyframe at frame 0.
4. Go to frame 70.
5. Move the object to Y: 1m, and set a keyframe (see Figure 15.22).
6. Save your scene.

Figure 15.22   Now the landing gear rises as the fighter flies away.

That's it! Now your fighter will rise off the ground, retract its gear, and fly away, all driven by the power of expressions! Create a preview and enjoy the fruits of your labors!

The Next Step

The project you've just completed is a good example of the power of expressions to greatly simplify and enhance your animations. The simplification comes from automating as many actions as possible, leaving you fewer objects to manipulate. The enhancement comes in being freed from the tedious work, to allow you to put more into your animations. It also is an example of a fairly typical setup that a technical director might run into at a production studio.

But don't think that this is the end of the animation. You should continue on from this point, fleshing it out in any way you can. Here are some suggestions:

- A camera shake as the engines run up to full power
- Lens flares in the engine nozzles
- An environment (airbase, field hangar, aircraft carrier)
- Dust and/or debris kicked up by the engines

Summary

This chapter has introduced you to the world of procedural animation. You've learned to use true expressions and their plug-in counterparts. You've seen how expressions can be used to simplify tasks that would otherwise be quite daunting, and to automate tasks that would otherwise become quite tedious. This chapter is but a scratch on the tip of the surface of a rather vast iceberg, but it should have given you a good solid understanding of the basics of expressions and procedural animation. From there, you can go on to test the boundaries of this seemingly limitless way of work. But remember, in the end, expressions are best used to make your job easier. Use the extra time they buy you to take your work to a whole new level!

Chapter 16

Nonlinear
Animation

You've heard the term. You know it's a big

deal. But what is it? Nonlinear animation in

LightWave is the ability to blend animation

motions in Layout. A common example is

to take a scene of a character walking and then perform a transition to a running character. The benefit of nonlinear animation is that you don't have to set up complex keyframing every time you animate. Instead, you can create a library of motions and use them later, just as you would a surface preset. Nonlinear animation is not just for character animation, or objects, for that matter. You can use this process on anything in your scene.

Project Overview

This chapter takes you full-speed ahead into LightWave's Motion Mixer feature (see Figure 16.1), used for nonlinear animation. Understanding how Motion Mixer works can inevitably help you when planning and executing animation.

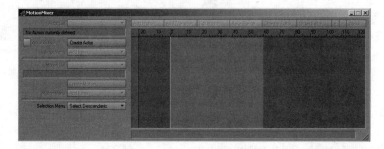

Figure 16.1   This is the Motion Mixer interface at startup. If you're familiar with nonlinear editing programs such as, in:sync's Speed Razor, Apple's Final Cut Pro, or Adobe Premiere, this timeline might look familiar to you.

The Motion Mixer timeline might look familiar if you've ever worked with nonlinear editing programs such as Adobe Premiere. However, although Adobe Premiere and others enable you to work with your video clips, Motion Mixer in LightWave lets you edit and create transitions to your animations, or better, your motions. Get it? Motion Mixer!

In this chapter, you'll learn how to begin using Motion Mixer, apply simple transitions, and set up a complex scene. Specifically, you'll learn how to do these tasks:

- Work with the Motion Mixer interface by creating an Actor and a simple transition
- Add Actors
- Add motions to the timeline
- Add transitions to motions
- Work with endomorphs in Motion Mixer

Motion Mixer

Motion Mixer was created by Mark Brown of Spatial Design (*www.spatial-design.com*). This much-needed addition to LightWave can and will help you expedite the creation of not only complex motions, but *any* motion. It begins by defining an Actor. All an Actor is to Motion Mixer is an object, light, or camera. The Actor contains Items, such as child objects in a hierarchy or bones.

Creating a Basic Motion Mixer Scene

For the first exercise, you'll need nothing more than a few simple objects, which are provided for you on the book's CD. The exercise will help you understand how to set up Motion Mixer and visualize how it interacts with the items in your Layout scene.

Exercise 16.1   Setting Up a Base Scene

The basis of Motion Mixer allows you to take one motion, such as a rotating finger, record it, and apply it somewhere else. You can do this with a quick cut or with a transition—much as you can with a nonlinear video editing program. What's more, you don't need to re-create keyframes for certain objects. One motion can be used over and over. The following exercise gets you going right away by showing you how to set up a base scene.

1. Open LightWave's Layout. Load the HandBone_Weighted scene from the book's CD.

   This scene is from a tutorial in Chapter 11, "Character Construction," that demonstrates weight maps. It also will serve well in this situation to demonstrate Motion Mixer.

2. Open Motion Mixer by clicking the button in the top left of Layout.

   Figure 16.2 shows the scene loaded. Notice that Layout has had its window scaled up to make room for Motion Mixer. For best results, set up your system like this when using Motion Mixer so that you can see everything you're doing.

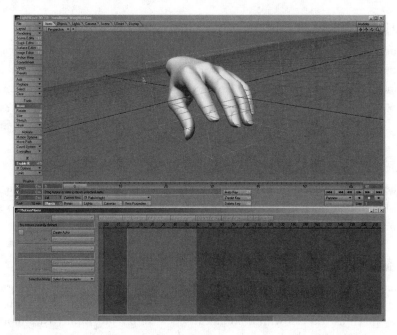

Figure 16.2   The weighted hand scene from Chapter 11 is a great place to start using Motion Mixer. The interfaces here have been adjusted so that all panels are visible.

3. In Layout, select the hand object. In Motion Mixer, click Create Actor, as shown in Figure 16.3.

Figure 16.3   Create Actor, the button at the left of the Motion Mixer interface, is the one you need to click to get the ball rolling.

4. In the panel that appears, name the Actor Hand (see Figure 16.4). If you had a more complex scene, such as a full body, you could give the Actor a more specific name, such as Right Hand or Left Hand. Click OK to close the panel.

Figure 16.4   Once you click the Create Actor button, you give your Actor a name—in this case, Hand.

Note

The Set Pose Frame value in the Actor Name field is for telling Motion Mixer the frame number at which the Actor object is in its rest position. In most cases, this will be zero.

At the top left of the Motion Mixer interface, you'll see your new Actor name. As you create other Actors, their names will be here as well. For now, you only need one Actor. Other Actors might be a body, other hands, or feet, for example.

5. Go to Layout, and select the base bone of the hand. In Motion Mixer, select Add Items from the Actor menu. This associates the bone item with the Actor that you named Hand, as shown in Figure 16.5.

Figure 16.5   Because the hand object has bones associated with it, which will be used to create motion, you need to add these items to the Actor menu.

6. Back in Layout, select the middle_finger_2 bone, and also select Add Items from the Actor menu.

7. Add one more item, the middle_finger_3 bone. Select it in Layout, and again, select Add Items from the Actor menu.

8. In Layout, select the hand object and rotate (**y**) it on its bank about 120 degrees. Create a keyframe at 60 to lock it in place.

9. Back in Motion Mixer, click the Create Motion button. In the panel that appears, name the new motion Bank_Rotate. If you like, you can be more descriptive by naming the motion BaseBone_Bank or something similar. This is a simple scene, so it's really not necessary to be more descriptive (see Figure 16.6). Be sure to save the scene!

Figure 16.6   Name your motion appropriately for its action.

There are a few settings in the Create Motion panel of which you should be aware:

• The Create Motion From selection can be set to Actor Items or Selected Items.

Choosing Actor Items tells Motion Mixer to take into account all that is within the Actor. For example, later you'll rotate a bone to bend the finger within the hand. Choosing to Create Motion From Actor Items for this bone would tell Motion Mixer to record the motion not only for the bone's movement in Layout, but also for the position of the Actor, or the hand. If, however, you choose Selected Items for the finger bone movement, Motion Mixer pays attention only to the motion of that bone.

In this exercise, and much of the work you'll do in Motion Mixer, you'll choose Actor Items.

• The next selection shows the listing Select XChannels. If you choose this, Motion Mixer allows you to select a channel for motion. Rotation channels, however, are not included in this list.

- The Start Frame and End Frame areas allow you to set the length of the motion you are creating. You don't have to change this here, because you can easily scale your motions in the Motion Mixer timeline.

- Lastly, the Clear Channels selection removes the channels of motion in Layout. You would choose this for things like full characters. For example, later in this chapter, you'll take an existing motion-captured walk cycle and record its motions. Using Clear Channels allows you to record the walk motion, but then be able to reposition the character's arm to create a wave motion in Layout. If you do not select Clear Channels, the motion will still be recorded in Motion Mixer; however, the items in Layout will still be moving, making it difficult to create and record new motions, such as an arm waving, because there are still existing keyframes.

  Motion Mixer will override your Layout motions when active. By leaving this unchecked, however, your Layout Motions will still exist, allowing you to create further motions for use in Motion Mixer. Generally, you'd uncheck this in much more complicated scenes in which objects and characters are performing a wide range of motions.

10. In Layout, select the middle_finger_2 bone. Rotate (y) it about 90 degrees on its Pitch, and create a keyframe at 60.

11. In Motion Mixer, click Create Motion, and name this object Finger_Bend, or something similar (see Figure 16.7). Then, be sure to choose Create Motion from Selected Items in the Create Motion panel. Otherwise, because this is a bone, when it is rotated it will affect surrounding transitions, such as the Bank_Rotate of the hand.

Figure 16.7   One more motion is created for the middle finger bone, with the Create Motion From option set to Selected Items.

You now have two motions for the Hand Actor in the Motion Mixer scene: Bank_Rotate and Finger_Bend. The reason you created these motions is so that you can edit the motions in Motion Mixer. You also can go back to the Hand object and rotate it on its pitch to create an additional motion, bank the bone, and so on.

Actors contain motions. Get it? And remember, bones, lights, cameras—all of them can be Actors as well.

12. Now you can begin having some fun. Drag the Layout time slider to frame 0. Because the Actor Active button is checked in the Motion Mixer panel, your Layout motions are turned off. Motion Mixer has taken control.

13. In Motion Mixer, select the Hand Actor. Any motions you've created will appear in the Motion List (see Figure 16.8). Right now, there are two motions in the list, so first select the Bank_Rotate motion.

Figure 16.8   When an Actor is selected, its available motions are visible in the Motion List.

14. With Bank_Rotate as the selected motion for the Hand Actor, click the Add Motion button above the timeline, and then click in the top bar of the timeline to add the motion, as shown in Figure 16.9.

Don't worry about precisely lining up the motion in the timeline, you can do that at any point. Just click in the top row and the motion will be added. You can now drag the motion back and forth, and adjust the timing! You can also click directly on the end of the motion clip and instantly scale the timing.

Figure 16.9   Once you've set up an Actor with its motions, you can click Add Motion and then click in the timeline to add the motion.

15. From the Motion List, select the Finger_Bend motion. Click Add Motion at the top of the mixer panel, and then click in the bar below the Bank Rotate motion, as Figure 16.10 shows. This bar, if you look very closely, is 01. The top line is 00 in the timeline.

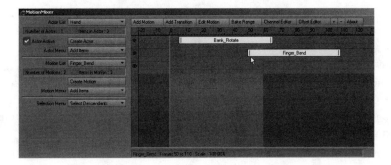

Figure 16.10   Now that you have made motions, you can simply click and add them to the timeline, just like a clip of video.

16. In the Motion Mixer panel, slowly drag the mouse in the numbered bar above the timeline, and you'll see your motions in Layout. Simpler items will update faster.

17. Select Bank_Rotate motion in the timeline. Click the Add Transition button at the top of the panel, and then click the Finger_Bend motion. A small blue bar will be added between the two motions, as shown in Figure 16.11.

Note

If you've ever worked with a nonlinear video editing system, you're familiar with having a "bin" of your clips, such as video clips, audio, or text. You take a clip from the bin and add it to the timeline for editing. In Motion Mixer, think of the Motion List as your bin. Select a motion from the bin, add it to the timeline, and edit.

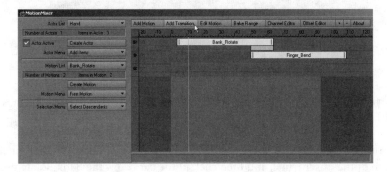

Figure 16.11   Once you place motions in the timeline, you can create a transition from one to the other.

18. Click the small dark line on the end of the Finger_Bend clip in the timeline, and drag it to the left. You're now scaling the timing of the motion. You'll notice that the transition will adjust accordingly.

19. In the top numbered area of the timeline, click and drag slowly through the clips. You'll see the hand rotate, and then the finger will begin to bend (see Figure 16.12). You'll also notice that once you extend behind the clip in the timeline, the hand jumps back to its original state. Read on to find out how to adjust the end behavior of a motion clip.

What you've done here is the basis for any Motion Mixer scene you will create. In review:

- Create an Actor for a Layout item.
- Add any items to that Actor, such as a bone.
- Keyframe a motion in Layout for any of the items.
- Create a Motion Mixer motion for the movement in Layout.
- Add the motion to the Motion Mixer timeline.
- Make transitions, and adjust.

Figure 16.12   With two motions and a transition in place, dragging the timeline in Motion Mixer shows the blending of two motions in Layout.

Adjusting a Motion Mixer Scene

You've set up a basic Motion Mixer scene and have seen how easy it is to add motions. But when you study the motion you created, you can see that there are subtleties that can be added. This section guides you through adjusting the motions you've created.

Exercise 16.2   Editing Motion Mixer Variables

The first exercise got you going with a Motion Mixer scene. It was simple, but effective. Control is what it's all about, and there's still more to explore. This next exercise shows you how you can use Motion Mixer to adjust the motions you've created.

1. Load the MM_Hand scene from the book's CD. This is the same scene created in Exercise 16.1.

2. Open Motion Mixer if it's not already open, and take a look at the timeline. The transition (the area between the two motions) is as long as the Finger_Bend clip (see Figure 16.13).

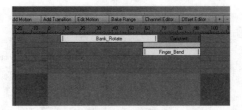

Figure 16.13   The motions loaded in Motion Mixer have a transition, but how do you edit it?

Perhaps you want this transition to be only 10 frames. What do you do? Although you can click and drag an actual motion to quickly adjust its timing and in and out points, you can't do that with a transition.

3. Right-click (hold the Apple key on the Mac) the transition. The Graph Editor opens with the transition curve loaded. Figure 16.14 shows the Graph Editor open.

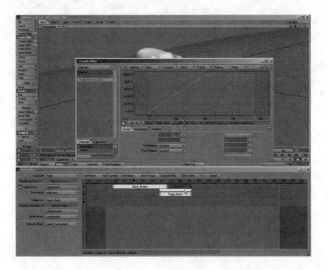

Figure 16.14   Right-clicking a transition opens the Graph Editor, allowing you to edit the transition.

If you've read through Chapter 5 "LightWave 7 Graphic Editor," you'll know about all the things you can do to a curve. In Figure 16.14, you can see that the curve value is from 0 to 100. You need to leave these keys here for the transition to work properly, but you can add more keys. Adding more will give you control over when the transition takes place and how long it is.

4. Create two additional keyframes at 10 and 30. Set the value at 10 to 0 percent to match frame 0. And set the value at frame 30 to match frame 100.

5. Hold the Shift key and double-click in the Curve window to select all keyframes. Set Tension to 1.0 to make the transition ease in and ease out. Figure 16.15 shows the new curve.

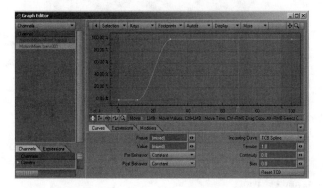

Figure 16.15   You can directly edit the transition curve in the Graph Editor, and even add new keyframes.

6. If you play through the Motion Mixer timeline at this point, you'll see the transition happen between 10 and 30 percent of the way through the existing transition. Although the transition representation in the timeline appears to be the same, and the transition happens originally at frames 60 through 90, the motion within it, now from the Graph Editor, works from 63 through 69.

7. Now go one step further and edit the timing of Bank_Rotate. In the Motion Mixer timeline, right-click the Bank_Rotate motion. The Motion Properties appear. Here, you can scale the motion, quickly set a start and end time, and add pre and post behaviors. Set the Local Start Frame to 30, and the Local End Frame to 40.

8. Set the Pre Behavior to [none], and the Post Behavior should be set to Constant. This will keep the motion's last frame. Figure 16.16 shows the panel.

Figure 16.16   Right-clicking a motion in the timeline opens the motion controls, allowing you to edit timing and behaviors.

9. In the timeline, click and drag the Finger_Bend motion so that the start of it is positioned at frame 30. You'll see the transition adjust along with it. Click and drag on the area between the dashed line and the right end of the Finger_Bend clip, and drag it in to frame 60, as shown in Figure 16.17.

 Tip
You can simply right-click and drag on a clip to change its length numerically.

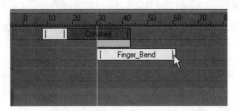

Figure 16.17   Clicking and dragging the space between the end of the clip and the dashed line lets you scale or stretch a clip.

10. If you drag the timeline slider now, you'll see the hand rotate within 10 frames, and then transition to the finger bending. However, if you look at the timeline, the post behavior of the Rotate_Bank motion ends before the Finger_Bend motion finishes. The result is the hand jumping back to its original position.

11. Grab the end of the Rotate_Bank clip and drag it out to frame 60 so that it matches the Finger_Bend end. Figure 16.18 shows the new position.

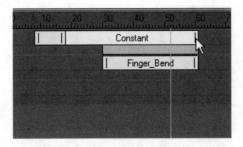

Figure 16.18   Although you set the Post Behavior of the Rotate_Bank to Constant, you need to tell that constant clip to live as long as the existing motions live.

12. Now drag across the timeline to play the motion and you'll see that the hand rotates and stays rotated through the duration of the finger bending. Save your scene.

Using Endomorphs with Motion Mixer

You might be wondering whether you can use endomorphs in Motion Mixer, and the answer is yes! You've seen how useful Motion Mixer is to blend, scale, and transition between motions, but you can do the same for endomorphs. For example, a character might have a number of different facial positions, as well as some lip sync action happening. Although the MorphMixer allows you a certain amount of flexibility, the Motion Mixer will take your control to the next level.

Exercise 16.3   Animating Endomorphs with Motion Mixer

This next exercise will show you how to take a 3D head object that has endomorphs made of different facial expressions. Using Motion Mixer, you can blend between those various expressions.

1. Load the HeadMorphs_Setup scene from the book's CD. This scene uses the head model from Chapter 12, "Deformations and Movements." Open the Object Properties panel, and the Motion Mixer panel. Figure 16.19 shows those panels open, along with the Spreadsheet Scene Manager.

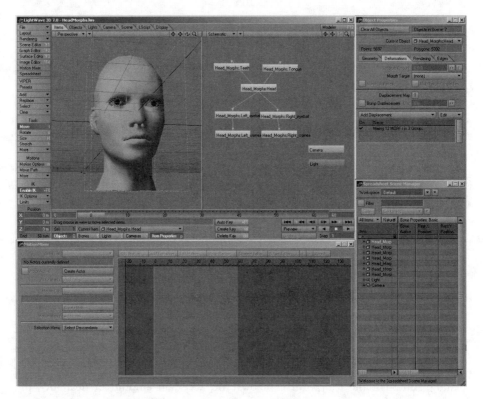

Figure 16.19   Using a 1280×1024 resolution, the various panels for the project are opened and arranged. The HeadMorphs_Setup scene has been loaded.

2. Select the HeadMorphs:Head object in Layout, and in the Motion Mixer, click Create Actor. Name this, appropriately, Head.

3. From the Object Properties panel, click the Deformations tab, and double-click the Mixing 12 Morphs listing to open the MorphMixer. Click the Face tab.

4. In the Layout timeline, bring the frame slider to frame 20. Then, back in the MorphMixer panel, move the Happy morph slider to 100 percent, as shown in Figure 16.20.

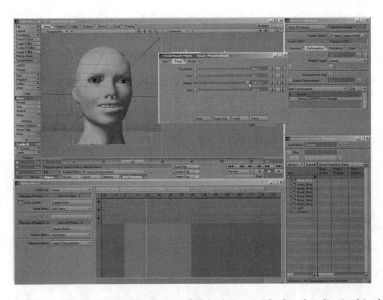

Figure 16.20   Just as you created keyframes for the bones in the hand earlier in this chapter, you need to create a keyframe for any of the endomorphs.

5. In the Motion Mixer, click Create Motion, and name the motion Happy. Set the last frame to 20. A motion of the Happy endomorph is now in Motion Mixer (see Figure 16.21). Click OK to close the panel.

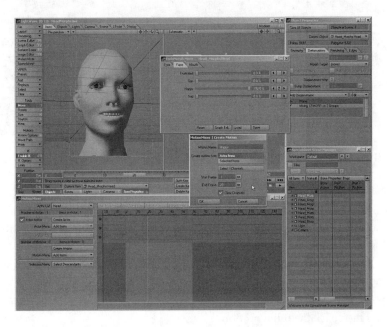

Figure 16.21   To keep things organized, create motions using the same names as their counterparts.

6. Back in Layout, select the Eyes tab of the MorphMixer. Bring the Blink slider to 100 percent. Create a motion for it in Motion Mixer.

7. Do the same for the Frustrated slider under the Face tab.

   You should now have three motions in Motion Mixer: Happy, Blink, and Frustrated.

8. Select Happy from the Motion List. Click Add Motion, and click in the timeline to add it to row 00. Figure 16.22 shows the motion added.

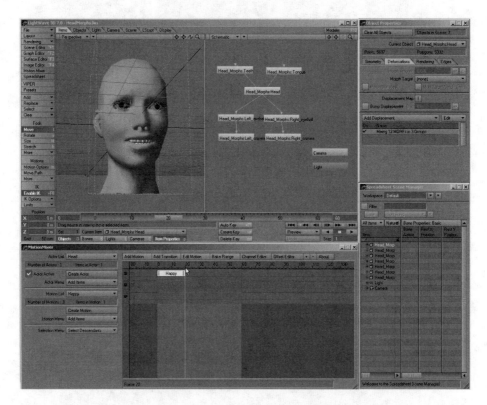

Figure 16.22   If you drag through the timeline, you'll see the smile appear on the character.

9. Select the Frustrated motion, and add it to row 01 of the timeline.

10. Finally, add the Blink motion to row 03 of the timeline. If you want to add more motions, you need to add more rows. Do this by clicking the plus (+) button at the top right of the Motion Mixer interface.

11. Select the Happy motion, click Add Transition, and then click the Frustrated motion.

12. Make sure that the Frustrated motion is highlighted and select Add Transition, and then click the Blink motion.

13. Drag the Frustrated motion so that the Happy motion overlaps it. Do the same for the Blink so that the Frustrated overlaps as well, as shown in Figure 16.23.

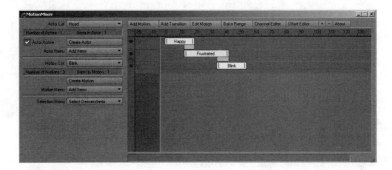

Figure 16.23   Two transitions are added to the three motions, and they are brought closer together so they blend.

14. Drag through the Motion Mixer timeline from above the motions, and you'll see the morphs changing. Remember to drag slowly and patiently so that your system has time to catch up and calculate.

15. But take a look at what happens when the blink morph occurs. The face went from Happy, to Frustrated, to a Blink. You would think that the frustrated face would stay looking frustrated, only with a blink, right? Instead, the face goes back to a neutral position. By default, Motion Mixer uses the absolute value of a motion, including an endomorph. You also can add some post behaviors to the motions by right-clicking them.

If you want Motion Mixer to pick up where the previous motion left off, you can use the Offset Editor.

16. To do this, select the Blink motion, and click the Offset Editor, found atop the Motion Mixer interface. You'll see the main object listed that contains the morphs. Click the Offset From list, and you'll see the motions you've created. Select Frustrated, because this is the motion preceding the Blink in the timeline. Set the Offset Type to Relative (see Figure 16.24).

17. Drag through your timeline. You'll see the face become happy, then blend to frustrated, stay frustrated, and blink.

18. Go one step further and select the Happy motion from the Motion List on the left side of the Motion Mixer interface. From the Motion menu just below, select Copy Motion, and name it Happy2.

19. Before you add this to the timeline, add another mixer row by clicking the small plus (+) at the top right of the panel next to the About button. Press it, and another row will be added to the timeline. Conversely, clicking the minus (–) will remove a row.

20. Click Add Motion and add the Happy2 motion to the time-line just after the Blink motion. Select the Blink motion, click Add Transition, and then select the Happy2 motion in the timeline. Your blink is now over and the face is once again happy.

Figure 16.24   Using the Offset Editor, you can tell one motion to pick up where another left off. This is great for mixing endomorphs.

As always, you can tweak and adjust and scale and experiment with the settings and values. But the goal here is to show you how the interface works and introduce you to the possibilities you can create.

Full Body Motions

There's one more area you should know about when working with Motion Mixer, and that's how to work with full figures. Although the techniques are the same as described in the rest of this chapter, it's always good to see how things are done. For example, suppose that you're animating a marching soldier. At certain intervals, the soldier needs to turn his head and look to his left for a certain amount of time. This would need to be repeated throughout the animation. Instead of keyframing the action, you can set it up once and use Motion Mixer to do the work for you. What if you have a walking character and at certain intervals, the character needs to raise his arms? Read on.

Exercise 16.4   Creating Full Body Motion Animations

This exercise will take a walking bone structure and show you how to blend and change the character's arms.

1. In Layout, load the DudeWalk scene from the book's CD. Open the Scene Editor, and select all of the bones. Open Motion Mixer. Click Create Actor and name the Actor Walk (see Figure 16.25). This adds all the bones as items to the Walk Actor.

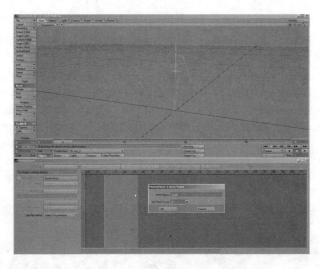

Figure 16.25   An Actor is created for the entire bone structure.

2. Back in the Scene Editor, select all of bones again, and then in the Motion Mixer, choose Create Motion. This will make one motion of all the selected motions. This looping walk cycle will now be easily editable in Motion Mixer.

3. If you drag through Layout's timeline, you'll see that there's no motion. Motion Mixer has taken over. In Motion Mixer, select Add Motion from the top of the timeline, and add the Walk motion to row 00 (see Figure 16.26).

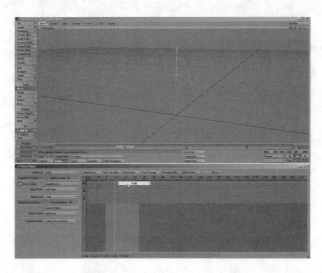

Figure 16.26   All the bone motions are recorded as a single motion and are then added to Motion Mixer's timeline.

4. Drag through the timeline in Motion Mixer, and you'll see the character walk.

5. Save the scene! Then in Motion Mixer, uncheck the Actor Active button on the left. This will reset the bone motions in Layout.

6. Now in Layout, go to frame 20. Select the R_Shoulder bone. Rotate the bone upward slightly, about 30 degrees. Then, select the right-upper arm bone (R_Upper_Ar) and rotate it into a waving position, about –20 degrees for the Heading, –16 for the Pitch, and –100 for the Bank, as shown in Figure 16.27. Remember to create a keyframe for each bone you reposition at frame 20. You also can try creating keyframes for the child bones of the arm a frame or two later, at, say 22. This will give a little more fluidity to the arm motion.

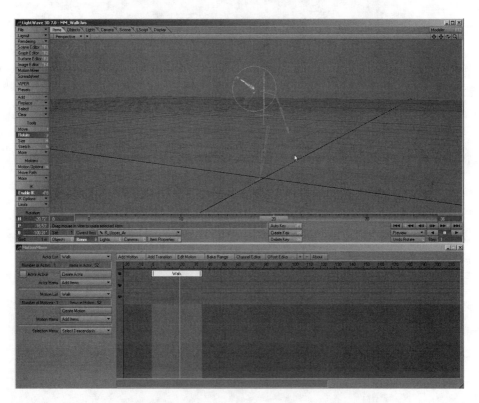

Figure 16.27   Once the bones' motions are added in Motion Mixer and the Actor Active is off, you can create additional motions.

7. Select all the bones of the right arm. You can easily do this through the Scene Editor. Once selected, choose Create Motion in Motion Mixer and name the motion Arm Wave. Make sure that the Create Motion From selection is set to Actor Items. Then add the motion to the timeline at about frame 30. Figure 16.28 shows the selections.

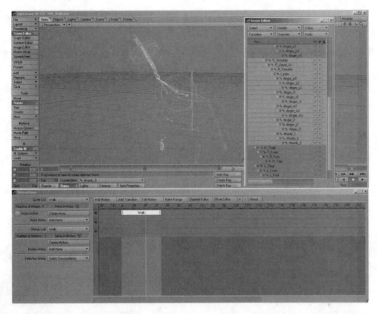

Figure 16.28   The bones of the right arm are selected in the Scene Editor, rotations are set, and a motion is created for them in Motion Mixer.

8. Make sure that Actor Active is checked on. Drag through the timeline from above the motions, and you'll see the walk motion, which then simply changes to the wave motion. There's no transition.

   Two things need to happen here. First, you need to turn off the other bones that aren't used for the wave motion. The next step is to create a transition.

9. Select the Arm_Wave motion in the timeline, and click the Channel Editor button. Here, you can turn any channel on or off. Figure 16.29 shows the panel.

Figure 16.29   The Channel Editor lets you turn off any channels for the motions you've created.

10. Starting from the left of the panel, select the Arm_Wave motion. Then to the right, under Motion Items, uncheck every item that is not part of the right arm, such as the neck, head, left shoulder, and so on. If you choose Selected Items when you create a motion, you may not need to use this panel.

11. You can even go a step further and select the motion item you are using, and turn off individual channels you won't need, such as Scale. For now, select the Walk motion in the timeline, click Add Transition, and then click the Arm_Wave to create the transition.

12. Now drag through the timeline. You'll see that by the time the wave happens, the walk stops. Uh-oh! Right-click the Walk motion and set Post Behavior to Repeat. Because the walk cycle was already created to loop perfectly over 36 frames, the repeat post behavior will work just fine (see Figure 16.30).

13. In the timeline, click the dash at the right side of the Walk's repeat motion and drag it out until it meets the end of the Arm_Wave motion.

14. Finally, select the Walk motion from the Motion List at the left of the panel and open the Motion Menu and select Copy Motion. Name the new motion Walk2.

Figure 16.30 Make sure the Walk motion is set to Repeat for Post Behavior.

15. Add the Walk2 motion to row 02 of the timeline, and transition to it from the Arm_Wave. Extend the Walk2 with a Post Behavior of Repeat, and drag that out a few seconds. The transition should create a smooth blend of the Arm_Wave coming down back into the walk cycle. If the arm suddenly jumps, adjust the transition to encompass more of the Arm_Wave. Figure 16.31 shows the final timeline. Remember to add some Post Behavior to the arm, something like Constant, so the arm will stay in the air as it waves.

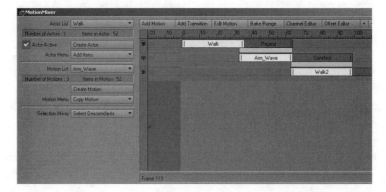

Figure 16.31 The figure now walks throughout the timeline, but in the middle it waves its arm. Simple, but effective!

From this point on, you can go further and add a head turn, a different walk style, a stop, a turn, whatever motion you'd like. Here are a few points you should keep in mind when working with Motion Mixer:

- The best course of action when working with Motion Mixer is to have a scene already set up from which all your motions are created. (This is what you did in the last exercise.)

- Add only the items that will be animated. Leave out any items that are controlled or driven by Inverse Kinematics (IK) or expressions.

- Use the Channel Editor to switch off channels that do not get animated. For example, in a character very rarely is any scaling animation done, so you can switch off all the scale channels for each item. Setting the Actor up this way is beneficial if you plan to do a lot of animation for a character. Switching off channels reduces the amount of calculations Motion Mixer performs and therefore increases performance, decreases memory usage, and reduces the size of saved motion files.

- Once you have a scene you like, you can use it as a starting point for your animations. When you've made another animation with new motions, open Motion Mixer and create a motion and then save it to disk. Do the same for subsequent animations. You'll soon have a library of motions on disk that you can load back into Motion Mixer by using the Motion menu; you then can add the motions to the timeline as needed.

- A motion does not need to contain all the items in an Actor. For example, you can create an animation of your character making a fist. Before making the motion, select only the bones in the hand that are animated, and in the Create Motion panel click Selected Items. This will create a motion containing only those bones that are needed to perform the action. This motion can then be added to the timeline below another motion and transitions then can be added so that the character makes a fist while walking, for example.

- Try saving different motions from different scenes. You can save the walk cycle example used in this scene and combine it later with a run cycle. When you load the motion from the Motion menu, a requester will appear asking you to assign each item motion to the current Actor. Because of this, it's useful to keep the same bone and body structure throughout your characters if possible. This will help make assigning preexisting motions much easier.

- Remember that you can use any item in Layout to create motions in Motion Mixer, not just bones. You can make a character spin or jump and have those as motions in conjunction with a walk cycle. In addition, you can select Bake Range within Motion Mixer to bake or "record" the motion you've mixed in Motion Mixer to the character in Layout. The benefit of this is that your mixed motions are applied to your Layout item, eliminating the need to have Motion Mixer running. Try it out!

The Next Step

There are many ways you can use Motion Mixer in your animations. The foremost is for character animation. Character animation can be tedious, as any animator can tell you. But by using Motion Mixer, not only can you save and reuse motions, but you also can control their timing and execution with the click of a mouse. Load the example scenes from the exercises in this chapter and study them, expanding on them. From there, create your own Motion Mixer animations to get the feel of it. Start with simple motions, even on a camera or light in your scene. Remember that Motion Mixer also can change motions in lights as well, so try that out! Before long, you'll be using Motion Mixer as part of your daily animation toolbox.

Summary

This chapter guided you through the setup of basic Motion Mixer nonlinear animation techniques. From here, you learn how to add more complex motions and edit them. It's your goal to use the power of this killer addition to LightWave 7. Enjoy it, because it is much fun! Now move on to Chapter 17, "Broadcast-Style Animation," and learn how to make dazzling text and backgrounds in LightWave.

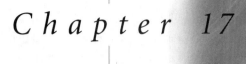

C h a p t e r   1 7

Broadcast-Style Animation

Anyone will tell you that the bread-and-butter animation jobs are flying logos. Although you might wince at the mere mention of the term, flying-logo animations *do* pay the bills in many animation studios around the globe. The task, however, can easily be misconstrued as "simple" or non-professional work; but you can rest assured that there are many companies and independent animators making a very good living creating these types of animations. Not every job is meant for broadcast television; there is a significant market for logos in corporate and industrial video environments. This chapter focuses on broadcast-style animations for television and corporate video.

Project Overview

This chapter takes you full-speed ahead into a complete broadcast-style animation that goes far beyond the typical chrome flying logo you might be used to. LightWave has a powerful rendering engine and tons of texture tools that will make your job easier, especially when you are creating logos. Figure 17.1 shows a still frame from the finished animation that you will create.

Figure 17.1   You can create a rich, colorful, broadcast-style animation using LightWave and following the steps in this chapter. Be sure to view the color figures for this chapter on the book's CD-ROM.

In this chapter, you'll learn how to model text and elements that can give your animations depth and character—all in LightWave. No one cares to see only a simple flying logo anymore, so it's your job to stay ahead of the curve. To do so, this chapter also instructs you on techniques used by professionals. You'll put things in constant motion, not simply move one text object from point A to point B. This chapter gives you the knowledge and, hopefully, the excitement to create stunning broadcast-style graphics and animations. It covers the following:

- Modeling text and elements for broadcast animation
- Creating a mood or feeling with color and style
- Using transparency, glow, and bloom enhancements
- Creating continuous and multiple motions

Broadcast-Style Graphics

News programs and entertainment television shows have one thing in common: broadcast-style graphics and animations. Such graphics and animations are bold, colorful, and downright cool to see. Creating graphics and animations for broadcast can be fun and lucrative. Major television markets have high budgets for animation packages, which consist of a main title and bumpers—short versions of the main title that are used to go in and out of commercial breaks. These packages also can include variations on the main title theme for weather segments and news segments for news television stations. Animation packages must represent the feeling and style the broadcaster is trying to convey. This could be serious and strong, classy and cute, or the best way—sharp! These treatment styles also work very well for corporate or industrial video. You can even use these methods to enhance wedding videos—the choice is yours.

Often, text and logo animation jobs are done in multiple passes and composited together in programs like Adobe's After Effects, NewTek's Aura, or more expensive systems like Discreet's Flame. But you know as well as the rest of us that those other tools are not always available. This chapter will show you how you can create moving backgrounds, animated text, and 3D elements all in a single program—LightWave. Pay those bills!

Creating a Broadcast-Style Treatment

Let's take an example. Suppose that for this project, your client wants you to create a bold and colorful animation treatment that represents a proud, growing news station. The term *treatment* refers to a full set of animations, such as a broadcast or corporate package. This animation treatment will include moving backgrounds and title and segue animations. The segue animation will be used as an opening to the news program, from which the logo spins around, revealing a white mask that the technical director will "key out" as a window to the news set. Another use for these animations is that they can be transferred to a nonlinear editor and blended together as added elements.

The company's colors are blue, black, and white. This color selection may feel limiting at first, but you can find creative ways around that. Blue is always the best color to work with, especially when it comes to graphics for videotape. It is not really a "hot" color like red, which tends to bleed or smear when recorded to tape. Blue doesn't smear when recorded to tape, and it is comfortable and soothing to look at. The client was smart in color choices when it comes to white and blue, but the black may pose a problem for seeing the depth of a 3D element. Nevertheless, it's up to you to bring it to life—time to be an animator.

Exercise 17.1   Creating the Main Identity Logo—Importing EPS Adobe Illustrator Files

Broadcast treatments vary animations based on a theme or an initial animation. This exercise shows you how to begin creating the elements for that main title animation. Follow these steps:

1. Open LightWave's Modeler.

   The main logo is a disc with three letters, abc, in the middle. Not too complex; but it needs to be exact and it must look cool in an animation. Figure 17.2 shows the logo you will create.

Figure 17.2   A simple logo is one of the focal points of this broadcast-style treatment. The elements you add will enhance it.

2. Click the File drop-down button, click Import, and then select EPSF_Loader. This will call up the encapsulated PostScript file (EPSF) importer, as shown in Figure 17.3.

Here, you can import vector artwork from programs such as Adobe Illustrator.

> **Note**
>
> You can use the most current version of Adobe Illustrator with LightWave. You will, however, need to export your Illustrator art to Adobe Illustrator Version 6 for reliable importing into LightWave. Avoid files with gradient colors for best results. Big thanks go out to Deuce (Jack Bennett II) of Creative Imagineering, Inc., for converting the logo in this exercise.

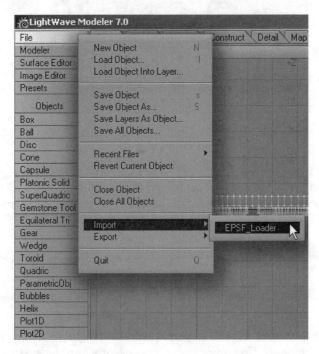

Figure 17.3   The EPSF_Loader will allow you to load and convert EPS and AI (Adobe Illustrator) files into LightWave 3D objects.

The hard part is over. Whew! That's a few hours you can bill your client right there! Just kidding—the idea here is to remember that this is so easy, you don't want your client to know. You client should always know that 3D logo animation is a complex, time-consuming art form that can't be rushed. While you're explaining that to your client, you can have this logo imported and built in no time. Read on!

3. Using the EPSF_Loader is simple, but there are a few things you should know. With the panel open, click the triangle to the right of the EPSF File listing. Do this to select the file to load. You can choose the abc_logo_6.ai file on the book's CD-ROM.

4. Set the Curve Division Level at the top of the EPSF_Loader to Fine for more detail (see Figure 17.4). For the Convert To listing, select Closed Polygons & PolyLines. This will turn your Illustrator file into the proper polygons ready for extrusion. Other choices are Spline Curve for additional manipulation, Closed Polygons, or Line Polygons.

Figure 17.4   Set the Curve Division Level to Fine for more detail.

5. Leave Auto Centering on. Scale can remain at the default 0.01.

6. The Auto Axis Drill setting is off by default. Click this on, and click OK. The abc logo is imported (see Figure 17.5). The process might take a few moments to complete.

Note

When working with imported Illustrator files, it's a good idea to save the import as is. Then once the object is separated into layers and the necessary holes are cut, save a flat version for use later in Layout.

You can see how easy it is to import artwork into LightWave, especially logos. Suppose, however, that your client wants each of the abc letters to be animated separately. What do you do?

7. Press the Delete key to get rid of this imported logo. Open the EPSF_Loader again (choose File, Import). Your previous settings should still be selected, so just uncheck the Auto Axis Drill. Click OK.

Your object now loads without the abc letters being cut out, as you see in Figure 17.6.

Figure 17.5   Importing the abc Illustrator file with Auto Axis Drill brings the logo in clean and flat, with the abc letters automatically cut out from the center.

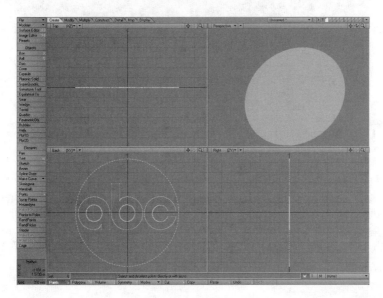

Figure 17.6   Importing the Illustrator file with the Auto Axis Drill off leaves the center letters as separate polygons.

Although it might look as though you have one flat object, the abc letters are really separate polygons, so don't judge the object by looking at Perspective view.

Notice that you can see the abc letters at the bottom left of the Back view. With these letters being separate objects, you cannot only cut out the center of the disc, but have the letters available for animation as well.

8. In the Perspective view, hold the Shift key and click to select the abc letters, totaling five polygons, as shown in Figure 17.7. (The abc letters, and the center of the a and b, make up five polygons.) Selecting the polygons might be a little tricky at first because you can't quite see the separation of the polygons. If this is difficult for you, you can select the polygons in one of the wireframe quad views.

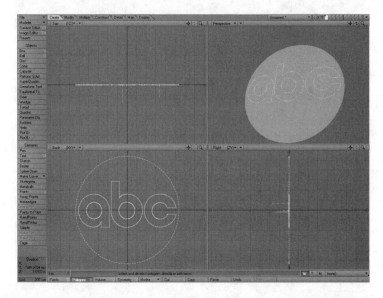

Figure 17.7   Although the Perspective view shows what looks like one big flat polygon, the abc letters are actually separate polygons.

If you try selecting in a wireframe view, however, you can't click directly on the face of the letter. You need to click and select the edge of the letter. Doing this might accidentally select the round disc behind the letters. If that happens, simply deselect the disc, hold the Shift key to continue in Selection mode, and select the next letters. Repeat if necessary.

9. With the abc polygons selected, cut (press x) and paste (press v) them into a new layer.

10. Now select the two polygons that make up the center of the letters a and b, as shown in Figure 17.8.

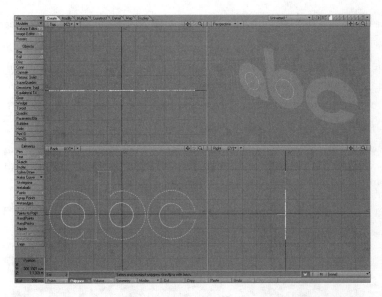

Figure 17.8   Select the two polygons that make up the center of the letters a and b so that you can use them as cutting tools.

With the two polygons selected, cut (x) and paste (v) them into a new layer. Now make the abc letters a foreground layer, leaving the two center polygons you just cut and pasted in a background layer, as Figure 17.9 shows.

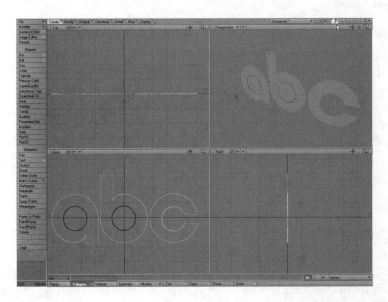

Figure 17.9   The two polygons are cut and pasted into a new layer, and then that layer is selected as a background layer. You can see the two polygons in the background as black outlines.

Exercise 17.2   Cutting Out a Background Object from the Foreground Object

Now it's time to cut the background object out of the foreground object, a step for which you will use LightWave's Template Drill command. Before you use the Template Drill command or any Boolean operation, make sure that the main object is in a foreground layer. Objects used to "cut" another object should reside in a background layer. Just follow these steps:

1. With the abc letters in a foreground layer and the a and b center polygons in a background layer, click the Multiply tab and select the Drill command (or Shift+r) to call up the Template Drill tool, as Figure 17.10 shows.

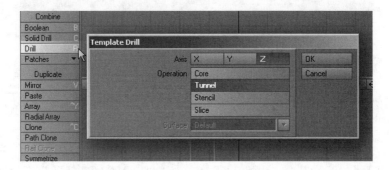

Figure 17.10   The Template Drill tool uses the background polygons to cut holes into the foreground polygons.

2. In the Template Drill panel, select Z for the axis because the direction of the operation should be performed on the visible axis—take a look at the Back view looking down the Z. If you look at the Right view, the object is flat.

3. Select Tunnel for the Operation setting. The Template Drill tool will take the background polygons and tunnel them through the foreground polygons. Click OK. Figure 17.11 shows the result of the Template Drill operation.

    If needed, you can subtract the abc letters from the disc in layer 1 using a Template Drill. However, for this project, the abc letters will be extruded and placed on the disc in layer one, so the operation is not needed.

4. At this point, delete the polygons used to cut the holes in the letters a and b. These are no longer needed.

5. Save your object!

    Next, you'll extrude the object to give it depth. This should be saved as another version. You want to be sure that at any point in the creation process, you can return to a previous version of the object if you need to. Better safe than sorry, as Mom always says!

Figure 17.11   A tunnel Template Drill operation cuts the background polygons from the foreground polygons.

Now you're ready to extrude and bevel the logo. But first, here are a few things you should know about Template Drill and its family of Boolean operations.

Under the Multiply tab, you'll see a listing of tools labeled Combine. These tools are all similar to the Template Drill tool you just used. The following list gives you an overview of these tools:

- Boolean is used like Template Drill, but it is meant for full 3D objects, such as cutting a ball out of a cow. (Why you would do that, who knows? But it's nice to know you could if you wanted to.) Figure 17.12 shows the Boolean Operations panel.

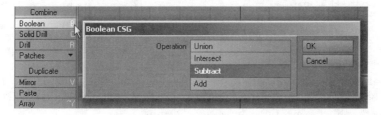

Figure 17.12   Boolean operations allow you to cut one object from another, when Subtract is selected.

- The Boolean CSG tool also allows you to create a union between two objects. Selecting this tool will weld a background layer object to a foreground layer object, while eliminating unneeded polygons. You also can use Intersect to create an object of two intersecting objects, using foreground and background layers.

  For example, take an extruded mantelpiece on the X, and Intersect it with an extruded mantelpiece on the Z, and you'll create a mitered corner. In addition, you can add a background object to a foreground object.

- The Solid Drill tool is similar to Template Drill, but whereas Template Drill works for flat objects, Solid Drill is used for three-dimensional objects (see Figure 17.13).

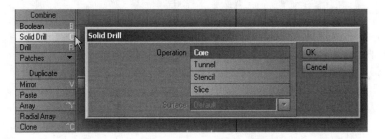

Figure 17.13   The Solid Drill tool is great for stenciling or slicing 3D objects with other objects.

You can choose to Core objects, a process similar to coring an apple. You can Tunnel, just as you did with Template Drill, but on all axes for a 3D object. In addition, there is the Stencil tool—perfect for branding irons! And, you can Slice an object as well, essentially using one object to cut another.

Note

Remember that any of the Combine tools require you to use objects between foreground and background layers. The tool is always in the background. For example, the holes to cut the letters earlier in step 14 of Exercise 17.1 were in a background layer.

Exercise 17.3   Extruding Imported Illustrator Objects

The main identity logo has been imported from an Adobe Illustrator 6.0 file. The necessary Boolean operations have been performed to put holes in the letters, so it's time to extrude the object to give three-dimensional depth.

1. Go back to the first layer where the Illustrator file was originally imported. You've cut and pasted the abc letters from it, so all that should remain is the disc.

2. Choose the Multiply tab, select Extrude (by pressing Shift+e), and in either Top or Right view, click and drag the text to the back of the logo, toward the positive z-axis. Drag out 1 grid length, which is 200mm. Note that this may vary a bit.

You'll notice that when you drag the extrusion, it shifts a little on the neighboring axis. You might be able to drag it straight right off the bat; or you might need to hold the Ctrl key while dragging to constrain the axis. Figure 17.14 shows the extruded disc.

Note

If you drag to the front of the logo toward the negative z-axis, your polygons will be facing inward—the object will be inside-out. If this happens, simply press the f key to flip polygons.

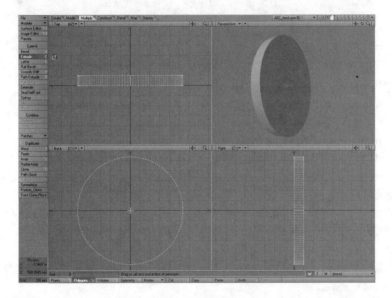

Figure 17.14   Holding the Ctrl key while using the Extrude tool constrains the position axis.

3. Once you've made the extrusion, press the spacebar to turn off the Extrude tool.

4. Go to the second layer, where the abc letters are placed. Extrude these 200mm as well.

5. Set the extruded disc layer as a background, while leaving the abc extruded letters in the foreground. Figure 17.15 shows the example. You'll see that the two objects, although on separate layers, are on top of each other.

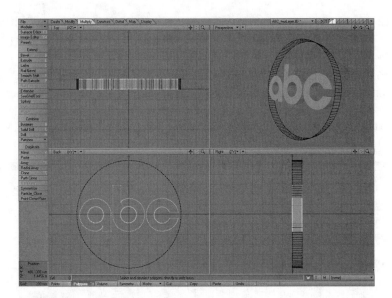

Figure 17.15   Both objects are placed within the same space, even though they're on separate layers. When this object is brought to Layout, the letters will be inside the disc.

Although you can easily move the abc letters in Layout away from the disc, it's best to set everything in place properly in Modeler first.

6. Under the Modify tab, press the t key to select-move and move the abc text forward on the negative z-axis from either the Top or Right view. Bring the object forward enough so that it is just sitting on the disc about 200mm, as you see in Figure 17.16.

> **Tip**
>
> Remember that you can hold the Ctrl key while using the Move tool to constrain movement on one axis.

7. Save the object!

Now you have your object converted and extruded direct from an EPS file. But there's a little more work you need to do before it becomes a usable animation element.

Exercise 17.4   Surfacing and Beveling the Objects

From here, you can surface and bevel the objects, following these steps:

1. Go to the abc object layer, and press the q key to call up the Change Surface command under the Detail tab.

2. Type the name ABC_Sides and uncheck Make Default. Leave the color selection alone at this point.

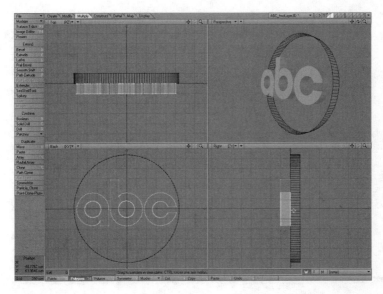

Figure 17.16   The benefit of working with layers—you can use one layer as a positioning reference for another.

Note

People get very confused by the Change Surface command and the color setting within it. The color selection here is simply given to help you identify the polygons you name. This panel is used to name polygons for proper surfacing later in the Surface Editor. When you want to change a surface, you do it from the Surface Editor—not here. Often, users will open this panel again and try to change a surface, only to get an error message stating "Color is Disabled." This means that the surface you're trying to adjust has already been created. Actual surfacing is done in the Surface Editor, either in Modeler or in Layout.

3. With the right mouse button in the Right view, drag around the front-facing polygons of the abc object (the negative z-axis). This is often referred to as *lasso selection*. (Before you do this, make sure that you are working in Polygon mode, at the bottom of the Modeler screen.) Figure 17.17 shows the example.

   Because you named the entire object ABC_Sides in step 2, you now need only to select the front polygons of the object to create the bevel and face surfaces. Selecting only the front polygons with the Lasso tool, as you just did, is much easier than trying to select all the side polygons of the object.

4. With the face of the abc object selected, press q again to access the Change Surface command, and name the selection ABC_Bevel.

5. Press b to activate the Bevel tool.

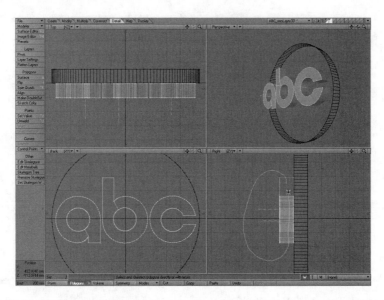

Figure 17.17   Using the right mouse button, you can select the front polygons by lassoing around them from Right view.

6. Click the face of the object in the Back view (Viewport BL), and drag to interactively bevel the abc object. Be careful not to overlap the bevels. You can undo what you did by pressing u.

   Moving the mouse up and down controls the shift of the bevel, while left and right movements control the inset of the bevel. You'll want to set a Shift and Inset value of roughly 20mm. You can do this numerically by pressing the n key to open the numeric panel. Figure 17.18 shows the beveled abc object.

7. While the front polygon is still selected, press q one more time, and name this surface ABC_Face. Press the spacebar to turn off the bevel tool, and then deselect the polygon by pressing the ? key, and save the object.

8. Perform the same selection and surfacing steps on the disc object in the other layer, but name the surfaces ABC_Disc_Sides, ABC_Disc_Bevel, and ABC_Disc_Face, or something similar.

9. When complete, click the Detail tab, and near the top-left side of the interface, click the Pivot tool. This allows you to set a rotational pivot for each layer.

   Because you moved the abc letters earlier in this chapter, the object's pivot now rests behind it at the original 0,0,0 axis. Move the pivot to the center of the abc object, as shown in Figure 17.19.

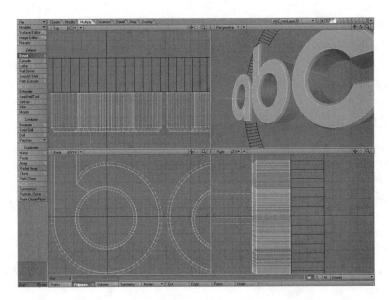

Figure 17.18   The Bevel tool is used to add a clean bevel to the abc object.

10. The disc should be centered at the 0,0,0 axis, so you don't need to change its
pivot. If the disc isn't centered there, select Center from the Modify tab (press
F2), then turn off the Pivot tool by clicking it, and save the object.

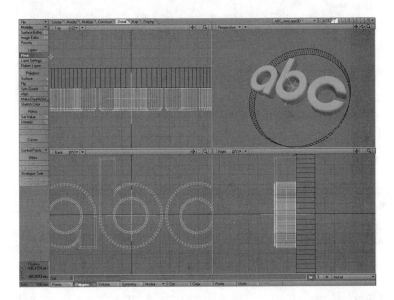

Figure 17.19   Using Modeler to prepare all variables of your objects, such as the pivot point,
helps later in Layout.

Exercise 17.5   LightWave-Generated Text Creation

From here, you need to add the letters that will animate next to the abc logo. These are the 3D NEWS letters. You'll often find it a big bonus when a client has a logo that includes standard typefaces. Both the Mac and PC versions of LightWave can create 3D text from basic system fonts. The Mac version uses PostScript fonts, while the PC version can use PostScript and TrueType fonts.

1. Go to a new blank layer, and save the object as ABC_with_text, or something similar. Saving the object now with a new name cuts down on the chance that you can make a mistake and overwrite the work you've already done.

2. From the Modeler drop-down list, select Options, and then choose Edit Font List. Here, you load fonts into LightWave Modeler, making them available for use (see Figure 17.20).

3. In the Edit Font List panel that appears, load a font based on your system: TrueType for the PC, or Type-1 PostScript for the Mac. Load a Times Roman-style font.

4. Click OK to close the panel.

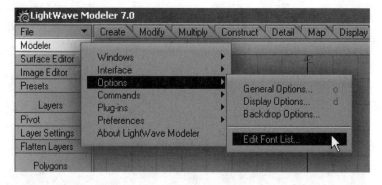

Figure 17.20   Before you can use fonts in Modeler, you need to load them into the program's memory.

 Tip

Using the Edit Font List panel, you can save various font lists if you load more than one font. Perhaps a client has a few set fonts he or she likes. You can load only those fonts, and then save the list to recall later.

5. Press the a key to reset your viewports. Then, under the Create tab, click the Text button (Shift+w) and you'll see a short vertical cursor appear. Click in Back view, and you'll see a blue shaded bracket.

6. Type the letters NEWS, in capital letters. You'll want the text to be in the 1m range of size, a good standard size for the text you create. Make the letters fit the screen, similar to what's shown in Figure 17.21. You can resize the lettering by grabbing and dragging the top end of the bracket. If you want to kern the letters, drag the crosshair at the bottom of the bracket.

Note

When you select the Text tool from the Objects tab, your keyboard essentially becomes a typewriter, enabling you to type and create fonts. Because of this, keyboard equivalents are temporarily suspended, requiring you to use the mouse to turn off the Text tool. You can press the ESC key, however, if you want to use a keyboard shortcut.

7. Once you have created the text, click the Text tool under the Create tab to turn it off.

8. Now go a step further and reshape the NEWS text slightly. Remember that these letters are polygons now, and they respond to selection and deselection just like the rest of 'em. Press h on the keyboard to select the Stretch tool.

9. Holding the Ctrl key to constrain an axis, click and drag to the left in Back view. You'll see the NEWS text begin to squeeze together. Stretch the selection in about 20mm to 50mm or so. You should see something similar to Figure 17.22.

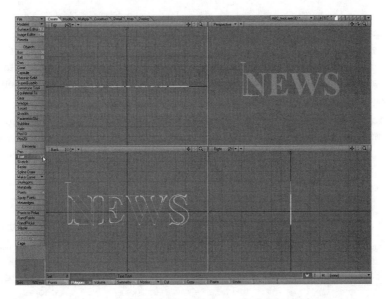

Figure 17.21   Once fonts are loaded into Modeler, you can begin creating text.

Remember that you can select and move the individual letters closer or farther apart so that they are perfectly spaced. Generally, a computer does not space text properly.

Figure 17.22   Even though the text is created, you still can manipulate its points and polygons the way you would any other object.

10. Save a copy of the NEWS text as News_Flat for later use in Layout. You can select Save Layers As Object from the File menu, or simply copy and paste the object to a new set of layers. Select Copy (c), press Shift+n for a new object, and then select Paste (v). This is now a separate copy of the original object. Copying and Pasting to a new layer does not create a new separate object, just a new object layer.

11. You've now created the main 3D text elements for the logo. You will need these on separate layers so that they can be animated independently, but first you must extrude and bevel them as you did the abc text in the earlier exercises. Be sure that the Face, Bevel, and Sides all have different surface names (select the polygon, press q, and name it).

Note

When you enter text, it will appear using the last font you loaded into your font list. Don't worry—just use the up arrow on your keyboard to cycle through the font list and click your desired font. You'll see your typed text change font styles, without having to go back into the Edit Font List. Open the Numeric window (n) while creating text for more precise control. You'll also be able to select between any loaded fonts.

12. Save, save, save!

13. Once you have surfaced and beveled the NEWS letters, cut and paste them so that they each occupy their own layer.

14. Select the Pivot tool from the Detail tab and center the pivot for each item with itself, so that each object will move and rotate in Layout as planned.

   In this case you don't want to use the Center command (F2) because that command will change the position of the object. Using Pivot changes the pivot point, while keeping the object in place.

15. You can open the Layers browser by pressing Ctrl+F5 or by choosing Modeler, Windows, and Layer Browser. Here, select each layer and name them accordingly for proper organization. You can do this by double-clicking on the listing.

The preceding exercises showed you how simple it is to create and model 3D text, whether it is from an Adobe Illustrator file or LightWave-generated text from system fonts. Although the fonts used were simple, beveling them adds a soft, subtle touch and even gives your models a touch of class. When it's time to surface this object later in this chapter, you'll see how the bevels you've created help make the logo stand out. But before you do that, you should create the background text elements that will make up the complete logo. The next exercise takes you through those steps.

Creating a Broadcast Animation Environment

The environment in which the animation takes place is just as important as the logo itself—sometimes more important! A simple logo on a black background is not nearly as effective as a logo with complementing objects, colorful backgrounds, and enhancement elements. This next exercise discusses how to create the enhancements that will give the full animation some depth.

Exercise 17.6   Creating Animation Elements

Broadcast-style animation elements are the extra pieces you'll need to help sell the logo concept. Remember that you're doing more than creating an animated logo; you're creating a theme, or mood, that needs to be conveyed to the viewer. Follow these steps:

1. In Modeler, make sure your work is saved, and press Shift+n to create a new object.

   Part of the company's logo is the broadcast identification WDMA. That's not much to go on, but there are ways to transform a four-letter acronym like this into a complex animation.

2. Use the same Times Roman-style font you used earlier for the NEWS letters.

3. Create the text WDMA by using the Text tool, but don't extrude and bevel it. Figure 17.23 shows the new text.

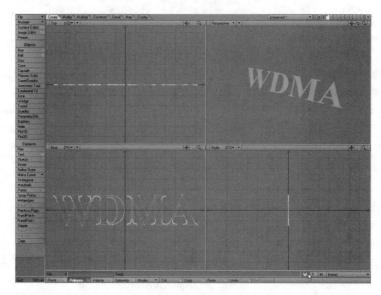

Figure 17.23   Additional text is created but left flat. This is an additional animation element.

Note

When you create new text with the Text tool and use fonts that are too large for the screen, you might have trouble grabbing the handle of the text cursor because it is outside the view. When this happens, use the Numeric window (press n). Remember that when you're in Text mode, however, typing n adds the letter n instead of activating a command; so to display the Numeric window, press Esc and then press n. To help avoid text not fitting into a view, always press the a key before you begin creating text.

4. Save the WMDA text.

   This is one element you'll use later. Because this is the only text or slogan in the animation, you need to copy it and modify it in some way to create additional elements, so don't close the object just yet. You'll come back to this text object in a moment.

5. Press the q key and give this object a surface name, WDMA_1. Save the object. Press the c key to copy the object.

6. Create a new object (Shift+n) and then paste (v) the WDMA object to create an additional font element; however, give this object a different surface name. Press q to call up the Change Surface requestor, and name the object WDMA_2.

   Believe it or not, two copies of the simple WDMA text objects will create a great-looking enhancement to the animation background. Now you'll need to create just a few more elements and the pieces will all be in place.

Exercise 17.7   Creating the Background for the Animation

Now that the main and background fonts have been created, you need to create something soft and transparent for the background of the animation. Follow these steps:

1. Create a new object, and using the Disc tool, create a large, flat disc in Back view, roughly 5m in size. You might not see the object in Perspective view—and that's fine.

   If you can't see the disc, your Perspective view is rotated or your object is simply facing backward. You can correct this by press the f key to flip the polygon forward after you create it.

2. Press the n key to open the Numeric panel. Change the default sides of 24 to 60. You also can use the up arrow while your mouse cursor is in the Back view to add sides interactively.

Note

While a primitive object is being created, you can use the up and right-arrow keys in a particular view to add segments to it. Using the down and left-arrow keys removes segments.

3. Press the spacebar to turn off the Disc tool. Change the surface name to Ring or something similar.

   You should now have a large, flat disc in the Back view with smooth edges, as shown in Figure 17.24.

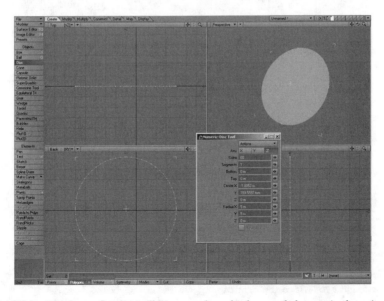

Figure 17.24   This large, flat disc will become a large background element in the animation.

4. Press F2 to center the disc on all axes.

   If you're on a Mac, the function keys might not work. On a Macintosh computer you might need to tell the system to apply function keys to the current application, rather than the system. Check your system manual for details. In the meantime, you can find the Center command under the Move heading under the Modify tab.

5. Copy the flat disc by pressing c on the keyboard. Select a new layer and paste (v) it in.

6. Select the Size tool from the Modify tab (Shift+h), and size the pasted disc down about 80 percent, with the original disc in a background layer for reference. Figure 17.25 shows the sizing with the Numeric window open.

7. Now move the smaller disc over and down to the right, so that the edge almost intersects with the edge of the larger disc, located in a background layer.

8. You want to cut the smaller disc out of the larger disc, so you'll need to reverse layers. You can do this quickly by pressing the single open quote key ('), which is usually found in the upper-left side of your keyboard.

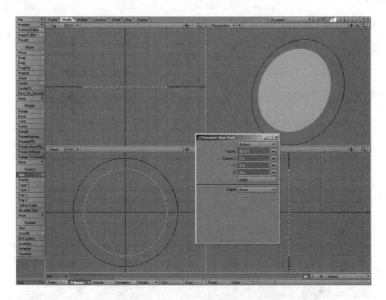

Figure 17.25   A copy of the 5m disc is pasted into a new layer and sized down 80 percent.

Tip

As you can see throughout this chapter and others in the book, you'll often move back and forth between two layers. This quick single-open-quote-key shortcut is handy and can be found two keys to the right of the l key on your keyboard.

9. Press Shift+r to call up the Template Drill tool. Select Z for the Axis, and Tunnel for the Operation. Click OK, and the small disc will be cut from the larger, as you see in Figure 17.26.

10. Press q to call up the Change Surface requester, and change the surface name to Ring or something similar. Save the object.

Now all you need to do is create one more element, and it's on to surfacing and animation.

11. Create a new object, press the a key to reset the views, and make a large rectangle using the Box tool, similar to the one shown in Figure 17.27.

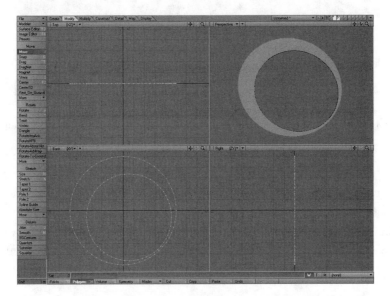

Figure 17.26   A simple disc, with a smaller copy used as a cutting tool, ends up making a very nice stylized element for the animation.

12. Give the rectangle a surface name (q) of TopBox. Save it as TopBox as well. Call up the Change Surface requester again (q) and rename the surface BottomBox. Save it as BottomBox. Whew! You're almost finished with the detail work.

You just made two copies of the same object, giving each its own unique surface name. You'll see in a moment why that's important.

Only a few more steps, and you'll be able to see how this all comes together. This next exercise guides you through the steps to set up the broadcast elements and prepare them for animation. You'll modify the original models so that they fit the final look of the animation, which in this case has some specific placement requirements. (To see the type of look you're shooting for, refer to Figure 17.1 at the beginning of the chapter.)

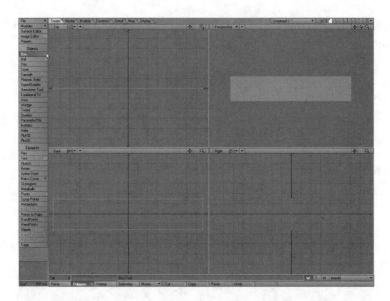

Figure 17.27   One last element, a flat rectangle, completes the modeling for the logo animation.

Broadcast Animation Setup

Setting up an animation can be simple or complex, depending on what you want to do. Broadcast-style animations generally have many parts that need to move, and stay moving, throughout the animation. You need to consider carefully which objects will move and how they will move. The following exercise helps you with that by leading you through the following tasks:

- Loading the objects you've created into Layout
- Positioning the objects
- Creating object surfaces

Exercise 17.8   Setting Up Broadcast-Style Animation Objects

Although you can load any object at any time into Layout, it's usually helpful to load the objects in the order you plan to use them. In this case, there are only a few objects to load, so you can simply load the objects in the order that they were created.

1. Open Layout and select Add, then Objects, and Load Object from the Items tab.
2. Load all the elements you've created up to this point—the extruded abc logo (on the disc) you first created in this chapter from the imported Illustrator file: the NEWS letters, flat and extruded, the WDMA call letters, the ring, and the top and bottom box. You can load all the elements at once because Layout lets you select and load multiple items.

Note

If you choose, you can use the objects on this book's CD for this tutorial. They are located in the Chapter 17 Objects folder of the Projects directory. There is a folder within the Objects folder labeled BlankObjects. These are final objects used to create the image in Figure 17.1 without surface properties.

3. Go to the Camera view (press 6), and you'll see just a pile of objects, similar to Figure 17.28.

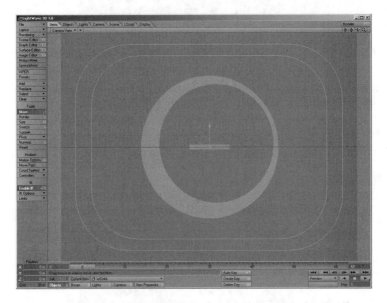

Figure 17.28   After you load all the objects into Layout, they just sit there until you position them and get them moving.

4. You now have to make a choice that you'll face continually with text and logo animations: Do you move the objects or the camera? In this case, you can move the objects. For now, leave the camera in place.

Note

Because the final animation piece will go to video for broadcast, you'll want to make sure that your elements are title-safe. So, from the Display Options tab within the Preferences panel, turn on Show Safe Areas. Title Safe means that the elements you create stay within a bounding region so that they remain visible when put to video.

5. Start setting up the scene by first going to the Camera panel and choosing the correct resolution. If you don't do this first, there's a chance that the image will change, and your objects will not appear exactly where you place them. Press the p key with the camera selected to call up the Camera Properties panel.

6. From the Resolution drop-down list, select the D1 NTSC preset for now. If you know exactly what resolution your output should be, whether it is PAL or perhaps a custom resolution for a digital editing system, set it now.

7. Leave the zoom factor to 3.2. Make sure that Antialiasing is off for the setup— you'll turn this on for the final render. Leave all other settings alone for now. Figure 17.29 shows the Camera Properties panel.

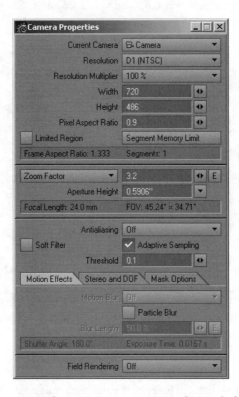

Figure 17.29   It's important to first set up your camera resolutions before setting up your animation.

8. At this point, it's tough to know where to begin with so many elements in the scene. Start by framing the shot. Select the TopBox object and move it down the z-axis toward the camera. Position it at the top of the frame, as shown in Figure 17.30.

Note

When you select your objects and move them, they might seem to move really fast. If so, you need to adjust Layout's Grid Square Size. Do this by pressing the left bracket key ([) to decrease the size of the grid. The right bracket key (]) increases the size of the grid. You also can manually set a grid size under the Display Options tab (d). A smaller grid enables you to move your objects with more control.

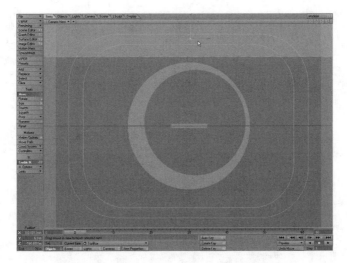

Figure 17.30   The first element, the TopBox object, is moved into place. The object just hangs into the frame.

9. Create a keyframe at zero to lock the position of the object.

10. Select the BottomBox object, move it forward, and position it in the lower portion of the frame, bleeding off the edge, just like the TopBox (see Figure 17.31).

11. Now take the Ring object and move it forward so that it rests slightly in front of the top and bottom boxes. It's probably going to be too large when brought close to the camera if you take a look at it from the Perspective view (see Figure 17.32). That's okay.

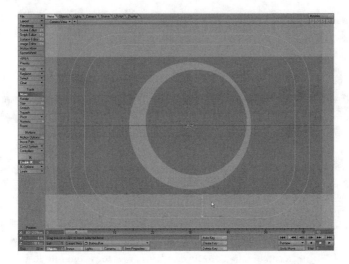

Figure 17.31   The BottomBox object is moved into place, mirroring the TopBox. It doesn't look like much, but that's the beauty of it.

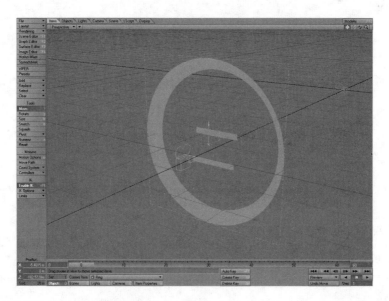

Figure 17.32   Moving the ring toward the camera shows that it's too large to view. You can use Size to scale it down.

12. Select Size, and then click and drag to size the ring down to fit into the frame. You will adjust it more precisely later when surfaces have been applied. For now, make sure that it fits the view, as shown in Figure 17.33.

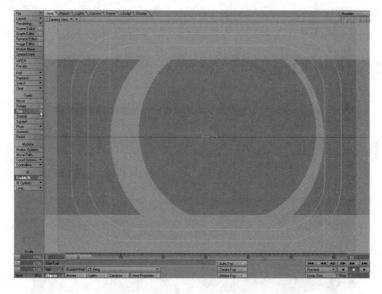

Figure 17.33   Using a combination of Move and Size, the ring is put into its initial position slightly in front of the top and bottom boxes.

13. At this point, save the scene. Give it any name you like.

14. Now select the flat NEWS object and the flat WDMA object. Instead of moving these objects close to the camera, select Size, and size up each so that they fill a little more than half the frame. Figure 17.34 shows the WDMA letters sized up.

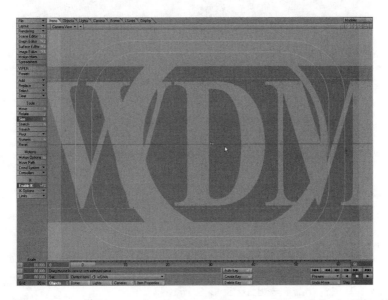

Figure 17.34   Because of the way the animation will be set up, you can use the Size tool to make the WDMA flat letters more visible.

15. Create a keyframe to lock the new size in place, and then size up the flat NEWS object as well. It can be a bit bigger, perhaps overlapping the WDMA letters slightly as well. Remember to create a keyframe to lock its new size in place as well.

The reason you've sized these up rather than moved them closer to the camera is for shadow control. By keeping them far behind the ring and box objects, they won't pick up shadows from the animated 3D letters you'll soon add. These larger flat letters will blend nicely with the background image without interference from the rest of the scene. Figure 17.35 shows the final elements in place.

There are still more elements to put into place, but it might help you visualize your final scene by setting up some surfaces.

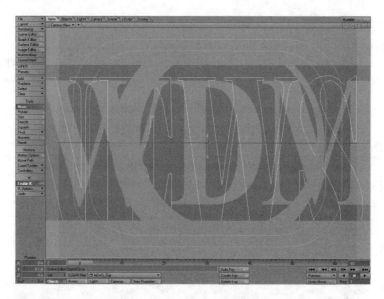

Figure 17.35   The flat NEWS object and WDMA call letters are both sized up, almost over-sized, and locked into place, awaiting surfacing. Note that the flat NEWS text has been set to a wireframe visibility for this screen shot.

Exercise 17.9   Creating Broadcast-Style Surfaces

This exercise takes the next step in your grand broadcast logo journey (all right, maybe not so grand) and sets up the surfaces for the broadcast animation you've been creating throughout this chapter. If you look at Figure 17.1 at the beginning of the chapter, you might notice that there is a lot of organic, natural surfacing going on. Bzzzzzt! Wrong, thanks for playing! One simple image, transparency, and glows are all you need. Read and learn:

1. With the scene you put together in the previous exercise still loaded, open the Image Editor. Click the Load button, and load the BlueSilk image from the book's CD-ROM (see Figure 17.36).

   This is a photograph of blue silk, slightly blurred in Adobe Photoshop. Although you can load images quickly within texture editors, it's a good idea to get into the habit of loading unfamiliar images directly in the Image Editor so that you can instantly adjust them—clone them, brighten them, darken them, etc.

2. Close the Image Editor and click the Scene tab. Open the Compositing tab within the Effects panel, and select BlueSilk as the Background Image (see Figure 17.37).

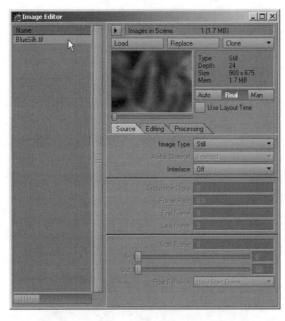

Figure 17.36   The Image Editor allows you to load images, delete them (by pressing the Delete key on the keyboard), and adjust their properties, such as contract, hue, saturation, and more.

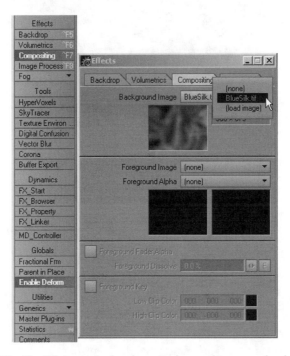

Figure 17.37   The BlueSilk image is placed as a Background Image under the Compositing tab of the Effects panel.

3. In Layout, press the d key to open the Display Options tab. Select Background Image as the Camera View Background at the bottom of the panel (see Figure 17.38)

4. You can see from Camera view that the blue silk image is visible behind the letters.

Using a background image is a great way to create a base for your animation. A background image can not be affected (except for Image Filters) by anything in your scene, such as lights or objects. It doesn't move and will always be in the Camera view. However, there's a deeper root to background images: front projection surfacing. Front Project allows you to "project" the background image onto objects, allowing you to create objects that blend with the background.

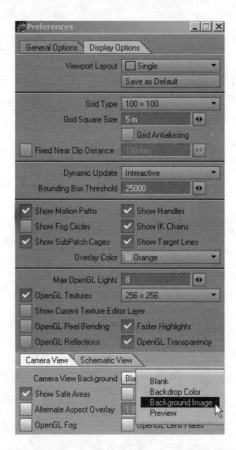

Figure 17.38   You can display the background image in Layout by telling LightWave to display it under the Display Options tab.

5. Open the Surface Editor and select the TopBox surface. Click the T button next to Color to open the Texture Editor. Set the following:

- Layer Type: Image Map
- Blending Mode: Normal
- Layer Opacity: 100%
- Projection: Front
- Fixed Projection: Off
- Image: BlueSilk
- Pixel Blending: On
- Texture Antialiasing: Off

6. Click Automatic Sizing, and then select Use Texture. Figure 17.39 shows Layout with the background image visible and the Texture Editor open. If you look closely, you'll see that the top box blends perfectly with the background image!

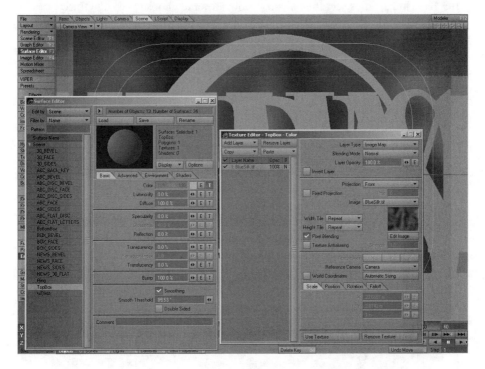

Figure 17.39   By applying the same image used as a background image to an object's surface as a Front Projection image, you'll see that the object seamlessly blends with the backdrop.

So you might be asking yourself, if you're creating a texture that seamlessly blends with the backdrop, why even have a surface at all? Good question. Look again at Figure 17.1 at the beginning of this chapter. Notice how the elements blend with the backdrop, but are sort of pulled out from it. There's a soft globe around them as well as a slightly brighter hue.

Using your background image as your surface texture is a quick and great-looking way to create stunning but not overpowering background graphics. Read on—you'll be rendering soon!

7. With an initial surface now applied to the TopBox, add a few more properties to make it stand out. Under the Basic tab, leave Luminosity set to 0 percent. Leave Diffuse set to 100 percent.

8. Bring the Specularity to 35 percent and Glossiness to around 40 percent. Reflection should be set to 0 percent, and finally bring the Transparency value to 35 percent. Leave all other settings alone.

9. Click the Shaders tab. Click the Add Shader drop-down list, and choose Edge_Transparency. Double-click it when loaded to access its controls. Set Edge Transparency to Transparent. Edge Threshold should be 1.0 (the maximum value).

10. Back in Layout, select the File drop-down list and choose Save All Objects to save the surfaces you've just applied. And while you're at it, save the scene.

11. You'll apply the exact same surface to the BottomBox, so you can easily make a preset. Or, right-click the surface listing, select Copy, and then select the new surface and click Paste. Figure 17.40 shows the Camera view at this point.

Figure 17.40   Front Projection maps and edge transparency are applied to the top and bottom boxes, framing the scene.

12. Next, select the Ring surface, and go to the Color Texture Editor. For this object, you're not going to use front projection mapping. You want this ring to stand out a bit more than the top and bottom boxes, but not too much more. So using

the same image, you can simply apply a planar image map. This will change the look of the pattern on the ring. Set the following:

- Layer Type: Image Map
- Blending Mode: Normal
- Layer Opacity: 100%
- Projection: Planar
- Texture Axis: Z
- Image: BlueSilk
- Pixel Blending: On
- Texture Antialiasing: Off

13. Click Automatic Sizing, and then select Use Texture.

Note

The Automatic Sizing function can help you set the surface manually. Because it's hard to guess what size parameters to enter for the x, y, and z-axes, Automatic Sizing can instantly find an approximate value for you to use.

14. Under the Basic tab for the Ring surface, set the following:

- Luminosity: 40%
- Diffuse: 100%
- Specularity: 20%
- Glossiness: 40%
- Reflection: 0%
- Transparency: 30%

15. Leave all other settings alone, and click the Advanced tab.

16. In the Advanced tab, set the Glow Intensity to 85 percent. All other settings should be set to their defaults. Close the Surface Editor.

Note

Look for more information on Glow toward the end of this chapter.

17. Click the Scene tab, and then click the Image Process button to open the Effects panel. Whenever a surface has Glow Intensity applied, you need to tell LightWave to globally turn the feature on for rendering. So far, you've only told a surface what value glow to have.

18. Under the Processing tab of the Effects panel, click Enable Glow. Set the Intensity to 60 percent, and the Glow Radius to 10 pixels. These two settings will create a slightly brighter and wider glow on any surface that has Glow Intensity set above 0 percent.

19. Back in Layout, click the Rendering drop-down list button, and select Render Options. In the Render Options panel, set Render Display to Image Viewer. Press F9 to render a test frame. As you can see from Figure 17.41, the top and bottom boxes now stand out from the background image and the ring pops a little more than the boxes.

Figure 17.41   When rendered, the front projection maps and glow surfaces show the blending created between object surfaces and the background image. You can see that not front-projecting the image on the ring, but rather using a Planar image map, gives it a slightly different look.

20. Save all objects at this point, and save the scene.

21. Guess what? That's it! There's nothing more to making a cool background. On your own, apply the same surface of the top and bottom boxes to the WDMA and NEWS letters.

22. Feel free to vary the transparency of each to give a slightly different look. Figure 17.42 shows the shot with the letters surfaced with a front projection map.

Now that you've set up simple but great-looking surfaces and a backdrop, you need to move on to the main portion of the animation—the logos. There's nothing too special about setting up a surface for a logo, but it's something that you might have to do over and over again in your job. The techniques here can be applied to all kinds of surfaces, not just logos. This next exercise guides you through the process of surfacing one of the main logos in the scene. From there, you'll light the scene and put everything into motion.

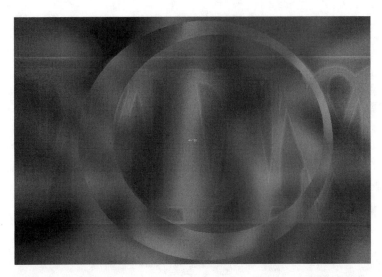

Figure 17.42   The same front projection map technique applied to the top and bottom box objects is applied to the flat letters of the scene. Here, the letters are 50 percent transparent, and the glow for the entire scene has been set a little lower, at 40 percent.

Exercise 17.10   Surfacing 3D Text Objects

You'll have to create text at one time or another during your career as an animator. Whether it's a main title animation, a broadcast logo, or credits for an animated movie you've created, text is an important element in 3D animation.

You can continue working with the scene you saved in the last exercise, or feel free to open the NoSurfacesLogo scene from the book's CD-ROM. If you use the scene from the CD, all the objects will be a default gray color without any surface attributes. You also can load the background animation scene only (BKD.lws), and then add the 3D text elements.

You'll surface the 3D NEWS letters first. These are a bit more challenging to surface because the client insists on using black. Black extruded letters can get lost visually during an animation. However, you can control that by applying the right surface.

You'll need to move the letters into view first.

1. From the Items tab, select Objects, and then choose Add Null. Name the object News_Mover. In the Scene Editor, parent the four letters N, E, W, and S to the null. Now you can move and size the letters equally as needed.

2. Select the News_Mover null object and move it toward the camera. Similar to the ring earlier in this chapter, you might need to size down the letters to fit them to view in front of the top and bottom boxes. Figure 17.43 shows the NEWS letters moved and sized.

Figure 17.43   The NEWS letters are parented to a null object and moved to fit into view in front of the camera.

3. Open the Surface Editor, select the News_Sides surface, and set color to 0,0,0 RGB.

   You can set the values to 0 quickly by dragging over the color square with your right mouse button.

   - Luminosity: 0%
   - Diffuse: 65%
   - Specularity: 60%
   - Glossiness: 40%
   - Reflection: 35%
   - Transparency: 0%
   - Bump: 100%
   - Smoothing: On
   - Smooth Threshold: 50%

4. Leave all other settings alone, click the Environment tab, and set the following for reflection properties:

   - Reflection Options: Spherical Map
   - Reflection Map: Foil
   - Image Seam Angle: 0
   - Reflection Blurring: 0

5. Leave all other settings alone and head back to Layout. Be sure to select Save All Objects from the File menu to save these surface settings to your objects. Press F9 for a test render. You'll see that the sides of the letters are black, but they show up because of the reflection map.

6. For the News_Face surface, you'll set up something similar:

   - Color: 0,0,0 RGB
   - Luminosity: 0%
   - Diffuse: 100%
   - Specularity: 30%
   - Glossiness: 40%
   - Reflection: 30%
   - Transparency: 0%
   - Translucency: 0%
   - Bump: 100%
   - Smoothing: Off

7. Leave all other settings alone, click the Environment tab, and set the following for reflection properties:

   - Reflection Options: Spherical Map
   - Reflection Map: Foil
   - Image Seam Angle: 0
   - Reflection Blurring: 0

Warning

Be sure to unclick Smoothing. Because the face of the object is flat, you don't need to apply smoothing. If you do, the surface of your object might appear streaked and cause oddities when rendered.

Figure 17.44 shows the surfaced sides and face of the text object.

The last part of the NEWS letters is the bevel surface. The bevel is used to make the object stand out, give it separation from the extruded sides, and help give it a more polished look. The bevel should not be the same color as the sides for the face of the object and should provide a contrast between the two.

8. Set the color of the News_Bevel surface to a soft grayish blue—about 227, 227, 253 RGB.

9. Change the Diffuse level to 45 percent and Reflection to 55 percent. Set Specularity to 30 percent and Glossiness to 40 percent. Smoothing should be on, with a Smooth Threshold of 40 percent so that the bevel doesn't bleed into the face surface.

This makes most of this surface appear as a reflection, like shiny metal.

Figure 17.44   You can use the same surface settings on the face of the object that you used on the side surfaces, with a few slight variances.

10. Go to the Environments tab and set a Reflection Image the way you did in Step 7, using the same reflection image, Foil.

   Often, using the same reflection on different colored surfaces helps give the full animation some diversity while keeping a consistency throughout.

11. When you have this surface set, be sure to save your work and remember to select Save All Objects to save the surface settings with the objects. Press F9 to do a test render. Figure 17.45 shows a close-up shot of the NEWS text now fully surfaced.

From this point, you can set the rest of the surfaces on your own, such as the abc logo. The other surfaces throughout the scene should be similar to the ones you just set in the previous exercise. The colors are black and blue, with some white (or metallic). You can add a metallic color like the News_Bevel surface to add some variation. For example, the abc surfaces can be set to a nice variation of the NEWS surfaces—the black sides can simply have the color changed to white, while keeping the same reflection maps. The same goes for the face, and the bevel can be identical to tie it all together. By setting up one surface, you can quickly and easily copy and adjust the surface to complete your scene. After you've surfaced all the objects, be sure to save them.

Figure 17.45   Although just black, the surfaces can stand out and look appealing with a slight bit of reflection and a nice metallic bevel.

Glowing Surfaces

The surfaces you set for the text in the previous sections are typical to the types of surfaces you would set for just about any kind of logo. Color, reflection, and some shininess would all be a part of it as well. But you can enhance the final look of the animation with glow. Glow softens any of the animations you create, especially broadcast-style animations, by creating a bright halo around the applied surface. Adding glows is easy—follow these tips to add glow to your scene:

- Set the amount of glow for each surface through the Advanced tab in the Surface Editor. You can set the Glow Intensity for the surface anywhere from 0 to 100 percent.

- Under the Scene tab in Layout, you can access the Image Process panel. Here, you must check Enable Glow to activate any Glow Intensities you've set.

- You can set the Intensity for all surfaces with Glow Intensity set through the Image Process panel. A typical glow setting is between 50 percent and 60 percent.

- Because Glow adds a soft haze when applied, you can set the amount of the Glow Radius through the Image Process panel as well. A good average to work with is 10 pixels.

Try adding glow to every surface in your scene, and then activate the Glow Intensity feature through the Image Process panel. Balancing Glow with transparent surfaces creates different looks as well. See what kind of results you come up with.

Applying Transparency

In addition to using glow to enhance a broadcast animation, you can add some transparency to further enhance the look. Figure 17.46 shows logo treatment. Notice the flat abc surface that forms a disc just off-center of the animation. The sides are soft and the surface slightly transparent. By not adding completely solid objects to the entire scene, all the elements start to work together. And, if the project you're creating is limited in color and depth, transparent objects can help add significant variances to any surface without changing any colors. You can add transparency by doing the following:

- Selecting the Shaders tab in the Surface Editor and adding a Shader modifier, such as Edge Transparency.

- Double-clicking the Edge Transparency shader to set Transparent edges to your surfaces.

- Setting the overall transparency of any surface by changing the 0 percent Transparency under the Basic tab to 100 percent Transparency.

Figure 17.46   Varying transparency settings can make each element stand out in an animation, while still enabling them to blend together nicely.

Adding a Fast Fresnel Shader

LightWave's Fast Fresnel shader (pronounced Fre-nel) offers you the ability to add more real-world surfacing properties to your animation. The Fresnel effect, which is universally known in studios, happens when certain surface properties such as reflection, light diffusion, or specularity appear changed based on the angle of viewing. A glass window, for example, will appear more or less reflective depending on the angle from which you are looking at it. The same can be said for reflective metallic objects, such as a logo. You can create the Fresnel effect in animation by adding the Fast Fresnel shader plug-in in the Surfaces panel. Then apply LightWave's Fast Fresnel shader through the Shaders tab to some of the surfaces in your scene to see the results.

Adding Bloom or Corona Shaders

One of the nicest touches you can add to a broadcast-style animation is additive bloom. A bloom, simply put, is that glare that comes off of a bright reflection. If you've ever taken a picture of a lake on a sunny day, or a shiny car, the hotspot of the sun is so bright that the hotspot glows. This is what adding the bloom and corona shaders will do to your logo animations. Corona is like bloom, but offers greater control over falloff values, allowing you to apply textures, and more. Load the NewsLogo scene from the book's CD and render a few frames to see the effects of these cool image filters.

You can find these shaders by going to the Scene tab, and then clicking Image Process. Select Add Image Filter, and take your pick.

Lighting Broadcast Animations

Lighting any scene in LightWave can be fun, but it also is time-consuming. If you're not familiar with traditional lighting techniques and principles, it might take you a bit longer to get up to speed. But lighting for broadcast-style graphics is not difficult. These types of animations can be lit with basic two- or three-point lighting schemes. Refer to Chapter 9, "Realistic Lighting Environments," for more information on lighting setups.

Exercise 17.11   Lighting Broadcast Animations

You can be as creative as you want with your lighting. Knowing a few simple rules, however, will help you with this exercise, as well as others. Good lighting produces an important element in your animations: shadows. Shadows are as important as the background elements you modeled for this project. By setting up the proper lights, you can create shadows throughout your scene which add depth and interest for the viewer. Follow along with this next exercise to set up lights in a broadcast text animation.

1. Load into Layout the scene you've been creating throughout this chapter. You also can use the LightMe scene from the CD-ROM.

   A default distant light is always in the scene. This scene has transparencies and glows, so adding a ray-traced shadow to the mix will not help with rendering. Instead, spotlights can add soft shadows with fast rendering.

2. Select the default light, and press p to display the Light Properties panel.

3. Change the Light Type to Spotlight. Make both the Spotlight Soft Edge Angle and Spotlight Cone Angle 40 degrees. Spotlights shine a round cone of light. The angle in degrees is the size of the cone, zero being no cone, and 40 about average.

   The Spotlight Soft Edge Angle will add a nice edge falloff to the light. This light will be the key light for the scene. The default color is white, but no light is ever a pure white.

4. Change the Light Color so that it is slightly off-white. The Light Intensity should be at 100 percent.

5. Because this is the main light for the scene, move it up and to the left, in front of the objects.

   This position also will help cast decent shadows from foreground elements to the background elements, helping to add depth to the animation. Figure 17.47 shows the position through Light view in Layout.

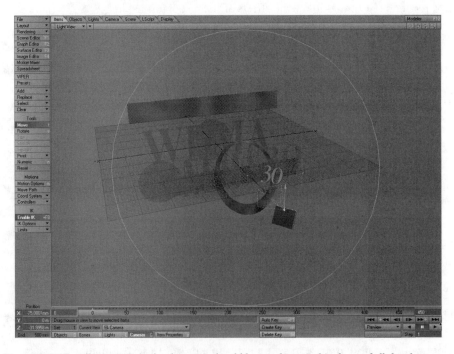

Figure 17.47   The main light for the scene should be set above and in front of all the elements. This is the view from the first light.

The next light can be added to help create some brightness on the main logos of the scene. You don't want it to look like there is just one big, hot light shining on the objects. By adding a soft white light off to the side, you enhance the feeling of distance and depth.

6. Add another spotlight and move it off to the right side of the elements. Use Light view to position and rotate the light into place. The light properties don't need to be specific; simply make sure that all the objects are lit. Make the color soft white, and set the Light Intensity to 75 percent or so—you don't want this light to overpower the main light.

   This light will focus on the 3D elements at they appear, and then follow them into place.

   You also can try the opposite position, below the objects to light the bottom. Test a few options to see which you like best.

   Lighting definitely can be a lot of fun when it comes to 3D animation, but the Ambient Intensity is also important. For this broadcast-style animation, this one last setting can make the elements pop off the screen more than they already do.

7. From the Lights tab, go to Global Illumination and set the Ambient Intensity to 0 percent (default 25 percent). Too much ambient light can flatten your scene and take away the effects of your lighting. Ambient light is the area in the animation not directly hit by any of your lights. As a rule, 0 percent to 5 percent is a good Ambient Intensity value.

There's only one more thing to do before you can render this animation—make it all move!

Movement and Timing

When it comes to broadcast-style animations, your goal should be to keep everything moving. Watch any of the major television productions—the titles are always moving. Perhaps the main title flies in and sits, but the background or foreground elements are in motion from the time the animation fades in from black, to the time it fades out. This is easy to do, especially on the animation you've created in this chapter.

Exercise 17.12   Putting Elements in Motion

Earlier in this chapter, you adjusted the positions of the objects in Modeler so they're viewed correctly when rendered. You also increased the size of the flat letters and left them far back into the scene so that they blend into the background, without being affected by the shadows of the 3D elements. Start by putting those two elements in motion.

1. Select the WDMA object in Layout from the elements and scene you've created in this chapter.

2. Press t on the keyboard to switch to Rotate mode. Move the WDMA object to the right, on the x-axis only. If Show Handles is turned on under the Display Options tab, you should be able to click and drag the red handle to constrain movement only on the x-axis. Create a keyframe at 0 for it.

3. Next, move the WDMA text to the left of the screen only on the x-axis, and create a keyframe at frame 450.

    This makes it move over the course of 15 seconds. Your animation might not be 15 seconds long, but the object will stay moving, so if you render 300 frames (10 seconds at 30 frames per second), your object will still be moving as the animation ends.

4. Select the flat NEWS text object. Move it to the left side of the screen and create a keyframe at 0 to lock it in place. This text object can hang out of the frame as well—remember, it's a background element. Move it to the right of the frame and create a keyframe at 500. This will change speed from the WDMA motion.

5. To add more elements to the scene, clone this object and move it to the top of the frame. Feel free to make it larger to add variation to it.

6. To continue adding movement, select the first 3D NEWS object, the N, and move it up close to the camera. Rotate it on its heading about 60 degrees, and rotate the pitch about 35 degrees. Create a keyframe at 0 for it, as shown in Figure 17.48.

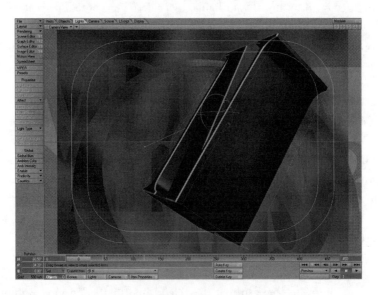

Figure 17.48   The first 3D element is rotated up close to the camera.

7. Rotate the N object to its original state and create a keyframe at 45. Then move it back into the scene at 120 slightly to the left, leaving room for the rest of the letters—E, W, and S—to come in, and make sure rotation stays the same (see Figure 17.49). Create a key to lock it in place.

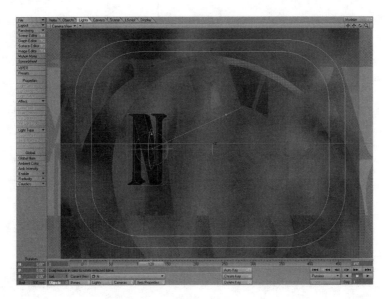

Figure 17.49   The 3D N object rotates in front of the camera and pulls back into the frame over 4 seconds.

8. Now for the E. This letter will perform the same move as the previous one, but instead of starting at frame zero, it will begin rotating at frame 45, right when the N object pulls back. Rotate the E about 45 degrees on its heading and 20 degrees on the pitch. Create one keyframe at 0 and one at 45 to lock it in place over those frames. Note that the letters should be in front of the camera when you create these initial keyframes.

9. Rotate the E back to 0 heading and pitch, and then create a keyframe at 85. Then, move the letter back into the scene, resting to the right of the N, at frame 150. Figure 17.50 shows the resting position of the E.

10. At this point, create the same motions for the W and the S, offsetting each about 44 frames or so.

11. Before you move on, there are a few things you can do to smooth out the motion of the letters. Select the N object and open the Graph Editor. Using the right mouse button (hold the Apple key on the Mac), drag out around the last keyframes at 120 for all channels. Set a Tension of 1.0 to make the N ease into its resting position. Figure 17.51 shows the panel.

12. Add another style element to the letters. Make them dissolve into view. Select the N object and press the p key to open the Object Properties for it.

13. Click to the Rendering tab, and then click the E button for Object Dissolve to enter the dissolve channel into the Graph Editor.

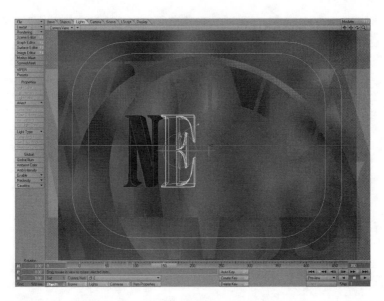

Figure 17.50   The 3D E object rotates in front of the camera and pulls back into the frame over 4 seconds, but doesn't start until the N performs its move.

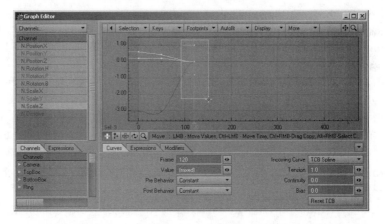

Figure 17.51   Using the Graph Editor, you can tweak any or all of your channels' motions for your objects.

14. You don't want the object to dissolve (or fade) on, rotate, and then move back. Instead, you want the dissolve to come on and see that the object is already in motion. So, set one keyframe in the Graph Editor at 10 and another at 45.

15. Set the Value at frames 0 and 10 to 100 percent, so the object is 100 percent dissolved for the first 10 frames of the animation. Give frame 45 a Value of 0 percent, so that the object is not dissolved at all at frame 45. (If you recall, it's at frame 45 that the object starts to pull back from the camera and move into position.) Add a Tension of 1.0 to all frames to ease in and ease out the dissolve. Figure 17.52 shows the Graph Editor at this point.

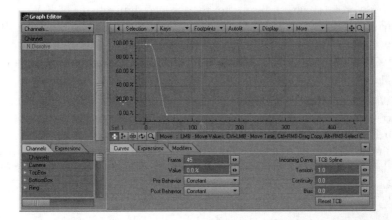

Figure 17.52   Create a dissolve envelope in the Graph Editor to make the N object dissolve as it is rotating.

16. Once you've set up the keyframes for the other letters, also set an object dissolve for them, but offset it 45 frames, just like the motion.

Note

If you'd like, you can use the Graph Editor to copy and paste all the motions of the N object to the other letters. From there, simply select all frames in the Graph Editor's curve window, hold the Ctrl key, and drag to the right to offset the motion. You can do the same with the Dissolve envelope. Read more about the Graph Editor in Chapter 5, "LightWave 7 Graph Editor." You can use expressions or the Follower plug-in to easily automate a single movement for multiple items.

Put one more element in motion: the abc logo. As the N, E, W, and S letters are rotating, dissolving, and animating in the scene, the abc logo has been waiting quietly in the background. Once the NEWS letters have been revealed, the abc logo can perform a similar move, by dissolving and rotating in place.

17. Move the abc 3D logo back into the scene next to the N object. Rotate it –90 degrees on its heading. Create a keyframe at 0, and another at 300. The object won't be revealed for 10 seconds, which allows enough time for the other elements to enter the scene.

18. At frame 370, rotate the abc logo back to 0 for the Heading. Create another keyframe in this same position at 400, so that the logo sits for 1 second. Then, rotate it 180 degrees on the heading, and move it up toward the camera so that it fills the frame.

19. Create a key at frame 450 for the abc logo.

   The back of the abc logo is 100 percent luminous white. By filling the frame with it, the client can use this animation as a wipe or transition to a video clip, using the bright white backing of the abc logo as a window or mask for the video.

20. Lastly, create an object dissolve for the abc logo similar to the N, E, W, and S letters, that stretches over 40 frames. The dissolve should start at frame 0 as 100 percent dissolved and then end 0 percent dissolved at frame 40. Save the scene.

   You can load the NewsLogo scene from the book's CD to see the final motions in place.

   What's important to understand here is that simple motions with object dissolves can create an appealing look for your animations. The trick you need to remember is to overlap the motions. Have the dissolve happening as the object is already in motion. As soon as one object is almost 0 percent dissolved, bring in the next object, and then the next. Make your animations flow. And then during all of this, the background animation is moving slowly, with a nice soft glowing look.

21. As an additional element, slowly rotate the ring object during the animation as well. In addition, you can move the main null object, the NewsMover object, slowly back into the frame as an added element.

Too often, animators feel the need to move things fast and furious. If you're keyframing, things should move fast, right? Well, not always. The most creative broadcast animations involve slow, colorful, moving elements, which is what you've created here. Remember to not overdo it. Subtle and classy is what you want for these types of animations. You can load the NewsLogo scene from the book's CD and take a look at the final scene with lights and movements. Something should always be moving, and movements should not be sudden. After you've set everything in motion, all you need to do is render it out.

Rendering for Broadcast

Rendering your animations is your final step to get this animation finished and out the door. The way in which you render it is crucial to the overall success of the project. Broadcast rendering needs to be of high quality, but not nearly the quality of that for film. Rendering for film requires almost four times the resolution than for broadcast. What does that mean to you as an animator? It means longer render times! Rendering for broadcast only requires you to set up a few key items within LightWave and does not take forever to render.

Resolution Settings

The first step to rendering for broadcast is to determine where your animation is going. In other words, are you going to use an animation recorder to play the animation to tape? Are you rendering directly to tape? Or is the animation going to stay digital and be edited together in a nonlinear editor? This is key to setting up the proper resolution for your animation. If you are rendering for an animation recorder, such as the Perception Video Recorder from Digital Processing Systems, you need to render in a different resolution than you would if you were rendering to a NewTek Video Toaster, an Avid system, or a Stratosphere nonlinear editor from Accom, to name a few.

Video resolution should be determined and set in the Camera Properties panel, as you did earlier in this chapter. You can choose a preset resolution from the drop-down list, such as D1 NTSC. This sets up your animation for a render with a pixel width of 720 and a pixel height of 486. It also sets the pixel aspect ratio to 0.9, which is the proper aspect ratio for NTSC video. If you are working with a PAL setup, you can select the D1 PAL Resolution setting, which sets a pixel width of 720 and a pixel height of 576. The pixel aspect ratio will change to 1.0667.

If you need to set a custom resolution, as you would for the Perception Video Recorder, you can manually adjust the width and height values to create a custom resolution. The PVR resolution setting is 720×480. To decide which resolution you need, it's best to check with your client or video editor. You also can check the documentation of the recording device you choose to use. They usually will list the resolution needed to bring in animations, video clips, and so on.

Antialiasing Settings

After you have determined a proper resolution, you need to set up antialiasing. Antialiasing is a smoothing process in LightWave Layout that ranges from Low and Enhanced Low to Extreme and Enhanced Extreme. For a broadcast-style animation, an Antialiasing setting of Enhanced Medium works well. This smoothing process takes away the sharp, jagged edges in the final rendered animation and makes the overall appearance clean.

Field Render and Motion Blur

When you're creating animations for film and special effects, you should always add a little motion blur. It makes your objects look more realistic and lifelike. But when it comes to broadcast-style animations, nothing works better for selling the whole package than field rendering. Field rendering draws two fields of video for every frame. What this means is that fast motions do not blur and textures remain visible. Field rendering keeps animated text in broadcast logos clean and smooth. Without field rendering the animation might not look as sharp—almost blurry if the motions are too fast. Be sure to apply Field Rendering to your broadcast and text animations for the best possible quality.

Field rendering is more than simply drawing two fields for each full frame; the frames are interlaced and every other line is 1/60th of a second later in time. This is just the way video is set up and the animation frame needs to mimic this to look correct. If your text isn't moving, field rendering doesn't do anything, because there is no motion between scan lines.

The Next Step

The techniques in this chapter can be applied to many everyday animations, from text, to effects, to image processing animations. You can modify the techniques in this chapter by using different text and different colors. By doing so, you suddenly have an entirely new animation.

After you have worked through the exercises and are comfortable with the techniques and principles applied here, try creating your own broadcast-style animation. Perhaps you can animate your company logo? Another way to practice these types of animations is to copy the big boys. Watch television; watch satellite and cable channels. Set a tape and start recording title animations for your own reference. There is a ton of high-quality work being broadcast every day, each example of which is a spark for a new idea for your next project.

Summary

When you can, experiment with different motions and adjust the timing of your animations. You can refer to Chapter 4, "LightWave 7 Layout," for more information on adjusting timing and keyframes. You can use the techniques in this chapter to go even further with multiple passes: one pass for the background, another for the logos. Toward that end, you might want to read Chapter 18, "Compositing and Rendering" to find out more about multi-pass rendering and compositing.

Part IV

Animation Post and Effects

Chapter 18

Compositing and Rendering

Compositing enables you to seamlessly
blend 3D computer-generated images either
with other 3D computer-generated images
or with 2D images, such as photographs

of real settings or people. Most of the visual effects created for film and video consist of 3D animation and digital effects composited over live-action. This can include photography, video, and film, as well as AVI or QuickTime movies. Using compositing, you can make it seem as though a 3D object is there when it actually isn't.

An important aspect of compositing with LightWave is that it enables you to do more, especially if your system is not as fast as you'd like it to be. Compositing in this sense enables you to blend multiple images together. Of course, before you can complete a composite in LightWave, you'll need to render! Later in this chapter, you'll learn about the steps needed to render your composite animations for many types of applications.

Understanding Compositing

Compositing is an art unto itself. Production houses often have entire departments devoted to the task and thousands of dollars invested in compositing software. From the optically composited spaceships of *Star Wars* to the digital apes of 20th Century Fox's *Planet of the Apes*, compositing has come a long way. Over the years, compositing technology has evolved from purely optical techniques such as matte paintings and frame-by-frame painting to completely digital methods, but compositing will always be an important part of animation and visual effects. It is its own unique art. That is the core of success for most Hollywood production studios.

Indeed, the enormous importance of compositing has led to the development of many high-powered, complex, and *expensive* programs dedicated to the task. But LightWave comes with its own, rather extensive set of tools both for compositing within the program and for exporting images to be composited in other software packages.

In this chapter, you will examine several different compositing techniques. You will use LightWave's compositing tools to do the following:

- Place a 3D object against a still background
- Place and move a 3D object in front of and behind a photograph
- Place a 3D spider on an image of a real table
- Examine the basic techniques for doing two-pass compositing
- Learn about LightWave's render engine and output options

Beginning Compositing: Background and Foreground Images

Compositing can be an extraordinarily complicated process, combining hundreds of separate 2D and 3D elements into one final image. However, many times it's just as simple as placing a 3D object against a background image.

A background image, or *background plate*, as it is commonly called, is a 2D image. It is usually a digitized photograph or sequence of film, though not necessarily so; sometimes other rendered 3D footage is used as the background image. A 3D object is placed against the background image to make it appear as though the 3D object was always a part of the background. An example of this would be the creatures in *Jurassic Park III*. Real settings were filmed with a regular camera, the footage was digitized, and then the 3D dinosaurs were composited into the footage to make them appear to be part of the picture.

Of course, compositing can be more complex than the simple explanation above. But regardless of how complex the composite, the background image is the beginning of every composited scene.

In LightWave, the background image has its place in the Effects panel, under the Compositing tab (see Figure 18.1). This is where you will begin the first exercise.

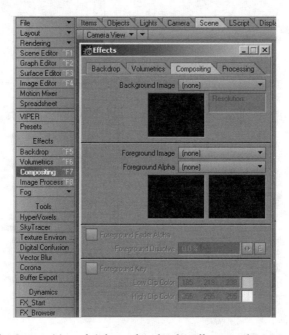

Figure 18.1   The Compositing tab is located under the Effects panel. Most everything needed for compositing in LightWave can be found here.

Exercise 18.1   Placing a 3D Object Against a Photograph

In this first exercise, you learn the basics for setting up just about any composited scene. You learn how to load a background plate, as well as a 3D object, and marry the two seamlessly. Study this process, because it will be the same for any composite you do in LightWave.

1. From Layout, click the Scene tab. Open the Compositing tab of the Effects panel by clicking the Compositing button.
2. Click the list beside Background Image, and select Load Image.
3. Load the Trees image from the book's CD-ROM, as shown in Figure 18.2.

Note

In addition to loading images directly from the Compositing tab, you also can go directly to the Image Editor and select Load Image. This enables you to load your image or sequence while having access to image-editing features.

Figure 18.2   A nice bright sky, complete with trees and clouds, acts as a backdrop for compositing.

4. Render a frame. You'll see the tree image and nothing else.

Only the tree image is displayed in the render, because nothing else has yet been added to the scene. There are a few important things to note at this point:

- When using a background image, this image overrides any backdrop color or gradient backdrop.
- The background image is not affected by fog, though it can be used as the fog color instead of a solid color.
- By default, the background image will not be refracted by transparent objects. However, you can set this option for each surface in the Surface Editor.
- The background image will always be centered and stretch itself to fill the camera's entire field of view. This also is true of the foreground image, which you'll get to shortly.
- The background image can be seen directly in Layout through Camera view if the Camera View Background is set to Background Image in the Display Options tab (d).

 Note

Special thanks to Ken VanBrocklin (*kvanbroc@qwest.net*) for the cool F16 aircraft model that we'll be using in this exercise.

The next step involves adding a 3D object into the scene.

5. Load the F16 object from the book's CD.

6. Select the F16 object, and press 6 on the numeric keypad to switch to Camera view. Make sure that Camera View Background is set to Background Image in the Display Options tab (d).

7. Move the F16 object back into the frame, and rotate it so that it is heading more toward the front right of the frame. Move it up so that it looks like it's resting just above the trees, as shown in Figure 18.3.

8. Press F9 and render a frame.

Now the 3D object is composited against the background image, the most basic of all compositing situations. Figure 18.4 shows the rendered image.

This technique will work for any situation in which a 3D object does not need to go behind a 2D image. In Chapter 17, "Broadcast-Style Animation," you learned to make a nice moving background, with large 3D letters animated in front. Using the techniques described in this first exercise, you can render that logo background as its own animation. That rendered animation then can be applied back into LightWave as a background image. The 3D letters would then be animated on top.

Figure 18.3   Move the F16 until it appears to be resting atop the trees.

Figure 18.4   A backdrop image has been set in LightWave and an object, the F16, has been loaded. When rendered, the F16 is composited over the background image.

The benefit of this is control. Not only do you have control over what you deliver your client for their needs, but you also have control over shadows, reflections, lights, shaders, and more. Rendering in passes is vital to proper compositing and is covered more fully later in this chapter.

Many times, however, you will need to use a foreground image for situations in which a 3D object *does* need to go behind a 2D image. For example, suppose that a 3D car driving down the street needs to pass by buildings that are in the footage. Using a combination of foreground images (the building) and a background image (the other parts of the footage), you can literally put a 3D element "into" your still or moving imagery.

The foreground image behaves in most ways like the background image. The main difference is that whereas the background image appears *behind* the 3D objects in the scene, the foreground image is applied *on top of* the 3D objects.

You've seen how easy it is to place a 3D object in front of a photograph. The look is convincing, and you can go further with moving images. But what if you need to make the F16 blend more with the photograph? What if it needs to come out from behind the trees? Exercise 18.2 shows you how to do just that.

Exercise 18.2   Applying Foreground Images

1. Continue in Layout from the previous exercise.
2. Under the Compositing tab of the Effects panel, set the tree image as the Background Image.
3. Load the F16 object from the book's CD, if it's not still loaded. Select Camera view.

   You should see the background image pop up into the Layout screen when you select Camera view.
4. Move and rotate the object until it appears, as you see in Figure 18.5. The exact positioning isn't very important at this point. What is important is that the object is placed so that it is roughly split across the top line of the trees—part of the image is across the trees and part is across the sky.

Figure 18.5   By setting the Camera View Background to see the backdrop image, you can easily position the F16 object in Layout. You can see the Layout Grid in this view as well—if it's in the way, you can turn it off through the Display Options tab (d).

5. Press F9 to render a frame.

You'll see that as in Exercise 18.1, the 3D object is pasted over the background image. But in this case it needs to be *behind* the trees! You might think that's a problem. Most compositing programs show you how to composite behind a solid object, like a rock or building, but what about something with various transparent areas, like trees? LightWave makes it easy.

Now you will add the foreground image and see how that changes your final output.

6. Under the Compositing tab of the Effects panel, set the same tree image to Foreground Image. Do not change the background image.

7. Press F9 to render a frame.

You'll see that the 3D object now appears to be gone. It's actually been covered by the foreground image, which in this case is the same as the background image, as shown in Figure 18.6.

Figure 18.6   The F16 object is obscured from view when a foreground image is applied under the Compositing tab.

As you also can see, this isn't terribly useful. All you end up with is the foreground image, which you already had as the background image without the F16 object. For the foreground image to be of any use, parts of the image must be *cut out* to reveal the 3D object behind it.

LightWave provides two means to accomplish this. The first is the Foreground Key and the second the Foreground Alpha.

Foreground Key and Foreground Alpha

In the next exercise, you'll start with the Foreground Key. The Foreground Key is nothing more than a color-keying system such as the blue and greenscreen systems used by TV weathermen and in visual effects throughout the industry. It works by *keying out*—removing—a range of colors that you specify. LightWave gives you two colors: a Low Clip Color and a High Clip Color.

The Low Clip Color is generally the darkest, most saturated color you would want to remove from your foreground image. The High Clip Color is the brightest, least saturated color you'd want to take out. Any colors between these two colors are removed from the foreground image before it's pasted over the rendering.

Exercise 18.3   Setting Up a Foreground Key

In this exercise, you will key out the sky and leave the trees. To do this, you want to pick the darkest, most saturated color in the sky and set this to be the Low Clip Color. And you'll set the brightest, least saturated color for the High Clip Color.

1. Starting where you left off in Exercise 18.2, under the Compositing tab of the Effects panel, check Foreground Key to On.

2. Set the Low Clip Color to R:140 G:180 B:240.

   Now, you're probably wondering where these values come from. Although you can use another image-editing program to determine the color value of the Low Clip (the sky in the tree image), you can do it directly in LightWave.

3. From the Rendering drop-down list at the top left of Layout, select Render Options. In the Render Options panel, set the Render Display to Image Viewer. You'll see two options there: Image Viewer and Image Viewer FP, or "floating point." The FP version is useful for determining values for HDR, or High Dynamic Range imagery. For this project, you want to use Image Viewer for RGB images. Figure 18.7 shows the selection.

Figure 18.7   Using Image Viewer from the Render Options panel can help you determine colors for a foreground key.

4. Press F9 to render a frame. After the frame is rendered, the Image Viewer opens. Move the mouse over the area of the sky where the F16 will appear. Click and hold the mouse, and look at the title bar of the Image Viewer panel.

Values appear there! Those are the RGB values of the image where the mouse is. You'll see four values—the Red, Green, Blue, and Alpha. The first two sets of numbers before the dashed line are the pixel number of the image.

The 140, 180, 240 RGB value for the Low Clip Color setting was determined using the Image Viewer. Cool, huh?

 Note
You can read more about render options later in this chapter.

5. Back under the Compositing tab of the Effects panel, set the High Clip Color to R:255 G:255 B:255.

Note

You can set color values quickly by dragging with the right mouse button directly over the color square.

6. In the Render Options panel, make sure that Show Rendering In Progress in checked on and that Image Viewer is still active.

7. Press F9 to render a frame and watch as it renders. Figure 18.8 shows the render.

As LightWave renders, you should see the foreground image render first, but you'll notice that it doesn't render all of the sky because those colors fall within the range between the Low Clip Color and High Clip Color that you specified. You'll then see the F16 object render in the blank area above the trees. Finally, the Background Image is put in behind that.

Figure 18.8   Using a Foreground Key and setting the Low and High Clip Colors drops out the sky of the Foreground Key, enabling you to see the object and the background image.

This is a good technique to use when your foreground image will support it. In this case, the image was a good candidate for this technique because the area you needed to key out was a large bright area with very little variation in color, and it was significantly different in color than the rest of the picture.

However, not all images are this easy. For images that are more complex, or for those times when you want more control, LightWave offers you the Foreground Alpha.

An *alpha* is a grayscale image that is used to tell a program where certain things should happen. In the case of a surface texture, an alpha image would tell the surface where to apply a texture map. It could tell a surface where to be transparent and where to be opaque. And in the case of a foreground image, the alpha image determines where the image will appear and where it won't.

Exercise 18.4   Using Foreground Alpha

This exercise will use a feature available in LightWave that enables you to key out portions of an image for foreground compositing. This technique uses the Foreground key features to remove parts of an image.

1. Continuing from the previous exercise, using the Image Editor, load the image TreesAlpha.tga from the book's CD. Turn off Foreground Key under the Compositing tab if it's still active.

2. Under the Compositing tab of the Effects panel, beside the Foreground Alpha image, click the selector and choose the TreesAlpha image. If you want, you can load an image from here as well.

3. Click the checkbox beside Foreground Fader Alpha.

   This tells LightWave to ignore the areas of the foreground image that the Foreground Alpha has marked pure black. Otherwise, those areas will be added to the image, making that part of the image much too bright.

4. Press F9 to render a frame. Figure 18.9 shows the rendered image.

Figure 18.9   Using a Foreground Alpha image gives you precise control over where the composited foreground image will be clipped. There also is a much cleaner edge between the leaves and the F16.

Now you can see that the rendered image appears much as it did with the Foreground Key, but this time using an alpha image. Using an alpha image gives you much more flexibility in determining where your foreground image appears. It also is more accurate than using a range of colors to clip the image. However, both methods are suitable depending on the project and the images at hand.

Using alpha images when compositing gives you the most control over your scene because the alpha image can be used to shape the foreground image into any shape you desire.

The situation outlined in the previous exercise would be fine if your 3D object needed only to be placed behind the trees and in front of the sky. But if your object needed to start out behind the trees, rise up above them, and then swoop down in front of them, it wouldn't work. The foreground image would be pasted on top, no matter what.

Another, more common situation is having a 3D object cast shadows and otherwise interact with your 2D images. This kind of seamless compositing is the mainstay of the visual effects industry. Without it, the movies and television shows you watch every day would be tremendously different.

As you might have guessed, LightWave has the answer to compositing and casting shadows—Front Projection Image Mapping.

Intermediate Compositing: Front Projection Image Mapping

Front Projection Image Mapping is one of the most powerful compositing tools LightWave has to offer. It enables your 3D objects to interact with your 2D images in almost every way that they can interact with other 3D objects.

Front Projection Image Mapping works by—you guessed it—projecting an image onto an object. The image is "projected" from the camera's point of view such that it would appear exactly as though it were a background or foreground image. This technique is difficult to explain but easy to understand when you see it for yourself—and you will, in the next exercise.

Exercise 18.5   Applying Front Projection Image Mapping

The methods of compositing you've learned in the previous exercises will be a staple for your compositing projects. This next exercise employs an additional method that enables you to cast shadows on background images.

1. Start with a clean workspace in Layout by selecting Clear Scene from the File menu.

2. Load the object HuronPolys object from the book's CD. This is a flat polygon with a picture of a cityscape applied.

3. Open the Surface Editor, and make sure that the HuronPolys surface is selected. Click the T button beside the Color channel to open the Texture Editor.

4. Select Load Image from the Image list, and Load the image HuronSt from the book's CD. This is a digital photograph of East Huron Street in Chicago.

5. In the Texture Editor, click the drop-down list beside Projection and select Front, as shown in Figure 18.10.

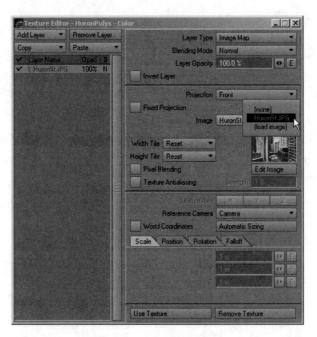

Figure 18.10   In the Texture Editor, you can tell LightWave to map an image as a Front Projection Image for compositing by selecting Front from the projection list.

6. Make sure that you have Image set to HuronSt.

7. Uncheck Pixel Blending and Texture Antialiasing to produce a cleaner rendered image. (Because you are going to match this mapped image with the same image in the background, you want them to match perfectly.) Set Width Tile and Height Tile to Reset. You do not want the image to repeat.

8. Click Use Texture and return to the Surface Editor.

9. Set the surface's Luminosity to 100 percent.

This will make the image self-illuminating and help you match the backdrop. LightWave can't cast light onto a backdrop image, but because the front projection image is on a polygon, you do not want LightWave's lights to be its only light source.

10. Set the surface's Diffuse to 0 percent to tell the surface not to accept any light from the scene. The Luminosity setting will make it visible.

11. Render a frame. Figure 18.11 shows the render thus far.

Figure 18.11   As it stands now, the render looks like nothing more than a regular image map on an odd polygon. But wait!

You can see that the 2D image of the hotel and sky appears wherever the object is. The image was mapped on the object from the point of view of the camera, exactly as a foreground or background image would appear. Moving the object does not move the image; it only moves that part of the image that is shown. Similar to rotating the object, the region defined by the shape of the object is the region of the image that will be shown, no matter what position it's in.

Note

To illustrate this point more fully, feel free to move, rotate, size, and stretch the object. Render a frame. It always will show a portion of the image no matter where you place it or what its angle is. Remember that by using OpenGL Textured Shaded Solid view, you'll be able to see your textures applied in real time, directly in Layout. Rendering an image will give you a more accurate idea of the setup with lighting.

Theoretically, if you were to set this same image to be the background image of the scene, the images should blend seamlessly. In fact, this is the case.

12. Under the Compositing tab of the Effects panel, click the selector beside Background Image and select HuronSt.

13. Press F9 to render a frame.

If you have Show Rendering In Progress still turned on from the Render Options panel, you will see LightWave render the object and then fill in the background image around it. Now you can't distinguish between the two. Figure 18.12 shows the example.

Figure 18.12   When the HuronSt image is placed as the background image, the front projection mapping seamlessly matches up with the image-mapped polygon.

It's this ability to blend seamlessly that gives Front Projection Image Mapping its power. In the next exercise, you'll examine how to really use that power.

Exercise 18.6   Creating Shadows for Compositing

Front Projection Image Mapping is unique in the way it maps the texture image, but in every other way it's just a normal surface texture. It can receive shadows, reflect other objects, and be transparent. By using these characteristics, you can make the objects appear to interact with the scene.

1. Picking up from Exercise 18.5, make sure that the HuronPolys object is still loaded.

2. Create a keyframe at 0 to lock the camera in place. If you don't do this, when you load the F16 object (which you will be instructed to do shortly), the camera will be in a different position due to LightWave's automatic grid size change based on the size of the F16 object. Once the camera's keyframe is set, load the F16 object into the scene.

   Now that you have the two components of the scene, you need to place them in the proper position.

   The HuronPolys object is a stand-in for the buildings you see in the image. Because you can't cast shadows on background images in LightWave, the

HuronPolys object is a flat polygon made to match the shapes of the building that will catch the shadows. Using Front Projection Image Mapping as in the previous exercise, you can match the polygon to the backdrop.

You don't have an exact 3D model of the hotel to use, and for what you're going to do, you don't need one. However, the F16 object here will do perfectly fine and really doesn't need to be more complex. The F16 object once again is going to be the subject.

3. The first step in doing a shot such as this is to establish your camera angle. There are various techniques you can use, and you'll find that there are entire programs dedicated to the task. However, you're going to start out with LightWave, and you'll see that in certain cases, it isn't even that difficult.

   When trying to match the camera to a real picture, you need to look for reference points first. Usually, the best reference points are those on the ground, or even the ground itself. But you'll notice that in this picture you do not see much ground at all. This is both bad and good; bad because it doesn't give you any easy reference, and good because if you don't have to see the ground, you don't have to be as preciese in the setup. Precision eats up time, and time is money. Hence, the less precision you can get away with, the better. The beauty is that the look and effect will be the same. As mentioned earlier, easy compositing all depends on the project at hand.

   Therefore, without the ground to use for reference, all you're left with are the buildings themselves. Looking at the angle, it's safe to say this picture was taken from another building, looking down the street. From counting the window divisions from the building on the right, which you can safely assume to be whole stories, you can guess that the building is somewhere on the order of 140–160 feet tall, given a story is about 10 feet. Again, precise measurements aren't necessary in this instance, so don't sweat the details. You just want a good idea to start with.

   Comparing the height of the building, which is about 140 feet, to the height of a human, which is about 5–6 feet, you see that the building on the right is about two orders of magnitude taller than a person. What does this mean to you? It means that the height of the camera in the scene doesn't really matter, as long as it's quite close to zero. As a matter of fact, you're going to leave it at zero and eliminate that variable altogether.

   So you have the coordinates for the camera's position: 0,0,0. The next thing to figure out is the angle at which the camera is pointed. You'll need a reference to do that. The perfect reference is the HuronPolys object.

   The HuronPolys object is going to be standing in for three of the walls of the buildings in the shot—the larger building on the left, the taller building on the right closest to the camera, and the ugly round buildings next to it. Because of this, you know that it has to be about 140 to 160 feet high. Knowing that the size of the HuronPolys object is 1 meter, you need to scale it up about twice its size.

4. Size the HuronPolys object to 1.6 on the x-, y-, and z-axes.

Once you size up the HuronPolys object, use the background image as a reference.

5. Make sure that Camera View Background under the Display tab is set to Background Image. In Camera view, you can see the HuronPolys object as well as the background image.

If it's hard to see the separation of the HuronPolys image and the background image, bring the luminosity on the surface down for setup, or open the Scene Editor and set the HuronPolys object to Wireframe Visibility mode. This will enable you to see the background image through the object.

If needed, you should position the HuronPolys object so that it's about the right size and angle to match the buildings.

As you can see in Figure 18.13, sizing up the HuronPolys object aligns the object with the top edge of the buildings.

Figure 18.13   Align the HuronPolys object with the background image, using Size and Move. Here the object has been darkened for you to see its alignment.

6. Move the F16 object back into the scene, and turn it around on the heading so that it's facing the camera.

Now you'll probably need to play with the positioning of the object so that it "feels" right.

Many times, animators are looking for a magic variable to set up composite shots. In actuality, nothing is better than your own eye and sense of judgment. Does the 3D object look too big for its environment? If so, make it smaller. Does the object look out of perspective? If it does, rotate and reposition it.

7. Do a test render by pressing F9 so that you'll have something to compare to, as shown in Figure 18.14. Save the scene.

Figure 18.14 After positioning the HuronPolys object, you'll see that it is more closely aligned with the top edge of the hotel. Notice how the polygon edge outline is lined up along the sides of the building. The F16 looks now as though it's behind the building.

With the Front Projection Image Map as it is now, the F16 could cast a slight shadow onto the sky—which is obviously not good. This effect could happen because it's difficult to perfectly line up polygon edges with the background image. To avoid this, you could tweak the scaling of the object until it fits perfectly to the building. The problem is, that's a lot of work, and there's still the issue of the irregular edge at the top of the buildings. No amount of tweaking and scaling would fit the square to that shape. To solve the problem, you need to call on the help of Clip Maps.

Clip Maps

A clip map is a special kind of image map. It can be applied every way a normal texture can, but it works in a much different way. A clip map is an image map that determines where an object will exist. It's very similar to transparency, but instead of determining where an object is clear or opaque, it actually determines whether the object is there.

Exercise 18.7   Working with Clip Maps

In this exercise, you're going to use a clip map to "trim away" the unwanted parts of the polygons and make the polygon conform to the shape of the building. You've got an image already prepared for this.

   1. Load the image HuronPolyAlpha from the book's CD.

      This image is much like the alpha image you used before. Like transparency, for a clip map, white denotes where the object *won't* be, and black shows where it *will* be. White denotes where an object is fully clipped out, and black shows where it's not clipped at all. To make sure that everything lines up perfectly, you're going to Front Projection Image Map the clip map onto the polygon.

2. Select the HuronPolys object and open the Object Properties panel (p) for it.

3. Click the Rendering tab.

4. Click the T beside Clip Map to open its Texture Editor.

5. Set the Projection type to Front.

6. Select HuronStAlpha as the Image.

7. Uncheck Pixel Blending and Texture Antialiasing to produce a cleaner rendered image. Set Width Tile and Height Tile to Reset. You do not want the image to repeat.

8. Check Invert Layer. You need to do this from time to time if your black areas are white and your white areas are black.

    The inversion makes it so that the white areas are left in and the black areas are clipped out. Notice that the white area in the preview image is the exact shape of the buildings. This assures you that the object behind the stand-in object, the F16 object, will appear behind the hotel when using Front Projection Image Mapping. The F16 will not be composited correctly if the stand-in object is not aligned with the backdrop image.

Note

To create the stand-in objects for compositing and Front Projection Image Mapping, you can load the desired backdrop image into Modeler and create polygons that are the exact size and shape, based on the image.

Tip

When using a clip map, the polygon shape can be a simple rectangle.

9. Press F9 to do a test render. Figure 18.15 shows the scene thus far.

    Now you should see the building image with an area of plain gray where the polygon is, and the polygon should be perfectly fit to the edge of the building. Behold the power of the clip map!

    Now you can put the F16 into place and continue on.

10. Move the F16 object toward the camera slightly, out from behind the building on the left.

11. Rotate the F16 on its bank about –25 degrees. You might want to size the F16 down a bit as well, so that you can move it in front of the building.

Figure 18.15   Position the stand-in object, and it's almost ready to catch some shadows!

Note

You might need to adjust the Grid size at this point to about 1m. Otherwise, you'll have some OpenGL clipping as the F16 nears the Camera view.

This will put the F16 a little bit out of realistic scale but make it a lot easier to see in the composite (see Figure 18.16). Feel free to adjust and position as needed, just so that the F16 sits in front of the building polygons.

Figure 18.16   Now the F16 hovers in front of the buildings, just waiting to be a part of the scene!

Exercise 18.8   Compositing Light Shadows

The next step is to match the virtual LightWave light to the real light in the scene. Like camera matching, there's no certain way you have to go about doing this, but there are generally much more obvious reference points for light matching, and they're called *shadows*. Let's take a look at how you can match them.

First, you need to be able to see both the real and virtual shadows.

1. Go back to the Object Properties panel for the HuronPolys object.

2. Set the Dissolve to 50 percent, under the Rendering tab. In the Surface Editor, make sure that the HuronPolys object surface has some Diffuse set, about 50 percent, and Luminosity is set to about 50 percent. This will allow the building to catch a shadow.

3. Check the Render Options panel. Make sure that Ray Trace Shadows is turned On.

4. Do a test render. Figure 18.17 shows the partially dissolved stand-in object.

Figure 18.17   The stand-in object is dissolved out 50 percent, enabling you to see the position of the sunlight to cast appropriate shadows from the F16 object.

Now you can see the large shadow on the side of the building cast by the F16 on the polygon. You should also be able to see that this shadow doesn't match the shadows on the ground and throughout the image. For the rest of the composite to hold up, it is essential that the shadows match very closely.

5. Move the light to –640mm on the X, 900mm on the Y, and –2m on the Z.

6. Rotate the Light to 20 degrees on its Heading and 30 degrees on its Pitch. Create a keyframe to lock it in place.

7. Save the scene and then do a test render. Figure 18.18 shows the shot with the light adjusted and the shadow of the jet in place.

Figure 18.18   When the light is adjusted to match the original building image and Ray Traced Shadows is set to On in the Render Options panel, the F16 casts a nice shadow on the stand-in object.

There, that's better. Now the shadow seems to line up nicely with the large one on the wall of the hotel.

You might be wondering why you haven't yet set up the Front Projection Image Map of the building onto the polygon. As you'll see, it will be necessary to balance precisely the diffuse and luminosity values of the polygon's surface to make the compositing seamless and the shadow values match. Because the brightness of the polygon is partly determined by the angle of the light in the scene, it is best to get the light situated first and only then begin to adjust the surface values.

Exercise 18.9   Matching Front Projection Images

This exercise guides you into the next step in this compositing project. You'll learn how to balance the brightness of the applied texture maps to match the background plate.

1. Continuing with the scene from the previous exercise, go back to the Object Properties panel for the HuronPolys object.

2. Under the Rendering tab, set the Object Dissolve back to 0 percent. Close the Object Properties panel.

3. Open the Global Illumination panel.

4. Set the Ambient Intensity to 10 percent.

   With the polygon fully back in place, it's time to surface it.

5. Open the Surface Editor. Select the HuronPolys surface.

6. Click the T beside the Color channel to open its Texture Editor.

7. Set the Projection type to Front.

8. Select HuronSt as the Image.

9. Uncheck Pixel Blending and Texture Antialiasing to produce a cleaner rendered image. Set Width Tile and Height Tile to Reset. You do not want the image to repeat.

10. Press F9 to render. Figure 18.19 shows the changes.

Figure 18.19   After the front projection mapping is applied to the HuronPolys object, the F16 looks like it's casting a shadow onto the building.

Now the building image is projected onto the polygon, matching up nicely with the rest of the image, but the brightness isn't quite right. Here's where you have to eyeball it. You have to play with the Diffuse and Luminosity values until the polygon matches the background image and the shadow values of the objects match those in the image.

11. Click Use Texture to exit the Texture Editor.

12. Set the Luminosity of the surface to 40 percent. Set Diffuse to 90 percent.

13. Do a test render. Figure 18.20 shows the change.

Now the values of the polygon surface and the background image match seamlessly. But the shadow is a little too light. You need to set the Luminosity lower and the Diffuse value higher.

14. Set the Luminosity to 10 percent.

15. Set the Diffuse to 153 percent.

You might need to play with the values slightly until you get the right balance of shadow and light.

16. Do a test render. Figure 18.21 shows the final render with matched shadows.

Figure 18.20   Adjusting the luminosity and diffuse of the HuronPolys object surface balances the brightness of the front projection image. But the shadow is lighter than the shadows on the building and ground.

Figure 18.21   Here is the finished render with properly matched shadows. You'll also notice that the building to the left of the F16 is casting a shadow, even though it's nothing more than a flat polygon. The F16 will now come through the buildings, picking up and casting shadows.

The shadow has a pretty nice value, closely matching the shadows the building casts on itself. This scene would be good enough for any situation in which the F16 flies down Huron Street in Chicago. Ever been to the annual Air and Water show?

This is as far as you're going to take this project, but there is a lot more you could do with it to flesh it out. For example, you could

- Set other walls in place to receive shadows or even model an entire stand-in of the other buildings on the street.

- Model the buildings' windows to receive not just shadows, but also reflections! Nice touch!

- Add more lights to more fully simulate the light in the scene, such as a light below the F16 to simulate bounced light.

- Add a bit of fog, or some blur, to help better blend the F16 into the background.

- Add post-processing filters such as film grain. A bit of film grain usually helps to really set in the objects. Right now, the object is too clean for the image.

Situations like you've just seen—casting shadows on vertical walls such as the buildings—are fairly common. But what's even more likely is what you'll examine next.

Exercise 18.10   Casting Compositing Ground Shadows

Having a 3D object cast a shadow onto "real" ground is probably the most common compositing situation you'll have to deal with. By *ground shadow*, we're referring to flat shadows on the y-axis. It's hard for people to comprehend at times how you can have a shadow below an object when the image is behind it. But it's a lot easier than it sounds. Most every principle you just learned will translate directly. You'll follow the exact steps you just followed:

- Position the camera.

- Position the stand-in 3D object.

- Position the 3D subject—in this case, a spider.

- Adjust the lighting.

- Adjust the surface of the ground plane.

In this exercise, you're going to place a 3D spider on a "real" table and make it fit right in. Figure 18.22 shows what you'll create, using a 3D spider and an extreme close-up picture of a patio table.

1. Clear the scene.

2. Load the tabletop image from the book's CD.

3. From the File drop-down menu, select Load, then the Load Items From Scene command. Select the MovingSpider scene. When asked also to load the lights, click No.

4. Load also the SpiderTableTop object.

Figure 18.22   Using the principles you've learned in this chapter and some creative lighting, you'll end up making an image like this.

5. Under the Compositing tab of the Effects panel, set the Background Image to Tabletop.

6. Under the Display tab of the Preferences panel, set the Camera View Background to Background Image. Figure 18.23 shows the scene at this point from Camera view.

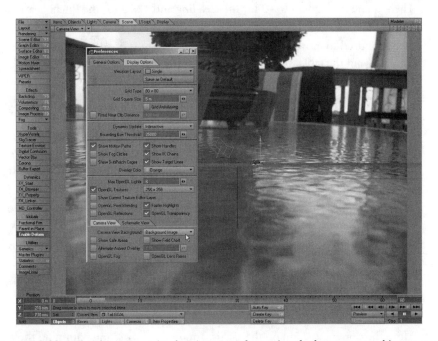

Figure 18.23   The elements are in place in Layout for casting shadows over a real image composited with a 3D spider.

7. Open the Scene Editor and select the SpiderTableTop object.

8. Click Visibility, and choose Show Selected Items As > Bounding Box.

This setting enables you to see where the ground plane and the tabletop object are positioned without obscuring the view of the background image.

Now you need to move the camera so that the spider lines up correctly with the elements in the background image. And like the previous example, there are no hard and fast rules on how to do it. You'll just eyeball it, following a good procedure.

The first thing to do is set the height of the camera. If you know the position the camera was in when the shot was taken, by all means, use that information when setting up the camera position. If you don't know the original camera position, you'll have to guess. Unlike the previous example, in this project, the height of the camera will matter a great deal. In this case, it is known that the picture was taken with a digital camera and that the camera was held low to the table. That means that the height of the camera should be about the height of a person's waist—about 4 feet up from the ground. A good combination of camera and object movement helps get things lined up.

This is just a quick reference—your eye will be the judge.

Move the camera to 2.5m on the x-axis, 1.3m on the y-axis, and –900mm on the z-axis.

Then, rotate the camera to –3 for the Heading and 12.50 for the Pitch. Leave the Bank at 0.

Now you need to move the camera so that the spider is lined up like the other elements and the table. But because you're using realistic measurements for the camera's height, you'll need to adjust the camera's zoom factor so that it's more realistic and matches the background image.

11. In the Camera Properties panel (p), set the Zoom Factor to 2.5. This is roughly equivalent to a 20mm camera lens, which also is an 18.7mm focal length.

Because you changed the camera's Zoom Factor, making a wider shot, you can perform the final tweaks to the view of the camera. This is one of two difficult parts in this type of composite, but here are some tips that might help you:

- Enlarge your grid size until the grid turns into just one line. This is your horizon line. Line this up with the real horizon first.

- Use your grid to help. Try to find straight lines on the ground in the picture and match the grid to those. In this case, you'll use the bumps in the table.

- The hardest part is matching the zoom. Unless you know the lens length from the real camera, you'll just have to guess and work it out through trial and error. Remember, use your best judgment!

12. Move the camera to 2.5m on the x-axis, 1m on the y-axis, and 50mm on the z-axis.

13. Rotate the camera to –2.20 degrees on its Heading and 12.70 degrees on its Pitch. Figure 18.24 shows Layout at this point.

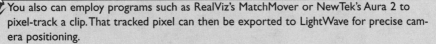

Note

You also can employ programs such as RealViz's MatchMover or NewTek's Aura 2 to pixel-track a clip. That tracked pixel can then be exported to LightWave for precise camera positioning.

Figure 18.24   The spider and camera are in position. Notice how the spider seems to fit in the scene already, and how the lines of perspective match. This is key. These settings were found through trial and error. And that's often the best way to do it. But after you've found that spot and all the lines of perspective are correct, you'll know it.

Now you need to move the ground under the spider. This is much easier.

14. Move the SpiderTableTop object to 10m on the x-axis and 380mm on the z-axis.

You won't need to size the object because it was built in Modeler to match the spider. If it didn't match, you can size it as needed. It is 1 single polygon.

Now that you've got the tabletop, you need to map on the image.

15. In the Surface Editor, select the SpiderTableTop surface.

16. Click the T beside the Color channel to open its Texture Editor.

17. Set the Projection type to Front.

18. Select Tabletop as the Image.

19. Turn off Pixel Blending, Width Repeat, Height Repeat, and Texture Antialiasing.

20. In the Render Options panel, make sure that Ray Trace Shadows is turned on.

21. Press F9 for a test render. Figure 18.25 shows the scene at this point.

Figure 18.25   With the camera aligned and the front projection map on the tabletop, the composited scene is coming together.

Now you've got the tabletop correctly mapped, so it's time to add the lights. To speed the process, there's a light kit already made for you. A light kit usually refers to a pre-made lighting setup that you will use by invoking the Load Items From Scene command. In this case, the light kit consists of two lights: a Key light and a Fill light. The Key light represents the main source of light in the shot, which in this case is the sun. The way to find the proper angle for the Key light is to line up the shadows cast by the 3D object with those already in the background plate, such as the shadows below the planter and candles. This is what you need to match. The Key light in the light kit should match nicely.

The Fill light is a light that generally is opposite of the Key light. It represents bounced light and/or the light from the sky or surrounding objects. Sometimes more than one Fill light is necessary if there are obvious sources of reflected light. Generally speaking, Fill lights should not affect specularity and should not have shadows of any kind, but they can have shadows if you like the look.

Note

It's good to be careful with the values of shadowless Fill lights. They can easily over-brighten your objects. Generally, they should be a very low value—25 percent or less is usually enough.

22. Select File, then Load, and then Load Items From Scene. Load the scene SpiderLights. When prompted, click Yes to "Load Lights from Scene." After this scene is loaded, you'll have two additional lights. Select the light named "light" and press the minus (–) key to delete it. This leaves just the Key_Light and Fill_Light.

Tip

You can Save and Load lights in LightWave. If you have set up a light that you like, you can save it for later use by selecting File, then Save, and Save Current Light.

23. Press F9 to do another test render.

    As you can see, the tabletop is now too bright with the added lights.

24. Open the Surface Editor.

25. Select the SpiderTableTop surface.

26. Set Luminosity to about 60 percent, and set the Diffuse value to 24 percent.

27. Do a test render. Figure 18.26 shows the spider composited on the table.

Figure 18.26   With proper lighting and diffuse settings for the tabletop, and with Ray Traced shadows turned on from the Render Options panel, the spider is starting to blend well with the surrounding.

Now that's more like it! The Front Projection Image Mapped tabletop plane blends seamlessly with the background image and still catches the shadow. A little more tweaking will have the shadows lined up and in place.

28. For the SpiderTableTop surface, set Reflection to 10 percent. Under the Environment tab, set the Reflection Options to Ray Tracing and Spherical Map. Make sure that Trace Reflection is set to On in the Render Options panel.

Note

Now, like the building example earlier in the chapter, this situation, although useful, is somewhat limited. Specifically, this trick would not work if the tabletop were not perfectly flat; an uneven surface would receive light unevenly, thereby keeping the tabletop from blending seamlessly with the background image.

29. At this point, you should save your work. Remember to click Save all Objects to save the surface settings you've applied to your objects.

30. From the File menu, load the SpiderComp_bumpy scene.

31. Press F9 to render, and take a look at Figure 18.27.

Figure 18.27   A bumpy ground is added for additional realism in the composite.

Examining this test render, you can see that the reflections look even more realistic and the shadow from the spider is more diffused. However, the shadow falls unevenly now. Unfortunately, there's no way to conquer this problem using anything you've learned up until now. To get around this, you're going to have to do a two-pass composite.

Note

Whenever possible, study the surroundings of the original image. Pay attention to light conditions, camera height, shadows, and other key elements. These references can help you when putting together composited images. The bumpy tabletop is a subpatched object with a procedural texture applied as a bump map. Bump Displacement is set to On in the Object Properties panel.

Advanced Compositing: Two-Pass Compositing

If it were possible only to "catch shadows" in the manner you had done in the previous exercises, you would be very limited in what you could accomplish with compositing in LightWave. Fortunately, LightWave has what you need to composite rendered shadows.

Exercise 18.11 Using Shadow Density for Compositing

1. In the Render Options panel, make sure that Render Display is set to Image Viewer.

2. Do another test render by pressing F9.

3. Now, in the Image Viewer, switch between viewing the Image and the Alpha. Figure 18.28 shows the example.

Figure 18.28 LightWave's Image Viewer from the Render Options panel enables you to view the alpha of any render image.

You'll see that in the alpha image, everything is black except for the area where the spider and tabletop plane are, where it's white.

4. Make sure that the SpiderTableTop_subd object is selected, and from the Items tab, select Replace, and then Replace With Object File.

5. Choose the SpiderTableTop object. There's nothing special about this object, only that it has a different surface name. This is set up to keep the different stages of objects in this tutorial organized.

6. In the Surface Editor, select the SpiderTableTop_Alpha surface.

7. Click the Advanced tab.

8. Beside Alpha Channel drop-down list, next to the Alpha Channel button, select Shadow Density, as shown in Figure 18.29.

9. Close the Surface Editor and make sure that Ray Trace Shadows is set to On in the Render Options panel as well as the Image Viewer. Render a frame.

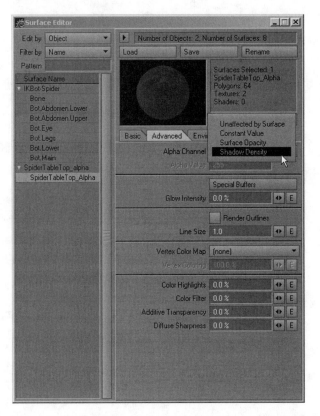

Figure 18.29   Here is the Surface Editor's Advanced tab. Setting the Alpha Channel to Shadow Density means that only the shadowed portion of the tabletop object will be a part of the alpha.

Now when you examine the alpha of the render, you'll see something very different! Instead of the ground plane being all white as it was before, it's now mostly black, except where the shadow of the spider hits. There it is a range of grays, as shown in Figure 18.30. You can view the alpha through the Image Viewer by selecting Alpha from the selection at the top-right corner of the panel.

What you've done is change the object surface so that the rendered alpha of the object is determined not by the opacity of the surface, as it would normally be, but by the density of the shadow hitting it. This means that in the alpha channel of the rendered image, only those parts of the object that are shadowed will show up and the strength of the alpha will depend on the strength of the shadows. Therefore, if you were to color the surface of the object black, the resulting render would have a black shadow with the proper shape and transparency levels.

Figure 18.30   Using the Shadow Density option will show the alpha shadow of the spider.

Exercise 18.12   Compositing Multiple Images

At this point, you could take the rendered image to another package, such as NewTek's Aura, Adobe's After Effects, or Eyeon's Digital Fusion for compositing. But the beauty is, you don't have to do that. You already know that you have the tools necessary to accomplish this composite in LightWave.

1. Continuing with the scene from the previous exercise, render and save both the RGB image and the alpha image.
2. Load the SpiderComp_bkdOnly scene. This scene consists of a background image of the table, the spider, and a flat polygon representing the tabletop.
3. Load the rendered RGB and alpha images back into LightWave Layout.
4. Go to the Compositing tab in the Effects panel.
5. For the Foreground Image, select your rendered RGB color image.
6. For the Foreground Alpha, select your rendered alpha image.
7. Check Foreground Fader Alpha On. In a moment, you'll see your render with the backdrop, spider, and his shadow!
8. Do a test render. Figure 18.31 shows the render.

If you watch the render, you'll see the foreground image overlaid on the background image. As predicted, the shadow looks correct, taking the shape of the object and the density of the shadow. And because no other part of the table is rendered, it's perfectly seamless. Remember, you took out the objects by loading the SpiderComp_bkdonly scene, and what you're seeing in the render are rendered images composited together.

Figure 18.31   When you use only a rendered color image and a rendered alpha image, you easily can composite the spider in LightWave over the background image.

This was a simple example with a single frame, but everything in it applies properly to image sequences and movies as well.

Rendering

After you set up your composites and animations, you must ask yourself at some point, "Now what?" This section shows you the methods and options available for rendering and outputting your animations. Specifically, this section provides you with information on the following:

- The LightWave 7 rendering engine
- Camera settings for rendering
- Rendering options

LightWave 7 gives you a variety of rendering methods, so dive right in. Figure 18.32 shows the LightWave Render Options panel in Layout.

Figure 18.32   Here is the Render Options panel in Layout.

The LightWave Render Engine

You will find that the LightWave render engine is one of the best in its class. It's fast, efficient, and, most importantly, good at what it does. As you can see from the cover of this book, the quality of the renders LightWave can produce is unparalleled. Through the software's radiosity rendering, area lighting, and shadow options, the LightWave rendering engine can deliver astonishing results (for more on lighting, see Chapter 9, "Realistic Lighting Environments"). Before you can get to this render level, it's good for you to know the process of setting up an animation to render.

Camera Settings for Rendering

Before long, the steps involved in rendering an animation will become second nature to you. You'll be jumping easily between the Render Options panel and the Camera Properties panel, making sure that you have all your settings in place. Figure 18.33 shows the Camera Properties panel. This panel is mentioned in this chapter because the settings here are directly related to the output of your animation.

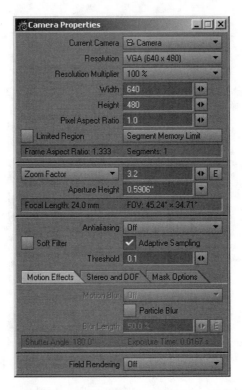

Figure 18.33 The Camera Properties panel goes hand-in-hand with the Render Options panel. Here you define the current camera's resolution for rendering, antialiasing settings, and aspect ratio.

When your animation is complete, open the Camera Properties panel and check out your settings. For proper camera placement, these values should be set up before you begin animating, and it's always a good idea to double-check them before you render. In addition, it is here that you set up any motion blur, field rendering, or antialiasing.

Exercise 18.13   Everyday Rendering: Part I

This exercise guides you through the kind of rendering most commonly used by LightWave animators: rendering that generates animations for video or computer work. If, however, you are using LightWave for rendering anything other than video or computer work, such as film or print, the information here still applies, and the difference is noted.

1. In Layout, load the RenderMe scene from the book's CD.

   This scene is set up with a few simple globe objects so that when you render, you'll have more than just a black screen. Figure 18.34 shows the scene setup.

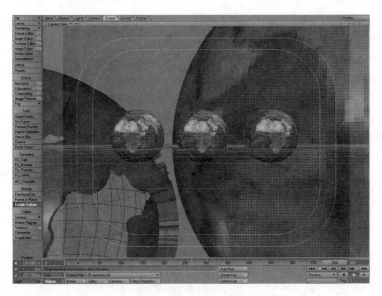

Figure 18.34   For rendering purposes, use the RenderMe scene from the book's CD.

The first thing to do when you're ready to render is display the Camera
Properties panel. You are ready to render when you have all your lighting,
textures, and motions in place. This scene has all of these in place.

2. Select the camera and press the p key to enter the Camera Properties panel.

    The Current Camera at the top of the panel should read Camera because only
    one camera is in the current scene.

3. Set the Resolution to D1 (NTSC) for video resolution. Change the Resolution
    Multiplier to 100 percent for equal size. You'll see the Width and Height values
    change when you do so.

    Figure 18.35 shows the information area in the Camera panel that displays the
    Frame Aspect Ratio and the Segments.

Figure 18.35   The information area within the Camera Properties panel shows how many
segments LightWave is currently using to render each frame.

4. Make sure that your Segments have a value of 1 by increasing the Segment
    Memory Limit to that value.

    If the Segments value is higher than 1, your render times could increase. Don't
    worry, though. If you are short on system memory, you can use less RAM for
    rendering. Therefore, the Segments will be greater than 1—say, 3 or 4.

At this point, you want to tell LightWave to use more RAM for rendering.

5. Click the Segment Memory Limit button and change the value to 20000000 (20MB).

   LightWave now has more memory with which to work and will render your frames in single segments.

6. When asked if you want this value set at default, click Yes. LightWave won't use this RAM until it needs it, so you can set it fairly high.

   The Zoom Factor should have been set up before you began creating your animation. If you change it now, you might have to change your shots and reset the keyframes.

7. Leave the Zoom Factor set to 6. The Aperture Height should be left at the original setting as well.

Note

While you're working, it's not necessary to have Antialiasing on. But you *definitely* want this on for your final renders. Although you have the choice of Low to Extreme settings, it's recommended that you render all your animations for video in at least Enhanced Low Antialiasing. Medium or Enhanced Medium Antialiasing can provide you with a cleaner render. High Antialiasing is overkill and a waste of render time for video. It might actually make your images look blurry.

8. Click Adaptive Sampling.

   Activating this setting tells LightWave to look for the edges to antialias in your scene. The Threshold value compares two neighboring pixels and a value of 0 sees the entire scene. A good working value is .12. You can set the value higher, which will lower rendering time. For this scene, you do not need any motion blur.

9. Do not change the Stereo and DOF settings or the Mask Options. This scene will not use these. You can read more on these settings in Chapter 6, "LightWave 7 Cameras."

10. Go back to the Motion Effects tab and select Even First for Field Rendering.

    Because the RenderMe scene has textures applied to the globe models and other elements, you want to keep these sharp during their motions. Field rendering will render two fields of video for every frame rendered, with the even field first. Figure 18.36 shows the selection.

11. Close the Camera panel and save your scene. All your settings will be saved along with it.

You should visit the Camera panel at least twice during an animation, if not more—once to set up the camera and zoom factors before beginning animation setup, and once before you are ready to render to set up antialiasing, motion blur, field rendering, and proper resolution size. From here, you can set up the Render panel.

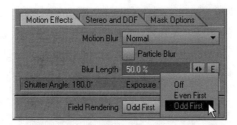

Figure 18.36   Field rendering is selected and set to Odd First in the Camera Properties panel. This tells LightWave to render the even fields of each frame first.

Exercise 18.14   Everyday Rendering: Part 2

The Camera and Rendering panels go hand in hand. This exercise continues where the first exercise left off.

1. With the RenderMe scene from the book's CD still loaded, go to the Render Options panel. You can find this panel by selecting the Render drop-down menu in Layout. The first selection in the list is Render Options.

    Figure 18.37 shows the Render Options panel. This is where you tell LightWave what to render and where to save it. You'll see Render First Frame, Render Last Frame, and Render Frame Step values. If your LightWave animation in Layout has a first frame of –30 and a last frame of 300, it will not render those frames unless they are entered here.

    The frame numbers you assign to your timeline in Layout do not automatically apply in the Render Panel.

2. Leave the First Frame set to 1, and make the Last Frame 300 (10 seconds). Frame Step should be at 1 to render every frame. A Frame Step of 2 would render every two frames, and so on.

3. Turn on Automatic Frame Advance.

    This tells LightWave to advance to the next frame and continue rendering. Very important for full animations!

Note

Frame End Beep is useful for monitoring the completion of your rendered frames, but is not necessary. It's kind of annoying after a while.

4. Uncheck Show Rendering in Progress to turn it off.

    Although it is useful for monitoring your rendering, Show Rendering in Progress will slow down the rendering process if left on for longer animations.

5. Turn off the Render Display.

Figure 18.37   The Render Options panel is home to all the controls you need for setting up renders.

> **Note**
>
> The Image Viewer and Image Viewer FP render display remembers your rendered frames. Turn this on while performing test renders on individual frames (F9), and leave it open. You can select any of your previously rendered images from its Layer list. You also can view the alpha channel in this viewer, and save an image.

6. Turn off Enable VIPER.

   VIPER is needed when setting up surfaces and other VIPER-ready features in Layout, but for final rendering this should not be applied. Leaving VIPER on while rendering multiple frames increases render times and memory usage. Learn more about VIPER in Chapter 2 "LightWave 7 Surface Editor," of the book.

   The Rendering tab is where you tell LightWave what parameters to use for rendering, such as ray tracing. Here, you can tell LightWave to calculate Ray Traced Shadows, Ray Traced Reflections, and Ray Traced Refraction.

7. Turn Off Ray Trace Shadows, as well as Ray Trace Reflections and Ray Traced Refraction. These options are not needed in this particular case. Unless you are applying Ray Traced Shadows with lights, reflections, or refraction to a surface, these options will increase render times.

   You also can add Ray Trace Transparency for objects that need to have a transparent surface reflect a certain way, such as a car window.

8. The Render Mode is usually set at Realistic and is not often changed. However, you do have the option to render Wireframe or Quickshade versions of your animations here.

9. Click Extra Ray Trace Optimization. Set the Ray Recursion Limit to 2. The higher the value, the longer LightWave will take to render, but the more accurate your Ray Tracing will be.

The Ray Recursion Limit, which doesn't often change, determines the number of times LightWave calculates the bounced rays in your scene. In the real world, this is infinite, but in LightWave, you can set a Ray Recursion Limit up to 24. Changing this setting increases render times. A good working value is 12. However, this can be a real timesaver while using the Ray Trace Reflection option, by setting a low value of 1 or 2.

10. If your computer has more than one processor, select 2, 4, or 8 for Multiprocessing. If you have only one processor, set the Multiprocessing to 1. And if you have multiple processors and have applied pixel filter plug-ins such as HyperVoxels, make your processors work for you by clicking Multithread Pixel Filters. Some plug-ins, however, may not be compatible with multithreading, so remember to check this setting if you find errors in your render.

11. Set Data Overlay to display the Frame Number, SMPTE Time Code, Film Key Code, or Time in Seconds in the bottom-right corner of your animation.

This is good for reference test renders. In addition, when one of these values is set, you can add a note in the Label area. This is good to do for test renders for clients that have a history of not paying and/or stealing your work. You can put a copyright notice in the upper corner, for example.

12. After you've set all the render options, be sure to save your scene. Saving regularly before any render—even a single-frame render—is a good habit to get into.

Those are the main parameters you need to set up to render an animation. But you still need to tell LightWave where to save the files and what type of files to save. The next section discusses the various file formats and procedures for saving your animations.

Saving Renders

Within the Render Options panel is another tabbed area entitled Output Files. This area is where you tell LightWave what type of file you want to save and in which format it should be saved. Figure 18.38 shows the Output Files tab within the Render Options panel.

The first area within the Output Files tab is the Save Animation selection. This confuses many people. You are creating an animation in LightWave, right? Save Animation! Makes sense—but it means something a little bit different. Clicking Save Animation enables you to save your rendered frames as one animation file, such as an AVI, QuickTime, or RTV (Video Toaster) format. It will save one complete file. You select different types of animations to save by using the Type selection option. Note that you'll need a Video Toaster board from NewTek for the RTV saver.

Figure 18.38   The Output Files tab within the Render Options panel is where you tell LightWave what type of file to save and where to save it.

Using Save Animation is great for previewing QuickTime movies or using Aura and Video Toaster. But you also can save individual frames—and at the same time. If you select the Save RGB button, you're telling LightWave to save the individual frames as they are rendered. Similar to Save Animation Type, you select from a variety of RGB formats in which to save your animations by selecting the one you want from the Type drop-down list, as pictured in Figure 18.39.

Finally, under the Output Files tab, you also can save the alpha channels of individual frames. Figure 18.40 shows the alpha channel of frame 100 of the RenderMe.lws animation.

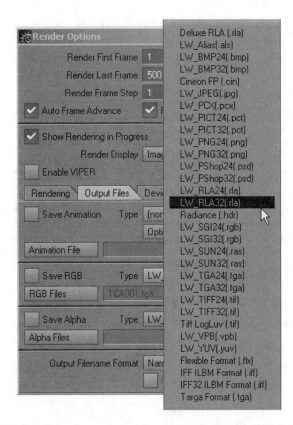

Figure 18.39   LightWave gives you a slew of formats for saving your RGB frames. This is the best way to render your animations if you do not use Video Toaster NT. The individual frames can later be imported into a variety of programs.

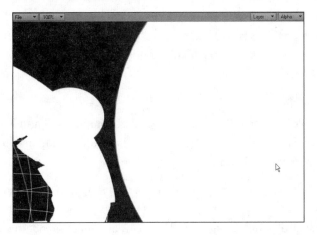

Figure 18.40   You can save the alpha channel information of individual frames in the Output Files tab.

Part IV   Animation Post and Effects

This is great for later compositing in a post-production environment. Remember that all these file types can be saved with one rendering. You can save a QuickTime or .AVI file, plus the RGB and alpha files all at once. Pretty cool, huh?

When all this is set—the camera resolutions, the rendering information, and the output file information—you're finally ready to render your animation. Pressing the F10 key will render your animation. Congratulations!

> **Tip**
>
> You might have a high-resolution frame that needs to render over a long period of time. You can tell LightWave to automatically save this frame by setting up the Render Options as though you were rendering a full-length animation. Set the RGB format, output filename, and location for saving, and then click Automatic Frame Advance. Make the First Frame and the Last Frame the same frame you want to render—say, frame 10. LightWave will render that frame and save the RGB, and because it's also the Last Frame, rendering will stop.

Render Selected Objects

If you click the Render drop-down list in Layout, you'll see the Render Selected Objects selection. Because LightWave enables you to select multiple objects, you can save significant rendering time with this option. In the Scene Editor or in Layout, you can select all objects at once by holding the Shift key and clicking the objects. Rendering selected objects has two useful functions:

- It saves render time by rendering only the objects you're interested in at the moment.

- It enables you to render multiple passes of the same animation with or without certain objects. This is great for special effects or compositing, or even for rendering before-and-after sorts of animations.

Network Rendering

LightWave enables you to render over a network of computers, not only the individual machine on which you're working. Whether you have a few computers or hundreds of computers at your location, you can use all of them for rendering the same animation.

LightWave 7 ships with some important network rendering software called ScreamerNet. ScreamerNet has been a part of LightWave for years. With ScreamerNet, LightWave needs to be installed on only a single machine. This distributive rendering can send your animations to other machines on your network that have a ScreamerNet process running. You don't have to use this feature, as it is used more by animators in larger studios who want maximize their time and their multiple computer environments. Please refer to your LightWave manuals for proper instruction.

ScreamerNet also is useful on a single machine for batch-processing your animations. Think about setting up four versions of your animated logo to render one right after the other. Because LightWave saves the Render Options information within a scene file, ScreamerNet knows where and what to save from your specific animations. You even can run ScreamerNet without running LightWave. Use ScreamerNet to batch-render animations without loading your scenes. The distributed rendering section of your LightWave manuals can instruct you further on the proper command lines needed to set up this process.

The Next Step

You can refer to this section of the book often when it's time to render your animations and images. But then you have to answer the question, "What's next?" When your animations are complete, the next step is to bring them into a digital animation recorder and lay them off to tape, or edit your final animations with audio and effects in a non-linear editor.

The exercises in this chapter have not only introduced you to the compositing tools in LightWave, but have also given you the knowledge to create your own composited images and animations. From here, you can build your own 3D objects, such as cars, spaceships, insects, or people, and experiment with compositing them into real-world images. You can use the color photographs on the book's CD for your projects. Take a look in the Extras folder, and you'll find royalty-free images, which you can use in the same manner as the images from the exercises in this chapter. Try using some of the city photographs to fly objects in front of and behind buildings while casting shadows. Use other images to make a 3D character walk down a long sidewalk or a flight of stairs. From here, experiment and practice whenever you can. If you have a digital camera, keep it with you at all times to create your own images for compositing.

Summary

Rendering your animations has to be done. Someday, you might not need to render, as processors and video cards become increasingly powerful. For now, though, LightWave still has to render, just like any other 3D application. But you'll find that the rendering engine inside LightWave is one of the best around. It's strong and stable, and most importantly, it produces beautifully rendered images.

NewTek has added many OpenGL enhancements. These speed up your workflow, but also give the poor F9 (Render Current Frame) key a break. Work through the exercises in this book, and make your own animations anytime you can. You can't be in front of your computer 24 hours a day—well, maybe you can, but you shouldn't. When you get ready to take a break, set up a render. Don't just wait until the animation is "perfect." Render often and see how your animation looks. You might find new ways to enhance it and make it even better. Or, you might just find that it's perfect the way it is.

As you've seen, LightWave has plenty of compositing power. These examples are only the tip of the iceberg, but hopefully they'll give you a good working knowledge of the fundamentals of compositing, from which you can learn further on your own. There's not much more to it, other than using moving images rather than stills. Use programs like NewTek's Aura or Adobe's After Effects for pixel tracking. If you use Aura to track movement in a real video clip, you can export that motion to LightWave! More tools! More power!

Chapter 19

Particle and Fur Animation

Particle animation is one of LightWave's

cooler capabilities. Particle FX, as it's

referred to in Layout, is LightWave's parti-

cle animation system. You can use Particle

FX for many types of animations, from simple sparks, to smoke, flames, blowing leaves, or even swarming bees. Add to particles the power to put fur onto your objects and these two features alone are worth the price of the software. But even more important than their value, these tools give you control and flexibility in the types of images and animations you can create.

Project Overview

This chapter takes you into the world of particle animation in LightWave. You'll start with the basics, so you can familiarize yourself with how the Particle FX controls integrate directly in Layout. From there, you'll apply surfacing to particles using Hypervoxels to create bubbles as in Figure 19.1. Then, you'll learn about SasLite, the lite version of Steve Worley's Sasquatch fur and hair plug-in. SasLite is a stripped-down version included with LightWave 7. You'll learn how to create basic fur on simple objects, and then step up to creating fields of grass. From there, you'll learn how to apply hair to different parts of a character's body. In this chapter, you will do the following:

- Create particle animations
- Add surfaces to particles with Hypervoxels
- Use Clip Maps to quickly and easily animate bubbles
- Use SasLite to create a grassy knoll
- Add hair to a full character

Figure 19.1   In this chapter, you'll use particles to make animated bubbles, and create a field of grass with SasLite.

Particles in LightWave

You've probably heard the term *particles* when watching behind-the-scenes or "making of" shows. Animators have been using particles for years to set up a wide range of dynamic animations, from water to smoke, to swarming objects and more. But before you get too deep into the particle world, take a few minutes and learn how the tools are integrated into LightWave 7.

Creating a Basic Motion Particle Scene

For the project in this chapter, you work with particles directly in Layout. There's no need for third-party plug-ins or expensive processing times. The particle engine in LightWave is robust and fast, as you'll see shortly.

Exercise 19.1   Setting Up the Emitter

In order for particles to "live" in a scene, they need an emitter. Think of the emitter as a faucet from which your particles spill out. The various controls within the ParticleFX Panel allow you to adjust how the particles come out, how many come out, how quickly they come out, and so on. An emitter also can be an object that emits particles, such as a bullet streaking through the air—the particles in this case would have Hypervoxels applied to the bullet as a smoke trail. There's no steadfast rule to using an object as an emitter rather than a standard particle emitter—the task at hand usually determines your needs.

In this exercise, you're not going to create anything with particles. Instead, you'll apply them to a scene to see how you can adjust parameters for instant feedback.

1. Open LightWave's Layout. That's all you need for this scene.
2. Click the Items tab and select Add, PFX, and Add Particle Emitter, as shown in Figure 19.2. When the Add Particle Emitter appears, you can change the name, or simply leave the default name, "emitter" (see Figure 19.3).

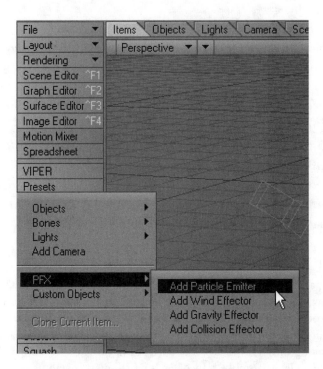

Figure 19.2   You add a particle emitter the same way you add null objects, 3D objects, lights, and so on. You can add a Particle emitter, Wind effector, Gravity effector, or Collision effector from the Add drop-down under the Items tab.

Figure 19.3   Once an emitter is added, you can apply a name to it.

Once the emitter is loaded, you'll see an outlined box in the Layout view, as shown in Figure 19.4.

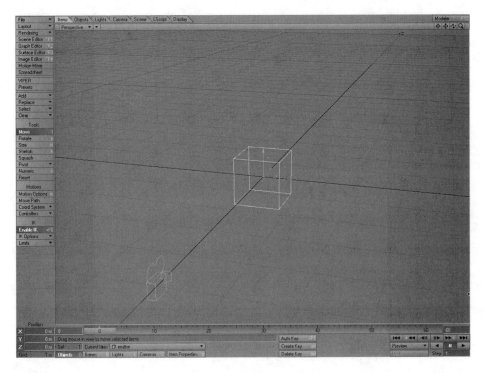

Figure 19.4   An added emitter in Layout is represented by a bounding box.

3. In the timeline at the lower right of the interface, set the last frame of the animation to 200.

4. Turn AutoKey on by clicking on the button below the timeline.

5. Press the o key to open the General Options tab within the Preferences panel. Make sure that the selector next to Auto Key Create is set to Modified Channels. The Auto Key button directly on the Layout interface will act as a remote control to turn Auto Key Create Modified Channels on or off. Close the General Options panel.

6. Back in Layout, make sure that the emitter is selected. Press t for Move.

7. Press the Play button, and move the emitter around in Layout. Look at that—instant particles (see Figure 19.5)!

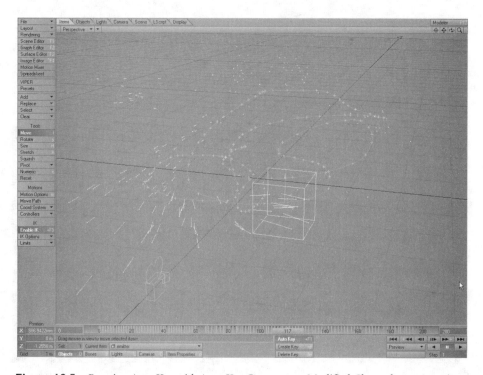

Figure 19.5   By using Auto Key with Auto Key Create set to Modified Channels, your motions can be recorded in real time in Layout. Moving the particle emitter around shows the spray of particles.

You can see that just by moving an emitter around, the particles fly about. This is great for sparks, sprays from wet hair, dust, and more. But it lacks control, so move on to the next exercise to learn how you can deliberately set up particle motions.

Exercise 19.2   Controlling an Emitter

You don't always need to create motions to see particles moving. They can move on their own in a variety of ways. This exercise shows you how to create a particle stream, good for water fountains, gushing oil wells, or smoke.

1. Select Clear Scene from the File menu in Layout.

2. From the Items tab, select Add, then PFX, and Add Particle Emitter. Name the emitter *Fountain* when the Add Particle Emitter requester appears.

Note

If you move too quickly and forget to rename your particle emitter, don't worry. Simply select Replace, and then choose Rename Current Item from the Items tab to rename the selected object.

3. Go to the Scene tab, and select FX_Property from the Dynamics listing, as you see in Figure 19.6.

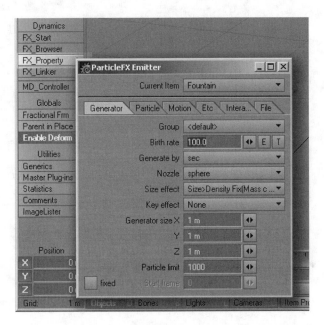

Figure 19.6   The Dynamics listing under the Scene tab in Layout is where you can access controls to regulate your particle effects. The FX_Property panel, labeled ParticleFX Emitter, shown here, is the control center for your Particle emitter.

4. Move the FX_Property panel off to one side of the Layout interface to see the actual emitter in the scene. Set the last frame of the animation to 300.

5. Press the Play button (right arrow) in Layout and begin adjusting the particles. What you'll see first looks like popcorn—just some particles popping within the emitter.

6. In the FX_Property panel, click the Motion tab, and bring the Vector Y value to 2.5, as shown in Figure 19.7.

7. You can see that when you adjust the value, the particles update in Layout. Note that you can click and drag the triangles to the right of a value for true interactivity. Play around with the Vector values for the X and Z to see how the particles will be affected.

8. Bring the Explosion value to 3.0. You'll see the particles spray outward, as Figure 19.8 shows.

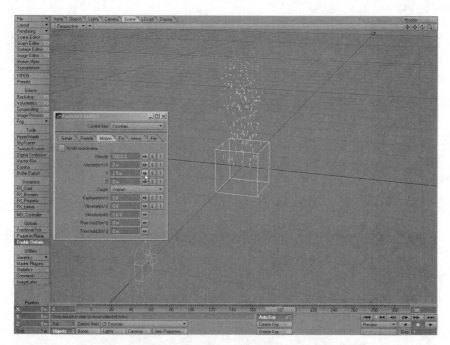

Figure 19.7   The Vector setting within the FX_Property panel for the emitter gives your particles movement on the xyz-axis.

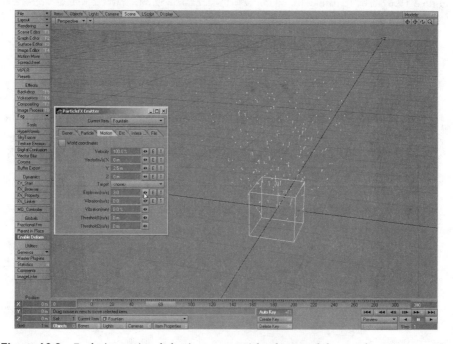

Figure 19.8   Explosion settings help give your particles the spread they need!

9. Try adding a little Vibration. Set the value to 10 and watch the particles freak out. They sort of scatter. Note that this is the first Vibration setting, with a meters-per-second (m/s) setting.

The second Vibration setting is a minimum percentage that you can apply as well.

10. Up at the top of the Motion tab, set the Velocity to 500 percent. This will help the particles move with a little more vigor. Figure 19.9 shows the settings.

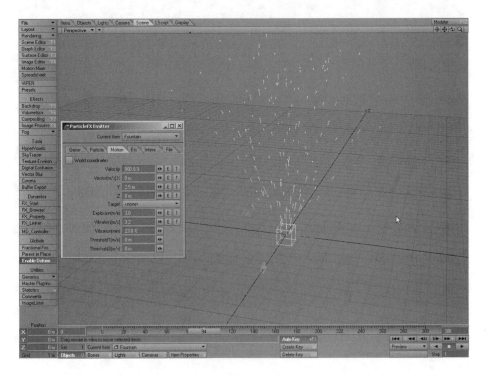

Figure 19.9   Increasing the Velocity for the particles makes them shoot out a little faster and more direct.

11. Click the Etc tab. Set the Y value for Gravity to –4. You're using a negative value because you want the particles to be pulled downward on the y-axis after they are emitted.

You might notice that the particles don't last very long after they've been emitted. You might also want them to spray from a tighter start.

12. Click the Particle tab, and set the Life Time value to 125. You set up a 300-frame animation earlier, so this will make the particles die out at 125, which lasts about 4 seconds. But they die evenly, so set the +/– setting, located just below the Life Time setting, to 20.

13. The particles are falling well, but you might want to see them emit from a smaller point. Click the Generator tab, and set each of the XYZ Generator sizes to 200mm. You'll see the particles spray out from a tight nozzle, as shown in Figure 19.10.

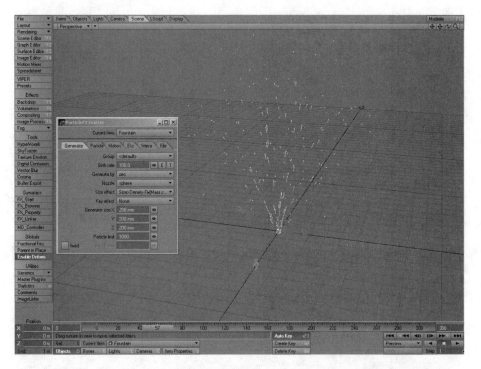

Figure 19.10   You can change the Generator size for the particle emitter. Here you changed it equally, but you also can flatten out and increase the size of the emitter for things like falling snow or rain.

The LightWave 7 manual gives a good description of the numerous settings and values available to you in the Particle FX_Property panel. This will be a helpful reference as you work with the tools. These first two exercises introduced you to particle emitters and the controls available to them. However, there's much more you can do with this system, so read on.

Exercise 19.3   Controlling an Emitter with Wind

If you're like most people, you want to see exactly how something is done using visual effects. Sure, it's good to know the theory and value settings for various mathematical properties, but often the best learning method is by doing. This next exercise takes the basic emitter example discussed in the previous exercise, expands on it, and changes its particle flow with a Wind Effector.

There is a different way to add particle emitters to Layout, and that's done through the Scene tab. The method used earlier through the Items tab is fine for simpler projects. But the Scene tab method is great for more advanced projects that will require more than just a single emitter.

1. Clear the scene. From the Scene tab, select the FX_Browser in the left side of the interface.

   This panel can remain open and allow you to not only add additional emitters of all types, but also open their properties panel.

2. Next to Add, you'll see HVEmitter. Click it once. You've just added an emitter. Figure 19.11 shows the browser open, with the emitter added in Layout.

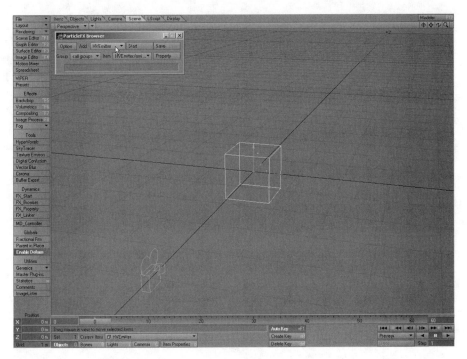

Figure 19.11   Using the FX_Browser, you can quickly add emitters and other effectors to your scene.

3. Also from the FX_Browser panel, click the Property button. This will open the property panel you saw earlier, FX_Property.

4. You're going to create a plume of smoke. Set the last frame of your animation to 250.

5. Under the Generator tab, set the Birth Rate to 20. The emitter will generate 20 particles over whatever you decide, such as frames or seconds. In the Generate By selector, the selection should default to sec, or second. Twenty particles will be generated per second, up to the set particle limit.

6. Set the Nozzle to Cone. Leave Size Effect alone for now.

7. Change the Generator Size to 500mm on the X, 100mm on the Y, and 500mm on the Z. This will create a relatively small, flat emitter, as you see in Figure 19.12.

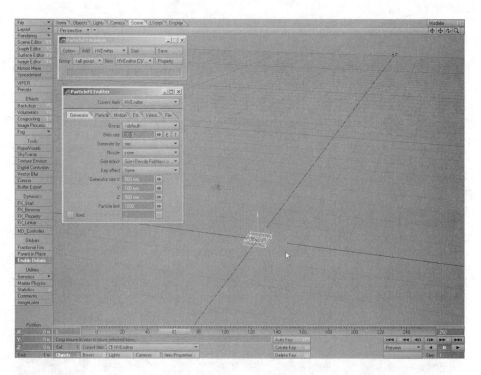

Figure 19.12   A simple generator is all you need to get started to make a plume of smoke.

8. Drag the timeline. You'll see particles generating, but going nowhere! That's okay—the wind will move them.

9. Back in the ParticleFX_Browser window, select Wind next to Add, as shown in Figure 19.13.

Figure 19.13   You easily can add a Wind effector from the ParticleFX_Browser panel.

10. The Wind effector looks like a bunch of dots, but don't let that fool you. Press the Play button. Remember those stagnant particles? They're moving upward now, thanks to the default Wind.

11. This is all fine and dandy, but it looks nothing like smoke. So, with the Wind effector selected in Layout, click the Property button in the FX_Browser panel to open the Wind controls. See how useful this FX_Browser panel is?

12. You'll notice that the particles end too soon. You need to change the length of their Life Time. Select the Particle Emitter, and open the Properties panel for it from the FX_Browser (if you had closed it).

13. Click the Particle tab, and set the Life Time frame info to 250, the length of the animation. Play the preview in Layout. The particles now go a little higher, but they just sort of hang in the air.

14. Just above the Life Time settings, set the Particle Resistance down to .2, from the default 1. You also can randomize the value using the +/– selector just below that. Set the random value to .1.

15. Lastly, randomize the Life Time by 60 frames. Figure 19.14 shows the setup.

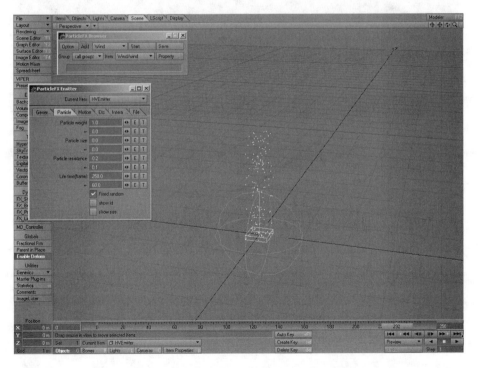

Figure 19.14   By changing the Particle Resistance and Life Time values, the particles, moved by the Wind effector, continue moving until they die off.

Now you could add another Wind effector to "push" the particles, but there's an easier way in LightWave 7, using the Path Wind mode.

16. Select the Wind effector in Layout. Move (t) it up on the y-axis about 1.5m.

17. Move it to the right, on the x-axis, about 800mm, and create a keyframe at 60. Figure 19.15 shows the keyframes.

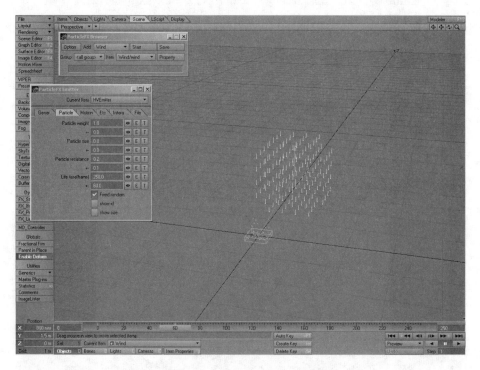

Figure 19.15   By keyframing the Wind effector, you'll add specific control to the Particle emitter.

18. Now move the Wind effector to –800mm on the X and up to 3m on the Y. Create a keyframe at 120, as shown in Figure 19.16.

19. Lastly, move the Wind effector one more time to 4.5m on the Y and 600mm on the X. Create a keyframe at 200.

20. Open the FX_Property panel for the Wind effector. For Wind mode, select Path. Drag the timeline slider in Layout, and the particles now follow the path (see Figure 19.17).

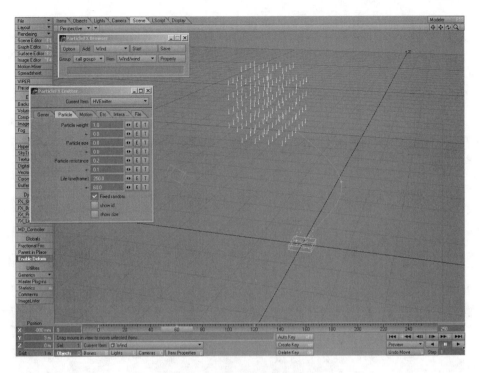

Figure 19.16   Here is another keyframe for the Wind effector.

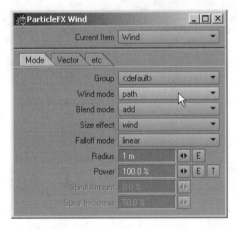

Figure 19.17   Changing the Wind effector's Wind mode to Path makes the particles follow the path of the wind.

21. There are a few more things you can do to make this even cooler. Select the Wind effector in Layout, and go to frame 120. Rotate the Wind about 200 degrees on the heading. Create the keyframe again at 120 to lock it in place (or use AutoKey).

22. Go to the last frame, 200, and rotate the Wind about −80 on its heading. Create the keyframe again to keep the change. Press the Play button at the bottom of Layout, and now you'll see the particles twist through the keyframes.

23. Another last setting: Select the particle emitter's property panel. Change the Vibration to .35 to randomize the emitting particles a bit. Figure 19.18 shows the final particle setup.

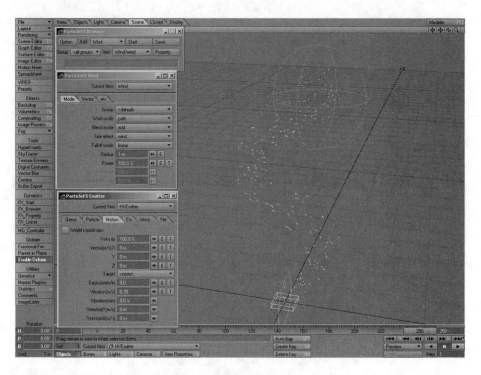

Figure 19.18   Here is the final particle emitter, controlled by wind.

Applying Smoke to Particles

As you can see, you have a ton of control over your particles, using things like wind and gravity. You can take the wind a step further and set up some crazy keyframes, fly it right past the camera, and beef up the particle emitter with more vibration and faster velocity for a cooler effect. There's even more you can do with collisions, but that's covered in Chapter 20, "Advanced Particle Animation." For now, these particles are great, but what good are they? If you render a frame, you'll see nothing. That's because these are Hypervoxel particles, meaning they need Hypervoxels applied to be visible.

Exercise 19.4   Surfacing Particles for Smoke

The particles you've been working with require Hypervoxels to be seen during a render. Another type of emitter you could add is a Partigon emitter. It works exactly the same way as an HVEmitter, only that it generates single point polygons that will show during a render. These are great for tiny sparks, water sprays, and even stars.

Hypervoxels have three surfacing options available: Surface for solid blobby objects, Volume for 3D clouds and smoke, and Sprite for a variation of a 3D volume. These are fast, great for smoke, easy to set up, and visible in Layout!

1. With the scene loaded from the previous exercise (or the WindEffector scene from the CD), click the Volumetrics button from the Scene tab. The Volumetrics tab of the Effect panel opens.

2. From the Add Volumetric drop-down list, select HyperVoxelsFilter. Double-click the name in the listing when loaded. The Hypervoxels panel opens. You also can open the HyperVoxels panel directly in Layout from the Scene tab.

    You'll see the name HVEmitter ghosted in the Object Name list, as shown in Figure 19.19.

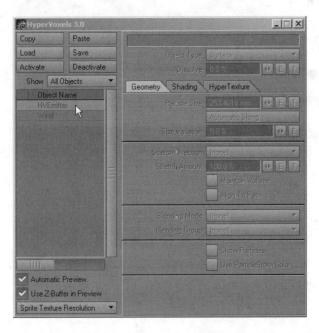

Figure 19.19   As soon as you load up Hypervoxels, your particle emitter is visible in the Object Name list, but it is inactive.

3. Either double-click the HVEmitter in the Object Name list, or select it once, and then click Activate. These both do the same thing—activate Hypervoxels for the Particle emitter.

4. The panel becomes active, and an automatic particle size is already in place. Now the best way to begin setting up smoke for these particles is to use VIPER. From the Layout interface, click the VIPER button. Because you're in Hypervoxels, VIPER shows your particles with the effect applied, as you see in Figure 19.20. You can learn more about VIPER in Chapter 2, "LightWave 7 Surface Editor."

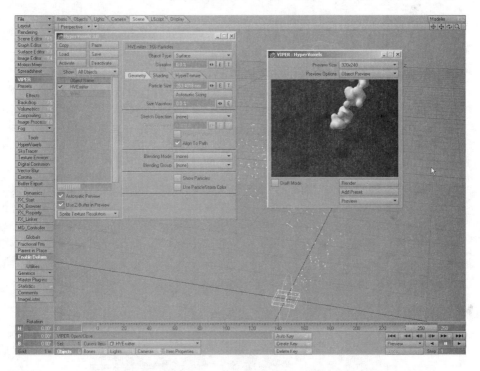

Figure 19.20   VIPER is the only way to go for setting up Hypervoxels interactively on your particles.

5. You'll see some white blobs. By default, Hypervoxels uses Surface as the Object Type. This is great for lava, water, shaving cream, and things of that nature; but it's not what you want here. From the Object Type listing at the top of the Hypervoxels panel, select Sprite.

Note

When using VIPER, you'll see your particles from Camera view, not the current view, which is Perspective. You can set your Camera view up to match Perspective view, if you like, for a full VIPER display.

If you take a look at Figure 19.21, you'll see that when you change Object Type to Sprite mode, VIPER shows the smoky change.

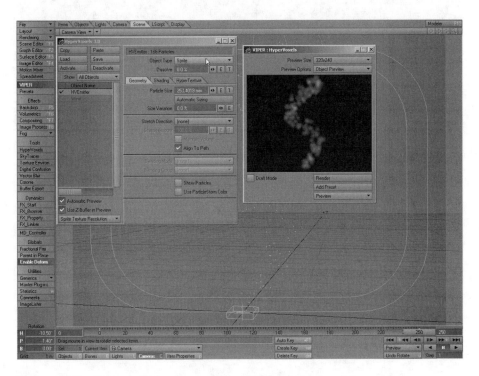

Figure 19.21   Sprite mode is not only fast, but it's also perfect for adding smoke.

6. Now all you need to do is tweak the settings. In the Hypevoxels panel, click the Show Particles button. Move the Hypervoxels panel and VIPER aside to see the Layout. Your Hypervoxel sprites are now visible in Layout (see Figure 19.22).

7. Back in the Hypervoxels panel, click and drag the arrow for Particle Size. Set the particles to 550mm.

8. Set Size variation to 50 percent to randomize the size of the Sprite particles a bit.

9. Set Stretch Direction to Velocity, so the particles stretch slightly based on their movement. Set Stretch Amount to 200 percent. Turn on Align to Path.

10. Click the Shading tab. Set the particle color to an earthy brown. Then, click the T button to add a texture.

11. Make the texture layer a procedural. The type of procedural should be Turbulence.

12. Change the Scale to about 800mm for the X, 800mm for the Y, and 260mm for the Z.

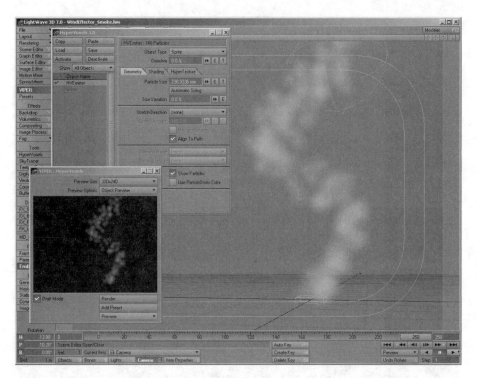

Figure 19.22   Turning on Show Particles in the Hypervoxels panel shows your sprites in Layout.

13. Next, add a new layer on top of the procedural, and make it a Gradient.

14. At the bottom of the gradient bar, set the End value to 250. This extends the range of the gradient.

15. Set the Input Parameter to Particle Age. Add three keys to the gradient bar. The initial key color should be brown, and then change to green and to gray for the additional keys, starting at the top of the bar. Figure 19.23 shows the panel.

Note

Remember that when you are using gradients, the up and down visibility of the gradient bar does not represent your surface. For this example, the top part of the gradient bar is the base of the particles because the Input Parameter is set to Particle Age.

16. Click Use Texture, and return to the Hypervoxels panel. Lastly, change the Number of Slices to 3 for a little more detail in the sprites. You'll see your color particle age directly in Layout.

17. In the VIPER window, select Preview from the drop-down list, and choose Make Preview. In a moment, you'll have a preview of your particle scene with textures applied.

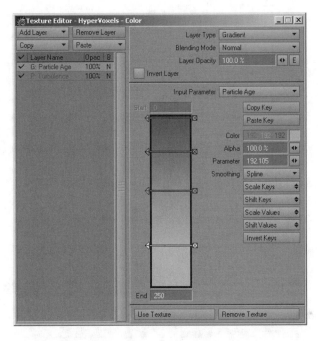

Figure 19.23   You can apply gradients to your hypervoxel textures on your particles.

What you've done here is basic, but also about as complex as it gets. Although that sounds contradictory, with the power of LightWave's particles in combination with HyperVoxel sprites, the texture editor, and gradients, the possibilities are endless. Endless how? Read on for another variation on these particles!

Exercise 19.5   Using Images on Particles

Yes, you read that heading correctly—using images on particles. Although it sounds odd, it's actually a very cool feature for all sorts of animations, from falling snow, blowing leaves, bubbles, pictures of your dog, whatever!

Check this out:

1. With the same scene loaded from the previous exercise, open the Image Editor. Load the Bubble image from the book's CD, as Figure 19.24 shows.

2. Back in the Hypervoxels panel, click the Shading tab. From there, click the Clips tab.

3. Select the Bubble image from the Add Sprite drop-down list. Watch what happens in Layout! You'll see the Bubble image applied to the particles, but grossly overlapping each other.

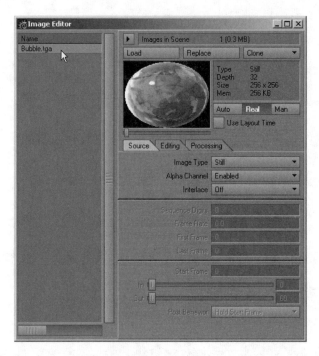

Figure 19.24   Use the Image Editor to load an image to be used with your particles. Remember that you can adjust any of the necessary properties in the Image Editor, such as hue, contrast, or brightness.

4. Click to the Basic tab for Shading, hold the Shift key, and click the T button for Color Texture to take off the gradient and procedural texture.

5. Go back to the Geometry tab, and bring the Particle Size to 55mm and Size Variation to 40 percent, and set Stretch Direction to None. Figure 19.25 shows Layout with the bubbles in place.

Note
You also can set the Sprite Texture Resolution from the bottom left of the Hypervoxels panel. At the bottom of the Clips tab where you applied the clip, you can tell LightWave how to use the Alpha, set a threshold, and choose a Frame Offset.

That's it! Hypervoxel sprites with clips are very cool, and quite useful. One of the reasons they're so useful is that you can take tiny images and animate them quickly, based on particles. You can see them directly in Layout so that you know what's happening with their size and color, and, they always face the camera.

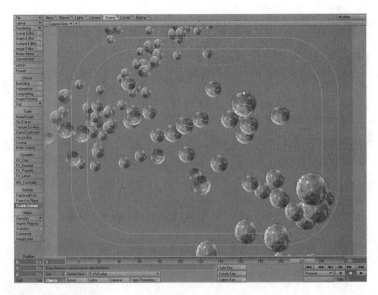

Figure 19.25   Using just a tiny image of a bubble applied to some particles with Hypervoxel sprites, you can create hundreds of bubbles.

Of course, you can adjust the motion of the particles—perhaps add another Wind effector at the top of the path to make the particles spread out as they reach their end. You also can change the emitter to a large, long, flat shape to emit sprite clips, such as the bubbles. The examples here should get you started with your own particle animations. There's more advanced particle information in the next chapter, but first, take a quick tour of SasLite, LightWave's hair and fur creation tool.

Exercise 19.6   Using SasLite to Create Grass

SasLite, a scaled-down version of Steve Worley's popular Sasquatch plug-in, comes standard with LightWave 7. Although many of the higher-end features in Sasquatch are missing from the Lite version, it has the same quality of look and ease of use as its big brother.

With SasLite, you can create fur, grass, and even long hair on anything you like. This first exercise shows you how to set up a grassy knoll.

1. In Layout, open the File menu, and load the GrassMe scene from the book's CD-ROM.

   This is a small scene using Skytracer2 for the sky (see the Backdrop tab of the Effects panel), and a large subpatched object for the ground.

2. The first thing you should do when working with SasLite is add the Pixel Filter. This plug-in generates the fibers you see in the render. From the Scene tab, click Image Process.

3. From the Add Pixel Filter drop-down list, select SasLite. Double-click to open the SasLite Pixel Filter. Figure 19.26 shows the panels.

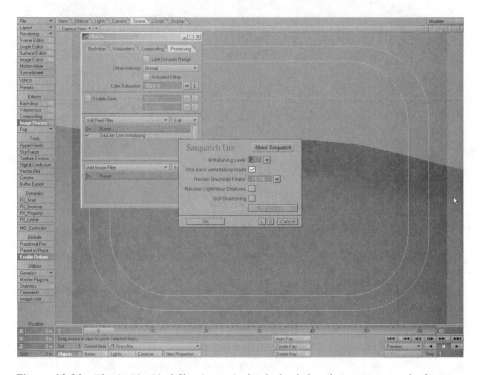

Figure 19.26   The SasLite Pixel filter is required to be loaded so that you can use the feature.

4. In this panel, you can set SasLite's antialising level and shadow options. For now, just click Receive LightWave Shadows, Self Shadowing, and Cast Shadows From All Spotlights. Click OK to close the panel.

5. Select the Grass object in Layout, and press the p key to open the Object Properties panel. Click the Deformations tab.

6. From the Add Displacement drop-down list, choose SasLite.

   This is the displacement plug-in that controls how the fur or hair will look on your object.

7. Double-click the listing to open the SasLite panel, as shown in Figure 19.27.

   Here you can see the default settings for the tool. The first rule of thumb is to tell the plug-in what you want to surface with SasLite. You can see in Figure 19.27 that the default setting is set to Apply Fur To All Surfaces. For the grass object in this scene, this setting is fine.

   If you have an object with multiple surfaces, such as the caveman character you'll surface in the next exercise, you need to specify a specific name.

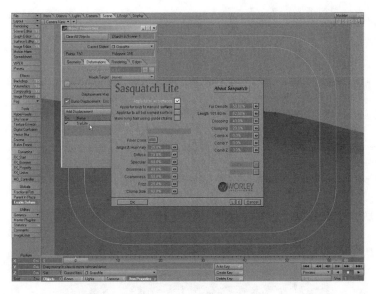

Figure 19.27 The SasLite displacement plug-in is where it all comes together for your object.

8. For Fiber Color, click the small brown swatch, and your systems' color requestor will open. Select a deep green, grassy color. Figure 19.28 shows the change.

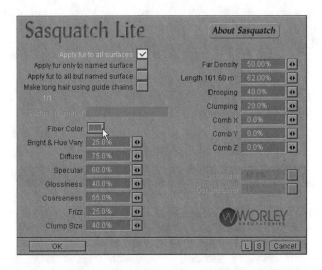

Figure 19.28 One of the first settings in the SasLite panel you need to change for grass is, of course, the color.

9. For now, click OK in the SasLite panel to close the interface. Press F9 to render a frame of your scene.

You'll see a progress window appear in a moment, informing you of SasLite's progress. Figure 19.29 shows the render. Yikes!

Figure 19.29   Well, you know SasLite is working, but the grass you just applied has totally obscured your landscape!

10. This is easy to correct. Go back to the SasLite displacement plug-in interface, and bring the Length to 20 percent. This will create blades of grass about 10.5m in length. Why this size? Because the object is about 900m. Figure 19.30 shows the change.

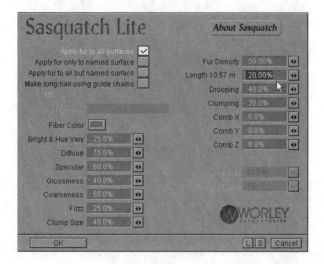

Figure 19.30   Changing the length to 20 percent will shorten the grass to about 10.5m.

11. Click OK to close the SasLite panel, and press F9 to render. Figure 19.31 shows the render. Much better.

Figure 19.31   Changing just the length of the fibers in SasLite brings the landscape back from the jungle.

12. Although the landscape isn't obscured, it now looks a bit sparse! Go back to SasLite and check that the parameters are set in the following way (See Figure 19.32):

- Bright and Hue Vary   25%
- Diffuse   75%
- Specular   60%
- Glossiness   40%
- Coarseness   55%
- Frizz   25%
- Clump Size   10%
- Fur Density   85%
- Length   20%
- Drooping   25%
- Clumping   10%
- Comb, XYZ   0%

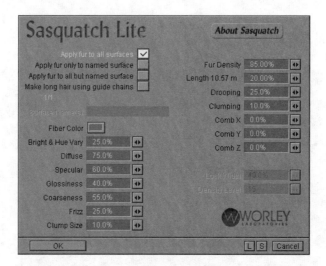

Figure 19.32   These settings applied to the simple landscape will create a grassy knoll.

13. Close the SasLite panel. Press F9 to render a frame. As you can see, with just a few settings, you now have a grassy knoll (see Figure 19.33).

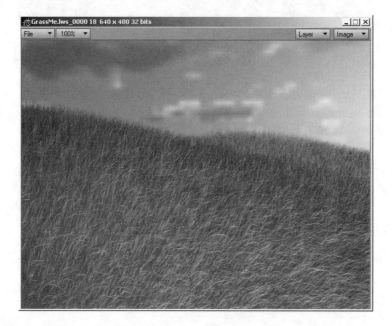

Figure 19.33   SasLite is at work on a grassy knoll. How nice.

14. You can go a step further with this grassy knoll. Go to the Object Properties panel and add another instance of SasLite to the object. Yes, you can load the plug-in multiple times! Multiple instances of the plug-in allow you to create varying levels of grass or fur.

15. You're going to add some secondary grass, weeds popping up in a few places. Open the new SasLite panel, give the Fur Color a brighter, more yellowish green color, and set the following (See Figure 19.34):

- Bright and Hue Vary   25%
- Diffuse   75%
- Specular   60%
- Glossiness   40%
- Coarseness   55%
- Frizz   25%
- Clump Size   30%
- Fur Density   15%
- Length   35%
- Drooping   20%
- Clumping   20%
- Comb, XYZ   0%

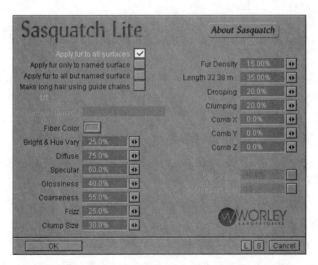

Figure 19.34 Input these settings in SasLite to add fibers to the grassy knoll.

Note

Remember that the Coarseness setting is tied to length. The shorter you make the grass, the more coarse it needs to be to maintain a grass-like look. You can set the Coarseness up to 400 percent.

16. Close the SasLite panel and press F9 to render a frame. You'll see sparse, coarse weeds, longer than the grass, but blended randomly throughout the grassy knoll, as shown in Figure 19.35.

Figure 19.35   By adding a second instance of SasLite with varied settings, the grassy knoll has more interest, and some weeds.

Guess what? You can even add more instances of SasLite for a crazy-looking image. Try it out!

Although the settings here are nothing more than a few percentages, the results are quite extraordinary, and fast. Take a moment and play with the various settings, one at a time, and render a frame so you can see the effect.

Here are a few key things to remember when working with SasLite:

- Be sure to tell SasLite properly to which surface you want the application applied.

- Using a wildcard, you can quickly set surface names. For example, if you named a surface hairybackguy, setting the Apply Fur Only To Named Surface to h* would apply the fur to any surface name that began with the letter h.

- Adjust one setting at a time between renders. The benefit of this is that you can see exactly the change that you've made before you make another one.

- Using the L and S buttons at the bottom of the SasLite panel, you can Load and Save your settings. If, however, you've used a specific surface name, SasLite will remember that when calling up saved surfaces. No problem; just tell SasLite the new name after you load the setting.

Exercise 19.7   Applying Hair to a Full Character

You've seen how easy it is to apply grass to a landscape. You've also seen how using multiple instances of SasLite can enhance your image and animation. This next exercise takes a full character and applies hair to various parts of the body. This character looks suspiciously like Bigfoot…hmmm.

1. In Layout, clear the scene from the File menu, and load the caveman object from the book's CD. Change to Camera view. Open the Surface Editor and take a closer look at the surfaces of the object. There are nine total, five of which need fur.

2. Click the Scene tab, select Image Process, and add the SasLite Pixel Filter.

3. Next, select the object in Layout and press the p key to open the Object Properties panel for the character. Click the Displacement tab.

4. Load the first instance of SasLite. Now, you can either load an instance, set up the surface, and then continue to load the next instance. Or, you can load five instances at once.

5. Open the SasLite panel by double-clicking the listing. Instead of using the default Apply Fur to All Surfaces, as in the previous exercise, click the second listing from the top, Apply Fur Only To Named Surface. The Surface Name requestor will become available.

6. Enter the name HeadHair. This will apply hair to the character around his beard, eyebrows, and head.

7. Set the Fur Color to a soft brown. Then, add the following settings (See Figure 19.36):

   - Bright and Hue Vary   25%
   - Diffuse   75%
   - Specular   60%
   - Glossiness   40%
   - Coarseness   40%
   - Frizz   10%
   - Clump Size   40%
   - Fur Density   75%
   - Length   38%
   - Drooping   80%
   - Clumping   20%
   - Comb X   0%
   - Comb Y   −45.5%
   - Comb Z   80%

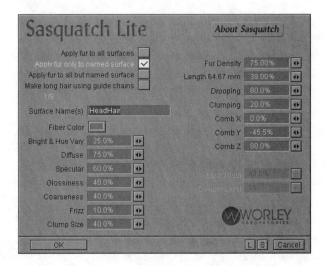

Figure 19.36   This is the first instance of SasLite applied to the character's head.

8. Close the SasLite panel. Press F9 to render a frame. In a moment, you'll see the hair generate for the character's head. Figure 19.37 shows the render.

Figure 19.37   You can apply multiple instances of SasLite to your characters. To start, one instance has been applied to the caveman's head.

Note

The render in Figure 19.37 has two lights set up: a bright orange from behind and left, and a soft blue from front right. The character is posed with a motion capture file. To learn more about applying motion capture to you characters in LightWave, check out Appendix A, "Motion Capture and LightWave."

9. You can tweak the settings and color to your liking, perhaps adding a gray-brown color. Now add another SasLite instance, and set the following for the ChestShoulderHair surface (See Figure 19.38):

   - Bright and Hue Vary   25%
   - Diffuse   75%
   - Specular   60%
   - Glossiness   40%
   - Coarseness   55%
   - Frizz   25%
   - Clump Size   40%
   - Fur Density   85%
   - Length   35%
   - Drooping   20%
   - Clumping   10%
   - Comb X   0%
   - Comb Y   0%
   - Comb Z   0%

10. Press F9 to render a frame. In a moment, you'll see the hair generate for the character's chest. Figure 19.39 shows the render.

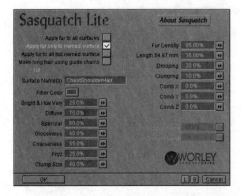

Figure 19.38   The second instance of SasLite is applied to the character to create longer hair around the chest. Remember, the chest, head, and other areas all have different surface names.

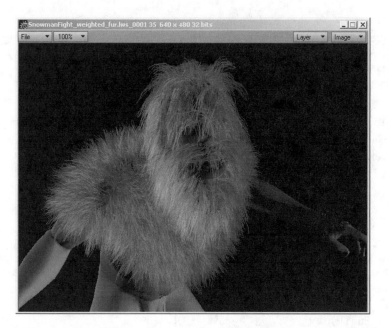

Figure 19.39   The second instance of SasLite adds hair around the caveman's chest.

11. Add one more instance of SasLite, and this time, apply the fur to the Body. Vary the color slightly, and add these values:

- Bright and Hue Vary   25%
- Diffuse   75%
- Specular   60%
- Glossiness   40%
- Coarseness   55%
- Frizz   50%
- Clump Size   40%
- Fur Density   100%
- Length   28%
- Drooping   20%
- Clumping   10%
- Comb X   0%
- Comb Y   0%
- Comb Z   0%

Figure 19.40 shows the panel.

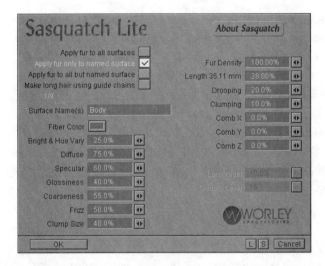

Figure 19.40   The third instance of SasLite is applied to the character to create shorter, less coarse hair around the body.

12. Press F9 to render a frame. In a moment, you'll see the hair generate for the character's chest. Figure 19.41 shows the render.

Figure 19.41   This guy needs to be introduced to a razor.

From this point on, add hair to the remaining two surfaces for the characters face and crotch. The settings can be very similar to the ones in the first three surfaces with slight variations in color and length.

The Next Step

Applying SasLite is easy once you know the steps—you might even find it addictive! The controls do what you think they would. Set a higher value for Coarseness, the hair will be coarser. Want the hair to droop? Increase the Drooping value. Does the hair need some direction? Use the Comb values. Within a couple of hours of experimentation, you'll have this down and will be scrambling for objects you think need fur and hair.

Summary

This chapter introduced you to some of the cooler additions to LightWave 7's arsenal of power. You easily can apply the information in these exercises to projects of your own, as well as projects for your clients. You'll find that both particles and SasLite are so fun to use that you'll be looking for projects that allow you to use them. Be careful, though—don't let your client know how easy it is to make objects look this good!

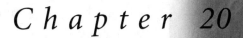

Chapter 20

Advanced Particle Animation

When you sit down in front of your computer and think about the things you can create with LightWave, you might be amazed by the number of possibilities

LightWave offers you as an animator. But don't think you're finished yet. Chapter 19, "Particle and Animation," gave you a good working knowledge of LightWave 7's particle system. This chapter ramps up the discussion of particle animation started in Chapter 19, and shows you how to incorporate even more objects and increase the interaction.

Project Overview

This chapter takes you through a number of projects that help you create more than just smoke. You'll use the particle system in LightWave as an animation tool to make liquid pour, leaves blow, and bats flock. But what will pour the liquid? Why are the leaves blowing? This chapter will answer those questions by teaching you the following:

- Using particles for fluid dynamics
- Using FX_Linker to animate blowing leaves
- Applying FX_Motion for colliding objects
- Creating a flock of bats

Particles for Animation Control

The particle system in LightWave, especially with visible Sprite mode in Layout, is fantastic. You have great possibilities in front of you for creating smoke, dust, sparks, and more. But did you know that the capabilities of the particle engine go much deeper, giving you the means of animating objects? Taking the particle animation system to the next level means using its collision properties and using the FX_Linker tool to replace particles with objects. Particles not only can interact with each other and be controlled by things like wind and gravity, but they also can be used for object animation.

Creating Liquids with Particles

There comes a time in every animator's career when some sort of fluid will need to be animated. Although a few third-party alternatives exist to help you with that task, the fastest and most integrated way of creating fluid animation is with LightWave's built-in particle engine.

As you'll learn in the first exercise, pouring liquid involves an emitter and at least one collision object.

Exercise 20.1   Pouring Liquid

This exercise uses a simple cup object found on the book's CD and a few particle controls. It also uses Hypervoxels to create a rendered look.

1. Open LightWave's Layout.

2. Click over to the Scene tab, and open the FX_Browser. Add an HVEMitter.

3. In Layout, move the emitter up on the y-axis about 2.5m, as shown in Figure 20.1.

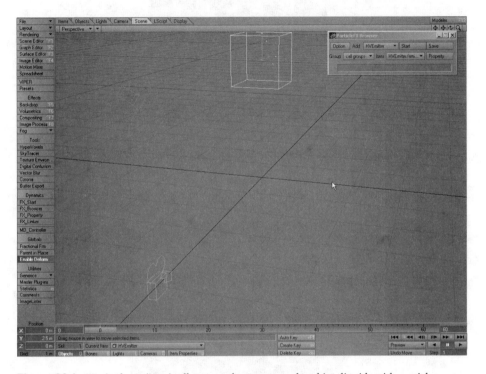

Figure 20.1   A single emitter is all you need to get started making liquids with particles.

4. Under the Items tab, load the cup object from the book's CD.

5. The cup loads to the 0 xyz-axis. Press the comma key a few times to zoom out or use the control in the top-right corner of the interface.

6. The default collision object is a sphere. That's fine for some things, but the goal here is to pour the particles into the cup. Make sure that the cup is selected in Layout, and press the p key to open the Object Properties panel. Click Add Custom Object and select FX_Collision (see Figure 20.2).

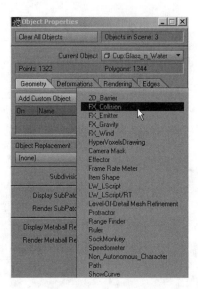

Figure 20.2   A collision object is added to the scene. This will serve as the colliding object, the cup.

7. Double-click the listing to open the Properties panel for the FX_Collision. In the Collision Properties panel, set the Type to Object. This change will slow your system down because LightWave is calculating all the vertices of the object, so be patient (see Figure 20.3).

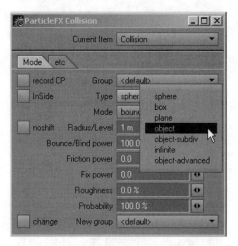

Figure 20.3   Instead of using a box or sphere for the collision object, you can turn the cup itself into the collision object.

8. When you set the Type to Object, your cup will highlight, almost appearing to be outlined, as shown in Figure 20.4.

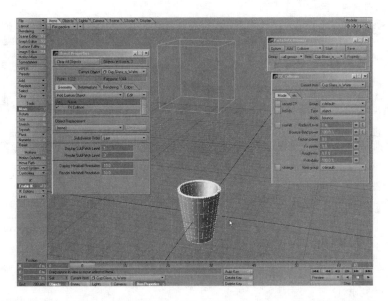

Figure 20.4   Once you set the cup object as the collision object, it is highlighted in Layout.

9. Select the ParticleFX Emitter, and open its properties. Click over to the Etc tab, and set the Y Gravity to –9.8. This is Earth's default gravity. Press the Play button in Layout. The particles fall but seem to collide with an invisible object, as you see in Figure 20.5!

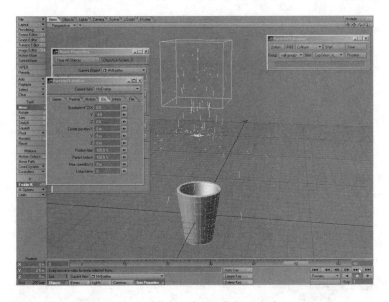

Figure 20.5   The particles begin to fall, but they collide with the cup too soon.

10. Set the last frame of the animation to 300 in Layout. In the ParticleFX Emitter properties panel, set the Life Time to 185 in the Particle tab.

11. Under the Generator tab of the ParticleFX Emitter panel, set the Birth Rate to 20. Set the XYZ size to 700mm each. Then, set the Particle Limit to 100.

    Because the Birth Rate is 20 and the limit is 100, all particles will be emitted within 5 seconds. (You've told the system to emit 20 particles every second, with a limit of 100, and 100 divided by 20 is 5.) Figure 20.6 shows the Generator tab.

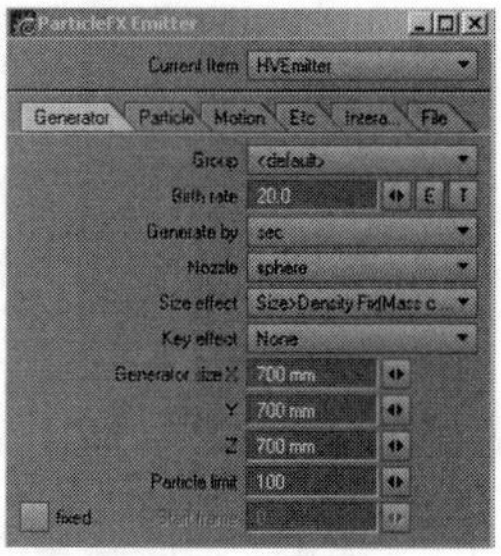

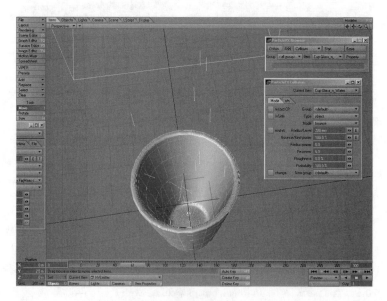

Figure 20.6   Enter a few settings under the Generator tab of the Particle Emitter properties, and you're on your way.

12. Do you know what to do now? RIGHT! Save the scene.

13. Go back to the Collision Properties panel, and take a look at the Radius Level. It's 1m. Your cup is only about half that size. Ah! That's why the particles collide way above the object.

    Think of this Radius as a force field. This is the area around the object that the particles understand to be the collision area. So, you need to adjust it based on the scale of your object.

14. Set the Radius of the Collision properties for the cup to 200mm. Move your view around to see the particles, and press the Play button in Layout. The particles now fall into the cup, hitting the sides and bouncing around (see Figure 20.7).

Figure 20.7   With the proper radius set for the collision object, the particles fall into the cup and bounce around.

15. You can play around with the other modes, such as Stick or Scatter, to see the various results. Select the cup object in Layout and create a keyframe at 160. This gives all the particles enough time to drop into the cup.

16. Rotate the cup on its Pitch about –120 degrees and create a keyframe at 170. Press the Play button. You'll see the particles fall into the cup. The cup slowly begins to rotate and then turns and dumps the few particles that are inside. The particles that don't quite make it into the cup hit the edges and bounce off.

This exercise completes the first part of creating fluid. The second part requires that you add a surface, and that's done with Hypervoxels.

Exercise 20.2   Surfacing Liquid

Depending on how you work, you might like to set up surfaces first, and then put things in motion. This chapter does the opposite, and for good reason. By putting the particles in motion first, applying Hypervoxels now will let you accurately see their interactions. If you did this before the motions, you would probably have to reset your size and various Hypervoxel parameters. This next exercise shows you how to create the liquid surface on the particles.

1. With the particle scene still loaded, click over to the Scene tab and select Volumetrics. Choose HypervoxelsFilter from the Add Volumetric drop-down list. Double-click the listing to open the panel.

2. In the Hypervoxels panel, double-click the HVEmitter listing to activate it. Change the Particle Size to 200mm.

3. In Layout, move the camera so that you have a good view of the cup and the particles falling into it. Create a keyframe to lock it in place.

4. Open VIPER by clicking the VIPER button on the toolbar on the left side of Layout. Move the Layout time slider to frame 110. Press F9 to render a frame of your scene to get the render information into LightWave's buffer. Press Render in the VIPER window. Figure 20.8 shows VIPER with the render.

Note

Remember that VIPER uses Camera view for information. If you've been setting up things in the Perspective view, be sure to move the camera into a good position for VIPER's information.

The particles look like big marshmallows, not really liquid. The tool's default Object Type is set to Surface, for a volume surface. This is fine for this project, but you need to tweak the settings.

5. In the Hypervoxels panel, click the Shading tab. Set the color to a light blue. Set Luminosity to 0, and Diffuse to 90 percent.

Figure 20.8 VIPER is essential to setting up Hypervoxels.

6. Bring Specularity up to 100 percent and Glossiness to 27 percent. Set Reflection to 10 percent. You'll set a reflection image in a moment.

7. Transparency is 0 percent, but click the T button to set a transparent texture.

8. Set the Layer Type to Gradient. Blending Mode should be Normal while Layer Opacity is 100 percent.

9. Change the Input Parameter to Incidence Angle. Create a key just above the middle of the gradient bar, and set its Value to about 10 percent, Alpha 100 percent, and Parameter about 19, as shown in Figure 20.9.

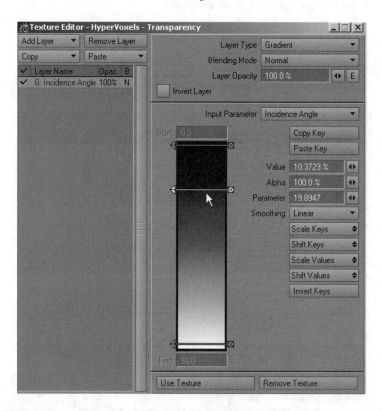

Figure 20.9   Create a key in the middle of the gradient by left clicking.

10. Create a key at the very bottom of the gradient, with a Value of 150 percent, Alpha of 100 percent, and Parameter of 89, as shown in Figure 20.10.

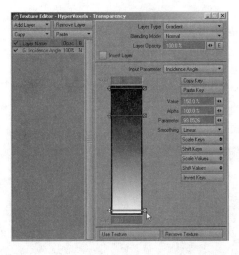

Figure 20.10   The bottom key in the gradient has a value of 150 percent.

11. For the first and fixed key in the Gradient at the top set the Value to 0 percent, Alpha to 100 percent, and finally Parameter to 0.0. Figure 20.11 shows the settings for the last key.

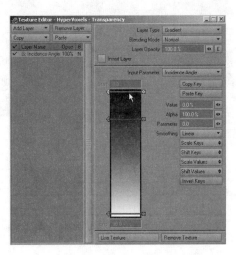

Figure 20.11   The top key, which is always fixed in the gradient, has a value of 0 percent, which is why it's represented by black.

12. Click Use Texture. Set about a 5 percent transparency, and then set the Refraction under the Basic tab to 1.33. Click over to the Environment tab.

13. Set Reflection Options to Spherical Map, with the Reflection Map being the 02Swamp.tga image on the book's CD.

14. Click back out to the Geometry tab, and change the Particle Size to 230mm for a little more volume.

15. Set Size Variation to 85 percent. Make sure that the Stretch Direction is set to Y for the flow of the liquid, and then set the Stretch Amount to 250 percent. Figure 20.12 shows the panel. Go ahead and make a preview with VIPER, and make any changes you like. Save the scene!

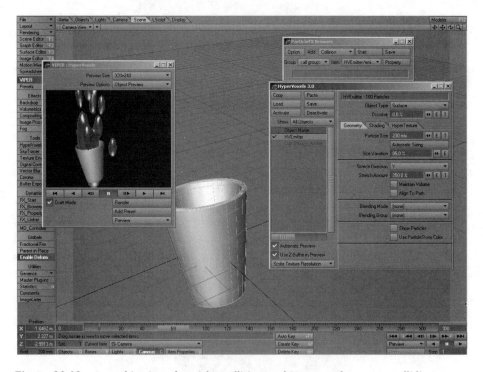

Figure 20.12 A combination of particles, collision, and Hypervoxels creates a colliding, flowing liquid.

At this point, you have a lot more you can play with and tweak. For example, go back out to the Particle emitter and increase the Birth Rate and Particle Limit for more particles. More particles will help create a better shape with Hypervoxels, but will take longer to render.

You also can try using this technique for particles falling over rock objects to create—you guessed it—a waterfall. But instead of using the Surface Volume Object Type for Hypervoxels, use LightWave 7's Sprite mode, as you did for the smoke in Chapter 19.

Now move on to another particle tutorial to create cool, natural-looking blowing leaves.

Multiple Objects Using FX_Linker

The FX_Linker is a tool that enables you to take any object and use it to replace particles. Think of flocking birds, falling dollar bills, or blowing leaves, to name a few. FX_Linker gives you the power to select one object and blend it with particle effects.

Exercise 20.3   Animating Blowing Leaves

Liquid is not the easiest thing to create in 3D, but the power of LightWave's particle engine and a fair amount of tweaking in Hypervoxels can get you the desired results. How about using particles to create blowing objects, like snow, rain, or leaves? This next exercise shows you how to create realistic-looking blowing leaves.

1. Clear Layout, and then add a HVEmitter and a wind controller.

2. Select Move from the Items tab (t), and move the wind out of the way to see your particles, making sure to create a keyframe for it, to lock it in place.

3. Open the Properties panel for the wind, and set the Falloff Mode to OFF. This will create a wind source for the particles, no matter where it is located.

   If you chose the Falloff Mode to be Linear, for example, the wind would need to intersect with the particles. Figure 20.13 shows the ParticleFX Wind panel.

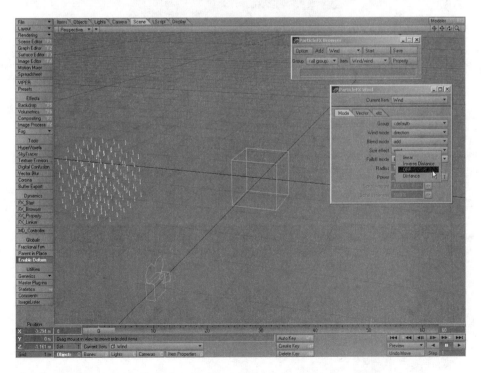

Figure 20.13   The Falloff Mode in the ParticleFX Wind panel is set to OFF so that the particles are affected no matter where the wind source is located in the scene.

4. Set Layout's last animation frame to 300 for a 10-second animation. Press the Play button. The particles drift upward. The wind by default is pushing up.

5. Select the Wind controller in Layout, rotate it 90 degrees on its bank, and create a keyframe at 0. Press Play again, and you'll see the particles pushed to the side.

6. The particles end too soon, so open the HVEmitter property panel. Set the Birth Rate to 30. Then under the Particle tab, set the Life Time to 300, and a random value (+/−) to 60. Figure 20.14 shows the settings.

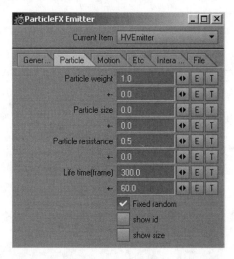

Figure 20.14   Make a few adjustments under the Particle tab, and the particles are almost ready for some leaves.

7. Bring the Particle Resistance down to 0.5 so the particles move throughout their lifetime. Then, click the Motion tab and set a Vibration of 1.0 to shake up the particles.

8. Lastly, click the Generator tab, and click the small button labeled Fixed in the bottom left. This allows you to set a specific start time for the particles. Set the value to −150.

   This entry will set the particles in motion 150 frames before 0, which is the start of the animation. The result is that the particles are already in motion from the emitter. They are not starting out from the emitter in the beginning of the animation.

9. Now back in Layout, under the Items tab load the Leaf_clipSub object from the accompanying CD. This is nothing more than a flat subpatched object with a clip map of a leaf. Figure 20.15 shows Layout. You might need to zoom out slightly after the object has been loaded.

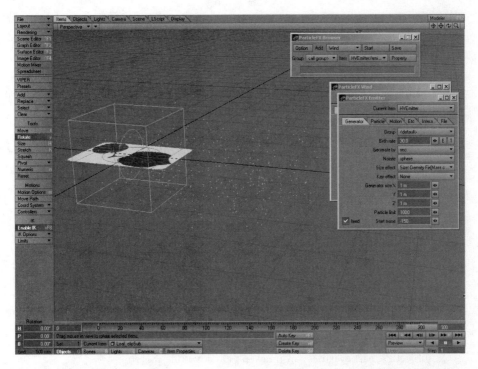

Figure 20.15   A flat polygon is all you need to begin creating a frame full of blowing leaves.

10. Select the leaf object and press the p key. Set the Subdivision Order to Last under the Geometry tab for the leaf object. Set Display SubPatch to 1, and leave Render SubPatch set at 3.

11. Click the Deformations tab, and then click the T button for Displacement Map to enter the Texture Displacement Map Editor.

12. Change the Layer Type to Procedural. The default Procedural Type is Turbulence, which is fine. Just change the Texture Value to 0.25. Lastly, click World Coordinates (see Figure 20.16).

What you've done here is put a fractal displacement map on the leaf object. This will rough it up a bit, so it's not perfectly flat. Setting World Coordinates will tell the object to move through the texture, rather than animate the texture on the object. You'll see how this affects the leaf shortly.

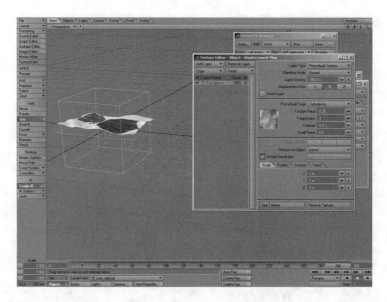

Figure 20.16   A procedural displacement map on the leaf object bends it up a bit.

13. Click Use Texture to close the Displacement Map Texture Editor. Close the Object Properties panel if you haven't already done so.

14. Now select the leaf object, and scale it down (Shift+h) to 0.2 for the X, Y, and Z. Create a keyframe for it to keep the new size. Figure 20.17 shows the change.

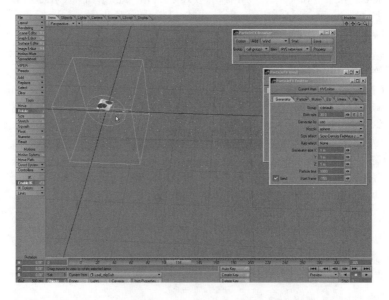

Figure 20.17   Sizing down the leaf object gets it ready for some blowin' in the wind.

15. Now the fun part begins. Make sure that the leaf object is selected, and from the Scene tab, click the FX_Linker button. The ParticleFX Linker panel appears, allowing you to replicate the leaf object for every particle in the scene. More importantly, it automatically adds the FX Link Motion modifier to each object (see Figure 20.18).

Note

Always save your scene before performing operations like this! There is no undo, which means that if you want to change anything after the fact, you'll have to go back and reset your particle scene.

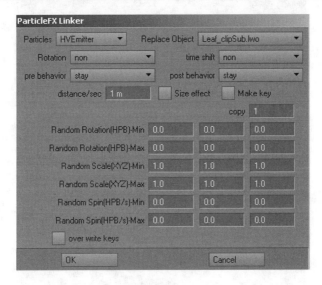

Figure 20.18   The FX_Linker panel allows you to replicate objects instantly to replace particles.

Because the leaf object was selected when you opened the FX_Linker panel, the object is automatically listed as the Replace Object in the upper-right corner of the interface.

The emitter in the scene has a maximum of 1,000 particles, emitting 30 of them every second. That's 30 leaves every second up to 1,000. The best option here is to go back to the emitter and lower the Birth Rate. But for now, you can just replicate fewer leaves. Too many might bring your system to a halt.

16. At the right side of the FX_Linker panel, the Copy area lets you add a value. Add 100. This will create 100 copies of the leaf object, replacing the first 100 particles with it (see Figure 20.19).

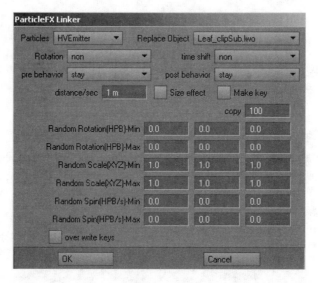

Figure 20.19   Set the Copy value to 100 for 100 leaves.

17. Set the Random Rotation Min values to –60. The three value areas from left to right are X, Y, and Z.

18. Set the Random Rotation Max values to 90 for the X, Y, and Z.

19. Leave Random Scale values all to the default 1.0.

20. Set the Random Spin Min to –60 for the X, Y, and Z, and the Random Spin Max to 90 for X, Y, and Z (see Figure 20.20).

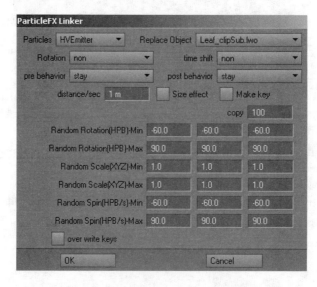

Figure 20.20   A few minimum and maximum rotation values in the FX_Linker panel will help the blowing leaf effect.

21. Click OK to close the panel. Your system will hang for a moment as LightWave calculates the changes. Figure 20.21 shows all the leaves now attached to the particles!

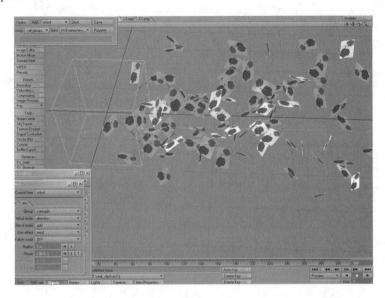

Figure 20.21   The FX_Linker easily replicated 100 leaves and attached them to particles.

22. Switch to Camera view, and move the camera into the frame so that it's filled up with leaves. Figure 20.22 shows the shot.

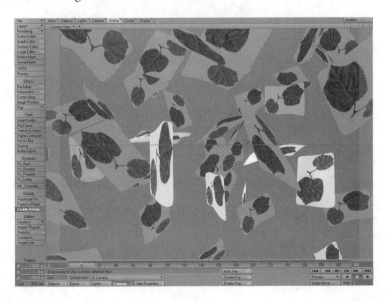

Figure 20.22   Because you set the particles to start at frame –150, the camera at frame 0 sees the leaves right away.

23. Move the timeline slider back and forth and take a close look at the leaves. They almost look like they're swimming through the air, sort of floating like a falling piece of paper. This is the World Coordinate setting for the Displacement Map you applied earlier. As the particles move the leaf objects, the leaf objects are moving through the displacement. This creates a nice, flowing look.

Note

Because the polygon count in the scene now has 100 copies of the leaf object, you'll need to crank up your Bounding Box Threshold to see some of the objects while moving the timeline slider.

24. Move the camera up and in to get a good view of the scene. Create a keyframe to lock it in place. Press F9 to render a test frame.

25. With the Leaf object selected, press the p key to open the Object Properties panel. From the Rendering tab, click the T button for Clip Map. Set an image map the way you normally would, using the leaf2.tga image. Add the image on the y-axis, and click Automatic Sizing.

26. Press F9 to render a frame. You'll see the leaf render, but not the white area! The image is clipped out (Clip Map, Object Properties panel). Figure 20.23 shows the rendered frame with SkyTracer2 added for a backdrop.

Figure 20.23   Using FX_Linker with a single clip mapped object, you suddenly have a view filled with blowing leaves.

From this point, you can enhance the animation with a little motion blur, more wind (such as wind gusts), and perhaps a secondary set of leaves of a different color. But the example here is a great way to get your multiple objects in motion. The FX_Linker is very straightforward as you've seen, and it is useful for replicating objects for your particles.

FX_linker allows you to add the FX_Link Motion modifier to a mass of objects and set randomized settings. You can use FX_Linker to create swarms of bees, bats, birds, whatever you like! The setup involves adding your Particle emitter and getting the particles to move the way you want them to. Then load the object, or use Load From Scene to load a scene of a bird flapping its wings. Select the main parent or root of that flapping bird, open FX_Linker, and set it up. The flapping bird, its wings, and so on, will be copied and assigned to the particles.

Now move on to another tutorial using FX_Linker and collision objects.

Exercise 20.4   Bowling with Particles

When you create animations that are more than just simple emitters for sparks, fireworks, or smoke, you'll often use the FX_Linker as you did in the previous exercise. This exercise expands further into another feature of particle effects called the FX_Motion. This is a motion plug-in that allows non-particle objects to be affected by particle effects, such as collision.

   1. Load the SinglePin scene from the book's CD. Drag the timeline slider and you'll see the bowling ball travel through the pin. Not zesty!

   2. Select the bowling ball, and press p to open the Object Properties for the object. Click the Geometry tab and from the Add Custom Object drop down, select FX_Collision, as shown in Figure 20.24. This will add a collision effector to the bowling ball.

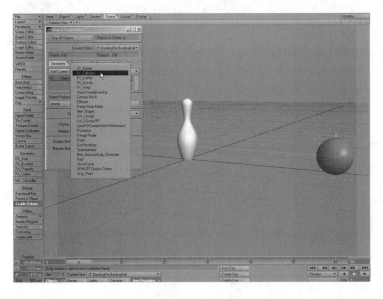

Figure 20.24   From the Object Properties panel, you can assign a collision effector to any object, such as a bowling ball.

3. Select the bowling pin in Layout, and press the m key to call up the Motion Options. From the Add Modifier drop-down list, select FX_Motion, as shown in Figure 20.25.

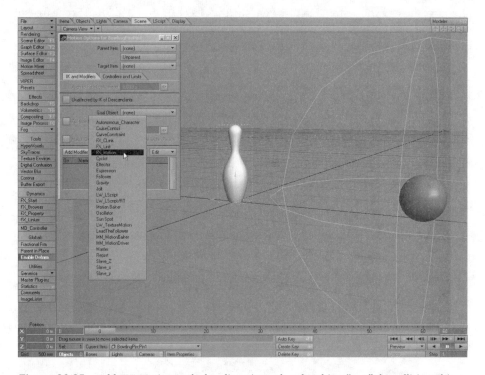

Figure 20.25   Add FX_Motion to the bowling pin so that the object "sees" the collision object.

This modifier tells the selected object to react with effectors in the scene; namely the collision effector, the bowling ball.

4. At this point, simply drag the timeline slider and watch the action. The bowling pin seems to be hit by the bowling ball long before the two objects actually meet.

5. Select the bowling ball, and from the Scene tab, select FX_Property to call up the collision properties. Change the Radius Level to 350mm.

6. The Bounce/Bind power should be 100 percent, while Friction power, Fix power, and Roughness are all set to 0.

7. The Probability default is 100 percent. This setting is fine. Figure 20.26 shows the panel.

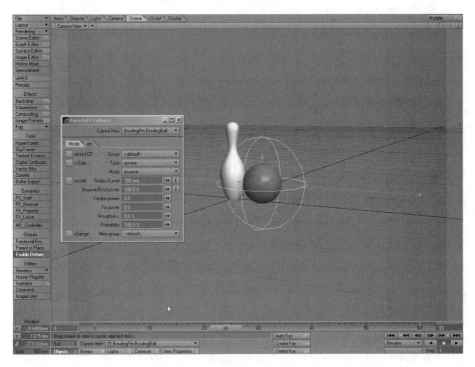

Figure 20.26   Changing the radius of the collision sphere changes the collision point.

8. Drag the timeline slider and you'll see that the ball now hits the pin just before collision. Now you need to change the way the pin reacts to the collision by opening the FX_Motion properties for the pin object.

9. Right now when the pin gets hit with the ball, it reacts but drifts downward unrealistically. Under the Mode tab of the FX_Motion panel, change the Mode to position+rotation. Set After Collision to random.

10. You want this random rotation action to happen at the point of impact. The point of impact is frame 24, which you can determine if you drag the timeline slider. Set the Start Frame to 24.

11. Set the Weight to 10.0.

12. Size should be 0. This setting can be increased to allow the collision to happen around a larger area of the object. For this particular object, increasing the size is not necessary, but if you had an object with large jagged edges, for example, you would increase the size value.

13. Resistance, Momentum, and Rotation resistance should all be set to 1.0. Increasing or decreasing these changes the parameter accordingly.

14. The z-Rotation by wind setting should be at 0, because there is no wind in the scene. Figure 20.27 shows the settings.

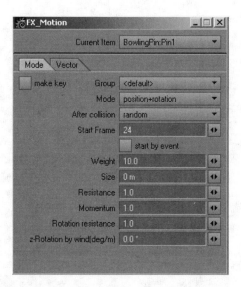

Figure 20.27   The Mode settings for FX_Motion control when and how the bowling pin will move at the point of collision.

15. Click the Vector tab and set the Y value for Initial Velocity to 2m. Keep the X and Z values at 0. This will help the bowling pin move up away from the collision. Velocity Coordinates should be set to Local for the single object.

16. Lastly, set the Initial Rotation for the Heading to 290 degrees. This will give some rotation to the pin when it gets hit by the ball, as shown in Figure 20.28.

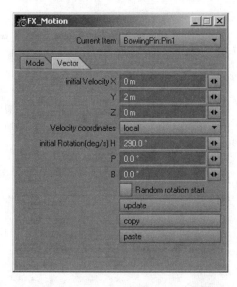

Figure 20.28   The Vector tab for FX_Motion is where you enter the initial rotation and velocity settings for the bowling pin.

17. Press the Play button and watch the action. Save the scene. Figure 20.29 shows the collision at frame 35.

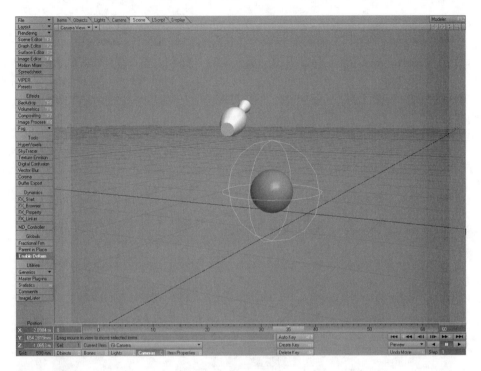

Figure 20.29   With the collision object set for the bowling ball and the FX_Motion in place for the bowling pin, the collision effect works, sending the pin spinning up into the air.

From here, you can add more pins, set FX_Motion to them, and have additional collisions. Then, try adding a gravity effector to the pins so that after they get hit, they fall to the ground. Add another collision as a flat plane, so the falling pins hit the ground and bounce. See how this works? Simply keep adding effectors for animation elements, and it will all come together.

Exercise 20.5   Flocking Bats with Particles

Similar to the blowing leaf tutorial earlier, this exercise shows you the techniques for creating a flock of bats. This technique is good for birds, bees, butterflies, or anything you want. And although this tutorial relies on FX_Linker to replicate an object, as the blowing leaf tutorial did, you'll be working with an object already in motion with a bone structure.

1. Load the PathFlockSetup scene from the book's CD. This is nothing more than an emitter with a wind object set up with three keyframes and path wind.

Note

Path wind is described in the smoke tutorial, Exercise 19.1, in Chapter 19.

2. Press the Play button to watch the flock of particles move toward the camera. There aren't many particles, and that's for good reason.

   While the blowing leaf tutorial earlier used hundreds of particles for hundreds of leaves, this tutorial only needs a few bats. In addition, applying FX_Linker to a few hundred bats might bring your system to a screeching halt. For now, you'll use just about 10 particles.

3. From the File menu, select Load, and then click Load Items From Scene. Choose the BatBone scene (see Figure 20.30).

   Essentially, this will load a scene into your scene.

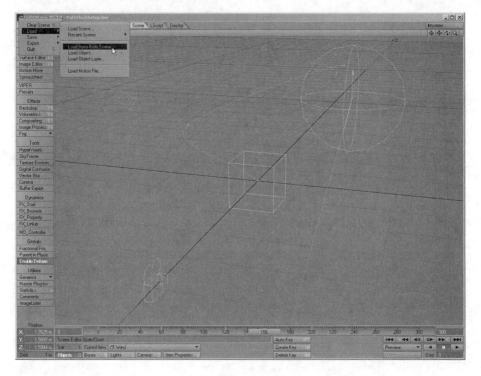

Figure 20.30   Load Items From Scene will allow you to load a complete scene into your existing scene.

4. When the requestor appears asking you whether you want to load the lights as well, click No. Figure 20.31 shows the bat scene loaded into Layout.

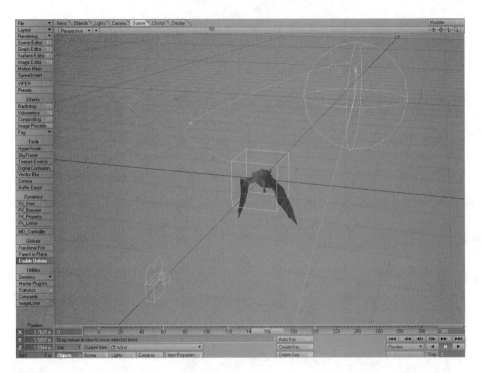

Figure 20.31   Once the scene is loaded, you can see the bat and its flapping wings in Layout.

5. If you drag the timeline slider, you'll see the bat flap its wings. That motion doesn't save with an object, but rather a scene. The benefit of Load Items From Scene is to load an object's motions along with the object.

6. Select the Bat_Mover object, which is a null object. Scale (by pressing Shift+h) the null to 0.3 for the X, Y, and Z. Create a keyframe to lock the size at frame 0.

7. With the Bat_Mover still selected, go to the Scene tab, and open the FX_Linker.

8. In the FX_Linker panel, set Rotation to align to path(hp) for heading and pitch. Set Pre Behavior to original. Set time shift to end shift, and post behavior to original. Because the Bat_Mover object was selected when you opened the FX_Linker, it's automatically added to the Replace Object setting.

9. Next to copy, select 10 to create 10 bats. You also can set some minimum and maximum rotations if you like. For now, leave the other settings at their defaults. Click OK. Figure 20.32 shows the panel.

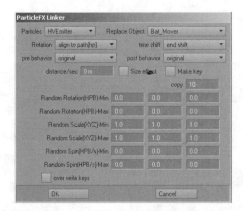

Figure 20.32   The FX_Linker panel lets you replicate the bat with its bones for the flocking particles.

10. Drag the timeline slider in Layout and you'll see your flock of bats! (See Figure 20.33.)

Figure 20.33   Using FX_Linker on a preexisting bat scene creates a flock of bats.

You need to consider a few variables with this scene. The first and foremost variable is the motion of the bat wings. Although the bats flock together nicely, they fly in unison. For some animations this is good, but not for bats. What you'll need to do is open the BatBone scene and scale the movements a few frames. Save that as another scene. Do this a few times so that you have various flapping scenes. Then, load those scenes using Load Items From Scene and then apply FX_Linker.

Another alternative is to save this scene you just created, but replicate only a few bats. Then, set the process up again with a few more bats of different speed. Then, combine the different FX_Linker scenes.

The Next Step

Clearly, we could go on and on with tutorials using LightWave's rich particle engine. The examples in this chapter have shown you how you can take your particle animations to the next level and really create scenes out of them, not just sparks and smoke. As you've seen, FX_Linker is great for replicating objects from particles, enabling you to create blowing leaves and flocking bats—you can even take it as far as crowd animations. The next step for you is to use these examples in your own work, and experiment with your own ideas.

Summary

FX_Linker, FX_Motion, and the other types of particle controls available to you in LightWave open up a world of possibilities. They're great for special effects, logo animations, industrial animations, and even real-world scenes. But before we run out of room talking about particles, read on to Chapter 21, "Motion Designer Creations," and learn how to create realistic cloth with Motion Designer.

C h a p t e r   21

Motion Designer Creations

No one would have guessed during the
mid-1990s that a program on your desktop
computer would have the power that
LightWave does today. The two preceding

chapters on particles demonstrated what this power can do—but this chapter will go a step further using Motion Designer. Motion Designer is a tool within LightWave that allows you to easily create cloth. Although this feature can be used for many applications, such as rippling water, turbulent clouds, or even Jell-O, the most common use is for creating animated cloth.

Project Overview

By following the exercises in this chapter, you will be up and running in Motion Designer in no time. The exercises here illustrate the tool's interactivity and demonstrate its functionality. The goal here is for you to gain from this chapter the knowledge you need to build even greater creations on your own. This chapter shows you how to do the following:

- Set up animated cloth from basic motion
- Apply object collisions
- Use Motion Designer to create cloth on full characters

Motion Designer

The interface controls for many of the tools within LightWave often are misleading. The Motion Designer interface is similar to these tools in that way. And although Motion Designer doesn't have too many controls for you to worry about, there are many important steps you need to understand so that you can properly use the tool.

Motion Designer is a displacement map plug-in, labeled MD_Plug. You access it by clicking the MD_Controller button, found in Layout under the Scene tab, just below the particle controls you used in the preceding two chapters. These are all part of the Dynamics listing on the toolbar.

Creating a Basic Motion Designer Scene

In the first exercise, you take a basic look at Motion Designer and set up a very simple blowing cloth. From there, you'll make an object collide with it.

Exercise 21.1   Building Cloth Objects

Starting out, you need to ask yourself, "Self, what sort of cloth should I animate?" The answer should be, "Any kind you want!" In all seriousness, you can animate any kind of cloth you like, such as cotton sheets, velvet drapes, or clothing—but you need to build it properly. Particularly, that means don't over-build it. Because you are able to use SubPatched objects in Layout, Motion Designer will understand this geometry. The result will be highly subdivided objects that bend and animate smoothly.

1. Open LightWave's Modeler.

    The object you'll create is nothing more than a large rectangle.

2. From the Create tab at the top of Layout, click the Box button. In the Back view, click and draw a large rectangle. Press the up arrow on your keyboard four times, and press the right arrow five times to create multiple segments.

3. Press the spacebar once to turn off the Box tool (or just click once on the Box tool), and your object has been created. Figure 21.1 shows the flat box.

Note

If your created box object does not appear in Perspective view, press the f key to flip the polygons forward.

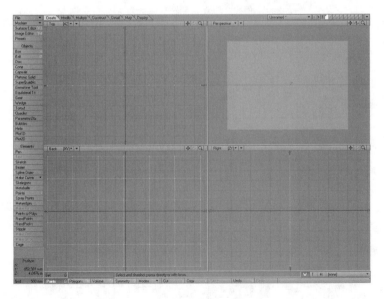

Figure 21.1   A flat box in the Back view in Modeler is all you need to get started using Motion Designer.

4. Before you move on to Layout, make a few adjustments to the flat box. First, select the top row of points. Remember to switch to Point mode at the bottom of Modeler. Figure 21.2 shows the selection.

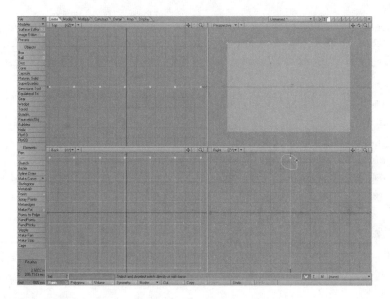

Figure 21.2   Select the top row of points.

5. Select Move (press t) and move the selected points down toward the second row of points, as shown in Figure 21.3.

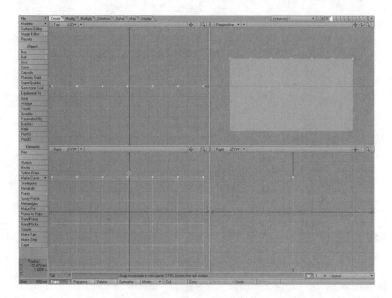

Figure 21.3   Move the points down toward the second row.

6. Deselect the points by first pressing the spacebar once to turn off the Move tool, and then either pressing the / key or clicking a blank area of the toolbar.

What you're doing here is creating a small top section that will be surfaced with a different name. Motion Designer uses surface names to understand where the deformations will occur. This tight top row of polygons will become a rigid surface, while the rest will become cloth. If this didn't happen, and the cloth object was not part of another object, applying Motion Designer to it would simply make it blow away!

7. In Polygon mode, select the small top row of polygons. Press q to call up the Change Surface requester and name the selected polygons Rigid. Figure 21.4 shows the setup.

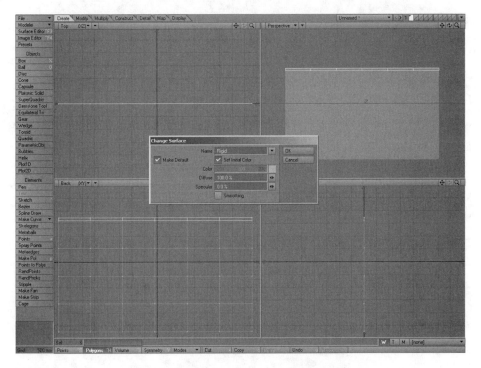

Figure 21.4   The top row of polygons is selected and named Rigid. This will become sort of a holder for the cloth when applying Motion Designer.

8. Now that the Rigid surface has been created, hold the Shift key and press the Single Quote key to reverse selections. This deselects the small top row and selects all the other polygons in one stroke.

9. Again, press q, and give these selected polygons the name Cloth, as you see in Figure 21.5.

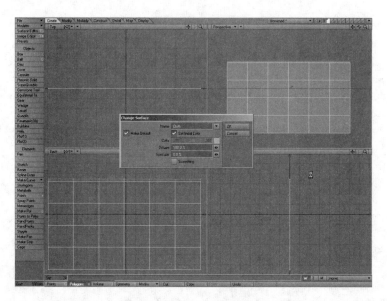

Figure 21.5   Give the main area of the object the surface name Cloth.

10. Deselect all polygons. Open the Surface Editor, and color both the Rigid and Cloth surfaces the same. Add a nice color of your liking, and apply a bit of specularity and glossiness. Click also on Smoothing and Double Sided (see Figure 21.6).

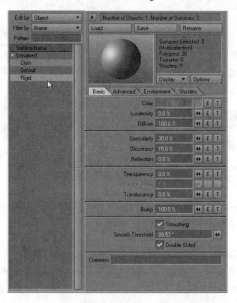

Figure 21.6   Apply surface properties to the newly named polygons. Be sure that both surfaces have the same properties.

11. Close the Surface Editor, and press the Tab key to activate SubPatch mode. Save the object, and give it a name like, oh, how about *Cloth*?

12. Up in the top-right corner of Modeler, select the tiny drop-down triangle and select Send Object to Layout. This will send the object directly to Layout without needing to load it from disc—the operation is automatic. (If your HUB is not activated, you'll see these controls ghosted. So, either activate your HUB or simply load the object directly from Layout.)

13. Press Alt+Tab to move over to Layout, and press 6 to switch to Camera view. Change the total length of the animation to 400 in the timeline.

14. Select the cloth, and move it back into the scene, up and to the right. Create a keyframe for it in this position at 60, as shown in Figure 21.7.

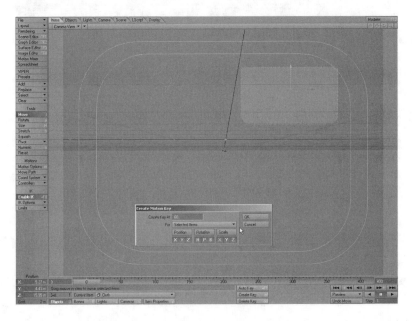

Figure 21.7   Create a keyframe for the cloth object back into the frame and up toward the right, at 60.

15. Move the cloth object to the left of the interface, maybe giving it a slight rotation, and create a keyframe at 120 to lock it in place (see Figure 21.8).

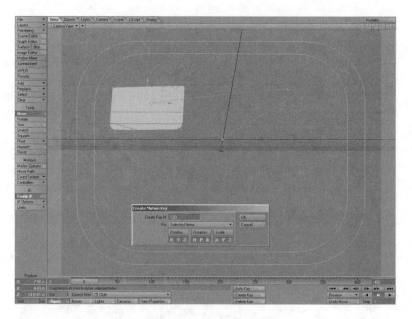

Figure 21.8   Create another keyframe to the left side of the screen with a slight rotation at frame 120.

16. Press the f key to display the Go To Frame requester. Enter 0 to go to the initial animation frame. Press Enter to create a keyframe, and when the Create Motion Key dialog appears, change the 0 frame value (your current frame) to 200. This takes the current state of the item at frame 0, but creates the key at frame 200. Click OK. You just copied a keyframe.

Note

The process performed in step 16 is great anywhere in your animation that you need to "copy" keyframes.

17. Do you know what to do now? Eeehh! Wrong! Save the scene!

18. Now you can play with Motion Designer. Under the Scene tab, click the MD_Controller. A small panel will open called Motion Designer Controller. On that panel, click the Property button. Figure 21.9 shows the selections.

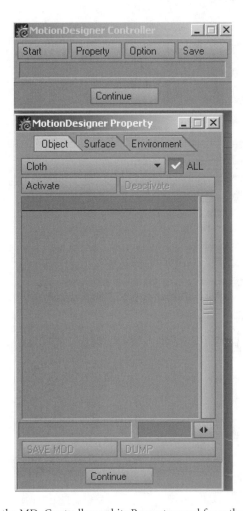

Figure 21.9   Open the MD_Controller and its Property panel from the Scene tab.

19. The MotionDesigner Property panel is where everything happens, so move it over to the side of the interface so that your cloth object in Layout is visible. Then click the Activate button. You'll see a few values added to the Property panel.

Note

In this particular case, only one object is in the scene. However, when you work with more than one object, be sure to have that particular item selected before you open up the MD_Controller. This will ensure you're telling Motion Designer to work with the correct object.

20. At the top of the Property panel, there is a selection list that shows Cloth, the name of your object—not the surface, but the name. If you had other objects in your scene, they would be listed here as well. The second information line in the panel reads Target. Double-click this. Your object is now active and identified as a Target Motion Designer item (see Figure 21.10).

21. More controls have appeared! For now, don't worry about setting any of the other controls. Most of the time, all you'll need to do under the Object tab is click Target as you've just done. Now click the Surface tab.

Figure 21.10 The first step to applying Motion Designer to your object is to activate it by double-clicking Target.

22. Under the Surface tab area, you'll see your object listed with a small white triangle. Click the object name to expand the triangle and display the object's settings. Do you see what's there? Remember those two surface names you created for the polygons in Modeler? Here they are. First select Rigid. Then in the lower portion of the interface, click next to Fixed. The word ON appears, as shown in Figure 21.11.

Setting Fixed for the surface will anchor the surface, basically telling Motion Designer to ignore it when deforming the object.

Note

When you set the Rigid surface to Fixed, the number 1 that appears at the bottom of the screen simply means the selection, Fixed, is on. Off, then, is 0.

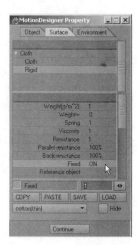

23. Now select the Cloth surface. Set a quick preset by choosing cotton(thick) from the drop-down list at the bottom left of the interface, as you see in Figure 21.12.

Figure 21.11 Setting the Rigid surface of the cloth object to Fixed will lock the surface from Motion Designer's deformations.

24. You've now set up your cloth object for animation. From the Motion Designer Controller panel, the first small panel that opened when you clicked the MD_Controller button, click the Start button (see Figure 21.13).

25. What happened? Nothing! That's because your object, if you remember, is a Subpatched object. Motion Designer is a deformation tool. This means that you need to tell your object when to subdivide. Under Layout, select the cloth object and press the p key to open the Object Properties panel. Under the Geometry tab, set the Subdivision order to Last, as shown in Figure 21.14.

Figure 21.12 A great way to get started setting up cloth surfaces is to use a preset, such as cotton (thick). From here, you can tweak to your liking.

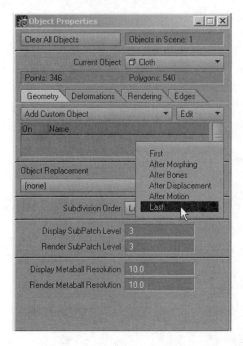

Figure 21.13 Clicking the Start button in the Motion Designer Controller panel begins the calculations.

Figure 21.14 The Subdivision order for the cloths should be set to Last from the Objects Properties panel.

26. Click the Play button at the bottom right of the Layout. Your object will move around, but it won't be displaced.

Among the key things you should know when setting up Motion Designer scenes is that your Bounding Box Threshold for your objects needs to be equal or greater than that of your object. For example, the cloth object in this exercise contains 540 polygons, with 346 points, at a SubPatch level of 3. Therefore, the Bounding Box Threshold Level (see Figure 21.15) should be 540 or higher. Whatever value you add will be saved when you quit LightWave. So set this to 10,000 in the Display Options tab (d).

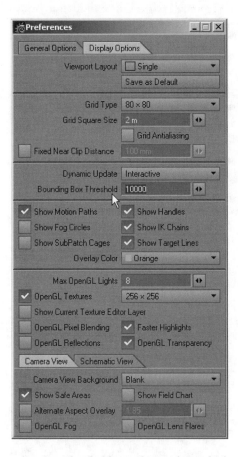

Figure 21.15   The Bounding Box Threshold must be equal to or higher than the point and polygon count of your object for Motion Designer to work properly.

Note

You quickly can check the point and polygon amount of your object from the Object Properties panel. Conversely, you can check the point and polygon count of your entire scene by pressing w to call up Scene Statistics.

27. Check your Bounding Box Threshold, and return to Layout. Press the Play button again. Your cloth object sways as it moves, as shown in Figure 21.16.

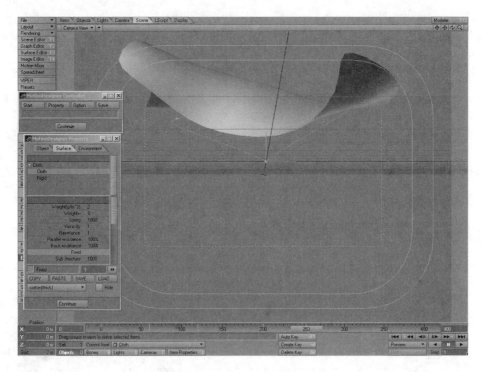

Figure 21.16   With the Bounding Box Threshold adjusted and the Subdivision Order set to Last, the cloth deformation is now visible.

As you can see, the object reacts to the keyframed movements you made earlier. But the object just sort of floats and has no weight.

Exercise 21.2   Adding Environment Variables to Cloth

You've set up a motion for a piece of cloth—these are the same basic principles you'll use for any Motion Designer creation. Motion Designer does its job well and your cloth flaps around as the object moves. But when the object comes to a rest, the cloth stays airborne! You need to use Motion Designer's Environment tab settings to add things like Wind, Turbulence, and Gravity.

I. With the cloth scene still loaded, click the Environment tab in the Motion Designer Property panel for the Cloth surface.

Here, you can set up various attributes for your cloth, such as Gravity. You'll see three entry areas next to the Gravity setting, representing X, Y, and Z, from left to right.

2. Set a Gravity value of –4.0 for the y-axis, as you see in Figure 21.17.

3. Now that you've made a change to the surface's properties, you need to tell Motion Designer to recalculate. Press the Start button again from the Motion Designer Controller.

   You'll see the cloth move around the keyframes again, but this time, it hangs a little. When the motion of the cloth ends, it falls and drapes naturally. But the cloth is a bit too smooth. You need to rough it up a bit.

4. Back under the Environment tab, set the Y Turbulence value to 10.0 and the Z to –20. This will add a sort of fractal interference up on the Y and toward the camera on the Z.

5. Set a 2.0 X Wind2 Value, and change the Wind Mode to Gust, so that the wind value gusts! Set the Random-ratio to 50. Cycle length should be 2.0, and Gust Length should be set to 1.0. Leave all other settings at their defaults. Save the scene. Figure 21.18 shows the panel.

Play around with the various settings, adding one value at a time, and pressing the Start button in the Motion Designer Controller interface after you've added a value.

Note

At any time after you've pressed the Start button, you can cancel the calculations by pressing the Ctrl key.

This exercise guided you through some of the necessary requirements for using Motion Designer. The next exercise shows you how you can set up collision objects with cloth.

Exercise 21.3   Adding Collision to Cloth

Now that you've put some cloth into motion, take it a step further by adding collision to it. This next exercise shows you how to take a human hand and make it interact with cloth.

1. Save anything you've been working on, and load the HitMe scene off the book's CD. This is a version of the cloth scene you created earlier in this chapter.

2. Under the Items tab in Layout, load the Fist object. You'll see the fist stick through the flat cloth object (see Figure 21.19).

Figure 21.17 Applying Gravity to the negative y-axis puts a little more weight and life into the cloth.

Figure 21.18 Adding a little Wind and Turbulence to the cloth surface helps set its freeform look. Random gusts can be added, too.

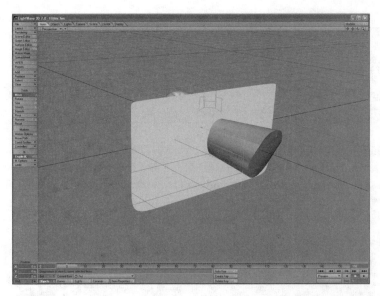

Figure 21.19   After loading the HitMe scene and the Fist object, both elements are seen easily in Perspective view.

3. If you click the Play button in Layout, you'll see the cloth move in the wind. This happens because the motion had already been set and saved with the scene. Select the Fist object and move it away from the cloth, to a point just in front of it. Create a keyframe at 0 to lock it in place.

 Note

Motion Designer calculations are not saved with a scene simply by saving that scene. If you reload a scene, you'll need to recalculate Motion Designer by pressing the Start button. You can record and save the Motion Designer file, however; it's the MDD file from the bottom Motion Designer Property panel. Saving here and then loading your scene again will load the calculated motion for your objects.

4. Open the MD_Controller from the Scene tab. Then open the Motion Designer Property panel by clicking the button from the Motion Designer Controller tab. Select the Fist object and click Activate in the Object tab. Then double-click Collision, as shown in Figure 21.20.

Figure 21.20   Activate the Fist object under the Object tab of the Motion Designer Property panel. Here, you tell Motion Designer that the Fist object is a collision object, not a target.

In case the cloth in your scene loaded from the CD looks odd when you apply the fist settings, set the following Motion Designer properties:

For the Cloth object's Rigid surface, be sure that FIXED is on.

For the Cloth objects Cloth surface, select the Cotton(thin) preset.

For the Fist surface, set the Skin Thickness to 0.4.

5. The fist is the collision object, while the cloth object will be the target. You can't have one object function as both a collision and target. Back in Layout, select the fist, and move it in toward the cloth so that it intersects into the hand. Create a keyframe at 20. Figure 21.21 shows the position.

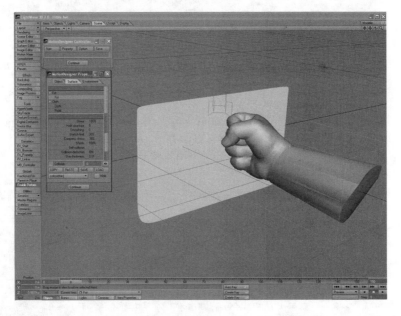

Figure 21.21   Begin creating keyframes for the fist so that Motion Designer can make the fist and the cloth interact.

6. Move the fist back to the 0 position and create a keyframe at 40. Then, in the Motion Designer Controller panel, press Start.

   Wow! The fist just moved back and forth. Aren't you proud?

7. Instead of the fist just traveling through the cloth, how about making it collide? Go to the Surface tab, and select the Fist surface from the Fist object. Set the Skin Thickness for the fist to 0.4. You'll need to drag the slider bar to access the controls in the Property panel. Press the Start button.

   Figure 21.22 shows frame 20 where the fist hits the cloth. Notice that the cloth now is pushed by the fist.

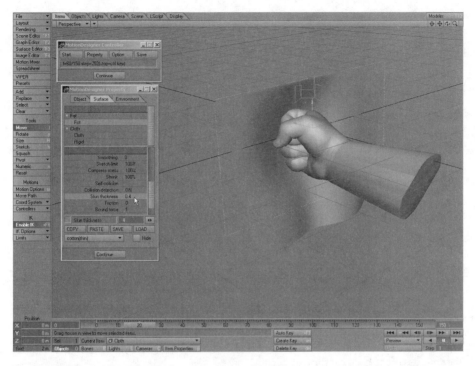

Figure 21.22   With a Skin Thickness applied to the collision object (the fist), it now appears to collide with the cloth.

The Skin Thickness for the fist object sets an invisible area around the fist, sort of like an influence. The larger it is, the farther away collision objects stay.

8. Rotate the view in Layout, and you'll see that the knuckles of the fist cut through the cloth (see Figure 21.23). In the Motion Designer Property panel, set the Friction for the fist surface to 250. Figure 21.24 shows the change with the effect. Press Start to calculate a new motion.

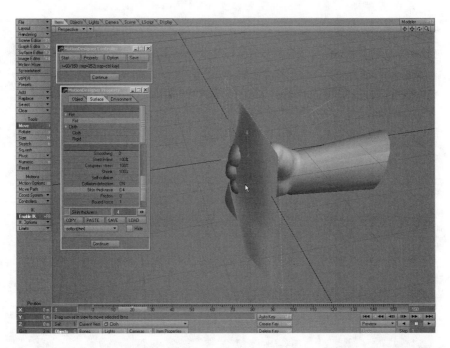

Figure 21.23   Although the Skin Thickness setting on the collision object pushes the cloth, the knuckles of the hand cut through slightly.

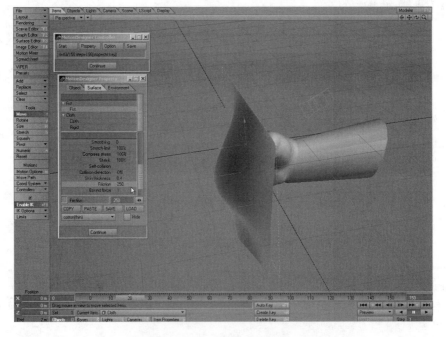

Figure 21.24   Increasing the collision object's Friction prevents it from cutting through the cloth.

From this point, adjust the Friction and Skin Thickness variables and press the Start button to calculate new motions and see the effects. You also can add some Gravity to the scene; something as much as –20 might work well. Take a look at the final scene, labeled fist.lws on the book's CD. From there, select the cloth surface and try using different presets, like Rubber and Silk, to see how the collision affects things.

Exercise 21.4   Adding Cloth to a Figure

So you've made it this far. You've seen basic cloth move, and you've punched the sucker, too. Now, take everything you've learned and apply it to a full character. Although not every button and value has been explained, the tools you're using in these tutorials can help you set up enough elements to physically see changes of any parameters you might choose to adjust. Adding cloth to a figure is a little more work than the previous exercises, and more calculation time is needed. Because of this, simple objects are used in this exercise to get you going.

1. Load the Chase_MoCap.lws scene into Layout. This is a short scene of a skeleton running and quickly turning left, like a football player.

2. Under the Items tab, click Add, then Objects, and Load Object. Load the Cape object from the book's CD. This is a subpatched object in the shape of a shiny red cape.

3. In Layout, parent the cape to the skeleton object. You can do this through the Scene Editor, Schematic view, or simply press m for the cape's motion options, and select WeightedSkeleton.

   If you click the Play button in Layout, the skeleton will run its course, and the cape will follow, sort of. There's one more thing you need to do, and that is to tell the cape object that it needs to be influenced by the skeleton's bones.

4. Select the cape, and then click the Bones button at the bottom of the Layout interface, telling LightWave you want to work with the cape's bones. If you look at the Current Item list (just above the Bones button), you'll see it reads "none." That's right, the cape has no bones. Click the Properties button to the right. Figure 21.25 shows the settings for the cape.

Figure 21.25   Although the cape does not have its own bone structure, it can share the bones of the skeleton character.

5. At the top of the Bones Properties panel, select Weighted Skeleton for the Use Bones From Object selection. Return to Layout.

6. Your cape now deforms and follows the skeleton, even though it's a separate object. Figure 21.26 shows the change.

Figure 21.26   Assigning the Use Bones From Object option in the Bones panel for the cape object tells the cape to be deformed with the bones from the skeleton.

7. From the Scene tab, open the MD_Controller. Click the Property button.

8. Under the Object tab of the property panel, select WeightedSkeleton, and click Activate. When the values appear in the information window, double-click Collision. You want the cape object to collide with this object (see Figure 21.27).

Figure 21.27   The body that any clothing would be attached to is the collision object. Motion Designer needs to have Collision set for the skeleton object.

9. Then, select the cape object, and activate it. Make this the Target, as shown in Figure 21.28.

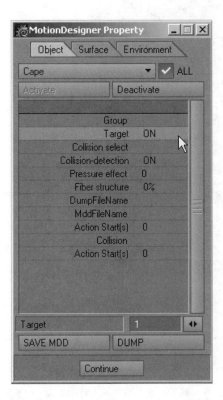

Figure 21.28   The cape object becomes the target for the collision object (the skeleton).

10. Click the Surface tab. Set the cape_fixed surface to Fixed ON (see Figure 21.29).

11. Set only the cape surface to a preset of cotton(thick). Then, under the Environment tab, set a –5 gravity.

12. Back under the Surface tab, select the Weighted Skeleton's bone surface. First, select a preset surface of cotton(thick) as well. Although you don't want the skeleton to move like cotton, doing this resets all the parameters to a workable value. Then, for the bone surface, select Fixed ON, as shown in Figure 21.30.

Figure 21.29   The top part of the cape, although parented to the skeleton, still needs to be fixed, just like the cloth in the first exercise of this chapter.

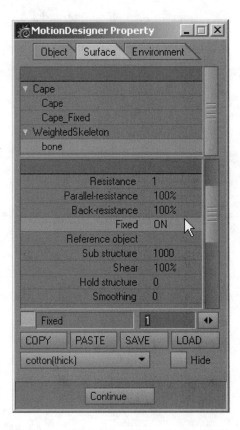

Figure 21.30   The bone surface of the skeleton also is a Fixed surface.

13. Press Start in the Motion Designer Controller panel. Depending on your system, the calculations might take some time.

14. The cape flows, but the elbows of the skeleton cut through it. So, similar to what you did in Exercise 21.2 to keep the fist from moving through the cloth, increase the Skin Thickness for the bone surface to 0.25, as you see in Figure 21.31.

15. You'll also want to set a Bound Force of about 2 for the bone surface (see Figure 21.32).

    Although the fist object in Exercise 21.2 might require a much higher value, any value about 2 begins to add great distortion to the cape.

Figure 21.31   The Skin Thickness setting of 0.25 for the bone surface will help keep the cape from folding into it.

16. Make sure that the Subdivision Order for the cape is set to Last in the Object properties panel. If you press the Start button again in the MD_Controller panel, you'll see the skeleton run, and the cape will now interact with the object. Figure 21.33 shows the cape motion.

Figure 21.32
Increasing the Bounding Force helps keep the shape of the cape during deformation.

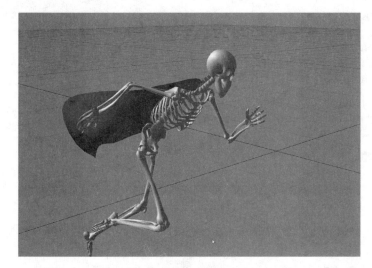

Figure 21.33 Changing a few settings now makes the cape object interact with the bones of the running skeleton.

Notes on Motion Designer

From this point on, you can tweak the settings and recalculate the motion. For example, the legs of the skeleton move quickly and sharply. They might cut through the cape, even with the settings you've applied. Here are a few very important tips to keep in mind when working with collision in Motion Designer:

- Make sure that the Bounding Box Threshold in Layout is set to (or higher than) than the point or polygon count of your object, whichever is greater.

- Objects that are colliding must have their surface normals facing each other. For example, the skeleton's surfaces face outward, while the cape faces inward, toward the skeleton's bones. Even though Double Sided is set for the cape in the Surfaces panel, the initial single surface must face toward the collision to properly deform.

- Balance Skin Thickness and Bound Force for collision objects.

- Set Viscosity for thicker, less fluid objects such as Jell-O. For example, in Exercise 21.2, you set a fist to punch a cloth. If you increase the Viscosity, the surface will be, of course, more viscous, giving it a thick softness, like a pillow.

- If your object has sharp movements, you should increase the Calculate Resolution setting in the Options panel, which you access from the Motion Designer Controller tab. Figure 21.34 shows the settings.

The Next Step

Experiment! Like Hypervoxels, there are only a few key settings in Motion Designer that you'll use all the time. Get those down, understand them, and create a working scene. From there, change some of the other values one at a time and see the results. There's no better way to see what changing those values can do! Be sure to check out the reference manual that came with your software for a listing of the other controls used less often in Motion Designer. Combine that knowledge with the practical examples in this chapter and you'll be on your way.

Figure 21.34 You can increase the Calculate Resolution setting for more accuracy if your object is fast moving. Longer calculation times are a result, of course.

Summary

Without becoming too technical, this chapter has provided a clear set of examples for working with Motion Designer. Although Motion Designer can be used for various types of animations, its purpose is to create cloth. Don't think of it as a physics simulator, but more as a cloth designer. With the information provided here, you can create just about anything from bedding, to drapes, to flowing hair, to flags, and more.

Part V

Appendixes

A p p e n d i x A

Motion Capture and LightWave

When you watch an animated television show or movie, the animated characters you see, more likely than not, have been put into motion using a process called *motion capture.*

Motion capture data can be used to drive the movements in the faces and bodies of humanlike characters, whimsical characters, and even animals. Although motion capture technology has become more affordable over the years, it's still an expensive and tedious process for animators. This appendix briefly introduces you to the process and provides ways you can work with motion capture affordably.

Overview

Motion capture is defined as "the creation of a 3D representation of a live performance" in Alberto Menache's *Understanding Motion Capture for Computer Animation and Video Games* by publisher by Morgan Kaufmann (October 1999, ISBN 0124906303). This is in contrast to animation that is created "by hand" through a process known as *keyframing*.

Motion capture is used in a wide range of applications, from computer animation, to medical imaging, to sports study. Although it's commonly thought that using motion capture is a "cheat" because it eliminates the tedious process of keyframing, as an animator, you should ignore this myth. Although the technology does eliminate the frame-by-frame setup you would normally perform for keyframe-based character animation, motion capture still requires a significant amount of work, often as much as or more than animating by hand.

Motion Capture Technology

Motion capture involves measuring an object's position and orientation in physical space. Motion capture sessions are usually conducted in a warehouse or garage, where the movement of real objects—usually humans and animals—is recorded in a usable computer form. Other objects you might want to capture in a motion capture session include facial expressions, camera or light positions, and other elements in a scene.

There are essentially two forms of motion capture: optical and magnetic. Both forms are widely used, but optical is more common. Optical motion capture requires that the performer whose motion is being captured wear discs on key points of his body, such as the head, shoulders, knees, etc. As the performer moves about, the motion capture system optically records the movements of these discs, and the computer remembers their position data in a set 3D space. This type of motion capture is used for television programs and movies. With magnetic motion capture, the performer dons a special suit that is tethered to the motion capture system, and his movements are recorded. This type of motion capture is often used for live performances.

Once the data is recorded, animators can use it to control elements in a computer-generated scene. With real-time motion capture devices, this data can be used interactively (with minimal transport delay) to provide real-time feedback regarding the character and quality of the captured data. You might see real-time motion capture being used at a trade show where an actor is acting out the part of an animated character. You'll often see a character that has been animated using this method on TechTV, which is found on cable and satellite television networks.

Other motion capture devices are nonreal-time, in that either the captured data requires additional post-processing for use in an animation or computer graphics display, or the captured data provides only a snapshot of measured objects.

Motion capture differs from synthetic or traditional animation in that traditional animation requires keyframing. With motion capture, keyframing is automated. Motion capture-based animation uses recorded motion to augment the hand-keyframed animation process by providing baseline information for object paths, event timing, or attribute control. Most animations that use motion capture do not rely strictly on motion capture data, however. Often, this data is tweaked by an animator. This combination of motion capture and synthetic animation produces the best possible animation movements.

Using Motion Capture in LightWave

Most motion capture systems cost somewhere in the neighborhood of $100,000 (US). As such, the everyday animator usually does not have access to this technology. However, you can buy just about any pre-made motion capture file from various sources (listed later in this chapter) and use them in LightWave. Credo Interactive's Life Forms software, for example, not only lets you edit and manipulate motion capture data, but also comes with hundreds of pre-made motions. These motions can be exported to LightWave and applied to a character.

Follow along with this exercise to see how easy it is to use a preexisting motion capture file on an object in LightWave.

Exercise A.1   Importing Motion Capture Files

Although setting up your own motion capture studio is ideal, it's not a plausible situation for most everyday animators. Luckily, you can purchase motion capture data and use it in your LightWave scenes. This next section guides you through importing and using a prerecorded motion capture file directly in LightWave Layout.

I. In Layout, load the Chase scene from the book's CD. Figure A.1 shows the loaded scene.

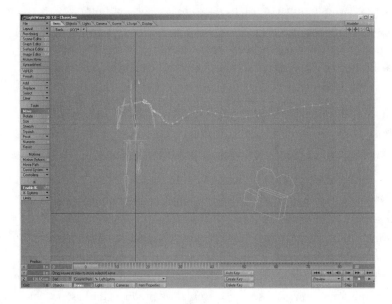

Figure A.1   The Chase scene is loaded into Layout.

2. If you take a close look at the setup of the model's hierarchy, you'll see that it's properly set up for Inverse Kinematics (IK) if needed, as described in Chapter 11, "Character Construction," (refer to Chapter 13, "Inverse Kinematics," for more information on IK). However, you don't need to use IK. The motion capture file will do the work.

You'll see that at the core, the parent item for the entire skeleton is a null object named Root.

3. Press the Play button at the bottom right of the Layout interface. You'll see the bone structure run and make a sharp turn. You can press the a key to fit the view (just like in Modeler).

As you might have guessed, keyframing something like this would be very difficult. But by using a motion capture file, your job is not to put it into a character.

4. Although this is not the easiest process in the world, it's fun to see the results, and your motions look great too. Select the Root null. From the Items tab, select Replace, abd then choose Replace with Object File. Select the WeightedSkeleton object.

5. As you can see in Figure A.2, the skeleton doesn't really match up with the bones. So, if you start moving the timeline slider, you'll see the object go through some hellish movements, as shown in Figure A.3. Ouch!

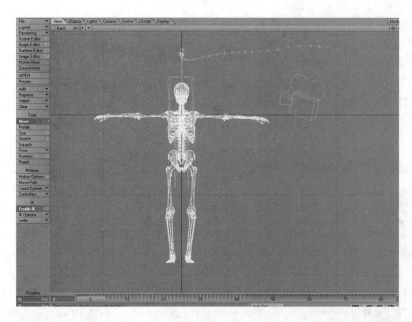

Figure A.2   The skeleton object has replaced the Root null of the motion capture file. This means that the bones now are associated with the skeleton, enabling it to deform.

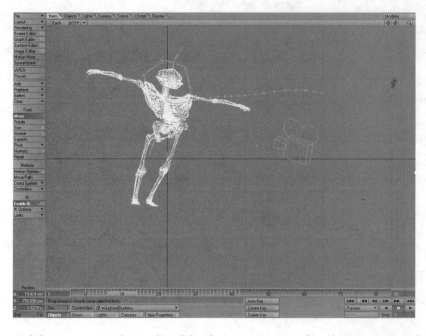

Figure A.3   Just moving the timeline slider shows a pretty messed up character! You need to reset the bones at frame 0.

6. Bring the timeline slider to 0.

You're going to deactivate all the bones and reset them so that they line up with the skeleton, and then activate them again.

7. Open the Spreadsheet Scene Manager, found in the top left of Layout.

8. Make sure that the Bone Properties: Basic listing is selected in the top right in the spreadsheet, as shown in Figure A.4.

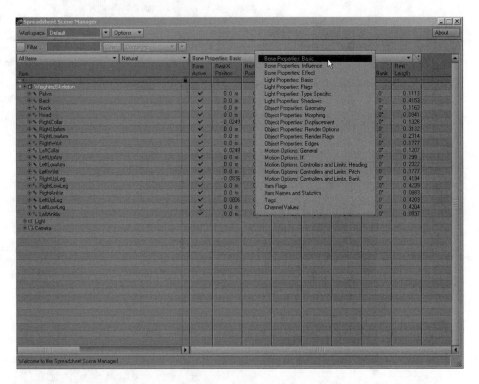

Figure A.4 The Spreadsheet Scene Manager gives you instant access to all of the skeleton's bones. You can choose to show the basic bone properties from the drop-down list at the top right of the panel.

9. With the basic bone information showing, you can see that the second column is titled Bone Active. There's a check mark next to every bone listing. Select the first check mark in the list (Pelvis), hold the Shift key, and then select the last check mark, as shown in Figure A.5.

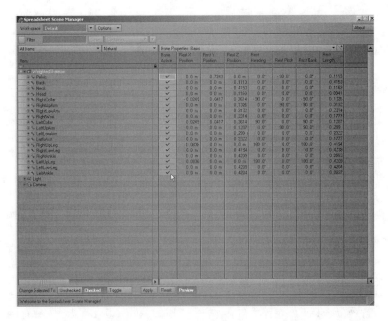

Figure A.5   Select the first check mark for Bone Active, hold the Shift key, and click the bottom check mark to select all.

10. You can see a yellow box around the first checkmark in the list. Right-click this (Mac users hold the Apple key) and choose Uncheck all selected cells, as shown in Figure A.6.

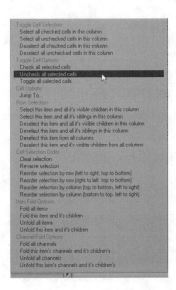

Figure A.6   By right-clicking the selection in the Spreadsheet Scene Manager, you can quickly deactivate all bones. No need for third party plug-ins anymore!

11. Now you'll see that the check marks under the Bone Active list are gone. The bones are inactive. Close the spreadsheet and return to Layout. If you like, you can save a copy of the scene at this point as Bone_Inactive for later use.

> **Note**
>
> Okay, now that you know how to deselect all bones in the Spreadsheet Scene Manager the hard way, take a look at the bottom of the panel in Figure A.5. There are buttons there labeled Unchecked and Checked. You could have simply clicked on Unchecked! Right-clicking gave you an idea of all the other tools and commands available to you in the Spreadsheet Scene Manager.

12. Back in Layout, drag your timeline slider back and forth—the skeleton will not deform as the bones move. This is what you wanted to accomplish by deactivating the bones.

13. Select the pelvis bone. Press p to open the Bone Properties panel. Set the Bone Weight Map to Pelvis. This skeleton has weight maps set up for its entire structure to help control bone influences.

14. In Layout, select Rest Length from the Objects tab. Click and drag on the pelvis bone until it fills the hip area of the skeleton, as shown in Figure A.7.

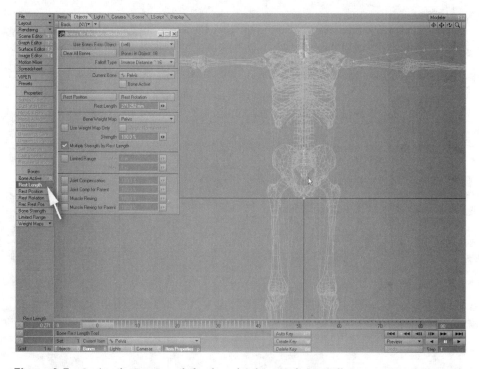

Figure A.7   Setting the Rest Length for the pelvis bone at frame 0 allows you to position properly the character's bone.

15. Using the down arrow, select the back bone. This controls the chest and back area of the model. Now that you've changed the rest length of the pelvis, the back bone is out of place. Move it up so that its base rests on top of the pelvis. You might need to unlock the axis controls at the bottom left of Layout as well. Grab the blue arrow and drag. Be sure to create a keyframe to lock the new position in place, or turn Auto Key on. Figure A.8 shows the new bone position.

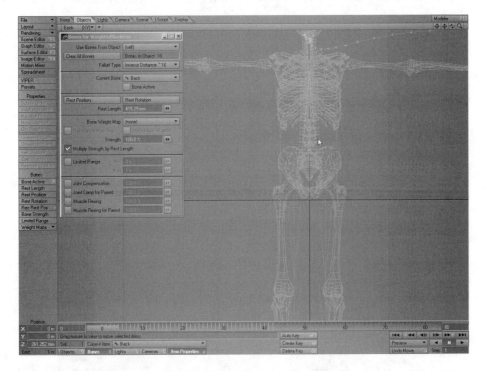

Figure A.8   Because the rest length of the pelvis bone, was adjusted, the corresponding child bone, the back bone, needs to be moved.

16. Set the Bone Weight to Chest, for the back bone, because this bone influences the chest and back.

17. Next, select the neck bone. Adjust its rest length to match the long neck of the skeleton object. Set its weight to Neck in the Bone Properties panel as well.

18. After the neck, select the head bone. Make sure that it's in place, and adjust the rest length for proper fit if needed, as you have done in the past few steps.

19. Set the appropriate weight maps in the Bone Properties panel. Continue adjusting and placing the bones, making sure to check the Front, Top, and Side views while doing so to ensure proper placement. Create keyframes at zero for the bones if you move or rotate them. There is no keyframe for rest length.

Use Perspective view to take a good look at bone placements.

20. Once the bones are all in place, save the scene.

21. Select the pelvis bone. Press r on the keyboard to activate the bone.

22. Press the down arrow on your keyboard. Press r to activate.

23. Continue the process to activate all bones. The display of each bone will change from a dashed line to a solid line when active. You can open the Spreadsheet Scene Manager and you'll see that the checkmarks have returned under the Bone Active list.

Activating bones in Layout directly from the root bone (the pelvis, in this example) is important. Activating all bones in the Spreadsheet doesn't allow for the initial proper deformation. This often confuses animators and their clients! Activate bones in Layout quickly and in order from parent to child by pressing first the r key and then the down arrow; then repeat the process.

On the CD, you'll find a scene called Chase_BonesSet that has all the bones in place. Use this scene file if you like. Remember to activate the bones in order, starting at the pelvis bone.

Play through the animation and watch what happens. It's working, but something's amiss! Can you see what it is? (See Figure A.9.)

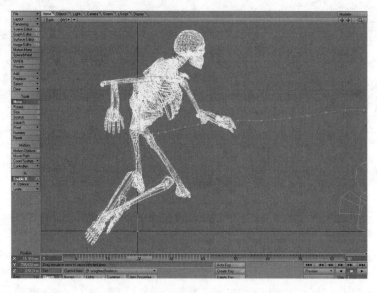

Figure A.9   While the bones seem to get things in motion, the limbs are overlapping! No problem—the original motion capture position channels need to be eliminated.

The bones after frame 0 are changing positions to what was set before you made the changes at frame 0! To fix this, you'll need to open the Graph Editor.

24. In the Graph Editor, clear any motion channels that might be in the Curve Bin. Select the first one, hold the Shift key, and then select the last. Right-click and select Remove From List.

25. Now click the white triangle to expand the channels of the WeightedSkeleton object in the scene display at the lower left.

26. Expand the Pelvis bone listing, and select only the Position.X, Position.Y, and Position.Z channels. Do this by selecting the first one, holding the Shift key, and selecting the third. Drag them up to the Curve Bin, as shown in Figure A.10.

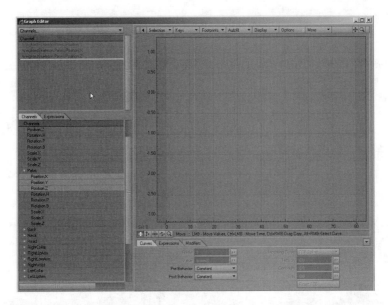

Figure A.10   To make the final tweaks to the motion capture files, you'll need to remove the XYZ position channel motions.

> **Note**
>
> You can remove the XYZ channels because only the Root (the skeleton) needs this movement information. The rest of the bones use only rotational values. This means that you can eliminate the keyframes that are causing your object to move improperly.

27. Now expand the Back bone list of channels, select the Position.X, Position.Y, and Position.Z, and bring them into the Curve Window as well.

Continue this process for all the bones' XYZ channels. Figure A.11 shows the Curve Window in the Graph Editor filled up with XYZ motion channels!

Tip

Here is a great way to work with the Graph Editor and multiple repeated operations, such as removing certain position channels from the bones. Collapse all bone groups in the Scene window of the Graph Editor. Select all the bones and drag them up to the Curve Bin. Once in the bin, select all the bone channels by selecting the first in the list, holding the Shift key, and clicking the last in the list. Then, under Selection at the top of the Graph Editor, choose Filter Position Channels. Everything except the position channels is removed from the bin. Now, edit the position motions in the Curve Window.

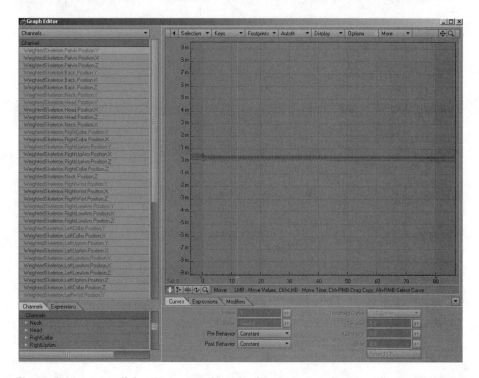

Figure A.11   Bring all the XYZ motion channels of the bones into the Curve Window for editing.

28. With all the XYZ channels of the bones in the Curve Window, select the first channel in the list, hold the Shift key, and select the last. Or, you can use the Ctrl and Up Arrow keys to select all. You may need to scroll down to see the bottom listing.

29. Once the channels are selected, press the a key to fit all to view. You'll see all the channels and their keyframes in the main Curve Edit window, as in Figure A.12.

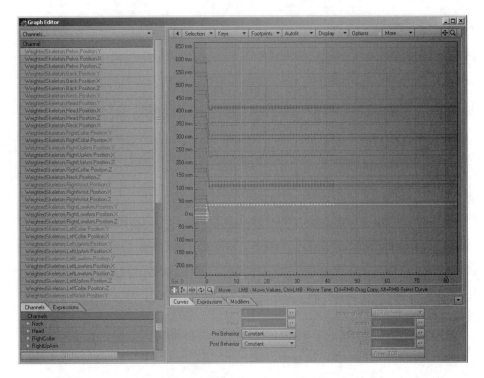

Figure A.12   You can edit all channels at once in the Graph Editor by simply selecting the necessary channels in the Curve Window.

30. With the right mouse button (Apple key on the Mac), click and drag around all of the keyframes for the XYZ channels in the Curve Window except for frame 0. This keyframe you need. Figure A.13 shows the selection.

Note

Depending on your screen resolution or preference, you might have trouble seeing all the keyframes at once in the Curve Window. If that's the case, simply delete a few sections at a time, and use the Zoom and Move tools in the upper right corner of the Graph Editor to get a closer and better look at your keyframes. Be sure not to delete frame 0!

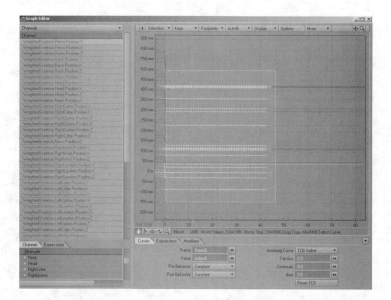

Figure A.13   With the right mouse button, you can select all the keyframes for all the channels at once.

31. Once all the keyframes are selected, press Delete on your keyboard.

32. Return to Layout, and drag your timeline. The skeleton runs, and the limbs no longer overlap, as Figure A.14 shows.

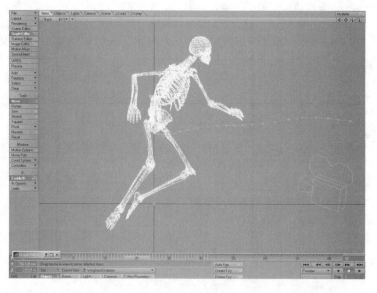

Figure A.14   Once the XYZ channels have been deleted, the limbs of the skeleton no longer overlap. The bones are not fighting for new positions in each keyframe—they are simply rotating.

You did it. Motion capture in LightWave is that easy. And although this exercise simply showed you a skeleton, this process can work with any of your characters. There's a nice snowman-type character from Zygote media on the book's CD, in this Appendix's project folder. Try using this model for more full-body movements.

Summary

Motion capture is appealing, no doubt. But it's not as simple as just plug and play, like many people believe. It's tedious work to clean up motion capture files, set bones and weights, adjust motion channels, and more. But the results in movement, combined with high-quality textures and lighting, can bring your animations to movie theater quality! Take a look at these vendor web sites for more information:

www.viewpoint.com

www.curiouslabs.com

www.charactermotion.com

www.biovision.com

www.moves.com

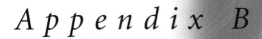

Appendix B

LightWave 7 Plug-in, Tool, and Technical List

You've gone through the book and played

with all the cool features, but there are still

a bunch of buttons you don't know about,

right? Of course. No single resource can

cover it all, but we certainly try! Because many of the plug-ins and commands in both Layout and Modeler perform very specific functions, it's difficult to incorporate their uses into every tutorial. We would need thousands of pages to create tutorials for every feature in LightWave. Because we don't have thousands of pages, the authors put together this Appendix, which lists all the plug-ins available in LightWave 7. We didn't want you to close the book and not at least get a glimpse of what's there for you to play around with!

Overview

This appendix introduces you to the Layout and Modeler plug-ins and tools that are available to you. These tools often are accessible through buttons directly on the interface, or buried somewhere within a menu or panel. Remember this section as reference anytime you come across a tool and you're not sure why it's there. This appendix is broken down into three parts:

- A complete alphabetical list of plug-ins list and their locations
- A list of Layout plug-ins
- A list of Modeler plug-ins

LightWave Plug-ins

LightWave has plug-ins in a few key places. Understanding these areas will help you understand what certain plug-ins do and also know how to locate them. The plug-in types within LightWave

- **Animation I/O.** Plug-ins used for input and output.
- **Channel Filter.** Plug-ins that perform direct control over channels, such as expressions and Motion Mixer.
- **Custom Object.** Plug-ins that are used for object control, such as particle effects.
- **Displacement.** Plug-ins that that can shape and deform objects, be it points or polygons.
- **Environment.** Plug-ins that add functionality to Layout environment variables, such as SkyTracer2.
- **Global.** Plug-ins that look at the entire scene, such as the Spreadsheet Scene Manager.

- **Image I/O.** Plug-ins for loading and saving images. Generally, you won't access these plug-ins directly, but you'll use their functions when loading or saving in both Layout and Modeler.

- **Image Processing.** Plug-ins that control the various image-related functions, such as pixel calculations for working with fur in SasLite and Image Filters for things like Bloom and Corona.

- **Modeling.** Plug-ins and tools used throughout LightWave Modeler.

- **Layout Command.** Plug-ins that are used in Layout to control the interaction of other plug-ins that use representation in Layout.

- **Motion.** Plug-ins for various motion operations, such as Jolt! or Gravity.

- **Object Importer.** Plug-ins for importing object formats other than LightWave.

- **Object Replacement.** Plug-ins used to replace objects during the course of an animation.

- **Rendering.** Plug-ins used for textures and shaders.

- **Scene Master.** Plug-ins for various scene-related functions, like Proxy Pic for item selection. These are similar to independent applications, like Motion Mixer.

- **Volumetric Effect.** Plug-ins that are good for things like ground fog.

Where to Find LightWave's Plug-ins

Finding the various plug-ins is easier in Layout than it is in Modeler. Modeler's plug-ins are accessible usually through a button added within the interface or a selection in a list. In Layout, most plug-ins must be selected from the various areas throughout the program. Those areas are

- Object Properties panel, for Custom Object plug-ins and Displacement Map plug-ins.

- Motion Options panel for a selected item's motion plug-ins.

- Effects panel, which is home to the plug-ins for the Environment (Backdrop tab), Volumetrics (Volumetrics tab), and Pixel Filter and Image Filter plug-ins (Processing tab).

- Graph Editor, under the Modifiers tab for plug-ins like Oscillator.

- Master plug-in list, found under the Scene tab.

- Generics, which is a drop-down list found under the Scene tab. These plug-ins range from basic system tools, to key functions, to third-party plug-ins.

Loading Plug-ins

When you install LightWave, your plug-ins already are loaded for you. However, there might come a time when you want to reload certain plug-ins or add third-party ones. You can do this through LightWave or Modeler, regardless of the plug-in. The information within the plug-in file is read by LightWave and it is installed in the proper place—to one of the areas listed above.

Loading plug-ins is very easy, and you need to do it only once. LightWave writes the information to a configuration file when you close the programs. In Layout, you can select the Layout drop-down list, then choose Plug-ins, and access various plug-in commands such as Add Plug-ins, Generic Plug-ins, Master Plug-ins, Activate Last Plug-in, or Edit Plug-ins. Figure B.1 shows the selection, while Figure B.2 shows the Edit Plug-ins interface. This same selection is available in Modeler from the Modeler drop-down list.

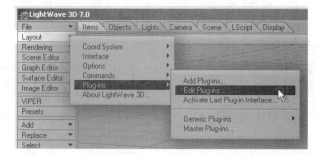

Figure B.1   Plug-in options and controls in Layout are accessible from the Layout drop-down list.

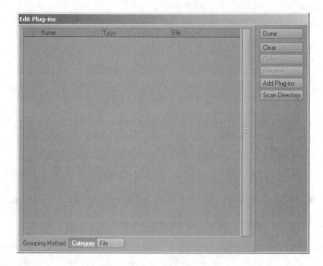

Figure B.2   The Edit Plug-ins interface is where you can add and edit plug-ins.

The easiest way to add plug-ins in LightWave is to use the Edit Plug-ins panel and select Scan Directory. Click this, and point your system to the Plug-ins folder. Select OK, and in a moment, a requester will appear telling you how many plug-ins were added, as shown in Figure B.3.

Figure B.3   The Scan Directory option in the Edit Plug-ins panel allows you to load all plug-ins in one click for both Layout and Modeler.

Clicking OK in the requester will display the plug-ins loaded, as shown in Figure B.4.

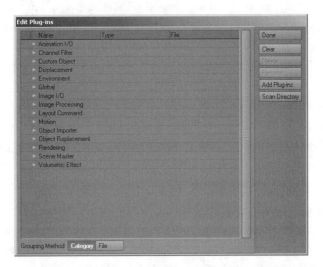

Figure B.4   Once loaded, the plug-ins will be displayed within their appropriate groupings. Notice that Modeler is not listed here, because these are all Layout or Global plug-ins.

Using the Scan Directory option to load plug-ins loads all plug-ins in the chosen directory. To add just a single plug-in file, select Add Plug-in, point your system to the plug-in, and click OK. You also can delete or rename plug-ins in the Edit Plug-in panel.

LScripts

LScripts, LightWave's custom scripting language, are also loaded as plug-ins, although they are slightly different. If you have an LScript you've written or one compiled from a third-party source, you can load it the same way you do a regular plug-in. Select Add Plug-in, and then select the LScript.

The Complete Plug-in List

In deciding on the best way to accomplish a plug-in reference, it seemed that an alphabetical listing would be best. However, you might have trouble locating the plug-ins this way. So, first the plug-ins are listed in alphabetical order, and then listed based on their locations.

Certain plug-ins such as LScript are available in more than one location. Image Filters are available in the Effects panel, as well as the Image Editor, and so on. Other plug-ins, however, are available only in specific locations, such as Pixel Filter or Modeler plug-ins. You'll also notice that plug-ins vary in name, based on their usage, such as a modifier, tool, command, or just generic plug-in.

Although many of these plug-ins are covered within the tutorials in this book, they are listed here for your reference. The information here will not provide working tutorials for these plug-ins, but at least give you an idea of what's there and what it's for! Ready? Here we go!

The Alphabetical Plug-in List

This is a complete list of plug-ins that ship with LightWave version 7. There are a few other plug-ins that install with your system for things like importing and saving images. These are plug-ins you don't directly access. They are functionality plug-ins more than they are tools, so they are not included in this list.

The list here is an alphabetical list containing both Layout and Modeler plug-ins. A few plug-ins are listed multiple times because they are used in multiple locations or groups. If you've ever used a tool or plug-in, or perhaps someone tells you to "just use the Rove tool," you can search through this list like an index, find out where the plug-in is located, and then find more information about that plug-in in the various sections on the following pages.

You should note that image importers and exporters are not listed here, as well as object exporters. These are basic load and save functions. In addition, procedural textures are plug-ins, but are covered in more detail through tutorials in this book. They are part of LightWave's Surface Editor.

Plug-in	Location or Group
Absolute Size	Modeler Plug-in
Add Camera Mask	Generic Plug-in
Add Collision Effector	Generic Plug-in
Add Effector	Generic Plug-in
Add Frame Rate Meter	Generic Plug-in
Add Gravity Effector	Generic Plug-in
Add Particle Emitter	Generic Plug-in
Add Range Finder	Generic Plug-in
Add Ruler	Generic Plug-in
Add Speedometer	Generic Plug-in
Add Wind Effector	Generic Plug-in
Adjust Polygon Map	Modeler Plug-in
Aligner	Modeler Plug-in
Anaglyph Stereo: Compose	Image Filter Plug-in
Anaglyph Stereo: Simulate	Image Filter Plug-in
Apply Morph	Modeler Plug-in
Audio Channel	Graph Editor Modifier
Auto Patcher	Modeler Plug-in
Auto PatcherMK	Modeler Plug-in
Background to Morph	Modeler Plug-in
Band Saw	Modeler Plug-in
BESM	Surface Shader Plug-in
Bezier Tool	Modeler Plug-in
BG Conform	Modeler Plug-in
BlackandWhite	Image Filter Plug-in
Bloom	Image Filter Plug-in

continues ▶

Plug-in	Location or Group
Blotch	Surface Shader Plug-in
Bone Weights	Modeler Plug-in
Bounding Box	Modeler Plug-in
BRDF	Surface Shader Plug-in
Bubbles	Modeler Plug-in
Buffer Export	Generic Plug-in
Cage	Modeler Plug-in
Calculate	Modeler Plug-in
Camera Mask	Custom Object Plug-in
Capsule Tool	Modeler Plug-in
Center 1D	Modeler Plug-in
Center Scale	Modeler Plug-in
Center Stretch	Modeler Plug-in
Channel Follower	Graph Editor Modifier
Chroma Depth	Image Filter Plug-in
Clear Polygon Map	Modeler Plug-in
Clone Hierarchy	Generic Plug-in
Color Map Adjust Tool	Modeler Plug-in
Comments	Generic Plug-in
Content Manager	Generic Plug-in
Corona	Image Filter Plug-in
Corona	Generic Plug-in
CruiseControl	Motion Modifier
Cull Map	Modeler Plug-in
Curve_Conform	Displacement Plug-in
Curve Constraint	Motion Modifier
Cut Curves	Modeler Plug-in
Cycler	Graph Editor Modifier
Cyclist	Motion Modifier
Dangle	Modeler Plug-in

continues ▶

Plug-in	Location or Group
Deform: Bend	Displacement Plug-in
Deform: Pole	Displacement Plug-in
Deform: Shear	Displacement Plug-in
Deform: Taper	Displacement Plug-in
Deform: Twist	Displacement Plug-in
Deform: Vortex	Displacement Plug-in
DeluxeRLA	Image Filter Plug-in
Demo All BG Layers	Modeler Plug-in
Demo Next Empty Layer	Modeler Plug-in
Depth-Of-Field Blur	Image Filter Plug-in
Digital Confusion	Image Filter Plug-in
Digital Confusion	Generic Plug-in
Draw Metaballs	Modeler Plug-in
Draw MetaEdges	Modeler Plug-in
Draw Skelegons	Modeler Plug-in
Edge	Image Filter Plug-in
Edge_Transparency	Surface Shader Plug-in
Edit Metaballs	Modeler Plug-in
Edit Skelegons	Modeler Plug-in
Effector	Motion Modifier
Effector	Custom Object Plug-in
Effector	Displacement Plug-in
EPSF Loader	Modeler Plug-in
Equilateral Tri	Modeler Plug-in
Export 3DS	Modeler Plug-in
Export DXF	Modeler Plug-in
Export Encapsulated PostScript	Modeler Plug-in
Export LightWave 5	Modeler Plug-in
Export OBJ	Modeler Plug-in
Export Scene As VRML97	Generic Plug-in

continues ▶

Plug-in	Location or Group
Expression	Graph Editor Modifier
Expression	Motion Modifier
Expression	Displacement Plug-in
Extended RLA Support	Image Filter Plug-in
Extender	Modeler Plug-in
Fast Fresnel	Surface Shader Plug-in
Fast Triple Fan	Modeler Plug-in
Fast Triple Traverse	Modeler Plug-in
Find Center	Modeler Plug-in
Flatten Layers	Modeler Plug-in
Flip UVs	Modeler Plug-in
Follower	Motion Modifier
Fractalize	Modeler Plug-in
Frame Rate Meter	Custom Object Plug-in
Full Precision Blur	Image Filter Plug-in
Full Precision Gamma	Image Filter Plug-in
FX_Browser	Generic Plug-in
FX_CLink	Graph Editor Modifier
FX_CLink	Motion Modifier
FX_Collision	Custom Object Plug-in
FX_Emitter	Custom Object Plug-in
FX_Gravity	Custom Object Plug-in
FX_Link	Graph Editor Modifier
FX_Link	Motion Modifier
FX_Linker	Generic Plug-in
FX_Motion	Motion Modifier
FX_Property	Generic Plug-in
FX_Start	Generic Plug-in
FX Wind	Custom Object Plug-in
Gear	Modeler Plug-in

continues ▶

Plug-in	Location or Group
Gears	Modeler Plug-in
Gemstone Tool	Modeler Plug-in
gMIL	Surface Shader Plug-in
Gravity	Motion Modifier
Ground Fog	Generic Plug-in
Ground Fog	Volumetric Plug-in
Halftone	Surface Shader Plug-in
Halftone	Pixel Filter Plug-in
HDR Exposure	Image Filter Plug-in
Helix	Modeler Plug-in
HyperVoxels	Generic Plug-in
HyperVoxels_Drawing	Custom Object Plug-in
HyperVoxels_Filter	Volumetric Plug-in
HyperVoxels_Particles	Displacement Plug-in
ImageLister	Generic Plug-in
Image World	Backdrop Environment Plug-in
Inertia	Displacement Plug-in
Interference	Surface Shader Plug-in
Item Picker	Master Plug-in
Item Shape	Custom Object Plug-in
Joint_Morph	Displacement Plug-in
Jolt	Motion Modifier
Julienne	Modeler Plug-in
Lazy_Points	Displacement Plug-in
LeadTheFollower	Motion Modifier
Level-Of-Detail Mesh Refinement	Custom Object Plug-in
Level Of Detail Object Replacement	Object Replacement Plug-in
Load Object Into Layer	Modeler Plug-in
Lock UVs to Polygon	Modeler Plug-in
Logo	Modeler Plug-in

continues ▶

Plug-in	Location or Group
LS Commander	Generic Plug-in
LW_DisplacementTexture	Displacement Plug-in
LW_LSCompiler	Generic Plug-in
LW_LScript	Surface Shader Plug-in
LW_LScript	Motion Modifier
LW_LScript	Image Filter Plug-in
LW_LScript	Custom Object Plug-in
LW_LScript	Object Replacement Plug-in
LW_LScript	Displacement Plug-in
LW_LScript	Generic Plug-in
LW_LScript	Master Plug-in
LW_LScript Commander	Master Plug-in
LW_LScript/RT	Surface Shader Plug-in
LW_LScript/RT	Motion Modifier
LW_LScript/RT	Image Filter Plug-in
LW_LScript/RT	Custom Object Plug-in
LW_LScript/RT	Object Replacement Plug-in
LW_LScript/RT	Displacement Plug-in
LW_LScript/RT	Generic Plug-in
LW_LScript/RT	Master Plug-in
LW_Macro Recorder	Master Plug-in
LW_NormalDisplacement	Displacement Plug-in
LW_Select Group	Generic Plug-in
LW_TextureChannel	Graph Editor Modifier
LW_TextureEnvironment	Backdrop Environment Plug-in
LW_TextureFilter	Image Filter Plug-in
LW_TextureMotion	Motion Modifier
LW_Texture VMap	Modeler Plug-in
LW_Xcommand	Modeler Plug-in
LW_LScript	Graph Editor Modifier

continues ▶

Plug-in	Location or Group
LW_LScript/RT	Graph Editor Modifier
Make 1 Point Polygons	Modeler Plug-in
Make DoubleSided	Modeler Plug-in
Make Metaballs	Modeler Plug-in
Make MetaEdges	Modeler Plug-in
Make Metafaces	Modeler Plug-in
Make Skelegons	Modeler Plug-in
Make Text	Modeler Plug-in
Master	Motion Modifier
Master Channel	Generic Plug-in
Master Channel	Master Plug-in
MD_Controller	Generic Plug-in
MD_MetaPlug	Displacement Plug-in
MD_MetaPlug_Morph	Displacement Plug-in
MD_Plug	Displacement Plug-in
MD_Scan	Displacement Plug-in
Mirror Item	Generic Plug-in
MM_ChannelBaker	Graph Editor Modifier
MM_ChannelDriver	Graph Editor Modifier
MM_MotionBaker	Motion Modifier
MM_MotionDriver	Motion Modifier
MorphMixer	Displacement Plug-in
Motion Baker	Motion Modifier
Motion Mixer	Generic Plug-in
Motion Mixer	Master Plug-in
Negative	Image Filter Plug-in
New Quad Polygon Map	Modeler Plug-in
Noisy Channel	Graph Editor Modifier
Normalize Map	Modeler Plug-in
Normal Baker	Modeler Plug-in

continues ▶

Plug-in	Location or Group
Object List	Object Replacement Plug-in
Object Sequence	Object Replacement Plug-in
Oscillator	Graph Editor Modifier
Oscillator	Motion Modifier
Parametric Obj	Modeler Plug-in
Particle Clone	Modeler Plug-in
Path To Motion	Modeler Plug-in
Platonic	Modeler Plug-in
Platonic Solid Tool	Modeler Plug-in
Plot 1D	Modeler Plug-in
Plot 2D	Modeler Plug-in
Point Center	Modeler Plug-in
Point Clone Plus	Modeler Plug-in
Point Color	Modeler Plug-in
Polygon Map to UVs	Modeler Plug-in
Polygon Normal UVs	Modeler Plug-in
Primitives	Modeler Plug-in
Protractor	Custom Object Plug-in
Proxy Pic	Master Plug-in
Pulse	Surface Shader Plug-in
qemLOSS2	Modeler Plug-in
Quadric	Modeler Plug-in
Quantize UVs	Modeler Plug-in
Radial Array	Modeler Plug-in
Radial Select	Modeler Plug-in
Rail Bevel	Modeler Plug-in
Rand Points	Modeler Plug-in
Rand Pricks	Modeler Plug-in
Range Finder	Custom Object Plug-in
Reduce Points	Modeler Plug-in

continues ▶

Plug-in	Location or Group
Real Fresnel	Surface Shader Plug-in
Reduce Polygons	Modeler Plug-in
Rename Skelegon	Modeler Plug-in
Render Buffer Export	Image Filter Plug-in
Render Buffer View	Image Filter Plug-in
Report	Motion Modifier
Rest On Ground	Modeler Plug-in
Rotate About Normal	Modeler Plug-in
Rotate Any Axis	Modeler Plug-in
Rotate Arbitrary Axis	Modeler Plug-in
Rotate HPB	Modeler Plug-in
Rotate Morph	Modeler Plug-in
Rotate To Ground	Modeler Plug-in
Rotate To Object	Modeler Plug-in
Router	Modeler Plug-in
Rove Tool	Modeler Plug-in
Ruler	Custom Object Plug-in
SasLite	Pixel Filter Plug-in
SasLite	Displacement Plug-in
Save Layers As Object	Modeler Plug-in
Save Object Section	Modeler Plug-in
Save Object Section Cut	Modeler Plug-in
Save Object Section Point Cut	Modeler Plug-in
Save Object Section Points	Modeler Plug-in
Scale Morph	Modeler Plug-in
Schematic View Tools	Generic Plug-in
Shockwave 3D_Export	Generic Plug-in
SeaShell Tool	Modeler Plug-in
Select By Map	Modeler Plug-in
Select By Map Influence	Modeler Plug-in

continues ▶

Plug-in	Location or Group
Select By Polygon Map	Modeler Plug-in
Select Child Skelegon	Modeler Plug-in
Select Children	Generic Plug-in
Select Hierarchy	Generic Plug-in
Select Parent Skelegon	Modeler Plug-in
Select Polygons from Select Set	Modeler Plug-in
Select UV Seam	Modeler Plug-in
Serpent	Displacement Plug-in
Set Driven Key	Graph Editor Modifier
Set Skelegon Weight	Modeler Plug-in
Show Curve	Custom Object Plug-in
Skelegons To Nulls	Generic Plug-in
SkyGen	Generic Plug-in
SkyTracer	Generic Plug-in
SkyTracer2	Backdrop Environment Plug-in
Slave_x	Motion Modifier
Slave_y	Motion Modifier
Slave_Z	Motion Modifier
Sock_Monkey	Custom Object Plug-in
Sock_Monkey	Displacement Plug-in
Soften Reflections	Image Filter Plug-in
Speedometer	Custom Object Plug-in
Spherize	Modeler Plug-in
Spikey Tool	Modeler Plug-in
Spin It	Modeler Plug-in
Spline Guide	Modeler Plug-in
Spline Draw	Modeler Plug-in
Split Skelegon	Modeler Plug-in
Spray Points Tool	Modeler Plug-in
Spread UVs	Modeler Plug-in

continues ▶

Plug-in	Location or Group
Spreadsheet	Generic Plug-in
Spreadsheet Manager	Master Plug-in
Squarize	Modeler Plug-in
Stipple	Modeler Plug-in
SubDivLOD Tool	Generic Plug-in
Sun Spot	Motion Modifier
Super Cel Shader	Surface Shader Plug-in
Super Quadric Tool	Modeler Plug-in
Surface Baker	Surface Shader Plug-in
Surfaces To Parts	Modeler Plug-in
Symmetrize	Modeler Plug-in
Teapot	Modeler Plug-in
Texture Environment	Generic Plug-in
Texture Guide	Modeler Plug-in
Thin Film	Surface Shader Plug-in
Throw	Modeler Plug-in
TM-P Motify Delete Motion Keys	Generic Plug-in
Toggle Metamesh	Modeler Plug-in
Toroid	Modeler Plug-in
Trail	Displacement Plug-in
UV Copy	Modeler Plug-in
UV Flip	Modeler Plug-in
UV Map Jitter	Modeler Plug-in
UV Paste	Modeler Plug-in
UV Rotate	Modeler Plug-in
UV to Weight	Modeler Plug-in
Vector Blur	Image Filter Plug-in
Vector Blur	Generic Plug-in
Vertex Paint	Modeler Plug-in
Video Legalize	Image Filter Plug-in

continues ▶

Plug-in	Location or Group
Video Tap	Image Filter Plug-in
Virtual Darkroom	Image Filter Plug-in
VRML97 Custom Object	Custom Object Plug-in
WaterMark	Image Filter Plug-in
WaveFilterImage	Image Filter Plug-in
Wedge	Modeler Plug-in
Wrap Sphere	Modeler Plug-in
Z Shader	Surface Shader Plug-in
Zor	Surface Shader Plug-in

Graph Editor Modifiers

The Graph Editor modifiers can be found within the Graph Editor in Layout. At the bottom of the interface there is a tab labeled Modifier. Figure B.5 shows the selection.

Figure B.5   The Graph Editor modifiers are plug-ins that allow control specifically for individual channels.

- **FX_CLink.** This allows you to apply the particle motion to children of an item, with a parent that has FX_Link added and is using the Time Shift option.

- **FX_Link.** This plug-in links the motion of particles to a specific channel in the curve window of the Graph Editor.

- **Audio Channel.** Using this modifier, you can load a .wav file into the Graph Editor and create a motion from it for a specific channel.

- **ChannelFollower.** Is a hard-coded expression. ChannelFollower utilizes the motion of one channel to drive another.

- **Cycler.** Cycler allows you to "cycle" a driven motion. The Motion Modifier Cyclist allows you to repeat motions based on a parent movement, such as the wheels of a car. Cycler in this case is a single-channel version of Cyclist.

- **Expression.** This is an advanced LightWave control allowing you to set controls mathematically for items in your scene. Expression use is seen best when a Layout item reacts to the effect of something else, such as gears rotating because of a moving chain.

- **LW_LScript.** If you have an LScript that you'd like to apply to a specific curve in the Graph Editor, run this plug-in.

- **LW_LScript/RT.** Use this plug-in if you have a compiled LScript that you'd like to apply to a specific curve in the Graph Editor.

- **Oscillator.** Oscillator will create an oscillating motion for a selected curve. You can adjust the timing, speed, and amount of motion. Oscillator creates a continuous wave pattern.

- **Set Driven Key.** Set Driven Key is also a Channel Follower, which allows you to enter a specific command and control that command with a parented item.

- **LW_TextureChannel.** Allows you to use any image map, procedural, or gradient to a create a motion. This is great for things like flying airplanes or swaying leaves in the wind.

- **MM_ChannelBaker.** MM, or Motion Mixer, allows you to bake, or permanently record, a motion to a curve created in Motion Mixer.

- **MM_ChannelDriver.** This plug-in takes motion created in Motion Mixer and allows you to apply it directly to a channel in the Curve Window of the Graph Editor.

- **Noisy Channel.** Noisy Channel will randomly change the values of a particular motion curve. This is useful for things like creating a camera shake or jittery letters.

Surface Shader Plug-ins

Surface Shader plug-ins can be found within the Surface Editor under the Shaders tab. These plug-ins add additional controls to your selected surface. Figure B.6 shows the selections.

Figure B.6   The Surface Shader plug-ins, found within the Surface Editor, add different variables to your selected surfaces.

- **BESM.** BESM, or Big Eyes Small Mouth, is a cartoon shader. This expanded control lets you turn a surface into the look of a cel-shaded animation, like a traditional cartoon.

- **BRDF.** This shader helps add realism to a surface by allowing you to create three layers of specular reflection for a surface, as well as anisotropic effects found in everyday surfaces.

- **Blotch.** This plug-in adds blotchy color to a surface that you determine.

- **Edge_Transparency.** This plug-in allows you to take the edge of a surface and make it transparent. Conversely, you can use Edge Transparency to make a surface more opaque.

- **Surface Baker.** Surface Baker enables you to "bake" or burn in a surface. The benefit of this is that LightWave only has to calculate the surface one time. Once it's "baked," LightWave no longer needs the applied surface's settings, resulting in less render times.

- **Fast Fresnel.** This plug-in adds the Fresnel (pronounced *fre-nel*) effect to surfaces. Fresnel is a real-world property. For example, you see less of a reflection on a glass window when you're looking directly at it and more when you're viewing it from the side. Without this plug-in, a reflective surface will maintain the same reflectivity no matter where the camera is positioned.

- **Halftone.** Halftone changes the tone of your image. This is great for giving your surfaces newspaper-like looks.

- **Interference.** Adds a color interference to your surfaces. It's great for things like rainbows, color film, or other transparent-type surfaces.

- **LW_LScript.** Allows you to add an LScript to a surface.

- **LW_LScript/RT.** Allows you to add a compiled LScript to a surface.

- **Real Fresnel.** Similar to Fast Fresnel, but gives you control only over the specular and reflective polarization of a surface.

- **Super Cel Shader.** Similar to BESM, Super Cel Shader gives you the power to give your selected surface a cartoon-like appearance.

- **Thin Film.** Adds a wavelength of color to a surface for things like—you guessed it—thin film.

- **Z Shader.** This is a distance-to-camera surface control that enables you to vary the specularity, luminosity, diffuse, transparency, and reflectivity of surface, based on the surface's position to the camera.

- **Pulse.** An LScript application that cycles the luminosity and diffusion (inversely) of a surface so that the surface appears to "pulse."

- **Zor.** This plug-in has no interface, but simply varies the opacity of your surface on the z-axis.

- **gMIL.** This is a surface occlusion plug-in, allowing you to control the occlusion of diffuse, specularity, and reflection on a selected surface.

Motion Modifiers

The Motion Modifiers are plug-ins that control certain motions of scene items, including individual channels. The plug-ins control an item's entire motion, rather than specific channels. Many of these plug-ins have counterparts in the Graph Editor modifiers for specific channel control. To access the Motion Modifiers, you select an item in Layout, and then press m for Motion Options, as shown in Figure B.7.

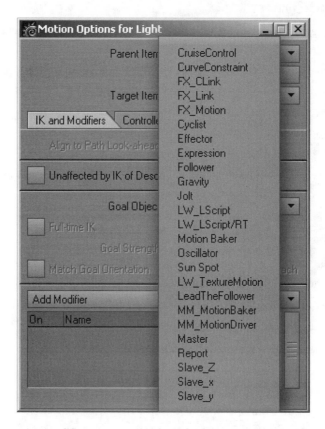

Figure B.7   Motion Modifiers are accessible from the Motion Options panel of a selected item, such as a light, camera, or object.

- **CruiseControl.** CruiseControl is an LScript that enables you to set the constant speed or motion of an item in Meters per Second, Kilometers per Hour, Miles per Hour, or Knots. If you set two key frames at 0 and 90, and then apply Cruise Control to, say, 1 Mile per Hour, the item will move at that speed based on that distance.

- **CurveConstraint.** CurveConstraint allows you move a specific item along a curve or motion path. You can use the Path To Motion command in Modeler to export out a spline curve, and then apply that to the item. CurveConstraint will give you control over how that item animates in that curve motion.

- **FX_CLink.** FX_CLink allows you to apply the particle motion to children of an item, whose parent has FX_Link added and is using the Time Shift option.

- **FX_Link.** This plug-in links the motion of particle effects to a selected item. For example, when you are working with particles, select a light, attach the FX_Link Motion Modifier, and the light will be attached to the Particle emitter.

- **FX_Motion.** Use FX_Motion to add particle-like movements and controls to a selected item.

- **Cyclist.** Cyclist allows you to set up a master control for an item that repeats a specific child movement. For example, a car driving down the road has wheels that are turning. The car stops, the wheels stop. The car backs up, the wheels back up. Apply Cyclist for this type of motion control. You also can apply it to characters such as spiders, people, etc.

- **Effector.** Effector is great for making the radius of an object affect that of another object. For example, suppose that you need a snake swallowing a big rat. Because snakes eat rats whole, you need to see the snake's body deform as the rat is eaten. Effector will allow you to do that.

- **Expression.** Expression enables you to apply a specific expression to a selected item. Learn more about expressions in Chapters 14, "Expression Applications," and 15, "Animation with Expression."

- **Follower.** Follower lets you animate one object and have others follow or copy it. For example, put a bone structure in a shark or fish. Rotate the parent bone. Apply Follower to the next bone in the chain with a slight offset. Repeat for the other child bones sequentially. Follower will tell the other bones to rotate, but it will offset them so you'll have a perfect swimming shark. Another example is the animation of a long set of letters. Rather than animating all the letters, animate one and then have Follower copy the motion with an offset for the others.

- **Gravity.** Select an item, apply Gravity, and that's it! So much for keyframing a bouncing ball! Let LightWave's Gravity Motion Modifier do it.

- **Jolt.** A cool plug-in from Bob Hood, this modifier allows you to set a reaction to an item that will "jolt" or shake the item based on the timing of other items or on a specific keyframe. For example, a big creature is walking. At every fourth frame, the character's left foot hits the ground. You can use Jolt to tell the camera to watch that foot movement and shake it every time it hits the ground.

- **LW_LScript.** Apply an LScript to a selected item.

- **LW_LScript/RT.** Apply a compiled LScript to a selected item.

- **Motion Baker.** Allows you to "bake" or freeze a motion to an object. This is also called a *virtual mocap modifier.*

- **Oscillator.** Set a repeating oscillating motion to a selected item.

- **Sun Spot.** Move an item based on real-world specifications, such as longitude and latitude, time of year, hour, minute, and second. There are a number of presets as well. This is great for simulating sunlight in, say, Chicago in August. A great plug-in if you never get outside.

- **LW_TextureMotion.** Use LightWave's texture editor to apply an image, procedural, or gradient texture to an item's motion.

- **LeadTheFollower.** An LScript plug-in that enables you to set up a specific range of movement to an item.

- **MM_MotionBaker.** Used with Motion Mixer, this motion modifier will "bake" or freeze the motion of an item that was created in Motion Mixer. The benefit is to use Motion Mixer to generate a new motion, and then bake it in for future scenes without applying the Motion Mixer application.

- **MM_MotionDriver.** If you create a motion in Motion Mixer, you can save that motion and then use it later on selected items with MM_MotionDriver.

- **Master.** This is a modifier that allows you to lock a channel of motion for a selected item.

- **Report.** This LScript enables you to save information about a selected item's motion.

- **Slave_z.** Lets you tell one item to trail a motion by a set number of frames on the z-axis.

- **Slave_x.** Lets you tell one item to trail a motion by a set number of frames on the x-axis.

- **Slave_y.** Lets you tell one item to trail a motion by a set number of frames on the y-axis.

Environment Plug-ins

The Environment plug-ins allow you to have control over a few things for your entire LightWave environment. Access this area by selecting the Scene tab, and then the Backdrop tab of the Effects panel, as shown in Figure B.8.

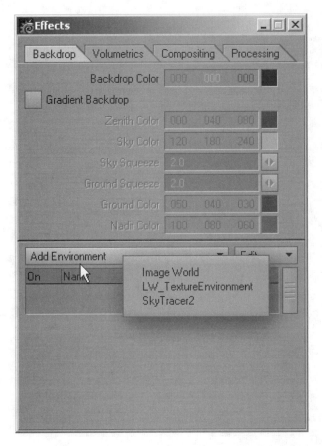

Figure B.8   Environment plug-ins, such as SkyTracer2 control full-scene environmental settings.

- **Image World.** This plug-in enables you to place an image, specifically a high dynamic range image, around your entire scene. It's great for radiosity.

- **LW_TextureEnvironment.** Use LightWave's texture editor to place an image or procedural texture around your entire scene. This is great for backgrounds of fractal patterns.

- **SkyTracer2.** SkyTracer2 allows you to create quick and easy full-scene skies. You can use VIPER to preview the sky as you're tweaking the settings.

Volumetric Plug-ins

Volumetric plug-ins are tools that use LightWave's powerful volumetric rendering engine. One of these powerful tools is HyperVoxels, which creates a physical volume for points in your scene for things like smoke, fire, and water. Access the plug-ins through the Effects panel's Volumetrics tab, as shown in Figure B.9.

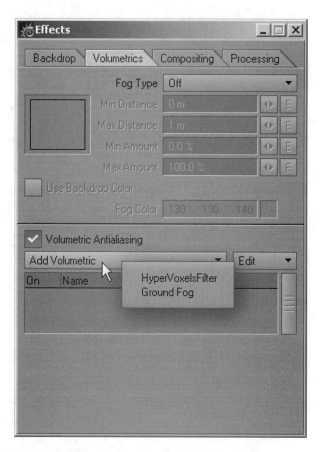

Figure B.9   Volumetric plug-ins are found under the Effects panel.

- **HyperVoxelsFilter.** HyperVoxelsFilter allow you to create surface, volume, or sprite animations based on the points or particles in your scene. This is great for creating oozing liquids, smoke, clouds, and more.

- **Ground Fog.** The Ground Fog plug-in does what you think—it creates a ground fog using volumetrics. The benefit of a volumetric ground fog is that you can fly right through it.

Pixel Filter Plug-ins

These essential plug-ins are used to generate pixels for certain plug-ins, such as SasLite for fur and hair rendering. Access the panel through the Effects panel's Processing tab, as shown in Figure B.10.

Figure B.10   The Pixel Filter plug-ins are found under the Processing tab of the Effects panel.

- **Halftone.** This Pixel Filter plug-in creates a halftone image of your render. Make this image black and white and it will look like newsprint.
- **SasLite.** In order to use SasLite, the lite version of the Sasquatch Fur and Hair plug-in that comes with LightWave 7, this pixel filter must be applied. It controls antialiasing and shadows.

Image Filter Plug-ins

These plug-ins are used to manipulate your rendered images, similar to filters in programs like Adobe Photoshop. Access the panel through the Effect panel's Processing tab, as shown in Figure B.11.

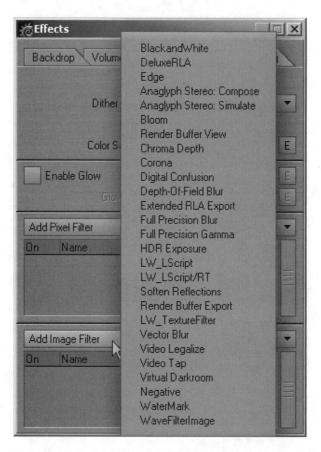

Figure B.11   The Image Filter plug-ins are found under the Processing tab of the Effects panel.

- **BlackandWhite.** Turn a rendered image into a black-and-white image.
- **DeluxeRLA.** Use this Image Filter plug-in to save out an RLA image that contains depth channel information for compositing in applications like Adobe's After Effects.
- **Edge.** Creates an edge around your rendered image based on the color values.
- **Anaglyph Stereo: Compose.** This Image Filter plug-in allows you to compose, or create, a stereo image. This is useful for creating rendered images to be viewed with 3D glasses.
- **Anaglyph Stereo: Simulate.** This Image Filter plug-in simulates the look of a rendered image used for viewing with 3D glasses.

- **Bloom.** Use Bloom to create highlights in your rendered images. For example, sunlight hits the hood of a car. The hotspot from the sun on the bright surface in the real world creates a glow or a halo. Bloom will add that effect.

- **Render Buffer View.** This Image Filter allows you to render and store a specific buffer of information for use elsewhere in LightWave, such as Specularity, Diffuse Shading, and more.

- **Chroma Depth.** This Image Filter plug-in creates a range or depth of color (chroma) in your rendered images. You can set this up to vary based on far or near z-depth information.

- **Corona.** Like Bloom, Corona lets you add halos or glows to your rendered image. However, Corona also lets you set a specific input parameter and falloff type, and then save the effect to a specific file.

- **Digital Confusion.** This image filter helps create very realistic depth-of-field renders. LightWave's built-in Depth-Of-Field renderer from the Camera panel tends to have banding if the antialiasing is not set high enough. Setting it higher means longer and often-unnecessary render times. Digital Confusion uses a blurring of the rendered image.

- **Depth-Of-Field Blur.** Use Depth-Of-Field Blur to blur various parts of the scene based on distance to the camera. You also can blur the background image.

- **Extended RLA Export.** This RLA saver allows you to save depth information, shadow, material, and object ID buffer information for later compositing in programs like Adobe's After Effects.

- **Full Precision Blur.** Use this image filter to blur your rendered image.

- **Full Precision Gamma.** This Image Filter plug-in allows you to vary the gamma of your rendered image. If you are familiar with ambient intensity, think of Full Precision Gamma as an ambient intensity for your rendered image.

- **HDR Exposure.** Use this Image Filter plug-in to normalize HDR data; that is, remove it.

- **LW_LScript.** Applies an LScript to a rendered image.

- **LW_LScript/RT.** Applies a compiled LScript to your rendered image.

- **Soften Reflections.** This filter enables you to set an amount of softness to the reflected images in a scene.

- **Render Buffer Export.** Use this image filter to save only the specularity of a rendered image or only the shadows of a rendered scene. In addition, you can use this plug-in to save any of the internal render buffers.

- **LW_TextureFilter.** Use LightWave's texture editor to apply an image, procedural, or gradient to your rendered images.

- **Vector Blur.** Similar to motion blur, this is a faster version, with limitations. Use it primarily for things that are linear.

- **Video Legalize.** Too often, the colors and lights in your scene might be too bright for broadcast when rendered. Use this to set gamma, pedestal, and IRE levels for NTSC and PAL video.

- **Video Tap.** This image filter allows you to save a copy of your image in a different format and resolution. Perhaps you have an animation that is rendering at 720×486 for broadcast. You can use Video Tap to save out a version at 320×240 for a QuickTime or AVI.

- **Virtual Darkroom.** Use this filter to change your rendered image or animation to the look of various film types, both color and black and white.

- **Negative.** Once you've rendered your scene, use this image filter to make the image negative (reversed).

- **WaterMark.** If you don't trust your client, you can add a watermark to your rendered image for copyright, identification, and so on.

- **WaveFilterImage.** Use WaveFilterImage to change many variables of your rendered image. If you open this plug-in interface, you'll see all the controls available to you, such as Posterize, Negative Image, Sharpen, Blur, Color Correction, and more. You can apply these effects to your entire rendered scene, only objects, only the shadows, and more.

Custom Object Plug-ins

The Custom Object plug-ins are tools that often are automatically applied to objects when other plug-ins are activated, such as particle effects or Hypervoxels. You access these plug-ins through the Object Properties panel of a selected object, as shown in Figure B.12.

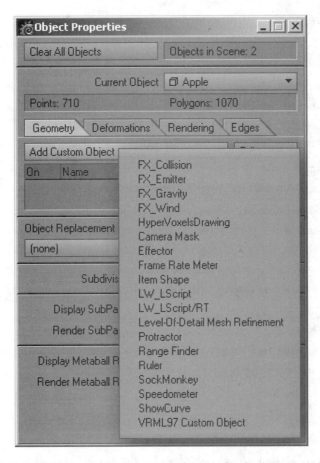

Figure B.12   Custom Object plug-ins are very useful and often load automatically with the access of other tools. These are found in the Object Properties panel of a selected object.

- **FX_Collision.** This makes a selected object a collision object when used with particle effects.

- **FX_Emitter.** This makes a selected object a Particle emitter used with particle effects.

- **FX_Gravity.** This makes a selected object a Gravity effector used with particle effects.

- **FX_Wind.** This makes a selected object a Wind effector used with particle effects.

- **HyperVoxelsDrawing.** When an object has Hypervoxels applied, such as a clump of particles, this custom plug-in is automatically applied to tell the object to work with Hypervoxels.

- **Camera Mask.** Camera Mask is useful for determining the exact Z distance of the camera to an object, usually a flat textured plane. Often, to simulate the look of a background image but with the ability to cast shadows and light, an image-mapped object is needed. Use Camera Mask to compute the exact distance.

- **Effector.** If you're using the Effector Displacement Map plug-in, you can use the Effector Custom Object plug-in to help visualize the effect in Layout.

- **Frame Rate Meter.** This custom object plug-in will add a visual frame rate meter to a scene. When you play the animation, you can see the frame rate of the playback. The benefit of this plug-in is for timing. Often, scenes with little information play back too fast, while scenes with larger amounts of information play back too slow. Frame Rate will help you determine how fast or slow a scene is playing back in OpenGL.

- **Item Shape.** Use the Item Shape custom object to add a shape to an object. For example, using null objects as goals for IK is great, but they're often hard to see. Apply an Item Shape to a null object for better visibility.

- **LW_LScript.** Applies an LScript to an object.

- **LW_LScript/RT.** Applies a compiled LScript to your object.

- **Level-Of-Detail Mesh Refinement.** This handy plug-in allows you to change the resolution level of your subpatched or metaball objects at set distances in your scene. For example, you can tell the object to have more detail closer to the camera and less detail (less subdivided) farther away from the camera.

- **Protractor.** This custom plug-in puts a protractor measurement in your scene, useful for measuring angles.

- **Range Finder.** Range Finder puts a measurement in your scene to display the distance of the object to the camera. This is great for determining focal lengths for things like depth of field, or perhaps Level of Detail Mesh Refinement.

- **Ruler.** Enables you to visually measure distance in Layout.

- **SockMonkey.** If you've applied SockMonkey (displacement plug-in) you can use this custom object to see the representations in Layout.

- **Speedometer.** Add this plug-in to an item, and you'll be able to see in Layout the speed of an item.

- **ShowCurve.** Displays the curve of an object in Layout, allowing you to set specific colors for it. You also can show the cage or points and set visual color for easy representation.

- **VRML97 Custom Object.** Use this custom object plug-in to create Virtual Reality Markup Language (VRML) information visible in Layout, for things like sound nodes, bounding boxes, and more.

Object Replacement Plug-ins

Object Replacement plug-ins also are found in the Object Properties panel of a selected object. The setting can be found just below the Custom Object selection.

- **LW_LScript.** Applies an LScript as an object replacement.

- **LW_LScript/RT.** Applies a compiled LScript as an object replacement.

- **Level-Of-Detail Mesh Refinement.** You can use this Object Replace plug-in to change an object beyond specific distances in your scene. When the selected object reaches a specific point, LightWave will replace the object.

- **Object List.** Use this plug-in to generate a list of the objects in your scene.

- **Object Sequence.** Certain animations require that you replace an object at every frame, such as a string of 3D letters. By having a named sequence of objects (just like a sequence of images—001, 002, and so on.) you can tell LightWave to replace that object every frame with the next object in the sequence.

Displacement Plug-ins

Displacement plug-ins are used often in LightWave because they change and deform objects in many ways. These plug-ins are found within the Object Properties panel of a selected item, under the Deformations tab, as shown in Figure B.13.

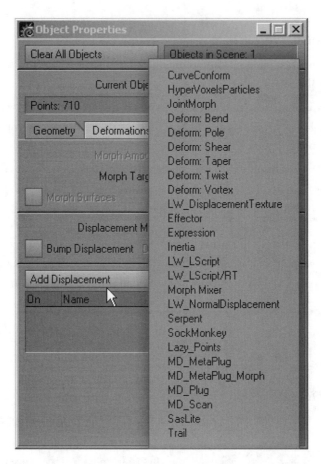

Figure B.13   The Displacement plug-ins can be found under the Deformations tab within the Object Properties panel.

- **CurveConform.** Use this displacement plug-in to conform a selected object to a specific curve. You can set an auto range and a specific axis. You also can align an object, stretch it, or flip it against a curve. Try this. Make a spline curve in Modeler—you can simply use the Spline Draw tool from the Create tab. Save that curve as an object. Load it in Layout, and use it with Curve Conform and apply an object to it.

- **HyperVoxelsParticles.** This plug-in usually is loaded automatically when an object has Hypervoxels applied. It has no interface.

- **JointMorph.** This plug-in takes a little work off your hands by automatically driving an endomorph, based on the rotation of a bone. For example, you can rotate bones in a face to make a smile, and have JointMorph tell the object to apply the puffy cheek endomorph you created to simulate a smile. This also is great for bulging or flexing muscles as well.

- **Deform: Bend.** The Deform displacement plug-ins all work in a similar fashion, based on two null objects. With Deform: Bend applied, you can perform a Modeler-type bend function on an object. One null acts as a base, while the other null acts as a control handle.

- **Deform: Pole.** With this plug-in applied, you can perform a Modeler-type pole function on an object. Pole is a sizing function, around an area of influence. The influence is controlled by the two nulls that the Deform tools use.

- **Deform: Shear.** With this plug-in applied, you can perform a Modeler-type shear function on an object. Shear is a move type function, with a fixed position. For example, you would use Shear to tilt a building to make the leaning tower of Pisa. One null is the fixed position, while the other null is set to be the control handle to "shear" the building.

- **Deform: Taper.** With this plug-in applied, you can perform a Modeler-type taper function on an object.

- **Deform: Twist.** With this plug-in applied, you can perform a Modeler-type twist function on an object.

- **Deform: Vortex.** With this plug-in applied, you can perform a Modeler-type vortex function on an object. Vortex is similar to twist, but it is applied to a specific area of influence using two null objects.

- **LW_DisplacementTexture.** Use LightWave's texture editor to displace an object based on an image, procedural, or gradient texture.

- **Effector.** Use the Effector displacement plug-in to make one object effectively deform another.

- **Expression.** Use this plug-in if you have an expression written to displace an object.

- **Inertia.** Inertia applies as inertia to an object's displacement. If an object is moving, you can set this to create a lag or falloff of movement. It's great for things like waving flags or flapping wings.

- **LW_LScript.** Applies an LScript to displace an object.

- **LW_LScript/RT.** Applies a compiled LScript to displace your object.

- **MorphMixer.** This plug-in is needed to directly access any endomorphs within an object. Endomorphs are created in Modeler.

- **LW_NormalDisplacement.** This plug-in allows you to set a basic displacement to an object based on an endomorph or on surface normals. You can use LightWave's texture editor to apply the type of displacement.

- **Serpent.** Using Serpent, you can conform an object to a path. This is great for things like snakes, worms, wires, and so on.

- **SockMonkey.** SockMonkey enables you to control a group of points or weighted area with an object, such as a null. These groups and weighted areas initially are created in Modeler. SockMonkey works very well with SubPatched objects.

- **Lazy_Points.** Use Lazy_Points to create a lag on your object. Perhaps you'd like to pick up a tablecloth and have the ends of the cloth follow slowly behind the pick-up point. Use Lazy_Points to do this. You also can use this to create things like warps or exaggerated character movements.

- **MD_MetaPlug.** Use MD_MetaPlug to apply a saved Motion Designer displacement to your object and also include a bounding box representation.

- **MD_MetaPlug_Morph.** Use MD_MetaPlug_Morph to apply a saved Motion Designer displacement to a morph, either one time, or every morph.

- **MD_Plug.** Use MD_Plug to apply a saved Motion Designer displacement to your object.

- **MD_Scan.** Apply MD_Scan to have Motion Designer scan your objects for calculations. This plug-in often is applied automatically with Motion Designer.

- **SasLite.** This is the Sasquatch Lite fur and hair plug-in interface. Apply this to objects on which you want fur and hair to grow.

- **Trail.** Trail is an LScript application that lets an object trail behind, similar to Lazy_Points.

Generic Plug-ins

Generic plug-in types might or might not be found in other locations throughout Layout. Some of these plug-ins also are accessed through specific panels, such as Custom Objects, so don't be confused by the double listing. LightWave has various plug-in "types" as described in the front of the chapter. When you click the Scene tab and select the Generics list, you'll find these plug-ins, as shown in Figure B.14.

Figure B.14   The Generic plug-ins might be listed elsewhere in Layout, but they are all shown here.

- **Add Camera Mask.** Add Camera Mask is useful for determining the exact Z distance of the camera to an object, usually a flat textured plane. Often you need an image-mapped object to simulate the look of a background image with the ability to cast shadows and light. Use Add Camera Mask to compute the exact distance.

- **Add Effector.** If you're using the Effector Displacement Map plug-in, you can use the Effector Generic plug-in to help visualize the effect in Layout.

- **Add Frame Rate Meter.** This generic plug-in will add a visual frame rate meter to a scene. When you play the animation, you can see the frame rate of the playback. The benefit of this plug-in is for timing. Often, scenes with little information play back too fast, while scenes with larger amounts of information play back too slow. Frame Rate will help you determine how fast or slow a scene is playing back in OpenGL.

- **Add Range Finder.** Add Range Finder puts a measurement in your scene to display the distance of the object to the camera. This is great for determining focal lengths for things like depth-of-field or perhaps Level of Detail Mesh Refinement.

- **Add Ruler.** Lets you visually measure distance in Layout.

- **Speedometer.** Add this to an item, and you'll be able to see the speed of an item in Layout.

- **Add Collision Effector.** Add a collision effector to your scene for particle effects.

- **Add Particle Emitter.** Add a Particle emitter to your scene for particle effects.

- **Add Gravity Effector.** Add a Gravity effector to your scene for particle effects.

- **Add Wind Effector.** Add a Wind effector to your scene for particle effects.

- **Buffer Export.** This LScript enables you to export out specific buffers of your rendered images.

- **Comments.** Have a lot going on in your scene? Don't have a notebook? Use the Comments tool to create comments on a scene. This information is a digital notepad that is saved with your scene file.

- **Content Manager.** If you ever need to export a scene and all of its components (such as images and objects) to a specific location—perhaps for backup or to send to another animator—use the Content Manger plug-in.

- **Corona.** Like Bloom, Corona lets you add halos or glows to your rendered image. However, Corona also lets you set a specific input parameter and falloff type and save the effect to a specific file.

- **Digital Confusion.** This image filter helps create very realistic depth-of-field renders. LightWave's built-in Depth-Of-Field renderer from the Camera panel tends to have banding if the antialiasing is not set high enough. Setting it higher means longer and often-unnecessary render times. Digital Confusion uses a blurring of the rendered image.

- **FX_Browser.** Clicking this (also a button under the Scene tab) opens the Browser window for particle effects.

- **FX_Linker.** Clicking this (also a button under the Scene tab) opens the FX Linker window for attaching objects to particles.

- **FX_Property.** Clicking this (also a button under the Scene tab) opens the Property window for selected particle effects.

- **FX_Start.** Often, your particle setups are too heavy to calculate on the fly. Use FX_Start to generate the calculations of your particle scenes for quick OpenGL playback.

- **Ground Fog.** The Ground Fog plug-in does what you think—it creates a ground fog using volumetrics. The benefit of a volumetric ground fog is that you can fly right through it.

- **HyperVoxels.** Hypervoxels allows you to create surface, volume, or sprite animations based on the points or particles in your scene. This is great for creating oozing liquids, smoke, clouds, and more.

- **ImageLister.** Have you ever wondered which images are in your scene? You can use ImageLister to save a text file of the images used in a scene.

- **LS Commander.** Use this LScript panel to access and edit your LScripts.

- **Skelegons To Nulls.** If your object has skelegons built (from Modeler), you can use this tool to create null objects from those skelegons. This is useful for creating goal objects for IK.

- **LW_LSCompiler.** Call up this tool to compile an LScript.

- **LW_LScript.** Select this to run an LScript.

- **LW_LScript/RT.** Select this to run a compiled LScript.

- **LW_Select Group.** If you've created a group of items in Layout, you can use this plug-in to instantly select the group.

- **MD_Controller.** Click this plug-in to access the Motion Designer panel for control over cloth animations in your scene.

- **Master Channel.** Adds custom user-defined channels to an item.

- **Motion Mixer.** This plug-in is LightWave's nonlinear animation control. Read more about this in Chapter 16, "Nonlinear Animation."

- **Schematic View Tools.** Any viewport in Layout can have a schematic view as an overview of the scene. Use Schematic View Tools for additional control.

- **Shockwave3D_Export.** Get ready for the web by exporting your LightWave scenes to Macromedia ShockWave format.

- **SkyGen.** Use SkyGen to create a quick sky backdrop using LightWave's powerful gradients.

- **SkyTracer.** SkyTracer, LightWave's built-in Sky generator, is useful for creating full environmental skies.

- **Spreadsheet.** The Spreadsheet Scene Manager is a great place to control and maintain just about every aspect of your scene. This tool has a button directly in Layout at the top left.

- **SubDivLOD Tool.** This handy plug-in allows you to change the resolution level of your subpatched or metaball objects at set distances in your scene. For example, you can tell the object to have more detail closer to the camera and less detail (less subdivided) farther away from the camera.

- **TM-P Mot-ify Delete Motion Keys.** The TM-P tool gives you advanced control over delete functions for keyframes. You can delete specific motions from a specific range of keys, for selected items, all items, or hierarchies. You can easily delete all keyframes for an item with this plug-in, but preserve frame 0, for example, for things like character animation.

- **Texture Environment.** Use LightWave's texture editor to place an image or procedural texture around your entire scene. This is great for backgrounds of fractal patterns.

- **Export Scene As VRML97.** Applying this plug-in allows you to save your scene to a VRML file.

- **Vector Blur.** Use this filter for fast motion blur effects.

- **Clone Hierarchy.** You can select just the parent of a hierarchy of items in Layout, and then run this plug-in to clone that hierarchy. This is great for things involving IK.

- **Mirror Item.** Pick an item or items in Layout, and choose this plug-in to mirror them across their axis. This will mirror an object's motions as well.

- **Select Children.** If an item has other items parented to it, you can choose this plug-in to select easily the children of the parent item.

- **Select Hierarchy.** If an item selected in Layout is part of a hierarchy, use this plug-in to select the entire hierarchy.

Master Plug-ins

Master Plug-ins, also found under the Scene tab just below the Generic listings, are plug-ins that control items on a more global scale. These plug-ins do things not related to a specific item, but rather, the whole scene.

- **Item Picker.** Use this plug-in to create a list of items in your scene for animation control. Perhaps you have a scene with 300 objects, but only 30 are used to animate. You can load those 30 items into the Item Picker and keep this panel open to easily select the specific items.

- **LW_LScript.** Use this to apply an LScript to the entire scene.

- **LW_LScript/RT.** Use this to apply a compiled LScript to the entire scene.

- **LW_LScript Commander.** The LScript Commander is a plug-in that allows you to edit and control LScripts for your scene.

- **LW_Macro Recorder.** Use the Macro Recorder plug-in to record a set of actions for your scene.

- **Master Channel.** Adds a user-defined channel for use in areas such as the Graph Editor.

- **Motion Mixer.** This is LightWave's nonlinear animation tool. There is a button on Layout's interface that directly runs this Master plug-in.

- **Proxy Pic.** This allows another object to act as a stand in (proxy) for easier selection of another object. Certain items are often very hard to select in a complex scene. You can use Proxy Pic to set callouts for specific items. For example, IK goals on a character often get lost when assigned to bones—use Proxy Pic to add a small selection dot outside of the character, making selection very easy.

- **Spreadsheet Manager.** LightWave's spreadsheet offers control over all aspects of your scene, from items loaded, their visibility, bone selections, light color, and more. A button is already on LightWave's Layout that directly runs this Master plug-in.

Modeler Plug-ins

Modeler's plug-ins, like many in Layout, already are assigned to buttons throughout the program. Unlike Layout, however, they are not "classified," but rather placed in their appropriate panels, such as Modify, Multiply, and so on. This section tells you briefly what they're used for. Some, like Layout, are very powerful; others are simple tools that come in handy, depending on the project.

- **Absolute Size.** Too often, when sizing an object, the object sizes based on the position of the mouse, origin, or other. You can use Absolute Size to size an object equally, negative or positive, on a specific axis. This tool is found under the Modify tab, under the Stretch heading.

- **Adjust Polygon Map.** When working with UV maps, use this plug-in to adjust the 2D movements of the UV coordinates. This also allows you to adjust the connection between the polygon's vertices and its texture points.

- **Aligner.** Use this plug-in to align geometry in 3D space and other objects. You can determine how to align geometry in Modeler's background or foreground layers, also employing scale. This plug-in is found under the Modify tab, under the Move heading.

- **Apply Morph.** You can use Apply Morph to merge a morph into the base endo-morph of an object. This is found under the Map tab, under the Morph heading.

- **Auto Patcher.** This plug-in patches a selected curve into polygons. You have the ability to set polygon level control as well.

- **Auto PatcherMK.** This plug-in also automatically patches a spline curve, but enables you to set a specific number of polygons per patch.

- **Background to Morph.** Use this plug-in to get an object in a background layer into an endomorph layer. This is great for taking pre-made endomorphs and applying them to another object.

- **Band Saw.** You can use Band Saw to slice up an object. To use it, you select polygons and run the command. Choose negative or positive and select how much you want the plug-in to "saw," or cut up your selection. This is great because it follows the path of the polygons.

- **Bezier Tool.** This plug-in allows you to create a spline curve with Bezier tools.

- **BG Conform.** This plug-in conforms the foreground object to the background object.

- **Bone Weights.** Bone Weights enable you to set up weight maps for objects based on your skelegons. Skelegons become bones in Layout, and when the Bone Weights are applied in Modeler, you'll have more control over movement in Layout.

- **Bounding Box.** This plug-in generates a bounding box for your objects. You use it for creating stand-in objects that exactly represent the volume of space your object has. Use a bounding box in place of a real object in Layout for quick and easy animation setup, and then replace the object with the real one before rendering.

- **Bubbles.** Use this tool to generate random 3D bubbles.

- **Cage.** If you like working with splines, this plug-in will create an instant spline cage for you to begin manipulating.

- **Calculate.** This plug-in allows you to enter an expression for either the x, y, or z-axis. This is found in the LScript drop down of the Construct tab.

- **Capsule Tool.** Found under the Create tab, this handy plug-in enables you to create a capsule-shaped object. Remember to use the numeric window for specific sizes, sides, and values.

- **Center 1D.** Found under the Modify tab, you can use this tool to quickly center an object on one axis.

- **Center Scale.** Use Center Scale to scale an object based on its center origin. You can find this tool under the Additional list of the Construct tab.

- **Center Stretch.** Also under the Additional list under the Construct tab, the Center Stretch command allows you to set a numeric value to stretch an object based on its pivot, for the x, y, or z-axis.

- **Clear Polygon Map.** Use Clear Polygon Map if you wish to remove a polygonally mapped texture, such as a UV. Don't confuse this with Clear Map. This tool is found under the Map tab, under the Texture heading.

- **Color Map Adjust Tool.** Use this tool to interactively adjust an existing color map for an object.

- **Cull Map.** To *cull* means to remove an inferior thing of a larger group. Given that this tool is under the Map tab, it allows you to remove a map from a group with maps already assigned.

- **Cut Curves.** Under the Construct tab, the Cut Curves command removes curves from a layer or selected polygons.

- **Dangle.** Dangle allows you to rotate an object based on its rotation center.
- **Demo All BG Layers.** This plug-in instantly selects background layers when you're working in a foreground layer. This is found under the Display tab.
- **Demo Next Empty Layer.** Click this button to instantly switch to the next empty layer. This is a good tool for creating a custom button. It is found under the Display tab.
- **Draw MetaEdges.** MetaEdges is a unique LightWave tool that builds multipoint metaballs. Metaballs are similar to Hypervoxels but are polygonal-based. When building these in Modeler, you can interactively see their shapes. This plug-in is found under the Create tab.
- **Draw Skelegons.** Use this tool to quickly and easily draw a skelegon, which later becomes a bone in Layout for object deformation. This command can be found under the Create tab.
- **Edit Metaballs.** If you've made metaballs, Edit Metaballs lets you modify them after they've been created. Edit Metaballs is found under the Detail tab.
- **Edit Skelegons.** Use Edit Skelegons to edit skelegons in your models. You can edit things like bone rotation (bone up tags) and you can also rename your skelegons with this tool. It is found under the Create tab.
- **EPSF Loader.** Use the EPSF Loader to load EPS or AI files from programs like Adobe Illustrator. This allows you to load the file and then convert it to a flat 3D object. Note that this plug-in does not like Adobe Illustrator files past version 6 or 7. This is found under the File drop down, under Import.
- **Equilateral Tri.** Use this handy tool from the Create tab to create instantly an equilateral triangle on the x, y, or z-axis at any size you like.
- **Export 3DS.** From the File menu, you can use Export 3DS to export a LightWave object to a 3D Studio format.
- **Export DXF.** From the File menu, you can use Export DXF to export a LightWave object to a DXF format.
- **Export Encapsulated PostScript.** From the File menu, you can use Export Encapsulated PostScript to export a LightWave object to an EPS file format.
- **Export LightWave 5.** From the File menu, you can use Export LightWave 5 to export a LightWave object to an object suitable for LightWave versions prior to 6.0.
- **Export OBJ.** From the File menu, you can use Export OBJ to export a LightWave object to a Wavefront OBJ format.

- **Extender.** Extender allows you to perform edge modeling. This tool is found under the Multiply tab.

- **Fast Triple Fan.** Fast Triple Fan triangulates your selected four-point polygon.

- **Fast Triple Traverse.** This plug-in also triangulates your selected four-point polygon, but with traverse effects.

- **Find Center.** This cool plug-in finds the center of a selected polygon and records it for you with a point. This is very useful for properly setting pivots. Find this tool under the Construct tab, under the Measure drop-down list.

- **Flatten Layers.** People often build single objects in multiple layers. If that's your method, rather than selecting all layers and then cutting and pasting, simply select Flatten Layers. Objects on all layers will be merged down to one. This is found under the Details tab.

- **Flip UVs.** If you have UV maps created, you can use Flip UVs to flip the direction of the maps. This is found under the Map tab, under the Texture heading.

- **Fractalize.** This plug-in allows you to subdivide your object, but do it unevenly in a fractal pattern. This is great for creating landscapes or rocks. This can be found under the Additional drop-down list of the Construct tab.

- **Gear.** A plug-in that allows you to generate. you guessed it—a gear. Find this one under the Create tab.

- **Gears.** Although not entirely different from Gear, Gears, found under the Additional list of the Construct tab, allows you to create a more detailed gear with more control over size and axis.

- **Gemstone Tool.** Found under the Create tab, this handy plug-in allows you to create gemstone-shaped objects. You can use the numeric window to vary the size and shape of the gemstone.

- **Helix.** This tool, found under the Create tab, generates a helix-based curve.

- **Julienne.** Julienne slices up your object—like Julienne potatoes—into little pieces. Find this command under the Construct tab. It slices your object in the number of pieces you specify, on the axis you choose.

- **Load Object Into Layer.** A great plug-in that lets you load an object into a specific layer of the current object. Find this tool in the File drop-down list.

- **Lock UVs to Polygon.** Found under the Map tab, Lock UVs to Polygon (or Poly Map) will keep the UV texture applied to the polygon, so that you can edit it without problems.

- **Logo.** Found under the Additional list of the Construct tab, the Logo command lets you load a font and create text. Essentially, this is a really quick way to make an extruded text logo.

- **LW_Texture VMap.** LW_Texture VMap allows you to apply a VMap texture to a particular axis, with offset and scale. It simply creates a VMap based on a texture. This tool is found under the Map tab.

- **LW_XCommand.** Found under the LScript selection of the Construct tab, LW_XCommand enables you the execute a command in Modeler. These commands are usually LScript-driven.

- **Make 1 Point Polygons.** There comes a point when every animator needs to make one-point polygons for things like stars. Use this plug-in to create one-point polygons.

- **Make Metaballs.** Similar to the Draw Metaballs command, Make Metaballs converts the points of an object to metaballs. You can find this tool under the Construct tab.

- **Make MetaEdges.** Similar to the Draw MetaEdges command, Make MetaEdges converts the points of an object to MetaEdges. You can find this tool under the Construct tab.

- **Make Metafaces.** Make Metafaces converts the points of an object to Metaface objects. You can find this tool under the Construct tab.

- **Make Skelegons.** Make Skelegons converts the points of an object to Skelegons, which later become bones in Layout. You can find this tool under the Construct tab.

- **Make DoubleSided.** Rather than using the DoubleSided shading option in the Surface Editor, it's often easy to use the Make DoubleSided command on selected polygons to make them two-sided. Polygons are normally one-sided by default. Find this command undere the Detail tab, within the Polygons heading.

- **Make Text.** Under the Construct tab, if you open the Additional drop-down list, you'll find the Make Text command. Use this to make a string or paragraph of text.

- **New Quad Polygon Map.** Found under the Map tab in the Texture heading, New Quad Polygon Map allows you to create a new vertex map (VMap) for a selected polygon.

- **Normal Baker.** Found under the Map tab, this plug-in bakes the normals of a selected object or polygon and generate a VMap. It creates two-point polygons based on each vertex normal of your object.

- **Nomalize Map.** Normalize means to scale something so that it is between a normal range. This just allows you to normalize any existing VMap. Find this command under the Map tab.

- **Parametric Obj.** Create an object based on a parametric mathematical equation. Find this tool under the Create tab.

- **Particle Clone.** This nifty little plug-in clones an object in the foreground to points in the background. Find this command under the Multiply tab.

- **Path To Motion.** Found under the Additional list within the Construct tab, Path To Motion allows you to create a curve in Modeler, and make it a motion path for use in Layout. For example, you can draw a curve, create a tunnel with it using Rail Extrude (Multiply tab), and then use Path To Clone for creating a perfect camera motion in Layout.

- **Platonic.** Under the Additional list of the Construct tab, Platonic creates geometric objects, such as tetrahedrons, octahedrons, and others.

- **Platonic Solid Tool.** Found under the Create tab, the Platonic Solid tool allows you interactively to create platonic shapes. Remember to use the numeric panel for more controls.

- **Plot 1D.** Using a mathematical function equation, you can create an object on a specific axis. Find this control under the Create tab.

- **Plot 2D.** Similar to Plot 1D, use Plot 2D to create an object based on a mathematical function equation in 3D space. Also find this tool under the Create tab.

- **Point Color.** Click the Map tab and under the Weight & Color heading, you can choose a point color for an RGBA VMap. A is for Alpha.

- **Point Clone Plus.** Point Clone Plus, similar to Point Clone, gives you specific control over the cloning of a foreground image to points in a background. You can control random values, such as centering, scale, and rotation. Find this tool under the Multiply tab.

- **Point Center.** Found under the Measure utility under the Construct tab, you can use this tool to find the average point value of an object or selected polygon, and its location to the 0 axis.

- **Polygon Map to UVs.** Use this plug-in to change polygon maps directly into UV maps. This is under the Map tab.

- **Polygon Normal UVs.** Use this plug-in to convert polygon normals directly into UV maps. This is found under the Map tab.

- **Primitives.** Under the Construct tab, the Primitives selection gives you the option to instantly create a donut, wedge, spline cage, random points, gear, or platonic solid object.

- **Quadric.** Use Quadric from the Create tab to build a quadric object such as a box with rounded edges.

- **Quantize UVs.** Under the Map tab, Quantize UVs enables you to quantize selected VMaps.

- **qemLOSS2.** Often, objects are overbuilt with too many points and polygons. Using qemLOSS2 allows you to decrease the number of points and polygons in an object while still maintaining the shape. You can find this tool under the Construct tab.

- **Radial Array.** You can array, or multiply, an object in a radial fashion with this command. This is great for things that need to be multiplied in a circular fashion. Find this tool under the Multiply tab.

- **Radial Select.** Found under the Display tab, Radial Select allows you to choose an XYZ origin, inner radius, and outer radius for point or polygon selection.

- **Rail Bevel.** A very useful tool, Rail Bevel allows you to create a curve in a background layer, and then select a polygon in a foreground layer—by applying Rail Bevel, the selected polygon will be beveled based on the curve. This tool is great for creating things like cabinets, carved surfaces, and more. Find Rail Bevel under the Multiply tab.

- **Rand Points.** Random Points generates a clump of points, useful for stars, Hypervoxels, point clones, etc. You can create the random points with falloff, as a sphere, or as a cube. Find this tool under the Create tab under the Elements heading.

- **Rand Pricks.** Random Pricks creates little prickly points from the selected surface of an object. You can find this tool under the Create tab.

- **Reduce Points.** Take a selection and apply Reduce Points from the Construct tab to reduce points. You have specific control over the reduction threshold in this plug-in.

- **Reduce Polygons.** Just like Reduce Points, you can take a selection and apply Reduce Polygons from the Construct tab to reduce points. You have specific controls over the reduction threshold in this plug-in as well.

- **Rename Skelegon.** By default, skelegons are named bone00, bone01, and so on. It's good practice to name them for organization. If you forget to name a skelegon while creating it, you can go back with the Rename Skelegon tool under the Detail tab and rename it.

- **Rest On Ground.** Use the Rest On Ground command from the Modify tab to bring a selected polygon or object to ground level, which is the 0 y-axis. This is the most common use; however, you can use this on any axis.

- **Rotate Morph.** This tool, found under the Modify tab, allows you to rotate all or a selected morph at a specific degree on a selected axis.

- **Rotate About Normal.** Take a selection and rotate it around its surface normal. This is found under the Modify tab.

- **Rotate Arbitrary Axis.** If you place a two-point polygon in a background layer and have an object in a foreground layer, Rotate Arbitrary Axis allows you to enter a rotational value for that object. It rotates around the two-point polygon in the background layer. This plug-in is found under the Modify tab.

- **Rotate To Ground.** Use this plug-in under the Modify tab to rotate an object based on the ground (0 y-axis) plane.

- **Rotate To Object.** Use this plug-in to rotate a selection of an object based on its own origin. Find this plug-in under the Modify tab.

- **Rotate Any Axis.** Also under the Modify tab, Rotate Any Axis rotates using BG two-point polygon. Similar to Rotate Arbitrary Axis, this plug-in uses the point on the axis closest to origin.

- **Rotate HPB.** Use Rotate HPB to rotate an object on specific Heading, Pitch, and Bank values.

- **Router.** The Router tool enables you to route the edges of an object or selection, making them rounded, hollow, or stair-stepped. Try making a ball and running this tool from the Additional list under the Construct tab to see it in action.

- **Rove Tool.** An excellent modeling control tool, the Rove tool allows you to move and rotate with one tool. Select it, and then click an object. Drag the lines to move, and the curve to rotate. Find it under the Modify tab.

- **Save Layers As Object.** From the File menu, you can choose the Save Layers As Object command to save selected layers as one object. Because each layer belongs to a single object, you might want a specific layer to be saved as a separate object.

- **Save Object Section.** From the Additional drop-down list under the Construct tab, you can use this plug-in to save a selected polygon as an object.

- **Save Object Section Cut.** Similar to Save Object Section, this plug-in saves the selected object section, and then cuts it from the object itself. Also found in the Additional list under the Construct tab.

- **Save Object Section Points.** From the Additional drop-down list under the Construct tab, you can use this plug-in to save selected points of an object.

- **Save Object Section Points Cut.** Similar to Save Object Section Points, this plug-in saves the selected points, and then cuts them from the object itself. Also found in the Additional list under the Construct tab.

- **Scale Morph.** Use this plug-in from the Modify tab to scale a selected or all endomorphs. You can adjust the X, Y, and Z values for Scale and Center.

- **SeaShell Tool.** Just in case you ever need to build a seashell, LightWave will do it for you. Select this plug-in from the Multiply tab. Create a flat simple object and run this command.

- **Select By Map Influence.** You can use this tool from the Display tab, under the Maps drop down to make a selection based on VMap values.

- **Select By Map.** You can use this tool from the Display tab, under the Maps drop down, to make a selection based on a VMaps.

- **Select By Polygon Map.** You can use this tool from the Display tab, under the Maps drop down, to make a selection based on polygon maps.

- **Select Child Skelegon.** Use the Select Child Skelegon to easily select skelegons that are lower in the hierarchy of your skelegon structure. Find this under the Display tab.

- **Select Parent Skelegon.** Use Select Parent Skelegon to easily select skelegons that are higher in the hierarchy of your skelegon structure. Find this under the Display tab.

- **Select Polygons from Selection Set.** If you've created a selection set, you quickly can select the polygons within it using the Select Polygons from Selection Set plug-in.

- **Select UV Seam.** From the Map tab, use this plug-in to select the seam of a UV map. This is useful for UV map editing.

- **Set Skelegon Weight.** When building characters with skelegons, it's often good practice to apply weights. This allows you to associate a weight map with selected skelegons. Found under the Detail tab under the Other heading.

- **Spherize.** Use Spherize to bring selected points or an object to a sphere. You can use this tool to turn your cow into a round ball, for example. Find this tool under the Modify tab.

- **Spikey Tool.** Use this tool from the Multiply tab to make spikes on your selected polygons. Choose the tool, and then click and drag on an object.

- **Spin It.** Select the Spin It tool from the Additional list under the Construct tab to spin an object on a specific axis and make a copy of it as you do so.

- **Spline Draw.** Under the Create tab, use the Spline Draw tool for great control over creating spline curves.

- **Spline Guide.** Spline Guide is similar to a lattice deformation tool. Select an object, even just a simple ball. Press the Tab key to activate SubPatch mode. Select Spline Guide from the Modify tab. Click your object in the desired axis view. Click and drag the points to shape and form your object. Remember to open the numeric window (n) for more control.

- **Split Skelegon.** Sometimes when you are building skelegons and they're in a complex hierarchy, you might need to split one. Choose this tool from the Construct tab, under the Subdivide heading.

- **Spray Points Tool.** From the Create tab, you can use the Spray Points tool to quickly create a spray of single-point polygons. Instant starfield!

- **Spread UVs.** You can choose this command from the Map tab to spread out a selected UV map, controlling each U and V.

- **Squarize.** Like Spherize, you can use Squarize to bring selected points of an object to a square shape. You can use this tool to turn your cow into a box, for example. Find this tool under the Modify tab.

- **Stipple.** Found under the Create tab, Stipple will allow you to create points within the regular points of an object or selection on an individual axis control.

- **Super Quadric Tool.** Like the Quadric tool, Super Quadric lets you interactively create geometric shapes. Be sure to use the numeric panel (n) for more control.

- **Surfaces To Parts.** For better control over your object in both Modeler and Layout, you can select polygons and create surface parts. This plug-in allows you to turn surface names into parts. This means you can name a group of polygons within an object that has various surfaces with this tool. Find it under the Grouping drop down from the Display tab.

- **Symmetrize.** This plug-in creates a range of Symmetry on a selected axis for an object. Find this tool under the Multiply tab.

- **Teapot.** Run this plug-in from the Additional list under the Construct tab to create a teapot.

- **Texture Guide.** From the Map tab, you can select and use the Texture Guide for specific control over projection textures and UV maps. You also can create UVs from existing projection textures.

- **Throw.** This nifty little gem allows you to create a motion path to throw an object. Of course, the controls available let you vary the type of motion, gravity, axis, and more. Find this under the Additional list of the Construct tab.

- **Toggle Metamesh.** Use Toggle Metamesh from the Construct tab to toggle any "meta" objects on or off. This helps for speed improvements and modeling control for visibility.

- **Toroid.** Use the Toroid plug-in from the Create tab to instantly create a torus shape. a donut.

- **UV Map Jitter.** Like the regular Jitter command (Shift+j), UV Map Jitter from the Map tab enables you to jitter the placement of a UV map.

- **UV to Weight.** Using this plug-in from the Map tab enables you to turn any UV map to a weight map.

- **UV Copy.** Copy a UV map with this tool, from the Map tab.

- **UV Flip.** Flip a UV map on a specific axis, from the Map tab.

- **UV Paste.** If you've copied a UV map, you can paste it with the UV Paste plug-in command. Also find this tool under the Map tab.

- **UV Rotate.** Rotate a UV map upon a specific axis. Do this from the Map tab.

- **Vertex Paint.** Vertex Paint can be a valuable asset to your modeling abilities. This plug-in is used for painting vertex color maps and weight maps on bones. With it, you can blend maps, change influences, and more. Be sure to check out the information on this tool in your LightWave reference guide.

- **Wedge.** From the Create tab, use the Wedge plug-in to create a wedge-shaped object. This object is similar to a torus, in that it's flat on its edges.

- **Wrap Sphere.** You can choose the Wrap Sphere plug-in from the Additional list under the Construct tab to wrap selected polygons or an object spherically, based on an inner and outer radius.

Learn Your Tools

LightWave's Layout and Modeler are extremely powerful creation tools. The tools within this program require a lot of time and experimentation. Hopefully, the information in the preceding pages has given you a good indication of what can be accomplished. There's nothing better than knowing the tools you have available to you.

Reference Charts

To expand on the powerful plug-ins throughout LightWave, here are a few more references for you to use when creating surfaces and rendering.

Technical Reference

This section consists of various charts and tables that come in handy when you're trying to find that particular property or specification that you swore you knew, but just can't seem to remember. You'll find information on the following:

- RGB color values
- Reflection properties
- Refraction properties
- Color temperatures of light
- Film and video output resolutions

It can't be stressed enough that the following information should be used as a guideline only! The scientific world routinely deals in absolutes. As animations, however, we do not. The information presented here should be used as a starting point only. Feel free to adjust anything as necessary to achieve the look you are going for. Don't worry that your diamond doesn't have the exact refraction value of a real diamond. If it looks better tweaked higher or lower, do it! If your banana looks kind of funky with the "proper" banana color, change it! There are no hard and fast rules, and in the end, the only thing that really matters is that you and/or your client are happy with the end result.

RGB Color Values

In this section, we provide a good mix of various RGB color values. The diffusion value and lighting scheme you use in a particular scene can have a pronounced effect on the visible color of an object, so keep that in mind. There are very few things in this world that have a 100 percent diffusion value. For most objects, except metals, 70–80 percent is a good starting point if you don't know an object's diffusion value.

RGB color values for common colors:

Base Color	R	G	B
Black, True	0	0	0
Base Color: Blue			
Blue, Cobalt	61	90	170
Blue, Dodger	30	144	255
Blue, Indigo	8	46	84
Blue, Manganese	3	168	158
Blue, Midnight	25	25	112
Blue, Navy	0	0	128
Blue, Pastel	131	147	202
Blue, Peacock	50	160	200
Blue, Powder	176	224	230
Blue, Royal	65	105	225
Blue, Slate	106	90	205
Blue, Sky	135	206	235
Blue, Steel	70	130	180
Blue, True	0	0	255
Blue, Turquoise	0	200	140
Blue, Ultramarine	20	10	143
Base Color: Brown			
Brown, Beige	163	148	128
Brown, Burnt Sienna	138	54	15
Brown, Burnt Umber	138	51	36
Brown, Chocolate	210	105	30
Brown, Flesh	255	125	64
Brown, Khaki	240	230	140
Brown, Raw Sienna	199	97	20
Brown, Raw Umber	115	74	18
Brown, Rosy	188	143	143

continues ▶

Base Color: Brown

Brown, Sepia	94	38	18
Brown, Sienna	160	82	45
Brown, Saddle	139	69	19
Brown, Sandy	244	164	96
Brown, Tan	210	180	140
Brown, True	128	42	42

Base Color: Cyan

Cyan, Aquamarine	127	255	212
Cyan, Pastel	109	207	246
Cyan, True	0	255	255
Cyan, Turquoise	64	224	208

Base Color: Green

Green, Chartreuse	127	255	0
Green, Cobalt	61	145	64
Green, Emerald	0	201	87
Green, Forest	34	139	34
Green, Lawn	124	252	0
Green, Lime	50	205	50
Green, Mint	189	252	200
Green, Olive Drab	107	142	35
Green, Pastel	130	202	156
Green, Sap	48	128	20
Green, Sea	45	140	87
Green, Spring	0	255	127
Green, Terre Verde	56	94	15
Green, True	0	255	0

Base Color: Gray

Gray, Cold	128	138	135
Gray, Slate	112	128	144
Gray, True, Medium	128	128	128
Gray, Warm	128	128	105

continues ▶

Base Color: Magenta

Magenta, Blue	138	43	226
Magenta, Orchid	218	112	214
Magenta, Pastel	244	154	193
Magenta, Plum	221	160	221
Magenta, Purple	160	32	240
Magenta, True	255	0	255
Magenta, Violet	143	94	153

Base Color: Orange

Orange, Cadmium	255	97	3
Orange, Carrot	237	145	33
Orange, Red	255	69	0
Orange, True	255	128	0

Base Color: Red

Red, Brick	156	102	31
Red, Cadmium	227	23	13
Red, Coral	255	127	80
Red, Firebrick	178	34	34
Red, Indian	176	23	31
Red, Maroon	176	48	96
Red, Pastel	246	150	121
Red, Pink	255	192	203
Red, Raspberry	135	38	87
Red, Salmon	250	128	114
Red, Tomato	255	99	71
Red, True	255	0	0

Base Color: White

White, Antique	250	235	215
White, Azure	240	255	255
White, Bisque	255	228	196

continues ▶

Base Color: White

White, Blanch	255	235	205
White, Corn silk	255	248	220
White, Eggshell	252	230	201
White, Floral	255	250	240
White, Gainesboro	220	220	220
White, Ghost	248	248	255
White, Honeydew	240	255	240
White, Ivory	255	255	240
White, Linen	250	240	230
White, Navajo	255	222	173
White, Old lace	253	245	230
White, Seashell	255	245	238
White, Smoke	245	245	245
White, Snow	255	250	250
White, True	255	255	255
White, Wheat	245	222	179

Base Color: Yellow

Yellow, Banana	227	207	87
Yellow, Cadmium	255	153	18
Yellow, Gold	255	215	0
Yellow, Goldenrod	218	165	32
Yellow, Melon	227	255	0
Yellow, Pastel	255	247	153
Yellow, Orange	247	148	29
Yellow, True	255	255	0

Metals

Aluminum	220	223	227
Brass	191	173	111
Copper	186	110	64

continues ▶

Metals

Gold	218	178	115
Graphite	87	33	77
Iron	115	115	120
Silver	230	230	215
Stainless Steel	125	125	120

Reflection Properties

Here is a good mix of materials and their basic reflective properties. There are a lot of factors that can affect an item's reflectivity, so again, use these values as starting points.

Percentage of incident light reflected by various materials:

Material	%
Aluminum	45
Aluminum Foil	65
Asphalt	14
Brass	40
Brick	30
Bronze	10
Chrome	70
Copper	71
Earth, Moist	08
Gold	84
Graphite	20
Green Leaf	21
Iron	15
Linen	81
Marble, White	53
Mercury	69
Paper, Newsprint	61
Paper, White	71
Pewter	20

continues ▶

Material	%
Platinum	64
Porcelain, White	72
Quartz	81
Rubber	02
Silicon	28
Silver	90
Slate	06
Stainless Steel	37
Steel	55
Tin Can	40
Vinyl	15
Wood, Pine	40

Refraction Properties

This is a rather extensive list of items. Chances are you may never need most of them until someone comes along from a scientific institution wanting work done that has to be scientifically accurate. You'll be glad you have this list then!

Indices of refraction for various elements, materials, liquids, and gases at STP (Standard Temperature and Pressure) in visible light are as follows:

Material	Index
Vacuum	1.000 (Exactly)
Acetone	1.360
Actinolite	1.618
Agalmatoite	1.550
Agate	1.544
Agate, Moss	1.540
Air	1.000
Alcohol	1.329
Alexandrite	1.745
Aluminum	1.440

continues ▶

Material	Index
Amber	1.546
Amblygonite	1.611
Amethyst	1.544
Amorphous Selenium	2.920
Anatase	2.490
Andalusite	1.641
Anhydrite	1.571
Apatite	1.632
Apophyllite	1.536
Aquamarine	1.577
Aragonite	1.530
Argon	1.000
Asphalt	1.635
Augelite	1.574
Axinite	1.675
Azurite	1.730
Barite	1.636
Barytocalcite	1.684
Benitoite	1.757
Benzene	1.501
Beryl	1.577
Beryllonite	1.553
Brazilianite	1.603
Bromine (liquid)	1.661
Bronze	1.180
Brownite	1.567
Calcite	1.486
Calspar1	1.660
Calspar2	1.486
Cancrinite	1.491

continues ▶

Material	Index
Carbon Dioxide (gas)	1.000
Carbon Dioxide (liquid)	1.200
Carbon Disulfide	1.628
Carbon Tetrachloride	1.460
Cassiterite	1.997
Celestite	1.622
Cerussite	1.804
Ceylanite	1.770
Chalcedony	1.530
Chalk	1.510
Chalybite	1.630
Chlorine (gas)	1.000
Chlorine (liquid)	1.385
Chrome Green	2.400
Chrome Red	2.420
Chrome Yellow	2.310
Chromium	2.970
Chromium Oxide	2.705
Chrysoberyl	1.745
Chrysocolla	1.500
Chrysoprase	1.534
Citrine	1.550
Clinozoisite	1.724
Cobalt Blue	1.740
Cobalt Green	1.970
Cobalt Violet	1.710
Colemanite	1.586
Copper	1.100
Copper Oxide	2.705
Coral	1.486

continues ▶

Material	Index
Cordierite	1.540
Corundum	1.766
Crocoite	2.310
Crown Glass	1.520
Crystal	2.000
Cuprite	2.850
Danburite	1.633
Diamond	2.417
Diopside	1.680
Dolomite	1.503
Dumortierite	1.686
Ebonite	1.660
Ekanite	1.600
Elaeolite	1.532
Emerald	1.576
Emerald, Synth flux	1.561
Emerald, Synth hydro	1.568
Enstatite	1.663
Epidote	1.733
Ethyl Alcohol (Ethanol)	1.360
Euclase	1.652
Fabulite	2.409
Feldspar, Adventurine	1.532
Feldspar, Albite	1.525
Feldspar, Amazonite	1.525
Feldspar, Labradorite	1.565
Feldspar, Microcline	1.525
Feldspar, Oligoclase	1.539
Feldspar, Orthoclase	1.525
Fluoride	1.560

continues ▶

Material	Index
Fluorite	1.434
Formica	1.470
Garnet, Almandine	1.760
Garnet, Almandite	1.790
Garnet, Andradite	1.820
Garnet, Demantoid	1.880
Garnet, Grossular	1.738
Garnet, Hessonite	1.745
Garnet, Rhodolite	1.760
Garnet, Spessartite	1.810
Gaylussite	1.517
Glass	1.517
Glass, Albite	1.489
Glass, Crown	1.520
Glass, Crown, Zinc	1.517
Glass, Flint, Dense	1.660
Glass, Flint, Heaviest	1.890
Glass, Flint, Heavy	1.655
Glass, Flint, Lanthanum	1.800
Glass, Flint, Light	1.580
Glass, Flint, Medium	1.627
Glycerine	1.473
Gold	0.470
Hambergite	1.559
Hauynite	1.502
Helium	1.000
Hematite	2.940
Hemimorphite	1.614
Hiddenite	1.655
Howlite	1.586

continues ▶

Material	Index
Hydrogen (gas)	1.000
Hydrogen (liquid)	1.097
Hypersthene	1.670
Ice	1.309
Idocrase	1.713
Iodine Crystal	3.340
Iolite	1.548
Iron	1.510
Ivory	1.540
Jade, Nephrite	1.610
Jadeite	1.665
Jasper	1.540
Jet	1.660
Kornerupine	1.665
Kunzite	1.655
Kyanite	1.715
Lapis Gem	1.500
Lapis Lazuli	1.610
Lazulite	1.615
Lead	2.010
Leucite	1.509
Magnesite	1.515
Malachite	1.655
Meerschaum	1.530
Mercury (liquid)	1.620
Methanol	1.329
Moldavite	1.500
Moonstone, Adularia	1.525
Moonstone, Albite	1.535
Natrolite	1.480

continues ▶

Material	Index
Nephrite	1.600
Nitrogen (gas)	1.000
Nitrogen (liquid)	1.205
Nylon	1.530
Obsidian	1.489
Olivine	1.670
Onyx	1.486
Opal	1.450
Oxygen (gas)	1.000
Oxygen (liquid)	1.221
Painite	1.787
Pearl	1.530
Periclase	1.740
Peridot	1.654
Peristerite	1.525
Petalite	1.502
Phenakite	1.650
Phosgenite	2.117
Plastic	1.460
Plexiglas	1.500
Polystyrene	1.550
Prase	1.540
Prasiolite	1.540
Prehnite	1.610
Proustite	2.790
Purpurite	1.840
Pyrite	1.810
Pyrope	1.740
Quartz	1.544
Quartz, Fused	1.458

continues ▶

Material	Index
Rhodizite	1.690
Rhodochrisite	1.600
Rhodonite	1.735
Rock Salt	1.544
Rubber, Natural	1.519
Ruby	1.760
Rutile	2.610
Sanidine	1.522
Sapphire	1.760
Scapolite	1.540
Scapolite, Yellow	1.555
Scheelite	1.920
Selenium, Amorphous	2.920
Serpentine	1.560
Shell	1.530
Silicon	4.240
Sillimanite	1.658
Silver	0.180
Sinhalite	1.699
Smaragdite	1.608
Smithsonite	1.621
Sodalite	1.483
Sodium Chloride	1.544
Sphalerite	2.368
Sphene	1.885
Spinel	1.712
Spodumene	1.650
Staurolite	1.739
Steatite	1.539
Steel	2.500

continues ▶

Material	Index
Stichtite	1.520
Strontium Titanate	2.410
Styrofoam	1.595
Sugar Solution (30 percent)	1.380
Sugar Solution (80 percent)	1.490
Sulphur	1.960
Synthetic Spinel	1.730
Taaffeite	1.720
Tantalite	2.240
Tanzanite	1.691
Teflon	1.350
Thomsonite	1.530
Tiger eye	1.544
Topaz	1.620
Topaz, Blue	1.610
Topaz, Pink	1.620
Topaz, White	1.630
Topaz, Yellow	1.620
Tourmaline	1.624
Tremolite	1.600
Tugtupite	1.496
Turpentine	1.472
Turquoise	1.610
Ulexite	1.490
Uvarovite	1.870
Variscite	1.550
Vivianite	1.580
Wardite	1.590
Water (gas)	1.000
Water 100°C	1.318

continues ▶

Material	Index
Water 20°C	1.333
Water 35°C (room temperature)	1.331
Willemite	1.690
Witherite	1.532
Wulfenite	2.300
Zinc Crown Glass	1.517
Zincite	2.010
Zircon, High	1.960
Zircon, Low	1.800
Zirconia, Cubic	2.170

Color Temperatures of Light

The color temperature of light is the temperature to which you would have to heat an object (a "black body") to produce light of similar spectral characteristics. Low color temperatures produce warmer (yellow/red) light, while higher temperatures produce colder (bluer) light.

The color of light is measured in Kelvins. LightWave has a handy Kelvin scale on its color picker, which makes it easy to plug in these values when you want an accurate starting point. For example, if you wanted to light your gunfight scene from "High Noon" you would select a starting temperature of 6000–6500 degrees Kelvin (noontime) for your skylight and adjust from there.

Temperature (degrees Kelvin)	Scene
1400–1930	Candlelight
2000–2500	Sunrise
2680	40W incandescent lamp
2800–2850	100W household (tungsten) bulb
2950	500W tungsten lamp
2960–3200	Tungsten studio lamp

continues ▶

Temperature (degrees Kelvin)	Scene
3000	Fluorescent light (warm white)
	200W incandescent lamp
	1000W tungsten lamp
3200	Halogen bulb, Nitraphot B
3400	Photoflood (floodlamp)
	Halogen bulb, Nitraphot A
3800–4000	Clear flashbulb
4000	Moonlight
4400	Sun two hours after rising
5000	Fluorescent light
5000–6000	Daylight at midday to noon sun
5500	Daylight (for photography)
5800	Electronic flash tube
5500–6000	Blue flashbulb
6000–7000	Electronic flash
6500	Daylight (sun and sky averaged)
7000	Overcast sky
8000	Cloudy sky, light shade
9000	Hazy sky, light shade
11000	Sky light without direct sun
13000	Blue sky, thin white clouds
16000	Average blue sky, medium shade
18000–19000	Clear blue sky, deep shade

Film Resolutions

The following chart represents the most common resolutions you are likely to run into when working with film. These numbers are not absolute, however. There are many factors that could change the final output resolution. The second rows under some of the formats represent alternate resolutions asked for by some postproduction facilities. Some facilities might also ask for rendered output resolutions not on this chart. It all depends on the particular needs of the project.

Film Resolutions	Image Aspect	Pixel Aspect	<1K	1K	1.5K	2K	4K
35mm Full Aperture	1.33	1.00	768×576	1024×768	1536×1152	2048×1536	4096×3072
				1024×778	1556×1182	2048×1556	4096×3112
35mm Academy	1.37	1.00		1024×747	1556×1134	2048×1494	4096×2987
				914×666	1536×1119	1828×1332	3656×2664
35mm Academy Projection	1.66	1.00	512×307	1024×614	1536×921	2048×1229	4096×2458
				914×551	1556×938	1828×1102	3656×2202
35mm 1.75:1	1.75	1.00	560×320	1120×640	1575×900	2048×1170	4096×2340
35mm 1.85:1	1.85	1.00	512×277	1024×554	1536×830	2048×1107	4096×2214
				914×494	1556×841	1828×988	3656×1976
35mm 2.35:1	2.35	1.00	512×218	1024×436	1536×654	2048×871	4096×1743
35mm Anamorphic 2.35:1	2.35	2.00	512×436	1024×871	1536×1307	2048×1743	4096×3486
70mm Panavision	2.20	1.00	880×400	1024×465	1536×698	2048×931	4096×1862
Panavision	2.35	1.00			1536×653	2048×871	4096×1742
						1828×777	3656×1555
70mm IMAX	1.36	1.00	512×375	1024×751	1536×1126	2048×1501	4096×3003
VistaVision	1.50	1.00	512×341	1024×683	1536×1024	2048×1365	4096×2731
						1828×1219	3072×2048
Cinemascope	1.17	1.00		1024×872	1536×1307	2048×1743	4096×3487
						1828×1556	3656×3112
Cinemascope	2.35	1.00			1536×653	2048×871	4096×1742
						1828×777	3656×1555
35mm (24mm×36mm) slide	1.50	1.00	512×341	1024×683	1536×1024	2048×1365	4096×2731
6cm×6cm slide	1.00	1.00	512×512	1024×1024	1536×1536	2048×2048	4096×4096
4"×5" or 8"×10" slide	1.33	1.00	768×576	1024×768	1536×1152	2048×1536	4096×3072

Video Resolutions

The following chart represents the most common video and computer resolutions for working with video. Although NTSC and PAL are interlaced formats, it is often a common practice today to render final output as frames rather than fields. Note that HDTV formats are still far from being standardized across various industries. Always find out from your clients which format they are using.

Video Resolutions	Image Aspect	Pixel Aspect	Resolution	Frames/Sec.
D1 NTSC	1.33	0.90	720×486	30i
D1 NTSC Widescreen	1.78 (16:9)	1.20	720×486	30i
D2 NTSC	1.35	0.86	752×480	30i
D2 NTSC Widescreen	1.87	1.15	752×480	30i
D1 PAL	1.33	1.07	720×576	25i
D1 PAL Widescreen	1.78 (16:9)	1.42	720×576	25i
D2 PAL	1.33	1.02	752×576	25i
HDTV	16:9	1.00	1920×1080	60i,30p,24p
	16:9	1.00	1280×720	60p,30p,24p
	16:9 (4:3)	1.00	704×480	60p,60i,30p,24p
	4:3	1.00	640×480	60p,60i,30p,24p
VGA	1.33	1.00	640×480	
SVGA	1.33	1.00	800×600	
XGA	1.33	1.00	1024×768	
SXGA*	1.25	1.00	1280×1024	
SXGA	1.33	1.00	1280×960	
UXGA	1.33	1.00	1600×1200	

*Note: 1280×1024 should be avoided because it is not the correct aspect ratio for video or computer monitors.

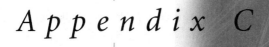

A p p e n d i x C

Reference
Materials
and Tools

LightWave gives you the power to create

just about anything you can imagine.

Some of that power comes from the

number of useful plug-ins that are

integrated into LightWave; however, there is life beyond the LightWave installation disc! There are many talented programmers out there who create plug-ins that can enhance your 3D experience. Furthermore, there are valuable references for additional learning and communication through the World Wide Web. This appendix introduces you to a number of third-party plug-in vendors and their tools and provides some useful references, including

- **Worley Labs.** The creative genius of Steve Worley is evident in his wide range of LightWave Plug-ins. Worley Labs produces plug-ins that are extremely useful to just about any LightWave animator.

- **MetroGrafx/Binary Arts, Inc.** A long time producer of plug-ins for LightWave, MetroGrafx has some tools for helping you animate.

- **Joe Alter, Inc.** Joe is a seasoned veteran of the effects industry and has created some useful plug-ins for various LightWave animation techniques.

- **BGT BioGraphic Technologies, Inc.** This company just might have created the perfect tool for your 3D character animation work.

- **Prem Subrahmanyan Graphic Design.** As an alternative to some of LightWave's expressions and features, Prem has created some of his own.

- **pmG: Project Messiah.** The popular add-on to LightWave 3D for character animation has been greatly enhanced with messiah:studio.

- **Internet resources.** One of the best places for up-to-date information on LightWave, tutorials, products, and more.

Third-Party Plug-ins

LightWave was written to be extensible through third-party plug-ins, which is a boon to artists and designers because it enables these users to further enhance and extend their creativity and productivity without ever having to leave the program. This section introduces you to a number of third-party vendors and highlights some of their more popular plug-ins.

Worley Laboratories

Often considered the best in the business, Worley Laboratories' plug-ins bring your animations to new levels of professionalism. The small price and huge toolset provided by owner Steve Worley are unprecedented in the 3D animation community. Read on to learn more about Worley's most popular plug-ins.

Sasquatch Hair and Grass

This long awaited plug-in took more than four years to develop. And while LightWave 7 comes with SasLite—a light version of Sasquatch that enables you to quickly and easily create fur and hair on surfaces and includes the same rendering engine as its counterpart but with fewer features—the full version of the plug-in enables you to apply hair and fibers to selected surfaces beyond what's included with your existing software. What's cool about the full version is that the fibers react to gravity, weight, wind, and more. They can receive shadows, and work with LightWave's surface settings. Network rendering is also possible. Figure C.1 shows the Sasquatch interface. Figures C.2 and C.3 show example renders.

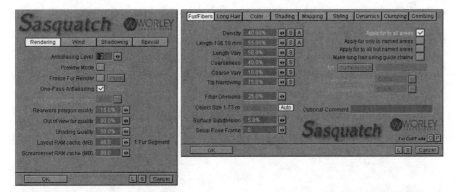

Figure C.1   The Sasquatch interface gives you all the control you'll need for creating just about any type of fiber.

Figure C.2 This cool-looking wolf was created with Sasquatch.

Figure C.3 Hairy animals aren't the only things you can create with Sasquatch. This jungle shot uses Sasquatch for leaves, grass, and general foliage.

The best thing about Sasquatch is that it is a pixel filter plug-in. This means that there is no geometry in your LightWave scene to slow down your workflow. The fibers are created during the render process. In addition, you can multithread pixel filter plug-ins in LightWave, so if you have two or more processors, you can render these effects even faster.

Another benefit of Sasquatch is the ability to have hair react to dynamics, such as wind and gravity. This is great for flowing hair or blowing grass. Another great benefit is the ability to add more color and texture to your furry creations.

From there, Sasquatch offers image styling controls, shadow control, compositing information, and much more. For a full, detailed list of the features in Sasquatch, visit *www.worley.com.*

The Taft Collection

The Taft Collection from Worley Labs is a set of six powerful plug-ins for LightWave Layout. The plug-ins enable you to do things that are nearly impossible otherwise.

- **Camera Match.** Aligning LightWave objects with photographs is much harder to do than it may seem. For example, if you render a LightWave object so that it matches the view of a camera in a photograph, you can perform many tricks including compositing and photo-texturing with Sticky Front Projection (explained next). But matching a photograph's view is much harder. Taft's Camera Match plug-in solves the task of matching a 3D object with a real photograph by using mathematical optimization. What it does is find the absolutely best match for your scene. If you ever composite, Camera Match will not only save you days of tedious frustration, but will enable you to do shots that are simply impossible manually. Camera Match is designed for use only with photographs, not animations. Animated camera tracking is significantly different and more specialized.

- **Sticky Front Projection.** A streak of dirt, a rust stain, or even a crack in plaster can add realism to your LightWave scenes, but they take time and effort to re-create. Image maps can help considerably, but simple mapping often is not enough. One answer to this problem is "image-based rendering," which uses real photographs and simple geometry to build photo-real objects. The difficult part is applying the photograph to the object to match its shape and surface. This is exactly the task of Worley's Sticky Front Projection. You also can build object surfaces with multiple photographs.

- **Whirley Points.** Many real-world objects bend and deform when they're moved, such as the way paper flutters when you drop it, the way a cloth wrinkles, or the way a person's double chin bounces when he walks. These effects of "soft dynamics" are everywhere in the real world, but not often seen in 3D animation. LightWave 7 comes with Motion Designer for full dynamics simulation, but often you will want something simpler, more interactive, and faster to apply, test, and tweak. Whirley Points applies fast, real-time dynamics to your object (or parts of your object). It features an interactive OpenGL preview of your object motion, showing the result of your settings in real time.

- **Tracer.** Imagine firing 100 shots out of an animated gun, one at a time—how long will it take you to set up those keyframes? And what happens when you want to change your aim later? And what if you wanted to add a second gun? As powerful as LightWave's Graph Editor is, there is no way to automate this process. Keyframing those simple shots can take days. Tracer is designed for automatic weapons fire enabling you to shoot thousands of rounds or launch fireballs, sizzling lasers, flame, or old-fashioned lead at your favorite targets.

- **HeatWave.** The real world has billions of details that people are used to seeing in any image or animation. Your goal as an animator is to re-create enough of those details to convince the viewer. One of the details that can add that subtle realism effect is air shimmer, often seen in hot environments. With HeatWave, you can make hot pavement, fires, jet exhaust, and deserts. Its animated effect is simple to apply and animate, and its real-time preview gives you instant feedback to design the exact effect you need.

- **Hoser.** It can be difficult to animate tubes, ropes, tails, cords, tentacles, antennae, strings, ducts, pipes, vines, cables, and hoses. The Hoser plug-in simplifies this process. Instead of wrestling with Inverse Kinematics (IK) and bones, just apply Hoser for instant, easy, interactive control of your object. You can move or rotate either end of the object and Hoser will make sure your tube behaves. Here are a few examples of the types of objects you can control:
  - Scuba air hoses
  - Car suspension springs
  - Octopus tentacles
  - Snakes
  - Animal tails
  - Telephone or electrical cords
  - Sailing ship rigging

The Taft Collection should be every LightWave animator's next purchase.

The James K. Polk Collection

This collection of useful plug-ins from Worley Labs will help you more than you can imagine. Like the Taft collection, the Polk collection is a set of plug-ins designed to take difficult to nearly impossible animation tasks and make them painless. Here's what this set of plug-ins can help you accomplish:

- **Acid.** A shader that enables you to change a surface's texture and bump mapping based on effectors.
- **Poke.** A displacement plug-in with history.
- **Blink.** Automates irregular, but periodic motion.
- **Parent.** Enables dynamic parenting of objects and bones over time.
- **Link.** Enables easy control of complex cycled motion.
- **Lens.** Corrects or adds lens distortions to LightWave imagery.
- **Wheelie.** Rotates wheels automatically.
- **Speedlimit.** Forces objects to stay within defined speeds.
- **Track.** Enables any object to be aligned to any axis, thereby enabling it to point at any other item.
- **Limiter.** Restricts object movement to prevent out-of-bounds motions.
- **Dangle.** Animates dangling chains, ropes, and cables automatically.
- **Flexor.** Allows smooth, dynamic bending of objects.
- **Diffuse.** Enables gaslike diffusion of particles over time.
- **HSVBoost.** This surface shader allows hue, saturation, and value manipulation.
- **Enviro.** Makes QuickTime Virtual Reality (QTVR) maps, as well as spherical, cubical, and orthogonal views of your scene.
- **Vfog.** Creates faster ground fog than LightWave's built-in fog.
- **DropShadow.** Creates simple 2D blurred shadows.
- **Confusion.** Renders depth-of-field effects in your scene.
- **Whip.** This is a simple physics simulator for adding dynamic hinges and joints.

Plus 10 other bonus plug-ins.

Gaffer

This plug-in from Worley Laboratories has been used by the LightWave community for years. Gaffer is a plug-in shader for LightWave 3D that performs a similar job as a real gaffer; it is a tool for controlling lighting and shading. It changes the algorithm LightWave uses to determine the appearance of a lit surface. Gaffer is not a minor change in the shading options of LightWave; it is a considerable extension. It adds new specular and diffuse shading options, per-surface light exclusion, boosting controls, area light shadows, bloom around bright reflections, and a new tool for compositing shadows into a background plate. Gaffer has been developed in close cooperation with several major Hollywood studios. Their need for photorealistic rendering drove the development of a tool to give them more control over their objects' appearance. Gaffer gives you control over the following:

- **Selective Lighting.** Exclusion of lights on any surface, negative lights, and new falloff options.

- **Advanced Specularity Control.** Multiple specular reflections, with independent intensity and color control.

- **Anisotropic Specularity.** Nonuniform specularity from brushed metals, hair, and threads.

- **Advanced Diffuse Shading.** Diffuse transmission, and a new model for rough surfaces such as rock.

- **Advanced Shadowing Options.** True photoreal area light shadows.

- **Shadow Compositing Modes.** Seamless integration of shadows into plates.

- **Specular Bloom.** Automatic glows around the brightest reflections.

For information on Gaffer, Polk, Taft, and Sasquatch, visit *www.worley.com* to find examples and buy online.

MetroGrafx/Binary Arts, Inc.

A long-time creator of cool plug-ins, such as FiberFactory, Wobbler, Sparks, PointAt, and ExtractAudio, MetroGrafx's Jon Tindal also offers FiberFactory3. This hair-generating plug-in for LightWave helps you build 3D hair in Modeler and render it in Layout. The trick is a Pixel Filter plug-in that doesn't require you to build enormous amounts of geometry—you only need very little.

For more information on MetroGrafx plug-ins, visit *www.metrografx.com*.

Joe Alter, Inc.

Prior to founding his company in 1999, Joe Alter worked in visual effects since 1985, starting at industry pioneer Robert Abel & Associates. Over the years Alter has done work for George Lucas's ILM, Steven Spielberg's Dreamworks SKG, Roland Emerich's Centropolis FX, Warner Bros., Boss Film, Metrolight Studios, and Phil Tippet Studios.

His most notable feature production (key shot) work includes "The Prince of Egypt," "Godzilla," "The Mask," "Star Trek: Generations," and "Cliffhanger."

Joe also makes valuable plug-ins for LightWave such as Shave and a Haircut, a fur and hair generating software; and LipService, a lip-syncing software application. For more info on Joe Alter and his products, visit *www.joealter.com*.

pmG

project:messiah, from pmG (formerly Station X Studios), is a user-focused character animation plug-in for LightWave. project:messiah has various elements. Some features include

- Fast IK
- Fast bones
- Fast expressions
- Easy character setup
- Real-time interactivity
- Local/world coordinates on-the-fly
- Forward/IK
- Procedural/keyframe animation blending
- Multitarget effects

Figure C.4 shows the project:messiah interface. New additions to the messiah family include messiah:animate, messiah:render, and messiah:develop, all are part of the messiah:studio. For more information, visit *www.projectmessiah.com*.

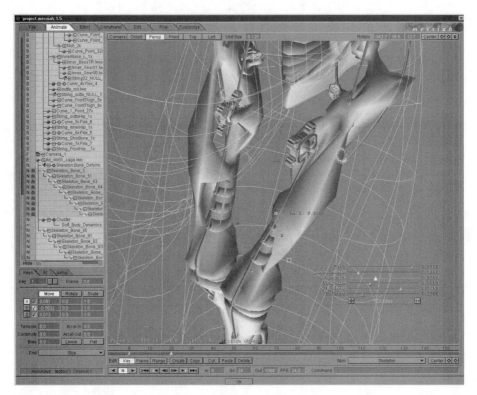

Figure C.4   Here is project:messiah's powerful interface.

BGT BioGraphic Technologies

The Autonomous Character plug-in by BGT BioGraphic Technologies allows animators to harness a sophisticated artificial intelligence (AI) engine to create natural-looking animations of large groups of interacting intelligent characters, such as race car drivers passing at high speeds, sharks hunting schools of fish, or disciplined Roman legions crushing hordes of barbarians.

With an efficient and intuitive workflow that is analogous to dynamics (physics-based animation) for physical objects, BGT's AI animation plug-in allows animators to create autonomous characters controlled by the AI solver directly in LightWave. The AI solver controls the character's motion path, orientation, and speed. Any LightWave object from a fully boned mech robot to a camera can be driven by the AI solver. There is an efficient collision detection feature, and surface hugging also is provided to keep characters properly grounded in their 3D worlds. The plug-in is real-time, supports large groups of characters, and can be exported into any game engine that uses the ACE SDK. The plug-in is completely artist-driven and requires no programming. Learn more about the plug-in by visiting *www.biographictech.com.*

Prem Subrahmanyam Graphic Design

A seasoned LightWave veteran, Prem's work can be seen throughout the state of Florida, and his plug-ins are used throughout the world. Prem's graphics and programming business are a great resource for LightWave animators looking to add to their LightWave skills. Check out Prem's plug-ins at *www.premdesign.com.*

Internet Resources

As you can see from the plug-in examples listed here, all references point to the Internet. As a LightWave animator, it is vital for you to be online. No matter how little or how often you animate, you are doing yourself a great disservice if you do not access resources on the Internet.

Here is a list of just a few LightWave-related sites to visit. There are many more, so search the web often!

www.flay.com	*www.sharbor.com*
www.newtek.com	*www.worley.com*
www.projectmessiah.com	*www.metrografx.com*
www.joealter.com	*www.danablan.com*
www.agadigital.com	*www.curiouslabs.com*
www.cgchannel.com	*www.3dluvr.com*
www.lightwave3d.com	*www.cgfocus.com*
menithings.com	*www.insidelightwave.com*

If you visit *www.flay.com*, you can always find the most up-to-date information on LightWave and the LightWave community. Over at the CG Channel, *www.cgchannel.com*, you can keep up-to-date with the latest 3D industry news. LightWave is a major player on this site. Also, take a look at your LightWave reference manual. The introduction area has a few great LightWave related web sites to visit.

Additionally, think about subscribing to the various LightWave 3D mailing lists. These lists have constant activity, and talk ranges anywhere from nonsense to serious technique. Visit *www.yahoogroups.com* and search for LightWave. You'll see which LightWave group is good for you. Lastly, if your Internet provider has a news service (which most do), visit comp.graphics.apps.lightwave for the LightWave newsgroup. Visitors often include representatives from NewTek and various high-profile studios. It's a great place for quick tips and techniques.

Summary

This appendix just skims the surface of the amount of information available to you. The tools for LightWave and 3D animation are plentiful, and you should gobble up whatever you can. Information is power.

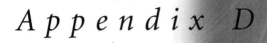

Appendix D

What's on the CD

The accompanying CD is packed with all of

the exercise files to help you work with this

book and LightWave 7. The following sec-

tions contain detailed descriptions of

the CD's contents. In addition, a number of "extras" have been provided for your enjoyment.

For more information about the use of this CD, please review the ReadMe.txt file in the CD's root directory. This file includes important disclaimer information as well as information about installation, system requirements, troubleshooting, and technical support.

Technical Support Issues

If you have any difficulties with this CD, please check out our tech support web site at *www.newriders.com.*

System Requirements

This CD was configured for use on systems running Windows NT Workstation, Windows 98, Windows ME, Windows 2000, Macintosh, SGI, or UNIX.

Loading the CD Files

To load the files from the CD, insert the disc into your CD-ROM drive. If Autoplay is enabled on your machine, the CD-ROM setup program starts automatically the first time you insert the disc. You may copy the files to your hard drive, or use them right off the disc.

Note

This CD uses long and mixed-case filenames, requiring the use of a protected mode CD-ROM driver.

Exercise Files

This CD contains all the files you'll need to complete the exercises in *Inside LightWave 7*. These files can be found in the root directory's Projects folder. Please note, however, that exercises in certain chapters do not require files from the CD. You may find, however, that some chapters have CD files that are not mentioned in the book; these are what we're calling "bonus stuff" and are variations on the book's projects. To properly access the project files, do the following:

1. In LightWave's Layout, press the o key to call up the General Options tab of the Preferences panel. You can do this in Layout or Modeler.

2. At the top of the panel, select the Content Directory button.

3. A system file dialog box titled Set Content Directory will open. Select your CD-ROM drive, go to the Projects folder, and click Open.

4. Your content directory is now set for working through the exercises. The content directory path should look something like this: \X:\Projects\, where *X* is your CD.

When you select Load Scene, LightWave will open to the Projects folder. There, you'll see folders named Scene, Objects, and Images. Within these folders are the individual chapter folders. Selecting Load Object within LightWave will point to the Objects folder within the Projects folder.

Third-Party Materials

This CD also contains third-party files and demos from leading industry artists and companies. These programs have been carefully selected to help you strengthen your professional LightWave skills.

Please note that some of the programs included on this CD-ROM are only demo versions of the particular software. Please support these independent vendors by purchasing or registering any shareware software you use for more than 30 days. Check the documentation provided with the software on where and how to register the product.

Here's what you'll find on the CD in addition to all the project files:

- A full-feature LightWave 7 demo for PC and MAC to get you up and running immediately!

- Poser (demo) from Curious Labs can help get you started posing and animating figures. Visit *www.curiouslabs.com* for information on using Poser Pro to work directly with LightWave.

- Tom Marlin, through his Marlin Studios Textures (*www.marlinstudios.com*), has provided a sample of many of his popular textures for you to use. You won't find these anywhere else!

- A few extra images from author, Dan Ablan, for reflection maps or compositing.

- All of the figures referenced in the book have been included on the accompanying CD in full color.

We've worked hard to make sure that the contents on this CD are just as useful as the content of this book. The combination of the two makes this a tremendous resource. Enjoy!

Index

H

X–Y–Z

HOW TO CONTACT US

VISIT OUR WEB SITE

WWW.NEWRIDERS.COM

On our web site, you'll find information about our other books, authors, tables of contents, and book errata. You will also find information about book registration and how to purchase our books, both domestically and internationally.

EMAIL US

Contact us at: **nrfeedback@newriders.com**

- If you have comments or questions about this book
- To report errors that you have found in this book
- If you have a book proposal to submit or are interested in writing for New Riders
- If you are an expert in a computer topic or technology and are interested in being a technical editor who reviews manuscripts for technical accuracy

Contact us at: **nreducation@newriders.com**

- If you are an instructor from an educational institution who wants to preview New Riders books for classroom use. Email should include your name, title, school, department, address, phone number, office days/hours, text in use, and enrollment, along with your request for desk/examination copies and/or additional information.

Contact us at: **nrmedia@newriders.com**

- If you are a member of the media who is interested in reviewing copies of New Riders books. Send your name, mailing address, and email address, along with the name of the publication or web site you work for.

BULK PURCHASES/CORPORATE SALES

If you are interested in buying 10 or more copies of a title or want to set up an account for your company to purchase directly from the publisher at a substantial discount, contact us at 800-382-3419 or email your contact information to corpsales@pearsontechgroup.com. A sales representative will contact you with more information.

WRITE TO US

New Riders Publishing
201 W. 103rd St.
Indianapolis, IN 46290-1097

CALL/FAX US

Toll-free (800) 571-5840
If outside U.S. (317) 581-3500
Ask for New Riders
FAX: (317) 581-4663

New Riders

VOICES THAT MATTER

Solutions from experts you know and trust.

www.informit.com

OPERATING SYSTEMS

WEB DEVELOPMENT

PROGRAMMING

NETWORKING

CERTIFICATION

AND MORE...

**Expert Access.
Free Content.**

New Riders has partnered with **InformIT.com** to bring technical information to your desktop. Drawing on New Riders authors and reviewers to provide additional information on topics you're interested in, **InformIT.com** has free, in-depth information you won't find anywhere else.

- **Master the skills you need, when you need them**

- **Call on resources from some of the best minds in the industry**

- **Get answers when you need them, using InformIT's comprehensive library or live experts online**

- **Go above and beyond what you find in New Riders books, extending your knowledge**

As an **InformIT** partner, **New Riders** has shared the wisdom and knowledge of our authors with you online. Visit **InformIT.com** to see what you're missing.

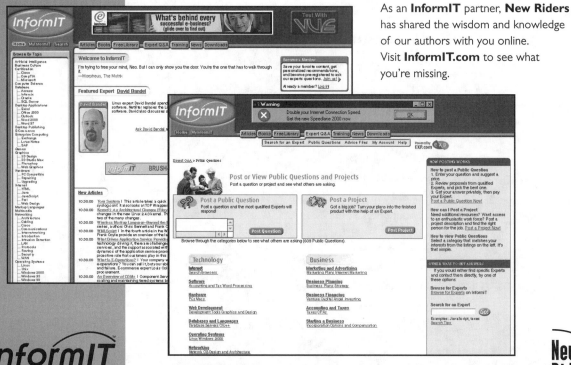

www.informit.com ■ **www.newriders.com**

Publishing
the Voices
that Matter

OUR BOOKS

OUR AUTHORS

SUPPORT

| web development | graphics & design | server technology | certification |

NEWS/EVENTS

PRESS ROOM

EDUCATORS

ABOUT US

CONTACT US

WRITE/REVIEW

You already know that New Riders brings you the Voices that Matter.

But what does that mean? It means that New Riders brings you the

Voices that challenge your assumptions, take your talents to the next

level, or simply help you better understand the complex technical world

we're all navigating.

Visit **www.newriders.com** to find:

► Never before published chapters

► Sample chapters and excerpts

► Author bios

► Contests

► Up-to-date industry event information

► Book reviews

► Special offers

► Info on how to join our User Group program

► Inspirational galleries where you can submit
your own masterpieces

► Ways to have your Voice heard

WWW.NEWRIDERS.COM

3D

The voices that

matter in a world

of technology.

New Riders

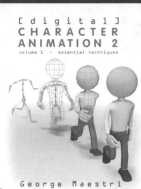
[digital]
CHARACTER
ANIMATION 2
volume 1 - essential techniques

George Maestri

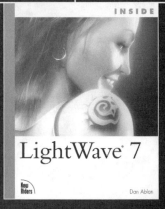
INSIDE

LightWave 7

New Riders

Dan Ablan

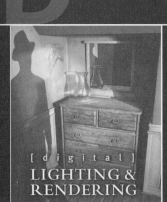
[digital]
LIGHTING &
RENDERING

JEREMY BIRN

[digital]
TEXTURING
& PAINTING

OWEN DEMERS

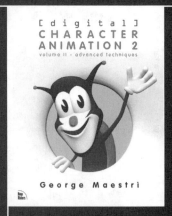
[digital]
CHARACTER
ANIMATION 2
volume II - advanced techniques

George Maestri

[digital] Character Animation 2,
Volume I: Essential Techniques
George Maestri
ISBN: 1562059300
$50.00

Inside Lightwave 7
Dan Ablan
ISBN: 0735711348
$59.99

[digital] Lighting & Rendering
Jeremy Birn
ISBN: 1562059548
$50.00

[digital] Texturing & Painting
Owen Demers
ISBN: 0735709181
$55.00

[digital] Character Animation 2
Volume II: Advanced Techniques
George Maestri
ISBN: 0735700443
$50.00

www.newriders.com

DON'T JACK AROUND WITH YOUR FUTURE

jordanWOLLMAN

A COMPUTER ART AND VIDEO MAGAZINE

Read *newtekPRO* for in-depth tutorials and the latest information on LightWave, Aura, and the Video Toaster.

SUBSCRIBE ONLINE	www.newtekpro.com
OR CALL	512-459-5099
OR WRITE	P.O. Box 5202
	Austin, TX 78763

newtekPRO
CREATIVITY IN MOTION

The *Inside LightWave 7* CD

The CD that accompanies this book contains valuable resources for anyone using LightWave 7, not the least of which are:

- **Project files.** All the example files provided by the author are here to help you with the step-by-step projects.
- **LightWave-related third-party software.** This includes several LightWave demos and plug-ins.

For a complete description of everything that's included, please see Appendix D, "What's on the CD."

Accessing the Project Files from the CD

To load the files from the CD, insert the disc into your CD-ROM drive. If Autoplay is enabled on your machine, the CD-ROM setup program starts automatically the first time you insert the disc. You may copy the files to your hard drive, or use them right off the disc.

NOTE: This CD-ROM uses long and mixed-case filenames, requiring the use of a protected mode CD-ROM driver.